6/5

RICE UNIVERSITY

SEMICENTENNIAL PUBLICATIONS

Restoration and
Eighteenth-Century
Literature

EDITOR

CARROLL CAMDEN

CONTRIBUTORS

RAE BLANCHARD
DONALD F. BOND
RICHMOND P. BOND
BENJAMIN BOYCE
REUBEN A. BROWER
JAMES L. CLIFFORD
DAVID DAICHES
HERBERT DAVIS
BONAMY DOBRÉE
IRVIN EHRENPREIS
ARTHUR FRIEDMAN
DONALD J. GREENE
JEAN H. HAGSTRUM
LEO HUGHES
RICHARD FOSTER JONES
WILLIAM R. KEAST
GWIN J. KOLB
LOUIS A. LANDA
MAYNARD MACK
DOUGALD MAC MILLAN
JOHN ROBERT MOORE
ERNEST CAMPBELL MOSSNER
FREDERICK A. POTTLE
RICARDO QUINTANA
GEORGE SHERBURN
JAMES SUTHERLAND
GEOFFREY TILLOTSON
AUBREY L. WILLIAMS
GEORGE WILLIAMS
STUART WILSON
W. K. WIMSATT, JR.

Restoration and Eighteenth-Century Literature

ESSAYS IN HONOR OF
ALAN DUGALD McKILLOP

PUBLISHED FOR

WILLIAM MARSH RICE UNIVERSITY

BY

THE UNIVERSITY OF CHICAGO PRESS

Standard Book Number: 226-09215-1
Library of Congress Catalog Card Number: 63-18853

THE UNIVERSITY OF CHICAGO PRESS, CHICAGO 60637
The University of Chicago Press, Ltd., London

ALAN DUGALD MCKILLOP

Contents

x   *Contents*

GEORGE WILLIAMS

Alan Dugald McKillop

EVERY MAN lives in several worlds simultaneously. Masefield doubtless had this truth in mind when he cast a cold eye on biographers who reduce the "golden instants and bright days" of a man's life to mere "lists of dates and facts." Alan Dugald McKillop's life has encompassed at least three worlds (personal, professorial, and scholarly) that even the biographer-in-brief must recognize.

The Personal World. All four of McKillop's grandparents were born on the Scottish Isle of Arran, in the Firth of Clyde; and both his parents, though born in Canada, bore thoroughly Scottish names: Dugald McKenzie McKillop and Catherine Jane McKinnon. This Dugald McKillop, Senior, wrote a history of the emigration and the settlement in Megantic County, Quebec, by the group of Arran Islanders that included his parents. Early in their married life, the older McKillops moved to Lynn, Massachusetts, where Alan Dugald was born 24 May 1892. He himself has always been proud of being derived one hundred per cent out of Scotland. His rich imitations of Scottish brogue and Lowland dialect and his readings of Burns have been a delight to those privileged to hear them.

McKillop attended the public schools of Lynn and was graduated, in 1909, from the Lynn Classical High School. He has said that he feels especially grateful for the training in languages that he received there. He matriculated at Harvard in the autumn of 1909, was elected to Phi Beta Kappa in 1912, and was graduated *summa cum laude* in 1913. His undergraduate major was philosophy; and he went on to receive his master's degree in philosophy at Harvard in 1914. But, as with some other graduate students before and since, money problems began to plague him, and he took time out from his studies to better his finances by teaching.

One of the places where he taught was the University of Illinois. Here he had the good fortune to meet Miss Lorel Pruitt, from Edin-

GEORGE WILLIAMS is Professor of English at Rice University.

1

burg, Indiana, who was working on her master's degree in English. The acquaintanceship grew into an engagement, and the two were married in Edinburg on 27 August 1921.

Meanwhile, McKillop had switched his scholarly interests from philosophy to English and had returned to Harvard (1916–17, 1919–20) to complete work on his doctorate in his new field. He received the degree in June 1920; and the following September he came to what was then the Rice Institute as an instructor in English.

Among his friends, Alan McKillop is known today as a superb mimic and story teller, as a ready and genial wit—one who can sometimes be devastating with an apt quotation, or parody of a quotation, that springs instantly from the prodigious storehouse of his memory. He reminds his friends a little of a Scottish Dr. Johnson (if such a combination is conceivable!)—the same wide learning, the drollery, the vigor, the common sense, but not the prejudices and the insularity. In what sometimes seems to be a science-dominated world, the personality of this man of letters has always elicited profound respect from the most hard-bitten of scientists, and it has been a bulwark of strength for the humanities at Rice for over forty years.

The Professorial World. Having received his master's degree at Harvard, McKillop became a full-fledged instructor in English at Colby College, Maine, the same year (1914) and retained this position till 1916. Then, after a year of further study at Harvard, he became an instructor in English at Trinity College, Hartford, Connecticut, for a year (1917–18). Next, he was an instructor in English at the University of Illinois for a year (1918–19). On receiving his doctor's degree in English at Harvard in 1920, he accepted an instructorship at the Rice Institute and went there in September 1920. He has been a member of the Rice faculty ever since—as an instructor until 1924, an assistant professor from 1924 to 1930, a professor from 1930 to 1962, and a Trustee Distinguished Professor since 1962.

The chairman of the English Department when McKillop arrived at Rice was Stockton Axson; but, as the years passed, Professor Axson's health began to fail, with the result that McKillop had frequently to act as chairman of the department. When Axson died in 1935, McKillop became chairman, and he retained that position until mandatory relinquishment at the age of sixty-five, in 1957.

He has served as a visiting professor on summer faculties at many other institutions: University of Chicago, 1925, 1961; Northwestern University, 1926; University of Texas, 1930, 1931, 1948; Johns Hopkins University, 1932, 1940; University of Minnesota, 1937, 1939, 1949; Harvard University, 1941, 1952; Indiana University, 1947; University of Colorado, 1950; Columbia University, 1962; Fellow of Newberry Library, 1955.

The subjects he has taught at Rice University have reflected not only his wide interests but also his versatility as a scholar. From his very first year at Rice, he has taught a course in the English novel; and for nearly thirty years he taught the survey course in English literature. In addition, he has regularly taught various courses in eighteenth-century English literature and, until the Second World War, a graduate course in Chaucer as well. On at least one occasion, he taught Shakespeare for a year, a course in American literature, and one in expository writing. He is one of those rare and ideal professors who enjoy both research and teaching. He actually gets pleasure out of grading student papers!

McKillop has been called on to give many public lectures at Rice, and these have been printed in the *Rice Pamphlet*. He has often read papers before the Rice Historical Society and the Houston Philosophical Society. He has been president of the Rice Historical Society, the Houston Philosophical Society, and the local chapters of the American Association of University Professors and Phi Beta Kappa. He has also served as president of the South-Central Modern Language Association (1950–51) and is an elected member of both the Texas Philosophical Society and the Texas Institute of Letters.

The Scholarly World. McKillop wrote his doctoral dissertation on the Spasmodic School of nineteenth-century poets, and his first published article concerned Philip James Bailey (author of *Festus*) and Dante Gabriel Rossetti. His next published article, however, dropped back to very early English literature. It appeared in the *Journal of English and Germanic Philology*, whose editors were apparently unusually well impressed, for they insisted that McKillop review books on Old English for some years thereafter, even though his interests had by then turned definitely toward much later periods of English literature.

Discounting this early flirtation with Old English, we might say, speaking very generally, that McKillop's first period of scholarship was a Collins-Smollett Period. Between 1922 and 1930, he published five items directly concerned with Collins (as well as several articles or reviews in which Collins figured) and four items on Smollett. Of course, his interest in Collins and Smollett did not cease at this time; he returned to them, and especially to Collins, repeatedly in later years. Moreover, even this Collins-Smollett Period was dotted with scattered writing on miscellaneous subjects.

As a matter of fact, the next period (which may be called the Richardson Period) was heralded as early as 1925 by an article on Richardson's influence on Young, and in 1929 by a review of a scholarly book on Richardson. Indeed, it was McKillop's projected research on Richardson that influenced the Guggenheim Foundation to grant him a fellowship, in 1928, for the express purpose of studying Richardson in the libraries of England. This period was crowned, in 1936, by the book *Samuel Richardson, Printer and Novelist*. Again, it must not be inferred that McKillop's involvement with Richardsonian problems lapsed with the publication of this work; but he did thenceforth divert his major activities toward other areas of scholarship.

The Thomson Period began in the late 1930's. The first book-length work of this period, *The Background of Thomson's Seasons*, appeared in 1942. Actually, the Thomson Period has not yet ended, for McKillop has yielded again and again, in articles, monographs, editorial comment, and books, to the fascination of his fellow Scotsman.

Nevertheless, the years since 1946 have seen a strong development of McKillop's interest in English prose fiction; and thus they might be said, with reservations, to constitute the Period of English Fiction. Though most of the earlier interests have been kept very much alive during these years, the book *The Early Masters of English Fiction* (1956) may well be remembered as the climactic achievement of this period.

On the other hand, every decade of McKillop's career since 1930 has been filled with so many outstanding scholarly achievements that singling out for special mention any one work in any one decade may give a false impression of his scholarly contributions as a whole. All his working life as a scholar, he has been making major contributions to scholarship. Moreover, his learning has "burned brightlier," if that were possible, in his later years than in his truly "flowering youth-time." For forty years, the light of his mind has played over English literature and has illuminated it with a brilliance rarely equaled in our time. The year in which this book appears in his honor finds him still as vigorous, alert, and intellectually active as ever; and the years ahead promise to add even greater luster to a name already great in scholarship.

RICHARD FOSTER JONES

The Rhetoric of Science in England of the Mid-Seventeenth Century

W HEN THE STATUTES of the Royal Society were drawn up some two years after its establishment, they included one which demanded that all reports of experiments presented to the society should be free of all "Prefaces, Apologies or Rhetorical Flourishes." In his history of the society published a few years later, Thomas Sprat, after expatiating upon the evils of rhetorical writing in general, with specific references to "this vicious abundance of *Phrase*, this trick of *Metaphor*, this volubility of *Tongue*," stated that the society had resolved to eschew all "amplifications, digressions, and swellings of style," and so "exacted from all . . . members, a close, naked, natural way of speaking," a clear, easy, plain style, in which the words employed should be those of artisans, farmers, and merchants rather than of scholars.[1] If there was any basis for this official requirement, some members must have been guilty of writing in a rhetorical and learned manner. If so, who were they? The present study attempts to answer that question.

In studying the rise of the scientific movement in seventeenth-century England, one can hardly fail to notice that the movement comprised two currents of thought, which, though alike in some particulars, differed widely in others: the mechanical philosophy and the experimental philosophy.[2] The mechanical philosophy asserted that all

RICHARD FOSTER JONES is Professor Emeritus of English at Stanford University.

[1] *The History of the Royal-Society of London for the Improving of Natural Knowledge* (1667), pp. 111–13.

[2] These differences will be described later in this article. Most of them were clearly pointed out by Robert Boyle, who was a thoroughgoing Baconian, or experimental philosopher, though he supported the mechanical philosophy as a hypothesis, frequently followed it in explaining natural phenomena, and strongly advanced it against the salt, sulphur, and mercury of the chemists. See R. F. Jones, *Ancients and Moderns* (2d ed., 1961), pp. 166–69, 185–91.

natural phenomena are due to matter and motion and that matter consists of minute parts, sometimes called particles, sometimes corpuscles, but generally atoms. In the seventeenth century, this theory was greatly stimulated by a revival of Greek atomic science, especially that of Democritus as presented in Jean Chrysostome Magnen's *Democritus Reviviscens*, published in Italy in 1646, and that of Epicurus as discussed by Pierre Gassendi in *Syntagma Phylosophiae Epicuri*, which appeared in France in 1649. Though there were differences, some of them important, between the various atomists,[3] they all participated in the belief that explanations of natural phenomena must be based on the size, shape, and motion of atoms. Whereas the Baconians experimented in order to find an explanation, the atomists experimented and observed in order to apply or verify an explanation. It was their task to observe carefully the nature of the phenomenon to be explained and then to show how atoms of a certain size and a certain shape, moving in a certain way, would produce that phenomenon. For this reason, the convincing power of their explanation depended as much upon the vividness as upon the accuracy with which they could visualize the action of the atoms. A few examples will make this clear.

In what is perhaps the most ambitious English atomic treatise of the period, and one heavily indebted to Gassendi, Dr. Walter Charleton, Dryden's friend, explains the coagulation of milk:

Hither also may we most congruously referr the Coagulation of milk, upon the injection of Rennet, Vinegre, juice of Limons, and the like Acid things. For, the Hamous [possessed of hooks] and invisicating [snaring] Atoms, whereof the Acid is mostly composed, meeting with the Ramous [branching like a plant] and Grosser particles of the milk, which constitute the Caseous and Butyrous parts thereof; instantly fasten upon them with their hooks, connect them, and so impeding their fluiditie, change their lax and moveable contexture into a close and immoveable or Firme; while the more exile and smooth particles of the milk, whereof the serum or whey is composed, escape those Entanglings and conserve their native Fluidity. This may be confirmed from hence; that whenever the Cheese, or Butter made of the Coagulation, is held to the fire, they recover their former Fluidity; because the tenacious particles of the Acid are disintangled and interrupted by the sphærical and superlatively agile Atoms of fire.

In another passage he explains how water, which is opposed to heat, will, when poured upon lime, produce it.

---

[3] Two of the most common had to do with the existence of vacuums and the infinite divisibility of atoms. Descartes, who did more than anyone to establish the mechanical hypothesis, held to the idea of a plenum, which made it necessary for him to postulate an all-embracing ether. Whereas the atomists generally considered light to be composed of atoms, Descartes held it to be motion in the ether.

... the Aqueous Humidity of the Lime-stone is indeed wholly evaporated by fire in its calcination; but yet the Pingous, or Unctuous for the most part remains, so that its Atoms of Fire lye still blended and incarcerated therein: and when those expede themselves, and by degrees expire into the ambient aer, if they be impeded and repelled by water affused, they recoyle upon the grumous masses of the Lime, and by the Circumobsistence [encompassing resistance] of the Humidity, become more congregated; and so upon the uniting of their forces make way for the Exsilition of the other Atoms of Fire, which otherwise could not have attained their liberty but slowly and by succession one after another. So that all the Atoms of Fire contained in the Lime, issuing forth together, they break through the water, calefie it, and make it bubble or boyle up; the calefied parts thereof being yet cohærunt to the uncalified.[4]

Certainly the diction employed in these two quotations is hardly that of "Artizans, Countrymen, and Merchants," but more of that anon. It is quite apparent that the atoms are the protagonists in the drama of nature, and sometimes they seem to act as rationally as human actors.[5] Sir Kenelm Digby, in attempting to explain the process by which the sun draws mists from the earth, describes what happens when the atoms of fire, which constitute its beams, strike the globe:

... he [the sun] shooting his little darts of fire, in multitudes, and in continued streames, from his owne center, against the Python the earth we live on; they do there overtake one an other, and cause some degree of heate as farre as they sinke in. But not being able (by reasons of their great expansion in their long iorney) to conuert it into their owne nature and sett it on fire, (which requireth a high degree of condensation of the beames) they do but pierce and diuide it very subtilely, and cutt some of the outward partes of it into extreme little atomes. Vnto which they sticking very close, and being in a manner incorporated with them (by reason of the moisture that is in them) they do in their rebound back from the earth carry them along with them; like a ball that struck against a moist wall, doth, in its returne from it, bring backe some of the mortar sticking upon it. For the distance of the earth from the sunne, is not the vtmost periode of these nimble bodies flight; so that, when by this solide body they are stopped in their course forwardes on, they leape backe from it, and carry some litle partes of it with them: some of them, a little farther; some of them, a shorter iorney; according as their littlenesse and rarity make them fitt to ascend.[6]

---

[4] *Physiologica Epicuro-Gassendo-Charltoniana* (1654), pp. 320–21, 293–315.

[5] Speaking of the fantasms that the outside world leaves in the imagination, Sir Kenelm Digby says, "... our braine is but the playhouse and scene, where all these faery maskes are acted." *Two Treatises. In the one of which, the nature of bodies is looked into; in the other, the nature of mans soule* (1644), p. 416.

[6] *Ibid.*, pp. 76–77. For another effort to visualize the atomic process, see Robert Boyle's explanation of the rarefaction of bodies by heat (*Works*, ed. T. Birch [1744], I, 113–16). Boyle was more of an experimental than a mechanical philosopher, but when he described atomic processes, he wrote like an atomist.

Imaginative visualization has throughout the ages played no inconsiderable part in the development of scientific theory, but probably never to such an extent as it did in the third quarter of the seventeenth century, when it was in fact the whole theory.[7] For this reason, the age clearly recognized the great importance of the imagination to science, and it was not until the romantic revival got under way that we find such homage paid to that mental power.[8] Charleton speaks of the imagination with great enthusiasm. If we keep in mind the selections quoted from him, we can well understand his calling his imagination "my laboratory." Though, like his contemporaries, he believed that the intellect should rule the fancy, as the imagination was sometimes called, he places the latter on the same level with reason, calling both instruments of the intellect, if either of which is defective, knowledge is false. He insists that he can "speculate," that is, think intently on, nothing

without the help of my imagination; . . . whatever I can think upon, comes to my mind in the dresse of Magnitude, Figure, Colour, and other the like conditions of Matter. . . . I alwaies found my Phansy so unseparably conjoined to my Intellect as if they were both one and the same Faculty. Nor am I yet able to distinguish betwixt my Imagination and Intellection.

He calls the imagination "the noblest part of the sensitive soul"[9] and emphatically asserts that he is very "apt to judge the Imagination to be the Escurial or imperial palace of the Rational Soul."[10]

[7] In arguing for the scientific nature of the magnetic cure of wounds (a hallucination that found strong support among the atomists), against those who superstitiously considered it a magic phenomenon, he cinches his argument with this statement: "what is more, it forestalls not the imagination," that is, it can be visualized. See his translation of J. B. van Helmont's *A Ternary of Paradoxes* (1650), p. 9. In *The Vanity of Dogmatizing* (1661), a work that makes extensive use of the mechanical philosophy, Joseph Glanvill says that when "the objects of thought are purely *material*, the judgment is made by the Imagination" (p. 97). Needless to say, the condition is fully met in atomic explanations.

[8] From a different point of view, of course, though there may have been some subterranean connection between the two attitudes via John Locke. See Ernest L. Tuveson, *The Imagination as a Means of Grace: Locke and the Aesthetics of Romanticism* (1960).

[9] A similar sentiment is expressed by the chemical atomist Samuel Boulton, who calls the imagination "the hand-maid of the soul" (*Medicina Magica Tamen Physica* [1656], p. 5).

[10] *The Darkness of Atheism* (1652), p. 20; *Natural History of the Passions* (1672), pp. 48, 65; *Immortality of the Human Soul* (1657), pp. 63–65; *ibid.,* pp. 66–67; *Natural History of the Passions,* pp. 61–64. In fact, Charleton appears to think that imagination incites visualization, when after visualizing the conduct of atoms in electric attraction, he adds, "the Itch of Phancy being soonest allayed by the liberty of ones singular Conjecture" (*Physiologia,* pp. 343–46).

Digby also emphasizes the importance of the imagination, even equating it with reason. The fact that quantity is infinitely divisible, he says, is "evident to him who shall consider with a profound imagination" the nature of quantity.[11] Indeed, the atomists frequently appear to mean imagination when they use the word reason. Robert Hooke was an enthusiastic experimental philosopher, but he is temporarily speaking as a mechanical one when he says that in drawing axioms from experiments one should use his imagination in order to trace the secret operations of nature in such phenomena as gravity and the loadstone.[12]

The age was quite aware of the tremendous part played by the faculty in atomic science, so much so, indeed, that an attempt was made to attribute to it some of the blame for the atheistic thought of the day. The fact that some of the Greek atomists believed that atoms had not been created but had always existed, that their motion was inherent, and that all things in the great void of the world had been formed by the accidental combining of atoms, together with the fact that Epicurus had banished the gods from the human world, repelled the Christian scientists of the day. Perhaps of even more influence on the thought of the times was the intractable dualism that Descartes had established with a material body and an immaterial soul. Few atomic scientists were content to express their ideas without attempting to explain the relationship between the two, but in most cases they were forced to declare that the problem had to be solved by faith rather than by intellect.[13] Not so Hobbes. He boldly declared that there was no such thing as an immaterial substance, which the soul had been considered, and the fat was in the fire. Seth Ward, Savilian Professor of Astronomy at Oxford and one of many who broke a lance against Hobbes in behalf of an immaterial soul, accused the philosopher of being a materialistic slave to his imagination. The trouble with Hobbes, says Ward, is his inability to distinguish between "imagination and Intellectual comprehension." In general, men can think of God and the angels in terms of their spiritual substance, but the Malmesbury philosopher can think of the latter only by images of "beautiful winged aery bodies." In short, he can think of nothing that his imagination does not clothe with material features. Ward was an

11 *Two Treatises*, pp. 90–91; *Of the Sympathetic Powder* (1669), p. 193. The latter treatise first appeared in 1658 under the title *A Late Discourse Touching the Cure of Wounds by the Powder of Sympathy*.

12 *Posthumous Works* (1705), pp. 44–45.

13 "For it is canonical, that no immaterial can Operate upon a Material, Physically; the inexplicable activity of the Rational Soul upon the body by the mediation of spirits and that of Angelical essences excepted" (Charleton, *Physiologia*, p. 235).

atomist as far as the material world was concerned, but he would not be a slave to the "shaping power" of his imagination.[14]

Even the most dedicated follower of the mechanical philosophy did not believe that his particular picture of the actions of atoms presented in every respect an accurate explanation of the phenomenon under investigation. The atomist was content if it was reasonably close to the truth. In his mind, the really important requirement of an explanation was that it employ material causation.[15] In the past, the habit of explaining phenomena, especially those of a more mysterious nature, by such terms as antipathy, sympathy, and occult qualities, mere verbalism which lulled ignorance rather than satisfying true scientific curiosity, was widespread.[16] The confidence of the mechanical philosophers rested on the corporeal nature of their explanations. Details were of minor consideration. Listen to Charleton:

We are *Men,* i.e. *Moles;* whose week and narrow Opticks are accommodated only to the inspection of the *exterior* and *low* parts of *Nature,* not perspicacious enough to penetrate and transfix her *interior* and *abstruse* Excellencies: nor can we speculate her glorious beauties in the direct and incident line of *Essences* and *Formal Causes,* but in the refracted and reflected one of *Effects;* nor that, without so much of obscurity, as leaves a manifest incertitude in our Apprehensions, and restrains our ambition of intimate and *apodictical Science,* to the humble and darksome region of mere superficial *Conjecture.* Such being the condition of our imperfect Intellectuals; when we cannot explore the profound recesses, and call forth the *Formal Properties* of some Natures, but find our disquisitive Faculties terminated in the some *Apparences,* or Effects of them: it can be no derogation to the dignity of *Humanity,* for as to rest contented, nay thankful to the *Bounty* of our *Creator,* that we are able to erect verisimilous Conjectures concerning their Causation, and to establish such rational Apprehensions or Notions thereupon, as may, without any incongruity, be laudably accommodated to the proba-

---

[14] *A Philosophicall Essay* (1652), p. 54. In his *Vanity of Dogmatizing* (as previously stated, a treatise in large part inspired by the mechanical philosophy), Joseph Glanvill finds similar fault with the use of the imagination in thinking about immaterial subjects (see especially chap. x). What Charleton says about his inability to think without imaginative images, quoted above, furnishes some support to Ward's charge against Hobbes.

[15] "Though peraduenture we shall not absolutely convince that euery effect is done iust as we sett it downe in euery particular, and that it may not as well be done by some other disposing of parts, vnder the same generall scope: for it is enough for our turne if we shew that such effects may be performed by corporeall agents, working as other bodies do; without confining ourselues to an exactnesse in euery linke of the long chaine that must be wound vp in the performance of them" (Digby, *Two Treatises,* pp. 203–4; see also pp. 322, 326–27, 341).

[16] Digby speaks scornfully of "that gentle and obedient Philosophy of Qualities" (*ibid.,* p. 341).

ble solution of other consimilar Effects, when we are required to yeild an account of the manner of their arise from their proper originals.[17]

We should consider this interpretation of scientific accuracy rather inadequate, if we did not realize that it was the corporeal nature, and not the exactness, of an explanation that was their chief objective. What is more to the point as far as this article is concerned, the imagination was thus given a wide liberty in its visualization.[18]

If in their calmer moments the mechanical philosophers realized that their visualizations were not likely to be circumstantially accurate, the realization must have made them all the more eager to make their pictures as vivid and effective as possible. The only limit their imagination had to observe was corporeality and the analogies and examples furnished by the mechanical actions of gross matter apparent to the senses. Not only, however, were the atomists remarkably free in their visualizations; they were also animated by a delightful feeling of getting inside nature. Again and again we find them expatiating on the labyrinths of nature, the innermost recesses forever closed to sensuous observation. Thomas Baker, a mathematician, expresses well this conception and, at the same time, one reason for the lack of a feeling of certitude regarding details.

There is nothing more common in nature, than matter and motion, or more easily distinguisht, but . . . if we speak of subtle matter and *intestine* motion, they escape the nicest scrutiny of Sense: And yet these are the secret Springs of most of the operations of nature, and as for gross matter and visible motion, they are rather of mechanical consideration. A Philosopher's business is to trace Nature in her inward Recesses and Latent motions, and how hid these are, is best known to those, who are most conversant in Philosophical Enquiries: Such men by looking deep [visualizing] into her and observing her in all her windings and mazes, find matter enough for Wonder, and reason to adore the Wisdom of God, but at the same time only meet with mortification to their own Wisdom and are forc'd to confess that the ways of Nature like those of God, are past Man's finding out.[19]

[17] *Physiologia*, pp. 50–51. In the conclusion of his treatise, he expresses the hope that he has led his readers to "the *Knowledge* of *Truth*, or what is so like the *truth* as to satisfy your Curiosity as fully." (See also pp. 127–28.)

[18] John Evelyn was an experimental philosopher, but at times he employed atomic explanations, as in *Fumifugium;* his first scientific publication was on atomism, and in it he presents a revealing and, naturally, a somewhat rhetorical picture of the imagination of the atomists: "It is very true, that a pregnant and mechanick imagination may in such a multifarious variety of some *variegated Achates,* and extravagantly veined *marbles,* fansie many pretty, and even wonderful things" (*An Essay on the First Book of T. Lucretius Carus De Rerum Natura. Interpreted and Made English Verse* [1656], pp. 173–74).

[19] *Reflections upon Learning* (1699), p. 76. The book must have been written not later than 1689, because Baker died in that year. We find the mechanical philosophers, far

But in spite of this last-quoted sentence, the spirit of the visualizers was free, happy, and confident; and this spirit, supported by the very nature of their scientific explanations, could find expression only in a rhetorical style. The effort to make their pictures clear placed a premium upon similitudes, examples, and analogies, while the desire to make them interesting and effective stimulated the use of metaphors. Charleton especially appreciated the value of the former. He remarks upon "the proper and significant Termes, illustrate with apposite Similes and prægnant Examples" of Descartes's discussion of vision; and after citing evidence for a theory of his own, he adds, "yet shall we further illustrate the same by certain Analogies and Similitudes."[20] Charleton emphasized the corporeal element in his idea of causation, and thus he felt the need to draw upon visible mechanical operations to explain invisible processes, such, for example, as the way in which atoms act in magnetic attraction. As usual in his explanations, he is drawn unerringly to a similitude:

Notwithstanding the perspicuity of these Arguments, we shall not supererogate, to heighten the lustre of so desirable a Truth, by the vernish of

---

more than the experimental, expressing belief in the power and wisdom of God, a belief fostered by their atomic insight into the innermost construction and workings of nature. Charleton calls God "the great Exemplar of all Mechanicks" (*Darkness of Atheism*, p. 111).

[20] *Physiologia*, pp. 152, 346. Though the very nature of atomic explanations calls for comparisons in making clear unseen processes, Charleton employs a rhetorical figure to introduce them, even when by his own word they are not necessary. In answering the question whether God created the world for fools or wise men, Charleton says, in his usual Latinistic manner, "The satisfactory force of this solution naturely perpended, it can be reputed neither incogitancy nor precipitation in me to omit the prolix appropriation of those pertinent *similitudes;* that the wary husbandman doth cultivate and prepare his field, as well for the fertility of Pulse, as Wheat; that the most skilfull Gardiner provides room in his nursery for the sprouting wild degenerous, and barren plants, as well as for the geniculation of wholesome, generous and fruitful; that Princes account Plebeians, as well as Nobles, members of their Commonwealth: and that *Apelles* prepared his Tables as well to receive the black of shadowing, as the finer touches of his Pencill, and the brighter gradualities of Colours, in emulation of the life. And this, not only because I conceive the objection already more than refuted, and therefore all that can be superadded may sound as nothing to the purpose: but chiefly because I understand, that the logick of *similes*, or the way of probation by *Comparatives*, is at best but *Analogisme;* and therefore inconsistent with my assumption of declining all but *Demonstrations*, or *Reasons* equally convictive." But he got them in just the same. See *Darkness of Atheism*, p. 90.

In another case, he adopts a different tack. In speaking of the repulsion that animals feel for some objects, he says, "though the Reasons and Manner of such *Fugation*, so far forth as concerns Animals, may be collected from our former Discourses of the Gratefulness and Offensiveness of Sensible Objects; yet shall we here farther illustrate the same by certain *Analogies* and *Similitudes*" (*Physiologia*, p. 346; see also p. 50). He also perceived that the power of similitudes could be used for deception. In one of his arguments he says he has no intention "by specious similitudes to impost upon the weaker credulities of the illiterate." See his translation of van Helmont's *A Ternary of Paradoxes*, p. 66.

a convenient and prægnant Simile, or two. If we attentively observe a *Chameleon* catching Gnats and other small Flyes in the Aer, for his food; we shall see him dart out a long and slender tongue, with a small recurvation at the tip, and birdlimed with a certain tenacious and inviscating moisture, wherewith, in a trice, laying hold of a fly, at some distance from his mouth, he conveys the same into it with such cleanly speed, as exceeds the Legerdemane of our cunningest Juglers, and may have been the cheif occasion of that popular Error, *that he lives merely upon Aer.* And when we see a peice of Amber, Jet, hard Wax, or other Electrique, after sufficient friction, to attract straws, shavings of wood, quils, and other festucous bodies of the same lightness, objected within the orbe of their Alliciency; and that with a cleanly and quick motion: Why should we not conceive, that this Electricity or Attraction may hold a very neer Analogy to that attraction of Gnats, by the exerted and nimbly retracted tongue of a Chamæleon. For . . . it is not improbable, that the Attraction of all Electriques is performed by the mediation of swarms of subtle Emanations, or Continued Rayes of exile particles, comparative to so many Chamæleons Tongues; which through the whole Sphere of their Virtue, in various points mutually intersecting, or decussating, and more especially toward their Extreams, doe not only insinuate themselves into the pores of those small and light festucous bodies occurrent, but lay hold upon several insensible Asperities in their superficies, and then returning (by way of *Retraction*) back to the Original or Source, bring them along in their twined Arms, and so long hold them fast in their Complicate embraces, as the warmth and radical Diffusion, excited by affriction, lasteth.[21]

The first sentence of this quotation, which speaks of heightening "the lustre of so desirable a Truth, by the vernish [varnish] of a convenient and prægnant Simile," indicates that Charleton is as much interested in the rhetorical effects of his similitudes as in their expository value, an attitude also expressed in his *Discourse Concerning the Wits of Men,* written in 1664. The last line shows how atomic narration naturally falls into metaphorical expressions, which seem almost necessary for a satisfactory completion of the picture and which here, as in innumerable other places, humanize the atoms. Of all rhetorical figures, metaphors were the most suspect in the seventeenth century, and much could be written about them. But it suffices to say that the atomists were quite fond of them.[22]

21 See *Physiologia*, pp. 343–46, which contain, besides the passage quoted above, a very clear description of the mechanical philosophy with its emphasis on materiality.

22 In *Darkness of Atheism*, p. 114, Charleton defended the use of metaphors. Thomas Hobbes furnishes a glaring exception to the association of a rhetorical style with the mechanical philosophers. He both preached and practiced verbal economy and precision and was especially severe in his criticism of metaphors. Though the present writer entertains some ideas regarding this exception, he is not now prepared to discuss the problem.

Digby felt a great respect for metaphors, as well as for rhetoric in general. The latter, he says, teaches how to "dispose" the arguments that logic furnishes and the words that grammar supplies for the purpose of persuasion. "Hence grow those encreases by metaphors, hyperboles, and other tropes and figures: hence those feruors by interrogation, exclamation, apostrophes, and the like; which when they are fitly placed, they carry the Auditor euen against his will." In using the word "encreases" with no hint of condemnation, he seems to be recommending the verbal superfluity that the Royal Society later condemned. Both he and Charleton, as well as other atomists like Nathaniel Highmore, strew their works with metaphors.[23] Charleton says, "By *Imagination* . . . we conceive some Similitude in objects really unlike, and pleasantly confound them in discourse: Which by its unexpected *Fineness* and allusion, surprising the hearer, renders him less curious of the truth of what is said." These words do not represent opposition to the use of rhetoric on the part of the atomists, for as long as they kept within the wide limits of corporeality, they felt that the readers need not consider their visualizations circumstantially accurate. In short, there was no exact truth in their explanations to be curious about. "This is very evident," he continues, "in the use of Similes, Metaphors, Allegories, and other Tropes and Figures of Rhetorick; which are therefore called Ornaments of speech, serving rather for plausability than for demonstration," a succinct statement of the express purpose of their atomic descriptions. In his scientific writings Digby freely employs metaphors. For example, in his description of the way in which the sun draws mists from the earth, which has been quoted above, the sun is Apollo shooting darts at the Python, the earth, and a little later the atoms from the sun that are carried by the detached atoms of earth are "the litle horsemen which rode vpon them."[24] Elsewhere atoms are ushers and cavaliers.[25]

[23] Dr. Highmore, a friend of Robert Boyle (see Boyle's *Works*, ed. Birch, I, 62, 67, 221) applied atomic explanations to biological phenomena. In tracing the development of a chick from its life in the egg to that outside, he says, "And now the Chick is perfectly fitted to come abroad, and seek his own provision; and indeed it is almost time, having spent his patrimony, he must seek other food" (*The History of Generation* [1651], p. 79). At the beginning of his treatise, Highmore lists and discusses what he considered nine fundamental laws of nature atomically interpreted.

[24] See Charleton, *A Brief Discourse Concerning the Wits of Men*, p. 20, and Digby, *Two Treatises*, pp. 76–78.

[25] "These atomes then are like Cavaliers, mounted on winged Coursers; who ride on still till the Sun, setting, takes them from their Pegasus and leaves them unmounted" (Digby, *Of the Sympathetic Powder*, p. 152). Can a metaphor be carried farther than Digby carries the following one in showing that when two bodies meet, both are affected: ". . . each of them beare before them some little quantity of a rarer body immediately ioyned vnto them: and consequently these more rare bodies must be the first to feele the power of the dense bodies and to receiue impressions from their motions; each of them, by the opposited rare body, which like an huissier [usher] goeth

Charleton is even more given to metaphors, for he came under the influence of Sir Thomas Browne, who, he asserted, together with Sir Francis Bacon, purified the English language and made it the equal of Latin.[26] Echoes of Browne's manner of expression are too audible in Charleton's to be considered accidental.[27] Sir Thomas exerted a subsidiary influence on the style of the atomists, but his own relation to the scientific movement needs to be worked out in more detail.[28] We see his influence on Charleton, however, not only in the use of tropes but also in such stylistic characteristics as balance, antithesis, and the condensation of terse metaphorical expressions, exemplified by "Plato himself, as lighting the tapor for us," and "the severe and præcise Dialect of truth."[29] But there are plenty of metaphors in him that

---

before to make way for his following master that obligeth him to this service. . . . Now when these rare vshers haue struggled a while like the first lightly armed rankes of two armies in the interiacent field between their maine battalies, that follow them close att the heeles; they must att the length yield, when they are ouerborne by a greater weight then they can sustaine; and then they recoyle backe, as it were to saue themselves by getting in among the files of the dense bodies that drove them on; which not opening to admitt them, and yet they still flying violently from the mastering force that pursueth them; they presse so hard vpon what att the first pressed them on, as not withstanding their density and strength they force them to retire back" (*Two Treatises*, p. 140).

26 See the dedication to Lord Brouncker in his translation of van Helmont's *A Ternary of Paradoxes*.

27 Consider, for example, this sentence, marginally described as "A pertinent (though short) Panegyrick on the sense of Touching": ". . . had not the Eternal Providence endowed the Organs official to the recruit of mankind, with a most exquisite and delicate sense of Touching, the titillation whereof transports a man beyond the severity of his reason, and charmes him to the act of Carnality; doubtless, the Deluge had been spared for the First age had been the Last, and Humanity been lost in the grave, as well as innocence in the fall of our first Parents" (*Physiologia*, p. 249). Consider also his comment on some divines who conceive "it a pitch sublime enough for the most aspiring thoughts of man to mount up to the Apostles O Altitudo! and soberly becalming the distractions of their Reason, by the Laudanum of Faith" (*ibid.*, pp. 341–42).

In his translation of van Helmont's *Deliramenta Catarrhi* (1650), we frequently hear echoes of Browne, as on page 17: "If so great a mist of *ignorance* hath surrounded the world in things *manifest* and *obvious* to the observations of *sense:* what Cimmerian blindnesse may not be suspected, in the common theory of such things as lye more *deep* and *abstruse*, and therefore have their Causalities onely discernable by the opticks of the most acute Reason?" This also sounds like the *Vanity of Dogmatizing*, and indeed Glanvill was much indebted to both Browne and Charleton.

The Anti-Ciceronian style and that of the mechanical philosophers have so much in common (for instance, their love for metaphors and Latinisms) that the second may well be considered related to the first. The late Professor Morris Croll would have been on much firmer ground had he maintained that the stylistic attitude of the Royal Society, instead of being an offspring of Anti-Ciceronianism, was indeed hostile to it. A number of years ago the present writer suggested as much (see Jones *et al.*, *The Seventeenth Century* [1951], pp. 104–7).

28 Though Digby did not always approve of Browne (see his *Observations on Religio Medici* [1643]), there are expressions in his writings that remind us of the doctor, such as "by a multiplication beyond the skill of Arithmetick." See *Two Treatises*, pp. 448–50, for Brownesque features.

29 *Physiologia*, pp. 237, 317.

spring from his exuberant and artistic temperament, such as "those radiant Centinels of night, the Stars," and "the large Captain of the watry regiments, the Whale."[30] Lack of space forbids more long quotations, yet one may rest assured that at almost every point at which he dips into Charleton's text, he will find rich rhetorical expressions. We may, however, take the liberty of quoting one example of his style. He is speaking of the way in which a power within us properly guides and controls all bodily processes.

If the oversight and regency of but half so many different operations, as that immaterial Empress, which keeps her invisible Court somewhere within us, doth every minute, even when we are fast lockt in the narcotick arms of Morpheus, and all our thoughts keep holy day, order and effect, while she maintains the œconomy of the body; were charged upon the hands of our understanding, but for one houre: without question, the burden would prove insupportable, nor could either the skill or strength of our limited reason, in any measure responsible, suffice to the due administration of so large a Province.[31]

Nothing is more characteristic of the mechanical philosophy than the purpose assigned to scientific activity, which is consistently and emphatically declared to be the satisfying of intellectual curiosity. Never has pure science been so vigorously emphasized. Not often are utilitarian notes struck in the scientific discussions of the atomists. "From the passion of Admiration," says Charleton, "comes *Curiosity* or desire for Knowledge" and also "all natural philosophy," and he emphasizes the power which this intellectual hunger wields over man. To gain knowledge, he says in his characteristic language, Eve's will was turned "from its indifferencie, or æquilibration, to an Appetition, and so to the Actual Degustation of the Forbidden Fruit."[32] Intellectual curiosity, declares Digby, is the noblest trait of man's nature, and the satisfying of it gives keenest delight, for "what can more powerfully delight, or more nobly entertaine an vnderstanding soule, then the search and discouery of those workes of nature, which being in

---

[30] *Darkness of Atheism*, pp. 62, 65.

[31] *Ibid.*, pp. 122–23. A good example of Charleton's use of the rhetorical figure of amplification, employed with considerable gusto, is seen in his development of the theme of the many kinds of destruction to which man is subject: "the ravenous appetite of wild Beasts, the deleterious punctures of Serpents [snake bites], the conflagration of Lightning, the Contusion of Thunderbolts, the eruptions of Earth-quakes, the arsenical eructations of Minerals, the epidemick contagion of Pestilential Diseases, kindled either by Anomalous seasons, Tempests, or malignant impressions in the aer; the invasion of intestine infirmities, upon the civil war often breaking out between the Heterogeneities of his bloud, or a meeting of his Elements; and though he escape all these, yet doth the Palsie Hand of Time soon shake down his ounce of sand, and then turn him to be devoured by oblivion" (*ibid.*, p. 85).

[32] *Natural History of the Passions*, p. 88; *Physiologia*, pp. 5–6.

their effects so plainly exposed to our eyes, are in their causes so abstruse and hidden from our comprehension, as (through despaire of successe) they deterre most men from inquiring into them?" He goes even further and declares that one of the chief joys of heaven will be the complete knowledge of nature that we shall enjoy there.[33]

Robert Boyle, the most truly representative English scientist of the third quarter of the seventeenth century, in a treatise which stresses the utilitarian value of the experimental philosophy, is somewhat skeptical of the joy of pure science. The acquisition of the knowledge of nature, he says, costs so much, and the pleasure gained thereby is so impaired by "the disquieting Curiosity" produced by this knowledge, that he is forced to the Biblical conclusion that he who increases knowledge, increases sorrow.[34] The more one knows, the more he wishes to know, and thus he is kept in a perpetual state of mental hunger.

The scientific spirit of the atomists is essentially aristocratic. They write as gentlemen for gentlemen. They make their appeal to the more highly educated levels of mankind.[35] In sharp contrast to the Baconian scientists, they have something in common with the humanists of the preceding century. Though opposed to the principle of authority, they are by no means hostile to the ancients. Their science was indeed based upon the Greek atomists, and they respect Aristotle, though severe with his "sectators," or followers. Their love for rhetoric, though its principal source was the imaginative nature of their scientific thought, was quite congenial with the humanistic emphasis upon eloquence. Especially were the mechanical philosophers true children of the Renaissance in their diction. They wrote under the strong impulse to use words drawn from the classics, not only when native words were lacking, but also to be eloquent, to write as educated gentlemen should. We may say that the diction of this group of scientists, composed of such men as Charleton, Digby, and Highmore, together with that of Sir Thomas Browne, represents the climax of

---

33 *Two Treatises*, dedication; p. 340; pp. 449–50. This last sentiment was echoed loudly by William Brent, a Catholic barrister, who was influenced by Digby's atomic theories. He emphasizes the delight that the soul in heaven shall feel in understanding the cause of the tides and the power of the loadstone (*A Discourse upon the Nature of Eternitie* [1655], p. 80). What a relief from Baconian utilitarianism this attitude is!

34 *Some Considerations Touching the Usefulnesse of Experimental Philosophy. The First Tome* (1663), p. 110. Charleton asserts that the illiterate, who are content with the simple information furnished by their senses, are "free from the disquiet of that curiosity, which occasions our delusion" (*The Immortality of the Human Soul*, pp. 5–6).

35 Speaking of his first published work, Charleton says that he intended his words for none "but the leading part of learning, and chiefly those who have more then looked into the mysterious Temple of Æsculapius" and "that no *English*, how plain soever, could have driven their ample meaning into those skulls, which are so thick, as not to admit it in *Latine*" (see his translation of van Helmont's *Deliramenta Catarrhi*, preface).

that strong neologizing movement, which arising in earlier generations reached its climax in the exuberant Elizabethan age.[36] Charleton's neologizing propensity was so pronounced in the first work he
published that it called down criticism upon his head, to which he
replied that he "would leave to any *educated* [italics mine] man" the
decision as to whether van Helmont's work, which he was translating,
*"might not have suffered a grosse Eclipse, if drest in a meer-English
veil?* Whether it be a Crime in me to trace the footsteps of those
Worthies, who have infinitely both enriched and ennobled our Language, by admitting and naturalizing thousands of forraigne Words,"
a true Elizabethan sentiment.[37]

Since the reader has already experienced Charleton's vocabulary in
these quotations, it seems a work of supererogation to give more samples of it, but it is hard to refrain from citing such gems as the following causal clause, a simple idea enveloped in billowing verbal
clouds: ". . . because the subingression of its contiguous parts into the
loculaments of the next vicine aer, is only perexile."[38] And shorter
but equally irresistible expressions are tardigradous incession, deob-
turated, proratarctick, the humectation of glass by any liquor affused,
antinobilism, anfracuous, alexipharmacal, transpecificated, obnubi-
lated, pathognomonick, and thousands of others. The reader who sits
down to peruse his works without a copy of the *Shorter Oxford
English Dictionary* at one elbow and a Latin lexicon at the other will
arise a frustrated man, but the linguist should find rich food for
thought in his vocabulary. Is it any wonder that the experimental
philosophers should have preferred "the language of Artizans, Countrymen and Merchants before that of Wits or Scholars"?

To a lesser degree, but still unmistakably, Digby found satisfaction
in hard words. It is true that near the beginning of his *Two Treatises*,
he expresses the wish that his style be plain, easy, and devoid of scholastic terms, and he discusses at length two kinds of words. In one,

[36] See the present writer's *Triumph of the English Language* (1953), chap. vi.

[37] See the preface to his translation of van Helmont's *Deliramenta Catarrhi*.

[38] *Physiologia*, p. 48. The following is his comment on the famous Torrecellian experiment regarding the barometric vacuum in a tube, the end of which is submerged in
mercury: ". . . the proportion of Compression from Gravity in the Quicksilver, may be
so equalized to the Resistance from Gravity in the Aer, as that both may remain
in statu quo, without any sensible yeilding on either side. Hence comes it, that at the
æquipondium of these two Antagonists, the space in the Tube, detracted from the
Aggregate of minute Inanities disseminate in the aer, is so small as not to be commensu-
rated by sense; and at the cessation of the *Aequilibrium*, or succeeding superiority of
the encreased weight of the Quicksilver, the parts of the Aer being compelled thereby
to a farther retrocession and subingression; the space detracted from the Aggregate
of Dissiminate Vacuities in the aer, becomes larger and consequently sensible, above the
Quicksilver in the upper region of the Tube" (*Physiologia*, pp. 49–50).

"the words expresse the thinges properly and plainely, according to naturall conceptions that all people agree in making of them." The other kind is terms of art intelligible only in the restricted domains of the trades and professions. He appears to show a preference for the first, yet a little later he hedges somewhat by saying that "the scarcity of our language is such, in subjects removed from ordinary Conversation (though in others, I think none is more copious) as affordeth vs not apt words of our own to expresse significantly such notions as I must busy myself about in this discourse. Therefore I will presume to borrow them from the Latine Schoole, where there is much adoe about them." But why does he use the last word in such as phrase as "under the search or Cognizance of a prudent indagation" when the more familiar "investigation" would have served his turn? And why did he not use "sufficient" for "adequated," "vaulted roof" for "Concameration," "excessive" for "exuperant," "wetting" for "humecting," "agreeing" for "*Consentaneous*," and so on with many other words to be found in his writings? He used his borrowed terms no more for lack of familiar words than because they were proper for the aristocratic science that made its appeal to the intellect.

By way of summary we may say that the style of the atomists, or mechanical philosophers, is quite rhetorical. It is characterized by a superfluity of similitudes and metaphors, rendered desirable by the very nature of the atomists' scientific thinking and visualization. Two factors especially made for the vigor and freedom of their imaginative activity. Their spirits were raised high by the feeling that they were getting on the inside of nature, that they were penetrating its innermost recesses and throwing light upon what had always been dark. Their imaginations also seized upon the liberty offered them by the realization that their visualizations could not be circumstantially accurate. This freedom Digby well describes as "that liberty of ranging about."[39] The only restraint placed upon this liberty was that of corporeality or the necessity of following analogically the mechanical processes of gross, or visible, matter. And finally, the fact that their science was pure science and made its appeal to the mind incited them to adopt a diction appropriate thereunto.

The experimental philosophers, true followers of Sir Francis Bacon, were in many respects diametrically opposed in attitudes and activi-

[39] In discussing the differences between the two treatises contained in the work of that name, the first devoted to material bodies and the second to the soul, Digby asserts that the difficulty of the latter subject and the nicety required by it made necessary a more succinct and concise style and "would not allow us that liberty of ranging about, as where we treated bodies." In a poem prefixed to *Two Treatises*, John Sargeant praises the beauty of Digby's "moving Rhetorick," especially "such enlightening Metaphors, as teach/What sense-deluded fancy could not reach."

ties to the mechanical philosophers.[40] They tended to view the imagination as a deceitful faculty, and they insisted upon accurate sensuous observation. They wished to become well acquainted with nature, with its outside rather than its inside. They emphasized experimentation, because it enlarged and enriched the field of observation. As Bacon said, nature best reveals herself when vexed. The ultimate goal of scientific activity, which Bacon presented to the experimenters and which they were sufficiently hypnotized by him to accept, was the accumulation, through a careful recording of observations and experiments, of an immense amount of data, which would enable the inductive thinkers of the future, of the rather far future, to arrive at a knowledge of the primary laws of nature, and all this not so much for the satisfying of intellectual curiosity as for the material benefits to which such knowledge might lead. The experimental philosophers were primarily utilitarian in their attitude toward science. Boyle emphasizes this fact in pointing out the difference between the two groups.[41] Furthermore, the Baconians were democratic, not aristocratic, in their attitude toward learning. Because they believed that those who were in closest and most constant contact with nature would know much about it, they paid considerable attention to the mechanic, the artisan, the farmer. They also believed that their own observations and experiments would furnish aid to the practical activities of their humble associates.[42]

The character itself of Baconian science gave rise to a definite stylistic creed, which found expression in the statutes of the Royal Society and was a few years later described in detail by Thomas Sprat in his history of the organization. The emphasis that the Baconians placed on accuracy in recording impressions made upon the senses forced them to advocate and employ a manner of expression that would, in their opinion, bring words and things as close together as

[40] One would not be guilty of much oversimplification if he described the experimental philosophy as a method of inquiry, and the mechanical as a method of explanation. In his address to the members of the Royal Society, prefixed to his *Scepsis Scientifica* (1665), Joseph Glanvill calls attention to their "experimental way of Enquiry, and mechanical Attempts for solving the Phænomena."

[41] See "A Poemial Essay," in *Certain Physiological Essays* (1661). In *Ancients and Moderns*, the present writer has traced in some detail the rise and development of the experimental philosophy in England. William Wotton, a true Baconian, maintained that "Knowledge not reduced to Pratice, when that is possible, is so far imperfect, that it loses its principal Use" (*Reflections upon Ancient and Modern Learning* [1694], pp. 247–48).

[42] This desire to make experimental discoveries useful to the worker is seen in the various agricultural treatises that, inspired partly by Bacon's *Sylva Sylvarum*, appeared with increasing frequency during the second and third quarters of the century. Agriculture was one of the chief interests of the young Royal Society. Cf. Dorothy Stimson, "Dr. Wilkins and the Royal Society," *J. Modern History*, III (1931), 552.

possible and thus give a true picture of material reality. They opposed the interposition of rhetorical devices and verbal superfluities between them and nature. They especially condemned metaphors, which call things by wrong names. In their diction, they insisted upon the use of simple, familiar words such as were employed by the working classes of society who were acquainted with nature, because these words afforded an unobstructed view of natural phenomena and also because they wished to reach the classes just mentioned with their writings.[43] Lastly, the experimental philosophers were utilitarians, and what utilitarian ever loved a rhetorician? Whatever the accuracy of the above analysis, we may be sure of the fact that the style upon which the experimenters insisted was a plain, simple, natural manner of expression both in diction and structure.

The experimental philosophers, under the lead of John Wilkins, were the dominant force in the formation of the Royal Society, a fact made perfectly clear in Sprat's *History*. The atomists, especially Charleton and Digby, were too prominent in the new science to be left out, even though their style must have caused some misgivings.[44] On two different occasions, one only a short time before the Restoration, Charleton's manner of writing had brought down criticism upon his head, we do not know from whom, but more likely than not from the Baconians, who were very sensitive to matters of style.[45] What then could have been more natural than for them to require that all reports made to the society be presented in the style that they considered so essential to the progress of science, especially after they had perhaps been subjected to a sample or two of the other in their meetings. One may well wonder whether this severe judgment had any influence on the style and stylistic views of the mechanical philosophers. Charleton was proposed as a member on 23 January 1661 and was

43 The prefaces of most of the treatises mentioned in note 42 stress the fact that the author is using a simple diction in order to be understood by agricultural workers. It was necessary to reach those who were working with nature if science was to achieve its utilitarian end.

44 Only three or four years after the founding of the Royal Society, Glanvill recognizes both experimental and mechanical philosophers as members of the society, and adds that some of the latter "publickly own the *Cartesian* and *Atomical* Hypotheseis" ("An Address to the Royal Society," prefixed to *Scepsis Scientifica*). Thomas Sprat (*Observations on M. Sorbière's "Voyage into England"* [1668], p. 206) says that among the members of the society, the men of general learning favored Gassendi, whereas the mathematicians favored Descartes. Speaking of the mechanical philosophers, whom he calls speculative naturalists, Boyle says the Cartesians among them were much fewer than the atomists (*Works*, ed. Birch, I, 227).

45 See the preface to Charleton's translation of van Helmont's *Deliramenta Catarrhi*, and his *Immortality of the Human Soul*, p. 10, in which he says that some condemned his *Physiologia* because of "too much youthful Heighth and Affection in the style."

admitted on 15 May.[46] In works published after this date, he gives some evidence of a desire to conform. Only three years later, he maintains that in all serious investigations, metaphors "are to be wholly excluded," though he allows some "convenient similitudes." At a later date, he goes so far as to state that he is expressing his thought "in a plain familiar Style (such with which I am always best pleas'd, especially in Discourses Philosophical)." But he retained much of his rhetoric, as for example in his description of the soul as "this Celestial guest in our frail and darksome Tabernacles of Flesh."[47] He became conscious of his Latinized diction and made some feeble efforts toward a simpler vocabulary. In his *Enquiries into Human Nature* (1680), he incorporated much of his *Natural History of Nutrition* (published in 1659), and a comparison of the two versions, shows that he made a stab at simplifying the diction of the earlier one.[48] Yet he could still retain such words as are contained in this sentence: "Nutrition consists of reparation or insaturation of what is absumed, by apposition and assimilation of similar or congerous matter." He was, however, sufficiently sensitive to his environment to apologize to his readers for his use of hard words, stating that his subject was of such a nature that it could not otherwise be properly treated "in our yet imperfect language."[49] Though Charleton made some efforts to adjust to his times, for the most part his inherently imaginative spirit refused to restrict its activities to the narrow limits required by the experimental philosophy, and it may have been responsible for his resigning from the Royal Society.[50]

After Digby joined the original group of scientists, he did not publish enough in the few remaining years of his life to indicate any

[46] See E. S. De Beer's valuable article "The Earliest Fellows of the Royal Society," *Notes and Records of the Royal Society of London*, VII (1950), 180. The organization which Charleton joined was that formed on 28 November 1660, two years later becoming the Royal Society. It was generally called the Philosophical Society, although, as we shall see in the next paragraph, the name was sometimes changed to emphasize the experimental philosophy.

[47] *The Natural History of the Passions*, pp. 2, 5.

[48] For example, he substitutes "made of" for "corporated of," "made up" for "fabricated," "watery" for "aqueous."

[49] If Charleton could not make the change in his style that his age seemed to demand, there was one who did reform in a most definite and decided manner. In 1661, Joseph Glanvill published his *Vanity of Dogmatizing*, a book written under the influence of the mechanical philosophy and in the style of Charleton and Sir Thomas Browne. Fifteen years later, after he had become a devoted member of the Royal Society, he published a second version in the approved style. See Jones *et al.*, *The Seventeenth Century*, pp. 88–97.

[50] The 1667 list of members was the last to contain his name. See De Beer, *op. cit.*, pp. 174–75, 180.

change in his way of writing.[51] Less than two months after he became a member, however, he was invited to read, and did read, a paper whose published title was *A Discourse Concerning the Vegetation of Plants. Spoken by Sir Kenelme Digby, at Gresham Colledge, on the 23d of January 1660* [1661]. *At a Meeting of the Society for promoting Philosophical Knowledge by Experiments.*[52] This is a description of the process by which a seed becomes the stem, branches, leaves, flowers, fruit, and seed of a plant or tree, and it represents Digby's nearest approach to a scientific discovery in that he points out that the air contains food for plants and trees. He describes the bursting of the seed through fermentation, the sending of roots down into the earth to tap its juices, and the sending of filaments up into the air, along which the juices are sublimed and acted upon by the sun and air. It is hard to conceive a more verbose narrative. He begins with an amplification of what he would say if he had time, enumerating rarefaction, concoction, the resurrection of dead bodies, and numerous other things, and concluding with an ambitious similitude. The treatise is strewn with similes and metaphors, some dragged in with much effort as, for example, reading the fate of nations in bursting seed. After speaking of the part that fermentation plays in the changing of a seed into a plant, he begins to talk in general about the power of fermentation, but catches himself up with the words, "But you do not expect . . . that I should discuss the Doctrine of Fermentation, to the utmost scope and extent of it." Yet he continues to talk about it until he finally reaches his conclusion, which he introduces with these words: "And lastly, (not to trouble you with too many particulars arising out of a digression)." Then after a few pages, he introduces another long digressive amplification on the virtues of saltpeter, which reaches a rhetorical climax in a swelling outburst:

Now in this Salt are enclosed the Seminary virtues of all things. For, what is it, but a pure extract, drawn by the Sunbeams from all the bodies that he darts his Rays on; sublimed up to such a height of place, as leavs all feculence behind it: and is there in that exalted Region of the Limbeck, baked and incorporated with those very beams themselves, which refined this extract out of its drossie Oar? Therefore, I wonder not to see any sort of Herb grow upon the highest Towers, where 'tis certain no man ever came to sow that *Plant*. And, the Loadstone or Magnes, of a like

[51] He was one of a list of forty-one prospective members drawn up by the twelve scientists who established the basic organization on which the Royal Society was founded (R. T. Petersson, *Sir Kenelm Digby* [1956], pp. 294–95). He was elected a member 12 December 1660 and served on the Council in 1662 and 1663 (De Beer, *op. cit.*, p. 181).

[52] All references are to the edition appended to the edition of *Two Treatises* entitled *Of Bodies* (1669).

substance, (though nothing near so pure) that is the Earth, the creeping Toad there, sucks and pulls down this flying Dragon to it, and both of them become one body.

One detects in Digby's account a suggestion of self-consciousness and apology, as if aware of a critical attitude in his hearers, and one is hardly surprised when, after a few more comments and references, he closes his expatiation on saltpeter with a confession and a defense: "Enough if not too much is said of these Curiosities by way of digression, and to entertain you with pleasing variety." The last four pages of his paper are devoted to a digression on the resurrection of human bodies, with no reference whatever to the vegetation of plants. Digby certainly passes by few opportunities to digress, though he tells us in one digression that he forbears more frequently than we realize: "But I should be too prolix if I hunted too far every Chase that arises before me in this copious Forest." When Sprat says that the members of the Royal Society resolved "to reject all amplifications, digressions, and swellings of style," he is giving a perfect description of Digby's treatise.[53]

The answer, then, to the question asked at the beginning of this study points toward the atomic scientists, especially Charleton and Digby. The manner of writing of these two men reveals all the stylistic vices that, according to Sprat's account, were reprehended by the experimental philosophers. Certainly the stylistic requirements of the Royal Society could with all justice have been directed squarely at them. The modes of expression of both the experimental and the mechanical philosophers sprang for the most part from the character and demands of their scientific objectives, and thus they do not represent a response to rhetorical models or authority, though the atomists were influenced to a certain extent by Sir Thomas Browne and so, perhaps, by the rhetoricians of the Anti-Ciceronian movement. The atomists felt the need of rhetoric to "persuade" their readers to accept as credible the imagined images of atoms in action. The Baconians, on the other hand, did not wish to persuade; their only care was to offer authentic data, based upon accurate sensuous impressions and free of any imaginative element. The style of the atomists was inimical to the objectives of the experimental philosophers and so indeed could have provoked the latter's earnest efforts to prohibit it.

[53] If Birch correctly records the attitude of Digby's fellow scientists, they took him with a grain of salt: "His abilities and learning were very considerable, but his character as a philosopher was much lessened by his credulity or want of veracity" (*History of the Royal Society* [1756–57], I, 82). Evelyn calls Digby a teller of strange things. *Diary*, ed. E. S. De Beer (1955), III, 550.

IRVIN EHRENPREIS

Personae

In an age when the nature of human identity has been examined by new and alarming procedures with new and alarming results, it was proper that we should interpret the monuments of literature as embodying that preoccupation. The works of many modern authors owed their conception to the same interests that directed the philosophers and psychologists. Quite spontaneously, therefore, the attempt to pursue such questions in literary studies began with contemporary reviews or studies of these authors. In the masks of Yeats and the auto-analysis of Proust's Marcel or Joyce's Bloom appeared poetic structures like the laminating egos that fascinated Freud and William James. Very soon, the gains accruing from such criticism of modern authors encouraged scholars to try parallel methods in historical research.

About this time, several young critics had also begun to enlarge their powers of interpretation by applying to one genre the terms developed for the study of another. Thus modern lyric poems found themselves treated as small dramas, modern novels as poems. When scholars again followed the procedures of these brave innovators, we had Shakespearean tragedy presented in the categories commonly reserved for lyric poetry and epics considered as tragedies.

The fruitful effect of these methods of dealing with literature has transformed what once threatened to be an increasingly sterile labor into the most adventurous of humanistic pursuits. Nevertheless, such methods, like any other way of disengaging the various elements that constitute a masterpiece, can never create values but can only reveal them. They can be applied as easily, therefore, in the support of entrenched opinion as in the establishment of new judgments. The former is what I think has sometimes occurred in the mingling of these rhetorical methods for the interpretation of works belonging to the age of Pope and Swift. Certain prejudices have been propped up by

IRVIN EHRENPREIS is Professor of English at Indiana University.

skillful carpentry instead of undergoing the probing that they deserve.

Yet these prejudices in turn were the outcome of an honest effort to rescue the Augustans from imprisonment in old Romantic commonplaces: Elwin's Pope, Thackeray's Swift, enacting mythical scandals before voyeurist literary societies. To effect the rescue, the scholars reversed the Romantic momentum and established an ideal of impersonal art as the distinguishing property of these writers. The *Essay on Man*, for example, became not a statement of Pope's own impressions but a reflection of traditional wisdom distinct from the beliefs or disbeliefs of the poet.

So successful did the first rescuers feel, that later salvage operations were mounted for the more remote parts of the authors' *œuvre*. Invoking now the principles of rhetoric to account for poetic effects and the emanations of a multiplied consciousness to account for apparently direct self-expression, a number of subtle, erudite scholars found impersonal art where it was earlier thought to be inaccessibly submerged.

The main instrument for these researches has been an elusive idea, rarely defined, which represents the compounding of two tendencies sketched above. In this compound, the terms of one genre are applied to another: narrative fiction is treated as drama; the didactic essay is treated as narrative fiction; lyric, didactic, and narrative poetry are treated as drama or rhetoric. To supply characters or debating sides for the story, play, or dialogue, the consciousness of the creator is divided up. Where a work once seemed to be the expression of an author's feelings or views, the scholars can separate the various tones heard in it and incarnate each as implying a change of speaker. Sometimes, more simply, the reader becomes a part of the action, and the work becomes a type of persuasive speech organized so as to alter his opinion: a *façon de parler* is transformed into an essential structure.

For almost a quarter-century, the concept thus constructed has been finding wider and wider employment in research dealing with Swift, Pope, and their contemporaries. To produce the concept now is to mark oneself as furnished with a sharp critical method. Most scholars call it *persona* or *mask*, but other labels are to be found. Rhetoricians speak of *ethical judgment* or *ethos*. Exegetical critics may prefer *implied dramatic speaker*. All those who like the method of study based on this concept seem to believe that if the structure of a poem involves a persona, the work deserves special praise on that account.

Although terminology may vary, the concept as normally invoked seems to imply certain common presuppositions. Fundamental is the principle that a literary work should be regarded not as an aspect of the author's personality but as a separate thing. As a consequence, the sentiments expressed in a literary work are not to be attributed to the author himself. In the room of the author, one is well advised to lodge an intermediate figure, the speaker or narrator created by him. It is to this persona that we may then assign the attitudes which seem implicit in a literary work. The persona again is not to be considered an aspect or revelation of the author but an independent creation, designed for its function as part of the self-contained work. The use of a persona by a writer is thus a mark of talent, a sign by which we may distinguish superior from mediocre achievement. In the critic, similarly, the method that concentrates on the persona is a sign of analytic skill. For any reader at all, an awareness of this concept will quicken his appreciation of a literary masterpiece. Or so (by implication) we are told.

II

The whole ground on which the search for the persona is based seems to me the belief that it is a device of art, that it belongs to the realm of peculiarly literary talent. There would be no profit in the attempt to identify it in imaginative literature if it were merely an inseparable part of language and communication: we do not praise an author for using participial phrases. Yet I believe that the persona or mask, as usually employed, has no status as art in itself, unless we admit such art to be congenital in humankind.

Thus, reasoning a fortiori, I should say the most subtle expression of the concept is that in which, according to the critic, an author pretends to be himself but acts a calculated role: Pope, for instance, in *An Epistle to Dr. Arbuthnot*. In so doing, the author—we are assured —gives his true name and supplies reliable information about his life. He suppresses or even distorts some of his honest views, however, so that the opinions and data presented in the work contribute to a rhetorical purpose; they do not necessarily conform with his private conversation or with his actual behavior. By this device, the author draws a public portrait, to be used on public occasions. It is argued that only a novice among scholars would confuse the portrait with the man.

Yet it seems that this kind of rhetorical pose is absolutely inseparable from all language and communication. One could never reveal the whole truth about oneself, even supposing one knew it. If one could, the effect would be chaos, for to reveal all is to hide all. One cannot speak without selecting a limited number of remarks from among possible remarks; and it is animal instinct to choose those which suit the occasion. A hound growls confidently at a spaniel but slinks without noise beside its own trainer. Children have the same talent, varying their characters according to the adult whom they must govern.

In every conversation, we misrepresent our nature. To the degree that the speaker in the *Epistle to Dr. Arbuthnot* does not stand for Alexander Pope, no man, in a single speech, can be wholly himself. If the effect produced by a speech gives a misleading or one-sided image of the speaker, the reason is that to be coherent, one must expose one side at a time. Misrepresentation in the vulgar sense is no issue in literary art. As audience, we try to discover what the real author means in the particular work. That he may possibly (without our knowing) deliver a different doctrine elsewhere, or that his life may exemplify the vices he begs us to avoid, is irrelevant. At the moment, in the poem, he says what we have to accept as his assertion if no evidence appears to the contrary.

To argue otherwise is to make the author defy the polite rules of language. We customarily hear a man's speech as revealing his character in the same way that his gestures and actions do so. Communication is impossible on any other basis. So long as there is no hint of deceitfulness, what a man says must be precisely what he means. In suggesting that we are not to take Pope at his word when he makes a statement in a poem, an essay, or a private letter, the critic is turning a genius into a fool. It is inconceivable that a writer as sensitive to overtones as Pope should deliver a proposition from his own lips and expect the reader to doubt that he feels responsible for it. Where, on the other hand, we find suggestions that the speech is ironical, or that the reasoning is suspended, or that a remark was intended to trick a specific correspondent, an intelligent reader will, of course, take warning from the cues.

For instance, it is sometimes argued that we are wrong to read the description of Sporus as the author's judgment on the historical Hervey: rather, we are told, it represents the imagined satirist-speaker's detestation of an example of evil. Such an analysis leaves Pope a pathetic fumbler. If it should hold, the poet would have described Hervey in epithets that force us to recall Queen Caroline's confidant; he would have endowed his own voice with the most vindictive harshness; yet he would have desired us to shut our ears to these thunderclaps and follow only the light patter of his pseudo-rhetorical design. True, the character of Sporus does erupt at an appropriate point in the poem; true, Hervey's career is treated by Pope as a type of radical evil; true, we are indebted to those scholars who demonstrated that far from expressing an odd fit of malice, the character has a significant position in a moral structure. But even more truly, in these verses we hear Pope attacking Hervey.

III

If there is any meaning in the concept of persona or mask, it must imply a difference between appearance and reality. The mask of Yeats is not the "true" Yeats; the "citizen" who writes Defoe's *Journal* is not "really" Defoe. Inevitably, the term implies that a genuine person does exist, could reveal himself, but chooses not to. It implies that while the work of the person is solid to the touch, it is not only distinguishable from him but essentially different from him. The more freely the term is employed, the more remote grows the being who lives behind its fence. Huckleberry Finn is not Mark Twain, who is not Samuel Clemens. By similar logic, even the speaker or narrator of a work is not traceable to the author but is a detached expression of his creative sensibility; and indeed any connection between the sensibility and the mask is haphazard.

Surely one appeal of these principles is that as artists Yeats, Defoe, and Clemens retain an extraordinary integrity throughout the operation of the method. Inept or distasteful aspects of their work can always be interpreted as revelations of the character of the "speaker," while the author remains deft and refined. Conrad, not to be confused with Marlow, can be anchored like the tortoise who supports the elephant on which the world rests. The more admiring but defensive we feel toward an author, the more reassurance we draw from this knowledge.

In studying the Augustans, an emphasis on masks offers us the special advantages of guarding their reputation for impersonality and eluding the charge of boastfulness. As it happens, Swift, Pope, Dryden, and Defoe often speak out boldly and directly. *Gulliver's Travels* is abundantly supplied with passages in which Swift gives the reader a piece of his mind, as when he denounces the English voters of his day for prostituting themselves by accepting bribes.[1] Pope's greatest powers appear in a work like the *Epilogue to the Satires*, which could not be more direct without turning ink to acid. But if we wish to ignore the violence of expression in such works and hunt only for a device to screen the author from his meaning, we may rouse up the concept of persona. Committed to the dogma of impersonal art, we may dismiss every evidence to the contrary as an attribute of the "speaker" alone; and having set this evidence aside, we may at last treat the poem as one more demonstration of Augustan impersonality.

By means of the same strategy, we can also dissipate the aura of vainglory that floats about any defense of one's own career. When an

[1] Part III, chap. viii.

author displays his moral virtue in public, he can scarcely avoid open-ing himself to the charge of vanity. *The Life and Genuine Character of Dr. Swift* embarrasses many of the Dean's admirers by its under-tone of self-approbation. This poem came out less than two years be-fore *An Epistle to Dr. Arbuthnot* and bore a long dedication to Pope, who may even have been involved in its publication. Because it also deals with the same autobiographical themes as the later work, I think Pope may have had it in mind when he was composing the *Epistle*. Certainly he commits the same blunder; for if Pope's poem remains a masterpiece, it does so in spite of the self-praise hinted in many lines. Once again, however, by introducing the persona and classifying the poetry as rhetoric, we can claim that not the author but the speaker is responsible for the praise and that his object is not Pope but the ideal satirist, the poet's so-called *ethos*.

Thus a further source of gratification is the analogy between artis-tic integrity and moral integrity. If the literary manifestation of a man may be isolated from the man, so may his nonliterary expression. Just as the narrator of the *Plague Year* is not Defoe, so also one might claim that the author of the obsequious letters to Oxford represents not so much Defoe as a pose assumed for the statesman by the jour-nalist. Similarly, whatever insinuation Pope may have written to Warburton against Swift, we may now deny that the attitude tells anything about the real Alexander Pope, for the remark could have been intended strictly to impress his correspondent. As we advance along these routes, language generally is transformed from a means of communication into a means of deceit and concealment. All that ap-pears as the expression of a man's feelings is available for analysis as the artful construction of a masked genius. Through such casuistry, however, not only is the literary status of a man's work enhanced, but his moral rectitude is barricaded.

Perhaps we are still further consoled by this critical method be-cause it inferentially secures the integrity of our own characters. By treating ourselves as we do the authors, we may sacrifice every ap-pearance to preserve the essence. In any regrettable act, we can say, "This is not the real me; my essential good nature remains hidden but genuine." During an age when the notion of the self is collapsing like the notion of the soul, the concept of persona enables us to cling a little longer to a substantial ego. For the glittering charm of the con-cept resides in its never leading us toward the issue but always send-ing us in the opposite direction. So quietly does it take for granted the pure "self," isolated and idealized, that we fail to observe the exist-ence of an assumption.

In such rationalizations, there would be little charm if we abandoned the postulate of an essence distinct from all its manifestations, if we admitted that not only communication but personality is impossible apart from learned, conventional behavior—"poses," if you like. When there is no audience, we act for ourselves. We cannot think or even dream without "posing." As long as a man's character is alive, it is trying out roles in language, in conduct. At the same time, although one "self" does continually displace another, each remains a form or mode of revelation of the real person. It is not illusory appearances that the real person sets before us: it is visible effluences, aspects, reflections—however indirect—of an inner being that cannot be defined apart from them. In order to understand any literary work, we must view it as a transaction between us and that inner being. If he tells a story, we must ask what he (not his emanation) means by the story; if he writes a play, we must ask what he intended to express through its action; if he talks by way of an intermediary figure, we must ask how he uses the intermediary; if he sounds ironical, we must discover the direct sense implied by the irony.

IV

Among the several benefits conferred upon a poem by the kind of rhetorical analysis that focuses itself on a persona, the most seductive is the apparent improvement in the merits of the work. This improvement is discovered first in the alleged appropriateness of the speaker to the design and secondly in the alleged persuasiveness of the reasoning. About thirty-five years ago, John Brooks Moore mistakenly described Gulliver as "an entirely credible and probable person at the same time that he is precisely the person to enforce Swift's demonstration."[2] Gulliver is none of these things, but Moore's comment foreshadowed similar judgments by other scholars on a wide range of Pope's and Swift's works. In each case, the brief follows the same line. We are told what the implicit purpose of the poem or essay is. We are then told what qualities an orator should possess if he is to execute the purpose. Finally, we are shown that the mask or persona employed exhibits just these traits and no others. *The Essay on Criticism*, the Digressions of *A Tale of a Tub*, the *Epistle to Bathurst*, the *Drapier's Letters*—all have rung true to this elaborate test.

What the analyst fails to notice is the source of his standard of judgment. In order to determine the implicit purpose of, say, *An Epistle to Dr. Arbuthnot*, one must examine the attitudes and sentiments of the speaker of the poem. From the clues contained therein, we find that it is a piece of argument intended by a high-minded poet to refute the accusations of his dishonest enemies: the purpose of the

2 "The Rôle of Gulliver," *Modern Philology*, XXV (1927–28), 469.

speech is the rehabilitation of the poet's character; the speech must prove the justice of his past actions to an audience that sits on the bench. Pope himself tells us as much, directly and covertly, in his verses. If we now examine the character of the persona, we see, naturally enough, that he is a high-minded author, harassed beyond patience by a gang of dishonest enemies. This is the ideal figure to speak the bill of complaint that constitutes the poem.

Transparently, such an analysis carries us around in a circle. If we deduce the intention of a poem from the attitudes implicit in the sentiments of the poet, we shall inevitably discover that the speaker of the poem has sentiments appropriate to its purpose. So long as intention and character are but different aspects of the same data, there is no breaking the circle.

But the rhetorical analysis moves on, to praise the argument of the poem as such. As before, the operation hinges upon the separation of the speaker from the author, for we could not regard the *Epistle* as an artful structure of persuasive devices if we left it in the category of a self-revelation. Once this split is accomplished, the connection of the poem with history is destroyed. Because its purpose is not to tell the truth but to appear truthful, the advocate must be divided from the defendant.

I have already suggested that if such an approach is valid, Pope has been inept, because the speaker of the *Epistle* appeals continuously to history, resting his defense upon the verifiable truth of his data. Now this appeal seems to me anterior to the surface of rhetorical persuasion. If the author of this poem were not the great poet of his age, if his relations with his parents were not well known to have been as he testifies, if Atticus and Sporus did not belong to public life, the force of the poem would dwindle.

I may further suggest that even the pseudo-rhetorical framework in which the poet chooses to deliver his self-defense belongs less to the realm of persuasive discourse than to the tradition of poetry. The "bill of complaint" form, of course, descends to Pope not from Aristotle's *Rhetoric* but from Horace. Between Pope's *Epistle* and such works of Horace as his *Satires*, Book I, Number 4, the parallels are so close that we may regard the Latin poems as authority for the English poem's structure.

The *Epistle to Dr. Arbuthnot* is cast in the form of a dialogue, and a persuasive line of reasoning has always been evident in it. But until recently, this form was assumed to be a *façon de parler*, a lucid figure of speech, allowing the poet to vary his poet of view and to avoid monotony. Nobody took it any more literally than the stroll-through-a-studio setting of *An Epistle to a Lady*. It was never doubted that the voice heard within the long speeches came from the throat of Pope himself. If we deny this principle and handle the surface of rhetoric as the essential form, we drive ourselves into the paradox I have already described: the poem must then be understood as irrelevant to the history and character of Pope, yet uttered by a speaker with his identity.

The benefits derived from this unnatural attitude are indeed great. Not only do we block, as extraliterary, any effort to interpret the poem as evidence of Pope's own sensibility. We also transform it into a flawless piece of ratiocination. The cause of this will be obvious. Every attempt to persuade a listener of the truth of a proposition involves not only the correct marshaling of logic, data, or sentiments but also a claim of truthfulness that can be judged by nothing but a reference to reality. If we classify a speech as rhetoric and in it, at the same time, refuse to admit any allusion to reality, we allow a man to prove a case by inventing whatever facts will support his demonstration: we free him from the responsibilities of rhetoric and endow him with the privileges of poetic. If in addition to these licenses, the debater possesses great eloquence, he will of course compose a masterpiece of argument. In the particular instance of the *Epistle to Dr. Arbuthnot*, as it happens, the argument itself urges us to look at the facts as verifiable. So we can ignore that element only by distorting the whole meaning of the speech.

As a specimen of imaginative art, the *Epistle*, therefore, is not simply rhetoric but an imitation of rhetoric. Like all Pope's satires in this form, it has a rhetorical scaffolding, but this is not the inner edifice. Yet even the light framework can be irritating. To the degree that we regard the verses not as complex poetry but as simple persuasion, we must feel annoyed by several flaws: by the fallacies in the poet's logic, by the improbable helpfulness of the questions planted in the friend's mouth, by the astonishing ease with which the friend accepts the poet's conclusions, by the unfair advantage that the poet grants his own intellect over his sympathizer's. When, however, we regard the pseudo-rhetorical form as a conventional means of giving life to the speaker-poet's expression of his own views, we moderate our annoyance and admire the art.

True, it would be absurd to read the whole of this poem, or the imitations of Horace, or the auto-analytical poems of Swift and Prior, as direct, literal statements of the author's principles. It is equally a mistake to read them as independent of those principles. Through his masterpieces a man defines—not hides—himself. By reading them, we are put in touch with him, not with a series of intermediaries. The nature of his communication may be subtle; his manner, devious. Ultimately, however, he is telling us his truth. If we about must and about must go, it is in order to reach that, and not some beautiful, self-contained, illusory Helen.

V

I think it would be a service to literature to distinguish the helpful from the misleading applications of the persona in methods of scholarship and criticism. The least illuminating applications seem those which treat mere personae as full, interesting characters. Swift's pseudonyms, for example, are sometimes treated this way; and yet they rarely depend on self-consistent "rounded" figures. Except when he uses what may be called the "ironical persona," Swift ignores the pseudonym and its few attached facts: in the body of the work, he speaks in his own way (ironical or direct), expounding his own views. In the creation of Gulliver, Swift cannot be recommended for consistency either of character or of fact. Again and again the veneer of probability is broken.

Broadly it can be said, on the other hand, that the most illuminating applications are made to works whose structure depends on the speaker's having an ambiguous character. I have claimed that any communication involves a kind of pose. But when this necessity is itself manipulated so as to become a method of communicating attitudes otherwise unacceptable to the reader, the result is a special form of art, the "ironical persona." I use this to designate a disguise that is intended to be seen through, a mask that the reader at first supposes to be genuine but at last sees removed. In such a literary structure, the author's fundamental tone also reverses itself: what sounded sober is transformed to mockery. For the device to succeed, the reader must be tricked during the early stages of the work and be undeceived during the later; and in his gradual apprehension of the meaning of the work, the process which removes the disguise must provide a dramatic turning point. Swift's *Modest Proposal* is an example.

The art of the employer of the ironical mask springs from his power to combine ambiguous moral sentiments with an ambiguous attitude toward what he is saying. The reader must assume that the doctrines to be expounded are proper, decent things. He must also assume that the author is serious in proposing them. The skill of the writer appears in his disclosing the wickedness of the doctrines before disclosing the irony of his manner. The longer the reader can be kept in suspense between the two revelations, the sharper is the effect. The greater the degree of fascinated ambivalence which results, the greater is the achievement of the satirist.

This effect, in turn, depends on the fact that we naturally sympathize with any speaker who sounds calm and well intentioned. It is a mistake to think that the skill of the author, in these maneuvers, should be measured by the ease with which he first leads the reader into associating himself with the speaker; for it is the instinctive, nonliterary tendency for all readers or listeners to commit themselves to the side of an unknown author, merely by embarking upon the effort of following a speech or essay. A persona need not be peculiarly designed to encourage the reader's identification of himself with the author; it need only be neutral enough not to discourage what amounts to a natural impulse. It would not matter whether Gulliver were a physician or a merchant, whether he studied at Emmanuel College, Cambridge, or Brasenose, Oxford, so long as none of his features would be likely to alienate the sympathy of the reader.

In the opening sections of the work, the reader assumes, therefore, that the moral character of the speaker is essentially like his own, and in this sense he identifies the two. What the man in the ironical mask must attempt is to retain this sympathy after the reader has contemplated the evil or absurdity of the recommendations. While, then, the reader is struggling to disengage his fellow-feeling—that is, while he still feels reluctant to admit that he was wrong to give a fair hearing to the author—it must grow obvious that the author himself is not in earnest, but is delivering a parody, acting out a caricature of a type of man he loathes or contemns. The effect on the reader is double, for he sees himself derided by the very person he has been straining to respect. At the same time, he feels that the author, by taking his initial sympathy for granted, has pinned the loathsome character on him. In fact, it is because of this sympathy that he is being ridiculed. If the maneuver is successful, the reader cannot help exerting himself to reject the character.

This sort of ironical mask has become a familiar prop in the theater of modern criticism. We have not only seen it fall from the face of Swift's Projector; we have watched a series of dressers trying to fit it over the face of Lemuel Gulliver. Far more insight than confusion, certainly, has emerged from these analyses. Yet I think they often suffer from an extension of the error associated above with the idea of a rhetorical pose, that is, the detachment of appearance from essence.

Scholars dealing with the ironical mask often assume that whenever it drops, the author remains hidden: only the speaker or narrator is revealed. Behind the sensible projector's advice there suddenly looms a monster; but behind the monster the author stands allegedly undefined. I believe, on the contrary, that *A Modest Proposal* makes sense only if we treat the voice as the author's throughout. Swift is so ambiguous that at first we think he is in earnest. At the moment of understanding, we realize that he has been speaking in parody. There is no intermediate person between the real author and us. Surly the inference we draw when a decent, intelligent man produces an abominable scheme is that he doesn't mean it, that he is ironical, that he speaks in parody. Surely we read the *Modest Proposal* as a wildly sarcastic fantasy delivered by the true author, whoever he may be. Surely the kind of literary disguise that is deliberately intended to be penetrated is a method of stating, not hiding, what one thinks.

As it happens, Swift corroborates this interpretation by using a third style in the essay, the mode of direct, bitter statement (like the vituperations that grow thick and frequent toward the end of *Gulliver's Travels*). To such outbursts both the noncommittal and ironic modes give way—in *A Modest Proposal*—when Swift says the landlords of Ireland have devoured the parents of the poor, or when he cuttingly attacks the frivolous young ladies, or when he lists real remedies for the condition of Ireland, or when he says England would gladly eat up the whole Irish nation. To maintain the hypothesis of an intermediate figure, one would have to claim either that the projector himself grows ironic in these passages or else that a third, angry person exists, creating an abominable projector who pretends to be a humane patriot.

Instead of multiplying entities so liberally, I suggest that we deal at once with the satirist. Whether or not he cracks the surface of the irony, an ironical hoaxer must show himself if his device is to succeed. Behind the author of the *Guardian* No. 40, on pastorals, the discriminating reader must meet not a silly critic blind to his own lacklogic, but a detester of Philips and an admirer of Pope. In ordinary conversation, when an intelligent friend suddenly utters absurdities in a sober tone, we do not conclude that he has changed his identity but that he is using dead-pan irony. If his wit grows so mocking that he seems to be imitating a particular fool or type of fool, we do not imagine that he has been metamorphosed. Surely we can deal as reasonably with a literary impersonation.

VI

In all speech, literary or nonliterary, it is as meaning only that there can be perceptible form. The primacy of meaning does not originate or end in the rhetorical persuasiveness of the speaker. It does not depend on our agreement or disagreement with him. Rather it springs from the power of his case to arouse us to intense contemplation one way or the other. Whether we say that the argument seems worth resisting, or we feel that it is the voice of our own mind, the meaning remains effective. If an author moves us to fight against his doctrines, he may have lost as a rhetorician, but he has won as a poet. It is when we feel that the case is worth neither entertaining nor refuting that the speech is negligible.

Only as a relationship between a real speaker and a real listener can meaning exist. In drama and prose fiction or epic, where separate speeches illustrate separate characters, the whole narrative must be read as a parable whose implications can be gathered from the light in which the various elements appear. The author is speaking this parable to the audience. In didactic or lyric poetry, as in the reflective or polemical essay, the author must be regarded as the speaker. He may talk ironically; he may imitate a man he despises; he may ask you to sneer at the fool he is copying; he may in mockery talk like his foolish audience. But unless we treat the material as indicating, however indirectly, what the author believes and is, we do not discover the meaning of the work; and if we miss its meaning, we cannot judge its form.

HERBERT DAVIS

A Modest Defence of "The Lady's Dressing Room"

W HEN POPE HAD COMPLAINED of the attacks made upon him after the publication of his *Epistle to the Right Honourable Richard Earl of Burlington* in December 1731, Bolingbroke had drawn his attention to Horace's *First Satire* in his *Second Book* and had observed how well it would hit his case, if he imitated it in English. In his dialogue, Horace asks his friend Trebatius what he should do in view of the protests made against his satires and takes the opportunity to defend himself and clear his character. This was the first of Pope's *Imitations of Horace*, the first of the poems in which he completely identifies himself with the Roman satirist and draws attention to the similarity in their circumstances and intentions and, indeed, in the very tone and manner of their verse by printing the Latin text opposite his own lines. He speaks of it as a trifle written in two mornings, with little care; yet he also refers to it as "the occasion of my imitating some other of the satires and epistles afterwards."

But the idea of imitating Horace was not at all novel, and Pope had recently included in *Miscellanies: The Last Volume* (1727) an *Imitation of Horace, Lib. 2, Sat. 6.*, which Swift had written in 1714. Later, in 1738, Pope printed the poem again separately, in folio, with an addition of nearly a hundred lines, containing the fable of the country mouse and the city mouse, written in imitation of the style of Swift. He also added a short Advertisement, which drew attention to the difference between their imitations, and he seems to have wished it to be clearly understood that their intentions were quite different: "The World may be assured, this Publication is no Way meant to interfere with the *Imitations of Horace* by Mr. *Pope*. His Manner, and that of Dr. Swift are so entirely different, that they can admit of no

HERBERT DAVIS was formerly Professor in the Faculty of English at Oxford University.

Invidious Comparison. The Design of the one being to sharpen the Satire, and open the Sense of the Poet; of the other to render his native *Ease* and *Familiarity* yet more easy and familiar."

It is perhaps less generally known that Pope's first *Imitation* of Horace had also been anticipated in a small eight-page pamphlet, printed in Dublin by George Faulkner, Swift's printer, in 1732, and entitled *A Modest Defence of a late Poem By an unknown Author, call'd "The Lady's Dressing-Room."*[1] For the whole defense is based upon the claim that "our Author hath observed to a Tittle, the precepts of his Master *Horace;* or, indeed, rather hath gone very far beyond him, in the Article of *Decency.*" To prove this, he quotes ten lines from the *Ars poetica* and then proceeds to give a "literal translation" in twenty lines of heroic verse, "purged . . . as much as could consist with preserving the true Sense of the Original": if this is compared with the whole poem called "The Lady's Dressing Room," he is ready to appeal to a committee of all the young ladies in the kingdom to decide upon the Article of Decency between the Hibernian Bard and "the great *Master of Politeness* in the *Roman* Empire, at the Time it flourished most in *Arts* and *Arms.*"

What the author has done, in fact, is to make his so-called "literal translation" a parody of ten perfectly innocent lines of Horace. This is Horace:

> Aut agitur res in scenis, aut acta refertur.
> Segnius irritant animos demissa per aurem,
> Quam quae sunt oculis subjecta fidelibus, & quae
> Ipse sibi tradit spectator. Non tamen intus
> Digna geri promes in scenam: Multaq; tolles
> Ex oculis, quae mox narret facundia praesens.

And this is the translation:

> Some Ladies *do their Need* before your Face;
> Some only tell the *Action,* and the *Place.*
> Our Mind is less provok'd by what it hears,
> Than when the *Fact* before our Eyes appears.
> In Closet dark, your *Cedar-box* be hid;
> Not in a Parlour shown without the Lid.
> Some *Actions* must be always out of Sight,
> Yet *elegantly told,* may give Delight.

A Modest Defence was reprinted by Faulkner in his edition of Swift's collected works, in the eighth volume, which first appeared in 1746, and in the subsequent Dublin reprints, with the following note: "The Poem on the LADY'S DRESSING ROOM having given Offence to a

[1] See Swift, *Works,* ed. Davis, Vol. V (1962), Appendix C.

few squeamish Ladies, and some *fine Gentlemen,* it was thought proper to publish the following DEFENCE." It was also accepted by John Nichols as Swift's and included by him in his *Supplement* (1779). In all these later reprints, a passage is omitted in which Swift disclaimed the authorship of *An Infallible Scheme To Pay the Nation's Debts, by a Tax upon Vice,* at the same time praising it and complimenting the true author, who "lyes yet concealed." Perhaps Faulkner omitted it after he learned that the author was the Reverend Matthew Pilkington, of whom Swift had written to Pope in the highest terms in 1732 as "the most hopeful young man we have," but whose subsequent conduct caused him to remove some favorable remarks about him in the Dublin reprint of his *Letters.* The fact that the same thing has happened to the compliments contained in this pamphlet seems to me to provide strong evidence in support of Swift's authorship.

I shall assume therefore that the argument put forward here in defense of "The Lady's Dressing Room" and other similar poems may be accepted as a humorous reply to the criticism that these poems had provoked.

Swift always maintained with some seriousness that it was the function of the satirist to deal with the vices of mankind and, by revealing them, to uphold the standards of virtue and good morals. And only an ill taste could fail to have discovered the "useful Satyr" running through every line of these poems, which were intended to inculcate the virtue of cleanliness, esteemed among the ancient poets to be "the chief corporeal Perfection in Women." Remembering some of the ugly, foul, and nauseating features of his descriptions, it must have given him a particular satisfaction to remind us of Horace's warning that some actions are not fit to be presented on the stage, but "they may be recited with *Pleasure* and *Elegance*"; indeed, many of his critics who protest most violently against this part of his satirical writing dislike him above all because he seems to recite with too much pleasure the nasty details he forces us to look at, and he often succeeds in shocking us by the use of a surprising epithet or an elegant conceit or by the effect of the rhyme:

> Should I the Queen of Love refuse,
> Because she rose from stinking Ooze?[2]

In his *Defence,* he makes fun of the sentiments of the romantic or heroic poet, by a sort of parody or imitation. For example, in the passage from the *Ars poetica,* wherein Horace illustrates the kind of actions that cannot be shown on the stage—

---

[2] *Swift's Poems,* ed. Harold Williams (Oxford, 1937), p. 530 (hereafter cited as *Poems*).

> Nec pueros coram populo Medea trucidet,
> Aut humana palam coquat exta nefarius Atreus,
> Aut in avem Procne vertetur, Cadmus in anguem—

and thus brings to our mind these figures from classical mythology
and drama, Swift seizes upon some detail and changes it into a humorous or disgusting image to debase or deflate the poetry of it and translates it thus:

> Nurse must not hold the Child, and cry *Eee, Hee,*
> When Madam and her Friends are o'er their Tea.
> Atreus, with Ladies by, mistakes his Wit,
> In new-born T——s to run a red-hot spit.
> Miss *Progne* must not cry, *a Bird, a Bird!*
> Before good Company, and shew a ——
> Cadmus, who voids out Worms of monst'rous Size,
> In mere good Manners should deceive our Eyes.[3]

Similarly, "The Lady's Dressing Room" is full of parodies of all the
overused and much repeated classical tags and stories and of words
and phrases in English poetry from Milton to Pope. It is as if he had
never tired of his vengeance on the Muse for forsaking him in his
twenties at Moor Park, when he had renounced forever her visionary
power:

> Say, whence it comes that thou art grown of late
> A poor amusement for my scorn and hate;
> The malice thou inspir'st I never fail
> On thee to wreak the tribute when I rail;
> Fools common-place thou art, their weak ensconcing fort,
> Th'appeal of dullness in the last resort.[4]

In the very opening lines, in which the weak rhymes give a tone of
scornful persiflage, we cannot help being just faintly reminded of that
other goddess, who issued forth from her dressing-room, where her
toilet had been so delicately described, inventoried as here in great
detail, before she was "Lanch'd on the Bosom of the Silver *Thames*."[5]

Swift is, of course, concerned only to report that Celia has gone
out, so that Strephon can make his investigations of her room:

> Five Hours, (and who can do it less in?)
> By haughty *Celia* spent in Dressing;
> The Goddess from her Chamber issues,
> Array'd in Lace, Brocades and Tissues.[6]

It is a little more startling to find that, when Strephon notices the
chest

[3] *Works*, V, 339–40.   [5] *Rape of the Lock*, Canto II, l. 4.
[4] *Poems*, p. 53.   [6] *Poems*, p. 525.

> With Rings and Hinges counterfeit
> To make it seem in this Disguise,
> A Cabinet to vulgar Eyes;[7]

and ventures to lift the lid, we are being given a parody of the classical simile by the introduction of the story of Pandora's box. At the
same time, we are perhaps expected to recognize in Celia a woman
fashioned out of earth and then endowed with beauty and the powers
of seduction, with cunning and the arts of flattery, a perfect symbol
for the real theme of Swift's poem, emphasized in the image of the
last line: "Such gaudy Tulips rais'd from Dung."

But the irrepressible spirit of parody bubbles up again immediately
and enables Swift to imitate his master Horace in reciting the worst
of Strephon's discoveries with elegance, by borrowing a whole line
from *Paradise Lost:* "Those Secrets of the hoary deep!"

There is an element of parody likewise in the ten-line simile, which
is built up so elaborately out of a detailed and vivid description of a
piece of meat roasting on the spit, which has been carefully prepared
as the laws of cookery require, but which is ruined if the fat drops on
a cinder—

> To stinking Smoak it turns the Flame
> Pois'ning the Flesh from whence it came.[8]

It is in this sort of verse that Swift seems most like himself; he shows
his mastery of it already in the early narrative poems like "Baucis and
Philemon" and "Vanbrug's House" and in the two well-known descriptive pieces that he contributed to the *Tatler*. The last volume of
the *Miscellanies* (1727) also contained a number of parodies, which
had been written probably in 1719 and 1720 for the amusement of
Stella, who had copied them out in her book, in which she had collected some of Swift's unpublished pieces. They might almost be described as short moral tales. The first, with the ironical title "A Quiet
Life and a good Name,"[9] addressed "to a Friend, who married a
Shrew," describes the bawling and the blows inflicted on the patient
Dick by his virago of a wife and the ill effects of his Christian for-
bearance:

> Scripture you know exhorts us to it,
> Bids us to seek Peace and ensue it.
>
> . . . .
>
> Lord! I should get so ill a Name
> The Neighbors round would cry out Shame.

[7] *Poems*, p. 528.

[8] *Poems*, p. 529.   [9] *Poems*, p. 219.

For he discovered that his behavior brought him small quiet and less credit:

> Within, his wife would break his Bones,
> Without, they pelted him with Stones,

And the moral of the story is that such Dicks are fools to their shame, victims of "false patience and mistaken pride."

"The Progress of Love"[10] is another moral tale of a prude, whose tricks, particularly in church, are knowingly described and who runs off with the butler. Their subsequent history is told with force and brevity: "their Journy long, their money short; . . . Their Vittels bad, their Lodging worse"—

> But what Adventures more befell 'um
> The Muse has now not time to tell 'um.

But the farce is finally brought to an end with exact poetic justice:

> They keep at Stains the old blue Boar
> Are Cat and Dog, and Rogue and Whore.

It should be noticed that with very few exceptions Swift does not attempt to imitate the different verse forms in his parodies, but is content to use the informality of the octosyllabic couplet and the possibilities of exactly balanced, trim-cut antitheses, which it so readily provides. It can also be sufficiently varied in pace and stress to bring out all the contrasts in that carefully wrought simile, in the first part of "The Progress of Poetry,"[11] between the Farmer's goose, grown fat with corn, and the Poet—

> [She] hardly waddles forth, to cool
> Her Belly in the neighb'ring Pool,

and afterward, grown lank and spare, straying on the barren common,

> Her Body light, she tries her Wings,
> And scorns the Ground, and upward springs,
> While all the Parish, as she flies,
> Hears Sounds harmonious from the Skies.

The moral is obvious.

> Deep sunk in Plenty, and Delight,
> What Poet e'er could take his Flight?

But, when all his drink is Hippocrene, when he is freed from all "incumbrances of food and clothes,"

> He singing flies, and flying sings,
> While from below all *Grub-street* rings.

---

[10] *Poems*, p. 221.   [11] *Poems*, p. 230.

It is surprising how easily Swift manages to adapt the octosyllabic couplet to all the various uses of compliment or light raillery as well as to savage political satire and the most stinging irony. He rarely has cause to try any other form; and when, in his lines "To Mr. Gay,"[12] he chooses heroic verse, it seems to be with the intention of increasing the mock-heroic effect:

> How cheaply had thy Liberty been sold
> To squire a Royal Girl of two Years old!
> In Leading strings her Infant-Steps to guide;
> Or, with her Go-Cart amble Side by Side.

And in the "Progress of Beauty,"[13] where for once he uses a four-line stanza, he still keeps the octosyllabic line throughout, though the rhymes are alternated. It has been suggested that Swift adopted his title from the well-known poem by George Granville, Lord Lansdown, which first appeared in Charles Gildon's *New Miscellany of Original Poems* (1701), but there is no attempt to parody Granville, and nothing to suggest the subject of his verses. Nevertheless, these "Progress" poems of Swift, which belong to 1719 and 1720, may very well have been prompted by his distaste for the kind of stuff to be found in such miscellanies, especially those poetic strains in praise of love and beauty and desire. He delights in smashing these false delusions and in turning upside down the usual romantic themes and images, whether they are applied to Diana or to earthly nymphs:

> When first Diana leaves her Bed
> Vapors and Steams her Looks disgrace,
> A frowsy dirty-colour'd red
> Sits on her cloudy wrinckled Face.
>
> But by degrees when mounted high
> Her artificiall Face appears
> Down from her window in the Sky,
> Her spots are gone, her Visage clears.

The parallel is then drawn between Diana and earthly females—like Celia:

> To see her from her Pillow rise
> All reeking in a cloudy Steam,
> Crackt Lips, foul Teeth, and gummy Eyes,
> Poor Strephon, how would he blaspheme!
>
> . . . .
>
> But Celia can with ease reduce
> By help of Pencil, Paint and Brush
> Each Colour to it's Place and Use
> And teach her Cheeks again to blush.

---

[12] *Poems*, p. 530.   [13] *Poems*, p. 225.

But she should not be too rash—the parallel is taken further:

> Take Pattern by your Sister Star
> Delude at once and Bless our Sight
> When you are seen, be seen from far
> And chiefly chuse to shine by Night.

There is a pretty stanza devoted to the praise of "white lead," which faintly recalls one of the most delicate strokes in Pope's satire and, at the same time, reveals the great contrasts in their way of parody. Swift removes very carefully and consciously any poetic diction, using only the flattest ordinary terms from the hardware store:

> Love with White lead cements his Wings,
> White Lead was sent us to repair
> Two brightest, brittlest earthly Things
> A Lady's Face, and China ware.

We may here observe how a line that might become poetic—"The brightest of all earthly things"—is broken by sticking in the middle of it the sharp exactness of a term like "brittlest"; and we may compare the effect of those lines of Pope where he is making use of the same image of the fragility of "China"—

> Whether the Nymph shall break Diana's Law
> Or some frail China Jar receive a Flaw—

or the complete rococo elegance of the other couplet—

> Or when rich China Vessels, fal'n from high,
> In glittring Dust and painted Fragments lie![14]

These "Progress" poems provided Swift with full scope for his gifts as a parodist and for indulgence in a pleasant, sly sort of humor, sometimes quite innocent of offense, like that of the little picture he gives of the elderly bridegroom in "The Progress of Marriage":

> A flourisht Night-cap on, to grace
> His ruddy, wrinckled, smirking Face,
> Like the faint red upon a Pippin
> Half wither'd by a Winters keeping.[15]

But he can't keep up his good behavior. He is not content to let the story of this foolish marriage between a rich old Dean and an extravagant young beauty carry its own obvious moral. The telling of it stirs his anger and fury; and as he leaves the rich young widow surrounded with swarms of new lovers, he pours out the filthiest curses upon her:

> Oh, may I see her soon dispensing
> Her Favors to some broken Ensign. . . .

---

[14] *Rape of the Lock*, Canto II, ll. 105–6; III, 159–60.   [15] *Poems*, p. 289.

But Swift's reputation has suffered most from a small quarto volume published in London in 1734, containing *A Beautiful young Nymph Going to Bed. Written for the Honour of the Fair Sex. To which are added, Strephon and Chloe and Cassinus and Peter.*[16] They were probably written in 1731, five years after the appearance of *Gulliver's Travels;* and they inevitably remind us of Gulliver's description of the Yahoos and of the violent disgust he felt for them and, because of their resemblance, for his fellows when he returned to his own country. Some recent critics have pointed out that we are very foolish if we think for a moment that Swift shared Gulliver's folly after he returned and behaved in such a strange fashion to his wife and children. But here in these poems there is no mask, no persona—only "the bashful Muse," who prevents him from going further, from trying to describe how the nymph puts herself together again after the horrors of the night, but who is not able to stop him from one last quick comment:

> *Corinna* in the Morning dizen'd,
> Who sees, will spew; who smells, be poison'd.[17]

I venture to suggest that it was Swift's intention in these poems to make every sense revolt with disgust, not, as is sometime said, because he could not bear to think that rational human beings should have excretory organs, but because of all the bestialities hidden beneath the surface of polite society, and because of his constant shock, as a moralist, at the insane pride of these miserable vermin, crawling about the face of the earth. These poems also betray paradoxically a certain fastidiousness in their author, outraged by the brutalities and insensitiveness of eighteenth-century manners, and therefore tempted to set forth his own conventions of decency and civilized behavior.

> On Sense and Wit your Passion found,
> By Decency cemented round;
> Let Prudence with Good Nature strive,
> To keep Esteem and Love alive.[18]

And, though we may sometimes feel that here too there is excess, a grim satisfaction in wielding Alecto's whip, a relentless fervor to expose everything that is rotten and foul, yet finally there is the humor of it all—especially in the "Tragical Elegy of Cassinus and Peter"; the nonsense of poor Cassy dying with his awful secret, in his madness, a college sophomore, seeing a vision of Virgil's hell, which Swift so frequently recalls:

16 *Poems*, pp. 581 f.

17 *Poems*, p. 583.   18 *Poems*, p. 593.

> And there—behold *Alecto* stand,
> A Whip of Scorpions in her Hand.
> Lo, *Charon* from his leaky Wherry,
> Beck'ning to waft me o'er the Ferry.
> I come, I come,—*Medusa*, see,
> Her Serpents hiss direct at me.
> Begone; unhand me, hellish Fry;
> Avaunt—ye cannot say 'twas I.[19]

For such a poem Swift is content to draw on the great tradition, on Virgil, on Shakespeare—he has a footnote drawing attention to the echo from *Macbeth*—and on Ovid as he tells further of poor Cassy struggling with his dreadful secret, and inevitably there comes to his mind the secret of Midas whispered to the reeds:

> Now, bend thine Ear; since out it must:
> But, when thou seest me laid in Dust,
> The Secret thou shalt ne'er impart;
> Not to the Nymph that keeps thy Heart;
>
> .   .   .   .
>
> Nor whisper to the tattling Reeds,
> The Blackest of all Female Deeds.[20]

And here, in accord with the methods of the new critics, let me point out that it was not Swift himself who was driven to madness at the revelation of Celia's infamy, as some of the psychoanalysts have striven to maintain, but only this innocent young Cambridge student Cassinus. Nor would Swift have thought it conceivable that it would be necessary to defend such a poem. For "The Lady's Dressing-Room" he had deigned to write an Apology in which he pointed out that his intentions were beyond reproach, as it was so obviously written with a moral purpose.

But the Celia poems were written for fun. And for them I believe he would have been content to be judged in the company of the sanest of his peers, standing by the side of Rabelais and Shakespeare.

[19] *Poems*, p. 596.   [20] *Poems*, p. 596.

LOUIS A. LANDA

The Shandean Homunculus: The Background of Sterne's "Little Gentleman"

I WISH there was not a clock in the kingdom."[1] This heartfelt lament from the lips of Mr. Shandy comes parenthetically as he is paraphrasing some of Locke's remarks on the succession of ideas. For Mr. Shandy, the word "clock" had associations, as it must have for even the least alert reader of *Tristram Shandy*, with Mrs. Shandy's untimely "silly question" (*"Pray, my dear . . . have you not forgot to wind up the clock?"*), uttered at the precise and fateful moment of Tristram's begetting, fateful because, as Mr. Shandy says, Tristram's misfortunes resulted from it: they *"began nine months before ever he came into the world."*[2] Tristram was indeed a "child of interruption."[3] But Mrs. Shandy, so culpable in the eyes of her husband, should be viewed with compassion. She was merely an innocent "victim" of the logical processes of the mind (as Locke viewed it), and her question

LOUIS A. LANDA is Professor of English at Princeton University.

[1] Laurence Sterne, *The Life and Opinions of Tristram Shandy, Gentleman,* ed. James Aiken Work (New York, 1940), III, xviii, 190. All references are to this edition. For designating chapters, I substitute roman numbers for the arabic in Work.

[2] I, iii, 7. As a gloss on the remarks of Tristram and his father concerning *tempore coitionis* (I, i, 4; II, xiv, 149), a subject that had received attention from the time of the ancients, one may turn to a controversy some three decades before Sterne published his novel. The chief antagonists were Dr. James Augustus Blondel and Dr. Daniel Turner, both members of the Royal College of Physicians. See Blondel's *The Power of the Mother's Imagination Examin'd, in Answer to Dr. Daniel Turner's Book* (London, 1729), pp. 9–10, 114, and Turner's *De Morbis Cutaneis* (3d ed.; London, 1726), pp. 161–62; *A Discourse concerning Gleets . . . to which is added A Defence of . . . the 12th Chapter of . . . De Morbis Cutaneis, in respect of the Spots and Marks impress'd upon the Skin of the Foetus* (London, 1729), pp. 69 ff. If certain current embryological views, defended in medical circles, had been valid, Tristram might well have been born with the image of a clock clearly defined on his body. See also Turner's *The Force of the Mother's Imagination upon her Foetus in Utero . . . in the Way of A Reply to Dr. Blondel's Last Book* (London, 1730), pp. 168, 170.

[3] IV, xix, 296.

was inevitable in terms of the theory of the association of ideas—and quite appropriate to the moment. It came on the first Sunday night of the month when Mr. Shandy, "one of the most regular men in every thing he did," followed his undeviating custom of winding the large house-clock and got out of the way at the same time "some other little family concernments [so as to] be no more plagued and pester'd with them the rest of the month."[4] Unlike Sterne, who once described himself as "totally spiritualized out of all form for connubial purposes,"[5] Tristram's father, aged between fifty and sixty at the time of his son's conception, was clearly not in that condition, even though he was rather abstemious; and the "sagacious *Locke*" would have been the first to understand the peculiar linkage of ideas in Mrs. Shandy's mind of two activities so ordinarily unrelated. As Tristram himself explained, "from an unhappy association of ideas which have no connection in nature . . . my poor mother could never hear the said clock wound up,—but the thoughts of some other things unavoidably popp'd into her head,—& *vice versa*."[6]

It may be thought that this witty, if somewhat indelicate, opening of *Tristram Shandy*, with its description of the homunculus, has received its full measure of attention; but it has, in fact, implications and complexities hitherto unexplored. Sterne's knowledgeable contemporaries would have read the opening chapters with special understanding in the context of eighteenth-century medical and biological science, and particularly in the light of a long continued controversy in the field of embryology. We have here one more example, actually one of the best examples, of what has frequently been remarked, Sterne's use of learning for purposes of wit. A clue to what an eighteenth-century reader found in Tristram's account of his begetting comes from a pamphlet published soon after the appearance of the first volume of *Tristram Shandy*—a brief, anonymous scribble titled *The Clockmaker's Outcry against the Author of the Life and Opinions of Tristram Shandy* (1760).[7] This is a pretense that Sterne, who is described as a "forerunner of Antichrist,"[8] has come close to destroying the clockmaker's trade because "no modest lady now dares to mention a word about *winding-up a clock*, without exposing herself to the sly leers and jokes of the family." The anonymous pam-

---

[4] I, iv, 8.

[5] *Letters of Laurence Sterne*, ed. Lewis Perry Curtis (Oxford, 1935), pp. 240–41. In this amusing and suggestive letter to Mrs. F., Sterne tells her: "I have not an ounce of carnality about me."

[6] I, iv, 9.

[7] I use the Second Edition, Corrected, London, 1760.

[8] *Ibid.*, p. 10.

phleteer complains that "hitherto harmless watches are degraded into agents of debauchery" and reputable hoary clocks excite to "acts of carnality."[9] Sterne is accused of beginning his novel "like one of Priapus's lecherous priests in Pagan times."[10] In the midst of the tirades are two significant relevant remarks, the insistence that most of what is said in *Tristram Shandy* about the homunculus is false and absurd[11] and that Sterne has contradicted himself by espousing two opposed hypotheses in embryology—a reference to the diametrical views of the ovists and the animalculists, whose controversy dominated that science.[12]

For our purposes the key passage in *Tristram Shandy* is the whole of Book I, chapter ii, in which Tristram complains that his mother's "unseasonable question" so ruffled the animal spirits that they failed to perform their function of conducting Homunculus safely "to the place destined for his reception." Then we are given an account of the homunculus:

The HOMUNCULUS, Sir, [is] to the eye of reason in scientific research . . . a Being guarded and circumscribed with rights:—the minutest philosophers . . . shew us incontestably That the HOMUNCULUS is created by the same hand,—engender'd in the same course of nature,—endowed with the same loco-motive powers and faculties with us:—That he consists, as we do, of skin, hair, fat, flesh, veins, arteries, ligaments, nerves, cartilages, bones, marrow, brains, glands, genitals, humours, and articulations:—is a Being of as much activity,—and, in all senses of the word, as much and as truly our fellow-creature as my Lord Chancellor of England.[13]

The witty context of this description and the humorous tone, as well as its remoteness from modern embryological theory, should not mislead us into believing that Sterne has greatly distorted certain scientific views of his time. Actually Tristram's account of the "little gentleman" is based on the microscopic investigations and the speculations of such respected biologists of the late seventeenth century as Harvey, Swammerdown, Malpighi, Leeuwenhoek, de Graaf, and others whose embryological views were accepted and disseminated in the eighteenth century. These views were reflected in a theory called "preformation" and in two schools of thought concerning human conception, the ovists and the animalculists, whose clashing ideas throw light on the opening chapters of *Tristram Shandy*.[14]

[9] *Ibid.*, pp. 42, 43.

[10] *Ibid.*, p. 11.

[11] *Ibid.*, p. 10.

[12] *Ibid.*, pp. 34–35.

[13] I, ii, 5.

[14] For the historical development of embryological theories, see R. C. Punnett, "Ovists and Animalculists," *American Naturalist*, LXII (1928), 481–507; F. J. Cole, *Early The-*

The school of ovists derived from the famous dictum enunciated by Harvey in 1651, *ex ovo omnium*, a principle further demonstrated by the work of Swammerdown and de Graaf, especially the latter's discovery of the mammalian egg. Scientists and others inclined to this school maintained the primacy of the female in generation and believed, with varying degrees of assurance, that "the first Bud of the future larger Animal [is] pre-existent . . . in the Egg of the Mother."[15] This "Ovarian Doctrine" was strongly challenged in the 1690's; and we find a continuous controversy between ovists and animalculists to the time of Sterne. The chief issue between the two groups was stated by one of Sterne's scientific contemporaries, whose details reveal at the same time that the homunculus of science closely resembles the homunculus of Sterne's novel:

But though Reason and Experience do now convince us, that all and every the most minute Part of every Animal, though ever so small, do really exist even to a single Artery, Vein, Nerve, Fibre; and all its Fluids were also in Motion, and circulated in the same, long before Generation: Yet whether this same Bud of Being, this *Minim* of Nature, this *Primordium Animalis*, this Principle of Body, this *Punctum vitae*, this *Stamen, Semen, Animalculum, Homunculus*, or *Manakin* in Miniature, was previously lodged in *Semine Masculino*, or in the *Ovum*, or Egg of the Female (for in one or the other it must needs be) is still Matter of Doubt and Dispute among Philosophers and Anatomists.[16]

---

ories of Sexual Generation (Oxford, 1930); Arthur W. Meyer, *The Rise of Embryology* (Stanford and London, 1939); Joseph Needham, *A History of Embryology* (2d ed.; New York, 1959). Cole and Needham include invaluable bibliographies. Good contemporary accounts of the ovist-animalculist controversy may be found in Dr. Daniel Turner's *The Force of the Mother's Imagination upon her Foetus in Utero . . . in the Way of a Reply to Dr. Blondel's Last Book,* pp. 89–105; and particularly in John Cooke's *An Anatomical and Mechanical Essay on the Whole Animal Oeconomy* (London, 1730), I, 1–29; II, 254 ff., where all the issues, scientific and religious, are examined. See also John Harris, *Lexicon Technicum* (London, 1710), Vol. II: "Generation."

15 J. C[ooke], *The New Theory of Generation, according to the Best and Latest Discoveries in Anatomy* (London, 1762), I, 15. See also I, 125: "The famous Lewenhoek and Hartsocker were the first, who . . . set this new Hypothesis of Animalcular Generation on Foot."

16 *Ibid.*, p. 14. The shift from the ovarian to the animalculist position in the early eighteenth century is made clear by James Drake, Fellow of the Royal College of Physicians and of the Royal Society: "It is agreed on all Hands, that there are in the *Ovaries* of *Women* little *Eggs*. These *Eggs*, most *Modern Anatomists*, and the most Able till very lately, have maintain'd to be the *material* and *formal* Rudiments of the Body of the *future Man*, which the *Seed* of the *Male* did only pregnate and vivifie. . . . This Opinion was first broach'd and laid down with Strength of Reason . . . by Dr. Harvey, in his book *De Generatione Animalium*. It procur'd almost universal Assent from the Writings of that Author; and seem'd perfectly establish'd by *De Graaf*, till the *Microscopical* Observations of Mr. Lewenhook grafted somewhat upon it, and took something from it" (*Anthropologia Nova, or, A New System of Anatomy* [London, 1707], I, 332).

The school of animalculists was inspired mainly by the work of three scientists, most extensively by that of Leeuwenhoek, the famous correspondent of the Royal Society, whose use of the microscope led to the discovery of spermatozoa, the *sine qua non* of the animalculist hypothesis. The other two scientists of influence were Nicholas Hartsoeker, the first to publish an illustration of a homunculus in the male sperm, and Francois de Plantades, secretary of the Montpellier Academy of Science, writing under the pseudonym of Dalenpatius. In his *Letter* on generation, which became widely known—it was reprinted in England in the *History of the Works of the Learned* (May 1699) and referred to by Leeuwenhoek in the *Philosophical Transactions* of the Royal Society (1699)—Dalenpatius helped to spread the animalculist hypothesis beyond any real merit in his investigations. His *Letter* was accompanied by illustrations depicting "little men" fully formed in human spermatozoa, allegedly seen under the microscope. These animalcules, he maintained, he had clearly observed, with tails "four or five times the length of their bodies":

They move with extraordinary agility, and by the lashings of their tails they produce and agitate the wavelets in which they swim. Who would have believed that in them was a human body? But I have seen this thing with my own eyes. For while I was examining them all with care one appeared which was larger than the others, and sloughed off the skin in which it had been enclosed, and clearly revealed, free from covering, both its shins, its legs, its breasts, and two arms, whilst the cast skin, when pulled further up, enveloped the head after the manner of a cowl. It was impossible to distinguish sexual characteristics on account of its small size. . . .[17]

The animalculist hypothesis received enthusiastic support from microscopic science in the eighteenth century. Typical is Henry Baker,

[17] See Cole, *Early Theories*, pp. 68–69, for this translation of the Latin; see also *History of the Works of the Learned*, I (May 1699), 269, for the *Letter* and the illustrations. Cole, who believes that Dalenpatius was perpetrating a hoax, says that the *Letter* was both accepted and attacked. By printing an account of the *Letter* in the *Philosophical Transactions*, XXI (August 1699), Leeuwenhoek seems to have furthered the cause of animalculism (see Cole, *Early Theories*, p. 70). It is true that Leeuwenhoek was skeptical that Dalenpatius had actually *seen* a fully formed being in the male sperm: "I put this down as a certain truth, that the shape of a Human Body is included in an Animal of the Masculine Seed, but that a Mans Reason shall dive or penetrate into this Mystery so far, that in the Anatomizing of one of these Animals of the Masculine Seed, we should be able to see or discover the intire shape of a Human Body, I cannot comprehend" ("Part of a Letter from Mr. Leuvenhook, Dated June 9th, 1699, Concerning the Animalcula in Semine Humano," in *Phil. Trans.*, XXI [August 1699], no. 255, p. 306). At another point in the same issue of the *Transactions*, Leeuwenhoek wrote: "Now if we know . . . the great Mystery that is included in the small Seed of an Apple, why might not we assert that in an Animal of the Masculine Seed of a Man, is locked up a whole Man, and that the Animals of the Seed are all descending from the first Created Man" (p. 27).

Fellow of the Royal Society and author of *The Microscope Made Easy* (1742). Like others who were fascinated by the world revealed through the microscope, Baker writes lyrically of the symmetry, beauty, and perfection found there—that whole world of nature so obviously the work of the Divine Artificer, which far surpasses the works of art, mean and rough by contrast. As one example of divine artifice, he refers to "those breathing Atoms"—the animalcules:

In them . . . we shall discover the same Organs of Body, Multiplicity of Parts, Variety of Motions, Diversity of Figures, and particular Ways of Living as in the larger Animals.—How amazingly curious must the Internal Structure of these Creatures be! The Heart, the Stomach, the Entrails, and the Brain! How minute and fine the Bones, Joints, Muscles and Tendons! How exquisitely delicate beyond all Conception the Arteries, Veins, and Nerves! What Multitudes of Vessels and Circulation must be contained within this narrow Compass! And yet, all have sufficient Room to perform their different Offices, and neither impede nor interfere with one another.[18]

Baker is of special interest because he was both a scientist and a man of letters—a poet, translator, and journalist. Well before Sterne he illustrates how literature in the period reflected embryological theory. Unlike Sterne, he makes serious use of the concept of preformation and, additionally, of the related concept of *emboitment* or encasement, in his poem, *The Universe* (1727).[19] This latter facet of embryological thought, concerned with the origin and transmission of the germ cells, had interesting implications for the actual physical transmission of original sin, and, as we shall see, for religion generally.[20] It held that all the germ cells of future generations were cre-

[18] *The Microscope Made Easy* (2d ed.; London, 1743), p. 298. Baker was widely read. In the 1750's, when Sir John Hill was attacking microscopic anatomy, he centered his fire to a considerable degree on Baker—that "Prince of Societarians." In 1751, Hill wrote: "We are to acknowledge Merit, great Merit indeed, in Lewenhoeck; he has the good Fortune to be one of the first People who worked at microscopical Observations, but we are to acknowledge at the same Time, That he has the Honour of having stocked the Philosophical Transactions with more Errours than any one Member of it, excepting his Successor in Peeping, Mr. *Baker*" (*A Review of the Works of the Royal Society of London* [London, 1751], p. 156).

[19] Additional contemporary comment on the concept of *emboitment* or encasement may be found in *Father Malebranche's Treatise concerning the Search after Truth*, trans. T. Taylor (Oxford, 1695), I, 15; John Ray, *The Wisdom of God Manifest in the Works of Creation* (1691; 10th ed.; London, 1735), p. 115; Nicola Andry, *An Account of the Breeding of Worms in Human Bodies* (London, 1701), pp. 190–91. See also Cole, *Early Theories*, pp. 50 ff. and *passim;* Meyer, *Rise of Embryology*, pp. 62 ff. and *passim.* For a vigorous attack on the concept, see Patrick Blair, *Botanick Essays* (London, 1720), pp. 304 ff. Blair was a Fellow of the Royal Society.

[20] The difficulty of reconciling the concept of encasement and Christian doctrines disturbed some contemporaries. See, for example, "Mr. Locke's Reply to the Bishop

ated at one and the same time by God and were contained in Eve (according to the ovists) or in Adam (according to the animalculists). "There is no necessity to think," wrote Dr. George Cheyne, the widely known physician and a Fellow of the Royal Society, "*God almighty* is confin'd to a new Creation, in ev'ry *generation* of an Animal." Since "these *Animals* Themselves are conspicuous in all male seeds hitherto examin'd, it is plain that they must be lodg'd in the Loyns of the Original Pairs of all the *species* of *Animal*." Or as one ardent expounder of the animalculist position said: ". . . you and I did once exist and swim together, in the real, corporeal, literal Loins of our first Parent *Adam*."²¹ The "preformed" beings waited, one generation encased in the other, "to be brought forth and disclosed to view in a certain time, and according to a certain order and economy" —so Ephraim Chambers reports, in his *Cyclopaedia: Or, An Universal Dictionary of Arts and Sciences* (1728). Thus "there is not properly any new *generation* . . . only augmentation and expansion of minute parts of the bodies of seeds; so that the whole species, to be afterwards produced, were really formed in the first, and inclosed therein. . . ."²²

Baker and his contemporaries, for whom the microscope had demonstrated the "Arithmetick of Infinites" and "the infinite Divisibility

---

of Worcester's Answer to his Second Letter," in *Works of John Locke* (London, 1812), IV, 303 ff. See also the reference to William Wollaston, note 57 below. In 1721, James Handley, in his *Mechanical Essays on the Animal Oeconomy*, disputed both the ovarian doctrine of Harvey and the animalcular hypothesis of Leeuwenhoek because if they are "absolutely in the Right, it must cause very great Doubts to arise in every Christian's Breast, and leave him in a very great Dilemma, as to the Truth of what the Bible contains: For if Harvey's *Hypothesis* be certain, how can our Saviour . . . be called the Seed of *Abraham* and *David?* Or if Lewenhoeck's were so, How can he be called the Seed of the Woman? Both which *we* know he most certainly was" (p. 38). See the answer to Handley by John Cooke, in *An Anatomical and Mechanical Essay*, I, 8–9. At another point in this work Cooke, after stating the case for encasement, wrote: ". . . so we may be said, in the literal Sense, actually to have fell with *Adam* in his first Transgression" (I, 13).

²¹ *Philosophical Principles of Religion, Natural and Revealed* (London, 1724), pp. 320–21; Cooke, *An Anatomical and Mechanical Essay*, II, 256.

²² Vol. I: "Generation." I use the edition of 1752. Sterne apparently owned the edition of 1738 (see *A Facsimile Reproduction of a Unique Catalogue of Laurence Sterne's Library* [London, 1930], p. 10, no. 236). See also B. L. Greenberg, "Sterne and Chambers Encyclopaedia," *MLN*, LXIX (1954), 560–62. For a passing reference to the concept of "a *primitive Ovum*" that contained the seeds of all future generations, see James Augustus Blondel, *The Power of the Mother's Imagination Examin'd*, p. 141. Cf. Cheyne: "*Generation* is nothing but *Accretion*, for it is beyond all Doubt, that all *Generation* is from a preceding little *Animal* lodg'd in the Male" (*Philosophical Principles*, p. 320). See also John Denne, *The Wisdom of God in the Vegetable Creation* (London, 1730), *passim*, an interesting example of a sermon in which the prevailing theories of generation are utilized.

of Matter," had no difficulty in believing "that all Mankind might once exist *in parvo* in Adam's loins":

> Each Seed includes a Plant: that Plant, again,
> Has other Seeds, which other Plants contain:
> Those other Plants have all their Seeds, and Those
> More Plants again, successively, inclose.
>
> Thus, ev'ry single Berry that we find,
> Has, really, in itself large Forests of its Kind.
> Empire and Wealth one Acorn may dispense,
> By Fleets to sail a thousand Ages hence.
> Each Myrtle Seed includes a thousand Groves,
> Where future Bards may warble forth their Loves.
> Thus Adam's Loins contain'd his large Posterity,
> All People that have been, and all that e'er shall be.[23]

Baker himself exclaims that this is an "Amazing Thought." Yet, he adds, "we must believe/What Reason tells."[24] It is indeed an amazing thought, but it had currency among scientists and laymen, poets and theologians. Sterne could have found it in many places, for instance (with ovist coloration) in his copy of Sir Richard Blackmore's *Creation* (1712),[25] where we are told that

> ev'ry foetus bears a secret hoard,
> With sleeping, unexpanded issue stor'd;
> Which num'rous, but unquicken'd progeny
> Clasp'd and inwrap'd within each other lie:
> Engendering heats these one by one unbind,
> Stretch their small tubes, and hamper'd nerves unwind;
> And thus when time shall drain each magazine
> Crowded with men unborn, unripe, unseen,
> Nor yet of parts unfolded, no increase
> Can follow, all prolific power must cease.[26]

---

[23] *The Universe, A Poem intended to Restrain the Pride of Man* (London, 1727[?]), p. 23. See also *Father Malebranche's Treatise*, p. 15; J. C[ooke], *New Theory of Generation*, I, 289. Malebranche, who was widely read in the period, relates microscopic revelations of the "invisible world" to the theory of preformation. "All the Bodies of Men and of Beasts," he wrote, "which shall be born or produc'd till the *End* of the World, were possibly created from the *Beginning* of it: I would say, That the Females of the Original Creatures were for aught we know, created together, with all those of the same *Species* which have been, or shall be, begotten or created whilst the World stands" (I, 15). On the subject of "the infinite Divisibility of Matter," see John Keill, *Introduction to Natural Philosophy, or, Philosophical Lectures Read in the University of Oxford, Anno Dom. 1700* (4th ed.; London, 1745), pp. 46, 53, and John Cooke, *An Anatomical and Mechanical Essay*, I, 11–14.

[24] *The Universe*, p. 23.

[25] *Catalogue of Sterne's Library*, p. 63, no. 1660. This lists the edition of 1715.

[26] VI, ll. 289–98.

Stated in the simplest terms the animalculist hypothesis maintained that the male sperm contained the animalcule or homunculus and that the act of conception involved the female only or primarily to the extent that she provides a proper nidus. She is not, as Mr. Shandy says of Mrs. Shandy, *"the principal agent."*[27] This is precisely what the animalculists were arguing, as we may see in a typical statement by John Cooke, who described himself as a "Student of Physick and Late of the College of Edinburgh." Writing in 1730, he maintained that "as the Earth seems a Nidus for all Seeds of Vegetables, so the Ova of the Female serve for the like Use":

. . . to think otherwise would be making Woman the chief Person in the Creation, in as much as she is supposed [i.e., by the ovists] to contain her Species, both materially and formally, in her self, and needs only a little of the Spirit of the Male Sperm to set those Animalcula in Motion; so that instead of God's giving Woman for a Help-mate to Man towards Procreation, he is thus made Womans Help-mate; and so hath the least share in this Action; whereas by Nature he was designed the chief Agent in it, and that from his Loins should proceed all Mankind . . . which the Text of St. *Paul* well alludes to, when he says of *Levi*, that he was yet in the Loins of his father, when Melchisedeck met him.[28]

This idea of the restricted function of the mother, in opposition to the ovist viewpoint, had profound implications reaching beyond the field of science, for example, into the realm of property rights. It is of more than passing interest that when James Boswell's father wished to entail the family estate on heirs general (i.e., both males and females), Boswell, who wished the entail to apply only to male heirs, thought he might rely on "the opinion of some distinguished naturalists"

that our species is transmitted through males only, the female being all along no more than a *nidus,* or nurse, as Mother Earth is to plants of every sort; which notion seems to be confirmed by that text of Scripture, "He was yet *in the loins of his* Father when Melchisedeck met him" (Heb. vii, 10); and consequently, that a man's grandson by a daughter, instead of being his *surest* descendant, as is vulgarly said, has, in reality, no connection whatever with his blood.[29]

---

[27] V, xxxi, 391.

[28] Cooke, *An Anatomical and Mechanical Essay,* I, 5. The animalculist view, stated by Cooke and reflected in Walter Shandy's remark that Mrs. Shandy is not "the principal agent," has ancient roots in Egypt and Greece. It was used by Aeschylus in *Eumenides.* Orestes, who revenged his father by killing Clytemnestra, is charged with matricide. Apollo, in defending Orestes, rejects this charge by maintaining, in effect, that the mother is not actually blood kin to her son, that she serves only as the nidus (ll. 637 ff. and note 2, in *Aeschylus* [Loeb Classical Library ed.], pp. 334–37). Euripides uses the same argument in his *Orestes* (ll. 552 ff.).

[29] *Life of Johnson,* ed. G. B. Hill, rev. L. F. Powell (Oxford, 1934), II, 414, n. 2. In the third decade of the eighteenth century a lively controversy broke out over the influence

Boswell's qualification, that this opinion was held by "some distinguished naturalists," hints at the controversial aspect of embryological thought and of the unwillingness of many contemporaries to press the animalculist viewpoint to its extreme. A report to the Royal Society in 1693, often quoted in the eighteenth century as a compromise, illustrates the cautious attitude. The author of the report, Dr. George Garden, glances at the discoveries of Harvey, Malpighi, and de Graaf, and the inferences drawn from them—that "the Rudiments of each Animal were originally in the respective Females"—to suggest that Leeuwenhoek's discovery of "an infinite number of *Animalcula in semine*" has cast doubt on "the Propagation of all Animals *ex ovo*." He therefore offers as probabilities: "1. That Animals are *ex Animalculo*. 2. That these Animalcules are originally in *semine Marium & non in Foeminis*. 3. That they can never come forward, nor be formed into Animals of the respective Kind, *without the Ova in Foeminis*."[30]

An occasional animalculist might be dogmatic, as, for example, Thomas Morgan, writing in 1735: "that all Generation is from an Animalculum pre-existing *in Semine Maris*, is so evident in fact, and so well confirm'd by Experience and Observation, that I know now of no Learned Men, who in the least doubt of it."[31] Nevertheless, such compendiums as Chambers' *Cyclopaedia* (1728) and Dr. James's *Medical Dictionary* (1745) presented both the ovist and the animalculist view. But the point for our purposes is that the homunculus was widely known, involved in vigorous controversy, and readily available for witty treatment. He had been fully visualized and introduced at Oxford by John Keill, Savilian Professor of Astronomy and Fellow of the Royal Society, as early as 1700, in his Philosophical Lectures. The "Subtility of Nature," he told his audience, "is wonderful beyond measure"; and he appealed to them to imagine the "organized

---

of the mother's imagination on the foetus. Dr. James Blondel, one of the chief controversialists and a convinced animalculist, argued that no such influence (in the usual sense of stigmata and deformities) was possible. He defended his position by reference to the new theories of generation: "If *Leewenhoeck's* or Dr. Gardener's Notion be true, by what right has the Mother's Fancy any Influence upon the Body of the *Foetus*, which comes from the *Semen virile*, and which is consequently a distinct and separate *Individuum* . . ." (*The Power of the Mother's Imagination Examin'd*, p. 111; see also pp. 128–29). Both Boswell and Walter Shandy would have found this view comforting. For Dr. Daniel Turner's answer, see *The Force of the Mother's Imagination*, pp. 102 ff. See above, note 2.

[30] Reprinted by William Derham; in *Miscellanea Curiosa* (3d ed.; London, 1736), I, 143.

[31] Thomas Morgan, *The Mechanical Practice of Physick* (London, 1735), p. 281. The ovist position was strongly asserted by Patrick Blair in 1720, in *Botanick Essays*, pp. 302–25.

Body" of the animalcules "beheld through a Microscope, floating in the Seed of Animals":

... the Heart that is the Fountain of its Life, the Muscles necessary to its Motions, the Glands for the Secretion of its Fluids, the Stomach and Bowels to digest its Food. ... But since every one of these Members is also an organical Body, they must have likewise Parts necessary to their Actions. For they consist of Fibres, Membranes, Coats, Veins, Arteries, Nerves, and an almost infinite number of fine Tubes. ... [32]

We find the homunculus again with the lineaments unchanged six decades later, as *Tristram Shandy* was in progress, a "Bud of Being ... *Punctum vitae* ... *Animalculum, Homunculus*, or *Manakin* in Miniature" whose "Arteries, Veins, Nerves, Lymphatics, and Fibres did every one pre-exist long before Conception ... and are after that ... as it were, blown up, enlarged, expanded, extended, unravelled, and augmented."[33] Conception occurs when "some of the animalcules lodge in the ova placed in the Matrix of the female as a proper *Nidus* for them."

Thus Tristram's description of the homunculus as consisting of "skin, hair, fat, flesh, veins, arteries, ligaments, nerves, cartilage, bones, marrow, brains, glands, genitals, humours, and articulation," though clearly set in a context of humor, is less a parody than an accurate reflection of aspects of contemporary embryological speculation. Similarly, Tristram's reference to the homunculus as "so young a traveller"—"my little gentleman had got to his journey's end miserably spent"[34]—reflects humorously the animalculist view of the homunculus seeking and finding "a proper *Nidus*." The image of the Shandean homunculus as a traveler undergoing the discomforts and fatigue of a journey tempts one to believe that Sterne had read and remembered the words of Patrick Blair, a Fellow of the Royal Society, who had vigorously opposed the animalcular position four decades earlier:

If [Blair wrote] *in an Animalcule of the Masculine Seed of a Man, a whole Man is lock'd up*, then the several Particles previously in the *Ovum*, are no more than the first Food to this Stranger; this new arriv'd Child (who after being fatigu'd by so long a Journey, and through so many difficult and unaccessible Roads, when all those in Company with him have been so wearied, that they were left behind and kill'd) had need of such Refreshment to rouse up his Spirits, and to make him grow up so as to become a brisk and lively Boy.[35]

---

[32] *An Introduction to Natural Philosophy*, p. 56.

[33] J. C[ooke], *New Theory of Generation*, I, 14, 41.

[34] I, ii, 6.

[35] *Botanick Essays*, p. 316.

Obviously Sterne saw the intrinsic comedy in such theories; and he is separated from the proponents of these views, scientists and others, by little more than the dimension of wit—from such a person, say, as Daniel de Superville, who reported in the *Philosophical Transactions* of the Royal Society (1740), that "each *Animalculum* . . . is a small Animal of the same Species with that which harbours it." It disengages itself, he adds, "from the Confinement in which it was, and in a Place where it meets with a Humour proper for its Vegetation and Expansion, it takes Root . . . swells like a Corn newly put into the Earth . . . spreads itself, its Members shape themselves . . . its Parts grow longer, and disentangle themselves. . . ."[36] Mr. Shandy himself reveals his animalcular prejudices in Book V. In conversing with Yorick concerning "the natural relation between a father and his child," he lists procreation as one means by which a father acquires jurisdiction over his offspring. To Yorick's remark that by this same means the mother has a similar claim to jurisdiction, Mr. Shandy gives the reply, already quoted, of a convinced animalculist: *"she is not the principal agent."*[37]

To anyone concerned with Sterne's reflection of contemporary embryological thought, the famous chapter (I, xx) on intra-uterine baptism is, of course, suggestive; and we do, in fact, find that here too the animalculist hypothesis serves comic purposes. It will be recalled that Sterne uses an actual instance, from the year 1733, in which a French obstetrical surgeon appealed to the Sorbonne for a theological opinion: the surgeon wished to know the validity of baptizing an unborn child, none of whose body could be made to appear.[38] Canon law and diocesan practice seemed to offer some flexibility. It was generally held, with Aquinas as authority, that a child fully retained in the mother's womb "cannot be counted among other men and thus cannot be the object of an external action in receiving through the ministry of men the sacraments necessary to salvation."[39] The surgeon asked whether a "conditional" baptism by means of a little injection-pipe (*"une petite canulle"*) might be permissible in this instance, giving his assurance that it could be done *"sans faire aucun tort à la mere."* Three learned doctors of theology at the Sorbonne, convinced that a child retained in the womb is capable of salvation or damnation,

[36] "Some Reflections on Generation and Monsters," *Phil. Trans.*, XLI (1744), 298 (no. 456, January–June 1740). De Superville was president of the College of Physicians in the Margravite of Brandenburg and a member of the Royal Society of Berlin.

[37] V, xxxi, 391.

[38] The letter of the surgeon and the response of the Doctors of Theology appeared in Henry de Deventer's *Observations importantes sur les Manuel des Accouchemens* (Paris, 1733), pp. 366–68.

[39] I, xx, 59.

approved (subject to assent by the bishop and the Pope) the surgeon's expedient—baptism conditionally *"par le moyen d'une petite canulle,"* or, as Sterne writes, "Anglicè *a squirt.*" This "Reply" inspired Tristram to raise an ingenious, and similar, point, which he addressed to the very same Doctors of the Sorbonne:

> . . . whether after the ceremony of marriage, and before that of con-summation, the baptizing all the HOMUNCULI at once, slap-dash, by in-jection, would not be a shorter and safer cut still; on condition as above, That if the HOMUNCULI do well and come safe into the world after this, That each and every [one] of them shall be baptized again (*sous condi-tion.*)[40]

The anonymous author of *The Clockmaker's Outcry* offered this passage in the novel as evidence that Sterne had abandoned the ani-malculist position of the early chapters for the ovist view that "all the *animalcula* are complete in the *ovaria* of the women."[41] But the Clock-maker's accusation is groundless. He ignored Tristram's all-important proviso, that baptism-by-injection be applied to the homunculi if "the thing can be done . . . *par le moyen d'une* petite canulle, and *sans faire aucun tort au pere.*"[42] The significant word, of course, is *"pere"*—involving a fully calculated change by Sterne from the phrase of the French surgeon, *"sans faire aucun tort à la mere,"* in order to maintain consistency with the animalculist position of the opening chapters. Tristram, therefore, is still reflecting the hypothesis that "Animalcules are originally in *semine Marium & non in Foeminis.*" It may be supererogation to point out that Sterne at this point in *Tris-tram Shandy* has put the homunculi into the context of long-contin-ued theological debate concerning the human embryo and its rela-tionship to the sacraments necessary for salvation. In effect, he has given to the homunculus the status of the unbaptized child in the mother's womb, whose damnation and torment, should it die, were so endlessly discussed from patristic and scholastic times to his own day. Sterne relies on his readers to be aware of certain issues implicit in his chapter on intra-uterine baptism, such matters as the precise moment the embryo was animated by a soul (thus becoming capable of salva-tion or damnation) and related considerations, as infant perdition and the mortal sin of abortion. A knowledge of these strengthens the im-pact of his profane wit. He did not miss the possibilities for Shandean humor in the weighty deliberations of the learned doctors of the Church; and, of course, as a child of the age, he had no delicacy or

40 I, xx, 62.

41 *The Clockmaker's Outcry*, pp. 34–35.

42 I, xx, 62.

restraint in treating them. But perhaps the cream of the Shandean jest in this notable chapter is the idea of homuncular baptism in the male, a sacramental procedure possible only if there is validity in the animalculist hypothesis.

We have not yet exhausted all of the subtleties resident in Tristram's proposal that the sacrament of baptism be given the homunculi collectively. Certain philosophical and additional religious considerations reached into the biological controversies; and these too add an extra intellectual dimension to the proposal and increase the wit. Here we must look again at one of the provisions Tristram included in his address to the doctors of the Sorbonne: "if the HOMUNCULI do well and come safe into the world after this [i.e., after the proposed baptism-by-injection in the father] . . . each and every one of them shall be baptized again."[43] This proviso reflects a fundamental and disturbing point for both opponents and proponents of the animalcular hypothesis. What, they asked, of those homunculi who do *not* "do well and come safe into the world"? Here, clearly, was a problem involving the providence of God and the rational structure of the universe. We must recall that for the animalculist, animalcules were not merely "originally *in semine Marium*"; they were there by the tens of thousands. Henry Baker reported with amazement that "the Eye, assisted by a good *Microscope,* can distinguish plainly, in the Semen masculinum of Animals, Myriads of *Animalcules,* alive and vigorous, though so exceedingly minute, that it is computed three thousand millions of them are not equal to a Grain of Sand, whose Diameter is but the one hundredth Part of an Inch."[44] Human semen under the microscope is observed to be "plentifully stocked with Life": Mr. Leeuwenhoek had seen "more than ten thousand living Creatures . . . moving in no larger a Quantity of the Fluid Part thereof than the Bigness of a Grain of Sand."[45] Thomas Morgan, in his *Mechanical Practice of Physick* (1735), calculated precisely the size of "one of the largest of these seminal Animalcula": the "solid content of one of these little People," he wrote, "is not more than 1/12000000000 Part of a Cubick Inch."[46] Leeuwenhoek, had he been alive in the eighteenth century, might well have failed to recognize some of his discoveries, but he had indeed startled his contemporaries and later generations by maintaining that "the Milt of a single Cod-Fish contained more living *Animalcules,*

---

[43] *Ibid.*

[44] *The Microscope Made Easy,* p. 149. See also James Handley, *Mechanical Essays on the Animal Oeconomy* (London, 1721), p. 35.

[45] *The Microscope Made Easy,* p. 163.

[46] *The Mechanical Practice of Physick,* p. 282.

than there are People alive upon the Face of the Whole Earth at one and the same Time."[47] His computation of three thousand millions compressed into a space smaller than "one single Grain of coarse Sand" is mentioned again and again in the period with awe and even with reverence. Perhaps no one expressed the idea better than John Keill, in his lectures at Oxford, in 1700: "what some Philosophers have dreamed concerning Angels," he declared, "is true of these Animalcules, *viz.* that many thousands of them may dance on the Point of a small Needle."[48]

But, as indicated, this "numerosity" of animalcula, when only an occasional one functioned in the act of generation, had some dark implications. It meant shocking wastefulness, a squandering of potential lives, the apparently wanton destruction, if we may use Tristram's words at the opening of the novel, of fellow creatures who have "the claims and rights of humanity." Quoting the "minutest philosophers" (a pejorative phrase, of course), Tristram describes the homunculus as created by the same hand as others, a being who may be benefited or injured, one with all of the immunities of any member of the human race. Once again Sterne's humor is achieved without an exaggerated distortion of prevailing views. At least, Tristram's remark—"if the HOMUNCULI do well and come safe into the world"—raises the question of living beings pointlessly created and destroyed, a very sensitive matter for Sterne's contemporaries and one that prevented some from accepting the animalculist hypothesis. For the physico-theologists and rationalists generally, who felt assured that the deity had created nothing in vain, that all the handiwork of God had a proper function in His orderly and harmonious universe, the wastefulness implied in the hypothesis was wholly unacceptable. As early as 1692, John Ray, in *Three Physico-Theological Discourses,* voiced his disagreement with Leeuwenhoek because "the necessary Loss of an incredible Multitude of animalcula seems not agreeable to the Wisdom and Providence of Nature."[49] Such compendiums as those of Chambers and James repeated this cogent objection in the eighteenth century. "It would be necessary," Chambers wrote, "for 9999 parts of the animalcules to be in vain, and perish, which is contrary to the

[47] *The Microscope Made Easy,* p. 155. Leeuwenhoek's remarkable calculation fascinated later scientists if repetition is an indication. See, for example, James Keill, *The Anatomy of the Human Body Abridg'd* (1698; 12th ed.; London, 1759), p. 109; Nicola Andry, *An Account of the Breeding of Worms in Human Bodies,* p. 180; Cooke, *An Anatomical and Mechanical Essay,* I, 11–13.

[48] *Introduction to Natural Philosophy,* pp. 55–56.

[49] 1713 ed., p. 59.

economy of nature in other Things."[50] In his *Medical Dictionary* (1745) James offered a similar refutation:

. . . if 3,000,000,000 Animalcules should be included in a Quantity of Male Sperm sufficient for the Production of one Animal only . . . all the rest are superfluous, and created for no End, but to be immediately destroy'd: Besides, we must suppose that Providence aims very ill, if oblig'd to load her Engine so enormously, in order to be able to hit the Mark propos'd. But in all other Instances we find that the Author of Nature perpetually adapts much less compounded Means, in order to arrive at destin'd Ends.[51]

Not everyone felt that a problem existed. J. Turberville Needham, Fellow of the Royal Society, a scientist of repute in France and England and later a correspondent of Voltaire, was skeptical of the existence of the spermatic animals described by his contemporaries; and he exercised some humor at the expense of their imaginary spectacle (in his view) of millions of animalcules competing to impregnate the egg, a privilege to be accorded only one: "Happy the first of these minute Beings," he wrote, "that could take Possession of this Cell, and shut the Door against contending Millions!"[52]

The defense offered by the animalculists lacked full conviction; and they relied to a considerable degree on the argument from man's ignorance of God's intentions. Since mysteries and miracles abound in the works of nature and Providence, who is presumptuous enough to question the deity's design in creating this "numerosity" of animalcules? Daniel de Superville, whose report to the Royal Society in 1740 has already been mentioned, exemplifies the uneasy animalculist facing this critical problem: "I own," he declared

[50] *Cyclopaedia*, Vol. I: "Generation."

[51] Vol. II: "Generation."

[52] "A Summary of Some Late Observations upon the Generation . . . of Animal and Vegetable Substances," *Phil. Trans.*, XLV (1748), 619 (no. 490, December 1748). For the curious mechanism involved in conception, one may turn to Nicola Andry: "A Friend of mine, a Physician of the Faculty of *Paris*, a Man of extraordinary skill in Physic, . . . is of opinion, that at the opening of the Egg there is a *Valvula*, which suffers the Worm [i.e., the spermatic worm, Andry's name for the animalculum] to enter the Egg, but hinders it to come out, because in the inside it shuts upon the outside. This *Valvula* is held fast by the Tail of the Worm which lies against it, so that it cannot open them neither without nor within. This is the cause that no other Worm can enter there, and this opinion seems very probable" (*An Account of the Breeding of Worms in Human Bodies*, pp. 184–85). This notion of competitive impregnation had been ridiculed earlier than Needham, by Daniel Turner, who thought it cunning of the animalculum "after he was thrown into the *Uterus*, to find his Way through the dark entry of the *Tuba*, and thence jump upon the particular *Ovum*, that is ready furnish'd for him, where finding out the Perforation, or putting by the Valve, he is to creep in, and make all fast after him, to prevent those millions of millions of his companions, who are beleaguering his Castle from entering after him . . ." (*The Force of the Mother's Imagination*, p. 104).

that the immense Number of *Animalcula* . . . in the Seminal Liquid of Man seems to oblige one to reject this Hypothesis, and particularly this Opinion, that every *Animalculum* is an *Embryo*. For it is certain, that in every Man there would be enough of them to people a vast Country, and of all that immense Quantity there are but a few that come to any thing. And so, there you have Millions of little Men, created never to exist; which seems directly contrary to the wise Intention of the Creator, who, in all Likelihood, made nothing in vain.[53]

After this statement of the difficulty inherent in the animalculist hypothesis, de Superville rests his case on "*Teleology* . . . one of those Parts of Philosophy, in which there has been but little Progress made." "Who dares presume," he asks, "so far as to pretend to penetrate into all the Designs of the Almighty, and into the divers Ends He has proposed to Himself in the Creation of the Universe?" De Superville saw a parallel in the rate of infant mortality. Why does "half of Mankind perish, before they come to the Age of one Year"? Clearly the deity might have saved himself the trouble of creating so "prodigious a Quantity of Creatures in order to precipitate them into nothing." But who can say that "creating so many Millions of Creatures has cost Him any more Pains" or that "all those *animalcula*, who do not come to the State of a Foetus, are annihilated"?[54]

The dilemma of the animalculists is revealed in de Superville's unwillingness to grant that superfluous animalcula were in fact created. Scientists were torn between the facts uncovered by the microscope, which implied in this instance a natural and divine order given to meaningless creativity, and the larger orientation of the age, which emphasized a rationally constructed universe with all parts meshed and functional. One edifying effort to solve the dilemma may be presented even though its relevance to Sterne is at best tenuous. This came from John Cooke, presenting his *New Theory of Generation*, in 1762. "It is very hard to conceive that Nature," he wrote, "is so idly luxurious of Seeds thus only to destroy them, and to make Myriads of them subservient to but a single one":

. . . all those other attending *Animalcula*, except that single one that is then conceived, evaporate away, and return back into the Atmosphere again, whence it is very likely they immediately proceeded; into the open Air, I say, the common Receptacle of all such disengaged minute sublunary Bodies; and do there circulate about with other *Semina*, where,

[53] *Phil. Trans.*, XLI (1744), 298–99 (no. 456, January–June 1740).

[54] *Ibid.*, pp. 299–300. De Superville points out that the principle of excess applies to the ovists as well: ". . . this seemingly useless Quantity of Animalcula equally affords an Argument against the Hypothesis of those, who believe the *Embryo* is in the Egg. One cannot maintain that all the Eggs in the *Ovaria* are fruitful" (p. 299).

perhaps, they do not absolutely die, but live a latent Life, in an insensible or dormant State, like Swallows in Winter . . . till [they] are received afresh into some other Male Body of the Proper Kind . . . to be afresh set in Motion, and ejected again in Coition as before, to run a fresh Chance for a lucky Conception. . . .[55]

Cooke had, in fact, offered this comforting viewpoint three decades earlier, when he gave assurances to his readers that though these animalcula come to nothing for the present, "Nature hath taken proper Care of them, and will in her own Time produce them all upon this Earth." "We need not wonder," he adds,

at their vast Number, since it is so necessary that they should be so, nor reckon them lost, since we know that provident Nature loses nothing, though we short-sighted Beings know not exactly how she manages them in that State in her secret chambers. And we know not but that we ourselves were once some of them . . . and that we underwent the like Circulation as they do. . . .[56]

Cooke's conception of widely dispersed animalcula in the air, risible as it may seem, is a traditional view with a long and respectable history in western thought. Latterly called panspermism, it maintained that all seminal elements, the primordial sperms, were formed simultaneously at creation and scattered over the universe, with each sperm or animalculum destined eventually to reach the genitals of the appropriate animal by means of air or food or water. "Equivocal generation," or the formation of monsters, was prevented by strainers in the recipient animal, which kept the primordial sperms or stamina of one species from finding their way into the wrong species. Panspermism in varied forms had exponents from the time of Virgil (*Georgics* III) to the middle of the eighteenth century; and Cooke's version may have struck contemporaries as unusual only by virtue of the speed with which his animalcula scrambled back into jostling competition for possible "lucky Conception."[57] But the historical fact seems to be that Cooke reflects the dying gasps of preformation and animalculism, as well as of panspermism. By 1750, dissenting views, which had never been silenced, appear to intensify. John Turberville Needham's vigor-

---

[55] *New Theory of Generation*, I, 85.

[56] *An Anatomical and Mechanical Essay*, II, 266, 268–69. Cf. I, 6.

[57] On the subject of panspermism, see Cole, pp. 169 ff., 208–9; Arthur W. Meyer, pp. 92 ff. For an interesting example of panspermism used in religious controversy, to prove the falsity of traducianism, see William Wollaston, *The Religion of Nature Delineated* (1722; 7th ed.; 1750), pp. 160 ff. Wollaston remarks on the "*animalcula* already formed; which being distributed about, especially in some opportune places and are *taken in* with aliment, or perhaps the very air; being separated in the bodies of the males by strainers proper to every kind, and then lodged in *their* seminal vessels. . . ."

ous attack of 1748 in scientific circles was followed in 1750 by Sir John Hill's satiric treatment of preformation and panspermism in a work amusingly called *Lucina sine concubitu*. Here the reader finds a machine invented to intercept the floating animalcula in the west wind, the *west* wind because Virgil's mares in *Georgics* III had snuffed the west wind and were impregnated; and Hill writes of the captive animalcula that "these small, original, unexpected minims of Existence" are revealed as "little Men and Women, exact in all their Limbs and Lineaments, and ready to offer themselves Candidates for Life, whenever they should happen to be . . . conveyed down into the Vessels of Generation."[58] Crudely interpreted and distorted, panspermism, with its hypothesis of the ubiquity of sperms—aliment, air, and water alive with them—offered embarrassing prospects if a wandering and unseemly animalculum found refuge without regard to the ethical and social codes of society. In the scientists themselves one senses a certain urgency to explain that the mechanism of conception does not and cannot go awry.[59] But Hill saw his opportunity; and I assume that no very great perceptiveness is required to realize from the title, *Lucina sine concubitu*, how he exploited humorously the concept of panspermism.

Thus a decade before the publication of *Tristram Shandy*, Sir John Hill, both scientist and literary man, had seen the possibilities for wit in the prevailing embryological theories, particularly in the homunculus. Indeed, it may well be that Sterne took his cue from Hill, of whom he had good reason to be aware;[60] and conceivably Tristram's remark—"The HOMUNCULUS, Sir, in how-ever low and ludicrous a light he may appear, in this age of levity, to the eye of folly or prejudice"[61]—is an allusion to *Lucina sine concubitu*. At any rate, Hill's

[58] Edited by Edmund Goldsmid (Edinburgh, 1885), p. 12. Hill makes a reference to both Virgil and Wollaston.

[59] Consider a serious variation of Hill's experiment of transferring a captured animalculum to a virgin, in Nicola Andry's *An Account of the Breeding of Worms in Human Bodies:* Andry presents the possible case of a married woman whose husband has died leaving behind an all too leisurely "spermatick worm," which does not enter the egg for several weeks. Thus, Andry warns, a woman may be "brought to bed without being criminal" (pp. 185-86). Isaac Watts gives a religious explanation for the perfect functioning of the reproductive mechanism: "Ever since that Week of creative Wonders God has ordered all these Creatures to fill the World with Inhabitants of their own kind, and they have obeyed him in a long Succession of almost six Thousand Years. He has granted . . . a divine Patent to each Creature for the sole Production of its own Likeness, with an utter Prohibition to all the rest" (*Philosophical Essays on Various Subjects* [London, 1733], p. 198).

[60] Wilbur L. Cross, *The Life and Times of Laurence Sterne* (New Haven, 1925), I, 202 ff.

[61] I, ii, 5.

pre-Shandean homunculus indicates that the time was ripe for Sterne.[62] Sterne's sortie into the microscopic world places him even more firmly than hitherto indicated in the tradition of preceding writers, including Swift, whose literary imagination found nourishment in science. The general resemblance to Swift, so often pointed out, is perhaps additionally demonstrated by the Shandean homunculus, but at the same time the difference becomes more evident. For Swift, the corruptions of science served as an emblem of the degeneracy of human nature and the entire environing culture; Sterne's treatment, though it has some implications for man's folly and the aberrations of the intellect, tends to be unleavened comic spectacle, all geniality, with no hint of that Juvenalian thunder characteristic of his great predecessor.

---

[62] I know of only one earlier instance of the comic use of animalculism, the casual mention in the *Memoirs of Scriblerus;* see the *Memoirs,* ed. Charles Kerby-Miller (New Haven, 1950), pp. 96–97, and n. 16, p. 189. A copy of the *Memoirs* is listed in the *Catalogue of Sterne's Library,* p. 93, no. 2664. Post-Shandean homunculi seem to have thrived. They appear several times in 1760, notably in two anonymous works, *Yorick's Meditations upon Various Subjects* and in what purports to be a third or supplementary volume to Sterne's novel. This latter work, attributed to John Carr, has the same title as Sterne's. In *Yorick's Meditations,* the author has brought Sterne and Shakespeare together, to demonstrate man's littleness and castigate his pride: "If imagination may trace the noble dust of Alexander, till it find it stopping a bung-whole [*sic*], why may not imagination trace that very Alexander, who conquered at Issus, Arbela, and Granicus, and who carried his presumption so far as to assume the title of son of Jupiter Ammon . . . why may not imagination trace that very Alexander, till it perceives him an homunculus in the genitalia of Philip, or, which seems rather more probable, of one of Philip's domestics . . ." (pp. 47–48; see also pp. 44–45). In the alleged third volume of *Tristram Shandy,* Walter Shandy tells Uncle Toby that "in generation the woman is but little different from being entirely passive. The disposition, figure, situation, number, activity, etc., etc., of the homunculi depend on the male. It is his business to adjust all these matters" (p. 11). He tried to convince Uncle Toby that "the science of generation depends on as certain and as reasonable rules as any other" (p. 13). When Uncle Toby perceives the relationship between his cherished science of fortifications and generation, he is convinced (p. 16).

MAYNARD MACK

"The Shadowy Cave": Some Speculations on a Twickenham Grotto

Pope's poetry, like the book he was accustomed to call Scripture, begins with a garden and ends with a city. To be sure, the city in Revelation is a holy city, whereas the city in the 1743 *Dunciad* is a version of Augustan London. Yet both are in an important sense visionary, and behind the *Dunciad*'s city looms another that is more abiding: the eternal City of man's recurring dream of the civilized community, only one of whose names is Rome.

As for the garden, no one today is ignorant of Pope's early and lasting association with settings horticultural and rural. First Binfield, then Chiswick, then the villa at Twickenham, and throughout his life, at home and on summer rambles, the landscaping and planting carried on by himself and his aristocratic friends. It is curious that this side of his personality and work should have gone almost unnoticed by nineteenth-century critics, who, following Warton, usually consigned him to the outer darkness of artificial and urban poets. Considering that he was a lifelong gardener of considerable renown, chatters continually in his letters of broccoli and pineapples, prospects and wildernesses, left behind him a considerable body of verse having to do with the natural scene, and was among the leaders of a landscaping movement that so modified the character of rural England that "in a sense," says E. K. Waterhouse, "the greatest English landscapes of the century are not the works of Lambert or Wilson or Gainsborough, but the gardens of Rousham (as they once were) and of Stourhead (as they are today),"[1] the oversight of the Romantic critics seems at first glance extraordinary. But only at first glance. Pope's interest in landscape was not their interest. His landscape had plenty of room in it for espaliers and kitchen-gardens, as theirs had not, and no room in it

MAYNARD MACK is Professor of English at Yale University.

[1] E. K. Waterhouse, *Painting in Britain: 1530–1790* (1953), p. 107.

whatever for Helvellyn or caverns measureless to man—a circumstance that seems to have rendered it unsuitable to Romantic needs and perhaps almost unrecognizable as "real" landscape. There, clearly enough, lies the crux of the matter. "As is the Gardener, so is the Garden," runs the adage set down by Thomas Fuller the physician in his *Gnomologia*,[2] summarizing an ancient topos that may be applied to periods as well as to men. The landscape that could mirror the sensibility of the Romantic generation tended in Renato Poggioli's phrase to be "as wild and boundless as the romantic view of the self"[3]— though Keats is an obvious exception. They could hardly be expected to thrill at the *paysages humanisés* of Rousham or Stourhead or even Stowe.

Furthermore, up to a point, the Romantic critics are right about Pope. He *is* a city poet, not simply in the obvious ways they saw, but in deeper ways they failed to see. His poetry has apocalyptic mutterings in it from his earliest years; it shapes itself again and again in patterns that exhibit loss converting into triumph or, for satiric ends (as in the fourth *Dunciad* and the first dialogue of the *Epilogue to the Satires*), triumph that in fact is loss. And always in Pope the thing that is being lost, or lost and recovered, or lost and recovered and lost again, is a vision of the civilized community, the City. To illustrate briefly: the *Essay on Criticism* moves from the glories of the past, through the errors and dissensions caused by pride, to the long line of "true" critics, in whom, each carrying like an Olympic torch-bearer his own portion of the "One *clear, unchang'd* and *Universal* Light," a way is shown that can reunite the critical and creative functions, the individual with tradition. Windsor Forest gives this pattern, based again on the loss and restoration of the good community, a larger bite. Beginning in "Peace and Plenty" because a Stuart reigns, the poem reverts to times of terror and desolation when usurpers ruled the land. These usurpers are the Norman Williams, but half-concealed in their shadow stands what Pope evidently regarded with the Jacobite half of his being as a more recent "usurpation," the accession of William III.[4] Then we return by way of a leisurely survey of native kings to

---

[2] Thomas Fuller, *Gnomologia: Adagies and Proverbs, with Sentences and Witty Sayings, Ancient and Modern, Foreign and British* (1732), No. 701.

[3] Renato Poggioli, "The Pastoral of the Self," *Daedalus*, LXXXVIII (1959), 699.

[4] J. R. Moore, 'Windsor Forest and William III," *MLN*, LXVI (1951), 451–54. It is not impossible that a further instance of Pope's private view of William emerges in the echo in *Imitations of Horace: Ep. II, ii*, 62–63:

> Hopes after Hopes of pious Papists fail'd,
> While mighty William's thundring Arm prevail'd

of Dryden's lines in *Palamon and Arcite*, III, 669–70:

> So laugh'd he, when the rightful Titan fail'd,
> And Jove's usurping arms in heav'n prevail'd.

"the great figure of the present, Anne, whose armies and fleets have won world-wide dominion, and whose ministers have brought about a Peace to which Pope attributes all the blessings of a Saturnian age of gold."[5]

This pattern became deeply rooted in Pope's thought; fragments and variants of it recur throughout his career. Particularly interesting, to my mind, is the form it takes in the *Epistle to Dr. Arbuthnot.* This poem begins, harried and breathless, as everyone remembers, with the figure of the tired literary lion bedeviled by his own success, totally caught up in a passing show that goads him into angry postures and tart replies. Gradually the argument expands to include considerations of far greater moment than "poetry and prate," reaching its climax in the juxtaposition of the slanderous and fawning Sporus with the staunch, firmly vertebrate, unflinching Satirist:

> Not proud, nor servile, be one Poet's praise
> That, if he pleas'd, he pleas'd by manly ways.[6]

The conclusion of the poem, which speedily follows this, brings a scene of restored perspective, where the poet recaptures in memory the solid virtues and natural pieties of his father's world at Binfield:

> Born to no Pride, inheriting no Strife,
> Nor marrying Discord in a Noble Wife,
> Stranger to Civil and Religious Rage,
> The good Man walk'd innoxious thro' his Age.
> No Courts he saw, no Suits would ever try,
> Nor dar'd an Oath, nor hazarded a Lye:
> Un-learn'd, he knew no Schoolman's subtile Art,
> No Language, but the Language of the Heart.
> By Nature honest, by Experience wise,
> Healthy by Temp'rance and by Exercise:
> His Life, tho' long, to sickness past unknown,
> His Death was instant, and without a groan.[7]

He recaptures these values in memory and by his prayer invokes their attendance upon his own future life at Twickenham: "Oh grant me thus to live, and thus to die!" Thus the epistle ends on a note of renewal and benediction, the child becoming father of the man in a sense that Wordsworth would have understood and approved as well

---

[5] Aubrey Williams, Introduction to *Pastoral Poetry and An Essay on Criticism* (ed. Audra and Williams; Twickenham Edition of the Poems of Alexander Pope), I, 142.

[6] Lines 336–37. In text and line-numbering of Pope's verse, this essay follows the Twickenham edition.

[7] Lines 392–403.

as in the very literal sense that summons the poet at this moment "To rock the Cradle of reposing Age."[8]

The *Epistle to Dr. Arbuthnot* is, of course, an urban poem by Romantic standards, and, like all Pope's works, it is ultimately about the City. Yet the evocation of Binfield at its end and the image of the invaded garden at its beginning

—What Walls can guard me, or what Shades can hide?
They pierce my Thickets, thro' my Grot they glide,
By land, by water, they renew their charge . . .[9]

together with all those other glimpses of garden, countryside, and landscape that come and go in the mature satires, remind us of a vein in Pope that his Romantic critics overlooked and our own critics have so far largely ignored.[10] In the remarks that follow, I have attempted a brief exploratory sounding of this vein, in the hope of clarifying somewhat its nature and its use.

To deal with it fully, one would of course need to speak at length of Pope's poetry, particularly of those characteristics of his interpretation of the natural world that seem to have as much in common with Renaissance conceptions as with the so-called century of Newton. One would have to note the extraordinary animism of nature in his poems; its continuing importance as a book of truths to be read, as a mirror reflecting human character and institutions; and the principles of reciprocity, retribution, and rehabilitation that still govern its relationships with men, as it heals the wounds they make in it and brings good out of the evil they do. One would also need to speak at length of Pope the man, of his youthful experiences in *Windsor Forest*, of the love of country scenes recorded so often in his letters, of his own gardens at Twickenham, and especially of the re-creating imagination that he brought to these and other aspects of his personal life. Since neither of these procedures is quite practicable in the pages at my disposal, I have chosen here to concentrate attention on one detail, a detail that is significant, however, in both the poetry and the life: the famous grotto.[11] By letting our imaginations linger lovingly upon this, we may just possibly catch a glimmering of some of the ways in which

[8] Line 409.

[9] Lines 7–9.

[10] A happy exception to this will be found in Geoffrey Tillotson's *Pope and Human Nature* (1958), chap. vii.

[11] For discussions of the grotto with a different end in view, see Helen S. Hughes, "Mr. Pope on His Grotto," *MP*, XXVIII (1930), 100–104; R. D. Altick, "Mr. Pope Expands His Grotto," *PQ*, XXI (1942), 427–30; R. W. Babcock, "Pope's Grotto Today," *South Atlantic Q.*, XLII (1943), 289–95; Frederick Bracher, "Pope's Grotto: The Maze of Fancy," *Huntington Library Q.*, XII (1949), 141–62.

—not only for Pope but other poets, and, indeed, in a degree for all of us—reality and dream converge and blur, each determining yet helping to transform the other.

II

Our earliest account of the grotto at Twickenham occurs in a letter of 1725, five years or thereabouts after Pope had begun work on it—the first of many occasions when he mistakenly believed that he had "put the last Hand to my works of this kind."[12] He has found a spring in the grotto, he tells Blount, "which falls in a perpetual Rill, that echoes thro' the Cavern day and night." This is an arresting circumstance, I think, because it comes from the man who had written from Lord Digby's gardens at Sherborne of "losing" his ears in the sound of water[13] and had placed among his Eloisa's aids to meditation in her convent "The grots that eccho to the tinkling rills."[14] One notices therefore with some interest that by 1740 he is able to speak of having conveyed into the grotto "three falls of water," which "murmur in a Cavern till they run out of sight."[15] One notices too that the anonymous correspondent who reports on the grotto to the *Newcastle General Magazine* in 1747, only three years after the poet's death, dwells ecstatically upon its waterworks:

Here it gurgles in a gushing Rill thro' fractur'd Ores and Flints; there it drips from depending Moss and Shells; here again, washing Beds of Sand and Pebbles, it rolls in Silver Streamlets; and there it rushes out in Jets and Fountains; while the Caverns of the Grot incessantly echo with a soothing Murmur of aquatick Sounds.[16]

Some of the possibilities of Pope's grotto as accessory to his Muse begin in these words dimly to emerge. Did its "soothing murmur" help induce in him, when solitary, states of concentration like those we know from the testimony of other poets—when one is "laid asleep" in body to become a "living soul," or sinks so deep in hearing music

> That it is not heard at all, but you are the music
> While the music lasts?

I am inclined to think it did. Pope was familiar with such states, as his correspondence shows. "Like a witch," he says, describing one such experience to his friend Caryll's son in his younger days,

[12] To Edward Blount, 2 June 1725, in *The Correspondence of Alexander Pope,* ed. George Sherburn (5 vols., 1956), II, 296. (Hereafter cited as *Correspondence.*)

[13] To Martha Blount, 22 June [1724], in *Correspondence,* II, 238.

[14] *Eloisa to Abelard,* l. 158.

[15] To Fortescue, 17 September 1740, in *Correspondence,* IV, 267.

[16] "To Mr. P—— T——, in Newcastle," *The Newcastle General Magazine, or Monthly Intelligencer,* I (January 1748), 26. The letter is signed "T," and dated 18 March 1747.

whose Carcase lies motionless on the floor, while she keeps her airy Sabbaths, and enjoys a thousand Imaginary Entertainments abroad, in this world, & in others, I seem to sleep in the midst of the Hurry, even as you would swear a Top stands still, when 'tis in the Whirle of its giddy motion. 'Tis no figure, but a serious truth I tell you when I say that my Days & Nights are so much alike, so equally insensible of any Moving Power but Fancy, that I have sometimes spoke of things in our family as Truths & real accidents, which I only Dreamt of; & again when something that actually happen'd came into my head, have thought (till I enquird) that I had only dream'd of them.[17]

Though the passage lacks Wordsworth's and Eliot's cathedral tone, its striking references to a seeming sleep that is actually profound agitation and to a turning wheel whose center is repose suggest that the natural history of poetic meditation may be in all ages much the same.

The next sentences in the letter to Blount equally deserve attention. The poet speaks first of the fact that his grotto permits an unbroken vista between his garden, which lies on one side of the public road dividing his property, and his parterre and the river Thames, which lie on the other. Then he turns to the chiaroscuro effects to be obtained by closing the grotto's doors and to the quite different effects when, with the doors still closed, he illuminates the interior with an alabaster lamp. The passage has been often quoted, but will bear repeating:

From the River *Thames* you see thro' my Arch up a Walk of the Wilderness to a kind of open Temple, wholly compos'd of Shells in the Rustic Manner; and from that distance under the Temple you look down thro' a sloping Arcade of Trees [lining the walk to the grotto on the garden side], and see the Sails on the River passing suddenly and vanishing, as thro' a Perspective Glass. When you shut the Doors of the Grotto, it becomes on the instant, from a luminous Room, a *Camera obscura;* on the Walls of which all the Objects of the River, Hills, Woods, and Boats, are forming a moving Picture in their visible Radiations: And when you have a mind to light it up, it affords you a very different Scene: it is

[17] To John Caryll, Jr., 5 December 1712, in *Correspondence*, I, 163. Cf. *ibid.*, I, 243 (To Jervas, 16 August 1714): "I have the greatest proof in nature at present of the amusing power of Poetry, for it takes me up so intirely that I scarce see what passes under my nose, and hear nothing that is said about me. To follow Poetry as one ought, one must forget father and mother, and cleave to it alone. My *Rêverie* has been so deep. . . ." Returning to the Scriptural analogy in a letter to Bolingbroke of 9 April 1724 (*Correspondence*, II, 227), Pope asks: "To write well, Immortally well, must not one leave Father and Mother and cleave unto the Muse? Must not one be prepared to endure the reproaches of Men, want and much Fasting, nay Martyrdom in its Cause? 'Tis such a Task as scarce leaves a Man time to be a good Neighbour, an useful Friend, nay to plant a Tree, much less to save his Soul." Pope has many matters in mind here, but poetry's "amusing power" is clearly one aspect of the problem, which as a whole continues to occupy him in some of the later satires.

finished with Shells interspersed with Pieces of Looking-glass in angular forms; and in the Cieling is a Star of the same Material, at which when a Lamp (of an orbicular Figure of thin Alabaster) is hung in the Middle, a thousand pointed Rays glitter and are reflected over the Place.[18]

This creation was obviously well suited to bring pleasure to one who is perhaps the acutest observer of effects of light among the English poets. Pope's eye loved light, and was capable of the most delicate discernments with respect to it.[19] His poems know the difference between effulgence and refulgence; between the "mild Lustre" of spring mornings[20] and the peculiarly "Purple Light" of autumn sunsets;[21] between the "glitter" of ice,[22] the "Gleam" of water,[23] the flame and "blaze" of diamonds,[24] the "shine" of fruits,[25] the "glow" of flowers.[26] They know how armor "beams" in lamplight,[27] "flashes" in firelight.[28] They know how moonlight on foliage yields a yellow radiance,[29] on stone a silver.[30] They know how, on a bright day when the sun is darkened by a passing cloud, the landscape momentarily loses its features, discomposes, "decays."[31] They know too that what we see depends as much upon the optics seeing as the object seen:[32] that the pheasant's breast "flames" most when we feel the pathos of its extinction,[33] the sun "glares" most when we are weary of it,[34] the lusters of a chandelier "double" and "dance" chiefly when we have had too much to drink.[35] And they know the telescope and microscope, the mirror and prism: how the obliquity of the latter can break a ray of light;[36] how the reflections in a mirror may falsify reality[37] or discover

[18] *Correspondence*, II, 296–97.

[19] For the delicacy of Pope's discernments with respect to color, a different but related topic, see "Mr. Alexander Pope: Painter," in Norman Ault's *New Light on Pope* (1949), Chap. V.

[20] "Spring," l. 74.

[21] "Autumn," l. 14.

[22] *Dunciad*, I, 75; *Temple of Fame*, l. 54.

[23] *Windsor Forest*, l. 215.

[24] *Temple of Fame*, l. 94; *Essay on Man*, IV, 10; *Epistle to Cobham*, l. 98.

[25] "Autumn," l. 73.

[26] *Epistle to Burlington*, l. 83. Cf. also "Spring," l. 31, and *Odyssey*, V, 94.

[27] *Epistle to Augustus*, l. 319.

[28] *Iliad*, VIII, 705.

[29] *Ibid.*, 693.

[30] *Ibid.*, 694. Cf. also *Imitations of Horace: Sat. II, vi*, 192.

[31] *Temple of Fame*, l. 20.

[32] *Epistle to Cobham*, l. 32.

[33] *Windsor Forest*, l. 118.

[34] *Epistle to a Lady*, l. 256.

[35] *Imitations of Horace: Sat. II, i*, 48.

[36] *Essay on Man*, III, 231.

[37] *Ibid.*, IV, 393.

it;[38] and how with the right kind of instruments, optical, dioptrical, and catoptrical, one may so manipulate a beam that it enlarges, multiplies, contracts, inverts, to say nothing of coloring, with "ten thousand dyes," all that we see.[39]

If we may believe the observer from Newcastle, the effects of this kind in Pope's grotto were even more spectacular than the waterworks. Just following the passage quoted earlier, he adds:

To multiply this Diversity, and still more increase the Delight, Mr. Pope's poetick Genius has introduced a kind of Machinery, which performs the same part in the Grotto that supernal Powers and incorporeal Beings act in the heroick Species of Poetry: This is effected by disposing Plates of Looking glass in the obscure Parts of the Roof and Sides of the Cave, where a sufficient Force of Light is wanting to discover the Deception, while the other Parts, the Rills, Fountains, Flints, Pebbles, &c. being duly illuminated, are so reflected by the various posited Mirrors, as, without exposing the Cause, every Object is multiplied, and its Position represented in a surprising Diversity. Cast your Eyes upward, and you half shudder to see Cataracts of Water precipitating over your Head, from impending Stones and Rocks, while salient Spouts rise in rapid Streams at your Feet: Around, you are equally surprized with flowing Rivulets and rolling Waters, that rush over airey Precipices, and break amid Heaps of ideal Flints and Spar. Thus, by a fine Taste and happy Management of Nature, you are presented with an undistinguishable Mixture of Realities and Imagery.[40]

This subterranean dark chamber, where, when the doors are shut, the outer world throws moving shadows on the walls and, when the lamp is lit, light sets all the contents glittering in "an undistinguishable Mixture of Realities and Imagery," is, of course, teasing to the modern imagination. On its dark side, reflecting images from elsewhere, it would appear to have analogues with Plato's cave and Locke's "dark room" of the understanding—"a closet," says Locke, "wholly shut from light, with only some little openings left, to let in external visible resemblances, or ideas of things without."[41] But viewed as possessing a lamp of its own that startles all it touches into "Imagery," it would appear to fall in equally with Plotinus's notion that the mind is a power, not simply a reflector, giving "a radiance out of its own store."[42] The latter notion is very much in keeping with Pope's re-

---

[38] *Epilogue to the Satires:* Dia. II, 78.

[39] *Epistle to Cobham,* ll. 25–29. See also *Temple of Fame,* ll. 132–34.

[40] *Op. cit.,* I, 26.

[41] *Essay Concerning Human Understanding,* II, xi, 17.

[42] *Enneads,* trans. Stephen MacKenna, IV, vi, 3.

current figuring of all forms of creativity as light derived from heaven, which *"Clears,* and *improves* whate'er it shines upon."[43]

How many, if any, of these analogies were savored or intended by the poet himself, we shall never know. One supposes he cannot have been oblivious of the associations between consciousness and caverns that are indicated in his own Cave of Spleen,[44] Cave of Poetry,[45] and Cave of Truth.[46] One supposes he was alert to the position his grotto occupied in the minds of his contemporaries, as a place "sacred" to poetry, dwelling place of his Muse. And one supposes that the long tradition that made grots and caverns the haunt of frugal virtue, philosophy, and true wisdom had not escaped the attention of one who could rally Queen Caroline on the incongruity of placing a bust of Dr. Samuel Clarke in her "Hermitage" at Richmond.[47] The tradition of the Sage in the holy cave was in any case widespread and so powerful that it persisted well into the nineteenth century. Coleridge in 1809 is impelled to make substantially the same point about Idoloclastes Satyrane, the hero of his "Tombless Epitaph"—

> Yea, oft alone
> Piercing the long-neglected holy cave,
> The haunt obscure of old Philosophy,
> He bade with lifted torch its starry walls
> Sparkle, as erst they sparkled to the flame
> Of odorous lamps tended by Saint and Sage—[48]

that Robert Dodsley had made in 1743 about future generations of visitors to the "Cave of Pope":

> With aweful Veneration shall they trace
> The steps which thou so long before hast trod;
> With reverend Wonder view the Solemn Place,
> From whence thy Genius soar'd to Nature's God.[49]

With his "odorous lamps" and "sparkling walls" Coleridge might almost be describing a visit to the Twickenham grotto itself.

Leaving all this aside, as we must, there was nevertheless a fine propriety for a poet in the grotto's character and situation. Between the ever-moving river with its transient scenes and figures and the garden with its quiet temple, the poet in his cave—whatever that cave may have represented to him—was intermediary. On the garden side, he had assembled all the instruments and emblems of the life of contem-

---

[43] *Essay on Criticism,* l. 316.

[44] *Rape of the Lock,* Canto IV.

[45] *Dunciad,* I, 34.

[46] *Ibid.,* IV, 641.

[47] *Epistle to Burlington,* l. 78.

[48] Lines 28–33.

[49] *The Cave of Pope: A Prophecy,* ll. 21–24.

plation: his shell temple; his "Large Mount" with its "Forest Seat or Chair, . . . overshaded with the Branches of a spreading Tree";[50] his serpentine walks leading in and out of "wildernesses"; and, from 1735, the obelisk to his mother—"a plain Stone Pillar resting upon a Pedestal," incised:

Ah Editha!
Matrum optima
Mulierum Amantissima
Vale.[51]

On the other side lay the traffic of the river, the great world seen in a passing show—"as thro' a perspective glass," says the letter to Edward Blount; the Heraclitean flowing away of all things; and, at a modest distance downstream, emblem of these and other impermanent delights: London.

III

That the grotto was related in some curious way to Pope's life and work as poet was instinctively understood by Pope's contemporaries. Dr. Oliver, for instance, offering to send more "Marble Spar or Diamonds," remarks that he is sure every diamond already sent "has acquired new Lustre from its artful Disposition."[52] "Artful disposition" was precisely the skill for which Pope's poetry was most admired, and Oliver intends the analogy he hints at between grotto-building and poem-building to be noticed. Swift too grasps intuitively a poetic affiliation of the grotto. He tells Pope that he has heard from Ford about the "Subterranean Passage to your Garden whereby you turned a blunder into a beauty, which is a Piece of Ars Poetica."[53] Johnson seems to be recalling this comment when he observes in the *Life of Pope*: "[His] excavation was requisite as an entrance to his garden, and, as some men try to be proud of their defects, he extracted an ornament from an inconvenience, and vanity produced a grotto where necessity enforced a passage."[54]

Johnson shows here his characteristic lack of sympathy with the *furor rusticus*, but his fine intelligence catches in passing at an ethical analogy that is highly characteristic of him and contains an important truth about Pope. Much in Pope's career, I think we must agree, *was* determined by the effort to extract ornament from inconvenience of a

---

[50] *Newcastle General Magazine*, I (January 1748), 27.

[51] *Ibid.*

[52] 15 October 1740, in *Correspondence*, IV, 281.

[53] 29 September 1725, in *ibid.*, II, 325–26.

[54] *Lives of the English Poets*, ed. G. B. Hill (1905), III, 135.

rather painful kind—to find, or make, some ground for pride in all too visible "defects." But had Johnson added "and deprivations," his remark would have touched a profounder truth. This comfortable estate at Twickenham, famous for its gardens, its grotto, and its distinguished visitors, famous particularly for its occupant, the man who was, in every sense of the phrase he had himself applied to the in-dwelling powers of nature, "the genius of the place"[55]—what was it all if not an exercise in extracting ornament from inconvenience? Barred by his religion from the ordinary routes to advancement and the normal kinds of patronage, largely self-educated, a retired merchant's son, physically a dwarf, he had plunged into the hurly-burly of literary London, bested the university-trained wits on their own classic ground, and, like another country boy a century and a quarter earlier, made his fortune. Indeed, he had made much more than his fortune: he was now one of whom it could be said that "His word alone gave Infamy or Fame,"[56] and of whom, though he lacked place or patron, Envy had to "own, I live among the Great."[57] Yet he had always, though he had friends on both sides, belonged more to the Outs than to the Ins. In the beginning, the Roman Catholic families of Binfield and its neighborhood. Later, his first literary advisers and well-wishers, all luminaries of the "last" age—Trumbull, Walsh, Wycherley, Sheffield, Cromwell, Congreve. Then the close friends of his young manhood and maturity, men sooner or later cast away by the government and court, driven into literal or at the least spiritual exile—Bolingbroke, Harley, Atterbury, Arbuthnot, Swift, Gay. And finally, even his latest friends, the new youth—Wyndham, Marchmont, Murray, Lyttelton, and the rest—who counted themselves on the side of the Patriot opposition till the fall of Walpole in 1743.

Hence the poet who declared himself "To VIRTUE ONLY and HER FRIENDS, A FRIEND"[58] had for his friends, in fact, and particularly during his formative years at Binfield, mostly alienated men—quite literally "Chiefs, out of War, and Statesmen, out of Place."[59] The communities he had known best were communities seeking to "dignify Disgrace" by retreat to "the silent Shade,"[60] to the country and the garden, to books and study and (inevitably) self-conscious virtue, the mind telling itself that it had served the world no worse, perhaps bet-

---

[55] *Epistle to Burlington*, l. 52.

[56] Dodsley, *op. cit.*, l. 16. Cf. *Correspondence*, IV, 245, n. 3.

[57] *Imitations of Horace: Sat. II, i*, 133.

[58] *Ibid.*, l. 121.

[59] *Ibid.*, l. 126.

[60] *Epistle to Oxford*, ll. 30, 28.

ter, than the run of mankind, yet the world, with its famed ingratitude, no longer having use for it:

> Awake, my St. John, leave all meaner things
> To low ambition, and the pride of Kings.[61]

For more than two hundred years of European and English history, as old causes crumbled, this plangent refrain had been recurring and would recur. John Evelyn, writing in 1658 and urging the satisfaction to be found in gardens now that "brutish and ambitious persons seeke themselves in the ruines of our miserable yet dearest country,"[62] sounds substantially the same note as Justus Lipsius in his *De constantia*, written when Lipsius was fleeing from his own war-ravaged country in the preceding century.[63] Likewise, Henry Vaughan, who published his *Flores Solitudinis* in 1654, "to bee," he tells us, "a companion of those wise *Hermits* who have withdrawne from the present generation, to confirme them in their solitude, and to make that rigid *necessity* their pleasant *Choyse*,"[64] says no more than Pope was to say again in the following century in the address to Bolingbroke in the *Essay on Man*. The antithesis of Vaughan's final phrase is, in fact, simply another way of putting the Senecan sentiment that Pope is reputed to have applied to his work on his grotto—and not, one may venture to fancy, without reference to wider issues—"What we cannot *overcome*, we must *undergo*."[65]

Pope's Twickenham estate, then, presents itself in two lights. On the one hand, it was evidence in its way of what a Roman Catholic, not to mention a hunchbacked, poet in Pope's society must undergo: the exclusions to which he might be subject at a moment's notice (for example, the ten-mile rule) and the alienations he might feel. To live secluded in this manner, to appear only on his own terms, as carefully arranged as when he sat for bust or portrait, was one way of meeting the problem of his ugly body, to which he was keenly sensitive, particularly when women were concerned. Seclusion likewise afforded a way of dealing with the practices of his religion, which, strictly speaking, were forbidden. He was not, to be sure, a devout man, and Augustan Catholic culture, cut away from its Continental root, would

---

[61] *Essay on Man*, I, 1–2.

[62] To Sir Thomas Browne [28 January 1658], in *Works of Sir Thomas Browne*, ed. Geoffrey Keynes (1931), VI, 302.

[63] *Two Bookes of Constancie*, trans. Stradling (1594), II, iii.

[64] "To the Reader," Leaf A6, verso.

[65] *Autobiography, Letters, and Literary Remains of Mrs. Piozzi*, ed. A. Hayward (1861), II, 154. Mrs. Piozzi's marginal note is not altogether unambiguous: it is possible she intends to assign the witticism to Johnson.

perhaps not have satisfied his sophisticated imagination if he had been so.

But the old usages must certainly to an extent have been kept up, at the very least while his mother lived, and there are indications in his grotto of the same resolution not to shrink from the consequences of his professed faith that he had shown in his reply to Atterbury when asked why he did not become an Anglican. An incised stone still surviving, affixed to the grotto's ceiling at the point where it is entered from the river side, represents one element of the *arma Christi*, the Crown of Thorns; another incised stone, three feet away, immediately above the entrance to the main passage, represents the Five Wounds.[66] These appear to be of stonework older than the grotto and were, one must suppose, made originally for some other situation, perhaps chapel or church, and contributed to the grotto by a Catholic friend or friends, as the spars and lignites were contributed by other friends. Their devotional significance should not be exaggerated. Yet their presence in this prominent position is not the work of one who would evade acknowledgment of his creed, and they may have served to remind Pope (as well as those who visited him) of the many circumstances that separated him from the ordinary pursuits and pastimes of the world. "All the beneficial circumstances of life, and all the shining ones," he had said in his reply to Atterbury, "lie on the part you would invite me to. But if I could bring myself to fancy, what I think you do but fancy, that I have any talents for active life, I want health for it; and besides it is a real truth, I have less Inclination (if possible) than Ability. Contemplative life is not only my scene, but it is my habit too."[67]

On the other hand—and this, as I have suggested, must have been the light in which Pope oftenest saw the matter himself—the Twickenham villa was visible and enormous proof of his success in overcoming what had to be undergone, extracting the ornament from the inconvenience. Here, in his own modern Tusculum, he could dispose of an affluence and independence that enemies might mock but must acknowledge:

> Sawney, a mimic Sage of high Renown,
> To Twickenham Bowers retired, enjoys his Wealth,
> His Malice, and his Muse: In Grottos cool,
> And cover'd Arbours dreams his Hours away.[68]

---

[66] On the history and use of the *arma Christi*, there is valuable information in Rudolf Berliner's "Arma Christi," *Munchener Jahrbuch der bildenden Kunst*, Dritte Folge, Band VI (1955), 35–152, and R. Wildhaber's "Der Feiertagschristus als ikonographischer Ausdruch der Sonntagsheiligung," *Zeitschrift für schweizerische Archäologie und Kunstgeschichte*, XVI (1956), 1–34. I owe these references to my friend Joseph Trapp of the Warburg and Courtauld Institute.

[67] 20 November 1717, in *Correspondence*, I, 454.

[68] James Ralph, *Sawney* (1728), p. 1.

Here he could introduce his friends, in language that may in fact spring from a conscious and whimsical evocation of the tradition[69] of the philosopher-king (the recluse whose kingdom is in his mind or lies all about him in nature), to the "triumphal arch, under which you shall be led into my garden,"[70] to the Large Mount, "in a point of view to shew you the glory of my little kingdom,"[71] to the new coat of stucco on "my palace, which you may now more truly style *Little Whitehall* than when last you saw it."[72] Here he could live at his sweet will, like those Eastern Kings to whom he has a habit of referring—

> I sought no homage from the Race that write,
> I kept, like *Asian* Monarchs, from their sight—[73]

and could set against the world beyond the thicket which hedged his property (the world of stratagem and compromise and money-grubbing and self-interest—into which he often entered because he had to and because it answered to the vein of stratagem and compromise and self-interest in his own nature), an imagined ideal community of patriarchal virtues and heroic friends: a community of the garden and the "grot." He pictures this community in one of the best-known passages of his first Horatian Imitation:

> Hear this, and tremble! you, who 'scape the Laws.
> Yes, while I live, no rich or noble knave
> Shall walk the World, in credit, to his grave.
> To VIRTUE ONLY, and HER FRIENDS, A FRIEND,

[69] A tradition with an interesting history, which has been little studied. It embraces a variety of formulations ranging from Edward Dyer's "My Mind to Me a Kingdom Is" to John Norris's "The Retirement" to Cowper's "Verses Supposed To Be Written by Alexander Selkirk" (which repudiate it); it coalesces at times with the tradition studied in Maren-Sofie Røstvig's *The Happy Man* (2 vols.; 1954, 1958), but is not identical with it. Pope's portrait of his father in the *Epistle to Dr. Arbuthnot* (above, p. 71) alludes to it overtly in a final couplet:

> Oh grant me thus to live, and thus to die!
> Who sprung from Kings shall know less joy than I—

which compresses the content of two of Dyer's:

> Lo! thus I triumph like a king,
> My mind content with anything. (23–24)

> Thus do I live, thus will I die,—
> Would all did so as well as I! (35–36)

[70] To Caryll, 20 March 1733, in *Correspondence*, III, 358.

[71] To Atterbury, 19 March 1722, in *ibid.*, II, 109.

[72] To Caryll, 19 April (1734), in *ibid.*, III, 406.

[73] *Epistle to Dr. Arbuthnot*, ll. 219–20. Cf. also l. 198, and "Elegy to the Memory of an Unfortunate Lady," 21–22:

> Like Eastern Kings a lazy state they keep,
> And close confin'd to their own palace sleep.

The World beside may murmur, or commend.
Know, all the distant Din that World can keep
Rolls o'er my Grotto, and but sooths my sleep.
There, my Retreat the best Companions grace,
Chiefs out of War, and Statesmen, out of Place.
There, St. John mingles with my friendly Bowl,
The feast of Reason and the Flow of Soul:
And He, whose lightning pierc'd th' Iberian Lines,
Now forms my Quincunx, and now ranks my Vines,
Or tames the Genius of the stubborn Plain,
Almost as quickly, as he conquer'd Spain.[74]

We have a contemporary dimension here, of course: Bolingbroke, Peterborough, and other chiefs out of war or statesmen out of place. We also have presumably a flick at Walpole in the implication that a great general of the past now lacks employment in an inglorious present.[75] But the full weight of the passage falls elsewhere. The ultimate object of its indictment is not Walpole's ministry, but "a Land of Hectors, / Thieves, Supercargoes, Sharpers, and Directors,"[76] of which Walpole is only a symptom, and behind that, "the way of the world," against which poets have always warred. Likewise, the indictment draws its strength less from the actual little cripple who lived at Twickenham than from a poet's generous vision of a possible true community. It is a community degreeless and heroic, where companions confer "grace" by their very presence; where (as among philosopher-kings) the taking of food has the dignity of a "Feast," the taking of drink the dignity of a "friendly Bowl" (both actions so transfigured by collations of another sort as to compose a "Feast of Reason" and a "Flow of Soul"); and where the same man, like that famous Roman Cincinnatus of the plow, now wields his battle "lightning" like a Jove, now wrestles with and tames the lesser godhead of the "stubborn Plain."

Swift perhaps spoke better than he knew when he compared the grotto to a piece of *ars poetica*. It was to become a place where not only had a beauty been snatched from blunder once, but where the world, having thrown its shadow on the walls, was continuously transformed by art into "an undistinguishable Mixture of Realities and Imagery." Actual great men came there, actual impassioned conversa-

---

[74] *Imitations of Horace: Sat. II, i,* 118–32.

[75] It is just possible that Pope's implication is more specific. There was already much unrest about Spanish interference among the City merchants by 1731–32, and Pope may conceivably imply that the man who mastered Spain before should be empowered to repeat his triumph.

[76] *Sat. II, i,* 71–72.

tions about the commonweal were evidently held there; but all that happened there was translated by the poetic imagination, of which it was itself the handiwork and possibly the conscious symbol, out of history into dream.

IV

This is the case in the lines at which we have just been looking, and it is notably the case in the lines which follow:

> Approach: But aweful! Lo th' Egerian Grott,
> Where nobly-pensive St. John sate and thought;
> Where British sighs from dying Wyndham stole,
> And the bright Flame was shot thro' Marchmont's soul.
> Let such, such only, tread this sacred Floor,
> Who dare to love their Country, and be poor.[77]

These are not among Pope's best lines. They are too much on the stretch in sense, and somewhat pompous in gait. But they illustrate the better for this reason the operation of that skill in multiplying and reflecting by which he achieved—in his grotto, as the Newcastle correspondent noticed, and also in a poetry apparently adjusted to the norms of common speech—effects analogous to those performed in epic discourse by a machinery of "Superior Powers and uncorporeal Beings." The phrase "Egerian Grott," like one of those "posited Mirrors" in the actual grotto, flashes upon the pensive figures of Bolingbroke, Wyndham, and Marchmont the almost archetypal image of the virtuous philosopher—"Saint and Sage"[78]—meditating in his cave, and also the particular variant of this image emanating from the legend of King Numa, who was credited with receiving the moral instruction that made his government memorable from the nymph Egeria. As Livy has it,

There was a grove watered by a perpetual spring which flowed through the midst of it, out of a dark cave. Thither Numa would often withdraw, without witness, as if to meet the goddess; so he dedicated the grove to the Camenae [a rather mysterious group of deities formerly identified with the Muses], alleging that they held council there with his wife Egeria.[79]

Plutarch's version of this story knows nothing of Egeria as wife to Numa, but is equally clear about the function of the Muses. "In like manner," says Plutarch, arguing that as the gods very probably approve men of virtue we should not judge it incongruous that "a like

---

[77] *Verses on a Grotto by the River Thames at Twickenham* (1743), ll. 9–14.

[78] From Coleridge's *Tombless Epitaph*, l. 33.

[79] I, xxi, 3.

spirit" should be presumed to have visited Minos, Zoroaster, Lycurgus, and Numa, "the controllers of kingdoms, and the legislators of commonwealths,"

Numa spoke of a certain goddess or mountain nymph that was in love with him, and met him in secret . . . ; and professed that he entertained familiar conversation with the Muses, to whose teaching he ascribed the greatest part of his revelations. . . .[80]

And on a later page, he adds:

His reign . . . [was] a living example and verification of that saying which Plato, long afterward, ventured to pronounce, that the sole and only hope of respite or remedy for human evils was in some happy conjunction of events which should unite in a single person the power of a king and the wisdom of a philosopher, so as to elevate virtue to control and mastery over vice.[81]

Numa's reign, in this notion of it, impressively anticipates much that Bolingbroke asks of his ideal monarch in his essay *On the Idea of a Patriot King*, a footnote in the long history of Plato's idea of philosopher-kings which Pope so admired that he had it privately printed.[82] Numa's deriving wisdom and inspiration from the Muse(s) likewise anticipates in its way the function that the younger Patriots in the late thirties and early forties sought to assign Pope vis-à-vis the Prince of Wales (their wan hope of that era) and in fact vis-à-vis the whole movement of reform. Thus Lyttelton writes to him in late 1738, speaking of the Prince:

Be therefore as much with him as you can, Animate him to Virtue, to the Virtue least known to Princes, though most necessary for them, Love of the Publick; and think that the Morals, the Liberty, the whole Happiness of this Country depends on your Success. If the sacred Fire, which by You and other Honest men has been kindled in his Mind, can be preserv'd, we may yet be safe. . . .[83]

Three years later he expands upon the theme:

I wish he [Bolingbroke] was in England upon many accounts, but for nothing more than to exhort and Animate You not to bury your excellent Talents in a Philosophical Indolence, but to Employ them, as you have so often done, in the Service of Virtue. . . . I believe they wou'd be of great Present Benefit; some sparks of Publick Virtue are yet Alive, which

---

[80] "Numa," in *Lives*, trans. Dryden-Clough (Modern Library ed.), p. 80.

[81] *Ibid.*, p. 91.

[82] Cf. Fannie E. Ratchford, *Pope and the Patriot King*, "University of Texas Studies in English," No. 6 (1926), pp. 157–77.

[83] 25 October, in *Correspondence*, IV, 138.

such a Spirit as Yours might blow into a Flame, among the Young men especially. . . .[84]

All this is comical enough now, as the politics of a past age is always comical if it escapes being tragic. Pope and his Muse in the role of Egeria, well-head of inspiration to a political movement that was no more disinterested than such movements always are, presents a hilarious picture of naiveté all around. Yet the conviction that the pursuits of every day should be shot through with the idealism and detachment of poetry, the arts of government lit by the imagination, intuition, and grace of heaven which we represent in the poet's Muse: there is nothing absurd in that. If we have come to think so, it is because we have lost the confidence that widely disparate areas of experience and instruments of knowing may interpenetrate to their mutual advantage.

Pope had not yet lost this confidence, and in the interval between the two passages of verse I have just quoted, a decade apart, went on to the career as a formal satirist which produced much of his best work. The issue of my observations is, I hope, now clear. To be a great satirist, a man must have, literally and figuratively, a place to stand, an angle of vision. For Pope, the garden and the grotto provided this. They supplied him, in fact as well as fiction, with a rallying point for his personal values and a focus for his conception of himself—as master of a poet's "kingdom," a counter-order to a court and ministry that set no store by poets, a community bound by ties quite other than those uniting the "pensioners" of St. Stephen, as he sardonically calls the members of Walpole's parliament.[85] In a sense, they supplied him with the materials of a *Selbstentwurf*, nourishing his feelings and imagination in much the way that at a later time the tower and the swan would do for Yeats.

Further, in Pope's case as in Yeats's, the elements of the self-projection were such that they enabled him, like Antaeus, to re-create his limited personal being by drawing on a large historical identity. This identity for Pope was that of the virtuous recluse, the Horatian *beatus ille* figure whom Professor Røstvig has lately studied with such fine attention.[86] Hence the position of sophisticated rusticity, which he had taken up at Twickenham in 1720 in order to give scope both to the worldliness of his literary inclinations and his genuine love of gardening and privacy, became of value to him during the 1730's in more

[84] 7 November 1741, in *ibid.*, p. 369.

[85] *Epistle to Bathurst*, l. 394.

[86] See above, n. 67. Some aspects of Pope's adaptation of this figure are examined in "The Muse of Satire," *Yale Review*, XLI (1951): 80–92 (reprinted in *Studies in the Literature of the Augustan Age*, ed. R. C. Boys [1952], and *Discussions of Pope*, ed. R. A. Blanshard [1960]).

ways than he could possibly have foreseen. As a visible practitioner of the retired life, in manners "easy" but in life "severe,"[87] he moved under the countenance of the most honorific public image of the age, an image that by 1720, though it had earlier been appropriated to Cavaliers and Tories,[88] was sought by men of all persuasions and so could aid a writer to survive the currents of public faction, whose threat to artistic independence Pope must have sensed sufficiently when hawking subscriptions to his Homer. Moreover, as himself a species of country "squire," occupant and improver of a small "estate," living off annuities, investments, a small inheritance, and other revenues not gained by commerce, he enjoyed at least fringe membership in the social group whose right to speak home about the condition of the nation was universally admitted and whose membership also comprehended the two parties in more or less equal shares—Walpole himself being no more than such a squire on a grander scale. Finally, through his interests as horticulturist and landscapist, experimenting with vegetables and fruits new to the English climate, studying Vitruvius and Palladio, building shell-temples, shaded walks, and grottoes in which to read Seneca and Plutarch, Cicero and Montaigne, he lived not only among the great, as he claimed, but like a number of them, and had access to a central vocabulary of assumptions about the practical means as well as ideal ends of living.

Apart from the happy circumstance of the Twickenham villa, offering an invitation to, and a suitable ambience for, a career that Reuben Brower rightly calls "progressively an *Imitatio Horati*,"[89] we may reasonably wonder whether Pope's work of the thirties might not have had a considerably different shape. The time was past when any serious writer could find his place to stand beside the throne. This Dryden had managed, and in his finest poems speaks as if the Establishment, with the monarchy its center, spoke through him—the last principle of order in a disintegrating world. For Pope, after the death of Anne, the throne as center of the dream of the civilized community has become absurd. What he gives us instead, in various versions, is intimations of a throne usurped, or a throne occupied by shadows. The throne of the *Epistle to Augustus* was once genuinely filled by Horace's Augustus. The throne of the first dialogue of the *Epilogue to the Satires* was formerly Virtue's, but is now seized by triumphant Vice.[90] The throne of the *Epistle to Burlington* awaits in vain a Bruns-

---

[87] Dodsley, *op. cit.*, l. 15.

[88] M.-S. Røstvig, *The Happy Man*, I, 60–62, 179–80.

[89] *Alexander Pope: The Poetry of Allusion* (1959), p. 165.

[90] Lines 141 ff.

wick who will fulfil in Britain the vision of law and government that
Anchises unfolds before his son in the sixth *Aeneid* and that Pope here
echoes.[91] And then there are the several thrones of the *Dunciad,* kept
supplied (in an England where "Dunce the Second reigns like Dunce
the First"[92]) with shadowy incumbents by a shadowy queen-mother.

Dryden's angle of vision was no longer available to a serious poet,
but there was a possible alternative. The one Roman poem that ran
perhaps deepest in the blood stream of Pope's age was Virgil's
Georgics, a poem whose distinctive achievement, as Sir Kenneth Clark
has shrewdly reminded us, lies in combining an almost absolute degree
of realism in its account of farming, with an almost absolute degree of
myth in its identification of the life of husbandmen with the innocence and felicity, hardihood and piety of the lost Golden Age before
Astraea left the earth.[93] Something of the same unlikely blend may be
observed in Pope's satires of the thirties.[94] They are all, in one dimension, entirely realistic, and this dimension has been authenticated sufficiently by the poet's editors, not to mention the poet's own frequent
notes. Yet in another dimension all play their part in an extended fiction (which is by no means all fiction) of the virtuous recluse who
ventures in and out of London to remind his contemporaries of the
City a little further up-river. Though the throne is empty, there remains an alternative center, and a power of a different kind: the poet-
king-philosopher in his grotto, midway between the garden and the
river. Under his magisterial wand, like the wrecked voyagers in *The
Tempest,* lords and rich men, ministers and society-wenches, kings,
courtiers, Quakers, clowns, and good Ralph Allens move through the
paces of an intricate satirical ballet, which combines the features of
reality and dream.

[91] Lines 191 ff.

[92] I, 6.

[93] *Landscape into Art* (1949), p. 54.

[94] The manifestations of Pope's role as rural sage in his *Satires* receive more extensive treatment (as several other topics touched on in this essay) in the Alexander
Lectures given at University College, Toronto, in March 1963, to be published under
the title *The Genius of the Place: Alexander Pope and the Theme of Retirement.*

WILLIAM R. KEAST

Johnson and "Cibber's" Lives
of the Poets, *1753*

AMONG THE BIOGRAPHICAL and critical collections dealing with English poetry published before Johnson's *Lives*, by far the most ambitious is *The Lives of the Poets of Great Britain and Ireland, to the Time of Dean Swift. Compiled from ample Materials Scattered in a Variety of Books, and especially from the MS. notes of the late ingenious Mr. Coxeter and others, collected for this Design, by Mr. Cibber*,[1] published in parts finally making five volumes by R. Griffiths in 1753. The collection contains 202 lives, ranging in time from Chaucer to John Banks (d. 1751). Although the work is largely derivative, being compiled, as the title page frankly acknowledges, from such existing sources as the *General Dictionary*, the *Muse's Library*, the *Biographia Britannica*, and a host of individual biographies, it nevertheless presents a certain amount of fresh information, evidently gleaned from unprinted papers, oral sources, and personal observation. Several of the lives, especially those of minor eighteenth-century writers like Samuel Boyse, Aaron Hill, and Elizabeth Rowe, are unusually full and interesting. The 1753 *Lives of the Poets* still justifies the judgment that Raleigh made half a century ago: "This important compilation, which probably suggested Johnson's great work, has had very little

WILLIAM R. KEAST is Professor of English and Dean of the College of Arts and Sciences at Cornell University.

[1] Thus the title page of Volume I, which adds that the work is to be "In Four Volumes." This phrase is dropped in subsequent volumes, evidently as a result of an expansion of the original design, and with it the phrase "to the Time of Dean Swift." After Volume I the publisher saw fit to identify the work as "By Mr. Cibber, and other Hands." The work was issued in (often delayed) weekly parts of 3 sheets (72 pages) each, 5 of the weekly parts to form a volume. No. I was published on 3 February 1753, and No. XXV, the last, on 21 December. Isaac Reed's copy of the *Lives*, with newspaper advertisements relating to the publishing history inserted, is in the British Museum.

justice done to it in literary history. It is seldom mentioned save in connexion with the dispute about its authorship."[2]

Because of this dispute about its authorship, the 1753 *Lives of the Poets* has always had some interest for students of Johnson. In beginning his *Life of Hammond,* Johnson wrote:

> Of Mr. Hammond, though he be well remembered as a man esteemed and caressed by the elegant and great, I was at first able to obtain no other memorials than such as are supplied by a book called Cibber's *Lives of the Poets;* of which I take this opportunity to testify that it was not written, nor, I believe, ever seen, by either of the Cibbers, but was the work of Robert Shiels, a native of Scotland, a man of very acute understanding, though with little scholastick education, who, not long after the publication of his work, died in London of a consumption. His life was virtuous, and his end was pious. Theophilus Cibber, then a prisoner for debt, imparted, as I was told, his name for ten guineas. The manuscript of Shiels is now in my possession.[3]

Although an attempt was made by Griffiths, the publisher, to discredit Johnson's allegations, the story of the composition and publication of the 1753 *Lives,* long since worked out by David Nichol Smith,[4] bears out, in general, Johnson's account of the matter. On 6 November 1752 Shiels contracted to prepare the work; a week later, Theophilus Cibber agreed, for £21, "to revise, correct, and improve" it, and to allow his name "to be made use of as the author of the said work, and be inserted accordingly in the title-pages thereof and in any advertisements relative to it." Except for the lives of Mrs. Chandler, Aaron Hill, and Eustace Budgell, which were supplied by others, Shiels wrote (that is, "compiled") the entire work. Cibber revised it—mainly, the publisher tells us, to moderate Shiels's Tory prejudices—and inserted a few notes, most of them designed to refute statements reflecting on his own character or acting ability that had been contained in Shiels's text. In the course of what must have been, to say the least, an uneasy collaboration, Shiels and Cibber quarreled; Shiels, who had been employed by Johnson as one of the amanuenses on the *Dictionary,* no doubt told his patron how he was being used by the publisher. Johnson, loyal to his friends, no friend to Whigs, and violent about actors, did what he could to insure that justice should be done to poor Shiels.

But Johnson had not waited until 1781, when his *Life of Hammond* was published, to assist Shiels with his project; and it may be that his role in the 1753 *Lives of the Poets* was large enough to make it espe-

---

[2] "Early Lives of the Poets," in *Six Essays on Johnson* (1910), p. 119.

[3] *Lives of the Poets,* ed. G. B. Hill (1905), II, 312.

[4] In an extended note to Raleigh's essay (Raleigh, *op. cit.,* pp. 120–25).

cially galling to him to see the book circulated and referred to as "Cibber's" *Lives*. Boswell tells us that "for Shiels, who died of a consumption, he had much tenderness; and it has been thought that some choice sentences in the Lives of the Poets were supplied by him."[5] Griffiths, the publisher, wrote to Edmund Cartwright in 1781 that "many of the best pieces of biography in that collection were not written by Shiells, but by superior hands."[6] Griffiths was attempting to supply Cartwright with ammunition to be used in a review rebutting Johnson's charge about the authorship of the 1753 *Lives*. But what he says here is substantially true, and one of the "superior hands" was Johnson's.

It has long been recognized that the *Life of Savage* included in Shiels's collection was derived from Johnson's own *Life of Savage* published in 1744; but the precise relation between the two has not been defined. Shiels's *Life of Savage* opens with a handsome acknowledgment to Johnson's work:

This unhappy gentleman [Savage], who led a course of life imbittered with the most severe calamities, was not yet destitute of a friend to close his eyes. It has been remarked of Cowley, who likewise experienced many of the vicissitudes of fortune, that he was happy in the acquaintance of the bishop of Rochester, who performed the last offices which can be paid to a poet, in the elegant Memorial he made of his Life. Though Mr. Savage was as much inferior to Cowley in genius, as in the rectitude of his life, yet, in some respect, he bears a resemblance to that great man. None of the poets have been more honoured in the commemoration of their history, than this gentleman. The life of Mr. Savage was written some years after his death by a gentleman, who knew him intimately, capable to distinguish between his follies, and those good qualities which were often concealed from the bulk of mankind by the abjectness of his condition. From this account we have compiled that which we now present to the reader.[7]

To this theme Shiels returns at the end of his *Life of Savage,* introducing Johnson's own concluding paragraph in this manner:

In the words of the celebrated writer of his life, from whom, as we observed in the beginning, we have extracted the account here given, we shall conclude this unfortunate person's Memoirs, which were so various as to afford large scope for an able biographer, and which, by this gentleman, have been represented with so great a mastery, and force of penetration, that the Life of Savage, as written by him, is an excellent model for this species of writing.[8]

[5] *Life*, I, 187.

[6] Raleigh, *op. cit.,* p. 122; cf. Boswell, *Life*, III, 30, n. 1.

[7] V, 32.　　　　　　　　　　　　[8] V, 65.

For Shiels to say that his *Life of Savage* is "compiled" and "extracted" from Johnson's perhaps leaves some ambiguity about the way in which he has used his source; but he seems to remove all doubt by concluding his account with "the words" of Johnson, which he puts in quotation marks. He gives the impression that he has quarried his material from Johnson but has cast it into his own words, except when he quotes Johnson directly. And this impression is reinforced by another quotation from Johnson midway in the *Life*, introduced by the phrase "says the author of his life."[9] But this impression, if it is indeed the one Shiels sought to convey, is wrong: Shiels's *Life of Savage* is not in this sense "compiled" from Johnson's. It is an abridgment of Johnson's. Except for the two paragraphs I have just quoted, a brief passage to which I will refer in a moment, and an occasional transition phrase or sentence, or trifling emendation, Shiels's *Life of Savage* is lifted directly from Johnson's biography. Shiels simply copied out Johnson's *Life*, omitting enough of it to fit the text to his space, providing a sentence or phrase from time to time to make splices required by his omissions, and putting quotation marks around two of the paragraphs. The following passages will give a fair sample of the relation between the two texts:

JOHNSON	SHIELS
Another part of his misconduct was the practice of prolonging his visits to unseasonable hours, and disconcerting all the families into which he was admitted. This was an error in a place of commerce which all the charms of his conversation could not compensate; for what trader would purchase such airy satisfaction by the loss of solid gain, which must be the consequence of midnight merriment, as those hours which were gained at night were generally lost in the morning? [Here are three paragraphs.]	Another part of his misconduct was, the practice of prolonging his visits to unseasonable hours, and disconcerting all the families into which he was admitted. This was an error in a place of commerce, which all the charms of his conversation could not compensate; for what trader would purchase such airy satisfaction, with the loss of solid gain, which must be the consequence of midnight merriment, as those hours which were gained at night were generally lost in the morning?
While he was thus spending the day in contriving a scheme for the morrow, distress stole upon him by imperceptible degrees. His conduct	Distress at last stole upon him by imperceptible degrees; his conduct had already wearied some of those who were at first enamoured of his

[9] V, 46–47.

had already wearied some of those who were at first enamoured of his conversation; but he might, perhaps, still have devolved to others, whom he might have entertained with equal success, had not the decay of his clothes made it no longer consistent with their vanity to admit him to their tables or to associate with him in publick places. He now began to find every man from home at whose house he called; and was therefore no longer able to procure the necessaries of life, but wandered about the town, slighted and neglected, in quest of a dinner, which he did not always obtain.

To complete his misery he was pursued by the officers for small debts which he had contracted; and was therefore obliged to withdraw from the small number of friends from whom he had still reason to hope for favours. His custom was to lie in bed the greatest part of the day and to go out in the dark with the utmost privacy, and after having paid his visit return again before morning to his lodging, which was in the garret of an obscure inn.[10]

conversation; but he still might have devolved to others, whom he might have entertained with equal success, had not the decay of his cloaths made it no longer consistent with decency to admit him to their tables, or to associate with him in public places. He now began to find every man from home, at whose house he called; and was therefore no longer able to procure the necessaries of life, but wandered about the town, slighted and neglected, in quest of a dinner, which he did not always obtain.

To compleat his misery,

he was obliged to withdraw from the small number of friends from whom he had still reason to hope for favours. His custom was to lie in bed the greatest part of the day, and to go out in the dark with the utmost privacy, and after having paid his visit, return again before morning to his lodging, which was in the garret of an obscure inn.[11]

At one point Shiels weaves into his own narrative sentences from a letter by Savage to the *Gentleman's Magazine*, which Johnson had quoted; the process of "compilation" reaches some sort of height when Shiels appropriates remarks that Savage—and Johnson—had quoted from the Queen's message to him! We ought in the future, therefore, to refer to the *Life of Savage* in the 1753 *Lives of the Poets* as an abridgment of Johnson's *Life*.

Apart from the two paragraphs that I have already quoted and the transitional sentences that Shiels added to bridge gaps, I find only one passage in Shiels's *Life of Savage* that is not transplanted from John-

---

[10] *Lives*, II, 417–19, pars. 287–92.　　　[11] V, 61.

son's.[12] In his summary judgment of the moral character of Savage, Johnson has the following paragraphs:

It cannot be said that he made use of his abilities for the direction of his own conduct: an irregular and dissipated manner of life had made him the slave of every passion that happened to be excited by the presence of its object, and that slavery to his passions reciprocally produced a life irregular and dissipated. He was not master of his own motions, nor could promise any thing for the next day.

With regard to his oeconomy nothing can be added to the relation of his life. He appeared to think himself born to be supported by others, and dispensed from all necessity of providing for himself; he therefore never prosecuted any scheme of advantage, nor endeavoured even to secure the profits which his writings might have afforded him. His temper was, in consequence of the dominion of his passions, uncertain and capricious: he was easily engaged, and easily disgusted; but he is accused of retaining his hatred more tenaciously than his benevolence.[13]

Shiels, who had been transcribing Johnson closely in this summary, substitutes this judgment:

He was born rather to bear misfortunes greatly, than to enjoy prosperity with moderation. He discovered an amazing firmness of spirit, in spurning those who presumed to dictate to him in the lowest circumstances of misery; but we never can reconcile the idea of true greatness of mind, with the perpetual inclination Savage discovered to live upon the bounty of his friends. To struggle for independence appears much more laudable, as well as a higher instance of spirit, than to be the pensioner of another.

As Savage had seen so much of the world, and was capable of so deep a penetration into nature, it was strange that he could not form some scheme of a livelihood, more honourable than that of a poetical mendicant: his prosecuting any plan of life with diligence, would have thrown more lustre on his character, than all his works, and have raised our ideas of the greatness of his spirit, much beyond the conduct we have already seen. If poverty is so great an evil as to expose a man to commit actions, at which he afterwards blushes, to avoid this poverty should be the continual care of every man; and he, who lets slip every opportunity of doing so, is more entitled to admiration than pity, should he bear his sufferings nobly.[14]

One or two of these sentences might be thought "choice" enough to have been supplied by Johnson, as Boswell suggested. But I think this

[12] In one or two places the account of the events of Savage's life is slightly more detailed than Johnson's (e.g., at V, 36, on the production of Savage's play *Woman's a Riddle*); here I suspect we have Cibber at work revising Shiels's manuscript. Cibber is responsible for two footnotes to Shiels's *Life of Savage.*

[13] II, 431.

[14] V, 64–65.

is more probably Shiels's own work, assisted by hints gathered from portions of Johnson's *Life* that he had omitted in his abridgment; the sentences are not in general Johnsonian, and the moral judgments are rather too flat.[15]

The *Life of Savage* was not the only work by Johnson that Shiels used in his collection. In May 1748, Johnson had published a brief life of Roscommon in the *Gentleman's Magazine*. This too Shiels appropriated for the 1753 *Lives of the Poets*. As published in the *Gentleman's Magazine*, Johnson's *Life of Roscommon* followed a scheme made famous by Bayle and familiarized in such works as the *General Dictionary* and the *Biographia Britannica:* it consisted of a very bare narrative of events, no more than a few lines per page, surmounting a heavy body of notes amplifying, illustrating, or documenting the narrative text; these notes were, in about equal proportions, quotations from Johnson's sources (chiefly Fenton's *Life of Waller*) and comments by Johnson himself. Despite its brevity and its heavy factual reliance on Fenton, who often led Johnson into inaccuracies, the *Life of Roscommon* is a fairly good short biography. When he came to do Roscommon for his own *Prefaces* in 1779, Johnson found that he could use virtually all of it, correcting some statements that he had found to be in error, expanding his discussion of Roscommon's project for an English Academy to fix and refine the language, and adding a few perfunctory paragraphs on minor poems about which he had said nothing in 1748. And, of course, since the *Prefaces* were to be continuous narratives rather than texts-with-notes after the Bayle manner, Johnson, as Boswell says, "indented the notes into the text" to produce a smooth piece of prose.

A similar conversion of the 1748 *Life of Roscommon* into a continuous narrative by indenting the notes into the text had in fact already been carried out by Shiels. Shiels reprinted Johnson's *Life* complete, not abbreviating it as he was to do with the *Savage*. In other respects, his treatment of this text is very similar to his treatment of the *Savage*. Thus, Shiels begins with a paragraph that is, except for a slightly modified opening sentence, taken verbatim from Johnson.

---

[15] Johnson's *Life of Savage* is used or referred to at several other points in the 1753 *Lives of the Poets*. In the *Life of Steele*, Shiels quotes two long passages from Johnson on Steele's "want of economy" (IV, 121–23; cf. Johnson's *Savage*, II, 331–33, pars. 31–34); these two passages were omitted from the abbreviated *Life of Savage*. Thomas Heywood's poverty is likened to Savage's, with a reference to Johnson's *Life* (I, 272). The reader of the *Life of Farquhar* is referred (III, 128) to Johnson's *Life* for a judgment on the moral character of Mrs. Oldfield (see Johnson, *Lives*, II, 336–37; this passage was also omitted by Shiels in his version, but it is contested in a note, obviously by Cibber, at the beginning of that *Life*, V, 32–33). Johnson's *Savage* is the target of a long defensive note by Cibber at V, 211–13, on Savage's opinion of Cibber's ability as an actor (cf. Johnson, *Lives*, II, 341).

Then he gives one of Johnson's notes, in quotation marks, introducing it with the formula "The ingenious author of lord Roscommon's life, publish'd in the *Gentleman's Magazine* for the month of May, 1748, has the following remarks. . . ." With this obeisance to Johnson, Shiels resumes his "own" account, which continues to be a literal transcription of Johnson's. Here, too, as in the *Savage*, Shiels brackets into his own text, without quotation marks, material that Johnson had quoted from Fenton, although, perhaps for the sake of variety, he retains the quotation marks for two of the Fenton passages and credits the source in a footnote. Apart from the occasional change of a phrase or sentence for editorial reasons, Shiels's only additions to Johnson's *Life of Roscommon* are two summary paragraphs (Johnson's 1748 *Life*, owing to its special form, ends rather abruptly), a final reference to Roscommon papers said to be in the Coxeter manuscripts, and a paragraph inserted midway in the *Life*.

This paragraph is by all odds the most interesting, for students of Johnson, in Shiels's *Life*, the rest of which is, of course, already familiar. Shiels has transcribed Johnson's account (including a quotation from Fenton) of Roscommon's proposal to set up an academy, modeled on those of France and Italy, to refine the English language—a proposal revived without success by Swift and others during the ministry of Oxford. Before resuming with Johnson's text, Shiels inserts this paragraph:

It will, no doubt, surprise many of the present age, and be a just cause of triumph to them, if they find that what Roscommon and Oxford attemped in vain, shall be carried into execution, in the most masterly manner, by a private gentleman, unassisted, and unpensioned. The world has just reason to hope this from the publication of an English Dictionary, long expected, by Mr. Johnson; and no doubt a design of this sort, executed by such a genius, will be a lasting monument of the nation's honour, and that writer's merit.[16]

This was certainly a handsome way of acknowledging his obligation to Johnson, and if it would have struck Johnson as hyperbolic, one must concede that in his last sentence, at any rate, poor Shiels's prediction was richly fulfilled.

In addition to printing texts of Johnson's *Life of Savage* and *Life of Roscommon* (the one abridged, the other reordered) and touting the "long expected" *Dictionary*, Shiels printed the text of one other Johnsonian piece. This was the Prologue for the benefit performance of Milton's *Comus*, on 5 April 1750, given by Garrick, at Johnson's suggestion, to raise a fund for Mrs. Foster, Milton's granddaughter. After reviewing the Lauder affair, Shiels concludes that "it is a pity so

[16] II, 348.

much classical knowledge should have been thus prostituted by Lauder, which might have been of service to his country; but party-zeal seldom knows any bounds."[17] But, he continues, "if Lauder is hot and furious, his passion soon subsides."

Upon hearing that the grand-daughter of Milton was living, in an obscure situation in Shoreditch, he readily embraced the opportunity, in his postscript, of recommending her to the public favour [this postscript was of course written by Johnson]; upon which, some gentlemen affected with the singularity of the circumstance, and ashamed that our country should suffer the grand-daughter of one from whom it derives its most lasting and brightest honour, to languish neglected, procured Milton's Comus to be performed for her benefit at Drury Lane, on the 5th of April, 1750: upon which, Mr. Garrick spoke a Prologue written by a gentleman, who zealously promoted the benefit, and who, at this time, holds the highest rank in literature.

This prologue will not, we are persuaded, be unacceptable to our readers.[18]

The Prologue as printed by Shiels[19] is textually identical, save for capitalization, with the original edition. This reprint of the Prologue, which may be added to the bibliography of the poem, seems to have been its only appearance between 1750, when it was published in two editions and in three magazines, and 1768, when it was included in Pearch's *Collection*.[20]

These are the only complete works of Johnson used by Shiels in the 1753 *Lives of the Poets*. But the compiler found several occasions, as many a later and better critic was to do, for quoting or referring to Johnson's Prologue for the Opening of Drury Lane Theater, 1747, and to the critical papers in the *Rambler*.

The *Drury Lane Prologue* appears seven times in the *Lives*. Discussing Shakespeare's genius, Shiels says, "I cannot forbear giving the character of Shakespear in the words of a great genius, in a prologue spoken by Mr. Garrick when he first opened Drury Lane as Manager."[21] Later in this volume, in the *Life of Jonson*, Shiels says that "we cannot better conclude his character as a poet, than in the nervous lines of the Prologue quoted in the Life of Shakespear."[22] A discussion of the closet dramas of William Alexander, Earl of Stirling, prompts Shiels to discourse on the declamatory style and lack of passion in contemporary drama, and he quotes[23] the couplet

17 II, 130–31.

18 II, 131.

19 II, 132–33.

20 *Poems*, ed. Smith and McAdam (1941), p. 55.

21 I, 123–24, quoting *Prologue*, ll. 1–6.

22 I, 249, quoting *Prologue*, ll. 9–14.

23 I, 316.

From bard, to bard, the frigid caution crept,
And declamation roared while passion slept

from Johnson's *Prologue*. This couplet is also quoted[24] in the *Life of Dryden* as the observation of "a living poet" on the style of modern plays.

In his *Life of Aphra Behn*, Shiels was driven to disagree with Johnson's reflections on that lady in the *Drury Lane Prologue*. He is forced to acknowledge that Mrs. Behn's plays contain a good many indecencies, but asks those who blame her to consider "that her's was the sad alternative to write or starve; the taste of the times was corrupt; and it is a true observation, that they who live to please, must please to live." With the *Prologue* in his mind, Shiels is aroused to quote its line about Aphra Behn; Johnson is now "another modern" (the first was Pope) speaking of the vicissitudes to which the stage is subjected:

Perhaps if skill could distant times explore,
New Behn's, new Durfey's, yet remain in store,

.   .   .   .

Perhaps, for who can guess th' effects of chance,
Here Hunt may box, and Mahomet may dance.[25]

This is too much for Shiels, even from Johnson:

This author cannot be well acquainted with Mrs. Behn's works, who makes a comparison between them and the productions of Durfey. There are marks of a fine understanding in the most unfinished piece of Mrs. Behn, and the very worst of this lady's compositions are preferable to Durfey's best. It is unpleasing to have the merit of any of the Fair Sex lessened.[26]

Shiels was incurably romantic and irrepressibly gallant; nothing aroused his fervor so much as the unfortunate female poets whose careers he recorded; his accounts of Mrs. Manley, Mrs. Thomas, and Mrs. Pilkington are frequently, but quite unconsciously, hilarious in their fussy, moralizing gallantry. Yet another couplet from the *Drury Lane Prologue* sees service in behalf of the Fair Sex in Shiels's *Life of Betterton*, where he quotes with approval Colley Cibber's praise of Mrs. Betterton and uses Johnson's observation—

That scenic virtue forms the rising age,
And truth displays her radiance from the stage—

to support his affirmation that persons of real worth may be reputable off the stage as well as on it.[27] Shiels's final use of this poem is in the

---

[24] III, 67.

[25] *Prologue*, ll. 41–42, 45–46.

[26] III, 27.

[27] III, 172, quoting *Prologue*, ll. 61–62.

Life of Blackmore, in which he quotes six lines (17–20, 25–26) from "an elegant writer having occasion to mention the state of wit in the reign of King Charles II. . . ."[28]

Shiels refers for support to the *Rambler* three times. The observations of "the ingenious author of the Rambler" (in *Rambler* 168) on the diction of *Macbeth* are cited in the life of Shakespeare;[29] Johnson, still "the ingenious author of the Rambler," is quoted on Raleigh's *History of the World* in the *Life of Raleigh;*[30] and in concluding his *Life of Milton* Shiels refers his readers to Addison's *Spectator* papers on *Paradise Lost* and to the *Rambler:*

A later critic, the ingenious author of the Rambler, has animadverted upon Milton's versification with great judgment; and has discovered in some measure that happy art, by which Milton has conducted so great a design, with such astonishing success.

From these two writers may be drawn all the necessary assistances for reading the Paridise Lost with taste and discernment; and as their works are in almost every body's hands, it would be needless to give any abstract of them here.[31]

These are the direct obligations of Shiels to Johnson in the 1753 *Lives of the Poets.* I do not imagine that anyone will wish to wade through the book in search of the "choice sentences" that Boswell said Johnson was thought to have supplied—if indeed Boswell was referring to anything beyond the very Johnsonian sentences in Shiels's lives of Savage and Roscommon. Sentences apart, however, it is clear that Johnson also supplied Shiels with information and with topics for comment:

1. Several of the facts in Shiels's interesting *Life of Samuel Boyse* were certainly provided by Johnson.[32]

2. Shiels apparently got from Johnson the story (which he tells at I, 130–31) about Shakespeare's employment holding gentlemen's horses outside the theater. Johnson later included the story in his own edition of Shakespeare as an addendum to Rowe's *Life,* and Steevens, in a note printed in the 1778 Shakespeare,[33] seems to suggest that Johnson was Shiels's source. This also was Chambers's opinion.[34]

[28] V, 178–79.

[29] I, 139.

[30] I, 202, quoting *Rambler* 122.

[31] II, 148.

[32] Compare "Cibber's" *Lives,* V, 160–76, and *Johnsonian Miscellanies,* I, 228, and II, 411; Nichols, *Library Anecdotes* (1815), IX, 277; Boswell, *Life,* IV, 408 n., 446; E. A. Bloom, *N & Q* (April 1954), pp. 163–65; Clifford, *Young Sam Johnson* (1955), p. 349, n. 2.

[33] I, 201–2.

[34] *William Shakespeare,* II, 285–86.

3. Shiels evidently had from Johnson (he simply says that he is presenting "authentic information") the explanation of Swift's animosity toward Dryden: when asked to read over some of Swift's early Pindaric odes, Dryden is said to have remarked, "Cousin Swift, turn your thoughts some other way, for nature has never formed you for a Pindaric poet."[35] In his own *Life of Swift* Johnson has Dryden say simply, "Cousin Swift, you will never be a poet."[36]

4. I suspect that Shiels's remarks on the uniformity of versification and the declamatory style of modern plays in his *Life of Rowe*[37] may have been prompted by Johnson's remarks on these topics at the end of *Rambler* 125, and that the *Rambler* is also drawn on for the definition of pastoral poetry in the *Life of Ambrose Philips*.[38] Diligent search would no doubt disclose other parallels.

Johnson has been credited with one contribution to the 1753 *Lives of the Poets* which we can be reasonably confident he did not make. James Crossley, in 1852, printed a long advertisement for the *Lives* from the London papers of 20 February 1753. The advertisement, he said, was written by Johnson: "the internal evidence is decisive."[39] There is of course no external evidence for the attribution, and it is on the face of it unlikely that Johnson would compose a long advertisement for a publication announced as "Cibber's" *Lives of the Poets;* he would have done so only out of friendship for Shiels, whose fee did not in fact depend on the sale of the volumes. The internal evidence, if decisive, is decisive against Johnson's authorship. Although many of the sentiments, on the value of literary biography and the like, are not uncharacteristic of Johnson, they have nothing peculiarly Johnsonian about them. And no one could suppose that Johnson wrote a sentence like the following, which is typical of the whole: "As there is no Reading at once so entertaining and instructive, as that of Biography, so none ought to have the Preference to it: It yields the most striking Pictures of Life, and shews us the many Vicissitudes to which we are exposed in the Course of that important Journey."

Johnson, for his part, made occasional use of Shiels's work when he came to write his own "little prefaces." How frequently he did so must await a fuller investigation of the sources of Johnson's *Lives* and a more systematic study of Shiels's book than I have attempted. In addition to Johnson's use of Shiels in the *Life of Hammond*, noted at the beginning of this chapter, he seems to have used the 1753 collec-

[35] *Lives,* V, 97–98.
[36] *Lives,* ed. Hill, III, 7–8, and n. 10.
[37] III, 274–75.
[38] V, 131; cf. *Rambler* 37.
[39] *N & Q,* 1st Ser., V (10 January 1852), 25.

tion in his accounts of Rowe, Fenton, Edmund Smith, Pitt, Ambrose Philips, and Thomson. There may be other borrowings more difficult to trace. Boyce has suggested that Johnson may have found in Shiels's *Life of Pope* hints for his famous comparison of Dryden and Pope.[40] What we do not know, in any of these cases, is whether Johnson, when he wrote his *Lives*, may not have been simply repossessing what he had given Shiels—or what he had allowed Shiels to use—a quarter of a century before. When Johnson seems to have borrowed from the 1753 *Lives of the Poets* and when we can find no other source for the information there, we must consider it as antecedently probable that Johnson was Shiels's source. Shiels's book is a collection of quotations, most of them unacknowledged; his association with Johnson was close; Johnson's sources of oral information on literary history were far more numerous than those of Shiels, and there is simply no comparison between them as critics; we have Boswell's testimony that Johnson gave Shiels valuable assistance. From what we have seen, if Johnson dug around in the 1753 *Lives of the Poets*, he was bound to find some of the very nuggets that he had earlier dropped there himself or that the virtuous Shiels had panned from one of Johnson's own claims.

[40] "Samuel Johnson's Criticism of Pope in the *Life of Pope*," *RES*, N.S., V (1954), 37–46.

RICHMOND P. BOND

Isaac Bickerstaff, Esq.

IT WAS EARLY in the year 1708 that Jonathan Swift gave the printer John Morphew the manuscript of a small pamphlet called *Predictions for the Year 1708*, "Written to prevent the People of *England* from being further impos'd on by vulgar Almanack-makers." The name of the author on the title page was Isaac Bickerstaff, Esq. This was the first appearance in the literary world of the eidolon called up by the master of irony to create a foolery on John Partridge, astrologer and quack and compiler of almanacs. How Swift's original Bickerstaff caught the whim of the Town, how other writers adopted his signature for their own use, how he was transformed by Steele and Addison and their associates into the celebrated Censor of the *Tatler*—these are matters that will be examined in the present study.

The time was well chosen for Swift's mockery. The Company of Stationers was then making a profitable business out of publishing and distributing large numbers of almanacs, many of which were obviously mischievous media of the astrologers, defrauding the people with pretended facts and false predictions. Moreover, London was at that time also witnessing the extravagant prophecies of the French, or Modern, Prophets, a new sect whose leaders went into physico-spiritual gyrations and relayed God's warnings of doom for nonbelievers. In December of 1707, by publicly assuring a dying follower that he would rise from the dead exactly five months after the day of his death, these enthusiastic impostors drew particular attention to their extreme predictions.[1]

It is small wonder that Jonathan Swift thought it would be well for quackery to feel the assault of his pen; after all, in a sense astrology

RICHMOND P. BOND is Kenan Professor of English at the University of North Carolina.

[1] For an essay on these spectacular enthusiasts, see James Sutherland, "John Lacy and the Modern Prophets," *Background for Queen Anne* (London, 1939), pp. 36–74. Swift, of course, was well acquainted with the phenomenon of these Prophets and made a prophecy upon them in his *Predictions*.

represented his constant two-headed foe, false learning and false religion. The best kind of weapon for effective censure would be a packet of mock-predictions; sham prognostications and facetious almanacs had long since proved their value,[2] and a sham prediction could well accommodate the devices and readily call for substantiating sequels. But should Swift's ironical prognostications be directed in general at the whole company of astrological pretenders or be aimed principally at one particular prognosticating rogue, a popular "Spy upon the Stars," who would serve as the representative of his vulnerable vocation? With Partridge at hand, Swift had little option.

What were the peculiar qualifications of this Augustan Merlin? He had written too stridently against the Church so close to Swift's interest. He had fought in print with other almanac makers and issued challenges that could be turned to advantage by a merry outsider.[3] He was alive and very well established, whereas some of the other almanacs were being written by men of no large reputation and some bore the names of writers long since dead. Also, Partridge wrote the kind of prediction that could be mocked with consequence, whereas some of his contemporaries were too specialized for general ridicule, and some indeed included no predictions at all. We cannot know whether Swift's primary purpose was to expose astrology or chastise Partridge, but we may be sure that in several respects Partridge was not merely a good candidate for satirical attention but the best among all the living makers of almanacs.

In the process of writing his satire Swift constructed an eidolon exactly sufficient to the occasion and a character suitable for further employ—Isaac Bickerstaff, Esq. Where did Swift find the name for his mask? The orthodox explanation appeared as an editorial report during his lifetime many years after the publication of the pamphlet. "It is said, that the Author, when he had writ the following Paper, and being at a Loss what Name to prefix to it; passing through *Long-*

---

[2] See Cornelius Walford, "Sham Almanacks and Prognostications," *Book-Lore*, II (1885), 67–71, 91–95, 136–43, 159–68; Carroll Camden, "Elizabethan Almanacs and Prognostications," *Library*, New Ser., XII (1931), 83–108, 194–207; F. P. Wilson, "Some English Mock-Prognostications," *Library*, 4th Ser., XIX (1939), 6–43; Don Cameron Allen, *The Star-Crossed Renaissance* (Durham, N.C., 1941), Chap. V.

The Infallible Astrologer, a journal of mock-predictions in 1700, has been proposed as an anticipation of Swift: William A. Eddy, "Tom Brown and Partridge the Astrologer," *MP*, XXVIII (1930), 163–68. For a discussion of this periodical and its imitation, *The Dutch Prophet*, in 1700, see Benjamin Boyce, *Tom Brown of Facetious Memory* (Cambridge, Mass., 1939), pp. 129–33.

[3] Herbert Davis, in his edition of Swift's prose, emphasizes the violence of Partridge's abuse of the clergy and quotes from the verses in the *Merlinus Liberatus* for 1706 and 1707 and also from the challenges by Partridge to his rivals (*Bickerstaff Papers* [Oxford, 1940], pp. x–xii).

Acre, observed a Sign over a House where a Locksmith dwelt, and found the Name *Bickerstaff* written under it: Which being a Name somewhat uncommon, he chose to call himself *Isaac Bickerstaff.*"[4] The substance of this clear description of a simple situation may doubtless have come from Swift himself, who lived when satirists regularly wrote with their eyes on living objects. And a plain locksmith named Bickerstaff dwelling in Long Acre during the winter of 1707–8 might well have left a dull record of himself to corroborate the memory of the brilliant clergyman. But no original locksmith has so far been proposed, and a recent though somewhat casual excursion into parish registers, legal records, rate books, poll and association lists, and other local archives has discovered no such Bickerstaff.

Perhaps an identification will in time appear, but it is presently certain that Bickerstaff(e) or Biggerstaff was indeed a name somewhat uncommon in London and England, but one not exceedingly rare. A John Bickerstaff had frequently been named among the players at Drury Lane, where Swift could have seen him perform.[5] It is possible that Swift had encountered the name earlier, and while practicing his own art of walking the streets of London was reminded of this proper name when he sought a memorable pseudonym; on the contrary he may have had no experience of that sort at all but later decided to create a history for his famous character by adding such an item of circumstance to the merry tale. Swift, in any event, remained safely humorous—if readers accepted his story and did not search out a locksmith who had not lived, they would be gullible; if they doubted his explanation and located the original locksmith, they verified the obvious; and if they looked for the man and found no record, they were naive to inquire after the nonexistent. Whether fact or fable, the joke is good enough. Here the historian gives the critic an amiably unimportant choice, and the great wit may now smile at our caring one

[4] Swift, *Works* (Dublin, 1735), I, 148. Probably the first allusion to the name occurred in a tract written perhaps in February 1708, *An Answer to Bickerstaff,* quite possibly by Swift himself. In his reflections on the *Predictions* a Person of Quality remarks, "But, it seems, although he hath joined an odd sirname to no very common Christian one, that in this large town there is a man found to own both the names, although I believe, not the paper" (*Bickerstaff Papers,* pp. 196–97). This tract was first published by Hawkesworth in 1765 in his edition of Swift. Is it only an interesting coincidence, or a possible source, or a jest within a jest?

[5] John Bickerstaff inevitably got connected with Isaac Bickerstaff. In *Tatler* No. 3 Isaac recommended attendance on a certain performance for the benefit of his "near Kinsman," and the *Daily Courant* of 4 February 1710 carried an advertisement of a performance of *Don Quixote* at Drury Lane "At the Desire of Isaac Bickerstaffe, Esq; For the Benefit of his Cousin, John Bickerstaff." In Mrs. Centlivre's *A Bickerstaff's Burying* (1710) the role of the Captain was taken by John in a striking example of theatrical decorum. For John's performances see Emmett L. Avery, *The London Stage 1660–1800. Part 2: 1706–1729* (2 vols.; Carbondale, Ill., 1960).

way or the other about an actual signboard in the broad and handsome Long Acre.[6]

Whatever the source of his name, Isaac Bickerstaff was without doubt contrived to lend substance to Swift's mockery of fraud. And to give sharpest point to his satire Swift chose as his butt John Partridge. In order the better to describe the comic role of Bickerstaff, we may first have a short view of the charlatan himself.[7]

Partridge was born in the sixteen forties in Surrey, somehow gained the elements of astrology, and entered the great sphere of science and letters. In the late seventies this "Fortune-Seller, a Retailer of Destiny, and petty Chapman to the Planets" issued his first works. By the end of the reign of Charles II the busy Partridge had made himself responsible for four different almanacs and sundry astrological publications. His anti-Catholic animation sent him to the Continent during the brief regal experiment of James the Jacobite, but he returned with Dutch William and in 1690 did honor to his fresh political freedom with a new almanac, *Merlinus Liberatus*, his ephemeris of greatest fame. Living in Henrietta Street in Covent Garden and later at the Blue Ball in Salisbury Street in the Strand, John Partridge grew to be a thriving dealer in falsehood and futurity. He died quite solvent in 1715, with bequests adding up to a good sum, and his will was printed in newspaper and pamphlet. In 1734 the library of "the late Celebrated Dr. *PARTRIDGE*" was sold, but among the listed titles there were no Bickerstaff tracts or *Tatler* papers.[8]

[6] It may be added that in the *Tenth Black List* of the names or reputed names of lewd and scandalous persons who had been convicted by the endeavors of the Society for Promoting a Reformation of Manners during 1704 there appeared both a Bickerstaff and a Partridge. This list also included such literary names as Blake, Chatterton, Collins, Goldsmith, Johnson, Pope, Richardson, Smart, Steele, Swift, Thomson, and Young. All these people were described as whores or disorderly persons. Incidentally, in 1710 a William Partridge, locksmith in Kensington Square, advertised goods to be sold (*Post-Man*, No. 1894, 27 July), and a Mrs. Bickerstaff promoted a sale of goods by way of lots, ten blanks to a prize (*Evening Post*, No. 162, 26 August). In 1712 a "Bickerstaff's Coffee-house" was available to let in Great Russell Street near the Piazza, Covent Garden (*Daily Courant*, No. 3269, 5 April). Was this establishment named before or after Isaac?

[7] The first sizable discussion of Partridge appeared in the Nichols edition of the *Tatler* in 1786 (V, 427–48) and long remained the standard treatment in spite of its many inadequacies. The essay by William Alfred Eddy, "The Wits vs. John Partridge, Astrologer" (*SP*, XXIX [1932], 29–40), is too often confused and unreliable. The article by George P. Mayhew, "The Early Life of John Partridge" (*SEL*, I [1961], iii, 31–42), is a careful and fruitful examination. The article by Richmond P. Bond, "John Partridge and the Company of Stationers" (*SB*, XVI [1963], 61–80), concerns Partridge's attempt to publish his almanac without legal authority.

[8] The will was printed in the *Weekly Journal, or British Gazetteer* for 10 December 1715 and the next year in a pamphlet, *The Last Wills and Testaments of J. Partridge, . . . and Dr. Burnett*. John Brindley, bookseller, issued the catalogue as *Librorum Patricii Eruditissimi, necnon Celeberrimi Astronomi, Catalogus*.

Partridge's pattern for his *Merlinus Liberatus* was not very different from the standard procedure in almanacs. The book was an octavo in three sheets, thus falling into the trade category of "blanks," and had its share of attractive rubrication. The title page was crowded with a list of contents and Partridge's triple method of dating—by the Incarnation, by the Creation, and by "our Deliverance by K. *William* from Popery and Arbitrary Government." With the 1708 issue as a specimen, we see at once that the Calendar was the core: each month occupied an opening, with verses at the top, and provided the vital statistics of the world, such as the days of the month and week, the "remarkable" days, astronomical data, weather forecasts, and monthly observations punctuated by the changes of the moon. All of this material required half of the forty-eight pages. "A General Judgment on the Four Quarters" took ten more pages for astrological interpretations, and further space was needed for the eclipses, a "Division of the Heavens," and a special nativity. The few remaining leaves were given to standard departments of information and entertainment like tables of the monarchs, tides, terms, interest rates, and the hours of the sun, a poor but patriotic poem, and a few advertisements, mostly of publications and nostrums.

The predictions in the astrological parts became the distinctive feature of Partridge's shrewdness. Dubious prognostications had never been a novelty, but the *Merlinus Liberatus* achieved superb vagueness. Although its predictions seemed to look toward the definite in time, place, and/or person, it actually said very little that was specific, predicting the palpable and speaking double, all in oracular terms and tone.[9] A few samples illustrate Partridge's skill in propounding the obvious and parading the equivocal and leaving loopholes:

The end of this month, or beginning of the next, will undoubtedly give Violence and violent Actions, and perhaps private murder and such like, *&c.* [January 1690]

Why may not some eminent Lady leave her Husbands Bed about this time? [June 1691]

Toward the end of the month we may expect some mighty News from the *Teutonick* Shoar. Is *Poland* quiet and in good order? [April 1700]

News from *France;* good enough if it prove true, though perhaps all may not be of my opinion. [February 1701]

The Weather cold and uncomfortable, Coughs and Colds common to almost every one. [December 1702]

. . . his [the French King's] ill Success will be increased, and his Life

---

[9] Even when Partridge produced an exact prophecy, he was apt to give himself ample protection. For instance, in November 1704: "A Girl born the 24*th* at 15 min. past 1 at Noon, will prove a publick-spirited Wench. Observe it!"

in danger, either by Discontent or Poyson. It would be strange, if he should die the common Death of all Men. [Summer 1707]

Some old Statesman dies; and some eminent Sea-Commander either call'd in question, or decently laid by. [October 1708]

A notable component in Partridge's wares, and apparently a popular one, remained the strident assaults on Popery and France: as a bitter Protestant and excitable Whig he went beyond the line of patriotism in crying destruction on Louis and rejoicing in Roman disorder and including the Pretender and High Church in the desired distress. But we must in justice deny the charge by his rival George Parker that he had "kill'd the French King too, more than 100 times over."[10] Partridge was sincerely eager for the tyrant to die and gave him good opportunities, but it would seem that he did not specifically foretell the end of the King. That kind of shortsightedness was not a part of his trade.

The prominence of Partridge is discovered in the substantial and casual current references to him as a kind of proto-astrologer and in the number of persons who read his works. If we may indulge in a loose estimate, we can say that the forty issues of his various ephemerides could have had an average annual printing of twenty-five thousand copies[11] and that on this basis the popular astrologer must have had hundreds of thousands of reader-users, many of whom bought or consulted his almanac year after year. Partridge was perhaps better known to the lowly, the provincial, the merely "practical" people than was either Swift or Steele, and he had indeed become the foremost man of his profession.

THE FIRST BICKERSTAFF

The Isaac Bickerstaff whose name appeared on the title page of *Predictions for the Year 1708* seemed to be an earnest, conscientious, educated gentleman who would save astrology from "a few mean illiterate Traders between us and the Stars." "I have long considered the gross Abuse of Astrology in this Kingdom," he writes, "and upon debating the Matter with my self, I could not possibly lay the Fault upon the Art, but upon those gross Imposters who set up to be the Artists." He mentions the long departed astrologer William Lilly once and his own contemporary John Partridge twice before beginning his predictions, of which the first reads thus:

---

[10] *Parker's Ephemeris For the Year of our Lord 1708*, p. 4.

[11] In 1687 the Company of Stationers printed twenty thousand copies of Partridge's almanac (Cyprian Blagden, "The Distribution of Almanacks in the Second Half of the Seventeenth Century," *SB*, XI [1958], Table I).

My first Prediction is but a Trifle, yet I will mention it, to shew how ignorant these Sottish Pretenders to Astrology are in their own Concerns: It relates to *Partridge* the Almanack-maker; I have consulted the Star of his Nativity by my own Rules, and find he will infallibly dye upon the 29th of *March* next, about Eleven at night, of a raging Feaver; therefore I advise him to consider of it, and settle his Affairs in time.

In this pamphlet, which was not an almanac and so had no Calendar, a few of the two score "great Events" predicted for the next six months are happy, but most are literally disastrous. Although in some cases Bickerstaff gives the time as only "this Month," he frequently provides the day and occasionally the hour.

MAY, against common Conjecture, will be no very busy Month in *Europe*, but very signal for the Death of the *Dauphin*, which will happen on the 7th, after a short Sickness, and grievous Torments with the Strangury.

He generally states the place and the specific nature of the action.

JUNE. This Month will be distinguish'd at home by the utter dispersing of those ridiculous deluded Enthusiasts, commonly call'd the *Prophets;* occasion'd chiefly by seeing the Time come that many of their Prophesies should be fulfill'd, and then finding themselves deceiv'd by contrary Events.

Some of the persons he identifies by rank, and a few are named—Partridge, the Dauphin, the King of France, and the Pope, all of whom will die at definite times of specified causes. Be it noted that Bickerstaff followed Partridge's prognosticative procedure in form but ridiculed the whole mummery of prophecy by making particular an event that could not be foreknown by anyone in any way. And he was impressive in his responsible manner and public spirit.

As to the particular Events I have mention'd, the Readers may judge by the fulfilling of 'em, whether I am of the Level with common Astrologers; who, with an old paultry Cant, and a few Pot-hooks for Planets to amuse the Vulgar, have, in my Opinion, too long been suffer'd to abuse the World: ... I hope I have some share of Reputation, which I would not willingly forfeit for a Frolick or Humour; And I believe no Gentleman, who reads this Paper, will look upon it to be of the same Last or Mould with the common Scribbles that are every Day hawk'd about.[12]

This slight publication gained an immediate and immense popularity if we may judge from allusions, piracies, translations, and imitations.[13] What was apparently the first reference in a periodical was

[12] These passages from the *Predictions* are on pp. 2, 2, 5, 5, 6, and 8.

[13] There have been a few dissidents among later readers. Leslie Stephen did not think that the joke had a "very exquisite flavour" (*Swift* [London, 1882], p. 59). And in a reference to the Partridge-Swift affair Ellen McCaffery pronounced the

particularly apt and early—the *Predictions* appeared as the subject of a question-and-answer in the *British Apollo* only four days after the extinction of Partridge.

> *Q. What think you of Esq;* Bickerstaff's *Prophecies, were they writ in jest or earnest?*
>
> *A.* In jest Man! fie, fie! In earnest you may lay your Life on't, Esq; *Bickerstaff's* a downright Conjurer: The Dumb man's a Fool to him. He's as great a Conjurer as Dr. *Faustus,* or the *Brazen-head* of *Friar Bacon,* and if you are one of those Unhappy Souls his Prophecies threaten Death to, e'en set your House in order, take leave of your Friends, and die without grumbling.[14]

And the ubiquitous Defoe followed soon in his *Review:*

> O *Bickerstaff, Bickerstaff,* wonderful *Bickerstaff,* Esq; here is work to puzzle your Oracle! you, in that so wonderful a manner, foretel the Fate of Men to Hours and Moments, no matter whether they come to pass or no, . . . wherefore, I humbly entreat this great Genius, that so exactly foretold the Death of Mr. *Partridge* the *Almanack*-maker, that his Elegy was cry'd about streets the very day, and you know, Men's Elegies are never made till they are dead: . . . .[15]

Consider the fact that it was all a piece of sport, a fiction from an unknown pen, not concerned with the hand of war or the posture of affairs in state and church, and Swift's jest becomes a prodigy in English letters.[16] Such a hoax, to be truly successful, has two essential movements—prophecy and fulfillment. The rest lies in the presentation of verisimilar circumstance, the detail that captures concurrence. Swift proceeded accordingly. First, his *Predictions*. Then, close to or on the very day of doom for the astrologer, there appeared *The Accomplishment Of the First of Mr. Bickerstaff's Predictions,* a letter (not of course from Bickerstaff, who certainly would not have been present) to a noble lord describing the last hours of the failing Partridge, who confessed to the deceits of astrology and declared himself

---

former "a man of infinitely superior mental equipment" (*Astrology: Its History and Influence in the Western World* [New York, 1942], p. 327). A popular imitation in America was that by Franklin (see John F. Ross, "The Character of Poor Richard: Its Source and Alteration," *PMLA,* LV [1940], 785–94).

[14] I, 15 (2 April 1708).

[15] V, 10 (20 April 1708); cf. V, 8 (15 April 1708).

[16] It has been suggested that Swift may have got the idea of the prank from Tirso de Molina's tale of the duped husband who believed himself dead (Rudolph Schevill, "Swift's Hoax on Partridge, the Astrologer, and Similar Jests in Fiction," *Transactions of the Connecticut Academy of Arts and Sciences,* XV [1909], 227–38).

a Nonconformist and then died on the twenty-ninth of March at about seven o'clock, four hours short of Bickerstaff's estimate. Synchronously Swift's *Elegy on Mr. Patrige* was hawked about London, a broadside with black borders and funereal figures purveying one-hundred-odd lines of street doggerel plus an epitaph on the "*Cobler, Starmonger*, and *Quack.*" This was the first dissolution of poor Partridge.

Promptly the literary wags saw good occasion to follow a leader. *Mr. Partridge's Answer to Esquire Bickerstaff's Strange and Wonderful Predictions* replied month by month to "Squire *Conjurer.*" Another Bickerstaff issued a *Continuation of the Predictions For the Remaining Part of the Year 1708* (Old Style). In *Bickerstaffe's Prediction Confirm'd*, prophecies were included for the last three months of 1708 together with an invitation to the whole clan of almanac makers to repair to Bickerstaff's house in Chelsea for free answers to all their questions. And *Squire Bickerstaff Detected*, as if by Partridge, gave amusement by relaying the effects of his death and funeral on Partridge himself and his household.

The *Merlinus Liberatus* for 1709 appeared almost a year after the provocative *Predictions*, and Partridge decided that this was the proper time for him to make a public answer. On the title page he used the phrase "A Lover of Truth" to replace his usual sobriquet of "Student in Physick and Astrology"; perhaps he designed this change as a rebuke to the mendacious Bickerstaff. And on the title page Partridge included in the list of contents this item: "Also to inform the World that I am Living, contrary to that base Paper said to be done by one *Bickerstaff, &c.*" In the February observations there was this entry: "Much lying News dispersed about this time; and also Scandalous Pamphlets. Perhaps we may have a second *Bickerstaff* appear." With this qualified prediction of the forthcoming *Tatler* Partridge was for once a true prophet. At the end of the judgments on the autumnal quarter he made a third reference: "This shews some Knavish Scribbler that would do mischief if he could; perhaps another *Bickerstaffe*, or a Rascal under that Name." These were but incidental answers; the full reply was set off in a kind of epilogue and phrased with all force and clarity.

You may remember there was a Paper publish'd predicting my Death on the 29th of *March* at Night, 1708. and after the day was past, the same Villain told the World I was dead, and how I died; and that he was with me at the time of my death. I thank God, by whose Mercy I have my Being, that I am still alive, and (excepting my Age) as well as ever I was in my Life; as I was also at that 29th of *March*. And that Paper was said to be done by one *Bickerstaffe*, Esq; but that was a Sham-Name; it was done by an *Impudent Lying Fellow*. But his Prediction did not prove true: What will he say to excuse that? For the Fool had consider'd the *Star of my Nativity*, as he said. Why the truth is, he will be hard put to it to find a *Salvo* for his Honor. It was a bold Touch, and he did not know but it might prove true.[17]

With this rebuttal Partridge demonstrated the ultimate in pointless, ingenuous denial, delivering himself into the clever hands of his adversaries and completing the triangle of prophecy-fulfillment-denial that makes of this hoax a perfection of foolery. We wonder how a man canny enough to win his way through three decades of public dealing could not see for himself the absurdity of soberly denying his own demise, could not foresee that the wits would rejoice over such naiveté and that even his most unsophisticated reader might smile at such an absurdity. Partridge must have been a literal-minded man devoid of the lighter arts.

No satirist could reject such an opening. In reply to the almanac Swift concocted a *Vindication of Isaac Bickerstaff*, by himself, citing his good reception in Europe, reprimanding Partridge for his poor manners, and giving arguments in proof of his death. The first response, he said, had come from gentlemen who read this new almanac and cried out, "betwixt Rage and Laughter, *They were sure no Man alive ever writ such damn'd Stuff as this*." He further contended that his prediction of Partridge's death had been "computed to something under half an Hour,"[18] and thus he had not erred by hours, as the *Accomplishment* tract had reported. One more small item—a pamphlet of verse and prose entitled *A Famous Prediction of Merlin, the British Wizard*—and Swift had finished with Partridge.

Of the four drolleries published by Swift only the famous *Predictions* and one sequel were signed by Bickerstaff, and the several early followers used both Bickerstaff and Partridge as putative authors. In his first piece Swift had created an eidolon proper for his purpose—an experienced astrologer sober, reliable, knowledgeable, whose good sense and good will would gain the interest of a reader. He added little to this assumed character, nor did the witlings in tow materially alter the mask. As to the individual who represented the cheats of astrology, the satirists major and minor concerned themselves more with fun than with fine strokes of characterization. They may not of

[17] Pages C7v–C8.

[18] Pages 6, 7. The phrase "No Man alive" appeared also in "A TESTIMONIAL of the Death of Mr. *Partridge*," signed Jeremy Wagstaff, which was included in *Bickerstaff's Almanack* for 1710. This almanac had no predictions but contained an essay against false astrologers, including Partridge. It was mentioned in *Tatler* No. 94 a week before its publication (see Bond, *SB*, 75–77).

course have known the man in person, and certainly such a jest did not demand a character beyond a stereotype. These writers made a farce in which a complex and true character might have spoiled it all.

THE SECOND BICKERSTAFF

When in April of 1709 Richard Steele established a triweekly half-sheet to "expose the false Arts of Life" and named it *The Tatler*, he created the second Bickerstaff by reviving Swift's putative author. In one year's time this signature had been raised "to as high a Pitch of Reputation as it could possibly arrive at," and it was plainly acknowledged that "By this good Fortune, the Name of *Isaac Bickerstaff* gained an Audience of all who had any Taste of Wit." Such a "sudden Acceptance" was in all likelihood Steele's initial purpose in once more presenting Isaac Bickerstaff as a mask.[19] The *Tatler* thus and then became the first essay journal to use in a subtle and substantial way the device of assumed author-editorship. Defoe had made small effort to give his Mr. Review a personality but remained content in his tremendous journal of comment on events and ideas to use the eidolon as a pale spokesman for himself. Bickerstaff became a person who conducted the *Tatler* and was the writer of all the words on his leaf of letterpress save for some of the epistles and of course the hundreds of advertisements; Steele and Addison and the others were, shall we say, his agents or amanuenses, or so we must allow if we are willing to play in the game of fictitious authorship by its most rigorous rules.

The persona as a device in periodical literature has not been so carefully studied as the eidolon in other types or media, and there are special characteristics for the mask in an essay journal. The putative writer of an essay sheet is, first, the creature of periodicity—he writes not chapters but separate issues each of two or three thousand words. The periodic persona must not neglect the situation of his reader either individual or corporate—this reader, whether in his domestic seat or semipublic chair, will suffer frequent or occasional interruption in his attendance on the experiences and observations of Squire Bickerstaff or Nestor Ironside or Mr. Spectator or the Rambler or Adventurer or Connoisseur, the hiatus of one day at least or one week at most. And the author must realize that the readers who miss an issue now and then, here or there, deserve no serious penalty in the loss of continuity. The assumed author, we remark, is not writing a book; he is writing an indefinite number of parts of a whole, and he must not forget the nature of this subdivided pseudonymity. Or to say it in Addison's way, "A Man who publishes his Works in a Volume, has

19 The dedication of the first octavo reprint of the *Tatler*, I (1710), iv.

an infinite Advantage over one who communicates his Writings to the World in loose Tracts and single Pieces."[20]

The eidolon of an essay paper, if he would have a long and good life, must be an interesting individual in his own right, with enough personality to attract and to preserve his band of followers. He should have admirable traits without ascending to the dull paragon, but he can wander from normality and typicality with quirks and eccentric wiles so long as he does not descend to such disconformities as will forfeit him the confidence and respect and even affection that his audience expects and desires to give him. Furthermore, he must not aspire to the status of a hero, for he is not the leading character of the piece, which may contain no such figure at all. He cannot permit himself the center of the stage or a role overly developed; he should not steal the show through an unnecessarily complex personality or excessive participation in the episodes and speculations that he presents in his serialized performance. Though he must be in a credible position to report or remark, he must not oppressively call attention to his person or his situation. The effective persona, we see, should establish himself in the minds and also the hearts of his day-to-week-to-month adherents as a man worthy of welcome acceptance, humanly constituted but not sacrosanct or enveloping, a participant in the current circus of mundane things but not its major end. If he can maintain the center road between the definite and the indefinite and wear his character mask to speak his lines with fictive sincerity and reasonable authority, he will promote his purpose, be it literary, social, political, philosophical.

But there is another role he must play—and play concurrently. The assumed author is also an editor, and surely his readers understand that he is conducting a periodic project. He has a printer, who takes in advertisements and demands editorial copy on the hour; he receives letters long and brief, sharp and friendly, polished and crude, percipient and silly, and he can share these messages in print with those who seldom direct their pens toward an editor. He can confide his editorial vexations to his subscribers and thus draw them closer. This function of editor is not so prominent as that of writer, but it is there and it is a part of the business of the periodical eidolon. The full persona furnishes the essential unity, the indispensable continuity to the publication, and it is his skill that helps in sizable degree to determine its success as an economic venture and its influence in a less material sphere.

When Steele borrowed from Swift the name of Bickerstaff, without doubt he understood that with the name went a personality and the

[20] *Spectator*, No. 124.

profession of astrologer, and to this inheritance there was attached the asset or liability of John Partridge. Steele and Addison adroitly altered and developed the character of their fictitious editor-author, but Partridge could hardly be transformed from the stubborn, stupid almanac maker who contradicted the fact of his own death. At the outset Steele may well have seen that the zest of the year-old game had begun to wane, for in his first Lucubration he made Partridge into a mere symbol by saying "his Art is gone, the Man is gone." This second Bickerstaff thereupon pledged that he would "proceed to confute other dead Men, who pretend to be in Being, that they are actually deceased," and gave "all Men fair Warning to mend their Manners" and promised that those "who are good for Nothing shall find themselves in the Number of the Deceas'd." Steele kept the joke going—after all it was his best and patent entree into the brains and pockets of the Town—kept it going for several months with a dozen references to the quack during the remainder of 1709. Thereafter Partridge was mentioned only thrice and was in a way succeeded by the Company of Upholders, whom Bickerstaff commissioned to bury the Walking Dead, thus reaffirming his first idea that worthless people are really defunct.[21] Bickerstaff himself remained an occult scientist in acceptable standing to the end of the *Tatler*, though most of his interest in the stars was only incidental and carried an obvious or implied irony.

No introduction of the persona was required in the *Tatler* and none was made, as was necessary later in the *Spectator*. But some further development of Isaac Bickerstaff, Esq. was of course essential, and his way of living was gradually unfolded in the numbers of the paper. Bickerstaff possessed a huge family. An unusually witty letter of thorough genealogy appeared in No. 11, by D. Distaff, a cousin in the Heralds' Office, but the blood relations were wider than that. Sir Isaac Bickerstaff had been a Knight of the Round Table; a great-grandmother was a Welsh woman, and other forebears were Irish. Sir Walter Bickerstaff some ages ago had married Maud the milkmaid, who had spoiled the Bickerstaffs' blood but mended their constitutions. Isaac's great-grandfather had been learned enough to write a treatise, and his great-aunt Margery had been so wealthy that her family had devised to keep her single and her wealth intact.[22] Bickerstaff is himself a single man, but he has a "grandson," godson,

---

[21] The papers containing references to Partridge during 1709 are Nos. 1, 7, 11, 14, 36, 44, 56, 59, 67, 73, 76, 96, and 99, and during 1710 Nos. 118, 124, and 216. The papers referring to the Living Dead and/or the Upholders are Nos. 46, 96, 99, 101, 103, 106, 109, 110, 113, 115, 118, 122, 162, 174, 205, and 261.

[22] Nos. 75; 140; 236; 75; 42; 151.

nephews, and cousins.[23] His half-sister Jenny we see the most—she writes several of the papers,[24] is the object of his affection and care, is married off to a tranquil husband, and is a kind of representative of womankind. Among all these family connections it is Isaac Bickerstaff the astrological adept who becomes the foremost member of the great house of Staffs.[25]

Bickerstaff is of a "Complexion truly amorous," according to Jenny; he has a face "tolerable oval" and a tall, lank body, a "hective Constitution," spindles for legs, spectacles for his eyes, and at least one bad tooth, as well as a shaking hand that causes errors in his text.[26] His most emphasized condition is his age—he is in the mid-sixties and past the grand climacteric, and he repeats rather often that he is an old man. He lives at the upper end of Shire Lane in modest circumstances; he is attended by a careless boy and careful maid and fond cat and dog.[27] He has spent thousands of hours with his club, now reduced to five members. He is abstemious, smokes a pipe, and abhors snuff. He practices at foils and even wears pistols after receiving threats.[28]

In his eighty-ninth paper Bickerstaff gives a very short account of his life, which must be supplemented by miscellaneous details throughout the journal. He was bred by hand, early nourished on pudding and potatoes, lost his father when a child, followed youthful sports, attended the Merchant Taylors' School and the University, was a cadet at Coldstream, and left soldiering for his scientific work.[29] He

---

23 Nos. 52; 95, 241; 30, 196, 207; 93, 169.

24 Nos. 10, 33, 36, 37, 38, 247.

25 The nominal kin of Bickerstaff contained ambitious authors—e.g., *A Character of Don Sacheverellio, Knight of the Firebrand: in a Letter to Isaac Bickerstaff Esq; Censor of Great Britain,* Dublin, was dated 16 March [1710] and signed John Distaff in a text slightly different from that of *Quixote Redivivus: Or, The Spiritual Knight Errant,* London, dated 20 January and signed Jack Touchwood; the same year J. Distaff, cousin to the Esquire, produced *Monarchy and Church,* a poem anti-Sacheverell; a folio half-sheet dated 16 October 1710, *Votes of the New Parliament of Women,* was authorized by Susanna Bickerstaffe, Speaker, and printed for Jacob Longstaffe; also in 1710 "Adam Addlestaff, Gent. Near Kinsman to the Bickerstaffs" made *The Indian's Petition;* the death of the Queen was mourned, and the new monarch welcomed, in *A Letter from Mr. Jacob Bickerstaffe,* nephew to Isaac Bickerstaff; in 1738 another nephew, Gabriel, published "An Important Meditation on a Staff," in pursuance of Isaac's last will; the *Tatler* was revived in 1753 for three numbers by a third nephew, William, who inherited from the famous man a trunk "crowded with rare Manuscripts"; and about 1720 there appeared a farce called *The Modern Poetasters: or, Directors no Conjurors,* by "Isaac Bickerstaff, jun. Esq."

26 Nos. 10; 75; 93; 34; 83; 88, 93, 103; 175, 176; 101.

27 Nos. 59, 162; 86; 117, 208; 83; 77, 124; 95, 112.

28 Nos. 89, 127, 132, 202; 240; 69; 35; 93, 164, 173.

29 Nos. 181; 68; 18, 197, 255; 87; 89.

belongs to the Society for the Reformation of Manners but apparently not the Royal Society. He has good literary experience and interests.[30] He takes walks for his health into the countryside and an occasional expedition (such as a trip to Oxford) and goes to such places of resort as Whitehall Gardens and the Abbey and the drawing of the national lottery, in which he has bought a ticket. But his favorite scenes of action are, he claims, the coffee-houses, the playhouses, and his own apartment.[31] He not infrequently visits old friends. Mr. Bickerstaff is really not a recluse; indeed, he seems quite active for a man who re-iterates his advanced age. He is somewhat talkative and knows it. He is an amiable, though learned, companion. He is a gentleman of intel-ligence and wit. He wishes to promote virtue and good sense and to expose vice and folly. He can be smooth, and he can be sharp. He is inclined toward whimsicality and certainly is not the embodiment of stuffy normality.

Bickerstaff has still another side. He has named his paper, as he says in its first paragraph, in honor of the fair sex, and he obviously hopes that the ladies will buy and read it and profit from his interest in them. Actually this has been a long continued interest. He describes the death of his first love, and he often states his devotion to the Fair. One Maria professes love to him by letter; he returns the passion from the head rather than the heart. Another lady has chosen him for her Val-entine, but is requested to make him a nightcap.[32] His age and his fame of being an odd fellow make him acceptable to the other sex, and he reports visits to and from them to demonstrate his credentials.

Steele and Addison used Bickerstaff's character and activities with considerable skill in the presentation of their essays. He tells what he has heard at the Grecian Coffee-House and Will's, at White's and the Trumpet. He meets someone, and the encounter leads him to obser-vations on life. His letters and friends and visits open doors of topic and character. Here are three famous examples—the character of Tom Folio, the learned idiot, was drawn as the result of a visit from him; the scene for the superb sketch of Ned Softly, that pretty poet, was laid at Will's, where Bickerstaff had gone to read the newspapers; and Sir Timothy Tittle, the dogmatic critic, entered the *Tatler* when the writer was engaged at a friend's in conversation with the family and Tittle arrived as the suitor of the eldest daughter of the house.[33] And so it goes, this frequent technique of introducing description and narrative and exposition by way of Bickerstaff and his friends and relations, his comings and doings. The use of the eidolon is in this way particularly rewarding.

[30] Nos. 3; 53, 60, 182.

[31] Nos. 34, 45; 39; 170, 167, 203; 18.

[32] Nos. 117; 83; 137.

[33] Nos. 158; 163; 165.

The final issue of the *Tatler* was signed by Steele, who there said that he had chosen to speak "in the Character of an old Man, a Philosopher, an Humorist, an Astrologer, and a Censor." That was the end of our famous Mr. Bickerstaff, though of course he was resurrected and exploited more than once. He had been a good persona with many suitable qualities in his nature and points of experience. He was certainly an attractive individual and well known; he could speak with authority in many fields; he was a witty man with worthy motives; and he had numerous and broad relationships. He could gather a large amount of respect and confidence and regard. He was, on the whole, a success, or so says the testimony of his fame, contemporary and posthumous. But he had disadvantages—his connection with astrology, however softened by the grace of irony, was not an ideal professional affiliation, and the Partridge business lost its value; he lacked the best unity by being too many things and becoming diffuse; he talked a bit too much and in time got involved in partisanship; he was not always tactful and urbane; and he went perhaps too far toward whimsicality and eccentricity.

Inevitably the question is proposed as to whether all the papers of the *Tatler* agree with the mask of its author. During its first half-year the hundred-odd short reports of society, literature, and learning from White's Chocolate-House, Will's Coffee-House, and the Grecian might be taken by the reader as pieces collected by the agents with whom Mr. Bickerstaff had "settled a Correspondence in all Parts of the Known and Knowing World,"[34] and thus as only edited by him. The mere news dispatches from St. James's Coffee-House would demand even less of a personal pen; these accounts of military and diplomatic deeds, usually on the Continent, could not by any sensible reader be assigned to an astrological Esquire whose forte was not to report events but to foretell them—a faculty he promises in the beginning to "use very sparingly." However, the essays dated from Bickerstaff's Own Apartment and from Shire Lane, two hundred and fifty of them and the majority occupying the whole of an issue, were likely to be more Bickerstaffian. Here the reader disagrees occasionally in the interpretation of the eidolon. One critic may conclude that this or that paper does not fit the nature of the humorous Isaac—like the essay on the death of his father or that on the death of Betterton[35]—but another may regard Bickerstaff's character as broad and deep enough to qualify him for such sentiments of affection and admiration. Without resorting to the simple reversal of irony or deviating into eccen-

[34] No. 1.

[35] Nos. 181; 167. See William Bragg Ewald, Jr., *The Masks of Jonathan Swift* (Cambridge, Mass., 1954), p. 5.

tric estimates, we can simply concede that some papers, in whole or in part, seem not suitable to Bickerstaff as he is generally presented, or at least less suitable than the reader may desire.

In one province of public discussion, that of politics, Bickerstaff stepped most definitely from his usual role. Of course, as an alert citizen he could be expected to observe and remark on various public men and matters without violation of character—the victorious Duke of Marlborough, the Act of Naturalization, the deathly battle of Malplaquet, the poor Palatines, the Woollen Act, the national lottery, the trial of Sacheverell.[36] And throughout the life of the journal a sizable number of papers contained casual allusions to or careful discussions of events, figures, and ideas closely or loosely associated with Whiggish doctrine; some of these references were sharp and timely, and some were not so pointed or partisan as to interrupt the character of Bickerstaff.[37] But as the political situation worsened for the Whigs in 1710 and they got caught in their own errors and the tides of British history, Steele somehow allowed his spokesman to write and edit like his creator, like a zealous Whig, in a series of anti-Tory papers that only angered the enemy without benefit to the Whigs or the art of his journal. The analogy of Hannibal and Hanno, the character of Polypragmon-Harley, and the Downes letter[38] convinced the Tories that the Tatler had exceeded his warrant as Censor, and the new Examiner blandly advised Bickerstaff to abandon partisanship in favor of literary decorum.[39]

Actually it is quite probable that in their experimental sheet, with its several editorial developments, Steele and Addison were too busy to worry about utter consistency or too wise to strive for it as imperative. And the tone of urbanity they fostered would hardly prosper under the application of very strict rules to the exercise of putative authorship. It would have been difficult to create a persona—a man of the proper age, social status, temperament, education, intellectual agility, and individuality—who would be fully and precisely qualified to present the diversity of topic in the variety of tone that the *Tatler* contained. We should be artless to hold that each paper is perfectly congenial to the pen of an aging astrologer with his unique knowledge, character, problems, and history. Rather it would appear the point of common sense and critical acumen to recognize how often

[36] Nos. 5; 9; 64; 111; 118; 124; 142.

[37] For example, Nos. 4, 8, 44, 50, 68, 90, 130, 214, 220, 237, 239, 257. See the thorough doctoral dissertation by Calhoun Winton, "Richard Steele: the Political Writer" (Princeton University, 1955).

[38] Nos. 187, 191, 193.

[39] *Examiner* No. 5 (31 August 1710).

and how clearly Bickerstaff acted the appropriate cicerone through Anne's England.

The successful conversion of the persona into a person calls forth several questions. Did the Esquire gain such a high place in the minds and hearts of his countrymen that they considered him to be an actual person, a man whom they even wished to see? Did they forget his fanciful being or only half-remember the illusion? Or did they accept all the rules of fabling and enjoy the sport of confusing the actual and the fictive? *Tatler* No. 120 (14 January 1710) had a note by Thomas Doggett the comedian inviting Mr. Bickerstaff to attend his benefit performance of *Love for Love* on the next Monday. Bickerstaff accepted and stated the time of his appearance at the theatre and the length of his stay. In No. 122 he reported his attendance and courteous reception by his host; and in the first collected edition of Addison's works Tickell asserted that "A Person dressed for *Isaac Bickerstaffe* did appear at the Play-house on this occasion."[40] In August of 1710 John Penkethman advertised a performance at his new theater in Greenwich "For the Entertainment of Esquire Bickerstaff, who will honour Mr. Penkethman with his Presence" but who "is oblig'd to be gone when the 3d Act is over."[41] The Bickerstaff who edited the third continuation of the *Tatler* in 1711 said in his first number that he had "more than once produc'd my Person in a crowded Theatre" and also referred to "the Person produced as mine in the Play-house last Winter."[42] Did Steele himself appear at Greenwich or Drury Lane or both? Or did he send a deputy and in what dress? Or were such accounts a public bubble?

Another attempt to see the man Bickerstaff took the form of a portrait of him at work. Bernard Lens the Elder drew the lines, and John Sturt engraved and sold the scene for sixpence in 1710. Isaac Bickerstaff, Esq. sits gowned and hatted at his desk, one hand to his brow and the other holding the quill; he looks toward the reader and appears to be less than his reputed age. Two shelves of folios face the writer; astrological instruments form the background; a cat and a dog romp at his feet amid dice, playing cards, and broken swords; Pacolet,

[40] *Works of . . . Addison* (1721), II, 266 n. Cf. *Tatler* No. 184 and *Examiner*, III, 46 (1 May 1713).

[41] *Daily Courant*, No. 2750 (16 August 1710); repeated the next day. Of the several entertainments between the acts, Mr. Bickerstaff the novice swordsman must have particularly enjoyed the first: "A young Gentlewoman, who never appear'd on a publick Stage, turns round upon one Foot 300 times, and as she is turning fixes 12 Swords points about her, 2 to her Eyes, 2 to her Eye-lashes, 2 to her Eye-brows, 2 to her Nose, 2 to her Lips, and 2 to her Breasts, &c."

[42] *Tatler*, Harrison continuation, No. 1 (13 January 1711, published by A. Baldwin) and No. 306 (24 March, Morphew).

his familiar, moves on small clouds toward the subject bearing a sealed message. It is all quite authentic, and it would all reinforce the rapport between the Tatler and his friends if they wished to change a phantom into a fact.[43]

THE TWO BICKERSTAFFS

But, in spite of the popularity of the Censor, the first Bickerstaff and the success of his *Predictions* concerning Partridge were not forgotten. Late in 1709, when the *Tatler* was the topic of the Town, the watchful, skillful *Female Tatler* demonstrated that it was not difficult to repeat the earlier satiric stratagem of asserting the death of a man who was still alive. Only this time it was the biter bit, for the rival paper recorded the death of the *Tatler*'s Bickerstaff and pointed out that recent issues, especially Nos. 107 and 108, confirmed the suspicion, for no *"Honest Pains-taking Man alive"* and no *"Virtuous Man alive"* could have written as the Squire had been writing, and when the qualities that recommend an author "are no more to be found in those Works that go under his Name, the Author is Dead, and the Papers are Spurious."[44]

In March of 1710 *Titt for Tatt,* a close follower of the *Tatler,* was credited to "Jo. Patridge, Esq.," who in the first number finds his old friend Bickerstaff entombed in a vault in Lincoln's Inn, the victim of "a Disease call'd *laborious Laziness.*" There is an epitaph to the memory of the great man whose "Wit and Life decay'd."

In September, Defoe's *Condoling Letter to The Tattler* used the reversal of roles to reprimand Steele, the self-chosen Censor of Britain, then a prisoner for debt.

Here's Poor Mr. *Bickerstaff,* it is not many Months since he incarcerated honest *Partridge,* and laid him, *dead or alive,* in the Earth without any Crime; of which the Living Spectrum of *John Partridge,* which *they say,* is all of him, that has ever since appear'd in the World, made loud Complaints; protested against the Injustice, and declar'd he receiv'd an Inexpressible Injury; having been murther'd a Way that no Man was ever kill'd before; contrary to the known Laws of *Man-Slaughter,* and the Laudable Usage and Custom of *Assassination;* But the Man complain'd in vain, Mr. *Bickerstaff,* protected by the *Mob,* continu'd to justify the Crime; and to this Day made him no Reparation: But now 'tis come Home to him, and the Alternative is visible: *Fortune* having turn'd her Wheel round, and the True Reverse of Things now appearing; Behold! He that imprisoned *Partridge* in the Grave, is himself bury'd in that worst of Graves,

---

[43] A reproduction of this portrait appears in the edition of the *Tatler* by George A. Aitken (London, 1898–99) as the frontispiece to Volume IV and in the *Bickerstaff Papers,* edited by Herbert Davis, facing p. 171.

[44] *Female Tatler,* No. 72 (21 December 1709).

a Jail; as *Partridge* was mercifully admitted to walk about after he was dead, so *Bickerstaff* is kindly suffer'd to *Tattle* after he is bury'd; *Partridge* had a Death without a Grave, *Bickerstaff* a Grave without Death.[45]

And the next month the Tory *Moderator* likewise identified Bickerstaff with Steele the spirited Whig and reported his death during the political crisis that brought the fall of the ministry.

This day the Ingenious *Isaac Bickerstaffe*, Esq; late Censor of *Great Britain* departed this Life at his own Apartment in *Sheer-lane*, much lamented by the Gentlemen of the *Kit-Cat-Club* and all true *Republican Spirits*, for his hearty Zeal to the good old Cause, his universal Learning, and particular Skill in the Laws of the Land.[46]

As a matter of fact, after Bickerstaff the Censor had retired, the first Isaac Bickerstaff, the prophetic astrologer, made two further appearances. *The British Visions: or, Isaac Bickerstaff, Sen. Being Twelve Prophesies for the Year 1711*, by Defoe, reviewed the successes of the prognosticator and proceeded to foretell the events of the next year, principally military and political on the Continent. This Bickerstaff surprised his readers with several accurate predictions, including that of the death of the Dauphin.[47]

One of the best publications involving Partridge was perhaps the octavo pamphlet called *Predictions For the Year, 1712*, signed by Bickerstaff and addressed to the author of the *Oxford Almanack*. In his prefatory remarks to satirical predictions for each month, Bickerstaff acknowledges a debt to Abul Pharage in attaining the ability "to particularise Circumstances." He goes on to record his successes four years earlier, including the death of Partridge, which had happened "exactly at the Time foretold," protests that "any one should have the Impudence to Personate a Man that is dead," and commends "the Impostor for his Remorse, which I suppose has been the Reason that we hear no more the Hawker's Voice imploy'd in crying *Partridge*'s *Almanack*."

And on this occasion I can't but express my Resentment against a Gentleman who personated me in a Paper call'd Mr. *Bickerstaff*'s Vindication. I'm griev'd to find the Times should be so very wicked, that one Impostor should set up to Reprove another, and that a false *Bickerstaff* should write against an imaginary *Partridge*. And I am heartily concern'd

---

[45] Pages 6–7.

[46] No. 42.

[47] Defoe recorded this success in his *Review*, VIII, 12, 14 (21, 26 April 1711). He continued his prophecies with *The Highland Visions* for 1712, in which he blamed a friend for setting to the first *Visions* "the Imaginary and Threadbare Name" of Bickerstaff, and also with *The Second-Sighted Highlander* for 1713 and for 1715.

that one who shews so much Wit, such extream Civility, and writes such a Gentleman-like Style, should prefix my Name to Writings, in which there appeart so little Solidity, and no Knowledge of the *Arabian* Philosophy.

This estimable wag, eying the completed *Tatler*, is distressed that his name has been signed to papers filled with amusement instead of prophecy; "seeing four Volumes of Writings pretended to be mine, and a serious Philosopher's Name prefix'd to Papers as free from my Solidity as they are full of Wit," he thought it fit to vindicate himself. He compounds the irony by having Bickerstaff commend the *Spectator*, which "not only diverts but instructs Mankind, and mixes so much true Morality and Philosophy with his Wit."[48] When this later Bickerstaff rejects the first and second Bickerstaffs and accepts Mr. Spectator, we have completed the circle.

Isaac Bickerstaff, Esq. made notable contributions as an eidolon: his large popularity as the hero in the Partridge affair gave the *Tatler* an excellent introduction to the reading public; he showed in general the varied and fruitful techniques of putative authorship in a periodical publication; he specifically illustrated the effectiveness of a persona with an engaging individuality and thus aided in the great success of the *Tatler*. Moreover, he acted as precursor to the even more successful and famous Mr. Spectator.

Eight weeks after the cessation of the triweekly Lucubrations of Mr. Bickerstaff, Steele and Addison began the daily speculations of Mr. Spectator, who carefully introduced himself and not infrequently remarked on his own character and background and actions. Mr. Spectator had many points in common with Mr. Bickerstaff, including the principal goal of reformation, but he was not astral or diffuse or political or capricious or very old. His main irregularity was taciturnity, a habit that brings a smile to the reader but not derision. His silence interferes not at all with his keenness of sight and hearing, his proper play of wit, his passion to be an observer of life and its commentator on paper. He personifies subjective objectivity, and he seems to avoid his predecessor's shortcomings. These alterations in the eidolon raise a question: when it was decided to fling up the *Tatler* and begin the *Spectator*, did a wish to change the persona have a place in the decision? Some of the reasons for the termination of the *Tatler* that were assigned at the time seem to us to have small value. Others are quite tenable—that Steele during the ministerial crisis of 1710 had antagonized the Tories with certain passages in the *Tatler* and that, having already lost the official Gazetteership and being anxious to save

---

48 These passages appear on pp. 4, 5, 5, 5, 5–6, 6, and 16.

his sinecure as one of the Commissioners of Stamps, he was willing to lay down the *Tatler*, as John Gay said, "as a sort of Submission to, and Composition with the Government for some past Offences." Moreover, we may accept the Town's conjectures as reported by Gay —that Steele "had a Mind to vary his Shape, and appear again in some new Light."[49] Appear again he did, and promptly, with another title and mask and a double frequency and nonpartisan promises. Had Steele or Addison been somewhat dissatisfied with the persona of Bickerstaff, and did they therefore make the best of near-necessity by altering the eidolon? There survives no word of correspondence or conversation by either of these two highly skillful literary journalists to answer these queries, but it would appear legitimate to suggest that some strong consideration was given to the nature of a new putative author when Mr. Spectator replaced Mr. Bickerstaff, that is, if we can believe that the second eidolon in all its excellence was not merely a glorious accident but grew out of its more experimental antecedent.

Thus was the Esquire created to foretell and record the unreal death of an all too real charlatan, then transferred to produce a popular journal of affable reformation, and finally retired in favor of a younger cousin-german who has never been overmatched in merit. When we cast the nativity of Isaac Bickerstaff, his own astrological scales reveal that he was born under the conjunction of Mercury and Momus in an hour of great good fortune for English letters.

[49] *The Present State of Wit* (1711), p. 11.

GWIN J. KOLB

Johnson's "Little Pompadour": A Textual Crux and a Hypothesis

An EDITOR of *Rasselas* must examine with special care Johnson's letter of Saturday, 20 January 1759, to William Strahan, for it contains much of our information about the composition and sale of the work. The distinguished scholars G. B. Hill, O. F. Emerson, and R. W. Chapman all reprint and discuss the letter in the introductions to their editions[1] of the tale; and Chapman summarizes his earlier comments in his recent edition (1952) of Johnson's letters. One must step very cautiously when walking where these men have trod; yet the contents of the letter present problems of interpretation, so it seems to me, that are not removed by Chapman's explanation nor even hinted at by the other two editors.

The text of the letter reads as follows:

SIR

When I was with you last night I told you of a thing which I was preparing for the press. The title will be

The choice of Life

or

The History of ——— Prince of Abissinia

It will make about two volumes like little Pompadour that is about one middling volume. The bargain which I made with Mr Johnston was seventy five pounds (or guineas) a volume, and twenty five pounds for the second Edition. I will sell this either at that price or for sixty the first

GWIN J. KOLB is Professor of English at the University of Chicago.

[1] (Oxford, 1887), pp. 23–24; (New York, 1895), pp. xi–xii; (Oxford, 1927), pp. xi–xii (cited hereafter as "Chapman").

edition of which he shall himself fix the number, and the property then to revert to me, or for forty pounds, and share the profit that is retain half the copy. I shall have occasion for thirty pounds on Monday night when I shall deliver the book which I must entreat you upon such delivery to procure me. I would have it offered to Mr Johnston, but have no doubt of selling it, on some of the terms mentioned.

I will not print my name, but expect it to be known.

I am Dear Sir Your most humble Servant

Jan. 20. 1759   SAM: JOHNSON
Get me the money if you can.[2]

The first and last paragraphs of the letter, as well as the postscript, pose no real difficulties. At a meeting on Friday, 19 January 1759, Johnson had mentioned *Rasselas* to Strahan, who may have suggested that Johnson send him a note describing the work and setting forth acceptable terms for its sale. In the letter, Johnson, as Chapman points out,[3] does not give the name of his hero, although he promises, in the second paragraph, to "deliver the book" the next "Monday night" (22 January). The omission may be due simply to Johnson's abbreviation of the title of the work. If not, then Johnson, unless he had already composed much of the tale without naming his prince (and this possibility seems very unlikely) or wrote with great speed (as he obviously could do) over the weekend, was probably unable to meet his self-imposed deadline.

Of the second paragraph, Chapman remarks: "The sense would be clearer if Johnson had written 'either at that price, or for sixty pounds the first edition, of which,' etc." He continues:

Apart from this minor obscurity the terms of the letter are clear enough. But why does Johnson reduce his demands? I imagine that, having contracted to produce a volume or volumes at the rate of £75 per volume, he found that his book was or would be more than one 'volume' but less than two, and proposed a compromise. His demand is, no doubt, for £120 (an improvement on £110),[4] or alternatively for £80, and not for half those sums. In the alternative he was to 'retain half the copy'; 'copy' means 'copy-right' or 'copy-money'; presumably, under this arrangement, if Johnston had printed a second edition of 1000 copies, Johnson would have been free to pay half the printer's bill and to dispose of 500 copies at his discretion.[5]

---

[2] I reproduce the text of the letter in Chapman's edition of *The Letters of Samuel Johnson*, I, 117–18 (cited hereafter as "*Letters*").

[3] Chapman, p. xi, n. 4.

[4] In the letter, as Chapman notes, Johnson first wrote "fifty five" and probably also "pounds," then erased both and substituted "sixty pounds."

[5] Pages xii–xiii.

This explanation is clearly expressed, and part of it is almost certainly correct. Specifically, the sums of sixty and forty pounds would each seem, as Chapman says, to be Johnson's price for a single volume of *Rasselas*, not of the whole work. Two things support this conclusion: (1) the inference that Johnson's first reference to the price—"seventy five pounds (or guineas)"—of "a volume" should also be understood as applying to the specific amounts given later; and (2) the improbability that Johnson, after stating one alternative involving seventy-five pounds per volume, would then propose two additional alternatives which would bring him in ready cash only sixty and forty pounds, respectively, for the complete tale.

But agreement about the prices per volume of the work forces us to reject another of Chapman's assumptions: whatever his intentions, Johnson is not necessarily reducing "his demands." On the contrary, he gives three alternative, and comparable, sets of terms, which appear to be about equally satisfactory to him. He tells Strahan, first of all, that he "will sell this" (obviously *Rasselas*) "at that price"—i.e., at "seventy five pounds (or guineas) a volume" for the first edition and "twenty five pounds for the second Edition" (presumably of both volumes). His second alternative would produce less money immediately (sixty pounds per volume of "the first edition") than the first but might bring him more eventually, because after the first edition the complete control of the "property" would "revert" to him. The third alternative reduces further the amount of cash ("forty pounds" per volume) for Johnson but guarantees to him half the profit—in contrast to the flat twenty-five pounds of the first alternative—on the sale of (presumably) the second edition. The approximate equality, in Johnson's view, of the three alternatives may be indicated, finally, (1) by the fact that the latter two, although assuring him smaller sums of money than the first, embody Johnson's known reluctance to surrender all rights concerning the publication of his works and (2) by Johnson's comment that he has "no doubt of selling" *Rasselas* "on some of the terms mentioned."

II

Recognition of the existence and rough parity of these alternatives does not clear up all the obscurities in the second paragraph of Johnson's letter. Indeed, such recognition serves only to emphasize other, more significant cruxes. According to Chapman's interpretation, Johnson had previously "contracted" with the bookseller William Johnston[6] "to produce" one or more volumes of *Rasselas* "at the

---

[6] According to H. R. Plomer's *Dictionary of . . . Printers and Booksellers . . . from 1726 to 1775* (Oxford, 1932; cited hereafter as "Plomer"), Johnston, "one of the fore-

rate of £75 per volume"; on discovering, however, "that his book was or would be more than one 'volume' but less than two," he "proposed a compromise" in his letter to Strahan. Yet this explanation is deficient, I submit, in several respects. To begin with, it overlooks Johnson's explicit statement, "I will sell this [*Rasselas*] . . . at that price" (i.e., seventy-five pounds a volume for the first edition). Secondly, it says nothing about the combination of "this" and "that price" in the same expression—a combination which, as I point out later, does not really harmonize with the explanation and is susceptible of another interpretation. Thirdly, Chapman's reading is inconsistent with the co-ordinate, noncompromising character of Johnson's three alternatives. And lastly, the explanation clashes with the final sentence in the paragraph: "I would have it [*Rasselas*] offered to Mr Johnston, but have no doubt of selling it, on some of the terms mentioned." Why, we must ask, should Johnson tell Strahan that he "would have" the work "offered" to Johnston if he and Johnston had already "made a bargain" concerning a version—even a longer version—of the identical work? If the two men had really agreed on, or even only discussed, terms for the sale of *Rasselas,* isn't it much more likely that Johnson, on becoming aware of the difference between the projected and the actual length of the tale, would have addressed himself directly to Johnston rather than writing Strahan that he "would have" the work "offered" to Johnston? And, assuming that Johnson and Johnston had lately reached an agreement on the terms for *Rasselas,* doesn't it seem rather odd that Johnson, in his letter to Strahan, cannot recall the precise terms (seventy-five pounds or guineas) of the agreement? Why, we must ask finally, should Johnson talk so confidently of "selling" *Rasselas* on "some of the terms mentioned"—the phrase certainly excludes no specific set of terms—if earlier in the same paragraph he really reduces "his demands" for the tale?

Granted, then, that Chapman's reading does not fit all the definite or probable facts, we are led to consider other interpretations which may account for the entire second paragraph of the letter. I can think of only one explanation that seems to make sense of everything Johnson says. As the first step in the presentation of my reading, it will be useful to examine again, in order, four of Johnson's remarks: (1) "It will make about two volumes like little Pompadour that is about one middling volume"; (2) "The bargain which I made with Mr Johnston was seventy five pounds (or guineas) a volume, and twenty five pounds for the second Edition"; (3) "I will sell this . . . at that price

---

. . ."; and (4) "I would have it offered to Mr Johnston, but have no doubt of selling it, on some of the terms mentioned."

(1) To make clear the final size of his still incomplete "history," Johnson compares it with another book, which he calls "little Pompadour" and which Strahan is presumably more or less familiar with. *Rasselas*, like this work, "will make about two volumes . . . that is about one middling volume." As I shall remark later in developing my hypothesis, Johnson's own knowledge of the book on Pompadour seems curiously exact—"two volumes," "that is about one middling volume." With respect to my inference concerning Strahan's knowledge of "little Pompadour," it is relevant to add that, as might be expected, this kind of comparative statement occurs elsewhere in the letters of Johnson and other eighteenth-century authors to members of the trade. For example, writing to Edward Cave about *London* in April of 1738, Johnson begins: "I waited on You to take the Copy to Dodsley's, as I remember the Number of Lines which it contains it will be longer than Eugenio with the Quotations. . . ." Chapman explicates the reference to *Eugenio* thus: "A poem by one Beach, published by Dodsley (and presumably printed by Cave, *who is assumed to know it*) in '37."[7] Similarly, writing to Robert Dodsley about *Tristram Shandy* in 1759, Sterne uses the recently published *Rasselas* itself as a basis for comparison: "I propose," he says, "to print a lean edition, in two small volumes, of the size of Rasselas, and on the same paper and type, at my own expense. . . ."[8] And again, Sterne clearly assumes that Dodsley, whose name appears, in fact, on the title-page as one of the publishers, is familiar with *Rasselas*.

(2) In raising objections to Chapman's explication of the second paragraph, I indicated above two possible interpretations of "The bargain which I made," etc. The obvious definition of *to make a bargain* is "to agree on a stated set of terms concerning the object under consideration"; therefore, Johnson appears to be saying that he and Johnston had arrived at a specific agreement regarding the first and second editions of a work supposedly by Johnson. A rare meaning of *bargain* as a substantive, however, is simply "discussion regarding terms"; thus, although the interpretation seems, on the face of it, highly improbable to me, Johnson might be saying that he and Johnston had merely talked about terms for the sale of the book.

Several pieces of external evidence provide clues to the probable meaning of Johnson's expression. From the *OED* we learn that *bargain* in the sense of "discussion between two parties of . . . terms . . . ," "chaffering," "bargaining," has long been obsolete, the last recorded

---

[7] *Letters*, I, 11, n. 1 (my italics).

[8] *Letters of Laurence Sterne*, ed. Lewis Perry Curtis (Oxford, 1935), p. 80.

use occurring in Shakespeare's *Henry IV, Part I* (1596); that *bargain* in the sense of ". . . agreement . . . between two parties . . . ," "compact," encompasses the phrase *to make a bargain;* and that one of the meanings of *make* is "To enter into, conclude (a bargain, contract)." In Johnson's own *Dictionary,* the only sense of *bargain* combining (in an illustrative quotation) the word with *make* reads as follows: "A contract or agreement concerning the sale of something." In the same work, the first meaning of *contract* is "An act whereby two parties are brought together; a bargain; a compact"; and the second definition of *to contract* reads: "To bring two parties together; to make a bargain." Lastly, the only other combination of *bargain* and *make* that I have noticed in Johnson's letters clearly denotes "agreement on terms": writing on 29 November 1760 to Thomas Percy about the sale of the *Reliques,* Johnson says: "If we had not had this Specimen I think we should have immediately bargained. Perhaps after all the bargain is made."[9]

These pieces of evidence thus strongly support the obvious meaning of the phrase in Johnson's letter and point insistently to this interpretation: I made an agreement with Johnston to sell him a two-volume work at seventy-five pounds or guineas (I am not certain which) a volume for the first edition, and "twenty five pounds for the second Edition."

(3) In the third statement, Johnson says he "will sell this"—i.e., *Rasselas*—"at that price"—i.e., the price that resulted from his earlier bargain with Johnston. Now Chapman, although not mentioning the first part of the third statement, "imagines" that the earlier bargain also concerned the sale of *Rasselas.* But the wording of Johnson's remark suggests, so it seems to me, a totally different meaning. Had the "bargain" between Johnson and Johnston actually referred to *Rasselas,* Johnson's statement might have run something like "I *am* still *willing* to sell *it* at that price." However, instead of using a verb in the present tense to signify his continued willingness to accept the terms agreed on earlier, Johnson writes: "I will sell"; and instead of repeating the pronoun *it* ("It will make," etc., in the first statement) as a synonym for *Rasselas,* he writes "this." Quite apart from the confirmatory statement discussed in (4) below, the combination of "this" and "that price" provides a tangible if admittedly slight basis for the following hypothesis concerning the first part of the second paragraph in Johnson's letter: at some time well before January 1759, Johnson made a bargain (as Strahan knows) with Johnston regarding a work that Johnson calls "little Pompadour." His new work, Johnson tells Strahan, "will make" a book approximately the size of "Pompadour."

9 *Letters,* I, 130.

He "will" therefore "sell this" new work at the same price he had accepted for "Pompadour."

(4) Johnson's fourth statement, which is irreconcilable with Chapman's explanation of the letter, provides stout support for the hypothesis advanced above. Acceptance of Chapman's reading, I repeat, requires us to believe the following: Johnson, after first telling Strahan the precise terms of his agreement with Johnston concerning *Rasselas*, concludes by saying that he "would have"—i.e., wishes to have—the book "offered to Mr Johnston" but that he also has "no doubt of selling it, on some of the terms mentioned," these terms, it should be stressed, including the very set which (according to Chapman's explanation) had already been agreed on earlier between Johnson and Johnston. My hypothesis, on the other hand, assumes only that Johnson is really saying what he seems to be saying—namely, having previously agreed with Johnston on terms for "little Pompadour" and having now in preparation another work about the same length as "Pompadour," he wishes to have the latter offered to Johnston. If Johnston is not interested, however, Johnson has "no doubt" he can sell *Rasselas* on some of the terms he has mentioned—these including the price Johnston had paid for "Pompadour."

III

Nothing more about the tantalizing "little Pompadour" can be inferred from Johnson's letter, the manuscript of which is in the Houghton Library at Harvard. Photostatic reproductions of the manuscript show that the phrase was written over a smeared erasure. In the hope of being able to decipher the original text, I secured from the Houghton an infrared photograph of the phrase. Unfortunately, the original wording remains wholly illegible.

Provided that my reading of the second paragraph is tenable, Johnson, it therefore follows, may have been intimately connected with a full-length work on Madame de Pompadour that has not previously been associated with his name. The next question is as easy to raise as it is hard to answer: Can we find a book possessing any of the marks of such a work?

We may begin the search by recalling the scanty clues in Johnson's letter. First of all, William Strahan must have known something about the work. Secondly, William Johnston, one of the "foremost" London booksellers and publishers, was evidently a proprietor, although not necessarily the sole owner, of the book. Johnston, we know from other sources, actually owned a one-third interest in *Rasselas;* may have paid Johnson for other literary labors in 1759; and in 1772 was named by Johnson as a possible purchaser of "translations from the

German Language."[10] Thirdly, if we assume, as I do, that "little Pompadour" refers to a published work, not simply a manuscript, we can also deduce the following conclusions: the book was certainly in print before 20 January 1759; it was apparently published in two volumes and possibly in "one middling volume" as well; and by 20 January 1759, it *may* have appeared in two editions ("twenty five pounds for the second Edition").

Hunting "little Pompadour" by the light of these uncertain beams has produced results that are decidedly more teasing than conclusive. So far as I am aware, only two relevant works were printed in English before the beginning of 1759. The earlier and rarer book is entitled *Advice to a Female Friend*. "By Madam de POMPADOUR" (London: "Printed for WILLIAM MEYER, in *May's Buildings*, and THOMAS WILCOX, in the *Strand*," 1750).[11] Of anonymous authorship (according to the British Museum Catalogue), the duodecimo volume—a supposed translation from the French of 225 pages and approximately 33,000 words—contains, so we are told in the preface, a record of the counsel on the prudential conduct of life given to a young girl by a wise and witty woman identified only as *"Madam De * * * ."* The lady's apothegms cover a variety of subjects, among them female education and learning, conversation ("Languages, Poetry, the Laws of the Kingdom, Matters of Religion, all these fine Things," she declares,[12] "are intolerable in a Woman, and so I warn them in the Name of all Men of Sense"), dress, piety, religion, courtship, love affairs, and marriage. They are often shrewd and always amusing. But neither the content nor the style of the *Advice* affords us any reason for connecting the work with the "little Pompadour" of Johnson's letter to Strahan.

The later, more intriguing book, entitled *The History of the Marchioness de Pompadour*, was written by Marianne Agnès de Fauques (or Falques), a rather prolific but decidedly minor lady of letters, whose other works include *Le Triomphe de l'amitié* (1751), *Abbassai* (1753), *Les Préjugés trop bravés et trop suivis* (1755), *La Dernière guerre des bêtes* (1758), *Frédéric le Grand au temple de l'immortalité* (1758), and *Dialogues moraux et amusants* (2 vols.; 1777). According to Michaud's *Biographie universelle* and Hoefer's *Nouvelle biographie générale*, Mademoiselle de Fauques (*c.* 1720–

[10] See my articles on *"Rasselas:* Purchase Price, Proprietors, and Printings," *SB*, XV (1962), 256–59, and "More Attributions to Dr. Johnson," *SEL*, I (1961), 86–87, in which I argue for Johnson's authorship of a notice concerning a new edition of *Pilgrim's Progress* published by Johnston; *Letters*, I, 277; III, 388.

[11] My description of the *Advice* is based on a microfilm of a copy of the work in the British Museum.

[12] Page 33.

c. 1777) was born in Avignon, reared in a convent, and forced by her family to take the veil. After ten years, however, she obtained an annulment of her vows and went to Paris. There she was seduced by a "seigneur anglais," who took her to London. Soon deserted, Mademoiselle de Fauques assumed the name of Fauques de Vaucluse (or de la Cépédès) and turned to writing as a profession; she also taught French to the daughters of Lady Craven, later "Margrave d'Anspach," and to Sir William Jones. As late as 1777, we are told, she was still living in London.

The British Museum Catalogue, the Library of Congress Catalogue, and Hoefer agree that *The History of the Marchioness de Pompadour* is a translation of Mademoiselle de Fauques's French original, although the title page of the English work contains no reference to its provenance and although extant French versions purport to be "traduite de l'anglais." The account in Hoefer distinguishes two early French editions. Count d'Affry, ambassador to Holland, acting on instructions from Louis XV, attempted to buy the whole of the first of these, which was ostensibly published in London, "aux dépens de S. Hooper, à la tête de César," but which really appeared in Holland in 1759. Inevitably, however, the ambassador failed to secure all the copies; and one of those that eluded him "servit à faire une nouvelle édition et une traduction anglaise." "Les deux éditions françaises," the account observes, "sont presque introuvables." Their rarity was tangibly indicated by the publication at Paris in 1879 of a reprint[13] of what was called "l'édition originale." At the close[14] of his introduction to this reprint, Lucien Faucou notes the existence of a total of three copies dated 1759—each copy, he infers from the differences in pagination, exemplifying a different French edition.

The connections among these three editions and between them and the putative English translation thus form a tangled bibliographical skein which I do not pretend to have unraveled satisfactorily. The *History*, as shown below, was first published in 1758; and it is possible that despite the dates on their title pages, one or more of the French editions also appeared the same year. Toward the end[15] of the book, Mademoiselle de Fauques, who presumably wrote the work while in London, makes a point of telling the reader the specific time of composition: "j'écris au milieu de l'été de l'an de grace 1758." And on the

---

[13] My remarks about, and quotations from, the French edition of the *History* are based on and refer to this reprint. A collation of the text of the reprint and that of a French edition, dated 1759, in the British Museum reveals only minor differences—consisting mainly of inadvertent (I surmise) omissions from the reprint—none of which affect the material presented in this essay.

[14] Page 14.

[15] Page 142; cf. p. 154.

following Christmas Day, Count d'Affry supposedly reported to Madame de Pompadour the appearance of a French edition in Holland and later received from her an undated reply saying that she had already heard of "cette belle histoire de la marquise de Pompadour qui se débite en Hollande," that she suspected it came from England, and that, moved by love of truth, she wished to see it suppressed; at any rate, Faucou, in his introduction to the 1879 reprint, quotes[16] relevant extracts from two such letters, which, however, he carefully labels "apocryphes."[17]

In spite of common agreement on the matter, I have not discovered absolute proof that the *History* is a translation of the *Histoire*. Three pieces of evidence seem, nevertheless, to support the accepted order of priority. In the first place, the English version condenses and combines—"epitomizes," as Johnson might say—numerous groups of sentences[18] in the French edition. Secondly, the English version contains many sentences of a pronounced un-English, "translated" cast. Thirdly, another work by Mademoiselle de Fauques, *La Dernière guerre des bêtes*, was published in French and then translated into English the same year (1758) in which the *History*, and quite possibly the *Histoire*, appeared. Another piece of evidence—namely, closer resemblances, in a number of passages, between the *Histoire* and the second, "corrected" (according to the title page) edition of the *History* than between it and the first edition—may be used to support two different conclusions: guided by the "corrected" on the title page of the second edition, we might conclude that the text was "corrected" by reference to the *Histoire*; impressed, on the other hand, by the "traduite de l'anglais" on the title page of the *Histoire*, we might infer that the French version derived from the second edition of the *History*.

Still another possible source of information—the publisher's "advertisement"[19] to the third part of the *History*, published together with the fourth edition (1760)[20] of the first two parts (i.e., the *History* proper)—provides only ambiguous references both to the authorship of the work and the connections between the French and English edi-

---

[16] Pages 10–11.

[17] I have not located the full text of Count d'Affry's letter. But Madame de Pompadour's answer appears not in the collection of her authentic correspondence (ed. M. A. P. -Malassis [Paris, 1878]) but in *Lettres de Madame la Marquise de Pompadour: Depuis MDCCLIII jusqu'a MDCCLXII* (London, 1771), I, 49–50, which has been dubbed fictional and attributed to François Barbé-Marbois.

[18] I have counted well over a hundred such groups.

[19] Pages [iii]–v.

[20] *The History of the Marchioness de Pompadour* (4th ed.; "LONDON printed, and DUBLIN reprinted/By JAMES HOEY at the *Mercury* in *Skinner-Row*, 1760"). I have examined a copy of the work in the Library of Congress.

tions. "The two first parts . . . ," says the publisher, "having greatly excited, and partly gratified, the just curiosity of the publick, in every thing relative to so extraordinary a personage, it was but natural for the publisher . . . to wish for a supplement. . . . But this wish was easier to form than to procure its accomplishment. *The writer of the first parts having exhausted his materials*, respected the publick too much to palm invention upon it for historical truth. He is then entirely out of the question in the supplemental part here offered"—a part, the advertisement goes on to add,[21] which has been translated from "the French original" by "*a gentleman not concerned in the former parts*" (my italics). One remains uncertain, therefore, as to the precise relationships among the French and English versions[22] of Mademoiselle de Fauques's work.

Compared to the obscurity of the Anglo-French affiliations, the record of the purely English *History* seems almost dazzlingly clear. A notice in the *Daily Advertiser* for Friday, 6 October 1758, informed the reader that "*Tomorrow will be published,/Price 3s. 6d./* The History of the Marchioness de Pompadour. In Two Parts. / Printed for S. Hooper . . ."; and a corroboratory "This Day is publish'd" appeared in the same paper for the next day. Probably to remove confusion regarding the price of the book, an advertisement on 26 October retained "*3s. 6d.*" but substituted "Two Volumes" for the "Two Parts" in the first notice. The "List of Books Published" in the *Gentleman's Magazine* for October 1758[23] proves that the *History* was also available in a single volume costing five shillings. Three months later, on 11 January 1759, a "New Edition" of the work was published "in Two Volumes."[24] Thus—to return momentarily to the

[21] Page v.

[22] The "Advertisement" to a later work—the fourth edition of *The Life of the Marchioness de Pompadour* (2 vols.; London: S. Hooper, n. d. [the year 1771 has been added in pencil at the bottom of the title pages of the Library of Congress copy]), "Revised and Enlarged," according to the title pages, "by the AUTHOR OF THE FIRST VOLUME" and containing a revised and extended version of the original *History*—refers to the publication, "in the year 1758," of "the memoirs" of Madame de Pompadour, which were "compiled as near the truth as the best authorities at that time would admit" and went through a large "number of editions," including translations "into most of the European languages" ("in Germany," we are told specifically, "it was re-printed fourteen times").

[23] XXVIII, 493.

[24] In their editions of *Rasselas*, Hill (p. 24, n. 1), Emerson (p. xi, n. 2), and Chapman (p. xii, n. 1) all suggest that Johnson's "little Pompadour" refers to the "second edition" of the *History*. Chapman adds: "The first edition was published in one volume in 1758. The second, though dated 1759, was noticed in *The Gentleman's Magazine* for November 1758 (p. 543)." Actually, however, as I point out in the text, the *History* was available from the outset in both one- and two-volume versions; and the second edition—described as a "New Edition"—was not published until January of 1759 (*Daily Advertiser* for 11 January).

key passage in Johnson's letter to Strahan—although they may be wholly fortuitous, the correspondences between the *History* and Johnson's "little Pompadour" seem startlingly exact: both certainly appeared in two small volumes; one, and maybe both, appeared in a single "middling" volume; and one, and maybe both, had reached two editions before Johnson wrote his letter to Strahan. Moreover, the resemblances in size between the *History* and *Rasselas* increase the possibility that the *History* is indeed "little Pompadour": the two volumes of *Rasselas* run to 159 and 165 pages, or a total of approximately 38,500 words; the two volumes of the *History* come to 117 and 145 pages printed in smaller type, or a total of approximately 32,000 words.[25]

The *History*,[26] praised by Voltaire and the de Goncourt brothers[27] for its element of accuracy, presents a fairly circumstantial, usually hostile, occasionally moralizing biography of the famous mistress to Louis XV. The first part (or volume) begins with an account of la Pompadour's parents, birth, childhood, courtship, and marriage; jumps back in time to summarize the "French King's" earlier "gallantries"; and then concentrates on the initiation and gradual consolidation of Madame de Pompadour's position as Louis's sole mistress and the most powerful woman in France. The second part (or volume) recounts the King's affair with the beautiful young girl, "of irish [sic] extraction," named Murphy—an affair that la Pompadour triumphantly survived; relates instance after instance of the mistress's supposed vanity, greed, arrogance, cunning, vindictiveness, and meanness; rather grudgingly admits and discusses her patronage of the arts; and concludes with an unflattering "description" of la Pompadour's "person" "at present, (one thousand seven hundred fifty eight)" when "she may be about thirty eight years of age."[28]

As I noted above, the prose of the *History* merges, shortens, and recasts—often in the form of longish periods—many passages that, individually, comprise two, three, or even more sentences in the *Histoire*. It also displays a substantial number of constructions that,

[25] Chapman's estimate (*Letters*, I, 118, n. 1) of the length of the two works is higher than mine—"some 35,000 words" for the *History*, "rather more than 40,000" for *Rasselas*.

[26] I am very grateful to Dr. Robert F. Metzdorf, of the Parke-Bernet Galleries, for the loan of his personal copy of the first edition of the *History*.

[27] In his introduction to the 1879 reprint of the *Histoire*, Lucien Faucou quotes Voltaire as remarking, "La moitié de l'ouvrage est un tissu de calomnies, mais ce qu'il y a de vrai fera passer de qu'il y a de faux à la postérité"; and the de Goncourt brothers as labeling the work the "seule histoire véritable de Mme de Pompadour, écrite de son vivant" (p. 14).

[28] II, 138, 142.

as I have already remarked, look and sound unidiomatic and "translated." These locutions, scattered rather evenly through the two parts of the work, include such expressions as the following:

To the execution itself it is left to decide on [I, 1]; These indeed the uncle, on the overture of his nephew's passion and intentions, from his fondness for the young Poisson, soon got over, as to himself [I, 6]; The king however proceded [sic] more and more intangling himself [I, 56]; Neither was this the only, by many, examples [I, 77]; appearance of liking in him to another woman [I, 81]; it would have shewn too gross, too indelicate in her, to be active in [II, 14]; whilst the Queen and the daughters of France were barely allowed for expences suitable to their rank [II, 57–58]; towards suppressing the more than murmurs at the actual system of things [II, 133].[29]

The *History* contains, thirdly, one long paragraph (plus the beginning of another) and several shorter passages that have no counterparts in the *Histoire*. The texts of the passages are given below; that of the paragraph reads:

On this occasion however a reflection rises too naturally here not to be pardoned the admission. Here was a wife openly torn from the arms of a husband distractedly fond of her, and kept in defiance of him; consequently his property violated in the most sacred and tender point. No redress for him but arbitrary punishment for daring to assert his right; no resource but that of a passive acquiescence. After this instance, and many more of the most grievous oppression might be produced from french [sic] history, must it not appear extreamly pleasant to an englishman [sic] to hear the subjects of that nation denying the existence of their despotic government, when reproached with it, for a reproach they admit it to be, and what is stranger yet, naturally and with all the simplicity of self-persuasion, inveighing against despotism, without seeming to know or dream that they themselves are crouching under the compleatest form of it in the known world? Their Courts of justice, their forms of procedure, their appearances of Laws and Magistracy are evidently all nothing but the masks of that Arbitrary Power, the face of which they hide, only to make that Power the more secure and permanent. The bulk of the People, rarely any where penetrating beneath the surface of things, does not see, though it is sure, at times, to feel the fangs of that monster despotism lurking behind all that dazzling pomp of Order and State; a tiranny politically mitigated, reduced, in short, into system, and only the more detestable for the being so. How much preferable is the franker, honester barbarism of a Turkish Government; disdaining all those refinements of artfull Policy, in which alone, the Grand-Signior at Versailles differs from the Grand-Signior in his seraglio at Constantinople? What pity would not be due from humanity to the French if their native

[29] Similar infelicities occur on I, 38, 46, 49, 55, 63, 67, 72, 75, 78, 111, 112, 113, 114; II, 6–7, 12, 16, 26–27, 45, 49, 72, 79, 87, 88, 111, 138.

slavishness of heart did not sink them beneath it? Yet that the very Court which has forged for the people, those chains surely not the less chains for the nicety of their make or the glare of their polish, is in some measure sensible of their misery, may be inferred from it's constant endeavors to procure them that cruel consolation the miserable find in having numbers share their wretched fate, as if too that could lessen the shame of it.

This may at least be one of the reasons to be given for the rage, in that Court, of propagating slavery by every art of conquest and extension of dominion, in the presumption of a readiness in other countries to receive those its chains, from its having already tried them with such success on subjects that seem born for them, are vain and fond of them, and most certainly deserve, since they can so gaily endure them [II, 101–5].

Assuming that this prose is original, not derived from an unknown French source, the only justifiable comment apropos of my hypothesis seems to be that, though the signs are both few and faint ("the nicety of their make or the glare of their polish" and "every art of conquest and extension of dominion" may be cited), Johnson *might* have added the general "reflection" to the text.

A fourth and, in the light of my hypothesis, most suggestive element in the prose embraces words, phrases, notions, and limited syntactical patterns that bear distinct affinities, as I think, to the characteristic Johnsonian mode and that either have no parallels in the *Histoire* or differ from the obvious translations of the corresponding French versions. Since the selection is based on one man's opinion and since every student of Johnson will want to weigh each piece of evidence on his own stylistic scales, I record here a total of thirty-five passages collected, as the references indicate, from both volumes of the *History:*

dismal instants of vacuity [I, 42; cf. "dismal vacuity in life" in Johnson's letter of 27 July 1778 to James Elphinston[30]]; the stamp of her contrivance, or the sanction of her approbation [I, 44]; It has been averred, and not without some color of probability [I, 50; "dit-on" is the only counterpart in the *Histoire*]; Nor was their rage a little exasperated [I, 51]; commodiously contrived [I, 57]; Of the soundness of this theory, La Pompadour, was, by the having adhered to it in practice, enabled to boast a victorious experience [I, 71]; this double infrigidation of her personal infirmity [I, 72; it is perhaps worthy of note that while Nathan Bailey's *Dictionarium Britannicum* of 1736 lists neither *infrigidation* nor *infrigidate*,[31] the latter appears in Johnson's own dictionary]; No symptoms of remission betrayed such a design [I, 74]; procure a revocation of his disgrace [I, 76]; But what is there that may not be believed of the servility of

---

[30] *Letters,* II, 253.

[31] The *OED* dates *infrigidation* as early as 1590 and as late as 1886; *infrigidate,* 1545 and 1885.

the subjects of that nation? [I, 80; this passage has no counterpart in the *Histoire*]; with what probability of succeeding is not said [I, 111; this passage has no counterpart in the *Histoire*]; from the deepest obscurity to the strongest glare of pomp and magnificence [II, 11]; frigidly symmetrized compartments [II, 18]; the pompous palace of Versailles [II, 20]; it is credibly averred [II, 23]; And even those few, so dangerous are all court-connexions, she could not see with impunity [II, 24]; But, besides the sacrifice of so able a general, in so critical a conjuncture, to a mistress, and that mistress a La Pompadour [II, 32]; It is easy to conceive what emotions such an accident must excite [II, 33]; To her compliments on his recovery, succeeded the most pathetic expostulations with him, for the treatment she had met with [II, 35–36]; without any mitigation of his disgrace [II, 37]; A claim that with many others scarce less impudently mad, are only fit to be dated from Bedlam, and can pass but on such as are duly qualified for an hospital of ideots [II, 45; this passage has no counterpart in the *Histoire*]; it may reasonably be supposed [II, 45; this passage has no counterpart in the *Histoire*]; by temporizing with both parties suffer neither to preponderate [II, 48]; The Parisians especially could not forbear giving her [II, 55]; digesting her grief [II, 78]; and indeed, what artifice can there be that is not strictly resolvable into a lie in action, or in words? [II, 81; this passage has no counterpart in the *Histoire*; cf. " 'Sir,' said he, 'don't tell me of deception; a lie, Sir, is a lie, whether it be a lie to the eye or a lie to the ear' "[32]]; In the mean time, La Pompadour continues reigning triumphant in plenitude of power [II, 105; the comparable passage in the *Histoire* reads: "Cependant Madame de Pompadour règne" (p. 134)]; these awfull certainties [of religion] [II, 108]; a certain propensity [II, 119]; Of this design she has already given broad indications [II, 120]; her gaunt eagerness after money [II, 122]; a mixture of acrimony and concern [II, 127]; Nor did this deadly blast of all ardor, and emulation for the service of the public, but run through all orders from the highest to the lowest [II, 131]; should any visitation of a plague or famine supervene [II, 132]; hitherto there appears no abatement of her favor with him [II, 138].

Once it has been conceived, a hypothesis, as we all know, sometimes makes its begetter find supporting evidence where none really exists. In an effort to provide a measure of objectivity for my impressions regarding the quotations assembled above, I have examined, on the one hand, the English translation of Mademoiselle de Fauques's *La Dernière guerre des bêtes*, which appeared, it will be recalled, in both French and English editions in 1758, and, on the other hand, Johnson's contribution ("A Dissertation upon the Greek Comedy" and "General Conclusion") to Mrs. Charlotte Lennox's translation, *The Greek Theatre of Father Brumoy* (1759). The former contains not a single phrase that strikes me as being even remotely "Johnson-

[32] *Johnsonian Miscellanies*, ed. G. B. Hill (Oxford, 1897), II, 428.

ian"; the latter—shorter, of course, than the *History of Pompadour*—contains fewer awkward, involved constructions but also, according to my count, fewer expressions reminiscent of Johnson's style.

The title page of the second edition of the *History* informs the reader, as I noted earlier, that the text has been "corrected." A collation of the two editions reveals at least thirty-nine alterations in diction, most of which fall under the usual headings of deletions, additions, and substitutions. Six changes, listed below opposite the original passages, seem to me to move perceptibly in the direction of the Johnsonian manner, with the shift being most evident in "open nearer and more alarming prospects of futurity" (cf. "prospects of futurity" in *Rasselas,* chapter xxvii). When considering these revisions, one should remember that readings in the second edition, as I have already observed, are frequently closer to the French versions[33] than are those in the first edition.

FIRST EDITION	SECOND EDITION
certain infirmities rather fit to disgust than to invite enjoyment [I, 17]	a coldness or indifference unfavorable to the claims of love [I, 25]
an order for [I, 101]	the royal mandate for [I, 117]
to all the air of graciousness and falsity [II, 31]	to a most placid air of graciousness with all the falsity [II, 32]
she has caressed, patronized, and essentially served many who had those titles [II, 66]	she has done herself the honor of caressing, patronizing and essentially serving many who had those titles [II, 65]
open nearer prospects of a future life [II, 109]	open nearer and more alarming prospects of futurity [II, 108]
as one of the infernal shades, on the banks of the Stygian Lake [II, 144]	as one of the infernal shades, beckoning the ferryboat, on the banks of the Stygian Lake [II, 143]

These revisions comprise the last piece of evidence I can submit in support of the *History*'s claim to be Johnson's "little Pompadour." Obviously a number of questions remain unanswered. To the readers who wonder whether Johnson would have agreed, even for money,

33 The six passages corresponding to the six printed in the text read as follows: (1) "une roideur ou une indifférence dont l'amour ne s'accommodoit pas" (p. 26); (2) "une ordonnance du Roi" (p. 71); (3) "à tout ce que la douceur a de plus gracieux et la fausseté de plus trompeur" (p. 98); (4) "Elle, dis-je, se fit toujours un honneur de les flater, de les protéger, et de leur rendre des services réels, dans toutes les occasions" (p. 116); "à ouvrir les portes du destin, pour jetter des regards timides

to translate the life of a royal whore, let me say only that the *History* contains nothing bawdy or prurient, that it was favorably noticed in the *Critical Review* and the *Monthly*,[34] and that long extracts were printed in the *London Magazine*,[35] the *Scots Magazine*,[36] the *Universal Magazine*,[37] and probably elsewhere. To those concerned over the difference between the hundred and fifty pounds (or guineas) that Johnson, according to my hypothesis, would have received for a translation and the hundred pounds that he actually received for *Rasselas*, I can offer only a guess that the bookseller, whoever he was, saw in the *History*, which seems to have reached a fourth edition in 1760,[38] a solidly profitable investment, hence was willing to pay a good price for a speedy translation by a distinguished literary figure. In response to queries about other connections between Johnson and books on Pompadour, I can cite only item 144—"11. Letters [sic] de Pompadour, 2t. &c."—in the *Sale Catalogue* (on page 8) of his library, point out that the *Lettres*, and the English translation, did not appear until 1771, and regret, like everybody else, the cataloguer's failure to describe Johnson's books adequately. To those who ask whether Strahan, who printed *Rasselas*, might have also printed the *History*, the reply is simple: Strahan's extant ledgers tell us nothing, but, it should be emphasized, they do not record all the printing he is known to have done. To inquirers about relations between William Johnston and works on Pompadour, I can respond only with the name of a book—the *Memoirs of the Marchioness de Pompadour*—that was admittedly translated from the French and published in 1766 by "P. Vaillant" and "W. Johnston," and go on to say that the date, length, and style of this work[39] preclude its nomination as Johnson's "little

---

et pleins d'inquiétude dans l'abime d'une vie à venir" (p. 136); (6) "Ses embrassemens ne sauroient diférer de ceux des ombres souterraines, qui atendent sur les bords du Styx, la barque fatale, qui doit les traverser" (p. 155).

[34] *Critical Review*, VI (1758), 317–23; *Monthly Review*, XIX (1758), 497–98. The notices in both magazines comment on the unusual prose of the *History*. "The stile is spirited, though in some places uncouth and affected," says (p. 317) the *Critical* writer. "The stile of the narrative is extremely unequal," the *Monthly* reviewer declares (p. 498), "in some places verbose, perplexed, and affectedly pretty; in others, it is well polished, and truly elegant."

[35] XXVII (1758), 511–13, 582–84, 617–19.

[36] XX (1758), 574–79, 642–49.

[37] XXIII (1758), 297–302, 339–45.

[38] See n. 20 above.

[39] My statement is based on an examination of a microfilm of a copy of the *Memoirs* in the Huntington Library. The *Monthly Review* for October 1766 (XXXV, 266–76) contains a review, together with substantial extracts, of the work. The *Memoirs*, it may be noted, includes an obvious reference to the earlier *History*: "A multitude of injurious reports have been propagated concerning my parents," Madame

Pompadour." And to queries about connections between Johnston and Samuel Hooper,[40] the ostensible publisher of the *History*, I must answer that I know of none, nor of any transactions between Johnson and Hooper.

IV

What, then, in conclusion, is the status of the hypothesis set forth in this essay? No more and no less than what I have implied more than once during the discussion. It rests on the only interpretation of Johnson's letter to Strahan that makes sense to me. It is neither proved nor disproved by the evidence that I have presented regarding *The History of the Marchioness de Pompadour*. It continues to be only a hypothesis, and, as such, badly in need of decisive nourishment or the *coup de grâce*. Being its parent, I naturally prefer sustenance to destruction; being at the same time more passionately devoted to an accurate Johnsonian canon than to even a favorite brainchild, I am prepared to observe its death with equanimity.

---

de Pompadour is represented as saying. "A wretched anonymous writer has gone even further, by publishing a scandalous book with the title of the history of my life. The Count D'Affry wrote to me from Holland, that this production was of the growth of Great-Britain" (I, 6).

[40] Plomer describes (p. 131) Hooper as "An important publisher with a large trade."

BENJAMIN BOYCE

Mr. Pope, in Bath, Improves the Design of His Grotto

I_N THE MIDDLE of November 1739, Alexander Pope arrived in the
West Country to drink the waters at Bristol and Bath for an old stomach complaint. This was not the most agreeable season for travel, and
the accommodations for taking the waters at Bristol were so unsatis-
factory in cold weather that after a fortnight there Pope returned to
Bath—or, rather, to the house of his friend Ralph Allen in Widcombe across the river from Bath. On the advice of Dr. Oliver and
Dr. Cheyne, Pope was to mix the less impregnated Bristol water
(brought over by carrier or on the Avon canal) with a small quantity
of hot Bath water fresh from the Pump (and therefore especially
"spiritous" and effective). If this prescription failed, he would try the
water of the Lyncombe Spa, discovered only a year before. This
water was thought to be of the nature of that at Gerunster in Germany, and the well was on the Lyncombe hillside not far from the
Allens' house.[1]
  Whatever the two weeks at Bristol did for Pope's physical health,
they had a stimulating effect on his aesthetic sensibilities. The hot
well was outside the town where rocky cliffs rise above the Avon and
where wooded banks, the high Down, the river "at a vast depth below, winding in & out," and the "Prospect" through the gorge toward
the sea seemed to Pope wonderfully picturesque.[2] In the descriptions
that he sent to Martha Blount, he particularly mentioned the steep and
rugged and multicolored rocks above the river, so unlike his own
riverside prospect in Twickenham. Looking out the door of the house

BENJAMIN BOYCE is Professor of English at Duke University.

[1] See *The Correspondence of Alexander Pope*, ed. George Sherburn (Oxford,
1956), IV, 200–206 (hereafter cited as *Correspondence*); John Wood, *An Essay towards a Description of Bath* (2d ed.; London, 1749), I, 79–81.

[2] *Correspondence*, IV, 201–2, 204.

of the hot well, he saw "a vast Rock of 100 foot high, of red, white, green, blue & yellowish Marbles, all blotch'd & variegated."[3]

When he returned to the comfortable quarters provided by the Allens, Pope had not left hills or rocks. Allen's present dwelling in Widcombe was high above Bath,[4] probably somewhere near the ancient Prior's Park in which Allen was in process of building a Palladian mansion. The great house, with its pavilions and wings on either side extending a thousand feet from end to end, required tons and tons of the white stone, cut in Allen's quarries on Combe Down a short distance above the mansion. Allen, now rich and also benevolent, was this very season opening up an additional, not really needed quarry just in order to give employment, Pope said,[5] to the people in neighboring parishes who might otherwise have died of want and cold.

A guest for two months in the house of a man whose quarries supplied stone in large amounts to Bath, Bristol, and London, Pope probably would have come to know something about the strata of rock under the surface of the hills around him. Perhaps during this visit he had a look into a quarry; at any rate a few months later he felt able to describe the pillars in his grotto as being "like supporters left in a Quarry" rather than architectural columns.[6] Eventually he must have

[3] *Correspondence*, IV, 201.

[4] *Correspondence*, IV, 206. As early as 1735 Allen was subscribing his letters from "Widcombe near Bath," but as late as May 1741, Pope was asking Allen if he had yet got into his "New House"—obviously Prior Park (*Correspondence*, IV, 344). Where in Widcombe, then, were the Allens living when Pope made long visits to them in 1739 and 1740?
The basement story of the Prior Park mansion was built by 1737 (according to one of John Wood's drawings, now in the Bath Reference Library) and before that the westward "wing of offices" (Wood, II, 427). But the "offices" contained a stable, hay-house, etc., and could hardly have been suitable for housing the Allens and their guest. We may feel sure, too, that they were not in the house at the foot of Lyncombe Hill that was said by James Tunstall a century later (*Rambles about Bath* [London, 1847], p. 114) to have been used by Pope, nor at the family home of Allen's recently acquired second wife, Hampton Manor, which is at some distance from Widcombe. The Widcombe Manor House below Prior Park had in 1727 been rebuilt by the Bennet family, who must still have been living there in 1739.
Two other possibilities suggest themselves. Thomas Thorpe's map, *An Actual Survey of the City of Bath . . . and of Five Miles Round* (1742), shows, halfway up the hill-road from the Bennets' Widcombe House to the Allens' Prior Park, something labeled "Park House," which looks in the drawing to be large enough for a residence. Still farther up the hill, eastward but on a line with the Prior Park mansion, is "the Lodge," seemingly larger than Park House. Both of these would be on the edge of Allen's property if not indeed actually on it. And both would have been perhaps no more than a mile from Lyncombe Spa which Pope said was "near Mr. Allen's" (*Correspondence*, IV, 206).

[5] *Correspondence*, IV, 221.

[6] *Correspondence*, IV, 246. See also Plate I.

learned about the crevices in the limestone in Allen's quarries where water ran and stalactites formed. Some of the stones, a visitor reported, were "like the jaspar-agate of Saxony; and some of the stalactites are mixed with the fine particles of the spar and the free stone, some of the strata of the former shoot like crystals and these the workmen call cockles, and are very beautiful for grottos."[7] Pope was already practically one of the family at the Allens' house: the previous May he had given Allen a Great Dane puppy, one of Bounce's progeny, and he was now helping his hosts with their planting (presumably at Prior Park). It may have been on a previous visit to Bath that he first met Allen's fellow Cornishman, Dr. William Oliver, by this time a prominent Bathonian. Oliver's kinsman, the Rev. William Borlase, still lived in Ludgvan, Cornwall.

Borlase, like Oliver, was almost identical in age with Allen, though all three were some dozen years Pope's junior and all properly his admirers. Borlase had visited Bath for his health in 1730 and had been Oliver's patient. A constantly studious man—antiquarian, scientist, painter, Latinist—Borlase made experiments, four years after taking the waters at Bath, into the nature of mineral wells in his own neighborhood and found "no great quantity of alkaline Salt,"[8] a discovery that anticipated a similar but most unwelcome analysis of the Bath waters announced by Dr. Oliver's hated critic, the interloping Dr. Charles Lucas, in 1756.[9] Borlase's devotion to science was astonishing, wrote his kinsman in an especially pleasant letter of 5 September 1738: "You prefer the Exuvia of one Periwinkle, found on the top of an high inland Mountain, to six live Lobsters just taken out of the Sea." Borlase's interest in geology was eventually to produce the many pages discussing Cornish rocks and the accompanying pictures of Cornish crystals, "Figur'd Mundicks," and figured copper and tin in his great folio volume, *The Natural History of Cornwall* (1758). If he and Pope had not met previously, they were now to be effectively introduced by correspondence—and both were indefatigable letter writers.

Pope's grotto, a tunnel that connected his house with his garden

---

[7] *The Travels through England of Dr. Richard Pococke*, ed. J. J. Cartwright (London, 1888), I, 157. Pococke visited Allen's quarries in 1750.

[8] Letter from Oliver to Borlase, 27 August 1734, in Vol. I of the Borlase Correspondence belonging to the Penzance Library, Morrab Gardens, Penzance. This and subsequent quotations from Oliver's letters from Bath to Borlase in Cornwall appear by kind permission of Professor J. Herbert Sleeman and the other officers of the Library. My thanks are due Mrs. M. Harvey, Librarian, for locating the Oliver letters for me.

[9] See his *Essay on Waters* (London, 1756), Part I, pp. 164, 322–25; Part III, p. ccxii.

just beyond the highway that separated them, had been "finished" about 1725.[10] Shells, flints and iron ore, a trickling rill of water, cleverly placed mirrors, sudden brief views of boats on the Thames, and a hanging alabaster lamp—these made of the tunnel a place of surprise; whimsy and the fanciful use of whatever came to hand had produced something more or less suggestive of the poetic grottoes imagined by Virgil and various Renaissance authors. It was a poet's plaything. But now in Bristol and Bath, with rocks and talk of rocks around him, Pope new-conceived his grotto as a cavernous place very much like an actual mine and an actual quarry.

Dr. Oliver must have been an important abettor in the new plan. A popular physician but also a dabbler in poetry, he was an eager friend of Pope's. Early in December (1739) the poet seems to have started talking to the doctor about his grotto, and Oliver saw that what they needed was the help of Borlase. So on 13 December, Oliver addressed to him the following letter:

DEAR SIR

I have a favour to beg of you which your own good Taste draws upon you, and will likewise make my Apology for giving you this trouble in behalf of a Man, for whom, I think you can't but have the greatest Regard. I don't know whether you are acquainted with the Situation of M^r. Pope's House at Twickenham, where so many fine Pieces have been composed to the immortal Honour of the English Nation, and I hope to the great Improvement of the Morals of all Succeeding Generations. It lies towards the Thames, and is divided from a Garden, most elegantly dispos'd, by a high way. He has made a Communication between this Garden and his House under this high way. He has a mind to make this Passage a beautiful Grotto, adorn'd with all the Several Productions of Nature, which are properly to be found under ground. I must therefore beg of you that you will let our Country have the honour to contribute all it can to the Beauty of this Grotto, where the greatest Geniuses of this Age will often contemplate, and admire the Riches of our native Soil. I beg therefore that you will Spare no Cost in collecting a quantity, three or four Tun, of the finest Spar, Mundick, Copper and Tin Oars, which you shall judge proper for such a work, and let them be packed up in Hogsheads, and sent to London by one of the Tinships, directed for Alexander Pope Esqr. He will be longing to receive them, and therefore I beg to know by the Return of the Post, by what time it may be probable that you shall have an Opportunity of transmitting this Spar, and Mundick, as they are very beautiful so they are cheap, and will make

---

[10] For a good account of Pope's grotto in its earliest phase and in its final phase see Frederick Bracher's "Pope's Grotto; the Maze of Fancy," *Huntington Library Q.,* XII (1948–49), 141–62.

a great Part of the Cargoe. But as you know the Design, and can so thoroughly enter into it, I need not be particular, and you will add whatever you think will contribute to the Beauty of such a work. Whatever the Cost is I will most thankfully repay, for I should be much pleased to contribute something to his Pleasure who has afforded me so much of a superior kind. I hope all your Family are well. My best wishes attend them, and you. I am with the truest Regard,

> dear Sir,
>
> > Your most affectionate and obedient Servant
> >
> > > W: OLIVER

While the two men in Bath waited for a reply, Christmas came and went. Pope kept up his correspondence with other people and continued planning the Allens' garden. He had an engagement to breakfast down the hill at Dr. Oliver's house in Westgate Street on Friday, 11 January, which the severe frost prevented his keeping;[11] so he proposed coming the next Monday. What happened on that occasion is indicated in another letter from Oliver to Borlase, dated 14 January 1739 (1740 N.S.).

DEAR SIR

I received your kind Letters this Morning, when M^r. Pope was at breakfast with me; as he did likewise that which you wrote to him at Twickenham. He was much pleased with your letters, and your Proceedings, and I believe will soon own his obligations to you himself. But that you might be fully apprized of the nature of his design, he has here given you a Sketch of his Grotto, and hopes a great Improvement of his design from that Taste which he plainly discovers you to be Master of. If it could be so contrived, he could wish to place all the Minerals in their several natural Strata. I suppose the Stallactites will be pendulous from the Roof. When you see his own Sentiments you will judge better; if ever you go to Twickenham I think I may assure you of a hearty welcome, not only to see his Gardens but himself, which is by much best worth seeing. He is the freest, humblest, most entertaining Creature you ever met with; He has sojourned these two months with our great Countryman M^r. Allen, at his country House, who needed only this lasting Testimony of so honourable, and distinguished a Friendship to deliver his Name in the most amiable light to Posterity. They are extremely happy in each other; the one feeling great Joy in the good Heart, and Strong Sense of his truly generous Host, while the other, with the most pleasing Attention, drinks in Rivers of Knowledge continually flowing from the Lipps of his delightful Stranger. They are much alone, and quite happy in each other, but they are so kind as to say that I do not interrupt them when I make a

---

[11] *Correspondence*, IV, 218.

third for an hour or two, which I believe you will not imagine to be very seldome.

I thank you for your Account of the Growth of Cornish diamonds, which I like extremely well; M^r. Pope put it in his Pocket this morning.

... W: OLIVER

M^r. Pope will stay here long enough for me to hear from you before he leaves me.[12]

Obviously Pope's imagination was greatly struck by the suggestions in Borlase's letters. The account of the "growth" of Cornish diamonds that Pope carried off to use in arranging the promised contributions in his grotto may have been something like (if not identical with) the description Borlase gave to Oliver of his laborious descent into a tiny cave near the tin mines:

We had two candles with us, by means of which we saw the roof, which might in the middle be about 5 feet from the floor, in other parts not near so much. It consisted entirely of spar shot into Cornish diamonds. I could not discern any in a perpendicular position, but in every other direction they pointed forth very plentifully, sometimes in groups and clusters, sometimes single, now crossing each other, and now standing by each other with parallel sides. Some were smooth and shining and clear; others rough and opaque; some veined with red, like porphyry; others speckled thick with the smallest spots of black and purple, and a blueish cast; but the finest of all were those which had innumerable little diamonds of the clearest water stuck upon their sides, and which by the candle had a lustre scarce to be conceived.[13]

The ink sketch[14] drawn by Pope at the top of Oliver's letter of 14 January provides specific information about the length (50 feet) of the whole grotto at this stage in its history, about its height (seven feet arching to ten in the middle chamber, six feet in the sections at either end), about the arched ceilings in the central "gloomy" chamber (where the alabaster lamp probably hung) and in the dark passage at the garden end and the flat ceiling at the river end under the house. The course followed by the spring into the "Basin" via "the small

---

[12] Borlase Correspondence (Penzance Library), Vol. I, fol. 119. A portion of this letter as well as other excerpts from the Borlase manuscripts was printed in an unsigned article, "MS. Collections at Castle Horneck. 1720–1772," *Quarterly Review*, CXXXIX (July–October, 1875), 367–95.

[13] *Quarterly Review*, CXXXIX, 382–83. In his *Natural History of Cornwall* (Oxford, 1758), pp. 127–28, Borlase again describes this little cave, repeating some of the wording in the account quoted above. On p. 128 n. he mentions an encrusted ammonite found in one of Ralph Allen's quarries.

[14] See Plate I. As far as I know, this sketch by Pope of his grotto has not previously been reproduced. It is presented here by kind permission of the officers of the Penzance Library.

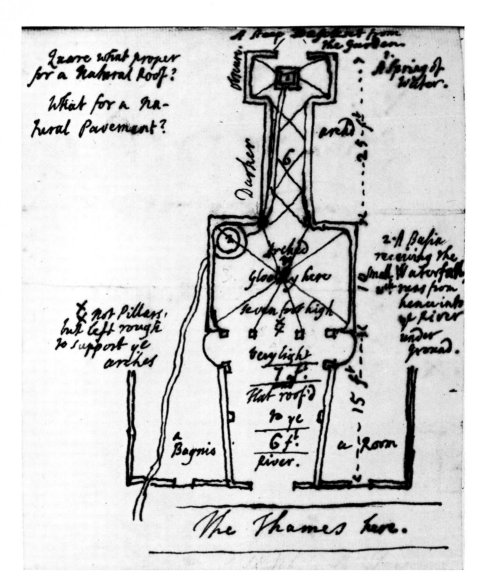

PLATE I. Pope's drawing (enlarged) of his grotto, made on 14 January 1739/40. (Courtesy of Penzance Library.)

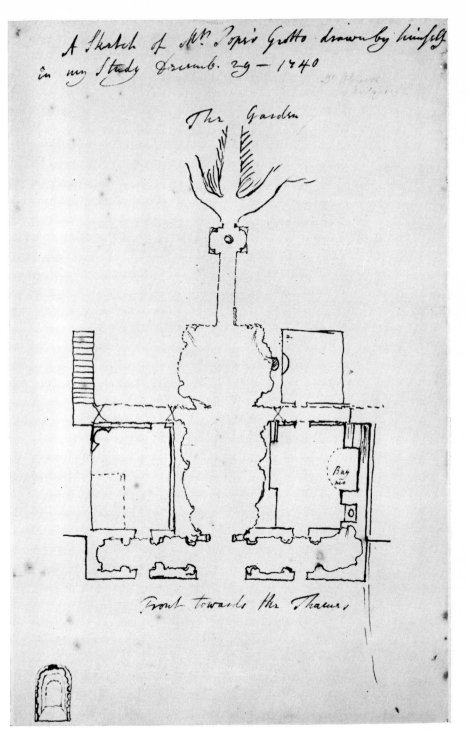

PLATE II. Pope's drawing of his grotto made on 29 December 1740. (Courtesy of Harvard College Library.)

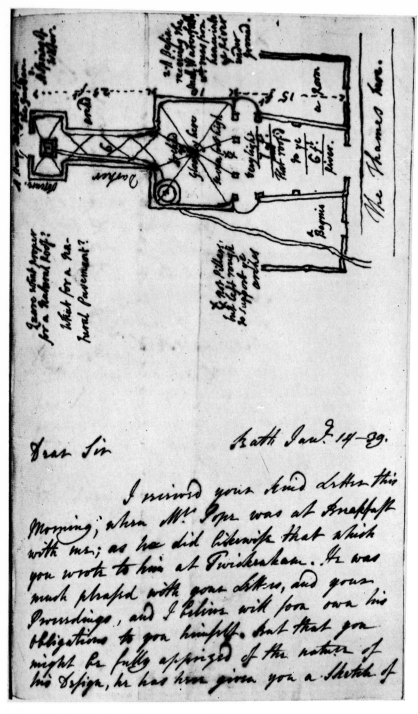

PLATE III. The drawing of 14 January 1739/40, at the top of Dr. Oliver's letter. (Courtesy of Penzance Library.)

Waterfall" and through a bagnio, thence underground to the Thames, is especially interesting. The pillars are "rough," as he said again in a letter of 8 June 1740. Pope's queries in the margins as to what would be proper for "a Natural Roof" and "a natural Pavement" are a key to his new conception of his grotto: not picturesque and playful fancy but nature itself was to be his guide.

Pope stayed on in Bath until February. Meanwhile, Borlase must have begun selecting and packing the "rich white Spars, interlaced with black Cockle," the yellow and blue and purple mundic, the Cornish diamonds and stalactites and other rocks that were to travel by water to Twickenham. On 9 March, Pope wrote to thank him for the first shipment, which contained apparently some of the rarer treasures in Borlase's collection. Pope once more asked him for instructions as to the position and direction of these stones in their native mines, for he wanted to make the grotto "resemble Nature in all her workings."[15] Presumably Borlase sent the needed information; in a letter of 8 June, Pope tells him that he has arranged the lodes of metal to run "East and West" between strata of beautiful but "rude" marbles,[16] an arrangement seemingly correct according to Borlase's chapter "Of the Fissures in which Metals are found"; for there one learns that the "course of fissures . . . is generally east and west in Cornwall."[17]

The queries about roof and pavement also seem to have been answered. At least Pope reported to Borlase that he had appropriated the stalactites for the ceiling and that the pavement alternated ore and marble, which ran east and west as the grotto happened to do.[18] In April, he thanked Allen for a shipment from his quarries including "Alabaster, Spars, & Snakestones."[19] In May, he asked him for a few "Bristol diamonds" and for more stones from his quarry; he thanked Oliver for Borlase's gift of his "finest discoveryes and richest treasures" as well as advice.[20] He really would like, now, a load of just common rocks from Cornwall.

Thus, throughout the spring and summer and fall of 1740, work went on apace, Pope continually adding mundics and crystals and shining ores and marble "cramp'd fast with iron to the walls." He kept wishing for the assistance of Mr. Omer, an expert on stone-work for-

---

[15] *Correspondence*, IV, 228.

[16] *Correspondence*, IV, 245–46.

[17] *Natural History of Cornwall*, p. 143. Likewise, we learn from Wood's *Essay* (I, 60) that soil in the Bath region has strata of rock beneath running east and west.

[18] *Correspondence*, IV, 228–29, 246.

[19] *Correspondence*, IV, 235.

[20] *Correspondence*, IV, 239, 244.

merly in the employ of the architect John Wood[21] and now in Allen's. Pope was thinking about using him as early as March, but his arrival was delayed, partly because in late May or early June he was conducting business for Allen with the Common Council of Bristol.[22] But by 17 June, Omer had come to Twickenham and gone.[23]

Although winter arrived before Pope could finish the new design—for still more stones were needed—the additions he had made to the layout as sketched the previous January were extensive. (See Plate II.) Two pillars had been removed from the central chamber, and a room had been added to the right of that chamber. A transverse passage had been constructed, which at the left ended in a stairway to the house above; the walls of the passage defined two rooms to left and right of the flat-roofed chamber leading toward the Thames. Also, a porch had been built facing the river. The "small Waterfall" in the central chamber had become "three falls of water, which break very naturally over two Rocks of Cornish Diamonds & Plymouth Marbles."[24] By some means—possibly by changing the course of the spring that originally ran underground below the left-hand chamber—a "Bagnio"[25] was provided in the right-hand chamber. In October, Pope told Oliver that he was placing the name of Oliver's other generous friend, Cooper, over the porch for which he had contributed the marble. In rather puzzling language, he adds: "And I design You [Oliver] a Bath (which is the Honour of a Physitian) to go by yours [i.e., your name] with a perennial Spring, by Mr Allen's."[26] When Borlase's neighbor, Sir John St. Aubyn, visited the grotto in December 1741, there he saw "Borlase" written in letters of gold.[27]

In all these changes (bating the gold letters), the effect sought, Pope insisted, was of a faithful representation of nature. Writing to Allen of his great indebtedness to Oliver and Borlase, he confessed how proud he would be "if they think I have imitated nature well."[28]

---

[21] See the manuscript letter from Wood to William Brydges, dated 27 April 1734, now in the Bath Reference Library.

[22] See the Minute Book of the Committee for building an Exchange and Market, 1738–50, in the Council House, Bristol. I am indebted to Elizabeth Ralph, City Archivist, for this information.

[23] *Correspondence*, IV, 247.

[24] *Correspondence*, IV, 267.

[25] Called a "Piece of Water," bordered by plants, in *A Plan of Mr. Pope's Garden, As it was left at his Death: with a Plan and Perspective View of the Grotto. All taken by J. Serle, his Gardener* (London, 1745). Serle also mentions a "Bason of Water" in the porch facing the Thames.

[26] *Correspondence*, IV, 278–79.

[27] Borlase Correspondence, Oliver to Borlase, 15 December 1741.

[28] *Correspondence*, IV, 254.

He had introduced into the grotto, he told Bolingbroke, "all the varieties of Natures works under ground—Spars Minerals & Marbles," so that the place was now "a Study for Virtuosi."[29] St. Aubyn reported to Borlase a year later that Pope had recently called on him in London and said, among other remarks, that in the grotto he had "strictly followed Nature."[30]

After all this work was done, Pope returned to Bath in December (1740). But he was by that time also at the climax of another enterprise, the prolonged and hazardous intrigue to get his correspondence with Swift into print without appearing to have approved the publication; the study of rocks was interrupted by the study of deviousness. Yet in Dr. Oliver's cheerful company he seemed at his best. The "divine Bard" breakfasted with Oliver on Christmas Day after being confined indoors at Widcombe for several days by snow and frost.[31] He had already given the doctor one version of his "Lines" on the grotto and later gave him another containing an extra couplet—

> Thou see'st that Island's Wealth, where only free,
> Earth to her Entrails feels not Tyranny—

which Oliver thought "a little dark," though he could not make Pope think so. Yet the poet eventually came round to accepting the doctor's judgment and dropped the obscure couplet.[32] Both versions of the poem, with mournful compliments to Bolingbroke, Marchmont, and Wyndham, recall unhappy aspects of current history and suggest anything but a cheerful frame of mind in the author. On the twenty-ninth of December, Pope, again in Oliver's house, drew another sketch of the grotto (Plate II)[33] to indicate how much had been accomplished in the year since the two of them had begun planning the transformation.

On 16 February 1741, Oliver wrote to Borlase that Pope, "that delightful little Man," had left Bath the previous week to return home.

[29] *Correspondence*, IV, 261–62.

[30] Borlase Correspondence, 5 May 1741.

[31] Borlase Correspondence, Oliver to Borlase, 25 December 1740.

[32] See Pope's *Minor Poems*, ed. Norman Ault and John Butt (London, 1954), pp. 382–85, for the intricate history of this small poem. The first version recorded for Borlase by Oliver in a letter of 4 December 1740, is what Ault and Butt call Stage B. The second, copied into Oliver's letter of 16 February 1741, is Stage C. Both letters are in the Borlase Correspondence.

[33] The drawing of the grotto bears at the top in Oliver's hand: "A Sketch of M^r. Pope's Grotto drawn by himself in my Study Decemb. 29–1740." The drawing, reproduced in Robert Carruthers, *The Life of Alexander Pope* (London, 1857), p. 175, now belongs to the Harvard College Library and is reproduced here from the original by permission.

The poet's preoccupation with securing "unauthorized" publication of the Swift letters had not spoiled the happiness and charm of his conversations with Oliver. "We talked over every Part of your Character," the doctor wrote to Borlase, "and found more beauty in it, and much more shining and durable ones, than all your Collection of Gems and Metals can afford. He charg'd me with his most grateful Acknowledgments to you for the decorations of his Grotto, and I believe the most agreeable Present you will receive from him, will be a Drawing of it in Perspective.[34] Writing is very troublesome to him, his Eyes being very tender," and Borlase was not to expect many letters from him.

In Pope's life, few things of the creative sort were likely ever to be positively finished; and during the summer of 1741 he continued "Grottofying," now drawing on Richard Owen Cambridge in Gloucestershire for "gold clift" and other stones.[35] Cambridge was told by an intermediary that one "wing" of the grotto was to be covered with shells.[36] For a time, too, in April and May, Pope thought of having something "of a Grotesque kind" painted in the grotto, though probably this idea was abandoned.[37] But if fantasy returned to the grotto in these ways, neither shell-room nor painting was mentioned in the detailed description included in the *Plan* of Pope's little estate published by his gardener Serle after his death. To be sure, lava from Vesuvius, gold ore from Peru and silver from Spain, Egyptian pebbles, coral from the West Indies, and varieties of Italian marble are all listed in Serle's description. Furthermore, the "Perspective View of the Grotto" published in his *Plan* shows a series of low, round arches all symmetrically bordered in rusticated stone, the walls

[34] Perhaps this drawing was the one by Serle that formed the basis of the full-page engraved "Perspective View of the Grotto" in Serle's *Plan of Mr. Pope's Garden*. A small, slightly modified version of that engraving was used to illustrate the text of Pope's lines "On a Grotto near the Thames" in Robert Dodsley's *Collection of Poems in Six Volumes. By Several Hands* (III, 1758, and later printings). Dodsley, who also published Serle's *Plan*, had a brother, Isaac, who was Ralph Allen's gardener. Robert was doubtless especially interested in the grotto. And Serle, after Pope's death, joined Isaac on Allen's staff in Widcombe.

[35] See Richard D. Altick, "Mr. Pope Expands His Grotto," *PQ*, XXI (1942), 427–30.

[36] In August, Pope asked Fortescue to send him a hogshead of scallop shells (*Correspondence*, IV, 356). It would be interesting to know the origin of a shell-roofed grotto built into the sloping earth about 450 yards downstream from Pope's grotto. Now within the garden of Thames Eyot, the grotto may have belonged to the house built by Dr. Batty after 1734 and later occupied by Earl Poulett (see Richard S. Cobbett, *Memorials of Twickenham* [London, 1872], p. 259). The shell-covered interior is ornamented by intersecting lines of red and bluish stones and probably gives one a fair idea of the *non*natural style of grotto. I owe my view of this grotto to the interest and kindness of Miss Irene Titcomb, F.R.C.S.

[37] *Correspondence*, IV, 340, 343.

neatly covered in smaller stones, all about the same size. There is no hint of stratification of spar and ore, of striking variations in color and texture and shape, of "two fine Rocks with Water distilling from them," of "shot" prisms or stones like "old broken Pillars," all of which are specified by Serle himself. Pope told Sir Hans Sloane in 1742 that his grotto consisted "wholly of Natural Productions, owing nothing to the Chissel, or Polish."[38] Probably the engraving made from Serle's drawing regularizes the prospect and suggests "the Chissel" too much. If the grotto was more domestic than Borlase's cave of Cornish crystals with a pool at the bottom, it was none the less lined with "Natures works under ground," placed, when Pope had information to follow, in natural directions; and its roof was supported by "a Diversity of Pillars and Jambs," which looked as if they had been "roughly hew'd out of Rocks and Beds of mineral Strata."[39] It was interestingly true to nature in the way Pope had planned it in the winter of 1739–40 with encouragement from a cheerful Bath doctor, an amateur Cornish geologist, and a generous Somerset quarry owner.[40]

[38] *Correspondence*, IV, 397. Pope ignores what Serle reports—that in the room to the right of the central chamber some "very natural Rock-work" was actually constructed out of the produce of glass-house furnaces.

[39] From a description of Pope's grotto in *The Newcastle General Magazine*, I (January 1748), 26, quoted by Bracher, p. 151.

[40] As Bracher notes, a diagram of "the Grotto of the late Alex^r. Pope Esqr. at Twickenham . . . 1785," published in some unidentified volume, is bound into the Hoe copy of Serle's *Plan* now in the Henry E. Huntington Library. It shows four statues, two busts, and two urns placed within the grotto. But neither Pope nor Serle mentions such "unnatural" intrusions, though Pope wanted urns to stand in the lawn. Because Pope bequeathed "the furniture" of his grotto and the urns in his garden to Martha Blount, we may assume at least that the pieces shown in the 1785 diagram were not his. The idea for them need not have been his. The Stanhopes, who took over Pope's villa after his death, greatly modified both house and garden; they may have tried to transform the grotto as well.

ARTHUR FRIEDMAN

The Time of Composition of Goldsmith's
Edwin and Angelina

Goldsmith's *Edwin and Angelina*—frequently called "The Hermit" and included in *The Vicar of Wakefield* simply as "A Ballad"—was first printed privately as an undated pamphlet "for the Amusement of the Countess of Northumberland." Of this edition Isaac Reed noted in his copy in 1775 that "a few Copies only were printed," and Reed's copy is now one of two known to exist.[1] Our only information concerning the circumstances of this printing is given by Thomas Percy in his Memoir of Goldsmith:

> In the year 1765, Dr. Goldsmith printed his beautiful ballad of the HERMIT; which he at first inscribed to the Countess of Northumberland, who had shown a partiality for poems of this kind, by patronizing the "Reliques of Ancient English Poetry," published in the same year.[2]

The date 1765 is almost certainly correct. Percy's memory could hardly have failed him in placing the printing of the ballad after the appearance of his *Reliques*, published 11 February 1765. Goldsmith would not have considered a private printing after he knew that the poem would soon be made public in *The Vicar of Wakefield*, and by the end of 1765 the decision to bring out the novel must finally have been made, for the first edition was published on 27 March 1766. The problem is whether *Edwin and Angelina* was composed shortly before its first publication in 1765 and then added to the manuscript of *The Vicar of Wakefield* just before the novel was printed or whether it

ARTHUR FRIEDMAN is Professor of English at the University of Chicago.

[1] It is now in the possession of Sir John Murray, who has kindly permitted me to collate it. A second copy was sold at Sothebys in June 1963.

[2] "The Life of Dr. Oliver Goldsmith," p. 74, in *The Miscellaneous Works of Oliver Goldsmith* (London, 1801), Vol. I.

was written early enough to form part of the manuscript of the *Vicar* when the copy for the novel was sold in the latter part of 1762.

Much of what is known about the composition of the ballad comes from Goldsmith and from Percy. A letter signed Detector in the *St. James's Chronicle* for 18–21 July 1767 charged Goldsmith with having borrowed "the Circumstances and Catastrophe" of his poem from Percy's ballad "The Friar of Orders Grey," published in *Reliques of Ancient English Poetry*. To this charge, Goldsmith replied in a letter in the same newspaper for 23–25 July:

> Another Correspondent of yours accuses me of having taken a Ballad, I published some Time ago, from one by the ingenious Mr. Percy. I do not think there is any great Resemblance between the two Pieces in Question. If there be any, his Ballad is taken from mine. I read it to Mr. Percy some Years ago, and he (as we both considered these Things as Trifles at best) told me, with his usual Good Humour, the next Time I saw him, that he had taken my Plan to form the Fragments of Shakespeare into a Ballad of his own. He then read me his little Cento, if I may so call it, and I highly approved it. Such petty Anecdotes as these are scarce worth printing, and were it not for the busy Disposition of your Correspondents, the Publick should never have known that he owes me the Hint of his Ballad, or that I am obliged to his Friendship and Learning for Communications of a much more important Nature.

Concerning this account Percy made no immediate comment, but in editions of the *Reliques* published after Goldsmith's death he gave in notes on "The Friar of Orders Grey" and "Gentle Heardsman" an explanation of the similarity between his ballad and Goldsmith's, and he returned to the subject in his Memoir of Goldsmith. He admitted that Goldsmith in his letter to the newspaper "justly vindicated the priority of his own poem." But, Percy continued:

> . . . in asserting that the plan of the other was taken from his, (in nothing else have they the most distant resemblance,) and in reporting the conversation on this subject, his memory must have failed him; for the story in them both was evidently taken from a very ancient ballad in that collection [*Reliques*], beginning thus, 'Gentle Heardsman,' &c. (Vol. II. No. 14,) as any one will be convinced who will but compare them. This Dr. Goldsmith had seen and admired long before it was printed. . . .[3]

These statements throw some light on the time of composition of *Edwin and Angelina*. "The Friar of Orders Grey" was composed by 12 February 1764, when Percy sent a copy of it to Farmer;[4] so Gold-

---

[3] *Ibid.,* pp. 74–75.

[4] *The Correspondence of Thomas Percy & Richard Farmer,* ed. Cleanth Brooks (Baton Rouge, Louisiana, 1946), p. 64.

smith's ballad, which—Percy and Goldsmith agree—was written first, goes back to an earlier date. Percy connects the composition of *Edwin and Angelina* with Goldsmith's knowledge of "Gentle Heardsman." Percy was sufficiently interested in this ballad in May 1761 to send a copy of it to Thomas Warton;[5] and because Goldsmith, Percy says, "had seen and admired" it "long before it was printed" in 1765, Percy may well have shown it to him when they were seeing each other in London at this same time.[6] *Edwin and Angelina*, then, was written no later than early 1764, over a year before it was printed; there is nothing in our very meager information about its composition to show that it was not written early enough to be included in Chapter VIII of *The Vicar of Wakefield* before Goldsmith sold the copy for the novel in the latter part of 1762; and textual evidence gives strong support for this early date of composition.

Between the text of the private printing of *Edwin and Angelina* (*65*) and the text in the first edition of *The Vicar of Wakefield* (*66a*), there are fifty-eight variant readings ranging in importance from a single word to three entire stanzas. The text in the second edition of the *Vicar* (*66b*) used *66a* as copy; and of the fifty-eight readings in which *65* and *66a* differ, *66b* agrees with *66a* against *65* in forty-two instances. In the remaining sixteen readings, however, *66b* agrees with *65* against *66a*. *66b* is thus a conflated text in which the readings of *66a* have been corrected by comparison with *65*. *66b* contains only three new readings not present in either *65* or *66a*.

As a conflated text representing Goldsmith's considered judgment concerning the ballad early in 1766,[7] *66b* provides the basis for inferences concerning the relationship between *65* and *66a*. First, it is highly probable that *66a* did not use *65* for copy. If we assume that it

[5] *The Correspondence of Thomas Percy & Thomas Warton*, ed. M. G. Robinson and Leah Dennis (Baton Rouge, Louisiana, 1951), p. 6, n. 18.

[6] Percy visited Goldsmith at Wine Office Court twice in May and four times in June 1761 (Alice C. C. Gaussen, *Percy: Prelate and Poet* [London, 1908], pp. 142, 144).

[7] *66b* cannot, however, be taken as representing in all respects Goldsmith's final intention, for later in 1766 he revised the poem again for inclusion in his anthology *Poems for Young Ladies* (dated 1767 but published 15 December 1766). This new text used *65* as copy and introduced fifteen substantive readings, twelve of them probably authorial, not found in any earlier edition. It also added a stanza, not present in *65*, from *66a* or *66b* and adopted one other reading of the *Vicar* texts, but it otherwise ignored the careful selection of readings made for *66b*. "As to my 'Hermit,'" Joseph Cradock reports Goldsmith to have said near the end of his life when he was considering the revision of some of his work, "that poem, Cradock, cannot be amended" (*Literary and Miscellaneous Memoirs* [London, 1828], IV, 286). Although an editor will not wish to quarrel with this statement, he will find himself puzzled in attempting to find or form a text of the poem that represents Goldsmith's final intention and is thus incapable of improvement.

did, then we must assume that Goldsmith introduced fifty-eight new substantive readings in revising *65* for *66a* and then returned to the readings of *65* in sixteen instances in revising *66a* for *66b;* we must assume, in other words, that—according to Goldsmith's later judgment and according to the judgment, I imagine, of most readers—over a quarter of his revisions for *66a* were faulty and later had to be given up for the readings they had displaced. Second, if *66a* did not use *65* as copy, then the manuscript from which *66a* was set probably was prepared before the printing of *65*, for it seems very unlikely that Goldsmith would have written out a manuscript copy if there had been available a printed text in which he could make his revisions. Third, the manuscript from which *65* was printed quite certainly did not derive from the manuscript from which *66a* was printed; if we assume that it did, then we must assume that Goldsmith first introduced fifty-eight new substantive readings into the manuscript of *65*[8] and then rejected nearly three-quarters of these readings in revising for *66b*. The most probable solution is that the manuscripts from which *65* and *66a* were printed were independent revisions of an earlier state of the text. The relationships between the manuscripts and editions may be shown, possibly in an oversimplified form, in the following diagram, in which the straight lines show the source of copy and the arrow shows the direction of influence when conflation occurs.

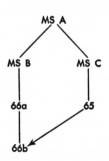

If this diagram is approximately correct, then certain inferences can be made concerning the dates of MSS A, B, and C. MS C was probably prepared at the time Goldsmith decided to print *Edwin and Angelina* for private circulation in 1765. MS B, which formed part of the manuscript from which the first edition of *The Vicar of Wakefield* was printed, was probably prepared a few years earlier, since copy for the novel, I think pretty much in its final form, was sold in the latter part of 1762. At the time of the sale, the manuscript of the

---

[8] This assumption is perhaps an oversimplification; some of the differences between *65* and *66a* may have been introduced in proofs.

novel very likely passed out of Goldsmith's hands, and no good reason
appears why he should have had any further concern with the work
until the owners of the copy finally decided to print it at the end of
1765 or the beginning of 1766. At this late date, MS B could not have
been prepared for insertion in the manuscript of the *Vicar*[9] if the
conclusion stated above is true that MS B was written before *65* was
printed. MS B, then, was probably written no later than the latter part
of 1762, and the original composition of the poem—represented in the
diagram by MS A—must be assigned to an earlier time.

[9] It may be noted that MS B could not have been inserted in the manuscript of the
Vicar after Chap. VIII was written without considerable revision, for if the ballad
and the paragraph introducing it are deleted, the two remaining paragraphs are quite
disconnected and are by no means long enough to comprise a separate chapter.

DONALD F. BOND

Armand de la Chapelle and the First French Version of the Tatler

IN 1724 THE PUBLISHING HOUSE of François Changuion brought out at Amsterdam a small duodecimo volume with the title *Le Babillard, ou le Nouvelliste philosophe*, "traduit de l'anglois par A.D.L.C." This French version of Steele's famous periodical is frequently cited in the two standard editions of the *Tatler*—by John Nichols (1786) and G. A. Aitken (1898).[1] And with justice, since the notes, intended for French readers, are done with intelligence and care, by a man who was living in England when the original sheets of the *Tatler* were appearing and who was obviously in sympathy with Isaac Bickerstaff's program of social reform. He was the Huguenot refugee, Armand Boisbeleau de la Chapelle, at the time (1709–11) pastor of the French church at Wandsworth. An active and controversial figure in the cosmopolitan world of journalism, scholarship, and theology, La Chapelle seems to have been well known both in London and on the Continent, where (in 1725) he became minister in the Walloon church at the Hague. The story of his translation of the *Tatler* forms an interesting episode in La Chapelle's own career and reveals in a striking manner the importance of this new genre, the periodical essay, in the early years of the eighteenth century.

Although there has been no full-scale biography of La Chapelle, brief notices of his career are to be found in the standard biographical collections,[2] and as a prominent Huguenot he appears in both editions

DONALD F. BOND is Professor of English at the University of Chicago.

[1] The second edition (1735) drops "Le Babillard" and alters the title to *Le Philosophe nouvelliste*, a change which has proved confusing to later editors and bibliographers. Aitken adds another element of error (*Life of Steele*, II, 405) by citing the second edition as *Le Babillard, ou Le Philosophe naturaliste*. Brunet had given the same erroneous title.

[2] Michaud, *Biographie universelle*; Hoefer, *Nouvelle biographie générale*; E. Hatin, *Bibliographie . . . de la presse périodique française* (1866), pp. 38–39; *Larousse du XIXe siècle*; etc.

of *La France protestante*.[3] Much of the material here is contradictory, however, and none of the reference works have much to say about La Chapelle's difficulties that arose out of his translation of the *Tatler*. Fortunately, there are abundant contemporary sources which enable us to see him more clearly as man and writer. Many of his letters are still in existence (though they have never been collected or edited), and these are of considerable value, since he had a wide acquaintance among the Huguenot refugees both in England and Holland and through his writing as journalist and polemicist came into contact—and conflict—with many of the leading theologians of his day.[4] La Chapelle also gives frequent autobiographical glimpses in his own books and in those he edited. This is notably true of the *Remarques historiques, critiques et philologiques, sur le Nouveau Testament*, of Isaac de Beausobre, which he brought out at the Hague in 1742. In the life of Beausobre appended to the *Remarques* (II, 253–320), La Chapelle recalls the situation of the French Protestants at the end of the seventeenth century and gives a revealing account of his own experiences in the persecutions which followed the Revocation of the Edict of Nantes.[5] For La Chapelle's career at the Hague (from 1725 until his death in 1746) we have the testimony of the *Lettres sérieuses et badines* of La Barre de Beaumarchais and, more important, the *Mémoires* of François Bruys, with an interesting discussion and "character" of La Chapelle. Finally, soon after his death (8 August 1746), a

[3] Eugène and Emile Haag, *La France protestante* (1846–59), 9 vols., s.v. "Boisbeleau." In the second edition (1877–88, Vols. I–VI [no more published]) several changes are made (Vol. II, cols. 693–98).

[4] Letters from La Chapelle to Pierre Desmaizeaux are among the Sloane MSS in the British Museum; others are to be found in the Bibliothèque publique et universitaire of Geneva, the Bibliothèque Wallonne at Leyden, and elsewhere. The Library of the Huguenot Society of London has a brief biographical sketch of La Chapelle in typescript, which has been of great value in the present investigation. (It was deposited in the Library in 1944, but the Society has no record of its authorship.) I am grateful to Mr. C. F. A. Marmoy, the Librarian of the Huguenot Society of London, for making available to me the books and manuscripts in the Library; to M. Daniel Anet of the Bibliothèque publique et universitaire of Geneva for securing photostats; to Mr. F. C. de Vries of the manuscript room of the Library of the University of Leyden; to Mr. H. Boeke, conservator of the Bibliothèque Wallonne at Leyden; as well as to the staffs of other libraries—the British Museum, the Bibliothèque Nationale, the National Libraries in Florence and Rome, the Bayrische Staatsbibliothek in Munich, the Austrian National Library and the University of Vienna Library in Vienna, the Royal Library in the Hague, the University of Basel Library, the University of California Library at Berkeley, as well as the Library of the University of Chicago.

[5] The British Museum copy was formerly owned by César de Missy and contains MS annotations in his hand.

short biography appeared in the *Bibliothèque raisonnée*,[6] which is of first importance, since La Chapelle was one of the regular writers for this journal and the other members of its staff knew him well.

La Chapelle was born at Ozillac, in the province of Saintonge (now Charente Inférieure) in 1677.[7] Although he signed himself Armand de la Chapelle, there seems to be no doubt that his surname was Boisbeleau. According to the biography in the *Bibliothèque raisonnée*, "ce nom *de la Chapelle* n'étoit qu'une Seigneurie qui lui avoit été donnée pour le distinguer de ses Frères." His father, the same notice continues," "étoit Avocat au Parlement de *Bourdeaux;* mais comme il étoit Protestant, la Persécution l'obligea à quiter le Barreau & à se retirer à la Campagne dans une de ses Terres où l'on venoit le consulter de plusieurs lieues à la ronde. Il eut cinq fils de Mlle *Dubourdieu* son Epouse; *Armand* étoit le troisième."[8] His mother, according to this biography, was a daughter of the famous Huguenot preacher Isaac DuBourdieu. "A l'âge de neuf ou dix ans ses Parens l'envoyèrent aux Ecoles à *Bourdeaux;* mais un an après, Madame sa Mère l'en retira par uns sage prévoyance des dangers qu'il couroit par raport à la Religion, & elle le mena en *Angleterre,* où elle le confia aux soins de son Père Mr. *Isaac Dubourdieu* Ministre à *Londres*."[9] Isaac DuBourdieu, who had served as pastor at Bergerac and later at Montpellier, had come to London shortly after the decree of the Parlement of Toulouse (15

---

[6] *Bibliothèque raisonnée des Ouvrages des Savans de l'Europe,* published at Amsterdam by J. Wetstein & Smith, 1728–53. The biographical sketch of La Chapelle is in Vol. XXXVIII (janvier-mars 1747), pp. 87–89.

[7] Beausobre, *Remarques,* II, 266.

[8] *Bibl. rais.,* p. 87. In the first edition of *La France protestante* the brothers Haag suggested that La Chapelle was probably son of "Boisbeleau ou Boisbellaud, dernier pasteur de Marennes avec Loquet" (II, 333). In the second edition (II, 693), they state categorically that his father was Jean, Sieur de La Chapelle. Both of these statements are clearly wrong. La Chapelle himself tells us (Beausobre, II, 266) that his father was not a pastor but a lawyer, a statement borne out by the obituary notice in the *Bibliothèque raisonnée.* The second conjecture is impossible because Jean, Sieur de La Chapelle, married (at 62) not Mlle DuBourdieu, but a widow, one Andrée Le Vallet. In his will, drawn up 29 August 1739 before Samuel Favon, notary, at the Hague and proved in September 1748 our La Chapelle is called Armand Boibellaud, Sieur de La Chapelle, Minister of the Walloon Church at the Hague. He mentions that his late father left him part of his estate in France, of which his two brothers Isaac and Pascal were then (1739) in possession, by virtue of the Edict of Louis XIV. This property is left to them, but all his possessions outside France are bequeathed to his wife, Anne Hebert. He mentions property in England, Holland, and elsewhere (manuscripts, household goods, etc.) and excludes all brothers and nephews who might claim. See Charles E. Lart, *Huguenot Pedigrees,* I (1924), 15.

[9] *Bibl. rais.,* p. 88.

November 1682), where he became minister at the French Savoy Church, dying at a very advanced age in 1699.[10]

La Chapelle retained to the end of his life the memory of the religious persecutions he had witnessed in his native land.

> J'ai vû [he wrote half a century later] les Dragons venir fondre sur le lieu de ma naissance; je les ai vû logés à discretion dans les maisons Reformées; je les ai vû dans la maison de mon Pere, qui étoit avocat, & malgré ma grande jeunesse, les desordres qu'ils y commirent, les desolations qu'ils y causerent, & les larmes qu'ils y firent repandre, firent alors sur moi une impression si profonde & si douloureuse, qu'encore, à l'heure qu'il est, & au bout de 56. ans, je ne puis me le rappeller sans frémir.[11]

In England, young La Chapelle studied theology and literature with Isaac DuBourdieu: "il n'eut point d'autre Maître, & ne fréquenta aucune Université."[12] Destined for the ministry, he began to preach at the age of seventeen or eighteen. Early in 1694 he appears as one of the two *proposants* or candidates for the ministry, assisting the Rev. Barthélemy Balaguier, pastor of the Bride Street Huguenot Church in Dublin, where he remained until July 1695.[13] From Ireland he went to the combined churches of the Tabernacle and Leicester Fields in London. He is first mentioned in the list of preachers in these churches in 1696; the "Registre des Actes du Consistoire de l'Eglise de Leicester Fields 1693 jusqu'à 1729" records the appointment of a paid *lecteur*—probably La Chapelle—on 5 April. Two years later the same register records (on 8 May 1698) a "Plainte portée au consistoire sur une Insulte faite dans leglise." A certain Mlle Unisenon had charged "que ce matin elle a este insultee dans ce temple par le sieur Lachapelle." The Consistory decided that the affair should be investigated and a report made on the following Sunday. On 15 May the report was duly

[10] One of his sons, Jean DuBourdieu (*ca.* 1642–1720), chaplain successively to the three Dukes of Schomberg, was also a minister at the French Savoy Church. Space is lacking here to go into the complicated genealogy of this famous Huguenot family. There were in fact four ministers named DuBourdieu who served as pastors at the French Savoy Church: in addition to the two just named there were Armand DuBourdieu (d. 1727) and Jean-Armand DuBourdieu (d. 1723). See D. C. A. Agnew, *Protestant Exiles from France* (3d ed.; London, 1886), II, 345–49. It is not certain that our La Chapelle's mother was a daughter of Isaac DuBourdieu; she may have been a sister or a niece. Jean DuBourdieu is said to have been related to Armand de La Chapelle through the latter's aunt (P. Corbière, "Une Controverse entre Bossuet et Jean DuBourdieu," *Bull. de la Soc. de l'Hist. du Protestantisme Français*, XIX–XX [1870–71], 436). The Rev. William J. DuBourdieu, of Maywood, Illinois, has generously placed at my disposal the materials which he has collected toward the history of the family, and I am greatly obliged to him for his help on these points.

[11] Beausobre, *Remarques*, II, 266–67.

[12] *Bibl. rais.*, p. 89.

[13] T. P. Le Fanu, "Libre de caisse pour l'église françoise de Dublin," *Proc. Huguenot Soc. of London*, XV (1933–37), 150.

presented; unfortunately it merely recorded that the affair had been satisfactorily ended and made no statement about the nature of the insult.[14] The incident is significant only in foreshadowing the difficulties which La Chapelle seemed destined to encounter throughout his life because of a certain "touch of satire" in his makeup.

During the next few years La Chapelle occupied various junior posts in the French Protestant churches of London. In 1703 his name occurs in the "List for the Distribution of Her Majestie's Bounty for the Relief and Support of such poor distressed French Ministers as are now residing within the Kingdom of England." Here he is registered as unmarried, about thirty years of age (actually he was twenty-six), and residing at Wandsworth.[15] He became minister of the French church at Wandsworth, just outside London, in 1707, where he remained until 1711, when he was called to serve as pastor of the Artillery Church in London.[16] It was apparently during his ministry at this church that he married. At any rate, the Calendar of Faculty Office Marriage Licences records that a license was issued to "Armand De la Chapel" and Anne Martin on 8 June 1712.[17] There is, however, no record of the marriage being performed in any of the Huguenot churches of London, and the name of his wife differs from that given in his will.[18] According to the somewhat malicious account of François Bruys, written many years later, La Chapelle had intended marrying another, but withdrew his suit at the request of a friend.

Il y avoit une maîtresse, qui comptoit sur lui pour le mariage; mais un de ses amis, devenu l'amant de cette Demoiselle, le pria de renoncer à ses prétentions; ce qu'il fit de bonne grace, blâmant la délicatesse de ceux qui ne peuvent souffrir de rivaux en amour. Il exhorta la Demoiselle à consentir au marché qu'il venoit de conclure; elle ne s'y opposa pas; & son mariage fut ainsi arrêté, & célébré avec l'ami de M. de la Chapelle.[19]

14 I quote here from the typescript mentioned in note 4 above.

15 *Proc. Huguenot Soc. of London*, I (1887), 241.

16 J. S. Burn, *History of Foreign Protestant Refugees Settled in England* (1846), pp. 118, 161. By this time, La Chapelle was minister in charge, for in the "Registre des Actes du Consistoire de l'Eglise de Leicesterfields 1698 jusqu'à 1729" are the minutes of a meeting held 6 December 1713 dealing with the election of elders and signed "Ar. De la Chapelle, Ministre." During this period he is also mentioned in the Registers of Rider Court Church, an annex of Leicester Fields; of Glasshouse Street Church; as well as of the Artillery Church. The latter church was formed from Glasshouse Street Church and shared its pastors. See *Pub. Huguenot Soc. of London*, XXX (1927), xi; *Proc. Huguenot Soc. of London*, VIII (1909), 26, 30.

17 *Calendar of Marriage Licences Issued by the Faculty Office, 1632–1714*, ed. G. E. Cokayne and E. A. Fry, Index Library, XXXIII (1905), 271.

18 See above, note 8.

19 *Mémoires historiques, critiques, et littéraires, par feu M. Bruys; avec la Vie de l'Auteur, et un Catalogue raisonné de ses Ouvrages* [ed. P. L. Joly] (Paris: Jean-Thomas Hérissant, 1751), I, 210.

By 1720, La Chapelle had become an important member of the refugee clergy of London. In the preceding year he took over the editorship of the *Bibliothèque Angloise*, begun in 1717 by Michel de la Roche and published at Amsterdam, "chez la Veuve de Paul Marrat."[20] La Roche, the first editor, seems to have been too lenient toward Catholicism and also to have stirred up some hostility in the Walloon circles of Amsterdam. "Je tâcherai de regler mon Goût sur celui du Public," wrote La Chapelle in an *Avertissement* to Volume VI (1719) as he took up the editorship, "& l'on peut s'assûrer par avance que mon inclination pacifique me sera d'un grand secours pour ne rien écrire qui soit contre les regles de la Justice, de l'Honnêteté, de la Bienséance & de la Charité Chrétienne." Two years later (in an *Avertissement* to Volume IX), he told his readers that he had hoped to remain anonymous because of the strong party feeling in London. "Quand on voit un Livre nouveau, la première question que l'on fait en *Angleterre* roule sur le Parti de l'Ecrivain: Est-il *Whig?* Est-il *Tory?* Est-il pour l'Evêque de *Bangor*, ou contre lui?" But, La Chapelle continues, his initials had been deciphered, and his name had become known as editor. He concludes by asking pardon for faults committed.

Il seroit à souhaiter, je l'avoüe, qu'un Journaliste fût toujours sur ses gardes, qu'il n'eût ni préjugés ni foiblesses, qu'il rendit une justice exacte à tous les Auteurs, & qu'il se bornât à faire simplement l'Office de Raporteur. Mais s'il y en a de tel dans le monde, je ne le considere pas avec moins d'admiration que d'envie.

Materials, meanwhile, are to be sent to the following address: "For the Reverend Mr. Armand de la Chapelle, in White Row, Spittlefields, London."

At about this time La Chapelle was appointed to the French Committee for the Distribution of the Royal Bounty. There were many complaints of inequities in allocating these charities, and La Chapelle came in for considerable unpopularity as a result. Several years later, when Aubrey de la Mottraye came to revise his *Travels through Europe*, he criticized La Chapelle for having attacked him, he says (in Volume XII of the *Bibliothèque Angloise* [1725]), because La Mottraye had cited "two or three Instances of the Division amongst the *Refugees,* and Complaints against the *French* Commissioners, or Distributers of the Royal Bounty and other Charity-Money given in *England* (one of whom he happen'd to be,) and [he] takes from hence

[20] At the time La Chapelle became editor, the publication was turned over to Mme Marrat's son, David Paul Marrat, and her son-in-law E. Valat. From Vol. VII (1720) it was published solely by D. P. Marrat, until Vol. XI (1724), when Pierre de Coup became publisher.

an Opportunity to cast the Venom of his Pen on my Person and Works. . . ."21

It was during this busy part of his London career that La Chapelle began to translate the *Tatler,* whether upon his own initiative or at the request of the French booksellers in Holland is not known. His work on the *Bibliothèque Angloise* undoubtedly had increased his interest in English books. Two editions of Volume I, containing *Tatlers* 1–35, appeared at Amsterdam in 1724.22 The first has a wood-engraving of Erasmus on the title page.23

Le / Babillard, / ou / Le Nouvelliste / Philosophe, / *Traduit de l'Anglois* / Par A. D. L. C. / Tome Premier. / [Figure of Erasmus.] / A Amsterdam, / Chez François Changuion, / M.DCC.XXIV. *4, A-T12, V2, X12, Y6. Pp. [vi], 460, [36].

The text of the *Tatler* begins on page 63. Preceding this are La Chapelle's *Epitre Dédicatoire* "a Mr. De F**" (pp. i–vi), La Chapelle's Preface (pp. 1–14), *Prédictions pour l'Année 1708* [by Swift] (pp. 15–34), *Accomplissement de la Prédiction de Mr. Bickerstaff, ou Relation de la Mort de Mr. Partridge . . .* [by Swift] (pp. 34–39), *Apologie du Sieur Isaac Bickerstaff* [= Swift's *Vindication of Isaac Bickerstaff*] (pp. 40–52), *Epitre Dédicatoire de l'Auteur* [= Steele's Dedication to Maynwaring] (pp. 52–55), and *Préface du IV. Volume imprimé en 1711* [by Steele] (pp. 56–62). Then follow the text of *Tatlers* 1–35 (pp. 63–460), a *Table des Matières* (pp. 461–95), and a list of *Errata* (p. 496) consisting of 15 items.

The other edition of 1724 omits "Tome Premier" from the title page, substitutes a wood-engraving of an armillary sphere for that of Erasmus, and omits certain passages from the text.

Le / Babillard, / ou / Le Nouvelliste / Philosophe. / *Traduit de l'Anglois* / Par A. D. L. C. / [Figure.] / A Amsterdam, / Chez François Changuion. / [Rule] / MDCCXXIV. *4, A-S12, T2. Pp. [vi], 404, [32].

This edition contains the same preliminary pieces and has no errata list at the end. It was reprinted in 1725 with a new title page, again with the engraving of an armillary sphere, this time supported by an arm and hand. These two "armillary" volumes are identical except for the title page.

From the start, La Chapelle had generally omitted Steele's articles

21 *Travels through Europe* (3 vols.; London, 1732), I, i. La Mottraye's defense occupies ten pages of an "Advertisement" prefixed to Volume I.

22 In the "Avis du Traducteur" in the second volume, published in 1735, La Chapelle speaks of the first volume as having appeared in 1723. It may have been published toward the close of the year 1723.

23 Designed by Bernard Picart.

headed "From St. James's Coffee-House," which were for the most part reports on the state of the war in Flanders, and also some of the articles "From My Own Apartment," especially when these turned on announcements of new stage performances or other matters of less permanent interest. From the "Armillary Sphere" edition of 1724 and its reprint in 1725, La Chapelle made further omissions, notably passages unusually anti-French in tone or particularly satiric upon Louis XIV. One of these was the article from St. James's Coffee-House (*Tatler* 19) containing the "authentic Letter from Madam Maintenon to Monsieur Torcy." In his first edition La Chapelle had added the following footnote to this letter: "Cette Lettre est purement d'invention. Je n'ai d'autre vûe en la traduisant que de faire voir de quelle maniere on parloit alors en *Angleterre* de l'état de la France, & de quelle maniere parlent tous les Peuples dans la prosperité."[24] Other passages omitted are the letter from Isaac Bickerstaff to Louis XIV (*Tatler* 22), Louis XIV's "reply," followed by Bickerstaff's reflections (*Tatler* 26), and the article from St. James's Coffee-House with the letter to Louis XIV (*Tatler* 29), containing the warning, "There is no governing any but Savages by any Methods but their own Consent."

The translation itself is straightforward and generally accurate, while the footnotes reveal La Chapelle as a well-informed and serious student of the subject matter dealt with in the *Tatler*. Although there is no evidence that he was personally acquainted with Steele, La Chapelle is obviously familiar with his writings and in sympathy with his political and religious views. The references to contemporary figures in the political and literary world of the time are about what we should expect from a regular frequenter of the coffeehouses of London. The footnotes are of interest since they were written within a decade after the first appearance of the *Tatler*. We know from his letters and other writings that La Chapelle was a friend of Desmaizeaux and that he knew Toland well,[25] while in *Le Babillard* itself the anecdotes introduced of Don Saltero are clearly derived from first-hand observation of the man and his famous coffeehouse in Chelsea.[26]

The value of the work which he is translating, La Chapelle writes in his preface, "peut être connu par la grande réputation de l'Auteur,

[24] I, 279.

[25] In a letter to Desmaizeaux of 4 February 1722 (MS. Sloane 4282.f.41) La Chapelle regrets being unable to meet him at the Rainbow Coffeehouse (the one in St. Martin's Lane) and refers to their friends Robethon and de Fonvive (the writer of the *Post-Man*). In the Life of Beausobre (*Remarques*, II, 289) La Chapelle recalls his association with Toland—"qu'il fréquenta long-tems un Caffé où j'allois moi-même, & que nous étions fréquemment en conversation à la même table."

[26] Note to *Tatler* 34: *Le Babillard* ("Erasmus" edition, 1724), I, 448–50.

& par le mérite du SPECTATEUR, dont le Public a si bien reçu l'excellente Traduction qui s'en est faite en *Hollande*." He then reviews the history of publication of the *Tatler* and Steele's reasons for concealing his name. "Courtisan, Soldat, Philosophe, Marchand, Critique, Galant, Censeur, jeune Homme, Vieillard, Fille, Esprit pur; que sai-je? Il pouvait être tout ce qu'il vouloit, pendant qu'on ne le connoissoit point." The pseudonym of Isaac Bickerstaff had been popularized by Swift: "Ce Mr. SWIFT est à présent Doïen de St. *Patrice* à *Dublin*, & depuis bien des années, il est fort connu en *Angleterre* par de petites Pièces qui sont presque toutes d'un tour assez singulier pour venir d'un Homme d'Eglise. Il se pique fort de penser & d'écrire en Cavalier & en Homme du bel air."

La Chapelle goes on to recount the story of the Partridge pamphlets composed by "cet Esprit colère & satiriquë" and the enjoyment of the town over the almanac maker's discomfiture. When Steele assumed the name of Bickerstaff and began to circulate the *Tatler* about London, his work met with universal applause.

Tout le monde voulut se faire honneur d'en sentir les beautez; & l'Auteur y avoit si bien attrapé le goût de son tems & de sa Nation, qu'au milieu d'une Guerre variée par un nombre presque infini d'événemens, tous plus importans les uns que les autres, l'impatience du Nouvelliste ne l'emportoit point sur la curiosité du Bel Esprit, & que l'on se consoloit de la disette qui regnoit quelquefois dans les Réflexions politiques des Gazetiers, par l'heureuse fecondité du BABILLARD, qui tiroit alors de son Imagination de quoi les entretenir agréablement. J'ai ouï dire que la Reine ANNE se faisoit lire le matin ces Feuilles volantes à mesure qu'elles étoient publiées, & que cette lecture lui fit toujours beaucoup de plaisir jusqu'à ce que Mr. STEELE se déclara trop ouvertement, au gré de cette Princesse, contre le changement du Ministere.

La Chapelle concludes by speaking of the difficulties in translating a paper like the *Tatler*, with its characteristic English flavor and its innumerable allusions to affairs of the day. Uncertain as he is of the reception which his translation may receive, he offers the present volume "comme un Essai pour en préssentir le jugement; prêt de ma part à continuer ou à discontinuer les autres, selon la reception qu'y trouvera celui-ci." As for the explanatory notes, "j'ai fait de mon mieux; & cependant je n'oserois me flater de n'être pas tombé dans la faute qu'on reproche aux Commentateurs, c'est-à-dire, d'expliquer les Endroits faciles, & de passer legerement sur les autres." If a second volume should see the light, he hopes to profit from the advice and criticism of readers of this first.

Meantime La Chapelle continued the *Bibliothèque Angloise*, even after his removal to Holland in 1725. An *Avertissement* prefixed to

Part II of Volume XIII (1726) speaks of the year's delay in bringing out this second part (Part I had appeared in 1725):

> L'Auteur de cette *Bibliothèque Angloise* ayant été appellé au service de l'Eglise *Wallonne* de la *Haye*, il ne lui a pas été possible de donner plutôt cette II. Partie du Tome XIII. A l'avenir, s'il plait à Dieu, sa regularité sera plus grande, & si quelques personnes ont des Avis, des Memoires, ou des Extraits à lui fournir, ils pourront s'adresser, en affranchissant les Paquets, ou à Mr. *Du Noyer* Libraire dans le *Strand* à *Londres*, ou à *P. de Coup* dans le *Kalverstraat* à *Amsterdam*, ou à l'Auteur, *Armand de la Chapelle*, Pasteur ordinaire de l'Eglise *Wallonne*, dans le *Kalver-markt*, a la *Haye*.

In 1728, the *Bibliothèque Angloise* was discontinued, and La Chapelle joined with Jean Barbeyrac and others in a new journal, not limited to reviews of English books, but (like the *Bibliothèque ancienne et moderne* of Jean Le Clerc, which had recently been discontinued) reviewing the world of scholarship of western Europe. This new journal, also published at Amsterdam (1728–53), was the *Bibliothèque raisonnée des Ouvrages des Savans de l'Europe*.

In the same year (1728), La Chapelle brought out a translation of another English work, *A Discourse concerning the Resurrection of Jesus Christ*, by the mathematician Humphrey Ditton (1712): *La Religion chrétienne démontrée par la Resurrection de notre Seigneur Jesus-Christ . . . traduit de l'anglois, par A.D.L.C. A Amsterdam chez J. Wetstein, 1728, 2 vols. in-8.* This received a favorable review in the very first number of the *Bibliothèque raisonnée*,[27] the journal published by Wetstein and in part edited by La Chapelle.

It was in the summer of 1725 (25 July) that La Chapelle had received an invitation from the Walloon Church at the Hague to become its pastor. His reasons for making the change are not known. Perhaps there was a combination of factors—the prospect of joining Huguenot friends in Holland, financial advancement,[28] and possibly increasing tension and personal unpopularity in London. At any rate, there seem to have been misgivings among his new parishioners at the Hague. A letter from Madeleine Amsincq (31 July 1725) to her sister Mme Israel Antoine Aufrère, "in Poland Street a Londres," inquires cautiously about the new minister.

> De mon costé je vous demande une grâce de tendre amie. C'est de me dire sincèrement et de bonne foy ce que c'est qu'un Monsieur de la Chapelle, que nous avons apelé pour quatrième ministre. Les sentimens sont si fort partagés sur son conte que je meurs d'envie d'en savoir

---

[27] July–September 1728, pp. 15–29.

[28] La Mottraye, in the "Advertisement" cited above (note 21), says he went to the Hague for the sake of £20 or £30 more per annum (*Travels*, I, ix).

l'exacte vérité, non pas pour en instruire les autres, mais pour me satisfaire moy même, car je vous promets un secret inviolable. Mais je demande le fort et le foible de tous les costés, tant pour son humeur et son âge que pour son génie et pour sa prédication.[29]

The information that Mme Aufrère supplied was evidently disturbing, for Madeleine Amsincq writes again, a month later (14 August):

Je vous tiens grand conte de celles que vous aves prises pour me donner une idée juste de nostre ministre et je vous réponds que cela demeurera uniquement entre vous et moy. Je compasserois aisément ses bonnes et ses mauvaises qualités sans son humeur satirique, mais j'avoue que cela me parâit jurer avec le caractère et que j'ay bien de la peine à croire qu'il puisse surmonter la prévention que nostre esglise paroit avoir contre lui; il n'i a que la main dont il nous vient qui puisse faire avaler la pillule.[30]

The *humeur satirique* of the new pastor was to find expression in controversies at the Hague, notably when Volume II of the *Tatler* came to be translated.

La Chapelle left London in the autumn of 1725. Pastor Chion, of the Hague, was commissioned to confirm him after the three usual proclamations, and he was duly installed pastor on 11 November. In spite of the rumors that had preceded him, La Chapelle seems at first to have enjoyed a considerable degree of success. At the opening of the Synod of Rotterdam (19 May 1729), he was chosen to preach the sermon. Two years later, the Consistory of the Hague church again selected La Chapelle as its deputy to the Synod to be held at Heusden (in September 1731). Charles-Pierre Chais was elected to replace him if necessary, and since Chais is recorded as having spoken in the assembly, La Chapelle did not, apparently, attend.[31] His absence from the Synod of Heusden suggests that difficulties were already arising between La Chapelle and some of his colleagues. During the last fifteen years of his life, he was in fact involved in more than one controversy waged both in the press and the pulpit by members—lay and clerical—of the Walloon churches.

The first of these, a dispute with the Rev. Paul Maty, minister and catechist of an Église de Charité at the Hague, arose over the publication in 1730 of Maty's *Lettre d'un théologien à un autre théologien, sur le mystère de la Trinité*, in which the author contended that there were three natures in Jesus Christ—divine, angelic, and human—and

[29] *The Aufrère Papers: Calendar and Selections*, ed. Winifred Turner (Publications Huguenot Society of London, XL, 1940), p. 141.

[30] *Ibid.*, p. 146.

[31] Articles of Synods of Walloon Churches: Synod of Heusden, September 1731, Art. XXIII (typescript in Library of Huguenot Society of London).

that He was thus God, Angel, and Man. Although Maty claimed to have consulted in advance the four Walloon pastors at the Hague—Theodore Huet, Chais, Chion, and La Chapelle—his book was immediately attacked by La Chapelle and the author officially censured by the Synod of Campen (in May 1730). In spite of Maty's charge that La Chapelle had persuaded his friend Jérémie Frescarode, pastor at Rotterdam, to prevent free discussion by intimidating the Synod, La Chapelle's position in condemning Maty was confirmed four months later by the Synod at the Hague, which condemned Maty's views.[32] In this controversy, La Chapelle clearly had majority support, but in some of the pamphlets which circulated at the time he was accused of intolerance and high-handed action.

La Chapelle soon became involved in another and more serious quarrel, this time with the eminent Huguenot preacher at the Hague, Jacques Saurin. In his large-scale *Discours historiques, critiques, théologiques & moraux, sur les Événemens les plus remarquables du Vieux & du Nouveau Testament,*[33] Saurin had somewhat imprudently inserted a long digression on the controversial topic of the "officious lie."[34] Commenting on the text from *I Samuel* in which the Lord seemed to authorize Samuel to conceal the truth concerning his mission to anoint David King of Israel,[35] Saurin reviewed the arguments supporting and opposing the *mensonge officieux* and, while not actually committing himself to either side, clearly implied that in this case the "lie" had a certain divine sanction.

Saurin's *Discours* had received high praise in the October–December 1728 issue of the *Bibliothèque raisonnée*,[36] but an article in the following number, for January–March 1729, obviously by a different writer, attacked both book and author.[37] The first writer, one Aymon, by submitting the manuscript of his review to Saurin for his approval,[38] had violated his agreement with the publishers of the journal, since all its contributors had agreed to remain anonymous. The pub-

---

[32] See the *Entretien entre MM. La Chapelle & Maty, au sujet de la Lettre d'un Théologien sur le Mystère de la Trinité* (La Haye, 1730).

[33] Two vols., folio; La Haye: Pierre de Hondt, 1728.

[34] Latin *mendacium officiosum,* "a lie told as an act of kindness to further another's interests" (*OED*).

[35] "And the Lord said unto Samuel, . . . I will send thee to Jesse the Beth-lehemite: for I have provided me a king among his sons. And Samuel said, How can I go? if Saul hear it, he will kill me. And the Lord said, Take an heifer with thee, and say, I am come to sacrifice to the Lord (I Samuel 16:1-2).

[36] *Bibl. rais.,* I, 400–16.

[37] *Ibid.,* II, 176–219.

[38] *Ibid.,* III (October–December 1729), 280.

lishers, Wetstein and Smith, accordingly rejected Aymon's second article and informed him that another and "more suitable" writer had been found. This was La Chapelle.

There was more behind the change, however, than this. Pierre de Hondt, the publisher of Saurin's *Discours*, had recently set up a subsidiary establishment in Frankfurt, which was seriously encroaching on the German trade of Wetstein and Smith, so that the latter saw that one of their best methods of revenge was to ruin the sale of Saurin's book. La Chapelle, moreover, who had aligned himself with the other Walloon ministers, Chion, Chais, and Huet (Saurin's clerical rivals at the Hague), and who seems himself to have regarded Saurin's popularity with distaste, if not envy, was ready to seize on the *mensonge officieux* dissertation as a method of embarrassing the much talked of preacher. "Ma faute, si c'en est une," La Chapelle remarked later, "est d'avoir dit haut ce que les Savans se disent tout bas, & de m'être hazardé à rompre la glace. Il y a 20. ans que cet Ecrivain se donne des airs de superiorité, qui ne lui appartiennent en aucune façon."[39]

La Chapelle's attack on Saurin occupies over forty pages of the January–March 1729 issue of the *Bibliothèque raisonnée*. It is in part a skillful and well-argued refutation of the doctrine of the "officious lie."

Il est visible que le but unique de sa *Dissertation* tend à prouver qu'il est des circonstances où le mensonge n'est pas criminel. Il est visible encore qu'il fait cette *Dissertation* au sujet d'un Mensonge où il pretend que Dieu est tombé. Il est visible par conséquent qu'il s'y propose d'y disculper Dieu de ce crime, non en niant l'accusation, mais en absolvant le Prevenu qu'il avoit mis comme sur la Sallette. Donc, selon lui, Dieu a pu, & peut mentir en certaines rencontres, parce qu'il est des rencontres où l'on peut recourir au Mensonge sans être coupable.[40]

But much of the article is less fair. In more than one place, La Chapelle just hints a fault and hesitates dislike. Saurin's reputation as a preacher, he suggests, is no guarantee of the soundness of his views. Saurin may be caressed by the great, and especially by the ladies, but his written words may be thin and silly. And there is more than a hint that false eloquence, borrowed learning, and an overinflated reputation in preaching may be responsible for Saurin's vogue.

La Chapelle followed this up with a second attack in the same journal exactly a year later (January–March 1730), apropos of a separate printing of the *Dissertation sur le mensonge*. La Chapelle's anonymity was well guarded, at least for a while, and Amsterdam and the Hague

[39] *Ibid.*   [40] Pages 215–16.

were both filled with speculations as to who the writer was. Saurin was ill at the time and made no rejoinder, but an anonymous defense appeared in Volume II (1729) of the *Lettres sérieuses & badines sur les Ouvrages des Savans & sur d'autres matières*, by La Barre de Beaumarchais, ironically dedicated "to the authors of the *Bibliothèque raisonnée*."

The noisiest defender of Saurin, however, was the young French traveler François Bruys (he was only 22 at the time), who threw himself into the quarrel with zest. Since Bruys had been a Roman Catholic—and was to return to the fold before the close of his short life—he may have relished the internecine struggles which he witnessed in the favored land of Bayle and Le Clerc. The tone of his letters, at any rate, is that of a delighted onlooker: now he speculates on the motives behind the quarrel, now he circulates an epigram on the affair, now he seeks an interview with Saurin himself to report his side of the controversy. Throughout the year 1730, he published a kind of periodical under the title *Critique désintéressée des journaux littéraires et des Ouvrages des Savans*, supposedly written "par une Societé de Gens de Lettres."[41] In the first volume, he identifies Saurin's adversary and names the motive behind the attacks:

> *Saurin* est un grand Orateur;
> On ne peut trop priser ses talens & son zele.
> Point, point; c'est un Blasphemateur,
> Repond brusquement L. C . . . /
> Effraié de ce nom, je m'informe en tous lieux,
> J'apprens enfin d'où vient le transport qui l'anime;
> Il a parbleu raison, sa haine est legitime;
> Le Public a jugé que *Saurin* prêche mieux.[42]

Although professing to be a friend of La Chapelle, Bruys constantly portrays him as the aggressor in the quarrel. "Ce n'étoit," he wrote several years later in his *Mémoires*, "que la jalousie qui fit naître cette querelle; & je proteste que M. de la Chapelle m'a dit qu'il n'avoit eu d'autre dessein que d'humilier son adversaire."[43] According to Bruys, it was at the home of Chion, "dans la gaieté d'un repas," that La Chapelle, Huet, Chais, and Chion conspired to get the question of Saurin's orthodoxy officially brought up before the Synod of Walloon churches meeting at the Hague in September; and he prints an amusing poem on the meeting of the four conspirators, with Mme Chion in the role of Pilate's wife, vainly protesting against the plot.[44] The outcome was

41 Three vols.; La Haye: Chrétien Van Lom, 1730.
42 *Critique désintéressée*, I (January–March 1730), 256.
43 *Mémoires*, I, 224. The *Mémoires* were written in 1737.
44 *Ibid.*, I, 235–36.

that Saurin did appear before the Synod and signed a declaration (7 September 1730) disclaiming any unorthodox interpretation of the "officious lie." Although the church at Leyden attempted to smooth over the affair, the warfare continued. Encouraged by what he said was an oral promise from Saurin, Bruys published a "defense" in the third volume of his *Critique désintéressée* but in such extreme language that Bruys felt it wise to flee to England for a time until the storm died down. La Chapelle also returned to the attack with an *Examen de la manière de precher des Protestans françois*,[45] a discussion in dialogue form on public worship and the style of sermons, with quotations from Saurin to illustrate the use of false rhetoric in the pulpit.

Saurin's death occurred while tension was at its height. Bruys, who found himself under fire from both sides, announced the news in a letter to Desmaizeaux, dated "La Haye le 2 Janvier 1731."

> Je vous apprends, avec douleur, la mort de Saurin. J'ai badiné avec vous tandis qu'il etoit en pleine santé; mais à present je ne vous dissimulerai point que je le regrette & que je le plains. On assure qu'il est mort de chagrin, & cela pourroit bien être vrai. Si M^r. De la Chapelle etoit le Theologien de la Bibliothèque Raisonnée, ne croiez-vous pas qu'il auroit de grands reproches à se faire?

La Chapelle, he continues, and the other three ministers (Chion, Chais, and Huet) are being publicly called Saurin's executioners, while Bruys himself is also coming in for a share of the blame.

> Mais ce qu'il y a de plus plaisant encore, c'est que je deviens le Bouc Hazaël. On me charge de toutes les iniquitez du Peuple de Dieu; car tandis que d'un côté les Amis de M^r. Saurin evaporent sur moi toute leur bile, nos Ministres publient que je parle mal d'eux. C'est ce que l'epouse de M^r. De La Chapelle a dit ce matin à Scheurleer [the bookseller]. Cependant, rien n'est plus faux; & je puis protester que depuis mon retour il ne m'est rien échapé de desobligeant sur le compte de ces Messieurs que j'estime reellement.[46]

Another letter from Bruys to Desmaizeaux (6 February 1731) comments on Saurin's death, in a somewhat light-hearted way, and reports that people are still wondering who wrote the articles in the *Bibliothèque raisonnée*. "Il faut d'absolue necessité qu'un Demon agite les trois quarts des gens à la Haye.[47] A week later he alludes to an intrigue that Saurin is alleged to have had with Mlle Frescarode [sister of Jérémie Frescarode, the minister at Rotterdam and friend of La

---

[45] Amsterdam: J. Cóvens & C. Mortier, 1730.

[46] MS Sloane 4281.f.330.

[47] *Ibid.* f.332.

Chapelle]: "le bruit est assez public ici que S. fit, dans l'occasion dont il s'agit, un bel enfant à la dite Demoiselle. Je ne voudrois pourtant pas garantir la verité de ce fait, car on publie tant de faussetés que cela fait pitié. . . ."[48] On 20 March he reports to Desmaizeaux that the author of the articles in the *Bibliothèque raisonnée* is known.

On vient de m'assurer que M[r]. D. L. C. est découvert à la Cour de Hollande pour etre cet Auteur Anonime qui [a] tant crié contre M. Saurin. Je serois mortifié que cette nouvelle fut veritable. M[r]. D. L. C. est un homme franc & droit pour qui j'ai beaucoup d'estime. Je le distingue infiniment de ses Collegues, & surtout de C[hio]n.[49]

In his *Mémoires*, Bruys probably exaggerates the extent of the reaction against La Chapelle ("On évitoit sa rencontre dans les rues; on s'absentoit de ses Sermons; on ne vouloit plus recevoir la Communion de ses mains"),[50] but there was doubtless a certain amount of ill feeling engendered against him. Bruys himself, however, had been summoned by the States General to court for some of the reckless statements he had made in the third volume of the *Critique désintéressée*. The process, which lasted for several months, ended in the condemnation of Bruys (July 1731), who soon after left Holland, never to return. The Consistory of the Hague, meeting in August, accepted an apology from La Chapelle for the violence of his language and declared the *mensonge officieux* controversy closed.

Peace now seemed at hand. Saurin was no longer living, Bruys had left the scene, and La Chapelle might—one would think—have allowed the matter to rest. But apparently he could not forget some of the ill feeling aroused against him in the charges and countercharges that arose from the controversy. He found his opportunity for revenge in bringing out, four years later, a second volume of his translation of the *Tatler*.

In the "Avis du Traducteur" prefixed to the new volume, La Chapelle explains that when *Le Babillard* had appeared, there were several sheets of manuscript left over, yet not enough to fill a second volume. Various "distractions" and lack of time had prevented him from going on with the task. Now that he has the necessary leisure, he has decided to revise the earlier volume and accompany it with a second, containing *Tatlers* 36–76. After a general statement on the laudable aims of Steele's writing ("la correction des Mœurs, & la connoissance de l'Homme"), La Chapelle disingenuously remarks that he has always welcomed criticism and only seeks to profit from it.

[48] *Ibid.* f.340 (to Desmaizeaux, 13 February 1731).

[49] *Ibid.* f.346.

[50] I, 284.

Je puis dire, qu'en bien des rencontres, la haine, que l'on m'a témoignée, ne m'a inspiré que des sentimens de reconnoissance. Souvent mes plus grands Ennemis m'ont fait appercevoir, dans ma Personne, & dans mes Écrits, des imperfections, que l'Amour propre, ou que l'Amitié m'y auroient, peut-être, caché toute ma vie. Je ne saurois donc me résoudre à vouloir aucun mal, à ceux qui me rendent de semblables services, & toute la Vengeance, que je tire de celui qu'ils ont voulu me faire, consiste à mettre à profit les sages conseils qu'ils me donnent, en faisant tout ce qui m'est possible pour me corriger. Aussi n'eurent-ils jamais de moi d'autre Réponse, & jamais n'en auront-ils d'autre.[51]

Far from receiving criticism in silence and profiting from it, La Chapelle went so far as to insert an attack on Saurin in this second volume of his translation of the *Tatler*. "Le Babillard, traduit de l'Anglois de Mr. Steel [in–] 12. Tome II," is announced as in press in the July–September 1734 issue of the *Bibliothèque raisonnée*, and a year later (July–September 1735) the same journal includes it in its list of "new books published." This second volume was issued by the same publisher, François Changuion:

Le / Babillard, / ou / Le Nouvelliste / Philosophe. / *Traduit de l'Anglois.* / Par A. D. L. C. / Tome Second. / [Ornament: figure of Erasmus.] / *A Amsterdam,* / Chez François Changuion, / M. DCC. XXXV. *[6], A-V[12], X[11]. Pp. [x], 487, [15].

The running title, however, was *Le Philosophe Nouvelliste*, which La Chapelle seems to have felt better expressed the spirit of Steele's work, and this he adopted as the title when both Volumes I and II were reissued later in the same year. Some copies of this edition retain the engraving of Erasmus on the title page, while others have a new one, showing a child seated in a garden, with the legend, *Tot pendebunt et ab Arbore Poma.* The title page of Volume I reads:

Le / Philosophe / Nouvelliste, / Traduit de l'Anglois / *De Mr. Steele,* / Par A. D. L. C. / *Seconde Edition revue & corrigee.* / *Tome Premier.* / [Ornament.] / *A Amsterdam,* / *Chez François Changuion.* / M. DCC. XXXV. *[4], A-V[12], X[10]. Pp. [vi], 476, [24].

Both copies of Volume II (*Le Babillard* and *Le Philosophe Nouvelliste*) are identical as far as Signature Q (page 361). The next 52 pages (pages 361–412) are from a different setting of type and in part (pages 373–410) contain entirely new matter. The reason for this was an attack on the memory of Saurin, which La Chapelle had inserted in the first edition of Volume II and which he found it desirable to withdraw in the second edition. This was Article XXXIV.

Article XXXIII had been based on *Tatler* 68, and the reader of

51 *5–*5v.

Article XXXIV would expect to find there a translation of No. 69, especially since it is dated "Du Jeudi 15. au Samedi 17. Septembre 1709" (the correct date for *Tatler* 69). Actually, however, it has nothing to do with Steelé's paper, but is an independent article by La Chapelle. It begins with a letter signed "Guillaume Bâtonfranc" warning Bickerstaff of a conspiracy against him, started by a certain Mlle Martin. (This was the name La Chapelle had used in Article XVII to translate Steele's "My Lady Courtly" of *Tatler* 62.) Bâton-franc proceeds to inform Bickerstaff that she had interpreted his praise of her as satire and that she was now offended. Crying out to the trees in St. James's Park "Biquerstaff est un Voleur! Biquerstaff est un Brigand!" she is stirring up ill will and even inducing a Member of Parliament to start proceedings against him as a Jacobite in disguise. She has also persuaded Madonelle and her "Cloître de Protestantes *Angloises*" to foster indignation against Bickerstaff. These Protestant nuns, who like to make vices seem virtues, try to make insipid orators (such as Saurin?) seem greater preachers than Barrow or Tillotson.[52] ("Madonelle" and her followers refer to Volume I of *Le Babillard* and *Tatler* 32, where Steele had in fact described one Madonella and an "Order of Platonick Ladies.")

The satire in this passage was too obvious to pass unnoticed by contemporary readers. Mlle Martin, here mentioned by name, was at once seen to be the daughter of David Martin (former pastor of the Walloon Church at Utrecht), a young woman known to be a friend and admirer of Saurin. As for Madonelle, a certain Mlle de Perai (or Peray) quickly recognized herself as the original of this character. In the declaration made against La Chapelle at the Synod of Flushing the following year, one of the charges read: "On sait qu'il y a une Societé de Dames Protestantes à La Haye connues sous le nom de Dames du Cloître à la tête desquelles est Mademoiselle de *Perai*, qui avoit témoigné une estime particulière pour Monsieur *Saurin*, aussi bien que Mademoiselle *Martin* fille de . . . Mr. *Martin* (en son vivant Pasteur d'Utrecht)."[53]

In the remainder of Article XXXIV,[54] Bickerstaff tells the story of a visit which he paid in his youth to a country village, where to his amazement he found the curate ostracized by the squire and most of the villagers. After a series of inquiries, he finally learns the reason for this state of affairs from the landlady at the inn. The squire's lady, it seems, owned a parrot, which was the darling of all the women of the

[52] II, 384–85.

[53] Articles of Synods, Flushing, May 1736, Art. LII (typescript in Library of the Huguenot Society of London).

[54] II, 391–411.

region. Even the landlady had succumbed to his charms. "Je ne dirai pas," she says to Bickerstaff, "que je fusse la seule; car je mentirois. Il aimoit le Sexe, & le Sexe l'aimoit. . . .

Son indifference même étoit piquante, parce qu'il avoit toujours, pour les plus abandonnées, certains petits coups d'œil, certains regards flatteurs, qui ne laissoient jamais éteindre le desir de lui plaire. Ajoutez à cela, Monsieur, qu'il avoit effectivement des charmes irresistibles, quand il vouloit se donner quelques soins pour se rendre maître d'un Cœur.[55]

The curate, waiting one day in the squire's anteroom, was insulted by some rude remarks made by the parrot, whereupon he took out a pencil and rapped the bird's claws. The parrot, who had hitherto known only caresses, raised an uproar in the house with his cries. All was in confusion; the squire's lady fainted; and soon the whole village—following the lead of the squire—turned against the unlucky curate. "Jugez à présent, Monsieur," the landlady concludes, "s'il y eut de ressentiment plus juste, & si un Pasteur qui a donné un si grand scandale à son Troupeau n'en mérite pas l'execration. Ha! Monsieur *Bickerstaff,* donner sur les pattes du beau Perroquet!"[56]

It seems an innocuous tale, but to contemporary readers there was no mistaking the allusion. Like Saurin, the parrot "eut le don de la parole . . . : il parloit bien, avec grace, avec esprit, avec finesse." Like Saurin, the parrot "s'emancipoit un peu quelquefois. . . . S'il lui arrivoit pourtant de dire des duretez, & même des choses choquantes [as Saurin had done over the *mensonge officieux*], nous disions tous qu'il étoit fort imprudent. Mais cela ne venoit que de la vivacité de son esprit."[57] Like Saurin (in La Chapelle's eyes), the parrot was a gallant. The landlady is in raptures as she recalls the parrot's caresses. "Il me baisoit si tendrement le bout des Doigts, les yeux, la Bouche, la Gorge, tout ce qu'il pouvoit! J'en suis encore dans les transports quand je me le rappelle. Les Caresses de mon Mari, même quand il n'étoit qu'Amant, n'en approcherent jamais."[58] And the curate of the village undoubtedly represents La Chapelle himself—one who did not apprecie the parrot's powers or popularity, one who dared to rap the bird on the knuckles, and one who in consequence suffered the boycott of the villagers, as La Chapelle had suffered for a time the resentment of Saurin's friends at the Hague.

Saurin's son Philippe—as well as Mademoiselles Martin and de Perai —was quick to protest to the Consistory of the Walloon church at the Hague. Receiving no answer, they complained (2 June 1736) to the Synod assembled at Flushing of this "ouvrage de Mr *de la Chapelle*

[55] II, 406–7.
[56] II, 410–11.
[57] II, 408–9.
[58] II, 405.

intitulé *le Babillard* ou *le Nouvelliste Philosophe* & de la conduite que l'Eglise de *la Haye* a tenue au sujet du dit Ouvrage.[59] There were additional complaints—from the churches at Dordrecht and Heusden, among others.

A committee of seven appointed by the Synod examined the book and reported later in June that "Mr. *Armand de la Chapelle* a rendu ses intentions suspectes, par l'Art. XXXIV. du 2. Tome, dont il n'y a pas un seul mot dans l'*Anglois*. . . ." It declared the work to be blasphemous and expressed disapproval of his whole attitude in translating the *Tatler*. Though he had suppressed passages likely to offend French ears, he should also have taken care to avoid personal satire.

Certainement Mr. *de la Chapelle* auroit bien dû avoir les même égards pour les idées des vrais Chrétiens & pour les oreilles chastes. Il auroit bien dû supprimer la profanation, avec laquelle il a mêlé les traits satyriques & les paroles libres qu'il s'est permis, avec . . . le sacré nom de Dieu, & des assurances de zele pour le service divin & pour l'observation du jour du repos.[60]

By Article LXI of the Acts of the Synod of Flushing, La Chapelle was automatically suspended from his ministerial duties, but actually the order could not be put into practice because the consent of the States General was not forthcoming. Although the Synod had officially condemned his book for "des impuretez, des profanations, des Railleries aux Orthodoxes, un air de Satyre violente,"[61] opinions were still divided, and La Chapelle continued his duties at the Hague in spite of his nominal suspension. It was not until August 1741 that he finally answered the summons which the Synod of Flushing had issued in 1736. Without offering any explanation of his five years' delay, he appeared before the Synod assembled at Rotterdam and submitted an apology for having written and published Article XXXIV. "Je suis vivement touché d'avoir donné du scandale par cette Pièce; je désavouë tout ce qui peut y avoir fait de la peine, de quelque nature que cela soit. . . ." By this time the Commissioners were willing to accept this as amply fulfilling the demands of the Synod of Flushing, and the churches that had complained agreed that it met their objection. The "suspension" was lifted and the commission disbanded.

During the early weeks of the storm which had been raised by the publication of his Volume II, La Chapelle compiled a new essay to replace the offending Article XXXIV. The substituted piece is a disquisition on the dangers of excessive drinking, with quotations from Horace and Erasmus, and with a number of anecdotes, drawn princi-

[59] Articles of Synods, Art. XXXVII.

[60] *Ibid.*, Art. LIII.

[61] *Ibid.*, Art. LIX.

pally from Grimarest's biography of Molière. There was, however, no official pressure brought upon the publisher to suppress the original article, and Changuion apparently made up copies of *Le Philosophe Nouvelliste* sometimes with the substituted article and at other times with the original essay.[62] Moreover, in two later editions of La Chapelle's translation—one published at Basel in 1737 and the other at Zurich in 1737–38—the first contains the original article satirizing Saurin while the second prints instead the substituted essay.[63]

For the remainder of his life, until his death in 1746, La Chapelle appears to have carried on his pastoral duties at the Hague without dissension among his parishioners or opposition from outside. He continued writing for the *Bibliothèque raisonnée;* the majority of the theological articles in this journal have been attributed to him. In 1738, Wetstein and Smith brought out his translation of another English work, Richard Bentley's *Remarks upon a Late Discourse of Freethinking* (1713), an attack upon Anthony Collins:

La Friponnerie laïque des prétendus esprits-forts d'Angleterre; ou remarques de Philaleuthère de Leipsick sur le Discours de la liberté de penser. Traduites de l'anglois sur la septième édition, par Mr. N. N. A Amsterdam: Chez J. Wetstein & G. Smith, 1738. Pp. xxxvi, 582.

Four years later, La Chapelle edited the *Remarques historiques, critiques et philologiques, sur le Nouveau Testament* of Isaac de Beausobre, to which he added a biography of Beausobre.[64] Much of this work was done in spite of declining health. Guillaume Smith (Wetstein's son-in-law and partner) wrote to Desmaizeaux from Amsterdam on 2 December 1738:

Je suis bien mortifié de vous devoir apprendre l'indisposition de notre digne Ami Monsr De la Chapelle, il a eu une Attaque de Paralisie, il y a environ quinse jours, laquelle l'a tellement ebranlé qu'il a eté obligé depuis ce tems là de ne travailler plus ni pour la Chaire ni pour le Public. Il se porte beaucoup mieux, mais ce vilain mal quand il attacque une Personne, qui ne doit pas etre loin de sa Climaterique [La Chapelle was in his sixty-second year], laisse presque toujours quelques cruelles traces de son pouvoir & de sa malignité. Esperons & faisons des Voeux pour un meilleur sort à notre digne & estimable Ami.[65]

[62] The copy of *Le Philosophe Nouvelliste*, Vol. II, in the Bayrische Staatsbibliothek at Munich (Per.170.h.2) has the offending Article XXXIV; the copy in the Bibliothèque publique et universitaire at Geneva (994.Hge) has the substituted article.

[63] *Le Babillard, ou Le Nouvelliste Philosophe* (Basel: J. Brandmuller & Fils, 1737, 2 vols.). *Le Philosophe Nouvelliste* (Zurich: Conrad Orell & Cie, 1737–38, 2 vols.).

[64] *Remarques historiques* (2 vols.; La Haye: Chez Pierre de Hondt, 1742), II, 253–320.

[65] MS Sloane 4288.f.150.

La Chapelle's last work, and the one for which he is still perhaps best known, was published the year of his death, which occurred on 8 August 1746. This was *La Nécessité du Culte public parmi les Chrétiens*,[66] an account of the sufferings of the French Protestants in the eighteenth century, a vindication of their loyalty to the French crown, and a defense of their right of assembly.

The *Bibliothèque raisonnée* summed up the character of its late writer with a judicious mixture of praise and criticism:

Ce qui mérite bien encore d'être admiré dans feu Mr. *de la Chapelle*, c'est qu'avec des connoissances très étendues il n'étoit point de ces Savans empesés & bourus, d'une humeur chagrine & pédantesque, qui ne plaisent que dans leurs Livres. Celui-ci étoit d'un caractère liant & d'un agréable commerce; sa conversation pleine d'esprit étoit enjouée & badine, & il se proportionnoit sans affectation au gout & à la portée de ceux avec qui il se trouvoit. Tout ce qu'on peut lui reprocher, c'est peut-être un peu trop de penchant à la Satyre. Heureux, s'il avoit toujours su le réprimer, & si, en voulant quelquefois mortifier les autres, il n'avoit pas répandu lui-même de l'amertume sur les plus beaux jours de sa vie![67]

Two other characterizations may be cited. The first, from Guillaume Smith, who had published much of La Chapelle's work, is from the letter (2 December 1738) cited above. Smith thought him "la personne de tout le Clergé françois dont je fais le plus de cas, en qualité d'Homme d'esprit, d'Homme Savant, & d'Homme d'honneur,—habile Journaliste & excellent Traducteur."[68] The second, from the hostile François Bruys, does not fail to mention La Chapelle's "satiric bent" but pays tribute to his more engaging qualities.

Ses écrits lui auroient fait une belle réputation, s'il avoit eu l'attention d'y marquer moins son penchant à la Satire. Son stile est agréable par les traits vifs dont il est rempli, quoiqu'il soit peu Académique. Il est sociable, & sans fierté. Il prétend que les cérémonies sont un effet de l'orgueil de ceux qui s'y assujétissent. Il a du sçavoir. Sa conversation est amusante & vive, son regard est sombre & malin. Il sourit d'une manière piquante & satirique.[69]

The greater part of La Chapelle's most important work—the editing of the *Bibliothèque Angloise*, the writing for the *Bibliothèque raisonnée*, and his translation of the *Tatler*—was done in an environment peculiarly suited to his talents. Holland had already become in the days of Bayle and Le Clerc one of the intellectual centers of western

[66] La Haye: Chez F. H. Scheurleer, 1746.

[67] XXXVIII (January–March 1747), 89.

[68] MS Sloane 4288.f.150.

[69] *Mémoires* (Paris, 1751), I, 209 (written in 1737).

Europe. Although he lacked the erudition of either of these men, La Chapelle had read widely in both French and English literature, and his journalistic work as well as his translations did much to spread a knowledge of English ideas on the Continent. His translation of the *Tatler* was reprinted, as we have seen, both in Basel and in Zurich. When J. D. Tietze came to translate the *Tatler* into German, some twenty years later, he not only made use of La Chapelle's footnotes but he also reprinted (in German) the two introductions from the 1724 and 1735 French versions of the *Tatler*.[70]

La Chapelle's footnotes were of course designed first of all to elucidate difficult passages for French readers. He not only explains many colloquial words and locutions, but he often stops to comment on English manners and customs. A typical example is his note on the sentence "I never saw above the First Act of a Play" in *Tatler* 26: "On rend l'argent à ceux qui sortent à la fin du I. Acte."[71] He often reports contemporary identifications of characters, such as Bentivolio in *Tatler* 7, who is regarded by some as Bentley and by others as Blackmore; or Timon in *Tatler* 9, who is spoken of as the Duke of Ormonde ("Bien des gens soupçonnerent qu'il désignoit le Duc d'O . . . . nd, dont tous les Domestiques se sont enrichis à ses dépens").[72] The dispute between Bishops Blackall and Hoadly, the ill feeling between Marlborough and Argyle—these and many other current topics find their place in La Chapelle's notes. For annotation, he draws on Tacitus, Horace, Suetonius, and of course the Bible, as well as such recent works as Browne's *Religio Medici* and Burnet's *History*. His comment on the first letter in *Tatler* 72 shows his own sympathy with Steele's political views:

> Le but secret de la Lettre & des Réflexions qui la suivent est de caractériser l'Esprit [du] Despotisme. Les Droits du Pouvoir absolu sont toujours les mêmes, & si tous les Princes, qui s'en trouvent revêtus, ne sont pas des *Nérons*, ce n'est pas qu'ils ne puissent l'être, s'ils veulent. Le grand Objet des *Whigs* est donc de faire envisager de ce côte-là le Gouvernement despotique, pour le rendre odieux.[73]

He also has interesting things to say of Steele the writer. One quotation must suffice. "On reprochoit à Mr. *Steel* de jetter souvent au hazard ses pensées, & de ne mettre aucune liaison sensible entre elles. La chose n'étoit que trop vraye. . . . Ce défaut n'est pas une des moin-

---

[70] *Der Schwätzer: Eine Sittenschrift, aus dem Englischen des Herrn Richard Steele* (2 vols.; Leipzig: In Lankischens Buchhandlung, 1756). Copy in University of California Library at Berkeley.

[71] *Le Babillard* (1724), i, 343.

[72] *Ibid.*, I, 156.

[73] *Le Philosophe Nouvelliste* (1735), II, 437.

dres peines que l'on trouve à traduire cet Ecrivain, & j'avoue que ma patience a été plus d'une fois mise à bout. . . ."[74]

In converting the *Tatler* into French, even if incompletely, La Chapelle was not merely introducing Steele to foreign readers—he was helping to initiate a new genre on the Continent, a literary form that was to have an enormous vogue not only in France but throughout western Europe. It is impossible to read La Chapelle's version, including introductions and notes, without feeling that here was a contemporary admirably suited to reproducing in another language the peculiar tone and spirit of Steele's periodical essay. In his fondness for new ideas, in his dislike of autocratic rule whether in church or state, and especially in his impulsive and even reckless behavior, La Chapelle seems almost like a French counterpart of Steele. An encounter between the two in the shades would have made an interesting addition to that other favorite genre of the eighteenth century, the *Dialogues des Morts*.

[74] *Ibid.*, II, 357 (*Tatler* 67).

BONAMY DOBRÉE

Horace Walpole

O<small>N</small> 20 A<small>UGUST</small> 1758, Horace Walpole wrote to George Montagu:

You cannot imagine how astonished a Mr. Seward, a learned clergyman, was, who came to Ragley while I was there. Strolling about the house, he saw me first sitting on the pavement of the lumber-room, with Louis, all over cobwebs and dirt and mortar; then found me in his own room on a ladder writing on a picture: and half an hour afterwards lying on the grass in the court with the dogs and the children, in my slippers and without my hat. He had some doubt whether I was the painter or the factotum of the family; but you would have died at his surprise when he saw me walk into dinner dressed and sit by Lady Hertford. Lord Lyttelton was there, and the conversation turned on literature: finding me not quite ignorant added to the parson's wonder; but he could not contain himself any longer, when after dinner he saw me go to romps and jumping with the two boys; he broke out to my Lady Hertford, and begged to know what sort of man I really was, for he had never met anything of the kind. Adieu!

Even today we can to some extent share the puzzlement of the worthy Canon of Lichfield as to the sort of man Horace Walpole really was. Not so long ago he was treated almost entirely as a provider of source material for historians of the eighteenth century. From Archdeacon Coxe onward, the earlier writers used him lavishly, some of them to the virtual exclusion of every other source, one later historian being heard to mutter bitterly: "Coxe—*et preteria nihil.*" Historians have their ways, but men of letters might well doubt how far it might be wise to accept the opinions of a man who declared that the finest writers of his day were Lords Chesterfield and Bath, with Soane Jenyns, Coventry, and even lesser others, as if at that date, 1753, Fielding, Richardson, Johnson, or Hume might not merit a little attention. We see, of course, what Walpole meant; good writing was to be like the best conversation of educated gentlemen. Historians today are, naturally, more cautious in relying on Walpole, and though

BONAMY DOBRÉE was formerly professor of English at the University of Leeds.

they will, with reservations, accept his statements, they look askance at his deductions and opinions. Romney Sedgwick is of the opinion that "a safe rule to go on is that his facts are first class, and his generalisations worthless."

This is an illuminating judgment, and accepting it, the reasons for it may perhaps come clear as we go along. To put one of them crudely, we can say that Walpole was at least this much of an artist: he could not leave facts alone: he had to mold them into a form, establish relations between them, give them significance, or wash them over with a color that made them seem congruous with the picture of society that he had formed. He worries at a fact, twists it and turns it, rationalizes, as we say, the motives of the actors until they suit his view. Sometimes he so much wanted a thing to be true that he forgot that he had invented it; as in his famous declaration that Stone, the Duke of Newcastle's secretary and "other self," and Murray, afterward Lord Mansfield, were Jacobites—whence the once generally believed notion that Bute had caused George III to be impregnated in his youth with certain of the "reactionary" ideas of Bolingbroke. At times he confuses himself, as in his attempts to make look as black as possible the relations between Bute and the Dowager Princess of Wales. In one passage of the second *Memoirs*—tactfully omitted in the edition of 1845—he is so convinced that he has made out his case that he forces one to assume either that the somewhat puritanical Bute was a minor Casanova, or that the charges against him are ludicrously false. In fact Walpole, without at all realizing that he has done so, convinces us that the Princess Dowager was guiltless on at least that count. However, it is not to the present purpose to consider him as a memoir writer, but to try to see him as a person.

Horace Warlpool, to give him the pronunciation he would recognize, was born in 1717, and lived to be over eighty. He grew up in what we call the Age of Walpole and died as Napoleon's star was rising; he spans the period from the heyday of Pope to the Romantic Revival. And through all that time he never changed; through all those years he was the battleground of two conflicting elements; or, to put it differently, two notions held equal balance within him. And it is because he holds these conflicting elements in him that, in a sense, he completely represents his age, or rather two aspects of it, the aspects which it wears according to the end from which you look at it. Seen from the early end of the eighteenth century, it is "the age of Reason," to adopt the common if somewhat misleading label; from the latter end, it is "the age of Romanticism." But let us look for a moment at the eighteenth century as though it were the age of Reason. Who, we may ask, were the reasonable people in it? There was, to be sure, Chesterfield—whom I shall touch on later. But who else? Pope could be furiously unreasonable; Swift was swayed by his passions; the Pitts were all mad (Chatham suffered from manic-depressive insanity); no one would deny that Dr. Johnson was on occasion as fine an example of unreasonable prejudice as you could wish to find —apart from his deep depressions and terror of death; among the poets, Collins, Smart, and Cowper were mentally afflicted, and Blake earned the name of Dippy Bill; Burke was as passionate as John Wesley—and those were among the great figures of the age. As for the mass of people, there were more unreasonable riots in that century than in any other before or since. The fact of the matter would seem to be that men early in the century were trying to define the limits of Reason and that after the forties the age became one of "uneasy Romanticism," as it has been called, a description supported by a cursory examination of the poets, from Gray, Collins, and the Wartons onward. Walpole, we can see, was a man in whom the reasonable was always struggling with something else: undoubtedly, he—if anyone— can be called an uneasy Romantic.

This is to suggest that he was of a dual nature—an understatement, perhaps. To Macaulay, at any rate, the description would have sounded much too simple. "His mind," we are informed, "was a bundle of inconsistent whims and affectations. His features were covered by mask within mask. When the obvious guise of affectation was removed, you were still as far as ever from seeing the real man." But if Macaulay *had* seen the real man, he would not have liked him any the better; he would have had the same robust contempt for him that he had for Steele or Boswell—men so different from himself. It amazed Macaulay that people who were, in his view, so inconsistent, could ever achieve anything; he did not see that it was precisely because they were not patterns of what he admired that they were able to pursue through life, with astonishing persistence, ends that they thought worth while. It was just because they had so little "character" that they were able to do what they did. Macaulay loved character: he himself was ninety-nine per cent character, and only one per cent of that other thing, "personality," which for certain purposes is more valuable than character. Bozzy, for him, had no character at all; yet what a superb piece of work he produced amid a vast mass, produced too by a persistence in hanging on which even the most bulldog "character" might envy.

I am using the terms "character" and "personality" in the sense now generally accepted. "Personality" is what we might call the bundle of impulses of which we are internally composed: it is the Freudian "ego"; but "character" is something we construct to enable us to live in the world; it is the Freudian "superego," the ideal social self. To achieve character involves a suppression of some of our impulses, a hacking about, a distortion of the more primitive instincts, and sometimes of the more advanced ones. The man of character is the man of the world, the man who has a picture of himself as, in his social circumstances, he would like to be. He becomes a strong silent man, or a man of power, a master of industry, a swayer of multitudes, a political or religious leader, or a genial companion. He may be a man of action or a Diogenes content to snarl from his tub. The one thing he rarely is, is an artist, for an artist is primarily a personality, a person of impulses and intuitions, open to the influence of thoughts and sensations, which he treasures for their own sakes and which, when enough have been accumulated, impel him by their pressure to create. Keats recognized this when he evolved his theory of the "negative capability" of a poet. Goethe expressed it when he wrote:

> Es bildet ein Talent sich in der Stille,
> Sich ein Charakter in dem Strom der Welt.

The man of character, then, is opposed to the man of personality. In the nature of things, living as we do in society, we all have to cramp our impulses and build up a character; the pity of it is that in the age of Macaulay character was considered so important that men distorted themselves unduly, and some who might have been artists became prophets instead: one thinks especially of Carlyle and Ruskin. The artist is the man who does not let his character swamp his personality unduly—assuming, of course, that he has a sufficiently impressive set of impulses to start with.

The force that in the eighteenth century was likely unduly to cramp impulses was this chimera of reason, the ideal of being a man of reason, which did to some extent afflict the time. Even if the men of that century were no more reasonable than those of any other, for the average educated man the ideal social self was that of the reasonable man, during the earlier years in a somewhat neo-classical style. "Mine be the little cot beside the hill," they quoted, warbling; or chanting "Happy the man whose wish and care/A few paternal acres bound," they built up enormous estates, enjoyed the whirl of "polite" society, ate food a Lucullus might envy, and erected superb country mansions.

So let us look for a moment at the society into which Horry Warlpool was born, at the people he would be thrown among—men of the world, men of power, men of action, of whom his father would be the supreme type: vociferous, hard-hitting, hard-drinking men, most of them, without much sensibility either moral or artistic, though they lived by a code and collected pictures. They might have brilliant intellects—not that Robert Walpole much encouraged these in his entourage—but they would be guided by worldly motives, for they were shrewd men of ambition, full of vitality; in short, men of character. What was a young man like Horace Walpole to do for himself in such society? He was brilliantly intelligent, but a weakling, a mother's darling. Moreover he had, after a childhood hatred of him, as W. S. Lewis shows, developed a great admiration for his father—it is now generally accepted that Robert Walpole really was his father—and never swerved from devoted loyalty to him. (Parenthetically, those asterisks printed in an early letter to Mann that led Stephen Gwynn to assume that he had said something derogatory of his father turn out to be nothing but a mildly improper anecdote about some quite insignificant person—such are the perils of prudish censorship.) His own personality shrank from the noisy Houghton-Downing Street world: his natural impulses were averse to the whole thing. But after all, one must live; one has to adapt oneself to one's surroundings; one has to build up some sort of character to present, if only to protect oneself.

So he too would be a man of the world, but of a different kind; or rather, one might say, of the *in*different kind, namely the aloof, amused, scoffing observer, understanding, oh all too well understanding, everything about it; condemning nobody, for the business of the man-of-the-world philosopher is to be utterly uncondemning, merely to be entertained by the folly of it all, perhaps enjoying the glitter, but despising the brute solidity. So very soon Horace Walpole clothed himself in his character as in a mantle.

Trust me [he wrote to Horace Mann as his father appeared at last to be tottering from his pinnacle], if we fall, all the grandeur, the envied grandeur, of our house will not cost me a sigh; it has given me no pleasure while we have it, and will give me no pain when I must part with it. My liberty, my ease, and choice of my own friends and company, will sufficiently counterbalance the crowds of Downing Street.

There already we get his "character," the cloak that was to cover him all his long life of nearly sixty years more. It ensured that nothing that could happen to him in the world of affairs, to which he was bound to belong, could hurt or humiliate him. He would mix with his world, since he was of it, but as the detached observer, as the "dancing senator," to steal his own self-description, who though he went to dances never danced, and who did nothing in his capacity of senator. The world would be tinsel; the happiest time of his life that which he had spent in Florence, when he took off his domino to get into bed and got out of bed to put on his domino.

But what of the personality? This begins to come to light still earlier in the letters. His impulses were not robust or crude; they were romantic. But we must be careful in the use of the word and use it as he used it. Writing to Charles Lyttelton from Cambridge in 1736, after saying that the country round Houghton is woody and full of delightful prospects, he adds: "I spent my time at Houghton for the first week almost alone; we have a charming garden all wilderness; much adapted to my romantic inclinations." "Romantic" meant seeing and feeling things through the eyes of the romance writers of the seventeenth and early eighteenth centuries. Just as "picturesque," as Logan Pearsall Smith pointed out, "was used to describe scenes that were like pictures and were seen through the medium of another art," so "romantic" meant "Nature seen through a literary medium." No more than that—no pantheistic flirtings, no high seriousness. For Walpole, the personality demanded an escape into fantasy, as Gray saw in the next year. Writing from Cambridge he told his friend:

You are in a confusion of wine and roaring and hunting and tobacco, and, heaven be praised, you too can pretty well bear it. . . . I imagine, however, you will rather choose to converse with the living dead, that adorn the walls of your apartments, than with the dead living that deck the middles of them; and prefer the picture of still life to the realities of a noisy one, and, as I guess, will imitate what you prefer, and for an hour or two at noon will stick yourself up as formal as if you had been fixed in your frame for these three hundred years, with a pink or rose in one hand, and a great seal ring on the other.

"You will imitate what you prefer"—the phrase is significant. It is equally significant that Walpole could not, in the end, get on with Gray. Gray became all character; the personality was crushed, and he grew to such a state that, in Matthew Arnold's famous phrase, "he never spoke out."

Let us pursue the personality a little further, to the Continent. Walpole, in terms made permissible by Blackmore and Thomson, inspired by Claude, Poussin, and Salvator Rosa, wrote to West during his journey, in September 1739:

Precipices, mountains, torrents, wolves, rumblings, Salvator Rosa . . . here we are, the lonely lords of glorious desolate prospects. I began this letter among the clouds; where I shall finish it my neighbour heaven probably knows; 'tis an odd wish in a mortal letter to hope not to finish it this side of the atmosphere. You will have a billet tumble to you from the stars when you least think of it; and that I should write it too! But I am to undergo many transmigrations before I come to "yours ever." Yesterday I was a shepherd of Dauphiné; to-day an Alpine savage; to-morrow a Carthusian monk; and Friday a Swiss Calvinist.

And two days later:

But the road, West, the road! Winding round a prodigious mountain, and surrounded with others, all shagged with hanging woods, obscured with pines, or lost in clouds! Below, a torrent breaking through cliffs, and tumbling through fragments of rocks! Sheets of cascades forcing their silver speed down channelled precipices, and hasting into the roughened river at the bottom! . . .

All this is vague enough, but the tangle of feelings was soon to be given a direction, that of the plastic arts. Florence and other towns offered a wealth of pictures for Horace Walpole to look at. We hear of the Corregios at Parma; at Bologna, "except pictures and statues we are not very fond of sights . . .": but this is not the place to study Walpole's education of himself. We must jump back to Houghton, after his father's fall. In 1743, we find Horace making a commented catalogue of the pictures, the *Ædes Walpolianae*, which gives a clear view of him as an ardent student of painting, and, what is surprising at this stage, endowed with a capacity for carrying through an arduous piece of work. His taste was his own. Unlike most of his contemporaries, he did not much admire Michelangelo; he "followed nature too closely"; he was "much too fond of muscles." The Dutch painters were "those drudging Mimicks of Nature's most uncomely coarseness." In many ways, naturally, he was with his age, but his final conclusion is independent: "In short, in my opinion, all the qualities of a perfect painter never met but in Raphael, Guido, and Annibal Carracci."

Now let us take another jump, which will bring me, so to speak, to the middle of my song. We may extract from a letter to Hanbury Williams, written in June 1745: "I like Mistley [the Rigby home] prodigiously; if it were not for the house, and the walks, and the avenues, which are all bad and *deplacées*, it would be a delightful place. I have built Roman porticos, Gothic spires, and Chinese galleries in plentiful ideas there." Two years later he rented Strawberry Hill, and soon after bought it. It began as a toy, straight out of Mrs. Chenevix's toy shop, as he declared; he played with the grounds, added to them, changed the shapes, and planted: and then in January 1750 he tells Mann: "I am going to build a little Gothic structure at Strawberry Hill."

And when we say Gothic in this connection, we must be as careful in our use of the word as we must be in saying that Walpole was romantic. By "Gothic" Walpole meant nothing awe-inspiring, nothing especially profound, certainly nothing of portentous spiritual significance. For him, at least at the beginning, to Gothicize was a game: it was about another century before it became, for anyone, a moral principle. The Gothic, in the first instance, was a decorative motif, and Walpole was not the only one at that time to begin playing with that motif, nor had the Gothic tradition entirely died out; even Vanbrugh used it. But with Walpole there was something else, and this something he could so easily hide under the pretense that it really was all a game; he could indulge his personality while everybody would think it was part of his character. He wrote very revealingly to Mann in April 1753:

I thank you a thousand times for thinking of procuring me some Gothic remains from Rome; but I believe there is no such thing there, I scarce remember any morsel in the true taste of it in Italy. Indeed, my dear Sir, kind as you are about it, I perceive you have no idea of what Gothic is; you have lived too long amidst true taste, to understand venerable barbarism. You say you suppose my garden to be Gothic too! That can't be; Gothic is merely architecture, and as one has the satisfaction in imprinting the gloomth of abbeys and cathedrals on one's house, so one's garden on the contrary is to be nothing but *riant*, and the gaiety of nature.

Venerable *barbarism*, we remark; the *gloomth* of abbeys and cathedrals. For Walpole this Gothic business was part of romance, in his sense of the term, and romance was itself the starting point of visions, visions of an existence in which mundane life could not hurt him. It was very real to him, because through the sham he could attain the reality of his visions. It may be true that, as Saintsbury said, he had "no real love for mediaeval things in general, and no real understanding of Romance in particular"; but the medieval was this starting-off place for him, and his romance not the portentous, prophetic, divine thing it was to become in the nineteenth century. He himself called Strawberry Hill, "a plaything, a vision, that has amused a poor transitory mortal for a few hours, and that will pass away like its master." And the word "vision" is not to be passed by lightly. "I hold visions," he wrote in 1779, "to be wisdom, and would deny them only to ambition, which exists only by the destruction of visions of everybody else." Life itself was "the great vision." But visions are for the personality; to have ambition, to pursue its ends, is a mark of character.

Let us for a moment look at Strawberry near the beginning of the process that was to make of it a considerable house, though still, indeed, a very small castle. Again he is writing to Mann, in June 1753, and extracts must be taken from his letter for brevity's sake, at the price of being jerky:

Now you shall walk into the house. The bow-window below leads into a little parlour hung with stone-colour Gothic paper and Jackson's Venetian prints, which I could never endure while they pretended, infamous as they are, to be after Titian etc: but when I gave them the air of barbarous bas-reliefs, they succeeded to a miracle; it is impossible at first sight not to conclude that they contain the history of Attila or Tottila, done about the very era. From hence, under two gloomy arches, you come to the hall and staircase, . . . the most particular and chief beauty of the castle. Imagine the walls covered with (I call it paper, but it is really paper painted in perspective to represent) Gothic fretwork; the lightest Gothic balustrade to the staircase, adorned with antelopes (our supporters) bearing shields, lean windows fatted with rich saints in painted glass, . . . niches full of trophies of old coats of mail. Indian shields made of rhinoceros hides, broadswords, quivers, long bows, arrows, and spears—all *supposed* to be taken by Sir Terry Robsart in the Holy Wars . . . and a bow-window commanding the prospect, and gloomed with limes that shade half each window, already darkened with painted glass in chiaroscuro, set in deep blue glass. Under this room is a cool little hall, where we generally dine, hung with paper to imitate Dutch tiles.

To us it sounds horrible enough, even as a fanciful game: but it soon became serious. Walpole became a "stickler for accuracy"; there was to be no more trumpery nonsense, and in 1761 we find him writing:

Went again to Mr. Charles Hamilton's . . . to see the Gothic building, and the Roman ruin. The former is taken from Batty Langley's book (which does not contain a single design of true or good Gothic) and is made worse by pendent ornaments in the arches, and by being closed in on two sides at bottom with cheeks that have no relation to the Gothic. The whole is an unnecessary edifice. In all Gothic designs they should be made to imitate something that was of that time, a part of a church, a castle, a convent, or a mansion. The Goths never built summer houses, or temples in a garden.

That is from his *Journals of Visits to Country Seats* (1751–84)—"note books," J. Steegman wrote, "filled with observations, ranging over more than thirty years, that suggest the professional scholar much more than the idle and flippant dilettante."

And indeed it must be insisted that at bottom Walpole was no dilettante, though he always protested strenuously that he was. Sometimes, however, the mask drops off, and we find him, in June 1770, writing to George Montagu about his *Anecdotes of Painting in England:*

I am very busy about the last volume of my Painters, but have lost my index, and am forced to turn over all my Vertues, forty volumes of miniature manuscripts; and this is the third time I shall have made an index to them. Don't say I am not persevering, and yet I thought I was grown idle. What pains one takes to be forgotten! Good night!

And what pains he took to pretend that his work was not work, simply a pastime on a level with his occasional verses (though they are polished enough). Take, for instance, what he once wrote to Mann about his *Royal and Noble Authors:*

I know nothing. How should I? I who have always lived in the big busy world; who lie abed all the morning, calling it morning as long as you please; who sups in company; who have played at faro half my life, and now at loo till two or three in the morning, who have always loved pleasure, haunted auctions. . . . How I have laughed when some of the Magazines have called me the learned gentleman. Pray don't be like the Magazines.

Macaulay, with his "inexperiencing mind," put this up as an Aunt Sally for his most boisterous coconut-shying: "This folly might be pardoned in a boy. But a man between forty and fifty years old, as Walpole then was, ought to be quite as much ashamed of playing at loo till three every morning as of being that vulgar thing, a learned gentleman." But, of course, the fear of being thought erudite—and Walpole was erudite according to the standards of his age—was part of the protective character, of the "I who have always lived in the big busy world." As a matter of sober fact, Walpole's literary output alone is prodigious. Besides the works already mentioned and others to be mentioned in another connection, there were the *Historic Doubts on the Reign of Richard III*, the first, and most ingenious, defense of that monarch; the *Description of Strawberry*, the *History of Taste in Gardens, Memoirs* of the reigns of George II and George III, and a considerable number of shorter things, mainly politico-satirical, together with an abundance of verses, some of which Dodsley did not disdain to reprint. All these besides the great letters, themselves a lifework, by which chiefly and most splendidly he lives. Moreover, as though all this were not enough, there was the printing press, which certainly did something to improve typography, and for some forty years involved considerable labor on his part, not only in the printing—one of its earliest productions was the first edition of Gray's *Odes*—but also in editing, which included the first edition of the delightful *Memoirs of Lord Herbert of Cherbury*. And concurrent with all this, there was the collection.

For Strawberry soon became a museum, so famous from an early date that before long Walpole was appointed one of the godfathers of the British Museum. It contained not only works of art—of various degrees of credit or discredit—but also a most astonishing number of things of no artistic or intrinsic value, but of great associative interest. Look, for instance, at a page of Harrison Ainsworth's description of the Tribune Room, printed in the sale catalogue of 1842, for a twenty-four day sale. I again make jerky extracts:

To detail the wonders contained in this beautiful room would claim a volume for itself. . . . There is a cabinet containing at least a hundred miniatures by Petitot, and others of the great masters; and glass cases on either hand, the shelves of which are loaded with relics, . . . the missal painted by Raffaelle and his scholars for Claude de France, the Queen of François Ier, . . . the famous Florentine boar, the Jupiter Serapis, the dagger worn by Henry VIII, snuff-boxes, medals, intaglios, rings, . . . the silver bell of Benvenuto Cellini, . . . Callot's battle-piece, the portrait of Madame de Sévigné, the letter written in her name from the Elysian Fields by Madame du Deffand, and pictures and bronzes without end, pass before us in succession, and leave us still amazed at the untiring perseverance of the man who heaped up all these treasures.

The untiring perseverance of the man! Yet we have been told that he was an idle dawdler, a heap of contradictions, a worthless simulacrum of a man. No doubt his character was lamentable.

Nevertheless the character, the ideal social self, still oppressed the personality. Strawberry itself became too serious; it had an unwanted gravity forced upon its sham stone wallpaper, its plaster battlements. It might have been the fault of Gray, the man of character, who had not looked very warmly upon the snug comforts the villa did after all provide. Why, he suggested, in ironic seriousness, did not Walpole go the whole hog, do it properly, and leave the windows unglazed, as in those happy early times after which, it seemed, the antiquaries hankered? And we may perhaps wonder whether Walpole himself was always altogether happy about Strawberry; it was, we may think, a little too *voulu;* so at least the Burneys thought when they visited it a short time after Walpole's death in 1797. "Strawberry Hill," we read, "with all its chequered and interesting variety of detail, had something in its whole of monotony, that cast, insensibly, over its visitors an indefinable species of secret constraint, and made cheerfulness rather the effect of effort than the spring of pleasure." Was there something of constraint about it for Walpole too, in spite of all the toys, the objects of art and *virtù,* the overfed lap dogs, the goldfish, and the soft round chairs? We may well incline to think "Yes."

For in the process of building up character, even if it pretends to the characterless, the impulses have to be suppressed, and they often take a strange revenge. Look, for instance, at Chesterfield, a man who, if man ever did, "created himself," to use Whibley's phrase. He, if anyone of that period, was the man of reason; and what happened? Romance got its own back by making him a slave, almost, to his passion for educating his son, a story at once ludicrous and pathetic. That is one way the thing may happen. Another is the case in which, by repression, the desire or the impulse is choked and clamped down, never allowed to appear on the conscious level, kept under lock and key by the censor: then it is only in dreams that the censor's vigilance is evaded; the impulse darts out, plays its pranks, reveals itself sometimes in symbols. And on one fateful night in 1764 Walpole had a dream, of which he wrote to his friend Cole on 8 March 1765:

I waked one morning in the beginning of last June from a dream, of which all I could recover was that I had thought myself in an ancient castle (a very natural dream for a head filled like mine with Gothic story) and that on the uppermost bannister of a great staircase I saw a gigantic hand in armour. In the evening I sat down and began to write, without knowing in the least what I intended to say or relate. The work grew on my hands, and I grew fond of it—add that I was very glad to think of anything rather than politics—in short I was so engrossed with my tale, which I completed in less than two months, that one evening I wrote from the time I had drunk my tea, about six o'clock, till half an hour after one in the morning, when my hand and fingers were so weary that I could not hold the pen to finish the sentence, but left Matilda and Isabella talking in the middle of a paragraph.

If that is not the passion of the artist, what is? The artist in the manufacture of *bibelots,* if you like. A kind of Strawberry Hill in literature. It duly appeared as *"The Castle of Otranto: a Story,* Translated by William Marshall, Gent, from the Original Italian of Onuphrio Muralto, Canon of the Church of St. Nicholas at Otranto." The translator remained anonymous, until, the work proving remarkably popular, it went into a second edition. Springing as it did from a dream, the writing was guided by impulse, by the subconscious, and by subconscious memory, Walpole recognizing when he later visited Cambridge that his Castle of Otranto was remarkably like Trinity College. But he certainly thought about it a good deal, with regard to both style and form, as the prefaces to the first two editions make plain. He was trying to wed the extravagancies of the old romance to the realism of the modern novel. He modeled his servant characters on Shakespeare's, and if that fact is not immediately apparent to the uninformed reader, we see what he means: he was thinking of Pompey and Lancelot Gobbo.

It is beautifully done; the machinery works with rapid smoothness, and it is astonishing how soon we accept the values of this fantastic world; sooner even than Manfred we become "almost hardened to preternatural appearances." As early as the first chapter we note without a tremor that "At that instant the portrait of his grandfather which hung over the bench where they had been sitting uttered a deep sigh and heaved its breast, . . ." but though in a sense we take all this "seriously," we are not allowed to be too serious. We have got to feel it and we do feel it (according to Gray, it made the Fellows of Pembroke cry a little and woo night fears); but at the same time we have to realize that it is all nonsense: " 'It is done,' replied Manfred; 'Frederick accepts Matilda's hand, and is content to waive his claim, unless

I have no male issue'—as he spoke those words, three drops of blood fell from the nose of Alfonso's statue. . . ."

The whole thing is saved from being ridiculous by a sense of situation, of the situation of this supposedly Gothic romance in polite society. When Theodore wants to hide Matilda from her pursuers "beyond the reach of danger" in the recesses of the labyrinthine cave, Matilda protests: "Alas! what mean you, sir? . . . Though all your actions are noble, though your sentiments speak the purity of your soul, is it fitting that I should accompany you into these perplexed retreats? Should we be found together, what would a censorious world think of my conduct?" Walpole was always in control of himself and, in his writing, possessed of that sense of his audience that is the mark of eighteenth-century civilization, an awareness that demanded sincerity and prevented you from fooling yourself.

Yet though he worked hard at it, since as a good amateur he knew that a man had no business to do a thing at all unless he did it as well as he possibly could, he was aware of its shortcomings as well as of its daring, as is shown by some lines in the sonnet addressed to Lady Mary Coke, which appeared in the second edition:

> Oh! guard the marvels I relate
> Of fell ambition scourg'd by fate,
> From reason's peevish blame.

And twenty years or so later, he wrote that "it was fit for nothing but the age in which it was written," an age, he added, which "rather wanted to be brought back to imagination, than to be led astray by it." But in trying to guess what sort of man Walpole really was, it is to be noted how wholly he put himself into the writing of it, as is revealed by his avowal to Madame du Deffand, that hardened old *salonnière*, who, though blind, fell deeply in love with him—with what, we ask? A voice? An emanation? However this may be, in one of the very few letters to her that remain, he wrote: "Je vous avoue, ma petite, et vous m'en trouverez plus fol que jamais, que de tous mes ouvrages, c'est l'unique où je me sois plu; j'ai laissé courir mon imagination; les visions et les passions m'échauffaient."

It is not a great work; Walpole was no grand creator: but it was a seminal work. One need not let it weigh one way or the other that the *surréalistes* in their day should have claimed it as an example of their school, a claim they could justifiably make in spite of the conscious portions; its importance is that it opened the floodgates of the whole torrent of "horror" or "Gothick" novels by Mrs. Reeve, Mrs. Radcliffe, Monk Lewis, and many others, including Mary Shelley, and these smoothed the way for novels of more genuine romance, such as the Waverley novels—just as Strawberry cleared the road for Abbotsford and more genuine resuscitations. And it reveals clearly what Walpole's personality really was, that of a dreamer, a minor visionary, not of the scale but of the same kind as Beckford, whose Fonthill as far outdid Strawberry as his *Visions* and his *Vathek* surpassed *The Castle of Otranto*.

Where, in his writing, Walpole was more conscious, he was less happy, in spite of the Gothic element. One may take his play, *The Mysterious Mother*, which (though not "of the highest order . . . the last tragedy in our language," as Byron declared it to be) has considerable skill. A certain Shakespearean "feel" has been ascribed to it, on the ground that he was an enthusiastic admirer of Shakespeare (as all the writers of the eighteenth century were), though well this side of bardolatry, and perhaps too because it bravely flaunts all neo-classical rules. But a little cursory reading may make us query that influence. Here, for example, a few lines from the first scene:

> What awful silence! How these antique towers
> And vacant courts chill the suspended soul,
> Till expectation wears the cast of fear;
> And fear, half ready to become devotion,
> Mumbles a kind of mental orison,
> It knows not wherefore.

That is not Shakespeare; it is Rowe or Young or Thomson beginning to become Gothic, while a later apostrophe:

> Globe of the World!
> If thy frame split not with such crimes as these,
> It is immortal . . .[1]

seems sheer Nat Lee; in fact the whole play seems a resuscitation of Lee, whose own work has been called Gothic. Again there are such things as *An Account of the Giants Lately Discovered*, a satirical squib on the state of England, or the more delightful *Hieroglyphic Tales*, designed for the Conway children, which, the preface to these whimsical stories tells us, "were undoubtedly written a little before the creation of the world."

It is in such things that the personality of Horace Walpole bursts out; it is visible throughout his life in his persistence as a builder and as an indefatigable collector; it peeps out again and again in his letters. Take an early one, written to Montagu in May 1736:

Were not the playing fields of Eton food for all manner of flights? No old maid's gown, though it had been tormented into all the fashions from

[1] Act V, scene v.

King James to King George, ever underwent so many transformations as those poor plains have in my idea. At first I was contented with tending a visionary flock, and sighing some pastoral name to the echo of the cascade under the bridge. How happy should I have been to have had a kingdom only for the pleasure of being driven from it, and living despised in an humble vale! As I got further from Virgil and Clelia, I found myself transported from Arcadia to the garden of Italy, and saw Windsor Castle in no other view than the *Capitoli immobile saxum.*

From the beginning we see the fanciful dreamer, and soon after, the man who loved solitude. It is all expressed many years later, in 1773, in an illuminating letter to Madame du Deffand, at a period when he found himself compelled to spend his time in looking after the affairs of his nephew, the then Lord Orford, who suffered from fits of insanity: "Je quitte le métier d'auteur pour celui de bailli. Mes songes ne me présenteront plus un château d'Otrante. C'est triste de troquer des visions contre des comptes. Je m'étais fait un monde qui ne ressemblait en rien à celui des affaires. Hélas! il faut apprendre des choses utiles." It is as melancholy as *The Castle of Otranto* itself.

For there, as plainly as anywhere, though it is often visible, Walpole reveals the perpetual conflict in him between the dreamer, even visionary personality, and the man-of-the-world character. It was a conflict that never ceased throughout his whole life, except perhaps at the very end, when the old fourth Earl of Orford, as he had now become, dreamed away his life with the Berry ladies, for whom he composed his *Reminiscences,* and wrote charming letters to the young Hannah More, wandering about Strawberry Hill, once his toy, now his "paradise," tasting his collection within doors, or rejoicing in the azaleas and the scent of lilac out in the grounds. Yet all through his life, the artist in him came out; there were times when the outer world, the silly trifling world of politics, which, to Macaulay's great scandal, he did not take seriously, made claims upon him, claims of sentiment or friendship. He hated the influence that the man of character aspires after; he loathed the power that made wars, was revolted by the general cruelty of the world of affairs. When it was proposed to him that he should become ambassador at Paris, he scouted the suggestion, protesting that he was a trifler. Yet he did his utmost to save Admiral Byng; and though he might be no active senator, he would sit for days in succession at wearisome all-night sittings of the House if anything involving his friends was in question.

Nothing remains of Strawberry but its husk.[2] *The Castle of Otranto* still carries on a faint, ghostlike existence (it has been twice reprinted

[2] Its interior has been remade to serve as a teachers' training college for Roman Catholic girls.

in the last thirty years), showing that it has something in it that appeals to what is enduring in the human make-up, for in that is revealed the conflict he himself was aware of between the dreamer personality and the man-of-the-world character. But it is the letters that are his enduring monument, for there actuality and fantasy came together without forcing, as though it were in that form that he could reconcile the personality and the character. They could blend, and work happily together in that realm. Throughout the fascinating series he selected, till they too become, in their way, a sort of fantasy. One feels this especially in his account of the Wilkes affair, or in the great set pieces, as, for instance, his account of the execution of Lord Balmerino (an occasion he shudderingly avoided), where he can end: "Balmerino certainly died with the intrepidity of a hero, but with the insensibility of one too. As he walked from his prison to execution, seeing every window and top of house filled with spectators, he cried out, 'Look, look, how they are all piled up like rotten oranges!' " Or again on the occasion of the funeral of George II, where he can mingle the sense of solemnity with the incongruous muddle, or contrast the melancholy figure of the Duke of Cumberland with the absurdities of "the burlesque Duke of Newcastle":

He fell into a fit of crying the moment he came into the chapel, and flung himself back in a stall, the Archbishop hovering over him with a smelling-bottle; but in two minutes his curiosity got the better of his hypocrisy, and he ran about the chapel with his glass to spy who was or who was not there, spying with one hand, and mopping his eyes with the other.

As Walpole wrote these letters, giving us the abstract, but by no means brief chronicle of the time, the dual being becomes one in a splendid unity. There the positive, protective character modified the not quite first-rate personality, prevented it from attempting the great work of art, and confined it to the smaller scope where it could work to perfection. For perfect within their kind Walpole's letters are. The mask gave freedom to the wit beneath it, so that it could play with fact or with the *esprit de Guermantes* of the time. The art there, so to speak, was to conceal the artist, so that the world in general could not see the serious visionary, or the man of extreme delicate sensibility, whom, he was terrified, it would turn into ridicule.[3]

---

[3] It is always supposed that it was this fear of ridicule that caused him to try to restrain the passionate expressions of Madame du Deffand, and to suppress most of his letters to her. But surely it is much more likely that he was trying to save her unnecessary anguish, and to shield her, not himself, from ridicule. There is no space to argue this here—and too little evidence.

GEORGE SHERBURN

"Writing to the Moment": One Aspect

SAMUEL RICHARDSON WAS justly proud of his lively technique of "writing to the moment"—a technique that transcribed emotional tensions instantly as they arose and not (to use a later phrase) when they were recollected in tranquillity. He used various devices for attaining this sense of presence, and perhaps the fact behind his success is that he had a naturally strong visual imagination: small details show that in his mind he actually *saw* the episodes that he depicted.

Obvious limitations to vividness in his work may be recalled. He wrote uneasily and at times did not clearly convey what he evidently saw. He had little interest in environmental detail or in objective description. Of the stately homes found in all three of the novels, only Grandison Hall got much description.[1] In general, interiors are furnished only with vague chairs and an occasional table—whatever the action really requires, but no more. Clarissa may sit in an "elbow-chair," but the piece is never described further. Persons tend to sit side by side, but practically always in chairs. There are almost no settees or sofas, and when one occurs, as at Mrs. Moor's in Hampstead, it is used as a stage property.[2] A very frequent arrangement places three persons in three chairs, with the principal person flanked, as in a court drawing-room, by subordinates of importance.[3]

Such details, given explicitly but not very vividly, seem in themselves of little interest to Richardson; but at times, curiously, he does pause for almost superfluous details—Lovelace's disguise at Hampstead,[4] or Singleton's appearance as a sailor,[5] or Clarissa's room at the

GEORGE SHERBURN was, before his recent death, Professor Emeritus of English at Harvard University.

[1] *Grandison*, VI, 21–27. All page references to the three novels here given refer to the Shakespeare Head Edition (Oxford: Blackwell [1930]).

[2] *Clarissa*, V, 260.

[3] *Pamela*, II, 73, 77; *Clarissa*, II, 217, 225; *Grandison*, III, 102; IV, 237, 342; V, 104.

[4] *Clarissa*, V, 74, 79.   [5] *Ibid.*, IV, 153.

bailiff's,[6] or Harriet Byron's masquerade gown[7] (Richardson's own creation?). These are useful but excessive details. Normally the focus is on emotional tensions, such as may be conveyed through physical or bodily attitudes. It is those that are here to be considered as one aspect of this method.

At first sight, these attitudes may not seem much particularized. Most of them have to be the physical reactions of gentlefolk of Richardson's day. A facility in fainting, in the shedding of tears (by either sex), and of bending what Shakespeare had called the pregnant knee are to be expected. All three novels are drawing-room dramas: it is even quaintly pathetic to find the dying Clarissa complaining of Lovelace's persistence in his persecutions: "He will not let me die decently! . . . He will not let me enter into my Maker's presence, with the composure that is required in entering into the drawing-room of an earthly prince!"[8] The decorum of the drawing-room implies conventional behavior, but Richardson usually modifies the demeanor of his persons nicely to suit the coloration of the moment.

One may observe that there are various small episodes in which the depiction of tensions seems awkward or false—at least at first sight. *Pamela* doubtless furnishes the best-known examples. Mr. B's first attempt at rape (Letter XXV), it will be remembered, is frustrated by a somewhat tardy fainting fit when Pamela becomes aware that, while Mr. B "expostulates" in her bed, his hand finds its way into forbidden regions. The failure here is less in imagination (Richardson has a pretty gift in imagining attempts at rape) than it is in expression. Almost any reader could improve the arrangement of details in this, Pamela's first real peril, but the disarrangement does not destroy the reader's avid attention.

Another episode that strains a pedestrian reader's sense of presence is the scene in which Pamela of an evening is ordered to wait upon her master at supper.[9] She is too tremulous to be efficient, and, upon wicked suggestions by Mrs. Jewkes, Pamela, while her master is at table, begs for mercy: "Sir, said I, and clasp'd his Knees with my Arms, not knowing what I did, and falling on my Knees, Have Mercy on me, and hear me. . . ." This may be writing to the moment, for if Mr. B's knees are under the table, clasping would be awkward. But if Mr. B is envisaged as sitting sidewise at a small round table—he is supping in a parlor—the acrobatics of this kneeling might be possible. Richardson normally *sees* what he is writing. He here imagines rather better than he writes. Another bit of strangeness with the knees oc-

6 *Ibid.*, VI, 296–98.

7 *Grandison*, I, 172–73.

8 *Clarissa*, VII, 413.

9 *Pamela*, I, 251.

curs in *Clarissa*, where Dorcas kneels hypocritically to Lovelace in order to win favor for and from Clarissa, "bustling on her knees about me."[10]

One again suspects a lack of attention to actuality in the scene toward the end of *Pamela* where, disbursing nuptial largesse to the servants, Pamela is encouraged by Mr. B, who "pulling out his Purse, said, Tell out, my Dear, Two hundred Guineas, and give me the rest."[11] One wonders from what part of his elegant attire a gentleman could "pull out" a purse containing well over two hundred gold coins. This problem of pockets is thus fascinating for men as well as for ladies. A damsel because of her long full skirt could be suspected of concealing voluminous correspondence in pockets (one had two) that (according to Lovelace) "are half as deep as she is high."[12] Pamela, fearing that a pocket might be too easily searched, had stitched her journal to her "under-coat" next to her linen.[13] Ordinarily, ladies placed their generous, tear-moistened handkerchiefs in their pockets.[14]

Much apparently casual imagining can be explained by attention to minute customs of the day, which have long since disappeared. Awkwardnesses among novelists who write with a flowing pen, as Richardson certainly did, may be frequent; but in the case of Richardson, the imagining is likely, upon examination, to be sound and evocative.

Facial expression is perhaps too overt an indication of emotion to require the author's closest attention. Yet see what may be done: Solmes "rising, with a countenance whitened over, as if with malice, his hollow eyes flashing fire, and biting his under-lip, to show he could be *manly*."[15] Clarissa, more conventionally, in the penknife scene, thanks God that she is saved from self-destruction, and "her charming cheeks [Lovelace tells us], that were all in a glow before, turned pale, as if terrified at her own purpose."[16] Clearly it is the emotional coloration that fixes the vividness in these cases. By implication, the same is true when Harriet Byron's desperate admirer, Greville, threatens, "You know what you have declared—Angel of a woman! said he again thro' his shut teeth."[17] Some emotions do not, as seen in a face, easily translate themselves into words. When Uncle Antony is firmly told by Clarissa that she values his money less than she would kind looks and kind words, he is stupidly nonplussed and angry: he falls into vague wonderment, and, in silence, "looked about him this way and that."[18]

[10] *Clarissa*, V, 377.

[11] *Pamela*, II, 312.

[12] *Clarissa*, IV, 46; cf. *Pamela*, I, 319.

[13] *Pamela*, I, 322.

[14] *Grandison*, II, 202; III, 156.

[15] *Clarissa*, II, 235.

[16] *Ibid.*, VI, 70.

[17] *Grandison*, I, 151.

[18] *Clarissa*, II, 218.

Small details are made to count, especially in the full-figure descriptions. Lovelace (19 June) records:

At day-dawn I looked thro' the key-hole of my Beloved's door. She had declared she would not put off her cloaths any more in this house. There I behold her in a sweet slumber . . . sitting in her elbow-chair, her apron over her head; her head supported by one sweet hand; the other hand hanging down upon her side, in a sleepy lifelessness; half of one pretty foot only visible.[19]

Again, when in prison, Clarissa is seen in a special posture: "Her face . . . was reclined, when we entered, upon her crossed arms; but so, as not more than one side of it to be hid."[20] The first view of her by Colonel Morden is of course similarly pathetic.[21] Stereotyped attitudes, but with variations, are bound thus to be frequent.

Not all Richardson's attitudes are stereotypes; and even stereotypes may express different emotions. In the *History of the English Stage* (1741), published as if by Thomas Betterton, it is specified that uses of hands may express "accusation, deprecation, threats, desire, &c."[22] Such emotions somewhat imply dramatic action. Richardson's more vivid passages are content to be pictorial and are tableaux rather than violently active situations. Clarissa, for example, reports with almost phenomenal explicitness: "My Father sat half-aside in his elbow-chair, that his head might be turned from me; his hands clasped, and waving, as it were, up and down; his fingers, poor dear gentleman! in motion, as if angry to the very ends of them."[23] This painful picture of the beginning of a family tea is paralleled by the family conclave (typical of the Harlowes and of Richardson) when Clarissa is on the carpet at her return from her stay with the Howes—where she had seen Lovelace, contrary to family injunctions. This scene, preserved to us by the brush of Highmore, shows the family seated in a long row listening to the harsh reproaches of brother James:

My Brother seemed ready to give a loose to his passion: My Father put on the countenance which always portends a gathering storm: My Uncles mutteringly whispered: and my Sister aggravatingly held up her hands. While I begged to be heard out;—and my Mother said, Let the *child*, that was her kind word, be heard.[24]

This brief passage (as first perceived by Duncan Eaves) furnished Highmore with sufficient matter so that he has depicted in color each attitude of every Harlowe, here given in words, even to the hands of Arabella.

[19] *Ibid.*, V, 357.
[20] *Clarissa*, VI, 298–99.
[21] *Ibid.*, VII, 449.

[22] Page 99.
[23] *Clarissa*, I, 51.
[24] *Clarissa*, I, 42–43.

Richardson is very fond of mentioning gestures involving raised hands. Arabella raises her hands more than once "aggravatingly" and frequently raised hands express vague or difficult emotions, such as might reflect the common "words-fail-me" reaction—or they are raised in prayer. Arabella's maid Betty is ironically "astonished (her hands and eyes lifted up)" that Clarissa objects to going to her Uncle Antony's house.[25] But normally sincere and prayerful emotions are thus expressed. Colonel Morden, for example, when, upon his arrival in London, he is informed that Clarissa is dying, exclaims "Good God! . . . with his hands and eyes lifted up."[26] Clementina similarly "prays . . . with lifted-up hands."[27] The Grandison sisters both pray with hands uplifted: Charlotte in gratitude to her brother,[28] and Caroline, earlier, in "pray-pray-fashion" to her unsympathetic father.[29] Clarissa, failing in an attempted escape from Mrs. Sinclair's establishment, raises the window sash and, "clasping her uplifted hands together," cries to the passers-by for help.[30] The raising of hands is indeed very common, but the emotional coloring is so varied and so appropriate that one can feel assured that Richardson saw the circumstance as he recorded it.

Prayers apart, hands are to be kissed and held—graciously or forcibly. When the two Grandison sisters try to lead Harriet Byron to confess that she loves their brother and are seated on either side of her, in sympathy with her speechless predicament, they "vouchsafed, each, to press with her lips the passive hand each held."[31] Pamela, naturally, gets kissed more often and more profusely than any of the ladies in the other novels. A late case is seen in the garden alcove to which Mr. B has led her: "For he began to be very tiezing, and made me sit on his Knee, and was so often kissing me, that I said, Sir, I don't like to be here at all, I assure you. Indeed you make me afraid."[32] This loving behavior doubtless amused Henry Fielding. Nothing like it occurs in the other two novels.

A gesture prized by Richardson, and evidently by him visualized, is the contemptuous *twirl* of a hand. Arabella grandly says to Clarissa, " 'Ask them; ask them, child,' with a twirl of her finger."[33] Later Clarissa in disparagement of Lovelace's rakish friends is reported as saying, " 'If ever again'—And there she stopt, with a twirl of her hand."[34] That the gesture is regarded as expressive is seen in Lovelace's added

[25] *Clarissa*, II, 39.

[26] *Ibid.*, VII, 447.

[27] *Grandison*, III, 60.

[28] *Ibid.*, II, 143.

[29] *Grandison*, II, 72.

[30] *Clarissa*, V, 360.

[31] *Grandison*, II, 204.

[32] *Pamela*, I, 285.

[33] *Clarissa*, I, 50.

[34] *Clarissa*, Ill. 360.

comment, "When we meet, I will, in her presence, tipping thee a wink, shew thee the motion; for it was a very pretty one."[35]

What has already been called the pregnant knee may also convey a considerable variety of emotion. Knees are possibly more active in Italian episodes (thanks to the emotional state of the Lady Clementina?) than in England; but even in England the twentieth-century reader is likely to think knees excessively flexible. Worship or entreaty is the common objective in kneeling, but within these limits there is much variation. Knees may give way as part of a total collapse, as in the case of Clarissa, where the fall adds a gruesome detail of a bleeding nose.[36] Kneeling may become a matter of policy. Mrs. Giffard, the exposed mistress of Lord W, kneels, as Sir Charles Grandison tells us, "Not from motives of contrition, as I apprehend; but from those of policy."[37] In such circumstance, the normally punctilious Sir Charles, far from helping the lady to rise, steps coldly back and lets her get up by herself. Lovelace, as Clarissa reports, "threw himself in the way at my feet," but the move purposed as much to keep Clarissa from leaving him as it did to express unselfish entreaty.[38]

Naturally there are examples of kneeling that are felt to be improper. A gentleman of Sir Rowland Meredith's age and status should not, Miss Byron felt, kneel to her in entreaty for his nephew.[39] Clarissa at St. Albans ironically reproves Lovelace for hypocritically kneeling: "That you are *your own mistress*, thro' *my* means [Lovelace says], is, I repeat, my boast. *As such*, I humbly implore your favour . . . *thus humbly* [the proud wretch falling on one knee] your forgiveness. . . . O Sir, pray rise!—Let the obliged kneel . . . !"[40]

Clementina, curiously, is on one occasion ashamed of kneeling to Sir Charles, for on many other occasions she feels no such qualm. Still imperfectly recovered from her madness, she is conscious of having caused much trouble. At first she begs forgiveness of her mother (kneeling): she then, Sir Charles tells us:

came to me; and to my great surprize, dropt down on one knee. . . . I raised her; and taking her hand, pressed it with my lips! . . . She hesitated a little; then turned round to Camilla, . . . and running to her, cast herself into her arms, hiding her face in her bosom—Hide me, hide me, Camilla!— What have I done!—I have kneeled to a man![41]

[35] The projected imitation is typical: Lovelace is practically always, with varying degrees of insincerity, acting a part. He is hardly ever and never for long truly sincere: his frequent outcries that he suffers more than Clarissa cannot, of course, be believed.

[36] *Clarissa*, V, 378.

[37] *Grandison*, II, 357.

[38] *Clarissa*, I, 258.

[39] *Grandison*, I, 132–33.

[40] *Clarissa*, III, 13.

[41] *Grandison*, IV, 164–65.

Later Clementina is involved in another tableau, one that is hard for the present-day reader to visualize, but evidently not too hard for Richardson: "Dropping down on one knee, God preserve and convert thee, best of Protestants. . . . I would have raised her; but she would not be raised. . . . I kneeled to her, clasping my arms about her: . . . I raised her, and arose; and kissing first one hand, then the other. . . ."[42] Here we have a theatrical picture of two eminently decorous but overwrought lovers both kneeling and both (one trusts Clementina co-operated!) clasping their arms about each other. It must be pure emotional drive or imagined Italian manners.

One may note that kneeling is almost sure to involve added gesture, or added detail, that may enrich the picture. When Emily Jervois is induced to ask her mother's blessing, she reports: "Down on my knees dropt I. . . . (And she kissed my hand, and bowed her face upon it). . . . And she kissed me *too*, and wept on my neck."[43] Complexity of mood as well as of detail is usual in Clarissa's private kneelings, witnessed perhaps through keyholes or by an onlooker in the sponging house, or often seen in filial-parent poses.[44] A final, most conventional kneeling is seen at the end of Harriet Byron's wedding ceremony: "Sir Charles . . . did credit to our Sex before the applauding multitude, by bending his knee to his sweet Bride, on taking her Hand, and saluting her."[45] "Applauding multitude" suggests a theater rather than a church, but the kneeling and the nuptial kiss were apparently the usual final touch for a "right" wedding before the couple left the altar. In this case, the applause was due: it recognized a suspense that had run through almost six volumes. It is fluently concluded: one feels that not even Sir Willoughby Patterne could have surpassed Sir Charles in grace when "making a leg."

Most readers will agree that Richardson is effective in the small detail, emotionally fused. Certainly it is the small bit that normally clinches the effect. When Betty rushes up to summon Clarissa to a meeting with Solmes: "Miss! Miss! Miss! cried she, as fast as she could speak, with her arms spread abroad, and all her fingers distended, and held up, will you be pleased to walk down into your own parlour?"[46] When asked who is there, Betty replies: "Why, Miss, holding out her left palm opened, and with a flourish, and a saucy leer, patting it with the forefinger of the other, at every mentioned person, There is your Papa!—There is your Mama!"[47] And she proceeds to pat off seven persons—including Solmes. The "arms spread abroad and fingers dis-

[42] *Ibid.*, IV, 407; cf. *Clarissa*, I, 342.

[43] *Ibid.*, III, 310.

[44] *Clarissa*, I, 53, 104; II, 221; V, 4; VI, 298.

[45] *Grandison*, V, 379.

[46] *Clarissa*, II, 200.

[47] *Clarissa*, II, 201.

tended" may seem awkward and superfluous, but the details (assuming the language to be competent) are very precisely what Richardson saw.

In the big scenes, it must be confessed that there is rather less physical detail expressed. In the famous penknife scene,[48] there are few vivid expressions of posture: it is all done in conversation. Yet one feels himself present. Actually more in accord with the technique here being emphasized is the scene between Lovelace and Clarissa after the terrifying cry of *Fire!*[49] Present-day readers sometimes feel that Clarissa was excessively outraged emotionally by the conduct of Lovelace here. They are wrong. Nowadays the language in novels may be more "realistic": four-letter words are in vogue, and we wish far less expostulation and argument. It remains true, however, that if one has merely a small part of the visual imagination that Richardson had, this scene is as lurid as anything in modern fiction.[50] The two persons are almost naked: Lovelace repeatedly clasps his arms about Clarissa, and he trusts that he has not "hurt the tenderest and loveliest of all her beauties." More than once she slides away through his encircling arms, and there is no reason to be surprised that she felt something like complete dishonor; the surprise is that (through romantic worship of innocence?) Lovelace allowed her to escape. He somewhat resembles Pamela's admirer in his frustrations. With the techniques at his disposal, Richardson made the scene impressive, but there are obviously too many words, too much emotional as well as physical and argumentative wrestling.

There is no end to the examples of vividly seen posture that might be cited. Most "uses" of arms and hands are conventional of necessity, but in these novels most uses are appropriately discriminated and varied in particular detail. Arms, for example, may be clasped by one female about another—and less often by a male; arms may be folded to show restraint or desperation; they may be akimbo to show arrogance; and they may be locked, as in Lovelace's dragging Clarissa from Harlowe Place[51] and again as in the chamber scene where Mrs. Jewkes (preparing to aid Mr. B) says to Pamela: "Here, . . . put your Arm under mine, and you shall find the [keys] about my wrist. . . . So I did, and the Abominable Designer held my Hand with her Right-hand, as my Right-arm was under her Left."[52] Here Richardson shows himself astonishingly knowledgeable.

There can be no doubt that even when Richardson's language is not

[48] *Ibid.*, VI, 65–71.

[49] *Ibid.*, IV, 388.

[50] *Ibid.*, IV, 393.

[51] *Clarissa*, II, 359.

[52] *Pamela*, I, 276.

quite clear, he saw with precision what he expressed with restraint or awkwardness. There were many other aids in his "writing to the moment." Perhaps the best as an aid to suspense is the one that he makes Belford specify in a letter of 4 August, which was adapted as part of the Preface of 1759. A mere memoir, Richardson thought, that shows a personage safe in port after various desperate experiences has less appeal than a story told in letters, where each letter is tentative, suspenseful, and inconclusive.

Much more lively and affecting . . . must be the Style of those who write in the height of a *present* distress; the mind tortured by the pangs of uncertainty (the Events then hidden in the womb of Fate); *than* the dry, narrative, unanimated Style of a person relating difficulties and dangers surmounted, can be; the relater perfectly at ease; and if himself unmoved by his own Story, not likely greatly to affect the Reader.[53]

In his central aim (if we discount that of moral instruction)—to be "lively and affecting"—Richardson was always trying to write to the moment. It is not difficult to see, though it is easy to overlook, the fact that he was much helped by a keen visual gift, commonly evident in the physical contacts and gestures of his persons.

[53] Preface to *Clarissa* (1759), I, xiv.

REUBEN A. BROWER

Dryden and the "Invention" of Pope

AFTER DRYDEN—it is tempting to say—if there had not been a Pope, it would have been necessary to invent him. It is a commonplace of literary history that Pope supplied the "correct" Augustan poet required by Dryden's most famous critical formula; and certainly "propriety of thoughts and words" fits Pope better than Dryden, and Pope was indeed the "well-weighed judicious" poet that the older writer saw in Virgil. The more obvious ways in which Dryden's practice prepared the ground for Pope's achievement are well known: his discovery of new couplet rhythms and a style appropriate for public address and manly debate, his development of a "true heroic" narrative manner, and, more important, his creation of the allusive mode that Pope later refined and elaborated for his special purposes as moralist and satirist. In general, Dryden is Pope's master in his more public roles of heroic poet and social and literary critic. Pope's mature style, his intimate and easy Horatian way, with its flexibility of tone and its range of sensuous and cultural reference, is distinctly his own. But in Dryden's latest phase, there are anticipations of this more truly Horatian style and of other Popeian modes less strictly Augustan —the pastoral and the descriptive[1] (frequently blended), and the style that we can describe roughly as "poetry of retirement."

It is the purpose of this essay to explore some of the ways in which Dryden's poetry from about 1685 until his death anticipated Pope and later poets in these various, often related, modes. It should be remembered that we shall be looking at aspects of Dryden's poetic personal-

REUBEN A. BROWER is Professor of English at Harvard University.

[1] "Descriptive" is used here of poetry in the "literary pictorial" style, not poetry of "enumerative description." See Jean H. Hagstrum, *The Sister Arts: The Tradition of Literary Pictorialism and English Poetry from Dryden to Gray* (Chicago, 1958), especially pp. xxi–xxii, 160, 161. Though I am concerned only with "description" of scenes in physical nature, the style is not limited to "nature poetry." As certain examples will show, the pictorial style is of great importance in heroic poetry. See also R. A. Brower, *Alexander Pope, the Poetry of Allusion* (Oxford, 1959), pp. 49–52, 130–34.

ity not characteristic of his whole career and at some kinds of poetry far from central in Pope's mature productions. But though Pope became a poet of "Sense" and "moral song," he began with "pure Description," and he had wandered in "Fancy's maze." He did not simply renounce his past,[2] but altered it to fit a more complex sense of himself and his world, while some of his contemporaries and many of his successors continued to develop styles that in their pure forms no longer interested him. Poets of the mid-century found it both easier and more congenial to follow Parnell and Thomson than the poet of the *Moral Essays* and the *Dunciad*. A further reason for looking into the byways of Dryden's poetry is that he—and Pope also—offered examples not only to writers surely in the Augustan line, like Swift, Johnson, and Crabbe, but also to writers who in the retrospective view of literary history tend to move outside the Augustan tradition, the poets of description and of melancholy meditation "mid rural shades," like Thomson and the Wartons, Gray and Collins, Blair and Akenside. The Augustans themselves, it has been said perhaps too often, were not always Augustan. Pope in his essay on gardens, cites Virgil and Homer as masters of "Painting" in poetry, but he also quotes *Il Penseroso*.

The figure of the "retired" poet, like that of Pope's urbane conversationalist, was a cultural metaphor, not a simple fact. Although Dryden never came as close as Pope to realizing the ideal in life or in art, in later years he enjoyed his glimpses and approximations, both in his personal life and in his practice as a poet. There are anticipations in the poetry of Pope's role of country-gentleman-Horace and signs of a change in temper that bring Dryden nearer to Pope and his contemporaries. Even during the reign of James, Dryden hardly seems the Court poet he was under Charles.[3] The well-known letter of 1687[4] in which he says that he had made his "court to the King once in seaven moneths" and that he "might probably get something at Court" does not sound, as Etherege suggests in his reply,[5] like the letter of a man who is a courtier or indeed of a man who is "in." *The Hind and the Panther* is an apologia for the King's religion, but it offers sharp criticism of Father Petre, the King's chaplain and adviser; and though Dryden speaks of being "gloriously lazy," he observes that James, un-

---

[2] Hagstrum, p. 234.

[3] For an uncharitable account of Dryden's changed position as defender of the Court, see Alexandre Beljame, *Men of Letters and the English Public in the Eighteenth Century*, trans. E. O. Lorimer (London, 1948), pp. 180–86. On James's failure to support Dryden and on his lack of interest in literature, see pp. 197–99.

[4] *The Letters of John Dryden*, ed. Charles E. Ward (Durham, N.C., 1942), pp. 26–27.

[5] Ward, *Letters*, p. 29.

like his brother "of blessed memory," is overeager to "advance his affairs by Stirring."

When in 1688 Dryden is surely "out," he does not retire to Binfield or the equivalent, but in losing royal support, he comes to the end of his life of "noble idleness." He still writes hopeful dedications to noble lords and occasionally receives handsome gifts in return, but he is now supporting himself in large part by fees from his publisher. He is well on the way to becoming a professional writer in the modern sense,[6] and the success of his Virgil must have shown Pope how an author might achieve financial independence. If in the last twelve years of his life, Dryden does not abandon the Town, he is a frequent visitor to the Country and often for considerable periods of time.[7] (But it is also probable that he had always made vacation journeys to his native Northamptonshire and elsewhere.) His letters show that he went often, that he did a good deal of writing during his visits, and that in spite of ill health, he enjoyed himself greatly.

In his later correspondence, there are many expressions of a warm interest in country matters: he worries lest "the few Damsins [on his place] should be gone," catches a "lusty pike," and finds a piece of "veneson . . . both fatt, large & sweet"; he praises his cousin's "Marrow Puddings," though he notes later that "a part of a chine of honest bacon wou'd please my appetite more than all the marrow puddings for I like them better plain; having a very vulgar stomach."[8] The tone of many of these letters to relatives and friends is very rural-domestic; and like others who have gone to the city and done well, he finds, on returning home, much to interest him (and occasionally bore him) in "characters" he meets in this simpler world. In one allusion, the writing of poetry—in particular, translating the *Fables*—becomes a country pleasure: ". . . so that it is not impossible, but ere the summer be pass'd I may come down to you with a volume in my hand, like a dog out of the water, with a duck in his mouth."[9]

In these years, Dryden also enjoyed more refined delights of retirement in scenes of some elegance and beauty. On three occasions, he stayed in "that delicious spot of ground," Denham Court, the house of Sir William Bowyer;[10] and on the two earlier visits, he worked on his translations of the *Georgics* and the *Aeneid*. He also stayed at

[6] Beljame, pp. 356–64.

[7] James M. Osborn, *John Dryden: Some Biographical Facts and Problems* (New York, 1940), "Dryden's Absences from London," pp. 198–209.

[8] Ward, *Letters*, p. 110.

[9] Ward, *Letters*, p. 109.

[10] Osborn, pp. 206, 207; Charles E. Ward, *The Life of John Dryden* (Chapel Hill, N.C., 1961), pp. 279, 288.

Burghley House[11] with Cecil while completing another part of his Virgil; and according to a strong tradition,[12] he was a visitor at Ugbrooke, the seat of the Lord Treasurer Clifford, while writing *The Hind and the Panther*. In view of the scarcity of biographical documents, there have come down a surprising number of impressions of the aging Dryden in country scenes with "study and ease / Together mix'd; sweet recreation. . . ." Although he did not attain the idyllic peace of Pope's Solitude, he approaches the life Pope actually led, of visiting great houses and mingling literary pursuits with country amusements. When he thanks Pope's friend Caryll for an invitation to Ladyholt, we almost hear the voice of his more delicate successor: "if I could promise my Self a year's Life, I might hope to be happy in so sweet a place, & in the Enjoyment of your good company."[13] But the same letter includes his hearty praise of "Veneson," and heartiness is the typical note in Dryden's talk of his country visits.

If Dryden's interest in country life had any effect on his style, it is to be seen in his increasing use of words of a vigorous and homely sort, terms often associated with simple and rustic life, like "lowly," "jolly," "cot" and "cottage," "honest," "homely," "sober," "poverty."[14] But it is well to remember, as Miss Miles has said, that Dryden's major vocabulary remains "an heroic one"[15] and that his "major words give us a view of his persistent subject: the state, the social order human and divine; emotional, moral, abstract in concept, yet in action imagible."[16] Although there is an increase in certain rural and descriptive elements in Dryden's later poetry, there is also, beginning with the translation of Virgil, an increase in the use of Latinized idioms and Virgilian allusions, especially when action or scene suggests the "heroic."[17]

With the death of Charles in 1685, no dramatic change takes place in Dryden's style any more than in his life. But in original poems and in translations he shows a growing fondness for certain kinds of country context and idiom, although intention is not always matched by

[11] Ward, *Life*, p. 275.

[12] Osborn, pp. 203–4.

[13] Ward, *Letters*, p. 100.

[14] For information on Dryden's "homely" vocabulary, I am indebted to an unpublished study, "Dryden's Late Narrative Style," by Neil Rudenstine, Harvard University.

[15] *Concordance to the Poetical Works of John Dryden*, ed. Guy Montgomery (Berkeley and Los Angeles, 1957), Preface by Josephine Miles.

[16] Josephine Miles, *Eras and Modes in English Poetry* (Berkeley and Los Angeles, 1957), p. 35.

[17] R. A. Brower, "Dryden's Epic Manner and Virgil," *PMLA*, LV (1940), 136–38.

performance. In the translations of Theocritus (1684, 1685), it is difficult to see much of the "Dorick Dialect" or of "that incomparable
sweetness in its Clownishness, like a fair Shepherdess in her Country
Russet, talking in a Yorkshire tone."[18] The "rusticity" of these
nymphs and swains at times reminds us too much of the hoydens and
bumpkins of the Restoration stage; and their "sweetness" is expressed
in the elegant and descriptive style that Pope sometimes adopts in his
Pastorals:

> Ah beauteous Nymph, can you forget your Love,
> The conscious *Grottos*, and the shady Grove. . . .
>
> (*Amaryllis*, 6, 7)

It is more surprising to find in Lucretius's prayer to Venus lines of
pastoral song similar in rhythm and idiom to songs in Pope's *Pastorals*
and similar in their scenic character to *Windsor Forest*:

> Thee, Goddess thee, the clouds and tempests fear,
> And at thy pleasing presence disappear:
> For thee the Land in fragrant Flow'rs is drest,
> For thee the Ocean smiles, and smooths her wavy breast;
> And Heav'n it self with more serene, and purer light is blest.
> For when the rising Spring adorns the Mead,
> And a new Scene of Nature stands display'd
> When teeming Budds, and chearful greens appear,
> And Western gales unlock the lazy year,
> The joyous Birds thy welcome first express,
> Whose native Songs thy genial fire confess. . . .
> O're barren Mountains, o're the flow'ry Plain,
> The leavy Forest, and the liquid Main
> Extends thy uncontroul'd and boundless reign.
>
> (Lucretius. *The Beginning of the First Book*, 7–17, 23–25)

The sweetly echoing repetitions of words and metrical units, the decorative and lightly sensuous epithets, and the pictorial as well as
rhythmic symmetry of the lines anticipate Pope's youthful pastoral
and descriptive style and also the style of various passages in the later
poetry of Dryden. The reminiscence of a passage in *The Faerie
Queene* and the use of Spenserian[19] epithets ("wavy," "flow'ry,"
"leavy") are also familiar features of Dryden's late style. "Cheerful"
appears only once before this in a landscape context, and then in lines

---

18 Preface to *Sylvae*, in *The Poems of John Dryden*, ed. James Kinsley (Oxford,
1958), p. 399. All quotations of Dryden's verse are taken from this edition.

19 "Spenserian," i.e., of a type used frequently by Spenser, not necessarily borrowed directly from his poetry. Neo-classical epithets in -y may have been formed
by analogy with scientific terms, according to John Arthos, *The Language of Natural
Description in English Poetry* (Ann Arbor, 1949), p. 33.

that are close in their rhythm and their extreme pastoral sentimentality to one of the songs in Pope's *Autumn:*

> For Her the weeping Heav'ns become serene,
> For Her the Ground is clad in cheerful green:
> For Her the Nightingales are taught to sing,
> And Nature has for her delay'd the Spring.

(*Prologue To the Dutchess on Her Return from Scotland*, 26–29)

Dryden's translation of Horace's second *Epode, Beatus ille*, also printed in the 1685 miscellany, is his first essay in the poetry of retirement. Although the rhyming betrays some Pindaric license, the octosyllabic meter and the classically just epithets for natural things connect the poem with the seventeenth-century tradition of retirement poetry,[20] familiar from Marvell's *Upon Appleton House* and *The Hill and Grove at Billborow:*

> How happy in his low degree,
> How rich in humble Poverty, is he,
> Who leads a quiet country life!
> Discharg'd of business, void of strife . . .
> And Court and state he wisely shuns,
> Nor brib'd with hopes nor dar'd with awe
> To servile Salutations runs:
> But either to the clasping Vine
> Does the supporting Poplar Wed,
> Or with his pruneing hook disjoyn
> Unbearing Branches from their Head,
> And grafts more happy in their stead:
> Or climbing to a hilly Steep
> He views his Herds in Vales afar . . .
> Or in the now declining year
> When bounteous *Autumn* rears his head,
> He joyes to pull the ripen'd Pear,
> And clustring Grapes with purple spread.

(1–4, 15–24, 28–31)

Toward the end of the translation Dryden the sportsman is heard in the rendering of *Afra avis* as *Heathpout* (the black grouse!). In the lines that follow, in which the rural delights have been greatly increased, Dryden's diction gives English sturdiness to a Latin idyll:

> Amidst these feasts of happy Swains,
> The jolly Shepheard smiles to see
> His flock returning from the Plains;
> The Farmer is as pleas'd as he
> To view his Oxen, sweating smoak,

---

[20] See R. A. Brower, "Lady Winchilsea and the Poetic Tradition of the Seventeenth Century," *Studies in Philology*, XLII (1945), pp. 72, 73, 79.

Bear on their Necks the loosen'd Yoke
To look upon his menial Crew,
   That sit around his cheerful hearth,
And bodies spent in toil renew
   With wholesome Food and Country Mirth.

(86–95)

It is no great distance from this scene to the nostalgic realism of *The Deserted Village*. (Note "jolly," "sweating," "wholesome," all of which are used by Dryden much more often after 1685.)

As Dr. Johnson observed, low language of this sort breaks into *The Hind and the Panther*, even in the First Part, where he was endeavoring to give his style "the majestic Turn of Heroic Poesie." Although the lowering of tone may be traced to the convention of the beast fable and in particular to the example of Chaucer, it also indicates Dryden's growing tendency to slip into a more familiar narrative style and to introduce natural scenes or bits of rural lore. Shortly after the "emblem" of the wolf that Dr. Johnson found "not very heroically majestic,"

His ragged tail betwixt his leggs he wears
Close clap'd for shame: . . .

(I, 163, 164)

come two similes that like some of Milton's bring in memories of country knowledge and speech:

As where in fields the fairy rounds are seen,
A rank sow'r herbage rises on the green,
So, springing where these mid-night Elves advance,
Rebellion prints the foot-steps of the Dance.

(I, 212–15)

So fulsome is their food, that flocks refuse
To bite, and onely dogs for physick use.
As where the lightning runs along the ground,
No husbandry can heal the blasting wound,
Nor bladed grass, nor bearded corn succeeds,
But scales of scurf, and putrefaction breeds. . . .

(I, 221–26)

The first of these lines combines in Pope's fashion rural fancy with topical satire:

Safe past the *Gnome* thro' this fantastick Band,
A Branch of healing *Spleenwort* in his hand.[21]

(*The Rape of the Lock*, IV, 55, 56)

[21] Tillotson, *Twickenham Edition*, II, quotes the parallel in the *Flower and the Leaf*, l. 188: "A Branch of *Agnus castus* in her Hand." The "branch" in this instance is carried by a "Sovereign Queen" in a "Fairy Place."

Near the end of Part II of *The Hind and the Panther*, Dryden descends—though more gracefully than Johnson's criticism suggests—to "Domestick Conversation":

> She thought good manners bound her to invite
> The stranger Dame to be her guest that night.
> 'Tis true, course dyet and a short repast,
> (She said) were weak inducements to the tast
> Of one so nicely bred, and so unus'd to fast.
> But what plain fare her cottage cou'd afford,
> A hearty welcome at a homely board
> Was freely hers; and, to supply the rest,
> An honest meaning and an open breast.
> Last, with content of mind, the poor man's Wealth;
> A grace-cup to their common Patron's health.
>
> (II, 670–80)

Again there are many examples of Dryden's "homely" idiom and, again, the combination of a simple country life with content of mind —familiar ingredients in an eighteenth-century retreat. The eighteenth-century quality appears especially in the tender references to poverty and in the tone and rhythm. For the first time in Dryden's career, I believe, the accent of private conversation is clearly heard in his verse, the tension of the couplet being relaxed to fit the run of gossipy speech—" 'Tis true . . . (She said) . . . one so nicely bred." The voice is feline and feminine, closer to "*The Spectator* tone" of the *Rape of the Lock* than to the heroic oratory of *Absalom and Achitophel*.

The more "Domestick" Third Part offers another sort of novelty. Early in the lines describing the country bumpkin Swifts, we read:

> These Lubbers, peeping through a broken pane,
> To suck fresh air, survey'd the neighbouring plain. . . .
>
> (III, 550–51)

After a heavy-handed transition, sounding like a parody of Pope's "Where-e'er you walk" lines,

> And saw (but scarcely cou'd believe their eyes)
> New blossoms flourish, and new flow'rs arise;
> As God had been abroad, and walking there,
> Had left his foot-steps, and reform'd the year . . .
>
> (III, 552–55)

comes a triplet of pretty, artificial description that might almost pass for an early bit of Pope.

> The sunny hills from far were seen to glow
> With glittering beams, and in the meads below
> The burnish'd brooks appear'd with liquid gold to flow.

We are reminded of "lakes of liquid gold, Elysian scenes" in the *Rape of the Lock* (IV, 45). "Glittering," which is used five times in the *Rape,* is a favorite adjective of Pope's. The lines on the Swallows' flight might serve as a study for the flight of the Sylphs:

> Who but the *Swallow* now triumphs alone,
> The Canopy of heaven is all her own,
> Her youthfull offspring to their haunts repair;
> And glide along in glades, and skim in air,
> And dip for insects in the purling springs,
> And stoop on rivers to refresh their wings.
>
> (III, 566–71)

Many of the words ("haunts," "glide," "glades," "purling," "beam") belong to Pope's pastoral-descriptive vocabulary, the kind of language he combines with the heroic in picturing Belinda's journey down the Thames.[22]

There is little place for "the fairy kind of writing"[23] in the translations of Juvenal and Persius (1693), and little opportunity for rural scene-painting either realistic or idyllic. One passage in the *Fourth Satyr* of Persius (II, 64–73)—if indeed the translation is by Dryden—has the same stalwart English flavor as the haying song from *King Arthur.* The *Fable of Acis, Polyphemus, and Galatea* (1693) gives an example of what very nearly becomes a rule in Dryden's translation of Virgil. Hints of description in the original are expanded into a fairly elaborate set piece, with much underlining of visual effects, especially of color:

> My Palace in the living Rock, is made
> By Nature's hand; a spacious pleasing Shade:
> Which neither heat can pierce, nor cold invade.
> My Garden fill'd with Fruits you may behold,
> And Grapes in clusters, imitating Gold;
> Some blushing Bunches of a purple hue:
> And these and those, are all reserv'd for you.
> Red Strawberries, in shades, expecting stand,
> Proud to be gather'd by so white a hand.
> *Autumnal* Cornels, latter Fruit provide;
> And Plumbs to tempt you, turn their glossy side:
> Not those of common kinds; but such alone
> As in *Phaeacian* Orchards might have grown:
> Nor Chestnuts shall be wanting to your Food,
> Nor Garden-fruits, nor Wildings of the Wood;
> The laden Boughs for you alone shall bear;

---

[22] For echoes of the lines on Philidel, the "Airy Spirit" of *King Arthur* (1691), see *Twickenham Edition*, II, *Rape of the Lock,* II, 78.

[23] The phrase was first used by Dryden in the Preface to *King Arthur.*

And yours shall be the product of the Year.
　The Flocks you see, are all my own; beside ⎫
The rest that Woods, and winding Vallies hide; ⎬
And those that folded in the Caves abide. ⎭

(103–22)

Again Dryden sets a model for Pope, who will, of course, surpass him in freshness of pictorial detail and in harmonious ordering of visual and sound patterns. Dryden's descriptive style turns Ovid's relatively bare and accurate list of country items into balanced pictorial and rhythmic sensations. Compare *auro similes . . . uvae* with

> Grapes in *clusters*, imitating Gold,

or *sunt et purpurae* with

> Some *blushing Bunches* of a purple *hue:*

or *nata sub umbra/mollia fraga* with

> *Red* Strawberries, in *shades*, expecting *stand*,
> Proud to be gather'd by so *white* a hand.

Ovid's natural caves, *sunt mihi, pars montis . . . antra*, become a Palace of Nature's art and inevitably, as in Pope, the grotto brings in a garden, and "a particular Picture of a Garden" is compared to the original of all such scenes, "Phaeacian Orchards." Only "Wildings of the Wood," like the "New Milk in Nut-brown Bowls" of the Cyclops's dairy, remind us of Dryden's England.

　Dryden was correct in saying that Virgil's Eclogues were "Coursely Translated" in his version. They offer plentiful examples of the "kind of Rusticity" he considered Theocritean, of that "Boorish Dialect" of Theocritus, which he confesses "has a secret charm in it." Though he was probably influenced by the *Shepherd's Calender* ("Spenser being Master of our Northern Dialect"), his use of barnyard language in his translations is boorish and not charming.[24] Unintentionally, Dryden writes lines worthy of a place in *The Shepherd's Week:*

> My Brinded Heifar to the Stake I lay. . . .

(*The Third Pastoral*, 40)

> To fold, my Flock; when Milk is dry'd with heat,
> In vain the Milk-maid tugs an empty Teat.

> How lank my Bulls from plenteous pasture come!
> But Love that drains the Herd, destroys the Groom.

(*The Third Pastoral*, 152–55)

---

[24] *Dedication of the Pastorals*, in Kinsley, II, 871–72.

The lesson was not lost on Pope, and though he "stole" freely from Dryden's versions, he did not imitate his rusticity. As we should expect, he borrows most often from lines and passages in Dryden's more artificial pastoral style, the style of natural description and echoing song. Study of the excellent notes in the Twickenham edition will show how he bettered all that he borrowed, how he found hints in Dryden of the sweet new style he was creating for himself. As we have seen and shall see again, Dryden came nearer to Pope's own pastoral style when he was not writing pastorals.

Dryden is more at home in translating the *Georgics*, where his accurate use of farming terms, like Virgil's, is seldom jarring. He anticipates Pope and the next two generations of poets by transforming Virgil's praise of country life into a celebration of a "Retreat from Human Race."[25] Many elements in Dryden's picture are Virgilian, but passionate love of the country and of poetry are replaced by a moderate mood of withdrawal from urban cares into a charming pastoral scene of "easie Quiet, a secure Retreat":

> Oh happy, if he knew his happy State!
> The Swain, who, free from Business and Debate . . .
> Unvex'd with Quarrels, undisturb'd with Noise,
> The Country King his peaceful Realm enjoys:
> Cool Grots and living Lakes, the Flow'ry Pride
> Of Meads, and Streams that thro' the Valley glide;
> And shady Groves that easie Sleep invite,
> And after toilsome Days, a soft repose at Night. . . .
> My next Desire is, void of Care and Strife,
> To lead a soft, secure, inglorious Life.
> A Country Cottage near a Crystal Flood,
> A winding Vally, and a lofty Wood.
>
> (639–40, 659–64, 688–91)

In rewriting Virgil in the manner of his own translation of *Beatus ille*, Dryden is thinking of the man of affairs (no Swain!) released from politics and blessed with the wisdom necessary for a life of retirement. What he has in mind is clear from his remarks to the Earl of Chesterfield in the *Dedication of the Georgics*:

You, my Lord, enjoy your quiet in a Garden, where you have not only the leisure of thinking, but the pleasure to think of nothing which can discompose your Mind. . . . [He then compares the man of good conscience to "the happy Old Corycian" of the Fourth *Georgic*.] Virgil seems to think that the Blessings of a Country Life are not compleat, without an improvement of Knowledge by Contemplation and Reading.

[25] To appreciate Dryden's success, the whole passage should be read (Book II, 639–794).

O Fortunatos nimiùm, bona si sua norint
Agricolas!

... Such only can enjoy the Country, who are capable of thinking when
they are there, and have left their Passions behind them in the Town.[26]

The weight given to "know" in *bona si sua norint* would have surprised Virgil: for the gentleman-farmer to understand his happiness,
it is necessary to have "A foundation of good Sense, and a cultivation
of Learning. . . ." A further requisite for a country life is a sizable inheritance. The farmer in Dryden's translation is like Chesterfield a
"rich Owner."

It would be agreeable to report that Dryden introduced distinct
and accurate images from the landscape around the country seats
where he composed parts of his translation. But if he was affected by
his surroundings, it was by the ordered nature of gardens, not by the
particular trees, flowers, and birds he may actually have seen. Wordsworth is in the main right: there are few "images from Nature" in
Dryden's Virgil, if we mean, as Wordsworth does, images that convince us that Dryden, like Virgil, had "his eye upon his object."[27]
But there are fewer images of this sort in Virgil than Wordsworth
seems to suppose, and when they occur they take their place in art-
fully designed scenes or in harmoniously fused impressions. Like his
"master," Dryden is writing in a tradition of literary "painting,"
though artifice often gets the better of nature. Pope, who did have an
"eye," more nearly restores the Virgilian balance.

The increase in this traditional descriptive quality appears in Dryden's addition of pictorial, often stock, epithets and in the elaboration
of scenes. Familiar elements are found in a familiar ordering in this
picture of a shepherd's retreat, from the third book of the *Georgics*
(with the principal additions italicized):

> In Summer's heat, some *bending* Valley find,
> Clos'd from the Sun, *but open to the Wind:*
> Or seek some ancient Oak, whose Arms extend
> In ample breadth, thy Cattle to defend:
> Or *solitary* Grove, or *gloomy Glade;*
> To shield 'em with its *venerable* Shade.

> (III, 512–17)

Although in the Fourth Book on the bees, Dryden cannot equal Virgil's light blend of comic and serious, he achieves at times a delicacy

---

[26] *Dedication of the Georgics,* in Kinsley, II, p. 917.

[27] Wordsworth says "not a single image from Nature in the whole body of his
works . . ." (*Early Letters of William and Dorothy Wordsworth,* ed. Ernest de
Selincourt [Oxford, 1935], p. 541). See L. Proudfoot, *Dryden's Aeneid and Its Seventeenth Century Predecessors* (Manchester, 1960), p. 196.

of image and rhythm that we associate with Pope in the *Rape of the Lock* and the *Pastorals:*

> The winged Nation wanders thro' the Skies,
> And o're the Plains, and shady Forrest flies:
> Then stooping on the Meads and leafy Bow'rs;
> They skim the Floods, and sip the purple Flow'rs. . . .
> Plains, Meads, and Orchards all the day he plies,
> The gleans of yellow Thime distend his Thighs:
> He spoils the Saffron Flow'rs, he sips the blues
> Of Vi'lets, wilding Blooms, and Willow Dews.
>
> (73–76, 266–69)

In his *Aeneis* Dryden finds further occasions to indulge in scenic description, sometimes with considerable success of a theatric kind. Virgil's descriptive touches in narratives of action, or in interludes of repose, or in epic similes are elaborated to produce more striking effects to eye and ear. There are numerous examples of groves and venerable woods, of night scenes and scenes of violence in nature—of storms, floods, and torrents.[28] Dryden's treatment of the great storm at the beginning of the *Aeneid,* when Aeolus lets forth the winds, is a good example:

> He said, and hurld against the Mountain side,
> His quiv'ring Spear; and all, the God apply'd.
> The raging Winds rush through the hollow Wound,
> And dance aloft in Air, and skim along the Ground:
> Then setling on the Sea, the Surges sweep;
> Raise liquid Mountains, and disclose the deep.
> South, East, and West, with mix'd Confusion roar,
> And rowl the foaming Billows to the Shoar.
> The Cables crack, the Sailors fearful Cries
> Ascend; and sable Night involves the Skies;
> And Heav'n it self is ravish'd from their Eyes.
> Loud Peals of Thunder from the Poles ensue,
> Then flashing Fires the transient Light renew:
> The Face of things a frightful Image bears,
> And present Death in various Forms appears.
>
> (I, 120–34)

Dryden is as usual longer, and long in his usual way. Where Virgil has seven adjectives, he has thirteen, and he adds many visual images of his own. He is always stepping up the already violent language of

---

28 For examples in addition to those cited see: 1. (*groves and woods*) VII, 88–91; IX, 98–101; XII, 1111–13; 2. (*night*) III, 761–67; IV, 757–68; VIII, 484; X, 306; 3. (*violence in nature*) II, 406–14; III, 747–60; IV, 231–38; IX, 903–13; X, 149–52; X, 566–75; XII, 760–67.

the original: *"quiv'ring* Spear," *"raging* Winds . . . *dance aloft and skim along,"* " raise liquid *Mountains," "Loud* Peals," *"flashing* Fires," *"frightful* Image." The increase in circumlocutions and the stock character of many of the epithets often blur sense impressions while making them seem vaguely tremendous. We are in the presence of "the sublime" as the eighteenth century will interpret it and attempt to evoke it in painting and poetry. Again the couplet lends itself to a balancing of images so that the shocks of imagery fall into a pattern of musical contrasts. The scene offers a good example of the verbal orchestration of Dryden's odes.

In the still more famous picture of the bay near Carthage, Dryden shows how he can "do up" a scene of perfect repose in a manner that could easily be transferred to a Restoration stage setting.

> Within a long Recess there lies a Bay,
> An Island shades it from the rowling Sea,
> And forms a Port secure for Ships to ride,
> Broke by the jutting Land on either side:
> In double Streams the briny Waters glide.
> Betwixt two rows of Rocks, a Sylvan Scene
> Appears above, and Groves for ever green:
> A Grott is form'd beneath, with Mossy Seats,
> To rest the *Nereids,* and exclude the Heats.
> Down thro' the Cranies of the living Walls
> The Crystal Streams descend in murm'ring Falls.
> No Haulsers need to bind the Vessels here,
> Nor bearded Anchors, for no Storms they fear.
>
> (I, 228–40)

William Frost rightly says that "what interests Dryden in the passage is the sense of order and well-being."[29] Dryden translates his "sense of order" into pictorial effects by emphasizing symmetries of rhythm and image: "on *either* side," "In *double* Streams," *"two rows* of Rocks," "To rest . . . and exclude." Virgil's metaphor, the *scaena,* the high back wall of the Roman theater, is muted by substituting the vague "Sylvan" for *silvis coruscis . . . horrenti umbra,* with its vivid suggestion of waving foliage and jagged shadows. The Miltonic echo recalls the artful landscape of *Paradise Lost,* Book IV, which is further suggested by "rows," "Grott," "form'd" and "Walls." ("Groves for ever green" looks ahead to the unfading Miltonic paradise of *Windsor Forest.*) Toward the end of the passage the scene becomes a Spenserian "port" of "rest" where "Crystal Streams descend in murm'ring Falls." Pope too was enamoured of murmuring streams and

[29] *Dryden and the Art of Translation* (New Haven, 1955), p. 43.

woods, and both he and Dryden have their place in the Spenserian and Miltonic revivals of the eighteenth century.

Many of the woods and groves of Dryden's *Aeneis* are of the gloomy, religiously awesome Ovidian type that Milton and other seventeenth-century writers had naturalized in English poetry.[30] (For a good example, see VIII, 791–94.) In Book IV, Dryden sets the temple of Sichaeus "Within a Grove" and paints a scene of nocturnal "horror" that looks beyond *Eloisa to Abelard* to the graveyard poetry of the next century. (Dryden's main additions are italicized.)

> Oft, when she visited this *lonely Dome*,
> *Strange* Voices issu'd from her husband's *Tomb:*
> She thought she heard him summon her away;
> Invite her to *his Grave;* and chide her stay.
> Hourly 'tis heard, when with a *bodeing* Note
> The solitary *Screech*-Owl strains her Throat:
> And on a *Chimney's* top, or *Turret's hight*,
> With Songs *obscene*, disturbs the *Silence* of the Night.
>
> (667–74)

There had been touches of this poetry of night and death, with its blend of Gothic and classical elements, in the fable style of *The Hind and the Panther*, for example:

> The birds obscene to forests wing'd their flight,
> And gaping graves receiv'd the wandring guilty spright. . . .
> I saw my self the lambent easie light
> Guild the brown horrour and dispell the night. . . .
>
> (II, 652–53, 658–59)

In the *Fables* proper, there are many scenes of the kind that are scattered here and there throughout the *Aeneis*. As might be expected, Ovid offers occasions for dark and melancholy descriptions of night, caves, and woods. "Brown," which first appears in *The Hind and the Panther* in the picturesque sense of "dusky" or "murky," now recurs in the "brown Cave" of *Ceyx and Alcyone* (line 301) and in the mysterious woodland scene of *Theodore and Honoria* (ll. 88–104). Dryden's fondness for this kind of thing leads him to expand the "forest syde" and "daunce" of "ladyes foure and twenty" in the *Wife of Bath's Tale* into:

> Lonely the Vale, and full of Horror stood
> Brown with the shade of a religious Wood:
> When full before him at the Noon of night
> (The Moon was up and shot a gleamy Light),
> He saw a Quire of Ladies in a round,

[30] See Tillotson, *Twickenham Edition*, II, 286–88.

> That featly footing seem'd to skim the Ground:
> Thus dancing Hand in Hand, so light they were,
> He knew not where they trod, on Earth or Air.

(211–18)

In *Palamon and Arcite*, Chaucer's "grove" and "nyght" become "A thick spred Forest" where Palamon

> meant to shun the Light,
> Till the brown Shadows of the friendly Night
> To *Thebes* might favour his intended Flight.

(II, 26–28)

The well-known melancholy scene in *Eloisa to Abelard* presents a variation on Dryden's gloomy manner, but with the addition of charming details of a more pastoral type of description.

In the *Fables* and other late works, Dryden too adds pastoral charms and images of garden-like beauty to his narratives, as in the May morning scene of *Palamon and Arcite*[31]

> *Aurora* had but newly chas'd the Night,
> And purpl'd o'er the Sky with blushing Light,
> When to the Garden-walk she took her way,
> To sport and trip along in Cool of Day . . .
> The Garden, which before he had not seen,
> In Springs new Livery clad of White and Green,
> Fresh Flow'rs in wide *Parterres*, and shady Walks between.

(I, 186–89, 220–22)

"Arcite's song," as Kinsley notes, "is freely embellished," and embellished with images and rhythmic effects of the kind Pope adopted in his pastoral lyrics:

> For thee, sweet Month, the Groves green Liv'ries wear:
> If not the first, the fairest of the Year:
> For thee the Graces lead the dancing Hours,
> And Nature's ready Pencil paints the Flow'rs:
> When thy short Reign is past, the Fev'rish Sun
> The sultry Tropick fears, and moves more slowly on.
> So may thy tender Blossoms fear no Blite,
> Nor Goats with venom'd Teeth thy Tendrils bite,
> As thou shalt guide my wandring Feet to find
> The fragrant Greens I seek, my Brows to bind.

(II, 53–62)

---

[31] For additions to descriptive passages in *Palamon and Arcite*, see headnotes to each book of the poem in Kinsley.

In describing the Temple of Diana,[32] Dryden introduces a landscape of the "ordered variety" of the opening scene in *Windsor Forest;* and like Pope's, it is adorned with decorative mythological figures:

> A Sylvan Scene with various Greens was drawn,
> Shades on the Sides, and on the midst a Lawn:
> The Silver *Cynthia*, with her Nymphs around,
> Pursu'd the flying Deer, the Woods with Horns resound. . . .
>
> (II, 619–22)

It is more curious to hear a pastoral strain coming from the lungs of Chanticleer, in a poem where Dryden, following Chaucer, writes in his most domestic and rustic vein:

> Then turning, said to Partlet, See, my Dear,
> How lavish Nature has adorn'd the Year;
> How the pale Primrose, and blue Violet spring,
> And Birds essay their Throats disus'd to sing. . . .
>
> (*The Cock and the Fox*, 455–58)

Though the parody was probably intentional, the joke seems to have escaped the youthful Pope, who follows one of Dryden's lines closely in his *Spring* pastoral (line 28).

Dryden's additions to the fairy element in his Chaucerian versions are less unexpected, though he might not be expected to write with lightness and grace. Along with the passage already quoted on the "Quire of Ladies in a round," consider these lines on the "airy Shapes" of nymphs in the *Flower and the Leaf:*

> This only Holiday of all the Year,
> We priviledg'd in Sun-shine may appear:
> With Songs and Dance we celebrate the Day,
> And with due Honours usher in the *May*.
> At other Times we reign by Night alone,
> And posting through the Skies pursue the Moon:
> But when the Morn arises, none are found;
> For cruel *Demogorgon* walks the round,
> And if he finds a Fairy lag in Light,
> He drives the Wretch before; and lashes into Night.
>
> (486–95)

Where Chaucer speaks casually of "th' olde days" when "this land" was "fulfild of fayerye" and

> The elf-queene, with hir joly compaignye
> Daunced full ofte in many a grene mede. . . .

---

32 On Dryden's elaboration of the painting of Diana, see Hagstrum, pp. 189, 190.

Dryden revives the fairy world of *A Midsummer Night's Dream:*

> The King of Elfs and little Fairy Queen
> Gamboll'd on Heaths, and danc'd on ev'ry Green.
> And where the jolly Troop had led the round
> The Grass unbidden rose, and mark'd the Ground:
> Nor darkling did they dance, the Silver Light
> Of *Phoebe* serv'd to guide their Steps aright,
> And, with their Tripping pleas'd prolong'd the Night.
> Her Beams they follow'd, where at full she plaid,
> Nor longer than she shed her Horns they staid,
> From thence with airy Flight to Foreign Lands convey'd.
>
> (*The Wife of Bath Her Tale*, 3–12)

As in Shakespeare and in Pope, this refined fantasy is linked with domestic lore of farm and countryside:

> I speak of ancient Times, for now the Swain
> Returning late may pass the Woods in vain,
> And never hope to see the nightly Train:
> In vain the Dairy now with Mints is dress'd,
> The Dairy-Maid expects no Fairy Guest,
> To skim the Bowls and after pay the Feast.
> She sighs and shakes her empty Shoes in vain,
> No Silver Penny to reward her Pain. . . .
>
> (16–23)

Although *Baucis and Philemon* cannot be translated without referring to household objects and rustic simplicity, Dryden again takes full advantage of his opportunity and fills the poem with "good English" home and country things and impressions. Here are two or three of many examples:

> A common Settle drew for either Guest . . .
> The Fire thus form'd, she sets the Kettle on,
> (Like burnish'd Gold the little Seether shone) . . .
> Then Curds and Cream, the Flow'r of Country-Fare,
> And new-laid Eggs, which *Baucis* busie Care
> Turn'd by a gentle Fire, and roasted rear.
>
> (44, 56–57, 96–98)

In general, Pope makes use of the language of household and farm only when he is satirizing excesses of wealth, taste, or self-indulgence, or middle-class success, or foulness of mind in courtiers and literateurs. But in his Horatian imitation addressed to Bethel, where he pictures himself in his most Horatian role of country-gentleman-poet, his vocabulary and idiom are almost as heartily English and rural as Dryden's:

Content with little, I can piddle here
On Broccoli and mutton, round the year;
But ancient friends, (tho' poor, or out of play)
That touch my Bell, I cannot turn away.
'Tis true, no Turbots dignify my boards,
But gudgeons, flounders, what my Thames affords.
To Hounslow-heath, I point, and Bansted-down,
Thence comes your mutton, and these chicks my own:
From yon old wallnut-tree a show'r shall fall;
And, grapes, long-lingring on my only wall,
And figs, from standard and Espalier join:
The dev'l is in you if you cannot dine.

(137–48)

We have seen some features of this role in various poems by Dryden, but little of the "true Horatian" tone and rhythm that mark Pope's mature conversational verse. But in this style, too, Dryden in his late phase offers an example to Pope.

Although Dryden cites Horace's "fineness of Raillery" as his model in *Absalom and Achitophel,* and though he says he preferred his manner to Juvenal's, the fineness of Dryden's allusive style is not Horace's. His satirical manner is both more "majestic" and more lusty than "that sharp, well-manner'd way of laughing Folly out of Countenance." In *Religio Laici,* he writes in something like Horace's "legislative" style, but he is much more combative in argument than Horace. In one rare passage, when he turns aside to speak to his friend, Henry Dickinson, Dryden anticipates his own later conversational manner and Pope's manner in his best epistles and satires:

Thus far my Charity this path has try'd;
(A much unskilfull, but well meaning guide:)
Yet what they are, ev'n these crude thoughts were bred
By reading that, which better thou hast read,
Thy Matchless Author's work: which thou, my Friend,
By well translating better dost commend:
Those youthfull hours which, of thy Equals most
In *Toys* have *squander'd,* or in *Vice* have *lost,*
Those hours hast thou to Nobler use employ'd;
And the severe Delights of Truth enjoy'd.

(224–33)

Dryden never wrote better than this, and Pope did not surpass these lines of urbane and just praise. Most notable is the skill with which Dryden manages his long and complex sentences, breaking them into not too obviously matched phrases in a way that satisfies easily the demands of meter and the normal pauses and accelerations of speech.

(The whole twenty-eight lines of the digression are composed with equal art.) Two features typical of Dryden's later manner and of Pope's Horatian "way" are the neatness with which the parenthetical aside is worked into the couplet and the polite intimacy of address.

Dryden had written epistles in verse early in his career, but in a style very different from this. In the lines (1660) to his "Honour'd Friend," Sir Robert Howard, with whom he was in fact on intimate terms, Dryden moves from conceit to conceit and witty point to point,[33] in a series of striking compliments that hardly give an illusion of talk between equals. The difference between Dryden's early and late epistles comes out in the contrast between *To my Honour'd Friend, Dr Charleton* of 1663 and *To my Ingenious Friend, Mr. Henry Higden, Esq.* of 1687. Dryden is, of course, adjusting his tone in both pieces to the occasion, in the first to the publication of an archeological treatise by an eminent man of science; in the second, to the publication of a translation of Juvenal by a fellow satirist. But while some allowance for the difference in occasions must be made, the lines to Higden exemplify the more relaxed, more personal, and more colloquial manner that Dryden achieves in his later epistles. For example, compare

> Nor are *You*, Learned Friend, the least renown'd . . .
>
> > > (*To . . . Charleton*, 33)

with

> Yet You, my Friend, have temper'd him so well,
> You make him Smile in spight of all his Zeal.
>
> > > (*To . . . Higden*, 18–19)

Or compare

> Such is the healing virtue of Your Pen,
> To perfect Cures on *Books*, as well as *Men*.
>
> > > (*To . . . Charleton*, 41–42)

with

> Suppose I had the better End o' th' Staff
> Why shou'd I help th' ill-natur'd World to laugh?
> 'Tis all alike to them, who gets the Day;
> They Love the Spight and Mischief of the *Fray*.
> No; I have Cur'd my Self of that *Disease;*
> Nor will I be provok'd, but when I please:
> But let me half that *Cure* to You restore;
> You gave the *Salve*, I laid it to the *Sore*.
>
> > > (*To . . . Higden*, 29–36)

[33] See James Kinsley, "Dryden and the Art of Praise," *English Studies*, XXXIV (1953), 58–60.

The declarative "I's" and the sharp "No" of these lines bring Dryden closer to Pope in his role of personal and defiant satirist.

The good-natured lines that follow look forward to the more elegant and surely the most perfect of Dryden's epistles, *To My Dear Friend, Mr. Congreve* (1694), a poem that best expresses the genial temper of Dryden in his last years and marks also his arrival at the true Horatian style. He begins with perfect casualness, moves to high compliment, goes on to objective comments on literary history, and returns easily to intimacy and greater warmth of feeling:

> Well then; the promis'd hour is come at last;
> The present Age of Wit obscures the past:
> Strong were our Syres; and as they Fought they Writ,
> Conqu'ring with force of Arms, and dint of Wit;
> Theirs was the Gyant Race, before the Flood;
> And thus, when *Charles* Return'd, our Empire stood.
> Like *Janus* he the stubborn Soil manur'd,
> With Rules of Husbandry the rankness cur'd:
> Tam'd us to manners, when the Stage was rude;
> And boistrous *English* Wit, with Art indu'd.
> Our Age was cultivated thus at length;
> But what we gain'd in skill we lost in strength. . . .
> In Him [Congreve] all Beauties of this Age we see;
> *Etherege* his Courtship, *Southern's* Purity;
> The Satire, Wit, and Strength of Manly *Witcherly*.
> All this in blooming Youth you have Atchiev'd;
> Nor are your foil'd Contemporaries griev'd;
> So much the sweetness of your manners move,
> We cannot envy you because we Love.
>
> (1–12, 28–34)

Later in the epistle, he qualifies a noble and witty compliment with a sufficiently offhand manner to make the transition easy to a biographical and even sentimental "I":

> Maintain Your Post: That's all the Fame You need;
> For 'tis impossible you shou'd proceed.
> Already I am worn with Cares and Age;
> And just abandoning th' Ungrateful Stage:
> Unprofitably kept at Heav'ns expense,
> I live a Rent-Charge on his Providence. . . .
>
> (64–69)

Note also the improvised effect of "That's all . . ." and the conversational turn of " 'tis impossible. . . ." In this poem, Dryden gives Pope a lesson in the Horatian art of "navigation" of which he was to become a master. The nearly contemporary lines to Kneller are stiffer and more majestic (possibly reflecting Dryden's feelings toward this rather pompous man), but they too have fine transitions and instances of natural but polite address. Dryden's skillful handling of the casual style appears again in the poem to Motteux (1698), where Dryden begins and ends with exactly Pope's effect of a conversation going on between craftsmen who share similar tastes and who confidently exchange criticism and praise.

But the poem that best sums up Dryden's late Horatian style and his appreciation of the life of retirement and of the even temper of Horace is the epistle *To my Honour'd Kinsman, John Driden, of Chesterton*. The first phase of the poem opens with an allusion to Horace,

> How Bless'd is He, who leads a Country Life,
> Unvex'd with anxious Cares, and void of Strife . . .

and continues in a vein of easy "converse" that rises from precise compliment to appreciation of Horatian *correctio animi:*

> Just, Good, and Wise, contending Neighbours come,
> From your Award, to wait their final Doom;
> And, Foes before, return in Friendship home.
> Without their Cost, you terminate the Cause;
> And save th' Expence of long Litigious Laws:
> Where Suits are travers'd; and so little won,
> That he who conquers, is but last undone:
> Such are not your Decrees; but so design'd,
> The Sanction leaves a lasting Peace behind;
> Like your own Soul, Serene; a Pattern of your Mind.
>
> (7–16)

The transition to the next section begins with an echo of Virgil's Second *Georgic,*

> So liv'd our Sires . . .

but the old satirist speaks out in the lines that follow,

> So liv'd our Sires, e'er Doctors learn'd to kill,
> And multiply'd with theirs, the Weekly Bill:
> The first Physicians by Debauch were made:
> Excess began, and Sloth sustains the Trade.
>
> (71–74)

From Physick he easily returns to the simple life of "our long-liv'd Fathers" in a passage recalling Horace's "Ofellus" *Satires*, II, ii.[34] After

[34] For an echo of Dryden's poem in the passage, see *Twickenham Edition*, I, note to *Windsor Forest*, 242.

the praise of "gen'rous" Garth, he pays his most direct tribute to his cousin, in lines that are direct and dignified and composed in the rare patriotic-moral vein of Pope's epistle to James Craggs. The ideal portrait of the patriot and man of affairs reflects in tone and statement Dryden's "mod'rate" political views and shows how his increased flexibility of style makes it possible for him to acknowledge a wider range of relations and values, both public and private:

> When, often urg'd, unwilling to be Great,
> Your Country calls you from your lov'd Retreat,
> And sends to Senates, charg'd with Common Care,
> Which none more shuns; and none can better bear.
> Where cou'd they find another form'd so fit,
> To poise, with solid Sense, a spritely Wit!
> Were these both wanting, (as they both abound)
> Where cou'd so firm Integrity be found?
>   Well-born, and Wealthy; wanting no Support,
> You steer betwixt the Country and the Court:
> Nor gratifie whate'er the Great desire,
> Nor grudging give, what Publick Needs require. . . .
>   A Patriot, both the King and Country serves;
> Prerogative, and Privilege preserves:
> Of Each, our Laws the certain Limit show;
> One must not ebb, nor t'other overflow:
> Betwixt the Prince and Parliament we stand;
> The Barriers of the State on either Hand:
> May neither overflow, for then they drown the Land.
> When both are full, they feed our bless'd Abode;
> Like those, that water'd once, the Paradise of God.
>
> (119–30, 171–79)

The blend in this epistle of patriotism and friendship, of "home-Felt Quiet," "Exercise and Ease," in country scenes will be renewed in the *Beatus ille* passage of Pope's *Windsor Forest*.[35] After the epistle to John Driden and the accompanying *Fables*, with their intimations of Pope's pastoral and descriptive styles, Dryden might well say that it was time for a new age and a new poet to begin.

[35] *Windsor Forest*, 235–58.

GEOFFREY TILLOTSON

The Methods of Description in Eighteenth- and Nineteenth-Century Poetry

D ESCRIBING IS AN IMPORTANT and necessary function of a poet, but great poets have done as little of it as possible, other necessary things being more important. In this brief chapter, I am concerned only with two methods of description used by some great poets of the eighteenth and nineteenth centuries, and only with one aspect—the syntax—even of those two. Nor shall I give them or suggest more than the minimum of analysis; I shall use syntax merely as a means of distinguishing methods, not attempting to point out differences within the sameness.

In the eighteenth century there is syntax applied to words describing external nature as Milton had applied it in *Paradise Lost*. The description of the Garden of Eden in Book IV makes three sentences stretching over sixty-two and a half lines, the syntactical pauses coming where they happen to fall, as it seems, and falling usually somewhere within the line. John Philips and Thomson apply syntax as Milton had applied it. Here are a few lines from the first edition of *Winter:*

> At last, the muddy Deluge pours along,
> Resistless, roaring; dreadful down it comes
> From the chapt[1] Mountain, and the mossy Wild,
> Tumbling thro' Rocks abrupt, and sounding far:
> Then o'er the sanded Valley, floating, spreads,
> Calm, sluggish, silent; till again constrain'd,
> Betwixt two meeting Hills, it bursts a Way,
> Where Rocks, and Woods o'erhang the turbid Stream.

Syntax like this fittingly contributes to rendering the external world in all its multitudinousness and turbulence. Pope never wanted to

GEOFFREY TILLOTSON is Professor of English in Birkbeck College at the University of London.

[1] Cracked, fissured.

highlight those aspects of it and could not well have done so in the couplet. When he surveys the creation at the beginning of *Windsor Forest*, it is the orderliness of it that he insists on:

> The Groves of *Eden*, vanish'd now so long,
> Live in Description, and look green in Song:
> *These*, were my Breast inspir'd with equal Flame,
> Like them in Beauty, should be like in Fame.
> Here Hills and Vales, the Woodland and the Plain,
> Here Earth and Water seem to strive again,
> Not *Chaos*-like, together crush'd and bruis'd,
> But as the World, harmoniously confus'd:
> Where Order in Variety we see,
> And where, tho' all things differ, all agree.
> Here waving Groves a checquer'd Scene display,
> And part admit and part exclude the Day,
> As some coy Nymph her Lover's warm Address
> Nor quite indulges, nor can quite repress.
> There, interspers'd in Lawns and opening Glades,
> Thin Trees arise that shun each others Shades.
> Here in full Light the russet Plains extend;
> There wrapt in Clouds, the bluish Hills ascend. . . .

There is wildness here but wildness behind bars. Another passage of description—one of the few others—shows him gaining his effect of absence of order by straining at the couplet. The syntax of a normal couplet by Pope has a comma at the end of the first line, and a heavier stop at the end of the second. That being so, the syntax of the passage in which Eloisa describes the surroundings of the Paraclete is most unusual:

> The darksom pines that o'er yon' rocks reclin'd
> Wave high, and murmur to the hollow wind,
> The wandring streams that shine between the hills,
> The grots that eccho to the tinkling rills,
> The dying gales that pant upon the trees,
> The lakes that quiver to the curling breeze;
> No more these scenes my meditation aid,
> Or lull to rest the visionary maid:
> But o'er the twilight groves, and dusky caves,
> Long-sounding isles, and intermingled graves,
> Black Melancholy sits, and round her throws
> A death-like silence, and a dread repose:
> Her gloomy presence saddens all the scene,
> Shades ev'ry flow'r, and darkens ev'ry green,
> Deepens the murmur of the falling floods,
> And breathes a browner horror on the woods.

(155–70)

The syntax in this passage falls as lightly as is possible in the couplet. Lines 155 and 165 show the first line of a couplet washing over onto the second. The commas at the end of lines 157–60 and 163–64 are all light because they merely detach the items in a list. Where we might expect a heavy stop—after "hills" (line 157), "sits" (line 165), "green" (line 168, because the "and" of that line suggests that the sentence will end with the clause it introduces)—we get light stops, commas instead of semicolons. In none of his poems does Pope allow the syntax of the normal couplet to interfere with the building-up of the paragraph—which is usually the unit he works to. Normally, the couplets remain plainly discernible as subsidiary units. Here, however, the separate couplets come near to being lost in the rhythm of the larger unit. We note that the description is given in a single sentence, in the manner of *Paradise Lost*. It is as near as Pope comes to writing Miltonic blank verse; when otherwise he wrote blank verse it was in the manner of contemporary plays.

The passage just quoted has four lines beginning with "The," the reason being that they form a list of equal items. Another method of description, as important in the later eighteenth and nineteenth centuries as the Miltonic method in the earlier eighteenth, seems to take its rise from that list, or from a fellow to it. But it goes one step further and makes the lines complete grammatical statements. Complete with their verb, they make sentences:

> The Curfew tolls the knell of parting day,
> The lowing herd wind slowly o'er the lea,
> The plowman homeward plods his weary way,
> And leaves the world to darkness and to me.

> Now fades the glimmering landscape on the sight. . . .

(I proceed beyond the first quatrain for a reason that will be clear later on.) Here the first two lines are virtually independent sentences (as items in a list such as Pope's cannot be), and the third line also until the fourth follows, showing retrospectively that it was in fact half a sentence. That first stanza of Gray's effected a revolution in descriptive method. He showed description proceeding by the laying-down of uniform strips, each a line in length, and each syntactically complete in itself. And he passed on the method to all the hundreds of poets who throughout the rest of the eighteenth, nineteenth, and much of the twentieth centuries (to count the verses of twentieth-century schoolboys figuring in their magazines) studiously parodied his "Elegy" or wrote independent poems in its manner. One of the latter poets is Wordsworth—for instance, in his "Hartleap Well," some of the stanzas of which have syntax like this:

> Now here is neither grass nor pleasant shade;
> The sun on drearier hollow never shone; . . .

But it is the opening of "Resolution and Independence" that shows Gray's method most strikingly:

> There was a roaring in the wind all night;
> The rain came heavily and fell in floods;
> But now the sun is rising calm and bright;
> The birds are singing in the distant woods;
> Over his own sweet voice the Stock-dove broods;
> The Jay makes answer as the Magpie chatters;
> And all the air is fill'd with pleasant noise of waters.

When quoting the opening of the "Elegy," I carried over to the fifth line because the line beginning with "Now" and making a complete sentence is another of Gray's innovations. It reappears in that most wonderful of all the songs Tennyson added to *The Princess*— we note also the syntactical completeness of other lines of the poem —the first stanza of which reads:

> Now sleeps the crimson petal, now the white;
> Nor waves the cypress in the palace walk;
> Nor winks the gold fin in the porphyry font:
> The fire-fly wakens: waken thou with me.

When Milton began paragraphs of description with "Now," his syntax remained true to the general system. For instance:

> Now came still Eevning on, and Twilight gray
> Had in her sober Liverie all things clad;
> Silence accompanied, for Beast and Bird,
> They to thir grassie Couch, they to thir Nests
> Were slunk, . . .

and so on to the end of the sentence twelve lines long.

LEO HUGHES

Theatrical Convention in Richardson: Some Observations on a Novelist's Technique

Puff. . . . Now enter Tilburina!
Sneer. Egad the business comes on quick here.
Puff. Yes, sir—now she comes in stark mad in white satin.
Sneer. Why in white satin?
Puff. O Lord, sir—when a heroine goes mad, she always goes into white satin—don't she, Dangle?
Dangle. Always—it's a rule.

W HEN, IN THE NOW FAMOUS LETTER of 20 March 1754 to Stinstra, Richardson professed to have had no idea "I had as much invention till I almost accidentally slid into the writing of Pamela," he was making one of the most fascinating, as well as amazing, pronouncements in literary annals. With very full evidence provided by his letters and by the records of his printing business, scholars, especially Professors McKillop and Sale, have been able to show in detail the curious process by which he did in effect slide into novel writing—and indeed into novel writing of an art so advanced in some ways that it required a century for others to overtake him.

It is my object here to examine into this "invention" so strangely disclosed by accident as it is revealed in Richardson's use of what might be called "stage business." What I hope to show is at least something of the method by which his imagination and observation operated.

Miss Tompkins has summed up very well the kind of thing I am here intent upon:

There is a great deal of what may be called stylized gesture in the sentimental parts of eighteenth-century novels and romances,—kneel-

LEO HUGHES is Professor of English and Associate Dean of the Graduate School at the University of Texas.

ings and raisings, and lifting up of fine eyes, and pressings of the benefactor's hand to one's heart in silent ecstasy, not to speak of the slapping of villainous brows and other handsome expressions of violent feeling. These may also claim to be dramatic in a bastard sense; that is, they are stagey; for they certainly include some shoddy fragments of the technique which tragic actors found necessary in the great theatre of the period, or rather of that technique as debased by strollers and barn-stormers. They can be accepted by the well-intentioned as a sort of emotional shorthand, but like all artificial tradition they tended to obscure the view of the real. . . .

And in another brief passage she indicates a possible source for such stylized materal, referring to "Richardsonian drawing-rooms" from which Lothario might abduct the heroine and carry her off to a deserted mansion, only to have the hero rescue her in a "clash of steel" and lead her to the altar, she being dressed for the occasion "in a white lutestring negligée with silver spots."[1]

By way of illustration it may be well to provide a brief sketch of the kind of stylized gesture Richardson used, especially when he was trying to develop high tragedy. Take one of the first listed by Miss Tompkins: the lifting up of fine eyes. We shall have to couple it with the lifting up of hands since Richardson often combined them. This gesture was a favorite. From Letter 19 of *Pamela*—"Mrs. Jervis lifted up her hands, and had her eyes full of tears"—to Letter LXVI of the final volume of *Grandison*[2]—"A man of honour, said [Clementina], her hands lifted up, is more valuable to a woman in trouble, than all the riches of the East!"—we get the same gesture over and over. Its use in *Pamela*, where I have marked fifteen occurrences, might be understandable enough considering Richardson's uncertainty in his apprentice work. But *Pamela* is only a faint suggestion of what is to come. Richardson became so enamored of the gesture that he used it nearly a hundred times in *Clarissa*. (I cannot vouch for the exact number. One can hardly justify reading so long a work merely to mark gestures. Besides, Richardson is prone to what might be called, to borrow his own coinage, *somnivolence*.) Appearing with increasing frequency as we get into the closing volumes, the gesture is symptomatic of the weakness of the later episodes, wherein Richardson, unwilling to let his heroine die with becoming dignity, insists on prolonging every scene of confrontation or edifying piety. *Grandison* begins more hopefully as far as the use of this particular gesture is

---

[1] J. M. S. Tompkins, *The Popular Novel in England, 1770–1800* (London, 1932), pp. 352–53, 208.

[2] Where letters are referred to by numbers the reference is to the edition by Leslie Stephen published by Henry Sotheran in 1883.

concerned. It seems clear that if the novelist had confined himself to drawing rooms in the homes of English gentility, he might have been able to avoid stylized gesture entirely; but with the Italian scenes and particularly with the temporary derangement of Clementina, he fell into his old ways. Uplifting hands and eyes recurs again and again, some thirty times.

Obviously the particular gesture I have been focusing on is not the only one. Miss Tompkins has suggested some of the others: kneelings, raisings, slapping of villainous brows. Richardson does not omit a single one. I have made no attempt to catalogue the kneeling or, more violently, the "flinging" of oneself at someone's feet. The posture had a contagious quality, for one character's kneeling led to another's. At one point in *Grandison*, we have three characters kneeling at once— and no really plausible reason for any of it. Stamping the feet or taking turns about the room, gestures of which Fielding was rather too fond, occurs with less frequency. Richardson seems to have been less than adept with the fan and snuff box, and, though these familiar comedy-of-manners props appear, they are not common. He does, however, make good use of the apron, a garment in high fashion at mid-century. And like Puff in *The Critic*, he has a nice sense of timing with the handkerchief.

Here, for example, is a brief passage from *Grandison*, with a far less stylized example than most of Richardson's gestures and actually suggestive of what he might have done had he chosen to develop his powers of observation:

The whole congregation was hushed and silent, as if nobody were in the church but persons immediately concerned to be there. Emily changed colour frequently. She had her handkerchief in her hand; and (pretty enough!) her sister bride-maids, little thinking that Emily had a reason for her emotions, none of them had, pulled out their handkerchiefs too, and *permitted* a gentle tear or two to steal down their glowing cheeks.

The handkerchief business is usually perfunctory, even mechanical. Here, for example, are three passages occurring in a space of ten pages in the heart of *Clarissa*: "She took out her handkerchief and put it to her eyes." "There the angel stopt; her handkerchief at her eyes," ". . . and down I dropt, her face all the time turned half from me, as she stood at the window, her handkerchief often at her eyes."

My mention of *The Critic* brings me back to the lines quoted at the beginning of this essay and to another theatrical convention that Richardson seems concerned to follow: the proper dress for his female characters. No great amount of attention is given to dress, but there is enough to suggest more than accident; Richardson seems to be conscious of a theatrical need.

The several references to clothes in *Pamela* are invariably tied to status: Pamela collects her "little all"—as Fielding was to parody it—and divides it into three parts, which she catalogues. Or Pamela dresses in homespun to prove to her master that she is not addicted to finery. Or Pamela, in "ordinary dress," after her triumph lords it over her genteel neighbors in fine attire. Or Pamela, now having climbed to the top of the social ladder, attends a masquerade, her Quaker costume and her strong disapprobation of the whole affair apparently intended to cancel out any effects of bad example. In short, there is nothing really theatrical in Richardson's references to dress in his first novel.

Clarissa is quite another story. The only detailed account of dress in the early volumes is casual enough, though interesting for what it reveals of another side of Richardson. Lovelace boasts to Belford of his critical taste in women's dress and then proceeds to demonstrate it, and the excellence of Clarissa's taste too, by describing in great detail the dress worn on the fateful day of her half-elopement, half-abduction: "Her morning gown was a pale primrose-coloured paduasoy: the cuffs and robins curiously embroidered by the fingers of this ever-charming Arachne," etc., etc. The theatrical note does not appear until after the tragedy, so long postponed, has occurred. After filling the interval following Clarissa's violation with incoherent bits and fragments—Clarissa's "papers" giving incomplete visions, condemnations of her violator, outbursts of self-pity—Richardson eventually brings us back to the more conventional epistolary narration and to the first big confrontation scene, which occurs on Sunday evening following the black Monday of Lovelace's crime. Lovelace, writing very much "to the moment," closes one letter at 6:00 P.M. on Sunday with "Here she comes." The next, dated simply "Sunday night," plunges into the theatrical:

> She was dressed in a white damask night-gown, with less negligence than for some days past. I was sitting with my pen in my fingers; and stood up when I first saw her, with great complaisance, as if the day were still her own. And so indeed it is.
>
> She entered with such dignity in her manner as struck me with great awe, and prepared me for the poor figure I made in the subsequent conversation.

Though Lovelace assured us that Clarissa has recovered from her recent negligence, the change does not seem to have been permanent, for she now resolves not to change her garments so long as she is a captive at Madame Sinclair's. We see the same white damask for days. We are told of her resolve in a letter from Lovelace to Belford on 19

June (the day following the theatrical scene mentioned above) and reminded of it on Thursday, 22 June. Belford informs us in a letter written 29 June that she was still wearing her white damask under the garments borrowed from Mabell, when she escaped on the preceding day.

Almost a month later, Monday, 17 July, Belford catches a dramatic picture of her kneeling in prayer in the corner of her room in the "horrid hole" of a bailiff's house, her finger marking her place in the Bible. "Her dress was white damask, exceedingly neat. . . . She had not been solicitous enough about her dress to send for others." His memory is a little short or his idea of neatness less exigent than a woman's, for he has forgotten reporting, in a long, long letter of the day before, Sally's suggestion to the poor prisoner that she was "a little soily."[3]

As the fateful Thursday, 7 September, inches nearer, when Clarissa will escape her prison through death, Richardson mercifully provides a change of attire; that is, he changes the dress and its material, but not the color. Clarissa herself prepares us for the change by assuring us, in a letter to Mrs. Norton, "My wedding garments are bought— and though not fine or gawdy to the sight, though not adorned with jewels, and set off with gold and silver (for I have no beholders' eyes to wish to glitter in), yet will they be the easiest, the *happiest* suit, that ever bridal maiden wore. . . ."

Again we can rely on the faithful Belford, who shows an increased fascination with dramatic tableaux. On Wednesday, 6 September, he reports another of these all-but-final scenes: "I found her up, and dressed in a white satin night-gown. Ever elegant, but now more so than I had seen her for a week past; her aspect serenely cheerful." Later the same evening Belford brings Colonel Morden to see his dying cousin. "We beheld the lady in a charming attitude. Dressed, as I told you before, in her virgin white. She was sitting in her elbow-chair, Mrs. Lovick close by her in another chair, with her left arm round her neck, supporting it, as it were. . . ."

Though *Grandison* leads us only to the brink of tragedy, it provides, in the highly theatrical scenes of Clementina's derangement, the full scope of female stage costume. Except for a noncommital "She [Clementina] was elegantly dressed" in an early scene I recall nothing on costuming before Richardson introduces his stilted attempt at high

---

[3] Dorothy Van Ghent refers to this scene with stress on Clarissa's "miraculously dirt-resistant white garments" since she is intent upon the mythic possibilities of the novel. Though such a reading is often enough completely oblivious of the author's intent, it must be admitted that Richardson's own stress on *virgin whiteness* does lend support to such a view (*The English Novel: Form and Function* [New York, 1953], p. 49).

tragedy, after Sir Charles returns from Bologna to visit the distracted girl. Having vainly tried a variety of devices to restore her to her senses, the della Porrettas resort to a form of shock treatment, "introducing her in full assembly, I [Sir Charles] one of it. But I could not forbear asking the marchioness, if Lady Clementina would not be too much startled at so much company? I wish, said the marquis, sighing, that she *may* be startled." After a few moments spent by the family in dispelling the doubts of the ever-considerate Sir Charles, the heroine enters: "Just then entered the sweet lady, leaning upon Camilla, Laura attending. Her movement was slow and solemn. Her eyes were cast on the ground. Her robes were black and flowing. A veil of black gauze half covered her face. What woe was there in it!"

Clementina does in time recover her senses and less than two months later is prepared to receive her English suitor again. Camilla lets him know what her mistress's striking recovery is owing to: the presence of Sir Charles himself. "Oh, sir, said the good woman, miracles!—we are all joy and hope!" And to symbolize the joy, the costume designer is again called into action: "My young lady is dressing in colours to receive you. She will no more *appear* to you, she says, in black. . . ."

The cheerful colors provide only a false dawn. No reconciliation of the religious differences between the fair Italian and the English paragon seems possible, and before the month is out we get a big rejection scene, a scene that so moves the imperturbable hero that he requires a second effort before his trembling hand is steady enough to record it. Again Camilla is called upon to prepare us for Clementina's entrance: "She was not to be pleased with her dress. Once she would be in black, then in colours; then her white and silver was taken out; but that, she said, would give her a bridal appearance: she at last chose her plain white satin. She looks like an angel."

On this celestial note I close my sketch of theatrical convention and turn to a study of the provenience of these items. To take the last item—costuming—first, it seems evident that the novelist combines with his own observation of life a generous mixture of theatrical tradition. The former ingredient is the more elusive. We know that Richardson was partial to the opposite sex, and though we lack conclusive evidence that this partiality extended to an interest in female fashions, we may assume so. The detailed account of the fugitive Clarissa's attire is done *con amore*. We also know, from evidence supplied by students of costume, that what he describes—actual garments, materials, colors—were then in high fashion. Take the apron, at times a badge of servitude. Nancy Bradfield tells us that the apron was fashionable from the end of the seventeenth century on through our period. She assures us too that "white, with embroidered or painted flowers, was very fashionable towards the end of the reign [of George II]."[4]

Concerning stage costume we can be a little more confident. This early in the period there is no wealth of detail to confirm the existence of the sort of tradition that Sheridan is amused over, but what little there is seems positive enough. It would be helpful if we could have such details as Oxberry gives in his collection of stock plays in the early nineteenth century. From him we learn that Lady Randolph in Home's *Douglas* wears "black velvet . . . trimmed with black bugles," whereas Viola in *Twelfth Night* survives a shipwreck in "white satin . . . trimmed with silver" and Olivia in the same piece wears a "white dress trimmed in black."[5]

In the absence of such helpful detail, we shall have to rely on the memoirs of George Anne Bellamy and Perdita Robinson. Miss Bellamy is especially helpful since she indicates both the existence of a tradition and something of its range. From an account of how she outwitted a rival actress in Dublin, we learn of a costuming tradition. The rival, playing Octavia in *All for Love*, had "just acquired taste enough to despise the black velvet in which those ladies [Roman matrons] were usually habited" and stole the gaudy dress with its "ground of . . . silver tissue" that George Anne had acquired for her role of Cleopatra. To shame her, the latter "to the surprise of the audience . . . appeared in white sattin." In a similar contest, this time with Peg Woffington in London, Miss Bellamy, now playing Octavia, dressed "again in white sattin; not indeed as I had then *improperly* done, as Antony's favourite mistress, but as his rejected wife." Later in her career, she allowed a local tradition rather than a contest with a rival to force her out of the common mode. Having lost her wardrobe in a fire in Glasgow, she at first refused to play Lady Macbeth, having no black dress, but the townspeople assured her that the legendary lady's ghost had often appeared at Dunsinane "dressed in *white* sat-

[4] Nancy Bradfield, *Historical Costumes of England* (London, 1958), pp. 120–21.

[5] Stage directions and even dialogue in standard plays provide meager help, but it is help. To give only token illustration, I call attention to the "sad solemn weeds" in Rowe's *Lady Jane Gray*, V, i, where Lady Jane is "discovered" on the drawing of the inner curtain "kneeling as at her devotion; a light, and a book placed on a table before her," a scene reminiscent, except for the color of the heroine's dress, of what Belford saw and described. Richardson must certainly have known this play, as well as the same author's *Fair Penitent*, where "Calista is discovered on a couch in black, her hair hanging loose and disordered" (V, i). He would have been equally familiar with Otway's *Caius Marius*, V: "Enter several old men in black with cypress wreaths, leading virgins in white with myrtle." One thinks of Lovelace's imaginary troop of "a dozen or two of young maidens all dressed in white" begging amnesty—"and what a pretty show they will make, with their white hoods, white gowns, white petticoats, white scarves, white gloves, kneeling for me, with their white handkerchiefs at their eyes, in two pretty rows . . ." (III, 190).

tin." With some misgivings, she "played the character, out of the usual form, in white sattin."[6] Perdita Robinson lends some confirmation to the tradition by recalling her own debut at Drury Lane as Juliet wearing "a pale pink sattin . . . and my monumental suit, for the last scene, was white sattin and completely plain. . . ."[7]

Other items in Richardson's limited stock of stage business may be traced to theatrical literature. By his own testimony he had too little leisure to read; yet he obviously knew some plays. We may feel sure, for example, that he knew the plays in the library Clarissa found at Madame Sinclair's: "Steel's, Rowe's, and Shakespeare's plays; that genteel comedy of Mr. Cibber, The Careless Husband, and others of the same author."[8]

From these plays alone he could have got cues for his own stage directions. His two favorites, the lifting of hands and eyes and the kneeling or throwing oneself at another's feet, are to be found here.[9] The former is not frequent, but it is to be found in Cibber's *Double Gallant* and *Provoked Husband* and in Rowe's *Biter*. Cibber was especially fond of "throwing himself at so-and-so's feet."[10] Both Cibber and Steele made frequent use of another gesture that Richardson used also: "flinging away" or "flinging off."

What Richardson may have learned from watching performances is much harder to recover. We know he attended plays, early in his career especially,[11] but we have no record of what he may have ob-

---

[6] *An Apology for the Life of George Anne Bellamy* (London, 1785), I, 132–35; II, 49; IV, 65.

[7] *Memoirs of the Late Mrs. Robinson* (London, 1930), p. 103.

[8] He most certainly knew Steele's *Tender Husband* well, though he has Pamela in her exalted, play-reading state give it a severe going-over. He almost certainly got his heroine's name from the play and not from Sidney. Twice he quotes Biddy Tipkin on the subject of "a good comfortable scheme," or I should say he misquotes her just enough to show that he depended on his memory of a favorite passage (*Clarissa*, V, 420; *Grandison*, II, 402). It is just possible that he got the name for his villain-hero from Cibber's Loveless in *Love's Last Shift*. Similarly his Belford-Belton is reminiscent of eighteenth-century theatrical names, such as Bellmour in *The Old Bachelor*, Bellmour in *Jane Shore*, Bellamant in *The Modern Husband*, Bellamy in *Caelia*—the roll is endless.

[9] The religious connotation of these gestures may have made them additionally attractive to Richardson. Defoe, who had much the same religious interest and background, used these gestures in *Robinson Crusoe* and *Journal of the Plague Year*, not notably theatrical works.

[10] In the prefatory material to *The Provoked Husband* (1728), poor Cibber committed a whole cluster of absurdities for his enemies to seize upon. Not only did he have Mrs. Oldfield "out-do her usual out-doing" and assign her "the paraphonalia of a woman of quality" in his preface; he also began his dedication to the queen with what must have seemed an overwhelming gesture: "The English theatre throws itself, with this play, at your Majesty's feet, for favour and support."

[11] A. D. McKillop, *Samuel Richardson* (Chapel Hill, N.C., 1936), pp. 141–42.

served of tragic action. We can best judge the possibilities of this influence by examining it in connection with a much more ponderable
kind of evidence, especially where Richardson the master printer is concerned: illustrations of plays. If he had never seen a performance, he
would still, by the demands of his trade, have been exposed to tragedy
queens in their most striking theatrical gestures. How accurately contemporary engravers reproduced them it is impossible to say; but
even assuming only approximations, we cannot avoid remarking on
the stylized nature of many of the gestures. Take for example a few
pieces printed in Richardson's own shop and therefore certainly observed by him. The frontispieces to Eliza Haywood's *Wife to be Lett*
(1735) and Aaron Hill's *Alzira* (1736) show characters, especially
women, gesturing in the approved fashion: kneeling, uplifting hands
and eyes, and dangling handkerchiefs or holding them to weeping
eyes.

Other examples of plays not traced to Richardson's shop add to this
story. Returning for a moment to Madame Sinclair's library, we find
additional evidence. The most recent edition of Shakespeare, for example, was the Hanmer, published at Oxford in 1744. There is a link,
admittedly casual, between Richardson and this edition in that Hay-
man and Gravelot, who had done the illustrations for the sixth edition
of *Pamela* two years earlier, illustrated the Shakespeare. These illustrations are anything but convincingly tragic, being soft, youthful,
even effeminate.[12] Still the gestures are the conventional ones: bended
knees, hands lifted in supplication. The most recent edition of Rowe's
plays, published by Feales in 1736, shows the same tendency of the
engraver to arrest dramatic scenes in tableaux, the characters frozen in
theatrical gesture.

What Richardson may have learned from association with professional dramatists is most conjectural of all. He had several playwright
friends, friends who could have given him advice if he had sought it.
Edward Young may be said to have advised Richardson publicly in
Conjectures on Original Composition,[13] but this particular advice
came after both had finished their work; it is also too general to have
any technical value. Although Young did give Richardson advice earlier and more privately, in his letter of 20 June 1744, it has nothing
to do with stage action but with the tragic ending of *Clarissa*. Three

---

[12] If, as Eaves maintains, "in 1741–42 these two artists were the best England could
offer," English art was in a bad way indeed (T. C. Duncan Eaves, "Graphic Illustration of the Novels of Samuel Richardson, 1740–1810," *Huntington Library Quarterly*, XIV [1950–51], 353).

[13] A. D. McKillop, in "Richardson, Young, and the *Conjectures*" (*Modern Philology*, XXII [1925], 393–99), tells the story of Richardson's share in this supposedly
revolutionary essay.

years later, 19 November 1747, we find Richardson regretting that he had ever "consulted anybody but Dr. Young."[14]

A far more eminent man of the theater had by this time become a close friend of Richardson, the venerable—though not excessively venerated—poet laureate, Colley Cibber. I have already suggested that Richardson might well have borrowed some of Cibber's stage business. Opportunity for advice of a more direct kind was even more readily available, for the two became fast friends. But very little in the way of exchange has been recorded, and this little suggests that the novelist neither sought nor received technical advice from the retired actor-playwright. Some curious nontechnical ideas do appear in the exchange. On one occasion, Richardson taunted Lady Bradshaigh for suggesting that the good man he was then picturing might be allowed a "moderate rakery" by recalling old Cibber's advice to allow Sir Charles a mistress.[15] Much earlier Cibber had revealed an unexpected side of his nature by urging Letitia Pilkington in violent terms to dissuade Richardson from allowing Clarissa's death.[16]

It may well be that Cibber and Richardson confined their discussion of the novels to just such emotional and moral problems. On the other hand, it is quite likely that Cibber, a shrewd judge of human nature, soon discovered how dangerous it was to offer advice to the oversensitive artist and did not allow himself to be trapped, as another friend did. I refer to Aaron Hill, whose friendship dated from a much earlier time and whose discussions with Richardson are much more fully recorded in published letters. Hill had very pronounced views on theatrical gestures and no aversion to sharing them with anyone who would listen. His letters include several to actors, from the obscure Miss Holliday to the already famous Garrick, urging them to adopt the system that he had developed. Though Richardson was not an actor, it seems hardly possible for him to have escaped completely from the system, for Hill was, as his own biographer admits, a colossal bore. We know that Richardson was exposed to at least one version, because he printed Hill's *Art of Acting* in 1746. Miss Brewster quotes a letter from Richardson to Hill describing the violent effects he felt on reading it.[17]

Two items on the art of gesture by Hill suggest possible connections with the novels. One has to do with lifting or extending the arms. In his gratuitous—and evidently wasted—advice to Miss Holli-

[14] *The Correspondence of Samuel Richardson* (London, 1804), II, 24–25.

[15] For the full story, see R. H. Barker, *Mr. Cibber of Drury Lane* (New York, 1939), pp. 252–55.

[16] *Ibid.*, pp. 250–52.

[17] Dorothy Brewster, *Aaron Hill* (New York, 1913), p. 257.

day, Hill urges her "to extend your arms, with an opener freedom as often as it is necessary." And in a long postscript he describes in detail a similar gesture used by Mrs. Porter, one of the most successful actresses of the day, as, in conveying a sense of horror, she "throws out her arms to their utmost extent. . . ."[18]

A second item has to do with the eyes, which Hill stresses repeatedly in his advice to actors. Both Clarissa and Lovelace make frequent mention of the eyes as expressive of emotion. "We are both great watchers of each other's eyes," says Clarissa, though at another point she takes umbrage at a similar suggestion from Lovelace: "You are an *observer of eyes*, my dear, said the villain; perhaps in secret insult. . . ." Even closer to Hill's system is the coaching that Lovelace gives the two abandoned women who are to impersonate his relatives. His greatest problem is to prevent their betraying their true nature by their eyes:

> Have I not told you that my beloved is a great observer of the eyes? . . . Once more suppose *me* to be my charmer.—Now you are to encounter my examining eye, and my doubting heart.
> That's my dear!
> Study that air in the pier-glass!

This last passage resembles one in *The Art of Acting*, which may well have been passing through Richardson's shop and hands at about the time he was busy with this section of his novel. Hill's comment reads:

> 'Tis but to look and will.—Th' imprinted *eye*
> Moves the struck *muscles*, and the limbs comply.
> . . . Find your smile's force, before some faithful glass,
> Heedful, to let no *faint* impression pass.[19]

In the long run, however, Hill was to discover the danger of advising Richardson, even when the latter sought advice. Fortunately Miss Brewster tells the story in detail[20] so that I need not repeat it all here. In briefest form it runs like this: In the summer of 1744 Hill had been favored, along with Young, by being asked to comment on the plan[21]

[18] *The Works of the Late Aaron Hill, Esq.* (London, 1753), I, 138–39, 144–45. It should be recalled that Pamela singles out Mrs. Porter as having "acted incomparably" in *The Distrest Mother*.

[19] Not having access to the 1746 version printed by Richardson, I have taken these lines from Hill's *Works* (1753), III, 395–96. I have also checked them against the lines quoted in the review of the 1746 version, *Gentleman's Magazine*, XVI (1746), 625–26.

[20] Brewster, *op. cit.,* pp. 260–68.

[21] McKillop, *Samuel Richardson*, p. 121.

for *Clarissa* and, along with Young, had approved: "It is impossible . . . to question your infallible success in this new, natural attempt." Anyone who assumes so superlative a send-off would be enough to content Richardson is unaware of that gentleman's insatiability, an insatiability which may have originated in diffidence but now fed upon itself. For months he kept sending Hill installments of the novel, always with pleas for suggestions. For months Hill's good sense held out, and he supplied what really was wanted: "I cannot improve you, would you have me frankly tell you why? It is, because I want the power to imitate you. You must be content to stand alone. . . ." Such lavish praise only increased Richardson's appetite and back he came for more until Hill, who may well have been growing apprehensive over the unconscionable length of the story, lost his grip and in October 1746 returned an elaborate set of suggestions not only for curtailment but also for character changes. Because like the timid man already determined to marry a shrew, Richardson had kept asking his friends for advice when all he wanted was reassurance, he was deeply offended and broke off all correspondence for almost a year, resuming it only on Hill's persistence.

Perhaps it is feasible then to suggest how Richardson's "invention" operated: His great strength, as he seems to have instinctively realized, lay in the analysis of motives and the consequences of certain kinds of conduct; when his own observation and intuition proved ample, he actually wanted no help, though he might ask for it. His greatest weakness lay in his desire for status, which forced him to venture into areas where his intuition had no check from his observation. And, as we have seen here, it forced him into the error of supposing that since the dramatic method was best adapted to showing the full range and depth of feeling—as it is—he was obliged, or privileged, to write in the manner of high tragedy, stage machinery and all.

JAMES SUTHERLAND

The Impact of Charles II on Restoration Literature

THE KING HAD LITTLE OR NO LITERATURE," said Bishop Burnet in his forthright Scotch way, "but true and good sense, and had got a right notion of style; for he was in France at a time when they were much set on reforming their language. It soon appeared that he had a true taste."[1] The context of this observation is a discussion of sermons and preachers; and what the Bishop has in mind is that Charles II was thoroughly modern and up to date, a man of his own time. The observation could be extended to most of the king's activities and to the whole cast of his mind. It is true that, unlike his grandfather James I, he had no literary ambitions: Horace Walpole could not find a niche for him among his Royal and Noble Authors and was forced to conclude that "the only genius of the line of Stuart, Charles the Second, was no author."[2] Charles had other interests: conversation, telling stories, sauntering in the Park, feeding the ducks, Newmarket, his elaboratory, his mistresses, the theater, and so on. He was, however, as Horace Walpole could hardly have known, an admirable letter writer; and once at least, on perhaps the only occasion when he was really in love,

(Never durst poet touch a pen to write
Until his ink were temper'd with love's sighs)

he may have written a rather touching song for La Belle Stuart, who had given him a new and bewildering experience by resisting his advances:

JAMES SUTHERLAND is Lord Northcliffe Professor of Modern English Literature in University College at the University of London.

[1] *Burnet's History of My Own Time*, ed. Osmund Airy (1897), I, 340.

[2] Horace Walpole, *A Catalogue of the Royal and Noble Authors of England . . .*, The Second Edition (1759), II, 50.

I pass all my hours in a shady old grove,
But I live not the day when I see not my love:
I survey ev'ry walk now my Phyllis is gone,
And sigh when I think we were there all alone.
   O then 'tis I think there's no hell
   Like loving too well.

And so on for three more stanzas—although it is by no means certain that they can be safely ascribed to the king.[3] If he wrote any more poetry, it has not survived. Charles was clearly of Sir Fopling Flutter's opinion that writing was a mechanic part of wit and that "a gentleman should never go beyond a song or a billet."

Nor, apparently, was he much of a reader. In September 1680, when the king was at Windsor, John Evelyn tipped a charwoman ("an antient woman who made these lodgings cleane") to let him spend several days in the king's private library at Whitehall. He found about a thousand volumes there, but "few of any greate importance, or which I had not perused before; they consisting chiefly of such books as had from time to time been dedicated, or presented him: Few Histories, some Traveles, & french bookes, Aboundance of *Mapps* & Sea-Charts: Entertainements and Pomps; buildings, and Pieces relating to the Navy. . . ."[4] The king was a desultory rather than a diligent reader. When we hear of him enjoying a book, it is one like Butler's *Hudibras* (which he carried around in his pocket), or Marvell's *Rehearsal Transprosed*, which his licenser L'Estrange wished to suppress, but which was allowed to reach a second edition through the personal intervention of the king.[5] For his more serious reading, we have Dryden's authority for it that he had read Louis Maimbourg's *History of the League* when it first appeared, and Burnet asserts that he had read D'Avila's *Storia delle Guerre civili di Francia* "more than any other book of history."[6] If he had also read all the various books that were presented or dedicated to him, from Hobbes's *Leviathan* to Sprat's *History of the Royal Society* and Evelyn's *Sylva*, he would

---

[3] This poem is printed in the edition of the *Royal and Noble Authors* "Enlarged and Continued to the Present Time. By Thomas Park, F.S.A." (1806), I, 154–55. The ascription is made on the authority of Sir John Hawkins and "on the negative testimony of lord Orford himself, who thought there was nothing in the following amatory song to contradict the report of its having been said in an old copy to be written by this witty prince." See Sir John Hawkins, *A General History of the Science and Practice of Music* (1853), II, 937.

[4] *The Diary of John Evelyn*, ed. E. S. DeBeer (1955), IV, 214–15.

[5] *The Critical Works of John Dennis*, ed. Edward Niles Hooker (1939), I, 413; George Kitchin, *Sir Roger L'Estrange* (1913), p. 192 n.

[6] See Dryden's dedication of his translation to the king in *The Works of John Dryden*, ed. Walter Scott (1808), XVII, 81; and Burnet, *op. cit.*, II, 266.

have had no lack of literature, but he probably read just enough to enable him to compliment the author intelligently. It may be recalled how gracefully he improved the occasion when, on 25 May 1660, as he set foot again on English soil and the Mayor of Dover presented him with a very rich Bible, he told the Mayor that it was the thing he loved above all things in the world.[7]

Yet however little he wrote, and however much or little he may have read, this leisurely and witty king had an influence on the literature of his country such as no other English monarch has had, with the exception of Elizabeth I. The writers of the Restoration period were conscious of Charles II less as the father of his people than as an easy-going uncle, who liked to be amused and who was very well able to distinguish good amusement from bad. Many of the best writers of the day, such as Buckingham, Rochester, Dorset, or Sedley, were his familiar companions; others, such as Dryden, Pepys, Evelyn, Wycherley, or Burnet, met and conversed with him fairly frequently. No king was ever more easy of access. Only a few days after he had returned to London in 1660, as his coach was passing along the Strand, he caught sight of the philosopher Hobbes, "putt of his hat very kindly to him, and asked him how he did." About a week later, while he was sitting for Samuel Cooper the miniature painter, he had a friendly chat with the old philosopher and later saw a good deal of him at court. When the king saw him approaching, he would say, "Here comes the bear to be baited," but Hobbes could hold his own in repartee with the witty young courtiers.[8] Such a state of affairs is typical of the king's attitude and of the freedom of his court: we can hardly imagine Bernard Shaw being given the same sort of liberty at the court of Edward VII or, still less, at that of George V.

Charles was prepared to be amused or interested by men of very different sorts, provided they had wit or talent. At the time of the Restoration he was only thirty, and many of the brightest ornaments of his court were men of his own age or younger: youth and high spirits set the tone for a good deal of the literature of the first decade. Later, in the 1670's, he was much attracted by the young Wycherley, and when Wycherley became ill of a fever, the king visited him at his lodgings near Covent Garden—"a Proof of his Esteem and Affection which never any Sovereign Prince before had given to an Author who was only a private Gentleman"—and promised him that as soon as he was fit to travel to the south of France, "he would order five

---

[7] *Diary and Correspondence of Samuel Pepys, F.R.S.*, ed. Richard, Lord Braybrooke (1828), I, 98. For further information on the king's reading, see Godfrey Davies, *Essays on the Later Stuarts* (1958), pp. 20–22.

[8] *Aubrey's Brief Lives*, ed. Oliver Lawson Dick (1949), pp. 152–53.

hundred Pounds to be paid him to defray the Expence."[9] About the same time, he was on familiar terms with Tom Durfey, at that time a very young man: Mr. Nestor Ironside could remember "King Charles the Second leaning on Tom d'Urfey's shoulder more than once, and humming over a song with him."[10] But he was just as likely to be seen conversing with John Evelyn about how to deal with London smog or with Sir William Petty on the subject of double-bottomed ships.

The familiarity with which the king was treated by his subjects, and especially by the writers of the day, is symptomatic of his easygoing tolerance. We need not, perhaps, be surprised that one of his own immediate circle like Rochester should produce witty epigrams at the king's expense, for satirical banter and repartee were looked upon as one of the chief graces of his court. We should remember, too, that although many obscene and wounding verses were written about the king, most of those circulated orally or in manuscript while he was still alive and found their way into print only after his death in such collections as *Poems on Affairs of State.* If Mulgrave, in his "Essay upon Satire," could write such lines as those upon "sauntering Charles between his beastly brace," he could not print them. Yet the freedom of reference in print to "His Sacred Majesty" has few parallels at any other period. Surely at no other time could the king's poet laureate have opened a poem as Dryden opened *Absalom and Achitophel,* with its free-and-easy allusions to the sexual vigor of his royal master, who, like Israel's monarch, had made

> Promiscuous Use of Concubine and Bride;
> . . . And, wide as his Command,
> Scatter'd his Maker's Image through the Land.

Dryden was not writing a lampoon to be circulated furtively by Captain Robert Julian, but a poem that was almost an official statement of the views held by the king's party, one that aimed at setting the king himself in the best possible light. The poem may well have been submitted to the king in manuscript. Even in the theater, which he was so fond of visiting, Charles might suddenly hear himself mentioned on the stage, not just in a prologue or epilogue, but in the dialogue of the play itself. In *The Country Wife,*[11] for example, Sparkish decides that it is too late in the day to go to Whitehall:

Sparkish. Another time. Faith, the king will have supped.

Harcourt. Not with the worse stomach for thy absence. Thou art one of those fools that think their attendance at the king's meals as necessary

---

[9] *Critical Works of John Dennis* (1943), II, 411.

[10] Sir Richard Steele, *The Guardian,* No. 67, 28 May 1713.

[11] Act III, scene i.

as his physicians, when you are more troublesome to him than his doctors or his dogs.

The king was perhaps the only person at court who really liked his spaniels, which wandered numerously everywhere and which, according to Evelyn, were allowed to "lie in his bed-Chamber, where often times he suffered the bitches to puppy & give suck, which rendred it very offensive, & indeed made the whole Court nasty & stinking."[12] Wycherley's allusion to the king's spaniels is not, indeed, malicious; but this public reference to the king's private life does bring out again how familiar a figure he was to his subjects and how they could risk a joke about him without fear of giving displeasure. Charles, in fact, would forgive much for a joke. We know, too, that he was "extremely fond" of Wycherley on account of his wit and that he often "chose him for a Companion at his leisure Hours, as Augustus did Horace."[13]

So far, then, as being *interested* went, Charles could be said to have encouraged literature and the arts, and also, of course, pure and applied science; the sympathetic and informed interest of such an intelligent ruler certainly counted for something. But it was when it came to translating this interest, or the promises that often accompanied it, into practical support that the king was apt to prove a broken reed. When he did authorize a pension or the payment of a sum of money, the Exchequer only too often failed to honor it. Indeed, we should know a good deal less about his pensions if the public archives did not contain so many letters suing for their payment. Hobbes was given a pension of £100, but it reached him so irregularly that he had to petition for it.[14] According to Pope, Charles gave Wycherley "now and then a hundred pounds, not often." Wycherley, in fact, spent the last four years of the king's reign in a debtor's prison and was not rescued from it until Charles's successor, James II, who "complained that he had not seen him for so many years and inquired what was become of him," paid his debts.[15] The neglect of Samuel Butler has become almost proverbial. "The King and Clarendon," John Aubrey noted, "both promised him great matters, but to this day he haz got *no* Employment, only the King gave him 300 pounds."[16]

[12] *Diary of John Evelyn*, IV, 410.

[13] *The Whole Works of Major Richardson Pack* (1729), p. 184; and Lord Lansdowne's "Character of Mr. Wycherley," *The Genuine Works in Verse and Prose* (1732), I, 435.

[14] *D.N.B.*: "Thomas Hobbes."

[15] Joseph Spence, *Anecdotes . . .* , ed. S. W. Singer (1820), pp. 17, 45.

[16] *Aubrey's Brief Lives*, p. 46.

As poet laureate, Dryden was naturally a target for the king's good-natured encouragement, but his relations with Charles are a long story of broken promises and salary unpaid. At some time in the 1670's, he had begun to meditate an epic poem. The first clear reference to this poem that he was never to write comes in the dedication of *Aureng-Zebe* (1676), where he tells the Earl of Mulgrave that he has never thought of himself as being especially fitted for writing plays and that he has no desire any longer to be the dramatic "Sisyphus of the age." He has still some hopes left that he may "make the world some part of amends for many ill plays by an heroic poem." Mulgrave, he continues, has long known that this is his intention and was, in fact, the first to give him the chance of talking about it to the king and the Duke of York, who "were then pleased, both to commend the design, and to encourage it by their commands." But that was as far as the king had gone, and unless Mulgrave can "stir up that remembrance in his majesty, which his many avocations of business have caused him, I fear, to lay aside," the epic will never be written. "As I am no successor to Homer in his wit, so neither do I desire to be in his poverty." Seventeen years later, when addressing another patron, the Earl of Dorset, he recalls his plans for an epic poem, now long abandoned, and gives a fuller account of what he had hoped to do. "But being encouraged only with fair words by King Charles II, my little salary ill paid, and no prospect of a future subsistence, I was then discouraged in the beginning of my attempt; and now age has overtaken me, and want, a more insufferable evil, through the change of the times, has wholly disenabled me."[17]

The king's treatment of his laureate could be paralleled, *mutatis mutandis*, in the lives of other Restoration authors: they had the fair words, and little else. As Dryden was to write in his funeral pindaric on Charles II, he was very casual in his bounty to the poets:

---

[17] Dryden, *Works*, V, 184; *Essays of John Dryden*, ed. W. P. Ker, II, 38. Dr. Charles E. Ward (*The Life of John Dryden* [1961], pp. 72–73) finds the first hints of this intention in the dedication of *Tyrannic Love* to the young Duke of Monmouth (1670), but although Dryden does there suggest as a possible alternative to his heroic play "an heroick poem, filled with the past glories of your ancestors," we can hardly assume that he had already considered writing such a poem himself. Again, in the dedication of *The Conquest of Granada* to the Duke of York (1672), after comparing Charles to Agamemnon and the Duke to Achilles, Dryden goes on to remark: "And I doubt not from both your actions, but to have abundant matter to fill the annals of a glorious reign, and to perform the part of a just historian to my royal master, without intermising with it anything of the poet." Dr. Ward takes this to be another reference to the projected epic and interprets Dryden's statement as meaning that "the abundance of heroic actions of the Stuart line will relieve him, as poet, of feigning actions that had no basis in history." It may, indeed, be so; but about eighteen months before this Dryden had been appointed historiographer-royal, and his words might equally well refer to a projected history of the reign of Charles II.

> Tho little was their Hire, and light their Gain,
> Yet somewhat to their share he threw;
> Fed from his hand, they sung and flew,
> Like Birds of Paradise that liv'd on morning dew.[18]

In other words, he treated them much as he treated the ducks in St. James's Park, when "somewhat to *their* share he threw."

No one today seems to regret very much that Dryden failed to write his epic poem, and even the poet himself was willing to think that it was enough for him to have *offered* to write one. "It may be to the advantage of my reputation," he suggested, "to have it refused me."[19] As for the king, it might be argued that he was behaving no worse than a publisher who assures an author that he will be glad to see his manuscript when it is finished. But on some occasions the initiative came from the king himself. It was he (according to an anonymous Catholic priest) who gave Dryden the plan for writing *The Medal;* and from Pope we further learn that he "obliged Dryden to put his Oxford speech into verse, and to insert it toward the close of *Absalom and Achitophel.*"[20] He certainly commanded Dryden's translation of Maimbourg's *History of the League,* and it was his desire for an English opera that involved Dryden in writing *Albion and Albanius* for the music of Lewis Grabu.[21] The king signified his royal wish that John Ogilby should make a survey of England and Wales, and the result of his labors appeared in the first (and only) volume of Ogilby's *Britannia* (1675).[22]

In 1669 he invited John Evelyn to write a history of the Dutch war, and Evelyn set about collecting materials. Almost exactly two years later the king remembered to ask how it was going along, but Evelyn never finished it. When, however, on 9 January 1674 the king sent for him and asked him to write something against the Dutch, he gave the king the preface that he had written for the projected history, and this was duly published with the title of *Navigation and Commerce.* . . . Unfortunately, events had caught up with the publication: a peace treaty had been signed with the Dutch some time before the book appeared, and the Dutch ambassador protested and asked for it to be withdrawn. The king, however, told Evelyn that he was exceedingly pleased with what he had done "and gave me many thanks. However . . . his Majestie told me, he must recall it for-

---

[18] *Threnodia Augustalis,* ll. 377–80.

[19] Dedication of *Aureng-Zebe,* in *Works,* V, 184.

[20] Spence, *Anecdotes,* pp. 171, 172.

[21] See Ward, *op. cit.,* pp. 203, 205.

[22] *Aubrey's Brief Lives,* p. 221.

maly, but gave order that what Copies should be publiquely seiz'd to pacifie the Ambassador should immediatly be restord to the Printer, & that neither he nor the *Vendor* should be molested."[23] No doubt a considerable number of works were written in this way in response to, or in anticipation of, a royal command (Dryden's *His Majesties Declaration Defended* is another example), but most of them, perhaps, would hardly rank as literature.

The impact of Charles II on the literature of his reign is seen most clearly in the drama. As a habitual playgoer he knew what he liked, and he took some trouble to see that he got what he wanted. What he usually wanted was comedy, which gave him "the greatest pleasure he had from the Stage."[24] From time to time he suggested to his dramatists where they could find a good plot. He drew the attention of Sir Samuel Tuke to the Spanish play from which he fashioned *The Adventures of Five Hours;*[25] and near the end of his life he gave Crowne the plot for his *Sir Courtly Nice* by advising him to read Moreto's *No Puede Ser.*[26] From one of Dryden's few surviving letters, we learn that he was at work on a comedy that was to be "almost such another piece of business as the fond Husband [i.e., Durfey's *The Fond Husband*, 1677], for such the King will have it, who is par-cell poet with me in the plott; one of the designes being a story he was pleasd formerly to tell me. . . ." Charles E. Ward is almost certainly right in identifying this comedy as *Mr. Limberham, or the Kind Keeper.*[27] No doubt there were other occasions when the king dropped a hint which a Tuke or a Crowne regarded as "a sacred command." Such evidence as is available certainly suggests that he had an eye for a good comic plot.

Left to himself, he might have been prepared to settle for comedy or opera; but he had to consider the tastes of the ladies of the court, and there is a good deal of evidence to show that the female part of a Restoration audience had a decided preference for tragedies and he-roic plays. So far as the establishment of the rhymed heroic play in England is concerned, the influence of the king appears to have been decisive, and it can be documented in some detail. His chief instru-ment in this palace revolution was Roger Boyle, Earl of Orrery. Ac-cording to Orrery's first biographer,

---

[23] *Diary of John Evelyn*, III, 523, 568; IV, 30, 41.

[24] John Crowne, Dedication of *Sir Courtly Nice* (1685).

[25] *Op. cit.*, Preface to the third edition (1671).

[26] *Op. cit.*, Dedication.

[27] *The Letters of John Dryden*, ed. Charles E. Ward (1942), pp. 11–12, 148.

King Charles was the first who put my lord upon writing plays, which his majesty did upon occasion of a dispute that arose in his royal presence about writing plays in rhyme: some affirmed it was not to be done; others said it would spoil the fancy to be so confined, but the Lord Orrery was of another opinion; and his majesty being willing a trial should be made, commanded his lordship to employ some of his leisure that way, which my lord readily did.[28]

To this may be added a statement by the earl himself that he had been commanded by the king to write a play for him and had thereupon written a tragi-comedy in rhyming verse, and "writt it in that manner . . . because I found his maj^{ty} Relish'd rather the French Fassion of Playes than the English. . . ."[29] As Orrery's editor makes clear, this play was *The Generall*, and Orrery must be given what credit is due to the author of the first rhymed heroic play in English. On 26 February 1663, the king wrote to him in encouraging terms:

I will now tell you, that I have read your first play, which I like very well, and doe intend to bring it upon the Stage, as Soone as my Company have their new Stage in order, that the Seanes may bee worthy the words they are to sett forth. . . .[30]

For reasons not entirely clear, *The Generall* was not produced at this time; but, as his editor claims, "the king's liking for Orrery's unique creation instigated the introduction of the heroic couplet and of disputative scenes concerned with love *vs.* honor, as new fashions in dramatic expression."[31] When, in the autumn of 1665, Orrery proceeded by the king's command to write another heroic play, *The Black Prince*, and sent the king a specimen of what he had already written, he was again encouraged by a letter that could only have come from Charles II. It was an open secret that Orrery's muse was only active when he had a fit of the gout, and in writing to him the king let him know that he was "very well pleased with that part of the Black Prince he had sent him, and conjured his lordship to go on and complete it, which if he could not do until he had a fit of gout, he wished him a fit presently, that he might the sooner finish it."[32]

One would like to think that the king was being no more than polite when he praised Orrery's plays; and certainly their high-flown sentiments, romantically generous motives, and long introspective debates are very far removed from the shrewd and cynical good sense

---

[28] *The Dramatic Works of Roger Boyle, Earl of Orrery*, ed. W. S. Clark (1937), I, 23. For what follows on Orrery's connection with the heroic play, I am indebted to Dr. Clark's "Historical Preface" to his edition of the *Works*.

[29] *Ibid.*

[30] *Ibid.*, p. 26.

[31] *Ibid.*, p. 30.

[32] *Ibid.*, p. 42.

of Charles II. But it may be that the heroic play with its autocratic and even tyrannical monarchs, its grandiose court settings, and its glorification of power and beauty, gratified a side of Charles II that is rarely noticed, but that became more obvious in the later and more Machiavellian years of his reign, when he ruled without a parliament and with the aid of such men as Sunderland and Jeffreys. However easy-going Charles might seem, there was something in his character which led him toward a more absolute form of government than the vast majority of his subjects would have approved; if he had not actually dreams of glory, he looked with approval, and perhaps envy, at the firm and undemocratic rule of the Grand Monarch across the Channel. His love of comedy may reflect the affable, and even democratic, aspects of the king's character; but his apparent interest in the heroic play (whose absurdities and unreality would seem to be so alien to his realistic appraisal of human character and motives) may reflect his desire for a world in which kings are not constantly checked and obstructed by their subjects.[33]

If we had, what we don't have, a record of all the plays performed at court during his reign and of those that he chose to attend in the public theaters, we should be able to say more confidently what his tastes in the drama really were and so discuss more precisely the influence that he exerted on the development of the Restoration theater. Even so, we should have to discount the influence of his mistresses. We know, for example, because Dryden himself tells us, that *The Wild Gallant*, which was apparently a flop with the ordinary playgoer, appealed to Lady Castlemaine and was acted at court, where it was "more than once the Divertisement of His Majesty, by His own Command."[34] Yet when Pepys saw it performed at court on 23 February 1663, he remarked that "the king did not seem pleased at all, the whole play, nor any body else" and that the only thing worth seeing in the whole evening was Lady Castlemaine.[35] Something, however, may be learned of the king's taste from a consideration of those plays which, on the evidence of their gratified authors, were his own special favorites. One such play was Dryden's *Secret Love; or, The Maiden-Queen*, which was "own'd in so particular a manner by His Majesty, that he has grac'd it with the Title of His Play."[36] What al-

---

[33] I owe this suggestion to my colleague, Basil Greenslade, who has also drawn my attention to the way in which the chronically impoverished king employed Hugh May the architect to refurbish Windsor Castle, together with the painter Verrio and a whole army of Italian and French craftsmen and the English Grinling Gibbons. Charles II was not indifferent to the pomp that should surround a monarch.

[34] *Works*, II, 17.

[35] Pepys, *Diary*, II, 9.   [36] *Works*, II, 383.

most certainly pleased the king most in this play was what also delighted Pepys—the gay, high-spirited pair of lovers, Celadon and Florimel, and more especially Florimel, who was played to perfection by Nell Gwyn. But he may also have enjoyed the emotional conflict in the heart of the young queen and the similar ambiguous agitations in the mind of Philocles. There is nothing particularly ingenious in the action of *Secret Love*, but a good comic plot was clearly one of the factors that counted most with the king. Nothing much else could explain his presence at three of the first five nights of Durfey's *The Fond Husband* (1677), a comedy full of intrigue and impudent contrivance and (as Durfey himself claims in the prologue) not depending for its effect on witty conversation and repartee.[37] Durfey was a favorite with the king, who also enjoyed another of his comedies acted some months earlier, *Madam Fickle: Or, The Witty False One*, and "according to His accustomed Royal and Excellent Temper, was pleas'd to descend so far, as to give it a particular Applause."[38] Again the situations, though often farcical and highly improbable, are contrived with considerable ingenuity, and both those comedies had droll parts specially written for two of the best comedians of the day, Nokes and Leigh. We learn again that in performing the Mamamouchi in Ravenscroft's *The Citizen Turn'd Gentleman*, Nokes "pleas'd the King and Court, next Sir Martin [i.e., Dryden's *Sir Martin Mar-All*] above all plays."[39] On such evidence of the king's taste, we could hardly venture to say more than that he "liked a good laugh"; but we must never forget that the character performances of men like Nokes and Leigh—as old dotards, blunderers, credulous cuckolds, country bumpkins, and the like—may have been superb in their kind.

There remains one other sphere in which, rather surprisingly, the king exerted a considerable influence. As Defender of the Faith, Charles could not escape listening fairly frequently to sermons, and he liked them to be "clear, plain, and short."[40] He had a pronounced dislike of sermons that were read from a manuscript in the pulpit, or even those preached from copious notes. Annoyed in October 1674 by a Cambridge don who preached before him in this manner while he was at Newmarket, he instructed the Duke of Monmouth, who was chancellor at the time, to give orders that all university preachers

[37] Steele, *The Guardian*, No. 82, 15 June 1713.

[38] *Op. cit.*, Dedication.

[39] John Downes, *Roscius Anglicanus*, ed. Montague Summers, p. 32. Downes adds: "This Comedy was looked upon by the Criticks for a Foolish Play: yet it continu'd Acting 9 Days with a full House."

[40] *Burnet's History of My Own Time*, I, 340.

should have their sermon *memoriter*. A similar direction was given to Oxford in the following month.[41] So far as Charles II was concerned, the ecclesiastical actor had to be perfect in his part. At all events, some of the greatest preachers of the day, like Burnet or South, delivered their sermons *ex tempore* or from memory, and the liveliness of the Restoration pulpit may be due in considerable measure to this practice. That the king's dislike of the written discourse was well known is suggested by the delightful story of a conversation he is said to have had with Stillingfleet. Why, the king asked, did Stillingfleet always read his sermons when he preached before him, although he invariably preached without notes on other occasions? Stillingfleet replied that "the awe of so noble an audience, where he saw nothing that was not greatly superior to him, but chiefly the seeing before him so great and wise a prince, made him afraid to trust himself." He then asked the king why, when he could have none of those reasons, he always read his speeches to Parliament. "I have asked them so often and for so much money," the king replied, "that I am ashamed to look them in the face."[42]

Whether this anecdote is true or false, it offers us a clue to the kind of influence Charles II must have had on the literature of his age. A king about whom such stories could be recorded—or made up—was clearly a source of inspiration to the writers of the day. So long as Charles II was alive, wit, humor, raillery, repartee, the droll remark, the well-turned phrase were all in demand and certain to be appreciated: the king and his court might be unfriendly to epic, but they were kind to epigram, and the stimulus of a king "who never said a foolish thing" radiated outward to coffee-house and tavern and to the writer in his study. Rightly or wrongly, Dryden gaves Charles much of the credit for reforming the conversation of Englishmen.

The desire of imitating so great a pattern first awakened the dull and heavy spirits of the English from their natural reservedness; loosened them from their stiff forms of conversation, and made them easy and pliant to each other in discourse. Thus, insensibly, our way of living became more free; and the fire of the English wit, which was being stifled under a constrained, melancholy way of breeding, began first to display its force, by mixing the solidity of our nation with the air and gaiety of our neighbours.[43]

The significance of this improved conversation and heightened wit for the drama, and more particularly for comedy, is sufficiently obvi-

[41] W. Fraser Mitchell, *English Pulpit Oratory*, 1932, pp. 23–24.

[42] *Richardsoniana*, 1776, p. 89.

[43] Dryden, *Essays*, I, 176.

ous, and Dryden goes on to make the point himself. The dramatists wrote better because they had the king and his court as models for imitation, as standards by which to test their own performance, and as judges of the finished work. It is equally true that the prestige of wit led to a swarm of amateur writers who, as Dryden put it, were "ambitious to distinguish themselves from the herd of gentlemen" by attempting a poem or even a play, and who would have done much better to be "contented with what fortune has done for them, and sit down quietly with their estates."[44] But that was the penalty that had to be paid in a period of wit and epigram. If there were inevitably many more Witwouds than Mirabells, the Mirabells were sometimes brilliant, and at least the Witwouds kept on trying.

[44] *Ibid.,* I, 196.

DOUGALD MacMILLAN

George Steevens's Contributions to Biographia Dramatica

Eccentric antiquarian and editor, George Steevens showed "exceptional diligence, method, and antiquarian knowledge of literature" in editing Shakespeare and made "valuable contributions" to Reed's revision of Baker's *Biographia Dramatica* in 1782.[1] Sidney Lee does not say what these contributions are except for an "appreciative notice of Garrick." The Hoe copy of *Biographia Dramatica* of 1812, in the Huntington Library, interleaved, does, however, identify Steevens's contributions to Volumes II and III. Facing the title page is a manuscript note by John Payne Collier: "With the assistance of Reed's original M. S. I have marked all the principal articles and passages furnished by Steevens up to 1782." In these two volumes, Collier's notes attribute substantial portions of fifty-three articles to Steevens. Reed's revisions were very extensive; and Steevens's contributions constitute, perhaps, the most interesting and original of these editions. Since *Biographia Dramatica* continues to be used as an authoritative reference work and is, indeed, the principal source of information about many plays and playwrights of the latter part of the eighteenth century, it may be instructive to examine these notes attributed to Steevens. Also, since many users of the work credit its information and opinions to Baker or Reed, though they frequently use the latest revision by Stephen Jones, which appeared in 1812, they may like to know who seems really to be responsible for some of the information and opinion there presented. First, some attention should be given to the development of the work.

David Erskine Baker's anonymous work, *The Companion to the Playhouse: or, An Historical Account of all the Dramatic Writers (and their Works) that have appeared in Great Britain and Ireland,*

DOUGALD MacMILLAN is Kenan Professor of English at the University of North Carolina and editor of *Studies in Philology*.

[1] Sidney Lee in *D.N.B.*

from the Commencement of our Theatrical Exhibitions down to the Present Year 1764, is in two volumes, the first containing criticism of individual plays, the second, the biographical sketches of the authors. Volume I contains a dedication to Garrick, an "Introduction. A brief View of the Rise and Progress of the English Stage" (pages v–xxvii), and "Critical Reflexions on the Old English Writers. Extracted from a Prefatory Discourse to the new Edition of Massinger's Works, printed in 1761; and addressed to David Garrick, Esq." (pages xxvii–xlii).[2] The remarks on the works, alphabetically by title, complete the volume. Baker took his "brief View of the Rise and Progress of the English Stage" from Robert Dodsley's Preface to his edition of *Old Plays.*[3] The "Critical Reflexions," from the edition of Massinger (1761), are by George Colman.[4] Reed dropped them from his revision of Baker.[5] He retained almost all of Dodsley's history of the stage; but, as he had already "added extensive biographical and bibliographical material"[6] to Dodsley when he edited the second edition of *Old Plays* in 1780, he also carried these revisions over to the new edition of Baker.

Reed changed the title to *Biographia Dramatica, or A Companion to the Playhouse;* and he put Baker's name (but not his own)[7] on the title page, where he states also that this is "A New Edition, carefully corrected; greatly enlarged; and continued from 1764 to 1782." He added an Advertisement (p. v), followed by the "Rise and Progress," Baker's version of Dodsley, corrected in a few places and greatly enlarged to cover the period from the closing of the theaters to 1782.[8] He then reversed the order of the parts, placing the biographical

[2] There is no pagination after p. xlii.

[3] *A Select Collection of Old Plays* (1744), I, vii–xxxiv.

[4] Attributed to him by B. M. *Catalogue of Printed Books.* See also *The Dramatic Works of Philip Massinger,* rev. T. Coxeter (4 vols.; London, 1761). The "Critical Reflexions" are reprinted in Massinger's *Works,* 1779.

[5] They are an address to Garrick on the excellence of Shakespeare and blank verse and a plea for the performance of other old plays, especially Massinger's. Baker's reprint is greatly reduced by omissions.

[6] *Isaac Reed Diaries, 1762–1804,* ed. Claude E. Jones (University of California Publication in English, X [1946], 5–6). See also *D.N.B.,* s.v. Dodsley. Reed's contributions survived in later editions of *Old Plays,* e.g., Collier's (1825–28) and W. C. Hazlitt's (1874–76).

[7] At the conclusion of his Introduction (I, li–lii), he says, "The present Editor has not been wanting in diligence to render the work as perfect as he was able, consistent with his attention to more important avocations. He desires, however to derive no credit from any part of it." The Introduction is not signed. On Reed's passion for anonymity, see Jones's Introduction to the *Diaries,* p. 5.

[8] Dodsley's account stops (p. xxxiv) with "the total Suppression of all Plays and Playhouses." Baker (pp. xxii–xxv) added to this in three pages a very sketchy account, closing with Garrick's becoming manager of Drury Lane.

sketches in the first volume. These biographies and the critical remarks on plays, which follow in Volume II, are corrected and expanded. Many earlier plays unknown to Baker are included as well as
those that had appeared after 1764. Steevens contributed critical remarks on plays in both groups.[9]

Steevens's hand is found by Collier in twenty-one discussions of
early plays that Baker had not known or knew only by title. Three
of these plays, or cycles, are medieval: the "Miracle Play of St. Katharine," "Coventry Plays," and "Cornish Interludes." Of St. Katharine
he cites Matthew Paris as source for the story of Geoffrey, later Ab-
bot of St. Albans, and the borrowed copes. He thinks this probably
"the first spectacle of this sort exhibited in these kingdoms," and it
"might have been the first attempt towards the revival of dramatic
entertainments in all Europe."

The "Cornish Interludes" he found rather puzzling; but he records
their existence in three manuscripts in the Bodleian, two on parchment
and "another, written on paper in the year 1611." He also refers to a
translation of the last in the British Museum (MSS. Harl. 1867.2). He
had found the *Ludus Coventriae* in the Cottonian manuscripts and
been shocked by the language—"as gross as that of some of the
Scotch dramatic writers before the year 1600." He hesitates to quote
from the plays lest he be accused of "prophaneness," but he does give
an extract "to show the indelicacy of the poets, as well as the ancient
audiences, of Coventry." He then quotes "this extraordinary stage
direction and dialogue" and concludes with references to the time
and manner of performance, citing Dugdale as his authority.

His disapproval of the early drama is further displayed in his contribution to the account of *Candlemas Day; or, The Killing of the
Children of Israel*.[10] Following a long quotation from Hawkins, Steevens remarks upon the impropriety of the treatment of this "sacred
drama," saying, "This tragical business is treated with the most ridiculous levity. The good women of Bethlehem attack our knight-errant
with their spinning wheels, break his head with their distaffs, abuse
him as a coward and a disgrace to chivalry, and send him home to

---

[9] We are not here concerned with the third and final revision of *Biographia Dramatica* by Stephen Jones (1812). It is probably the most easily accessible and, because
of Jones's corrections and additions, the best for general reference use. It is in three
volumes, the first issued in two parts often bound separately. Volume I contains
the biographies, Volumes II and III, the accounts of plays. Stephens's contributions
to the 1782 edition have usually been retained unchanged by Jones, though in some
cases additions have been made.

[10] The first two paragraphs consist mostly of quotation from Hawkins's *Origin
of the English Drama*, doubtless contributed by Reed, who habitually quoted at
length from others: Johnson, Warton, Percy, as well as Hawkins. The play was not
recorded by Baker.

Herod with much ignominy." But he concludes, agreeing with War-ton, that "our ancestors" were not aware of the impropriety of such incongruities.

Steevens knew *Everyman* in the edition printed by John Skot, whose colophon he quotes. He quotes the introductory statement and the dramatis personae and proposes a date of publication "early in the reign of Henry VIII." "The design of it," he says, "was to inculcate great reverence for old mother church and her popish superstitions." He agrees with Percy that it is "not without some rude attempts to excite terror and pity, and therefore may not improperly be referred to the class of tragedy." In conclusion, he refers the reader to Haw-kins's reprint in *The Origin of the English Drama* (Oxford, 1773), where will also be found "Dr. Percy's Analysis of this early drama."

In the same spirit, he approaches other dramas of the sixteenth cen-tury, which he finds generally crude and vulgar. *The Nigromansir* [*sic*], "by Maister Skelton, laureat," is described with some scorn in a passage ending, "the Devil trips up the Necromancer's heels and dis-appears in fire and smoke." Steevens comments sarcastically, "Great must have been the edification and entertainment which King Henry VII. and his court derived from so elegant and rational a drama!"

Gammer Gurton's Needle (the final paragraph is assigned to Stee-vens) provides him with an opportunity to disagree, with considera-ble asperity, with persons who "have persuaded themselves" that "the rude poetry of our early writers" possesses merit beyond that claimed as records of early customs or examples of obsolete language.

We therefore sieze [*sic*] this opportunity to disclaim all pretention to the like partialities in favour of Bishop Still's performance.[11] Could we deceive ourselves so far in respect to that, or the pieces of Heywood, as to imagine they exhibit any traits of the *beautiful simplicity* [his italics] for which many an insipid ballad, like *Chevy Chase*, has been loudly celebrated, our wiser readers would detect our weakness, and punish it with the ridicule it deserved. When Rowe, in his prologue to *Jane Shore*, without exception declared that

> *These venerable ancient song-enditers*
> *Soar'd many a pitch above our modern writers,*

he certainly said what he neither believed himself, nor could wish any part of his audience or his readers to believe.

He does, however, find a good word to say about a few of these early plays. *Hycke-scorner* he thinks approaches comedy, and the

---

[11] Reed and Steevens had identified the author (wrongly, of course) as "John Still, afterwards bishop of Bath and Wells." See the biographical sketch of Still, pos-sibly also written by Steevens.

characters resemble real people. He approves of *Necromantia*, a dialogue printed by John Rastell, who if he was not the author, "we might fairly enough ascribe it to the festive genius of his brother-in-law, Sir Thos. More." In *The Nature of the iiij Elements*, he finds enough merit to suggest that it, too, was written by Rastell or More. If they did not write it, however, "at least they are not disgraced by the supposition," since it is an improvement over similar pieces earlier and is "rendered the vehicle of science and philosophy."

The remarks on ten other plays belonging roughly to this period appear among those attributed by Collier to Steevens. Generally they give titles, dates of publication, and other information, but little critical comment. *The Troublesome Raign of King John* is attributed to Marlowe; *Lusty Juventus* is described as Protestant propaganda; *The Misfortunes of Arthur* is regarded as a great curiosity; *Philotus* (Edinburgh, 1603) is "the most offensive drama ever produced."[12]

Among the critiques assigned by Collier to Steevens none is of an important Elizabethan, Jacobean, or Restoration drama.[13] Reed's method of handling most of these plays is to give a minimum of information and to quote, often at great length, from Dryden (on *Epicoene* and *Bussy d'Ambois*, for example), Steele (on *The Alchemist*, *Tatler* No. 14), and others, including Steevens himself. Most of the remarks on Shakespeare's plays consist largely of quotations from Johnson. Of course, it is possible that Steevens, too, concurred in these judgments.

One seventeenth-century production that Steevens did criticize in *Biographia Dramatica* is *Comus*,[14] and he did not like it. Granting that it is "truly poetical," he concludes, "As a drama it is deficient"; and he demonstrates its deficiencies at some length. They are summed up in two sentences: "Throughout the whole, the figures are too bold, and the language too luxuriant, for dialogue. It is a drama in the epic style, inelegantly splendid, and tediously instructive."

He tackled five adaptations of Shakespeare, two of *Cymbeline*, one each of *A Midsummer Night's Dream*, *Macbeth*, and *Hamlet*. Of Charles Marsh's unacted version of *Cymbeline* (1756), he says, somewhat irrelevantly, "Though Mr. Marsh was not at that time a magistrate, the dullness he displayed in the present undertaking, afforded strong presumptions of his future rise to a seat on the bench at Guildhall, Westminster." He is less severe on Garrick's version of

---

[12] The others are: *King Daryus* (1565); *The Longer thou livest, the more Foole thou art;* Skelton's *Magnificence;* Richard Edwards's *Palæmon and Arcyte; The Three Ladies of London;* and *The Tryall of Treasure.*

[13] Some late stage versions of Shakespeare are discussed, as will be shown below.

[14] It is to be found under the title *A Masque.*

Cymbeline (D. L. 1761): "This alteration, being less violent, is less defective than many similar attempts on the dramas of Shakespeare." He objects, however, to the omission in the performance of the "physician's soliloquy in the first act," since this leaves the audience "utterly unprepared for the recovery of Imogen after she had swallowed the potion." Of *A Midsummer Night's Dream* with alterations and additional songs by Garrick (1763), later reduced to two acts by Colman, Steevens merely comments on its complete failure. The version of *Macbeth* treated by Steevens is that by John Lee (Edinburgh, 1753). He begins, "Language is not strong enough to express our contempt of Mr. Lee's performance," and concludes by quoting Lee's attempt to improve the incantation of the witches at the beginning of the fourth act.

The attack in *Biographia Dramatica* on Garrick's version of *Hamlet* (1772) has often been quoted.[15] James Boaden thought it was written by Reed,[16] but Collier's note assigns it to Steevens. The remarks begin, "This alteration was made in the true spirit of *Bottom the Weaver*, who wishes to play not only the part assigned to him, but all the rest in the piece." It comments on Garrick's omission of some characters and the reduction in importance of others until the manager "contrived to monopolize the attention of the audience. . . . In short, no bribe but his own inimitable performance, could have prevailed on an English audience to sit patiently, and behold the martyrdom of their favourite author." It also states that after Garrick's death the public forced the restoration of *Hamlet* to its former state. The tone of this is quite unlike that of Steevens's correspondence with Garrick on the subject. Steevens had been for some years associated with Garrick in the purchase of old plays and in cataloguing Garrick's collection. In a letter (dated by Boaden 1771) he expressed approval of the plan for an alteration, and he sent Garrick some "Remarks As to the *text* of Shakspear's play" (Boaden's heading).[17] These latter concern the text and punctuation of a number of passages in the alteration. With the letter, however, they show that Steevens was aware of Garrick's plans and that he probably saw the text of the alteration and, almost certainly, a performance. The comment on Garrick's acting certainly implies that the author of the published

[15] The whole question of this alteration was answered by George Winchester Stone, Jr., in "Garrick's Long Lost Alteration of *Hamlet*," *PMLA*, XLIX (1934), 890–921. Stone assumed that Reed was the author of this criticism, which he cites (pp. 890, 893).

[16] See James Boaden (ed.), *The Private Correspondence of David Garrick* (1831), I, 451.

[17] *Private Correspondence*, I, 453–54. Boaden's note, at this point, expresses his "eternal astonishment" that Steevens "concurred with Mr. Garrick in this desperate mutilation."

note had seen the play acted by Garrick, and Reed probably had not. His *Diaries* record many of his visits to the theater, but they contain no mention of *Hamlet* between the first performance of this alteration in 1772 and Garrick's retirement in 1776.[18] So, in spite of the incongruity of letters and the remarks on *Hamlet*, it seems that Steevens was probably the author of the latter, which is, in fact, in agreement with other of his comments on Garrick's productions.

Collier attributes the article on *The Mourning Bride* to Steevens, but he appears to be wrong in this case. The opening comment is found in Baker's 1764 edition; the middle portion consists of quotations from Johnson, in Reed's usual manner of expanding Baker.

The account of *The Fair Penitent*, on the other hand, contains some acute observations, which might justly be given more consideration than they have received. It begins with an approving reference to Johnson's praise of the fable and the language and notices that Richardson had "expanded" Lothario into Lovelace. But: "Lothario, with gaiety which cannot be hated, and bravery which cannot be dispised, retains too much of the spectator's kindness." "The fifth act," Steevens observes, "is not equal to the former"; the action is over, and "little remains but to talk of what is past." Developing a comment previously made by Baker on the unsuitability of the title and on the character of Calista, he continues, "Calista . . . at last shows no evident signs of repentance, but may be reasonably suspected of feeling pain from detection rather than from guilt, and expresses more shame than sorrow, and more rage than shame."

Steevens's contribution to the account of *Jane Shore* consists of the portion immediately following the reference to Johnson's remark that he cannot easily conceive "in what [Rowe] thought he was imitating Shakespeare." Steevens here remarks upon the great difference from Shakespeare in the "numbers, the diction, the sentiments, and the conduct" of the action. He then comments on the domestic character of the play and on its popularity. The article is concluded in the edition of 1782 with the long quotation from Joseph Warton's *Essay* on Pope.

Two of Young's tragedies, both written about 1720, though *The Brothers* was not performed until 1753, appear among Steevens's contributions. Baker had made no comment on *Busiris, King of Egypt,* beyond saying that it was founded on history and had been a success. Steevens expands this with references to the "glaring ambitious style, like that which we probably should have met with in the dramas of Statius, had any of them escaped the wreck of Roman literature."

[18] He did see Henderson in *Hamlet* at the Haymarket on 27 June, and at Drury Lane on 30 September 1777 (*Diaries,* pp. 96, 98).

He notes that the message from Busiris to the Persian ambassador is taken from Herodotus and that the dialogue "contains many striking beauties of sentiment and description," but it is not affecting. Calling attention to the circumstance that three of Young's tragedies are concluded with suicides in pairs, he quotes Dryden to the effect that a poet can always kill a hero when he "wants the brains to save him."

Collier's note says that the second and third paragraphs of the article on *The Brothers* were contributed by Steevens.[19] In them, Steevens asserts that the fine speeches of the brothers "are in great measure translations from Livy" and that the play was "coldly received." He objects, moreover, to the vulgarity and ribaldry of the epilogue by Mallett, which makes fun of Young's charitable intentions in giving his profits to the Society for the Propagation of the Gospel. He also cites Young's anger with Garrick for the "instigation" of it and for giving it to Mrs. Clive to speak "in her broadest manner."

In the article on Home's *Douglas*, three of the last four paragraphs are assigned by Collier to Steevens. One paragraph quotes Mason's observation on the similarity of a line in Ossian to a line in *Douglas*, concluding, "Quere, Did Mr. Home take this sublime image from Ossian, or has the translator of Ossian borrowed it from Mr. Home?" He then quotes with approval Gray's praise of the language and of the scene "between Matilda [Lady Randolph] and the Old Peasant."

Home's *The Fatal Discovery* gives Steevens a chance to repeat his scorn of primitive poetry and to denounce the bad taste of spectators and managers: "This play is a disgrace to the talents that produced the beautiful tragedy of *Douglas*. It is indeed little better than Fingal in verse." Garrick's poor judgment is shown by his performing this tragedy after he had refused *Douglas*, and the staging is marred by "anachronisms and absurdities," which are pointed out in some detail. "Surely a manager should bring with him to his task a perspicacity that will enable him to distinguish real merit."

The articles on six other tragedies of the sixties and seventies Collier assigns to Steevens, who has little good to say about any of them.[20] It seems unnecessary to go into detail, but they add to the impression that a group of contributions to *Biographia Dramatica* were written in a spirit different from the major parts of the work and probably all by the same man.

Steevens also appears to have written for Reed remarks on a num-

---

[19] The first paragraph is in Baker's original edition; the last was added in 1812.

[20] They are: *Euridice*, by David Mallett, as revived in 1870; *The Countess of Salisbury*, by Hall Harston, 1767; *Emilia*, by Mark Anthony Meilau, 1771 (?); *Sethona*, by Alexander Dow, 1774; *Semiramis*, by G. E. Ayscough, from Voltaire, 1776; and *Buthred*, anonymous, 1778.

ber of odds and ends. *The Death of Bucephalus*, a burlesque tragedy, by Dr. Schomberg, "is not without humour, but it is indecent."[21] Henry Carey's *Chrononhotonthologos* served to ridicule bombastic tragedy in its day; but it "would produce no effect on modern audiences, who have beheld *Zingis, Sethona*,[22] and *The Fatal Discovery*, which every way excell it in tumour, meanness and improbability." Garrick's *A Christmas Tale* is "a performance yet more contemptible than *Cymon*"; and it provides opportunity for a long and violent denunciation of "the public taste" and censure of the manager (and author) for catering to it. Of Garrick's Stratford *Ode*, Steevens says, "Minute criticism would be misemployed on a work to which no man will afford a second reading." He does acknowledge Garrick's success as a comic writer but regards him as unqualified to write odes.[23]

In 1764, Baker had praised Congreve's *The Old Bachelor* without qualification. Steevens views it with less wholehearted approval. He admits that it is a remarkable play to have been written by a boy, but closer examination shows that it is imitated from other writers rather than derived from the author's experience or knowledge. "The dialogue is one constant reciprocation of conceits, or clash of wit, in which nothing flows necessarily from the occasion, or is dictated by nature." The characters are "fictitious and artificial," and the catastrophe is improbable. "Yet this gay comedy, when all these deductions are made, will still remain the work of a very powerful and fertile mind: the dialogue is quick and sparkling, the incidents . . . sieze the attention, and the wit is so exuberant that it *o'er-informs its tenement*."

Steevens supports Goldsmith in defense of *The Good-Natured Man* saying, "Many parts of this play exhibit the strongest indications of our author's comic talents." He praises the character of Croaker and the incident of the letter. Following Goldsmith, he notes that the audience, "exalted on the sentimental stilts of *False Delicacy*," thought some of the scenes were too low; and the comedy succeeded less than it deserved to do.[24]

Finally, Steevens briefly but enthusiastically praises *The Duenna*,

---

21 See *Catalogue of the Larpent Plays in the Huntington Library* (1939), No. 293, under the title *The Rival Favourites*.

22 It seems to me likely that Steevens wrote the comments on these two tragedies as well.

23 Also attributed to Steevens are articles on *The Genius of Nonsense* (1780) and *The Monument in Arcadia*, by George Keate (1773).

24 The note on *False Delicacy*, not attributed by Collier to Steevens, ignores the "sentimental stilts" and, after stating that Garrick is thought to have made some "improvements" in it, merely records its success in England and, in translations, abroad.

which "exhibits so happy a mixture of true humour and musical excellence, that it deservedly stands second on the lists of its kindred performances. The *Beggar's Opera* perhaps will always remain the first."[25]

Generally these critical comments differ in tone and method from most of the remarks in *Biographia Dramatica*, which tend to cite sources, to abstract plots, and to quote at length from other critics. On the other hand, those assigned by Collier to Steevens are often severe denunciations, which display throughout the same decided opinions and prejudices. If one may accept Collier's identifications, Steevens disapproved of what he saw and expressed his disapproval in testy, sarcastic terms, which seem to have been characteristic of him. He deplored the bad taste of audiences in the theater and censured Garrick for catering to it in such deplorable exhibitions as the vulgar epilogue to *The Brothers*, in the staging of *The Fatal Discovery*, and in his own pieces like *A Christmas Tale* and the Stratford *Ode*. He condemned the treatment of Shakespeare revivals and the alterations of earlier alterations that he saw on the London stage. His attack on the alteration of *Hamlet* and some of Garrick's other pieces entered the stream of theatrical history to influence Charles Dibdin, Percy Fitzgerald, F. A. Hedgcock, and others, as Stone has pointed out.[26] In many other cases, his judgment has been sustained. His criticism of *The Old Bachelor* is judicious, and his remarks on *The Fair Penitent* are perspicuous. His evaluation of the tragedies of Rowe, Young, and Home is also just in its discrimination between what he thought poetical excellence and the lack of true dramatic force. He shows a strong prejudice against the Scotch and a scorn of primitive poetry. Of course, he cannot be expected to understand those examples of medieval drama that he encountered, and it is perhaps natural that he held a prejudice against the "popish superstitions" that he detected in them and in some later moralities. Moreover, these works, from his point of view, are indeed crude and vulgar; and he would not yield to the fashion then coming in of finding excellence in the early plays or in the ballads simply because they represent the crude manners and language of an early period of English literature.

[25] Collier also assigns the last paragraph on *The Critic* to Steevens. It remarks on the supposed representation of "a well-known author" in Sir Fretful Plagiary, and "Dangle is said to have been drawn from Mr. Thomas Vaughan."

[26] *PMLA*, XLIX (1934), 890–92.

JAMES L. CLIFFORD

Roger North and the Art of Biography

In any history of the rise of English biography, Roger North is certain to be mentioned. "In an age of seriousness," Sir Harold Nicolson remarks, North "wrote with humor, frankness, and great graphic and dramatic skill. It is he, far more than Mason, who links the 'actuality' of Aubrey with the 'actuality' of Boswell."[1] Attempting to tell the truth as he saw it, North wrote in a vivid, racy, and colloquial style. He introduced letters and written memoranda with the avowed purpose of showing his subject's inner thoughts, and he anticipated later biographers in the use of other technical devices.

Only recently has it become apparent that North was also one of the first serious students of biography. The final versions of his lives were not the result of chance, but of careful revision; they show that he thought more deeply about the process involved than any writer before Johnson. Why, then, has this not hitherto been recognized? The reason is the same that explains the attitude of nineteenth-century critics toward Boswell's methods. All the evidence had not come to light. Now all that is changed. With the opening of the ebony cabinet and the croquet box, the search of the loft in the cattle barn at Malahide Castle and of the attic at Fettercairn House, it is possible to see clearly just how Boswell worked and why. But the enormous mass of Roger North's surviving manuscripts has remained virtually untouched by literary scholars. It is time that they too should receive serious study.

Born in 1653, Roger was the youngest of six sons of the fourth Lord North. Like his elder brother, Francis, he was educated for the law, but because of his ardent royalist sympathies and his refusal to take the oaths of allegiance to William and Mary, his career at the bar came to an early end. In 1690 he bought an estate in Norfolk and lived

JAMES L. CLIFFORD is Professor of English at Columbia University.

[1] Harold Nicolson, *The Development of English Biography* (London: Hogarth Press, 1927), pp. 75–76.

there quietly until his death in 1734. In retirement North gave himself over to his passion for writing, though he lacked a corresponding desire to carry his works into print. Indeed, none of his major books was published during his lifetime.

There are still extant masses of manuscript material connected with the Norths, which may be consulted in the British Museum, the Bodleian Library, the Library of Hereford Cathedral, and recently in the Library of St. John's College, Cambridge—unpublished essays on music and the arts, transcripts of law cases, miscellaneous notes on a variety of topics, along with holograph versions of the lives of Roger's brothers. For a recent volume concerned with North's writings on music, the editor, John Wilson, had at his disposal manuscripts extending to some half a million words.[2] And this only about music!

It is not quite clear when Roger first thought of writing biographies of his three brothers, but he probably began that of Francis, Lord Keeper Guilford, shortly after the appearance in 1706 of White Kennett's *Compleat History*.[3] Like the *Examen*, also published after his death, it was planned to correct what North thought to be the distorted interpretations of the Whig historian. The last volume of another distasteful work, Laurence Eachard's *History of England*, appearing in 1718, only strengthened his determination to vindicate his family's reputation. Although there is a date, 1728, on one manuscript of the life of his brother John, it is likely that he was working on all three biographies until the time of his death. It might be added that scholars now believe that North began his autobiography, referred to as "Notes of Me" in the manuscript, long before the lives, with some portions going back as far as the 1690's.[4]

Little has been written about the various versions of the biographies to be found among North's papers. Yet even a cursory examination shows how vigorously he labored, expanding and contracting, revising and rewording. The early drafts may be more verbose and rambling than the printed versions, but they are often more revealing and amusing. Moreover, the extent to which his son Montagu censored and mangled the texts even further before allowing them to be printed has not been sufficiently recognized. In preparing copy for the printers of the first editions in 1742 and 1744, Montagu North omit-

---

[2] *Roger North on Music* (London: Novello, 1959).

[3] See Edward Almack, "Roger North's Life of His Brother: and Other Seventeenth-century MSS.," *N & Q*, 14 March 1908, pp. 201–3. Part of the manuscript is dated 1708.

[4] For example, see Lois G. Schwoerer, "The Chronology of Roger North's Major Works," *History of Ideas News Letter*, III (October 1957), 73–78; and R. W. Ketton-Cremer, "Roger North," *Essays and Studies by Members of the English Association* (1959), pp. 73–86.

ted large sections and shifted and changed others.[5] The more decorous final version may have been more suitable for formal publication, but it is not so appealing to twentieth-century readers.

The process of excision, to be sure, cannot all be blamed on Montagu. In earlier versions, his father had done considerable pruning himself. Like James Boswell, years later, Roger seemed often uncertain about just what to put in or how to describe a particular event. In the recently discovered original manuscript of the *Life of Johnson*, we can see Boswell struggling with phraseology, experimenting with the placing of anecdotes—an expert craftsman molding his material into a work of art. It is possible on occasion to see the same kind of struggle going on in Roger North's composition. But, as a few facts should make clear, to discover the exact order of the various versions, and to follow each shifting point of view, would require enormous labor.

In the British Museum, there are two manuscript versions of the life of his elder brother, Lord Guilford, one occupying some 374 pages, the other 308. The second is closer to the printed version, though it too contains numerous passages marked for excision. There are also separate volumes of recollections and miscellaneous material. In addition to these, there is a much longer third version at St. John's College, Cambridge, occupying ten quarto notebooks of over 3,000 pages.[6] Filled with extraneous material—law cases, documents, essays— this version apparently is earlier than the two in the British Museum, but the exact relationship of the three has never been carefully worked out. Similarly, there are three versions of the shorter life of his brother John, the first stage of about 178 pages, the second of 236, and the third of 454. The last version is very close to the printed text in places, though it too contains passages marked for omission.

These facts are cited merely to emphasize the complexity of the textual problems involved. What is more important for any short analysis of North's biographical techniques is what these various versions tell us of his handling of anecdotes. It will be remembered that Boswell's early accounts of Johnson's conversation were often re-

[5] See note 3. See also Edward Almack, "Johniana," *The Eagle* [St. John's College, Cambridge], XXX (1909), 112–13. Almack's generalizations, however, cannot all be accepted. See note 6.

[6] This manuscript was sold at Sotheby's on 23 June 1947. It was there described as "The Life of the Ld. Keeper North, the Author's Holograph Manuscript, 1708–1709, clearly written on over 3,000 pp. 4.to, sheepskin, some covers loose." For descriptions of the manuscript, see articles by Edward Almack cited in notes 3 and 5. It is now catalogued in the St. John's College Library as "James, No. 613." Almack apparently assumed that the passages in this version that do not appear in the printed volume were excised by Montagu North, but this is not at all certain. Much more work needs to be done on the exact nature of the editing by father and son.

corded as indirect discourse and later turned into dramatic dialogue. It is interesting to find Roger North, some fifty years earlier, experimenting with the same kind of change.

There is an example near the end of the life of John North. In telling of his brother's apoplectic seizure, Roger described the determination of the attending physicians to keep John awake at all costs—how they kept up a continual clangor, hitting the tongs, firegate, and wainscoting, and shaking the curtain rings—and the defiance of his mother, who insisted that he be allowed to go to sleep. On her own authority she took charge and saw to it that he was not disturbed for two hours. In the first manuscript version which has survived, this is how Roger tells of what followed:

And after the two hours were Expired She Called in the learned, and opening the Curtaines, shewd them in what good order he lay, with a breathing discharge from his body, wch was before parcht, & his Countenance fryed, as of one stark madd. Then she applyed to wake him, and gently jogged his arme, upon wch he opened his Eyes, & looking about, he knew most of the Company, & spoke to them. The learned were surprised at this Amendment, for they concluded they should have had much adoe to have waked him if Ever.[7]

In what appears to be another version, perhaps later, there is a slight variation at one point. After describing the patient's breathing, Roger added:

Now Drs sayd she, what think yee? Fy Madame, sayd one of them, but doth ye hapn think he will wake? you shall see, sayd she, and after a gentle jogging of his arm, he opened his Eyes, & knew those that were about him & spoke to severall of them. . . .[8]

The final version renders the scene with dramatic vividness:

After this she opened the Curtains, and called in the Physicians and the rest that had a Mind to be there, and shewed them how easy and quietly he lay, and breathing as Nature required. His Countenance had a good Colour, and his Face was composed, which, before, was distorted in diverse Manners with his Eyes staring like one of the Furies. *Now, Doctors*, said she, *what think ye? But, Madam*, said one, *will he wake? You shall see*, said she, and gently jogging him by the Arm as he lay, he woke, and, opening his Eyes, knew several there and spoke to them. The Phy-

[7] B.M. Add. MS. 32,515, f. 73. In this and in following quotations, spelling, capitalization, and punctuation have not been normalized, though superior letters have been lowered. Common contractions for "the" and "that" have been expanded, since they cannot be represented accurately in ordinary type.

[8] B.M. Add. MS. 32,516, f. 107.

sicians were exceedingly surprised; for they expected great Difficulty in waking him, and had been consulting of Methods how to do it.[9]

This same anecdote shows the way North sometimes censored his own remarks as he prepared later versions. In the earliest manuscript, following the description of his mother's triumph over the doctors, Roger added:

I must owne here an Impotence, wch is that I cannot forbear on this occasion to Reflect on the Infelicity of medicall practise, and how much better a kinder Parent is then Senertus, Riverius, &c. Here a patient was to be skillfully killed, for fear he should dye: and there being two ways one Easy, & the other with cruel torment; the latter is preferred, because it is secundum artem. The phisitians durst not let the patient Repose, for If he had dyed, then their fame had suffered, because the Method prescribd is to forstall all sleep.[10]

In addition to minor excisions and to changes in wording, North kept putting in and taking out whole anecdotes. What follows is a typical canceled passage:

And he could not bear the thought of being layd forth when he should be Dead. I have heard him say that when he went fresh to Cambridg, he had a severe feavour, and his good Mother Came over to Nurse him, and she seeing his legg's, as commonly with young folks, say'd fye Johnne, what makes yr Leggs so durty, what will they say If you should come to be lay'd forth. That speech, wch was Indeed a little cours, as he sayd, sunk so deep in his Imagination, that he Never after Could Endure the thought of that same Laying forth. Some years after, at his fathers hous, he had another acute feavour, and his mother was his tendor Nurse. I have heard her say that he had fancy's so Extravagant, that she concluded him to be delirous. once he desir'd her to come and hear two Notions, very fine Notions. his mother snapp't him up, and bid him goe to sleep with his notions. No she must needs come & hear them, Well! What are they? Beer & Beer—Maddame the fnest Notions In the World. Beer & Beer.[11]

Although such casual and intimate stories may amuse us, two centuries later, it is easy to see why they were omitted in the first published text.

[9] *The Life of the Honourable Sir Dudley North Knt . . . And of the Honourable and Reverend Dr. John North* (1744), p. 282. Printed from B.M. Add. MS. 32,514, with only minor changes of spelling and punctuation.

[10] B.M. Add. MS. 32,515, f. 73. The references are to Daniel Sennert (Sennertus), 1572–1637, and Lazare Rivière (Riverius), 1589–1655, well-known medical authorities.

[11] B.M. Add. MS. 32,514, f. 135. The passage immediately follows "remain undefaced" (1744 edition, p. 268).

Another example is the discussion of John's fear that he might go blind and his reflections on the later years of Milton. In an early version, Roger recorded:

> The Dr. once travelled with his best freind, & some other Compa. and his freind thought fitt to take a merry opportunity to make him better conceipted of himself: Mr. N. say'd he, is not that a very fine windmill (when none was in sight) the Dr. looked about, and seeing none. I protest & as I am a living man, sayd he, I verily beleiv I shall now soon be quite blind. For I cannot discerne so much as that windmill, at wch his freind and the compa made a stout laugh upon him. And at all times In Compy he mett with Raillery Enough: to have created In him a better opinion of himself, and If he had lived much amongst them such free conversation would have had its Effect. but retiring to his study's at the university the black vail came over his fancy, as If it had never been clear. . . . It is certain that he was overmuch addicted to thinking. . . .[12]

Probably at first he put in everything he could remember, later eliminating what seemed foolish or out of place. There is, for example, an anecdote about his brother Francis and the college barber:

> (And if I may have leave to Mention such trifles) he was a Dr. at a sort of minor witt, called quibbling: wch not a little prevailed among the youth in the university; the Colledge-Barber by long provocation, & exercise was become a tolerable Punster; and once barbering this little Gentleman, he was much Piqued at an affront put upon his Bason, for the little fellow commoner (for so he was call'd in the Colledge) said it was a Base-one, the Barber thus Irritated looks him in the face, & how! said he, is not your Name North? Yes said the fellow Commoner, and what then? I thought so, sd the Barber, because the wise men come out of the East. His Lordship was at that time a great Thorn in the sides of Fools, & Humourists, for he with his little Eyes observed every Body, & used to gather remarks for his own, all the vain and Rediculous actions of those, who in that way fell obnoxious to him: and then made the fellows merry with his Relating them; & they, for their diversion, encouraged him; and he never failed to Seis upon every foolish Behaviour, & described it, not in the satirical, but in such a veritable manner, as if the thing had been seen, as well as told.[13]

Certainly the story is silly enough and hardly worth preserving, but the accompanying description of Francis's sharp, rather cruel, propensity for taking off his fellow students for the delight of the Fellows is very revealing. Roger's inclination as a biographer was to tell all—to show the weaknesses as well as the merits of his brothers—but the

[12] B.M. Add. MS. 32,514, ff. 137–138.

[13] B.M. Add. MS. 32,508, f. 17. The passage follows "and the sciences called liberal" (1744 edition, p. 13).

combination of his own natural taste and the temerity of his son ultimately lessened the intimate candor of the lives.

In addition to such personal anecdotes, it may be asked, what other kinds of remarks were censored? In the life of Francis, Lord Guilford, there are episodes concerning the king, the lord mayor, and other worthies that he evidently thought better not to print, but they may fascinate modern historians; there are examples of how the Lord Keeper detected fraud and forgery and how he settled various law cases. There is even a long digression having to do with the use of legal French. In the life of John, his scholar brother, there are apologies for the philosophic excursions, diagrams, and other extraneous comments.

Not only were whole sections excised, but again and again a phrase or a sentence was removed in order to render the account in general more acceptable: references to "Phisicians, Quacks & Astrologers," casual remarks about people and events in the manner of Aubrey, or side comments like the one which concluded his account of his brother's admission to the Middle Temple—"but his father went away, and at home told (merrily) how Frank had cheated him of Three pounds, Ten shillings."[14] One is tempted to go on citing instances. *The Lives of the Norths* has always been noted as one of the earliest informal and frank biographies. Had all Roger's stories and incidental comments been included in the printed versions, the work would have had even more of a reputation for being indiscreet and hilarious.

As pointed out elsewhere,[15] the early versions are significant for us in still another way. Prefixed to the St. John's College version of the life of Lord Guilford are two drafts of what is called a "General Preface," the first of sixty-four handwritten pages, with numerous changes and corrections, and the second, more carefully copied in a smaller script, of forty-four pages. For some reason, Roger or his son thought this not worth printing, yet for students of biography today it is perhaps the most interesting part of all.

In his "General Preface," Roger North discourses at length about the difficulties of writing a life, carefully feeling his way, justifying the type of honest and candid account he wished to write. Although obviously shaped by the general sensibility of his day, this Preface is, notwithstanding, a remarkable document. Particularly is this so when

---

[14] Compare 1744 edition, p. 14.

[15] In *Biography as an Art* (Oxford University Press, 1962), pp. xii–xiii. Included in this volume (pp. 27–37) are extensive quotations from the second version of the "General Preface," made with the kind permission of the Master and Fellows of St. John's College, Cambridge. Since these are readily available, only a few sample excerpts will be reprinted here, enough to show the nature and style of North's comments.

one remembers the state of biographical art in the early eighteenth century.

The discovery of any extended discussion of the problems of life-writing written before 1750 would be important, but to find one of such length, so fresh and modern, is truly exciting. Consider how little there is of a critical nature about this genre before Johnson's *Rambler* essay No. 60. Yet it is now apparent that in his retirement Roger North was mulling over the whole problem of effective re-creation of character, jotting down his thoughts, revising and smoothing his phrases, happily unaware that all his labors would remain unknown for over two centuries, while the kind of biography he longed to see was slowly becoming popular.

Over and over again, North's comments anticipate the later thoughts of Johnson and Boswell. Many of the points which Johnson was to make in his *Rambler* essay and in *Idler* No. 84 were anticipated by North in his private jottings thirty years earlier. And almost all of his requirements for the perfect biographer were to be fulfilled by James Boswell.

Like Johnson, Roger North preferred the lives of ordinary individuals to general history and argued that any man's life, however unexciting on the surface, could be made interesting. He stressed the importance of the fullest coverage of a man's private affairs. And throughout he insisted on the necessity for complete truth and impartiality. Like Johnson, too, he was oppressed by the deficiencies of his contemporaries who claimed to be writing biography.

North's criterion for judgment is not, to be sure, revolutionary; in brief, he looks for moral instruction as well as entertainment. The history of private lives is more useful than formal accounts of great men, because it is more applicable to everyday concerns. Great actions, he points out, are often basically immoral and should not be used as models by a good man. Consequently, those who are sincerely trying to do right will tend to escape active public service (perhaps a rationalization of his own retirement!).

North is quite aware of the arguments on the other side. Most people enjoy reading about kings and spectacular affairs. They like to stretch their imaginations, to escape for a time from their own narrow existence. Moreover, domestic details are likely to make dull reading. What pleasure, it may be asked, can there be in reading about a private man's affairs—how he was educated, how he conducted his business, and how he passed his leisure time? With this position North refuses to agree. "After all a dullness is never to be charged on a subject but on the author, who should find spirit enough in himself to give relish to every thing he writes, whether of low, or of lofty matters." And then he adds a comment startlingly modern in tone. "I answer that the same ingredients that are usually brought to adorn fiction, may come foreward, and be as well applied to the setting forth of truths; that is choice of words, charming periods, invention of figures, interspersion of sentences, and facetious expressions." In other words, as some critics have recently been insisting, once the facts are discovered, the biographer and the novelist have similar problems. It is not the amassing of facts, North continues, that sometimes makes a biography tedious, but the skill with which they are used by the writer.

North is unsparing in his adverse criticism of the ancient biographers and of the ordinary practitioners of his own time. Having given the place and date of birth of their subject, they usually hurry over the formative years to get into spectacular intrigues of state. Or they are too eager to show their own learning and put in too much extraneous material. None of them gives enough personal information. Obviously North realizes that most ancient writers did not have available the proper details from which to produce rounded characterizations.

And how should Plutarch or any one gather the privacies of so many men remote in time, and place from him, but from loose fame, wch is but a poor instruction. . . . As for the many Scetches or profiles of great mens lives, pretended to be synopticall or multum in parvo, we are sure there is nothing we look for in them. One may walk in a Gallery, and extract as fair an account from the air of their Countenances or the cut of their whiskers. What signifies it to us, how many battells Alexander fought, it were more to the purpose to say how often he was drunk, and then we might from the ill consequences to him incline to be sober.

North is just as scornful of slanted biographies, written to prove some special point. "Some have wrote lives purely for favour of certain Theses, opinions, or facts"—and he mentions particularly religious lives, which give no true account of the subject's private affairs.

Not that North is unaware of the difficulties standing in the way of producing the kind of three-dimensional portrait he desires. "In education friendship, conversation, and all commerce of life," the biographer ought to be "nearest of any allyed to his subject, and not a contingent gatherer, or compiler." Repeatedly North makes the same claim: only a person who is in close contact with his subject is qualified to write a life. Yet how few biographers, he laments, have the opportunity for such intimate association. And how few people ever think of writing down daily accounts of their friends until it is too late. "And then for want of notes, as to all that may be recollected there is nothing but frail memory to trust to; wch must needs be very imperfect both as to times and matters transacted."

There is also the matter of personal loyalty, the desire to praise, and all the other pressures which bear down on every would-be biographer. Ordinarily a life is written by either a friend or relation, "whose very design is praise." How difficult to find a biographer who can be purely objective about his subject! Not only must he try to find the truth, but he must be free from all outside pressures, such as the desire for preferment or financial gain. Most abuses of history, North points out, are the result of such temptations.

What is to be expected from an history, that comes with a flattering preface, and there's 300 Guineas for that, or articled with a Bookseller to contain—sheets, for 100 £, besides dignitys in the Sequal, to encourage the family of corrupters; nay the very luere of selling a Copy is a corrupt interest, that taints an historical work, for the sale of the book must not be spoyld, by the dampness of overmuch truth, but rather be made vivacious, and compleat by overmuch lying.

It is easy to see why North was so continually disappointed with what he read. His standards were too high. Nevertheless, despite his pessimism about ever finding a perfect biographer, he set down much good advice for anyone who had a mind to try—advice unfortunately never read by those who might have profited from it. Boswell, with Johnson's advice, was able to work out his own technique. It is tempting to speculate on what might have been his reactions to North's remarks, which so clearly paralleled his own.

Of major importance, North insists, is the keeping of a journal, not only as an aid and encouragement to oneself, but as a help in writing biography. The practice of keeping a journal is useful to a man, he adds, in that he may "retrospect his actions, and seeing his errours, and failings, endeavor to mend them." And it should serve as a check on bad inclinations and "exorbitancys," "that being set down, they would stain his reputation."

After mentioning the necessity for honest and accurate reporting concerning the subject's character, North stresses the usefulness of selections from his writings: "a mans character is not, and scarce can be, justly represented, by words in the way of history, without some specimens derived from himself." "Friends may, but things will not prevaricate, or falsifye; and no description can come up to the force and expression of them." Only through the reciprocal reaction of factual material and just interpretation can true biography be written.

If an author commends a man for being a good Poet, and produceth none but silly verses; if for a good Orator and makes him speak obscurely or nonsense; if for a good soldier, and yet tells that for the most part he is beaten and the like, I doubt both Author and subject will suffer contempt alike: as on the one side all the Eulogys in the world will not sustain a character agst the real testimony of fact. . . .

Of course, when represented by judicious quotations, Roger North's disquisition may appear better organized and more coherent than it actually is. As one might expect, there are rambling digressions and wordy repetitions. North was not an orderly or disciplined writer. Yet for all its defects, North's "General Preface" abounds in valuable insights and fresh suggestions. In the meager accumulation of critical discussions of biography before the mid-eighteenth century it deserves a prominent place.

Even from this short discussion, it should be obvious that Roger North's achievement as a biographer and critic needs re-examination. He is a more important figure than one would guess from the treatment accorded him in the older histories of English literature. But any valid re-estimate can come only after a thorough study of all his surviving manuscripts, and that is a task which will require the labors of many devoted scholars.

RAE BLANCHARD

Richard Steele and the Secretary of the SPCK

U NTIL A SHORT TIME AGO one wondered how it came about that
Henry Newman would take the liberty of rebuking Steele—even
though as an "affectionate," if shocked, friend—for "the scandalous,
unaccountable, diabolical sin of profane swearing," which, he wrote,
"a Marlborough, a Stanhope, a Walpole, or an Addison" would never
be found guilty of. Equally puzzling was the fact that Steele seemed
to take the scolding for his "swearing tongue" meekly in the lines
scribbled on the back of Newman's letter, dated 1 March 1714 [1713–
14] and signed "R. S.," assuring "Brother Ch"[ristian?] that he had
"very much left off that vice, but the times are the worst that ever
were for reforming that sin above all others." The unaddressed (except for the salutation "Hon^d Sir"), unsigned, undated letter by
Newman is preserved in a collection of his papers in the Bodleian
Library, where is also found a brief signed note to him from Steele
dated 28 September 1711 with the request, also mystifying to the
annotator, for "the names of the boys and the places to inquire for
them."[1]

A background has now been provided for understanding these letters and for adding a few strokes to the picture of Steele as a benevo-
list. A recent biography of Newman based on records of the Society
for Promoting Christian Knowledge, of which he was Secretary for
many years, contains several references to Steele; and further examination of the *Letter Books* of the Society in London has brought to
light the drafts (or copies) of half a dozen letters that Newman
wrote to Steele over a period of fifteen years, between 1711 and
1726.[2] They bear witness to a mutual regard between two kindred

RAE BLANCHARD is Professor Emeritus of English at Goucher College.

[1] *The Correspondence of Richard Steele*, ed. Blanchard (1941), No. 50, p. 51,
Steele to Newman, 28 September 1711; No. 89, p. 87, Newman to Steele [February
or March 1714]; No. 90, p. 89, Steele to Newman, 1 March 1714.

[2] Leonard W. Cowie, *Henry Newman: An American in England 1708–45* (1956).
Another recent book with interesting observations on Newman is by W. K. Lowther

287

spirits working together for the public welfare. How long before 1711 this partnership began we do not know, but Newman was still writing after Steele's retirement into Wales. He wrote with the easy assurance of one who knew that his ideas and proposals would get a fair hearing—asking favors of Steele on behalf of the Society, requesting the publicity of a *Spectator*, a *Guardian*, or a *Lover* paper, showering political and religious pamphlets upon him, counseling with him on their common concerns, and even on one occasion, as we see in the "swearing tongue" letter, admonishing him freely. Except in the two instances mentioned above, what Steele said in return we can only infer, but it is apparent that he was responsive to a number of Newman's suggestions.

Without a doubt, Steele admired Newman for the generous soul that he was—a devoted servant of the SPCK, working tirelessly, selflessly for many humane causes during his long tenure as Secretary. We can speculate with a degree of certainty on the beginning of their friendship. Newman, a native of Massachusetts and a graduate of Harvard College, came to London in the early years of the century; and they may have become known to each other through Newman's American friend, Colonel (afterward Governor) Joseph Dudley, who served for a time with Steele on the staff of Lord Cutts. It is a matter of record that Steele and Dudley were on friendly terms. Another person closely connected with the association of Newman and Dudley was almost certainly well known to Steele—John Chamberlayne, Secretary of the Society for the Propagation of the Gospel in Foreign Parts. Friendship with the leaders of these two Anglican Societies of far-reaching influence undoubtedly gave Steele a less provincial point of view and broadened his sympathies. To judge from entries in the *Letter Books* of the SPCK, Newman had correspondents not only in England but also on the continent and in the American colonies.

Three of Newman's draft letters to Steele—dated 11 September 1711, 2 September 1712, and 21 May 1714—have to do with charity schools. This notable social experiment affording hundreds of poor children their only means of instruction had been conceived and or-

---

Clarke, *A History of the S.P.C.K.* (1959). The transcription of Newman's letters was made for me in August 1958 by John C. Stephens of Emory University, to whom I am gratefully indebted. The material relating to Steele is found in the archives of the Society in London in volumes labeled "Society's Letters." The letters are in rough draft form with considerable lining out and alteration. In the opinion of Mr. Stephens they were composed and written by Newman himself and then made the basis for fair copies. The letters to Steele are found in Vol. II, pp. 7, 74; Vol. III, pp. 51, 54; Vol. IV, p. 46; Vol XVII, p. 26; to Derham, in Vol. III, p. 65. Several of them are mentioned or excerpted by Cowie, pp. 80, 156–57, 158. Permission to print was very kindly given me by the Director of the Society, F. N. Davey.

ganized by the SPCK at the turn of the century and for many decades continued to be one of its chief projects. Though there is extant no letter in any form to prove it, we can now be reasonably certain in the light of these draft letters that Steele's two *Spectator* papers on charity schools were written at the request of none other than Newman. "I fall into this discourse from a letter sent to me . . . ," "a generous mind like that of him who writ to me . . . ," "my correspondent seems to expect from a publication of it in this paper . . . ," Steele wrote in No. 294 (6 February 1712), where he endorses charity schools as "the greatest instances of public spirit the age has produced." The statistical facts in No. 294—the date of the beginning of the movement, the amount of money subscribed by voluntary donors, the number of boys and girls thus far instructed—were doubtless supplied in a pamphlet or paper (or in the sermon Steele did mention as an enclosure), which seems characteristically to have accompanied a Newman letter. A second *Spectator* paper, No. 380 (16 May 1712), gives publicity to the charity-school movement by the inclusion of a short letter signed "The Sexton," announcing a special church service for a group of schoolgirls at St. Bride's; and this, we can plainly see, has all the earmarks of a Newman letter.

The specific points that Mr. Spectator was expected to publicize in No. 294 are obvious. In addition to an appeal for funds and a notice for an anniversary sermon for schoolboys at St. Bride's, Steele makes a special plea that suitable employment be found for these young students, "who will make a race of good and useful servants." He recommends the utilitarian value of charity schools, which not only give instruction in the three R's and the tenets of the Anglican faith but also provide training for efficient domestic servants. Indeed several months before Steele wrote this paper, he himself had taken steps to engage a charity schoolboy as a servant. This we learn from a clue in the draft letter dated 11 September 1711, where Newman speaks of interviewing boys from different schools—"but I can't say I like one of 'em so perfectly as I could for your Service." He has, however, made the choice of a boy from St. Martin's School "to wait upon you when you please to command him." So it is now possible to annotate without guesswork Steele's letter to Newman of 28 September asking for "the names of the boys and the places to inquire for them." As a moralist, Steele often took special note of the human relationship between master and servant, as he did here in this *Spectator* paper; and whether or not his small personal venture was successful, at least he was willing to test his theories.

In the letter of 2 September 1712, Newman addressed Steele as a Commissioner of the Stamp Office. He wanted to know whether the

Society's printed circular letter on the subject of charity schools was taxable under the new law for sheets and half-sheets. He explained that this printed document with a personal postscript signed by the Secretary was sent annually by post "to most parts of the Kingdom." To be sure, the inquiry was a legitimate one, but the indefatigable Newman also made use of the opportunity to air his propaganda by enclosing "a rough draft" of the report to be spread before the Board of Commissioners. Two years later, it was a *Lover* paper he was asking for, and he seemed to feel sure of a sympathetic response. "When you are at leisure to bestow a Lover on the Charity Schools," he wrote on 21 May 1714, "you will very much oblige the wellwishers to them." He went on to say with undisguised pride that Steele would have been pleased "yesterday" at St. Sepulchre's at the sight of "above four thousand children in their best cloathes at their Devotions," assembled for the annual anniversary sermon. And Steele, who shared Newman's satisfaction at the success of the charity-school project, probably would have obliged the well-wishers had he not have been ending *The Lover* the following week.

The date of this letter, 21 May 1714, and indeed the mention of *The Lover* give rise to a purely speculative question related only indirectly to the draft letters: Was Newman the person who gave Steele—or introduced the person who gave him—the facts of the incident that he related in *Lover* No. 36 on 18 May? "One of my friends told me," he said in the paper, "lately." It is a pathetic story of forlorn Negro slaves living on a Maryland plantation, who despite their ignorance and harsh servitude show a disposition for humanized conduct. Both Anglican Societies—for Promoting Christian Knowledge and for the Propagation of the Gospel in Foreign Parts—had from their beginnings shown concern for the plight of the American Indian and Negro. And increasingly of late, they had intensified their propaganda by sermons preached and published and by pamphlets circulated to enlist the sympathy of the English public as well as of the colonials, who questioned the propriety of Christianizing Negro slaves. This Maryland story is the kind of thing Newman, himself a colonial agent, would be likely to hear from planter, merchant, or traveler and to recognize as illustrative of what he considered colonial injustice. What more effective medium for its circulation could the Secretary of the SPCK have found than *The Lover?* And, hypothetically speaking, may not the printed appearance of the story, which Steele had related with imaginative sympathy, have encouraged him to ask for another "Lover" three days later?[3]

---

[3] Before these letters were brought to my attention, I analyzed the story in the *American Quarterly*, X (Spring 1958), 78–82.

But to return to the draft letters and a common interest of the two men: politics. Both were Hanoverian Whigs and both extremely partisan. Whether they saw eye to eye on all issues and on the many angles of practical politics it is impossible to say; but they were agreed on one point: the menace to the Church and to the Revolution Settlement of Catholicism, the religion of the Stuart Pretender. We are well aware of the direction often taken by Steele's pamphleteering. And we are informed by the biographer of Newman that in addition to his activities in distributing anti-Catholic material for the Society, he was secretary from 1712 to 1715 for a separate organization that dispensed such pamphlets. He was also active under the aegis of the Society in assisting the Protestant refugees from Europe, and apparently he had connections with their underground leaders. Newman had his eye on Steele and Steele's pen, and it is probably not a coincidence that a letter was dispatched to him in August 1713, the month when he was burning his bridges to prepare for running for Parliament and plunging into active politics—and when *The Guardian* was taking on a political cast. Newman's letter is dated 4 August and comes straight to the point: "Some of your friends would be very well pleased to see a Guardian now and then bestowed on the world against Popery and the Persecuting Spirit." The letter continues with a comment arresting to anyone who may have wondered about the source of Steele's subject matter in several of his forthcoming *Englishman* papers and in his anti-Catholic pamphlets of 1714 and 1715: "If the books accompanying this may furnish any materials for such an Entertainment you are requested to accept of them."

Politics in part motivated the benefactions bestowed by Newman and Steele in 1713 upon William Whiston, clergyman and mathematician; but on Newman's side, gratitude for Whiston's help with the charity school of Cambridge and on Steele's, respect for his scientific attainments probably were motives, as was also their Christian charity. The story of Whiston need not be retold here. Since his banishment from a Cambridge professorship in 1710, he had given his heterodox views a thorough airing and in the late summer of 1713 had become a controversial figure in religious and political circles, his heterodoxy under scrutiny by officials of the Church and himself the target of contemptuous satire by high-church Tories. The theme of bitter articles in *The Examiner* was that he was trying "to lead a Party as *Arrian* did of old," and Swift declared that he "hated *Wh——n* like a toad."

During the years 1710 to 1713, Whiston had continued his work in mathematics and astronomy; it was known, however, that he and his family were living in London in great need. From Newman's draft letter to Steele of 10 August 1713, we learn that these two churchmen and fellow Whigs had previously conferred on finding a way to give Whiston moral and monetary support. Steele, it appears, may have been the first to suggest lectures at the Coffee House, and Newman was acting as intermediary. The letter gives the answers to two questions long parried or answered incorrectly: when Whiston's lectures began and who his benefactors were.

Wh[ite Hall] 10 Aug. [1713][4]

Mr Steele
HONd & DEAR SIR

I thank you for yr Kindness to Mr Whiston as it is a Charitie not only to him but to the Publick in putting him upon an Amusement which may divert him from those Studies that have made him so obnoxious to the reproach of Good Men. I gave him notice immediately of yor favour, & suppose he will wait upon you for yr Commands. I only beg leave to suggest one thing to you when he does, because it will come with more authority from you than perhaps any man in ye Kingdom beside, and yt is that you will be pleas'd to conjure him Silence upon all Topicks foreign to the Mathematicks in his Conversation or Lectures at ye Coffeehouse. He has an Itch to be venting his Notions about Baptism & the Arrian Doctrine but yor authority can restrain him at least whilst he is under your Guardianship. I am Sr yr most obliged

[H.N.]

Addison is usually credited with the arrangement and the date conjectured as 1711, presumably soon after Whiston came from Cambridge to London. Indeed, Whiston himself, thirty-five years later in his *Memoirs*, remembered that it was Addison who came to his aid, assisted, he said, by Steele. It is true that Addison had shown his good will in July 1713 by including Whiston's letter on his longitude invention, with a generous preface, in his *Guardian* paper No. 107; and his assent to lectures at Button's Coffee House was probably granted willingly. It is plain to see, however, that Steele and Newman thought of the plan and carried it out in August 1713; and we know that Steele continued his support in *The Englishman* (1713–14) with advertisements of Whiston's lectures on astronomy at Button's and elsewhere and notices of his mathematical experiments. There is an ironical twist to the affair. Sometime before these happenings, Whiston had placed himself outside the good offices of Newman: on coming to London in 1710, he had resigned his membership in the SPCK, telling Mr. Secretary Newman that he could no longer belong to a Society

---

[4] Though the year is not stated in the manuscript, the order of the letter in sequence indicates 1713 as the correct date.

affiliated with the Anglican Church. Of Steele he said in his *Memoirs,* "He was a Christian in Principle but not in Practice."[5]

Another clergyman-scientist, we learn from the *Letter Books* of the SPCK, was given a publicity notice in *The Guardian* on the recommendation of Newman. In a draft letter to the Reverend William Derham dated 24 September 1713, Newman commented: "I wrote to Mr Steele last week to recommend your book and he has since promis'd me that he will do it very heartily. I look upon his Guardian of this day to be a Prelude to it [169]." Steele kept his promise in the final number on 1 October, where he reviewed Derham's recently published book, *Physico-Theology or a Demonstration of the Being and Attributes of God from His Works of Creation.* This rather famous book (incorporating Derham's Boyle Lectures for 1711 and 1712) was destined to run through many editions and to be translated into several European languages. It has always been considered a credit to Steele that he marked its importance by a prompt commendation in *The Guardian* and by notices of the second edition "with additions" in *The Englishman* during the following November and December; but it has not been known until now that he was keeping a promise to Newman.

In August 1726, though Steele had been living in retirement in South Wales for two years, he still was within reach of his old friend's pen. As Newman had found out, he was indeed working on a play, intermittently, *The School of Action* [Acting], which survives as a fragment. Possibly Newman had seen newspaper accounts in 1723 and 1724 of a new play in the making; undoubtedly he had caught wind of a deposition Steele had made recently, in June, for use in a London court. In it, he spoke of the "new Comedy" which God willing he hoped to finish by the next season; and he described the plot as "formed for the reformation of the theatre and restoring the credit and good sense of theatrical entertainments."[6] But Steele in his deposition and Newman in his letter had in mind two entirely different abuses of the theater. The reforming purpose in *The School of Action*

[5] *Memoirs of the Life and Writings of Mr. William Whiston* (1749), pp. 302, 303, and Whiston's letter to Newman dated 18 December 1710, p. 175; Whiston, *An Account of the Charity School lately Erected at Cambridge,* 16 February 1704–5; *The Guardian,* No. 107, 10 July 1713; *The Englishman,* ed. Blanchard (1955), pp. 119–20 (No. 29, 10 December 1713), 425–26, 436, 440, 485; *The Examiner,* IV, 41, 26 October 1713, and V, 12, 8 January 1713–14; Swift, *Part of the Seventh Epistle of the First Book of Horace Imitated,* 23 October 1713; Steele, *Periodical Journalism 1714–1716,* ed. Blanchard (1959), pp. 262, 312 (*Chit Chat,* No. 2, 1716). I do not know whether Addison's *Guardian* papers of July 1713, No. 105 on charity schools and No. 107 containing Whiston's letter on the longitude invention, were written at the solicitation of Newman.

[6] George A. Aitken, *The Life of Richard Steele* (1889), II, 312; and John Loftis, *Steele at Drury Lane* (1952), p. 231.

was to be aesthetic—to check the "non-rational" elements of spectacle and buffoonery plaguing the London stage. Though Newman may have misconstrued the deposition, he could hardly have forgotten that Steele had written all his plays under the influence of Jeremy Collier's moralistic strictures. But here was an opportunity to encourage an old confederate in well-doing; and Steele, in declining health and far removed from the scene of battle, would doubtless welcome the letter and would read the accompanying pamphlet by the "Learned & Pious Author," which may well have been a belated document in the Collier controversy, still after three decades very much alive.

Mid. Temple
16 Aug. 1726

To Sr Richd Steele at Carmarthen
Hon^d Sir

I gladly embrace any occasion of Saluting you; and being inform'd that you was preparing an Entertainm't for the Stage the approaching winter I thought it might not be unacceptable to you to present you with the reflections of a Learned & Pious Author on that Subject.

If his arguments are weighty I am persuaded you are too great a friend to virtue & honour to be an Advocate or promoter of the contrary and that you will always do justice to Sacred Truth whatever may be the consequence of it. I have sent the Pamphlet in 2 packets by this Post that it may be sure of going from

S^r Y^r most obed. humble Ser^t
H.N.

The discovery of a handful of Henry Newman's draft letters to Steele is not earth-shaking in importance. They do, however, enable us to annotate correctly several of his periodical papers and a letter or two, and they encourage fresh speculation on the possible sources of his anti-Catholic pamphlets. Moreover they reveal a relationship and an influence not before suspected, which have sidelights of interest. The inference has always been that the essay in which Steele first discussed his ethical and social ideas, *The Christian Hero* (1701), was in a general way related to a powerfully organized movement of reform, religious and social in purpose. What has not been surmised is his association afterward, as he tried to put his ideas into practice, with the influential "executive" Secretary of one of the reforming Societies, national in scope and indeed international in its work. The few letters surviving seem to be samples only; but from them can be assessed, if not the extent, the nature and spirit of the correspondence.

Those we have imply a give and take between two men of good will, their minds teeming with humanitarian projects. Secretary Newman possessed strong backing from a Society affiliated with the Church, and though self-effacing in personality, he had prestige and power; he was a shrewd observer of men and affairs; he worked single-mindedly and laboriously. It appears from his letters that he was impressed with the usefulness of Steele as a publicist and a politician and that he considered it his province in their alliance to suggest, inform, assist. He was in a position to put Steele in the way of meeting persons of wide-ranging interests, to supply him with timely information for working up in paper or pamphlet, and to maneuver for his political advantage. One instance of political aid is on record: shortly after Steele was elected to the Commons in 1713, Newman, sensing his political danger, solicited help from friends to prevent his being unseated.[7] And he once declared (in the "swearing tongue" letter), "I have been an advocate for you . . . and fought your battles upon occasion to the best of my capacity." Though he coveted the publicity of *Spectator, Guardian,* and *Lover,* there is never a hint of his having made a suggestion with anything but deference. The brilliance and goodness of Steele at his best were not lost upon Newman.

On his side, as far as we can judge from the charity-school *Spectators,* the Whiston episode, and the book notice for Derham in *The Guardian,* Steele's response to Newman's overtures was generous and hearty. That he would value the opportunities for mutual aid in such an alliance seems certain. He must have been appreciative of his friend's durable qualities, perhaps even suspecting that in comparison with himself as a projector in the art of the possible Newman was less visionary and better able to channel his energies.

As for us, in these eighteenth-century letters we catch a glimpse of an American and an Irishman, both loyal, public-spirited Englishmen, together practicing their philanthropies in the name of Christian charity.

[7] Letter from Newman to James Lowther dated 8 October 1713: *Hist. MSS. Commission,* Lonsdale (1893), p. 247.

ERNEST CAMPBELL MOSSNER

Adam Ferguson's "Dialogue on a Highland Jaunt" with Robert Adam, William Cleghorn, David Hume, and William Wilkie

I N THE BRILLIANT LITERARY CIRCLE of Edinburgh in the second half of the eighteenth century, that "hot-bed of genius" in the words of Smollett, Adam Ferguson was widely regarded as one of the most brilliant. That judgment, however, was never fully justified, as there was always something superficial in Ferguson that was perhaps less evident in his conversation than in his publications. Nevertheless, he was the intimate friend of David Hume and Adam Smith. A sizable body of unpublished writings by Ferguson has recently come to light, the publication of which might conceivably have enhanced his reputation in later times. One of these, first printed in 1960, displays some dexterity in its smashing attacks on Hume's theory of utility and, more particularly, on Smith's theory of sympathy.[1]

A second unpublished work, "Dialogue on a Highland Jaunt," although relatively brief, bears some affinity to both Dr. Johnson's *Journey to the Western Islands of Scotland* (1775) and Boswell's *Journal of a Tour to the Hebrides* (1786)—the philosophical inquiries

ERNEST CAMPBELL MOSSNER is Professor of English at the University of Texas.

[1] "Of the Principle of Moral Estimation: A Discourse between David Hume, Robert Clerk, and Adam Smith: An unpublished MS by Adam Ferguson," ed. with a Foreword by E. C. Mossner, *Journal of the History of Ideas*, XXI (1960), 222–32. Ferguson himself does not participate in the discourse; it is General Clerk who attacks the other two. At the time of publication, I was unaware of the dialogue discussed in this chapter.

of Johnson and the conversational reporting of Boswell.[2] Besides Ferguson himself, the speakers and travelers are Robert Adam, William Cleghorn, David Hume, and William Wilkie, all Scots, and with the exception of Ferguson, all Lowlanders. Hume is too well known to require even the briefest biographical mention, but a few words are in order about the others.

Adam Ferguson (1723–1816), a Highlander by birth (Logierait, Perthshire), had a varied career as clergyman, chaplain in the Black Watch, librarian, politician, tutor, professor, philosopher, moralist, historian, and general man of letters. It was probably Hume who arranged for Ferguson to succeed him as Keeper of the Advocates' Library in Edinburgh (now the National Library of Scotland), and it was certainly Hume who later helped maneuver him into a professorship—the first of three held successively at Edinburgh University: Natural Philosophy, Pneumatics and Moral Philosophy, Mathematics. In regard to the first professorship, the Reverend Alexander "Jupiter" Carlyle observes that "David Hume said Ferguson had more genius than any of them, as he had made himself so much master of a difficult science—viz., Natural Philosophy, which he had never studied but when at college—in three months, so as to be able to teach it."[3] Hume also remembered Ferguson in his will, along with D'Alembert and Adam Smith, leaving each a legacy of £200, a tribute of affection and admiration. In character, Ferguson always remained an irascible but beloved Highlander, a good friend of many of the truly great, and a man of the world in the best sense of that term. It was at Ferguson's Sciennes Hill House near Edinburgh that the very young Walter Scott in 1787 met for the first and only time the young Robert Burns.

Robert Adam (1728–92) descended from a well-to-do family of architects and became the most distinguished of them all, lending his name to the Adam or light classical style. His several books on architecture, as well as his various buildings and interior decorations, brought him the honor of burial in Westminster Abbey and undying fame. To mention but a few examples of his architectural achievements: in Edinburgh, he drew the designs for the University and the Register House; in London, he laid out Portland Place and Adelphi

---

[2] I am happy to express my thanks to C. P. Finlayson, Keeper of MSS, Edinburgh University Library, for calling my attention to this dialogue (E.U.L., MS Dc 1. 42. No. 5) and for providing information about it. Permission to publish has been generously granted by Edinburgh University Library. Professor Ian S. Ross of the University of British Columbia has been invaluable in the reading and transcribing of the MS and in the interpretation of certain passages. To him, my deepest gratitude.

[3] *The Autobiography of Dr. Alexander Carlyle of Inveresk, 1722–1805,* ed. J. H. Burton (London and Edinburgh, 1910), pp. 297–98.

Terrace; and, in the country, he designed Syon House. It was also Adam who planned the New Bridge of Burns's "The Brigs of Ayr." Adam had been associated with Ferguson at school and university and is said to have had the "advantage of having [Ferguson] as his particular friend." They remained mutual admirers through life. "Jupiter" Carlyle relates how Hume came to be accepted into the Adam family. "When Mr. Robert Adam, the celebrated architect, and his brother, lived in Edinburgh with their mother, . . . a very respectable woman, she said to her son, 'I shall be glad to see any of your companions to dinner, but I hope you will never bring the Atheist [Hume] here to disturb my peace.' But Robert soon fell on a method to reconcile her to him, for he introduced him under another name, or concealed it carefully from her. When the company parted she said to her son, 'I must confess that you bring very agreeable companions about you, but the large jolly man who sat next me is the most agreeable of them all.' 'This was the very Atheist,' said he, 'mother, that you was so much afraid of.' 'Well,' says she, 'you may bring him here as much as you please, for he's the most innocent, agreeable, facetious man I ever met with.'"[4] In 1764 Hume was happy to acknowledge: "That Family [the Adam] is one of the few to whose Civilities I have been much beholden, and I retain a lively Sense of them."

William Cleghorn (1718–54), clergyman and professor, is remembered today, if he is remembered at all, only because he was appointed Professor of Pneumatics and Moral Philosophy at Edinburgh University in 1745 over the candidacy of David Hume. "His colleagues and contemporaries," writes the historian of that university, "considered him as a young man of the most promising talents." Nevertheless, there is no evidence that Cleghorn ever published; but, to be sure, he died at a relatively early age. On his deathbed, after resigning from the University, Cleghorn said of Ferguson, "he has my dying voice" for the professorship.[5] It was not, however, until ten years later that Ferguson was elected to that particular chair. In the present dialogue, Ferguson allots considerably more space to Cleghorn than to Hume; Hume, in fact, is accorded the least of all.

Finally, there is William Wilkie (1721–72), farmer ("Potato Wilkie"), clergyman, poet, and professor, whose epic, the *Epigoniad* (1757), was well received in Edinburgh, though severely castigated in London. In a fervor of Scottish patriotism, Hume went so far as to name it "the second Epic Poem in our Language." The eccentric

---

4 *Ibid.*, pp. 285–86.

5 Alexander Grant, *Story of the University of Edinburgh* (London, 1884), II, 338–39.

"Homer of the Lowlands" was dearly loved by his friends. A perfect specimen of the absent-minded professor, Wilkie, it is reported, met a student in the street one day and inquired:

"I am sorry to hear, my dear boy, that you have had the fever in your family. Was it you or your brother who died of it?"

"It was I, Sir."

"Ah, dear me, I thought so. Very sorry for it."[6]

This, then, is the group of cronies assembled by Ferguson for the Highland jaunt—"originals" all. At the outset, it is fitting to inquire whether the dialogue is a work of pure fiction or, in some wise, a Boswellian reconstruction of an actual journey. Considering the fact that Cleghorn died in 1754 "after a tedious illness"[7] and that the paper on which the dialogue exists is watermarked 1799, when Ferguson was aged seventy-six, the latter, or Boswellian, hypothesis will hardly stand scrutiny—but, of course, the present draft may not have been the first. Yet when we bear in mind that 1754 is the latest possible date for an actual discussion, anachronisms are obvious in references to Johnson's *Dictionary of the English Language* (1755), Smith's *The Theory of Moral Sentiments* (1759), and Watt's steam engine (patented, 1769). All in all, the dialogue is probably best regarded as a fiction devised by an elderly scholar recollecting various philosophical discussions with intimate friends of some distinction, all of whom were dead at the time of writing.[8]

Lord Cockburn has left an incomparable description of Ferguson, "a spectacle well worth beholding," at about the period when presumably he was composing the dialogue. "His hair was silky and white; his eyes animated and light blue; his cheeks sprinkled with broken red, like autumnal apples, but fresh and healthy; his lips thin, and the under one curled. A severe paralytic attack had reduced his animal vitality, though it left no external appearance, and he required considerable artificial heat. His raiment consisted of half boots lined with fur, cloth breeches, a long cloth waistcoat with capacious pockets, a single-breasted coat, a cloth greatcoat also lined with fur, and a felt hat commonly tied by a ribbon below the chin. His boots were black; but with this exception the whole coverings, including the hat,

---

[6] Harold Thompson, *A Scottish Man of Feeling: Henry Mackenzie* (Oxford, 1931), pp. 46–47.

[7] *Scots Magazine*, XVI (1754), 404, gives the date of death as 23 August.

[8] This is as good a place as any for a true confession. In my Foreword to Ferguson's other unpublished dialogue, I argued that it might very well actually have taken place at London in 1761. The watermark on the paper, unhappily not then examined, turns out to be 1800! But, to repeat, the copy may not have been the first draft. In any event, I can only cry *Peccavi!*

were of a Quaker grey colour, or of a whitish brown. He generally wore the furred greatcoat even within doors. When he walked forth, he used a tall staff, which he commonly held at arm's length towards the right side; and his two coats, each buttoned by only the upper button, flowed open below, and exposed the whole of his curious and venerable figure. Ferguson's gait and air were noble; his gesture slow; his look full of dignity and composed fire. He looked like a philosopher from Lapland."[9]

Ferguson's manuscript of the dialogue is incomplete: the first two pages are missing, as are pages 21–24, and the ending on page 58 is somewhat abrupt. Many passages are corrupt and some indecipherable. Clearly, the manuscript was not prepared for publication.[10]

As a work of art, however, the dialogue does not fare badly. The setting is authentic because Ferguson is describing Highland scenes familiar to him. Specifically, the scene is set at midsummer in the deer forest of the Duke of Atholl in the extreme northern region of Perthshire, which includes the central Grampians. The birds mentioned are common in the Highlands, the moor cock (or male grouse) and the plover. The talk of guns, a dog, and a stag fit a typical Highland setting. So, too, does the diction: *Gilly whitfoot* (a servant or beater for game, customarily going barefoot to allow him to carry his chieftain across a stream); *Shealing* (a hut of rough construction); *Stalker* (a guide who stalks game; also, a fowler); *Strath* (a valley traversed by a stream and bounded by hills); *Whittering* (chirping, twittering).

"I am not sure," observes Ferguson toward the beginning of the dialogue, "but [that] the most learned are the most apt [to] espy Barbarity in every thing different from themselves, And something like the Chinese Map of the World is to be found in every European head. My friends, however," he continues, "were not insensible to the Natural Beauties of the Country: Its Woods, Waters, Lofty Hills, & Precipices; and my heart overflowed with pleasure in a Company to which I was so much attached & from whom I had taken my first Draughts of Moral Science. Having already Rode or Walked through every Road or by-Path among the Woods & Banks of the River, We agreed one Evening that next day we should ascend the mountains & enjoy a Pleasure which I had often talked of to them of Sauntering amidst the Solemnity of Lone & Empty Vales among the mountains

---

[9] *Memoirs of His Time by Lord Cockburn,* abridged and ed. W. Forbes Gray (Edinburgh, 1946), pp. 40–41.

[10] I have silently added necessary punctuation and expanded abbreviated words; otherwise, I have retained the original spelling and capitalization. Essential additions to the text are placed within brackets.

with nothing to see but heath, towering hills, & Magestick Rock & not a Sound but of the Whittering Plover or Moor Cock when he springs [from] the Heath.

"But that we might appear to have some meaning in our Walks & not pass for Madmen in the Country," Ferguson "undertook to Arm them all with some sort of Guns & procure a Dog to give us the appearance of Sportsmen." Accordingly, at four o'clock the following morning the Lowlanders were awakened by the firing of a gun by their host "under the Window [of] the Place where they Slept." Soon the company set off with a "Gilly whitfoot," bearing "a bag of provisions to stay hunger which," Ferguson shrewdly observes, "never fails to make itself felt through the day in Such excursions." It was not long, however, before the Lowlanders began to complain of the unaccustomed mountain climbing and would have thrown away their guns "but for Shame." A "Stalker" or deer hunter, an acquaintance of Ferguson, whom they had met, flushed two or three coveys of birds and was much vexed when no one fired a shot except Ferguson, who cheerfully admitted that he was no marksman.

Trying to make the best of the situation, Ferguson led the way "to a Spring & Rivulet with which I was well acquainted where I proposed we should take some Rest and Refreshment. The Stalker . . . took a different way towards a Shealing from which he said he would meet us round the hill with some Supply of Milk & what else the Shealing could supply. We had accordingly scarce got sight of our Rivulet when our Friend appeard accompanyed with a herdsman & two young Women carrying Pitchers of Milk, Cream, & Whey with Barley Cakes of the most delicious, as every one of the Company owned at this time, tho at any other perhaps, they would scarcely have tasted such fare."

Replete with the simple and wholesome food, the company began discussing "what sort of pleasure Sportsmen could have in killing poor birds." In the midst of the discussion, the Stalker whispered to them to be silent, "pointing to Windward with his face almost touching the Ground." Then "We Spyed a Stag coming at speed over a height beyond us." The Stalker prepared to take a shot. "For your Life," cried Cleghorn, "don't shoot him. I would not forgo the pleasure of seeing him pass for all the Venison in your Duke's Forrest." Sensing danger, the stag sprang away, much to the relief of all except the Stalker who, obviously enraged, immediately made a silent departure. What became of the "Gilly whitfoot" remains a mystery, for he is not mentioned thereafter.

Left alone and entranced with the grace of the stag, the philosophical Nimrods—Wilkie had already lost his powder horn—are led into a discussion of the meaning of pleasure, freedom of choice, humanitarianism, and beauty. Plato, Aristotle, Epicurus, Zeno, and Cicero are cited or alluded to among the Ancients; Samuel Clarke, Shaftesbury, Hutcheson, Montesquieu, Hogarth, Johnson, and Smith among the Moderns. Needless to say, the five disputants vent their own opinions, Ferguson judiciously apportioning the most space to himself. The "Dialogue on a Highland Jaunt" now really becomes a dialogue. The episode of the stag is referred to time and time again, Ferguson employing it as a symbolic device to enter into philosophic discourse, a means of discussing the nature of beauty and happiness.

The grand debate opens with the consideration of whether the stag has acted by instinct or by thought. "I believe that all animals," says Wilkie, "do what is agreeable to them & Man among the rest." Cleghorn suggests that man differs from other animals in that he has freedom of choice through reason. Adam acts as the gadfly: "What a Mighty Vista you would open for so short sighted a Creature!" Cleghorn contends that there is another principle in man by which he may act without taking time for deliberation. This is "the distinguishing principle of right & Wrong, Innocent & Guilt, Honour & dishonour." "I believe," he goes on, "we are more effectually Supported in acting . . . through Sentiments of Integrity & honour than any mere consideration of future Interest or safety. . . . Virtue, it should seem by this account, to be the greatest Pleasure And the Systems of Epicurus & Zeno were the same."

The last point is illustrated thus: "Epicurus says that Pleasure is the Chief Good. Zeno says that Virtue, his Chief Good, is Supremely pleasant. Here the only difference seems to be that the Adjective and Substantive are differently placed. Strange that so slight a difference should have occasioned so much Controversy or that in the effect there should be any difference!"

Neither Adam nor Wilkie, however, is much impressed, the latter scoffing, "I am affraid that if the World is to be governed by the Choice of names we have little to expect from Philosophy at least." Cleghorn reiterates his emphasis on "the Principle of Estimation in the human mind." To which Wilkie gibes: "What a Mysterious and Indefineable Principle you open upon us! And Plato himself, I believe, with his One in Many or his many in one could hardly make Sense of it. What is it, Vanity, Ambition, or Pride? The fashionable point of honour, Dress or Beauty, Politeness, Education, Science, Fortune or Birth, or any thing else which mankind affect to set themselves off?"

Driven by the taunts of Adam and Wilkie against the contention that the principle of estimation can include or explain all of the foregoing, Cleghorn turns to Ferguson for support. The latter rallies to the defense. "It is a certain disposition to Esteem the Excellent or Perfect in Contradistinction to Imperfection or defect. In what Relates to our own attainments, I would call it Ambition, A term in common use, for the most part united to the desire of Power." He cites the authority of Johnson's *Dictionary:* "The desire of something higher & better than the present."[11] Consequently, he concludes, "We may venture to call the desire of Excellence *Ambition,* As we call the Love of Animal Pleasure Sensuality." On this note the debate breaks off with a gap in the manuscript. When it resumes after four missing pages, the topic of discussion has shifted to the nature of beauty.

Wilkie observes that all those present have something to do with the arts that contribute to pleasure as well as to profit and suggests that, "if each will specify what he aims at for Beauty in his Way, we may possibly find some point in which to Agree." Entering the discussion for the first time, Hume pins his faith on "Bob Adam," the distinguished creator of architectural beauty. "I shall," declares Hume, "desire no other account of Beauty than what he will give."

Adam, for his part, is more than a little cynical. "In our Professsion, we have less to do with Beauty than People imagine. We must humour our Imployers; they have each Crotchets and think only how they may be lodged at the least Expense."

Hume accepts Adam's reply as an exposition of "the very summit of Beauty: Utility in which every one is entitled to judge for himself." So the debate turns to the relation between utility and beauty, Adam and Hume agreeing that the contemporary world can find the best instances of the union of the two in the "Remains of Antiquity." To this Ferguson retorts that "utility wherever found should have the same Effect, And a Dunghill be more admired than the Pantheon of Agrippa or the Dome of St Peters." The issue is partially conceded by Hume: "I grant you that Utility without art or Design, especially if it offend our other Senses, is not admitted for Beauty."

Wilkie will have none even of this, sardonically commenting, "We have let the Deer escape and I suspect we must let the game you are in pursuit of escape also. It is too nimble, I doubt, for our speculations. . . . What connection can Beauty or matters of Fancy and lovely conceit have with Utility, the dullest of all Considerations, or with great Schemes of Contrivance however beneficent? . . . Beauty has always appeared to me a matter of Surface & Delight, not of internal Solidity

---

[11] In the first edition of 1755 Johnson's definition was: "AMBITION—The desire of any thing great or excellent."

or depth of thought." He instances "a Pair of Boots bespattered with Dirt," which "should be beautiful because of the Use they were of in keeping a traveller clean." The steam engine is a similar case. Taking a new tack, Wilkie challenges, "What is the Use or Design of a Tulip or a Rose?" A "Note of Music?" "Hogarth's line?" "A Circle . . . than any Angular Figure?"

Ferguson now enters the fray again, holding forth on the semantics of the word *beauty*. "There are some things in their own Nature agreeable or Admirable. Others are so only by association with something else. A Fine Morning or Evening is pleasant in itself. The Rise of the Curtain at the Playhouse is pleasant on account of the Entertainment expected to follow." With Plato, he is desirous to ascend from sensory objects to esteem, admiration, ecstasy, even to the "Divine Artist." Cleghorn elaborates on the concept that the Almighty had superadded intelligence to man in order to give him the "Power of discriminating Excellence & Defect" and of leading up to ideal perfection.

Hume and Wilkie are by no means convinced that "Intelligence alone is requird for this Purpose," stipulating the "moral sense, The Sense of Beauty, The Sense of Ridicule, and so forth. Understanding or Intelligence is employed in discovering Truth or refuting Error. But in judging of Merit or Demerit there is sensation as well as reasoning."

Cleghorn replies that the moral sense is "a mere Metaphor and, as Metaphors frequently do, tends to Mislead our Conception." He, therefore, turns the discussion back to the topic of beauty. "The Question," he proceeds, "may be divided into two:

"1st, What it is in the Nature or Form of Things that thus affects the Observer of Beauty?

"2nd, By what faculty in the Observer this Perception or Sentiment is obtained?"

In answer to the first question, Cleghorn argues against Hutcheson's theory of "Uniformity amidst Variety" and Hogarth's "gently flowing Lines or Surfaces."[12]

Hutcheson is dispatched swiftly. "This scene is undoubtedly Beautiful: but whether [it] is so from its mere variety and analogy may be doubted. These circumstances may be conceived to take place in scenes of which the Effect will be quite the Reverse. Suppose, for instance, [different forms] of Torture but analogous in the manner of their application by Machinery or by fire. The Hell produced with

12 Francis Hutcheson, *An Inquiry into the Original of Our Ideas of Beauty and Virtue: In Two Treatises* (London, 1725); William Hogarth, *The Analysis of Beauty. Written with a View of Fixing the Fluctuating Ideas of Taste* (London, 1753).

all variety & analogy would be a scene of Horror and Detestation, not of Delight or Admiration. It is, therefore, not the mere analogy of Various Classes and orders of things that Constitutes their Beauty, But the Beneficient Intention that appears throughout, and still appears in all the Variation of unexhaustible Invention."

Hogarth's "line of beauty" also gets short shrift. Indeed, it has "something childish" about it, which "would tempt us to believe he had never looked for Beauty beyond the Folliage which decorates the Frame of a Picture. In Architecture the Streight line and plane surface are as Necessary to beauty as foliage is to the Festoon or . . . a serpentine Walk to the Pleasure [garden]. Give Hogarth's line of Beauty to the Column & his Waving Surface to his paviment in the portico, I imagine his Beauty will disgust or offend the Taste it is meant to Gratify."

The second question concerning that faculty in the observer by which beauty is obtained leads to a discussion of esteem, happiness, and perfection. Ferguson, taking over from Cleghorn, postulates a scale of being in which there is a gradation of happiness. "I am not affraid to offer a Conjecture that the Frame of Nature is presented to our Observation As the Aliment of Intelligence, [just] As the Fields on this Globe are Covered with the Verdure for the Aliment of Pasturing animals. I am ready to contend that still matter in any form has no Value but in its Relation to living Nature and, on this Earth, chiefly to the Living and Intelligent Nature of Man. The Huntsman finds his game even on these Barren & Towering mountains and, if the Stag were ten times more cautious & swift than his pursuers, [they] would find out ways to overtake & seize. The Game for Contemplation & Thought is spread over all from the Earth on which we tread to the Gallaxy and the sparkling Suns that do but now reach us with their Ray. We may err in the order in which we employ our thoughts, and our opinions be no better than matter for Correction; but even our mistakes are still an Approach to our End. To the Progress of Intelligence this is peculiar that the experience of [a] Mistake & its consequences lead to the discovery of Truth. We are not, therefore, to be deterred from the use of Reason for it is in using it that we render ourselves fit to enter the higher scenes of Being to which our progression may lead."

Wilkie grants the likelihood of the progress of intelligence in all species but insists that "how far one species in the System of Nature [is] of an order superior to others may be questioned or, at least, the grounds of any such superiority may be considered."

From this point on to the end of the manuscript (pp. 48–58), the "dialogue" becomes a monologue with Ferguson doing the talking.

His general topic is man's "Powers of Progression" and his intelligence or reason. The monologue is a development of the major points he has already postulated and, consequently, need not be presented in detail. Progressivism is an axiom in all Ferguson's publications, but the present emphasis on reason or intellectualism comes as something of a surprise.

"Omnipotence," he opens, "is that to which there is no resemblance or approach in any Contingent Being. Even contingent Intelligence, however, is of a prominent Rank in the Order of Created Being. There is Will directed to happiness and, in proportion as this is approached, there is Will to bestow it. The Will to be Good, to be Wise, Intrepid, orderly is happiness and is also the Will to Bestow it." The faculty that enables us to discern wisdom and goodness is intelligence. "Beauty too, a less Respected Name than Wisdom and Goodness, still points at Perfection & Excellence and cannot long delight where these are found to be wanting. The commendation of Beauty, tho meant of Excellence, is given on the first Appearance of it, while that excellence is reserved as matter of deliberate Judgment . . . [and] it may with Confidence be said that mind alone is truly happy, Excellent, and Fair."

In an analogous way, the "Principal of moral approbation" is fixed and rational, a dictum already advanced by Dr. Samuel Clarke and President Montesquieu.[13] This, we cannot question, declares Ferguson, "but the Enunciation is too general. We must ask, what things & Relations?" To which question he supplies his own answer: "Undoubtedly the things & Relations to which moral Laws refer, That is, human Mind and the Relations of Man to Man and to his Maker." Those who merely say "Truth" or "Utility" are begging the question. "Benevolence is in itself highly Estimable, but to call it useful is a mere abuse of words."

"Others in treating of this Subject confound two questions together as different as Wisdom is from folly and Candour from Partiality."

The first question is, "From what Principle may we Safely & truly decide of Action and Character?"

The second question is, "On what Principle do men actually decide or entertain Sentiments of Praise or Blame?"

Ferguson's answers are speedily forthcoming.

"To the first Question we have now endeavoured to Answer that Wisdom & Goodness, the Excellence of Intelligent Being, is the Test

---

[13] Samuel Clarke, *Boyle Lectures 1691–1732*, ed. Letsome and Nicholl (London, 1739), under the years 1704 and 1705; Charles de Secondat, Baron de Montesquieu, *De l'esprit des lois* (Paris, 1748).

of moral Rectitude & Felicity and that well Informed Intelligence is competent to judge of such Merits.

"To the second Question we may admit that men frequently consult their own Interest in judging of merit in others.

"To others we may admit that what they are pleased to call sympathy or even coincidence of Sentiment or [the] reverse is the ordinary or frequent ground of Estimation of praise or Censure. But we cannot admit that either is a safe ground of Estimation, much less the only Ground which Nature has laid for the distinction of Right & Wrong. And every attempt to Instruct us on the Subject without distinguishing the Questions is not only Nugatory and Perplexing to the unwary but actually tending to explain away distinctions of the utmost importance to Mankind, turning Zeal for Morals into a mere selfish Interest or into a mere coincidence of sentiment which may take place among Knaves and Fools as well as among honest Men." He concludes that mankind may make mistakes concerning others; but the individual, relying on his wisdom or intelligence or reason, is seldom mistaken about himself. Indeed, his "Wisdom or Intelligence" is "a Watch that seldom slumbers or sleeps or mistakes whatever the Party concerned may plead or pretend to others."

On this triumphant note of intellectualism or rationalism, of the idea of necessary progress, and of the doctrine of final causes, Ferguson, to his own satisfaction, routs the antirationalism of both Hume's theory of utility and Smith's theory of sympathy. And, although everyone present has had his say, even though only Cleghorn would agree with Ferguson, it is Ferguson who takes an author's prerogative and gives himself the last word. So ends Ferguson's dialogue on a jaunt to the Highlands with his Lowland friends, a jaunt more notable for talking than walking.

AUBREY L. WILLIAMS

Pope and Horace: The Second Epistle
of the Second Book

Aｌｅｘａｎｄｅｒ Pｏｐｅ's *Imitations of Horace*, not surprisingly perhaps, have been the most neglected of the poet's later and maturest work. Such critical comment as they have received has ranged from delight to entire dissatisfaction, but more often than not they have been brushed only lightly in studies of Pope.[1] From the very beginning, moreover, there has been an inclination to measure Pope's work against that of Horace almost solely in terms of one or another isolated passage lifted out of context. Such an inclination is most baldly displayed in the commentaries of Pope's early editors, whose notes declare now that "These four lines [are] greatly superior to any thing in the Original," now that a passage "is much inferior to the original." And a variation on this mode of criticism was firmly established, though not originated, by Dr. Johnson, who judged such "imitations" to be pleasing "when the thoughts are unexpectedly applicable and the parallels lucky."[2] In either case, whether approached by way of scattered passages found to be superior or inferior to the original, or by way of occasional "lucky parallels" between Roman and English scenes, the *Imitations* have usually been measured by the "Exactness of peculiar Parts."

The inclination to such criticism derives, possibly, from a disquiet with works that seem to fall, vaguely, somewhere between translation

AUBREY L. WILLIAMS is Professor of English at the University of Florida.

[1] Several valuable studies of the *Imitations* have recently been published and suggest a growth of interest in these poems: Reuben A. Brower, *Alexander Pope: The Poetry of Allusion* (Oxford, 1959), esp. Chap. IX; G. K. Hunter, "The 'Romanticism' of Pope's Horace," *Essays in Criticism*, X (1960), 390–404; John M. Aden, "Pope and the Satiric Adversary," *SEL*, II (1962), 267–86; R. E. Hughes, "Pope's *Imitations of Horace* and the Ethical Focus," *MLN*, 71 (1956), 569–74.

[2] *Lives of the English Poets*, ed. G. B. Hill (3 vols.; Oxford, 1905), III, 176.

and original composition. And oddly or not, it was again the author of *London* and *The Vanity of Human Wishes* who early formulated a generally depreciatory attitude toward Pope's *Imitations* and also defined a dissatisfaction with them as a species of "middle composition":

> The *Imitations of Horace* seem to have been written as relaxations of his genius. This employment became his favourite by its facility; the plan was ready to his hand, and nothing was required but to accommodate as he could the sentiments of an old author to recent facts or familiar images; but what is easy is seldom excellent: such imitations cannot give pleasure to common readers.[3] The man of learning may be sometimes surprised and delighted by an unexpected parallel; but the comparison requires knowledge of the original, which will likewise often detect strained applications. Between Roman images and English manners there will be an irreconcileable dissimilitude, and the work will be generally uncouth and party-coloured; neither original nor translated, neither ancient nor modern.[4]

Confronted with works neither quite original nor quite translated, scholars have in effect simplified the main critical issue by adopting the essentially invidious procedure of comparing discrete passages. A natural but unfortunate result of this procedure has been the inclination to value Pope's work most highly when it is closest to the original (that is, when it is closest to what can be called a "spirited translation"), or when sheer historical coincidence has provided a lucky parallel between Roman and English scenes. But when Pope varies or departs widely from Horace, critics of his performance have too often been content to observe merely that a certain passage is "not Horace" or "not out of Horace."

From all we know of Pope's labors on his translations of Homer—his care and energy in the consultation of texts, his assiduous search for comment on his author—it seems reasonable to assume that, for his work on the *Imitations*, he familiarized himself with at least some of the Renaissance and contemporary editions of Horace. He was obviously familiar with Bentley's Horace and would hardly have failed to consider the kinds of critical discussion of Horace's poetic

---

[3] Johnson's view here has been contested by several critics. Cf. John Conington, *Miscellaneous Writings*, ed. J. A. Symonds (London, 1872), I, 69: "Yet I am mistaken if a common reader may not enjoy these imitations nearly as much as any of Pope's more original satires. . . ." Cf. also J. W. Tupper, "A Study of Pope's Imitations of Horace," *PMLA*, XV (1900), 181–215.

[4] *Lives of the English Poets*, III, 246–47. Dryden's remarks on the three kinds of translation (metaphrase, paraphrase, and imitation) have a bearing, of course, on what Pope himself may have meant by the term "imitation."

strategies and meaning to be found in the editions of such men as Johannis Bond, André Dacier, and Noël-Étienne Sanadon (to mention only a few).[5] Critical exegesis of the structure and meaning of Horace's work was too readily available, and too pertinent to his own work, for one such as Pope to ignore. When, therefore, he deviates widely from the Horatian originals, it would again seem reasonable to assume that he has specific and conscious reasons for doing so and that the chief of these is his desire to create in English a poem with its own new unity and design.

Evidence and notice of deliberate departures from Horace are given by Pope in the Latin texts of the original he provided for his readers. Printed on pages facing his own English texts, these Latin texts are studded with italicized words or phrases,[6] which are obviously designed for the reader's particular attention and which seem to have had one of two purposes: first, they signal moments when Pope apparently wishes it remarked that he is following hard upon Horace, perhaps in order that the dignity and weight of Horace's authority might be attributed to his own position, perhaps in order to gain consent to what in the *Imitation* might seem a novel idea or phrasing; second, but equally important, the italics signal moments when Pope wishes it to be noticed that he has deliberately forsaken the original.

The number, the quality, and the design of Pope's departures from Horace in such a poem as the *Imitation of the Second Epistle of the Second Book* may be more readily measured and appreciated if they are placed against contemporary scholarly accounts of the structure and development of the Horatian original. In two massive contemporary editions of Horace, for example, those of Dacier and Sanadon,[7] the structure of *Epistle II ii* is specifically discussed and disagreement about the co-ordination of the epistle's various parts is aired. And while these two critics lose no opportunity to attack each other in their commentaries, still they are in general agreement about the

---

[5] For discussion of editions of Horace in Pope's library and of his use of them in constructing the Latin text he provided his readers, see Lillian D. Bloom, "Pope as Textual Critic: A Bibliographical Study of His Horatian Text," *JEGP*, XLVII (1948), 150–55, and the review of Mrs. Bloom's article by Robert W. Rogers, *PQ*, XXVIII (1949), 397–98; also Ralph Hagedorn, "Pope and Horace," *N & Q*, 194 (1949), 144–45.

[6] Early editions of the *Imitations* print the body of the Latin text in italic type and stressed words or phrases in roman type. In discussion of the stressed passages, it seems to me less confusing to modern readers to apply the term "italic" to them.

[7] André Dacier, *Œuvres D'Horace En Latin et en François, avec Des Remarques Critiques et Historiques* (3d ed., 10 vols.; Paris, 1709); and Noël-Étienne Sanadon, *Les Poésies D'Horace, Disposées Suivant L'Ordre Cronologique, et Traduites en François: Avec des Remarques et des Dissertations Critiques* (2 vols.; Paris, 1728). Sanadon displaces *Ep. II ii* from its normal position; in his edition it becomes *Ep. I ix*.

course of Horace's poem. Thus Dacier points out that Horace offers
to Florus five reasons or excuses for his failure to write to him: first,
Horace, like the slave boy offered for sale at the start of his poem, is
lazy and flees from work; second (lines 55 ff.), age is creeping up
upon him; third (lines 58 ff.), there is difficulty in satisfying the
diversitiis of taste among readers; fourth (lines 65 ff.), there is the
difficulty of writing amidst the bustle and confusion of Rome; fifth
(lines 87 ff.), vanity and unhappiness generally attend upon anyone
who attempts poetry. Sanadon in effect accepts Dacier's five reasons,
but specifies two more: the episode of the soldier of Lucullus shows
that when a man has enough, he is foolish to strive for more, whether
in the taking of citadels or in the writing of epistles; beginning at line
141, and continuing till the end of the poem, Horace shows there
comes a time when the art of the good life is more important than the
art of poetry.[8]

Of all the ways in which Pope departs from the development of
Horace's poem as it was perceived by these two French critics, none
is more broad and obvious than that displayed in the opening scene
of his *Imitation*. For the Roman slave trader who employs the wiles
and jargon ("Fiet erítque tuus"[9]) of the market place to palm off a
worthless young slave, Pope substitutes a Frenchman who attempts,
with Gallic floridity and obsequiousness, to place his worthless son in
an English gentleman's service. In addition, Pope abandons almost
completely, it should be observed, the highly legalistic and commercial terminology and imagery used throughout the opening scene of
the original, the precise quality and dramatic use of which were
stressed repeatedly in seventeenth- and eighteenth-century commentaries on the Horatian text.[10]

Most important, however, is the very specific change in the fault
of the youth offered for service, a change Pope carefully emphasized
by the italicization of a single word in the text of the original he
provided. Horace's slave merchant says (line 16), "Des nummos,
excepta nihil te si *fuga* lædat" ("Give me the sum asked, if his run-

[8] The seven reasons pointed out by the French critics are reiterated by Warton
in his note to line 27 of Pope's *Imitation of the Second Epistle of the Second Book.*

[9] The Latin text cited here and elsewhere is that which Pope provided his readers
and which has been reproduced in Vol. IV of *The Twickenham Edition of the
Poems of Alexander Pope*, ed. John Butt (New York, 1946). As stated earlier, however, I reverse Pope's use of roman and italic type faces.

[10] See, for example, the comment by Johannis Bond (*Q. Horativs Flaccus, Cum
commentariis selectissimis Variorum* [Leiden, 1670]) on line 3 of Horace's poem:
"*Tecum sic agat, &c.*] Μίμησις longe pulcherrima, qua mangonem summo artificio
exprimet."

ning off, duly noted, does not trouble you"[11]). The analogous passage by Pope reads:

> The Fault he has I fairly shall reveal,
> (Cou'd you o'erlook but that)—it is, to steal.

In the notes to his edition of Pope's works, Warton remarked on the change thus: "The fault of the Slave-seller's Boy is *only* [italics mine] his having run away; but the young Frenchman has been guilty of stealing; this makes his behaviour more unpardonable, and less likely to be overlooked by the purchaser: a circumstance that alters the nature of the allusion, and the probability of the bargain." Warton's observation is, of course, anachronistic, for in a slave-owning economy one can imagine no greater fault, in a slaveowner's eyes, than a slave's flight. Indeed, as seventeenth- and eighteenth-century commentaries on the original stress, running off was regarded by the Romans as so considerable a fault that a slave merchant was specifically obliged by law to mention any occurrence of it (as Horace's merchant does, though almost in a jesting aside), else the merchant could be punished and the sale of a slave voided. Thus, as far as Pope's alteration of the circumstances is concerned, Warton's comment is beside the mark: stealing in the eighteenth century was no more considerable a fault, in all probability, than running away would have seemed in the first century B.C., and so the relative credibility of the respective bargains is hardly in question.

The actual significance of Pope's change would seem to be defined by considerations quite different from those raised by Warton, for here the poet is to be seen introducing the controlling metaphor of his poem—thievery. Images and episodes of thievery suffuse and dominate the first half of the *Imitation* (and guide one's responses to the material of the second half) in a way not paralleled in the original, and by means of them Pope establishes and controls the central themes of his poem. These themes are, first, the decays and losses to which men are subjected by the inexorable passage of time, and, second, the proper attitude with which these decays and losses are to be faced. The decisive importance of the change Pope made so early and so pointedly in his *Imitation* lies in his deployment of images of thievery to suggest that the greatest of thieves is Time, which robs man of everything.

Images of thievery do occur in Horace's poem, and certainly Horace is primarily concerned with the establishment of individual equanimity in the face of losses brought by Time. But much of

---

[11] *Satires, Epistles and Ars Poetica*, ed. and trans. H. R. Fairclough (The Loeb Classical Library; Cambridge, 1947), p. 425.

Horace's argument draws its metaphoric terms from legal or commercial or political contexts (contexts either minimized or abandoned by Pope[12]), and he does not create as single-mindedly or as pervasively as Pope an awareness of the relentless and insatiable encroachments of Time. Thus, as we have seen from contemporary accounts of the structure of Horace's poem, Horace in his opening scene specifies the faults of the slave boy as being those of laziness and truancy, and these faults then serve, by analogy, to excuse Horace's failure (or refusal) to send a letter to Florus. And whereas Horace says that Florus unjustly accuses him of being false to his word and leaves the matter at that for the moment, Pope abandons this circumstance of the original in favor of an exclamation that insists upon the predicament of a man trying to save his soul in the midst of demands not only from importunate friends but from Time itself:

> Nay worse, to ask for Verse at such a time!
> D'ye think me good for nothing but to rhime?[13]

The insistent way in which Pope expands or adds to the few scattered references to thievery found in the original, and thereby creates for his poem a metaphor whose ascendancy and influence has no exact counterpart in the original, results no doubt in a reduction of the sheer range and variety of metaphor employed by Horace. But by his changes, Pope gives his poem a new unity and focus, and he may even convey, to an English reader at least, a deeper and more poignant awareness of the losses brought by Time.

The course of Pope's changes and the development of his metaphoric pattern of thievery are easily followed. Immediately after the conspicuous change made in the opening incident of his poem, he introduces four lines having no parallel in Horace:

> Faith, in such case, if you should prosecute,
> I think Sir Godfry should decide the Suit;
> Who sent the Thief that stole the Cash, away,
> And punish'd him that put it in his way.[14]

---

[12] On occasion, Pope may actually introduce a political context not found in Horace (ll. 184–97 of the *Imitation*, for example). But such contexts never overshadow Pope's central themes and metaphor.

[13] Pope's theme is actually anticipated in the second line of his *Imitation*, where he says to the "Col'nel": "You love a Verse, take such as I can send." The force of *such* gets Pope's argument off to an early start by suggesting that he has reached the age when there are more important things than verse. Pope's line 2 has no counterpart in Horace, who plunges directly into the story of the slave boy.

[14] Lines 23–26. Although Pope introduces some circumstances not to be found in the original, it is also true that he does not even attempt to "imitate" portions of the original (thus he offers no counterpart to lines 97–98 of Horace).

These lines are then followed by Pope's story of the "Soldier poor and old" who, in the time of "Anna's Wars," had his purse stolen "one luckless night." The story closely parallels that of Horace's plain "soldier of Lucullus," who also had his purse stolen. But the story in the Latin poem does not follow hard upon two other accounts of thievery as it does in Pope, and so the English poem establishes, with some persistence, a suite of metaphors, and thereby an emphasis, not to be found in the original.

Both Pope and Horace next recount, in autobiographical terms, their early years and circumstances. But while Horace relates the loss of his paternal estate to Caesar Augustus in such neutral terms as to imply little or no recrimination against the confiscatory power,[15] Pope leaves no doubt that he regarded the penal laws against Catholics as little more than legalized thievery:

> But knottier Points we knew not half so well,
> Depriv'd us soon of our Paternal Cell;
> And certain Laws, by Suff'rers thought unjust,
> Deny'd all Posts of Profit or of Trust:
> Hopes after Hopes of pious Papists fail'd,
> While mighty William's thundring Arm prevail'd.
> For Right Hereditary tax'd and fin'd,
> He [Pope's father] stuck to Poverty with Peace of Mind;
> And me, the Muses help'd to undergo it;
> Convict a Papist He, and I a Poet.[16]

It is in the next verse paragraph that Pope's metaphor of thievery rises to that meridian whence it will exert a quiet but powerful influence over all subsequent events and affairs in the *Imitation*. Previous instances of thievery in the poem have partaken of the accidental or exceptional (all men do not hire thievish servants, lose purses, or have their estates confiscated), and losses to such thievery seem in some sense recoverable. But in this sequence of thievish events Pope has risen from an instance of petty larceny to grand theft on a national scale, and now his order of thievery culminates with the presentation of that cunning and universal thief to whom all men are prey—and with losses that are irreparable:

> Years foll'wing Years, steal something ev'ry day,
> At last they steal us from our selves away;
> In one our Frolicks, one Amusements end,
> In one a Mistress drops, in one a Friend:

---

[15] Compare Dacier's comment on line 49 of *Ep. II ii:* Il fait ici un aveu sincere de son malheur, & de la misere qui l'avoit obligé à faire des vers; & il le fait d'autant plus volontiers que cet aveu tourne à la gloire d'Auguste."

[16] Lines 58–67.

This subtle Thief of Life, this paltry Time,
What will it leave me, if it snatch my Rhime?
If ev'ry Wheel of that unweary'd Mill
That turn'd ten thousand Verses, now stands still.[17]

These eight lines of the *Imitation* are based on two and one-half lines
in Horace:

Singula de nobis anni *prædantur* euntes;
Eripuere *jocos, venerem, convivia, ludum;*
Tendunt extorquere poemata.

And justly famous as the original is, one may feel that in range and
subtlety it is no match for the *Imitation*, that Pope has developed the
image of Time's thievishness (note his italicization of *prædantur*) far
beyond Horace.

Maynard Mack has pointed to Dryden's *State of Innocence*, to
Montaigne, and to a portion of the *Odyssey* perhaps translated by
Broome,[18] as possible sources for the second line ("At last they steal
us from our selves away") of Pope's verse paragraph. All of these,
as well as passages in Pope's letters also cited by Mack, may have
helped to create the mystery and sadness of the line. But of even more
direct help to Pope may have been the following passage from Dryden's *All for Love*, which at one point offers a word-for-word analogy
to Pope's line. Cleopatra, the instant before her death, addresses the
asp:

Welcome, thou kind deceiver!
Thou best of thieves, who, with an easy key,
Dost open life, and, unperceived by us,
Ev'n *steal us from ourselves*,[19] discharging so
Death's dreadful office, better than himself;
Touching our limbs so gently into slumber,
That Death stands by, deceived by his own image,
And thinks himself but Sleep.

The echoes of Shakespeare ("Nay, [Time's] a thief too. Have you
not heard men say / That Time comes stealing on by night and
day?"[20]), of Milton ("How soon hath Time the suttle theef of youth
. . ."), of Creech's translation of Lucretius ("When Age steals softly

---

[17] Lines 72–79.

[18] Review article in *PQ*, XXXVI (1957), 398–99.

[19] My italics.

[20] *Comedy of Errors*, IV, ii, 58–59.

on, and Things decay"[21]), of Dryden and other sources pointed out by Mack, all invest Pope's verses with a sadness and weight that English readers may not find in Horace's lines. By the very expansion of the original into eight lines, furthermore, Pope is able to create a rhythm and a mood of somber yet stately pathos hardly possible in the shorter space of the original. The effect he gains is partly due to the climactic couplet of his verse paragraph: without parallel in Horace, this couplet, with its subdued pun on "turn'd" and its final measured spondee, carries Pope's thought to a perfectly modulated stop.

With Time so unforgettably established, in the first third of his poem, as that supreme thief who steals everything—even ourselves—away from us, Pope now uses the middle section of his poem to dramatize the rush and press of Time amid the turmoil of London. Horace had also dramatized the difficulites of leading, amid the turmoil of Rome, a tranquil and useful life, but he does not direct the reader's attention to the encroachments of Time in the pervasive, almost exclusive, fashion of Pope. Thus Pope asks "can *London* be the Place" to attend one's "Muse, or Self, or Soul," and then, in a passage which quietly reorients the original (where Horace simply mentions inconveniently distant *places* within Rome), goes on to say:

> My Counsel sends to execute a Deed:
> A Poet begs me, I will hear him read:
> In Palace-Yard *at Nine* you'll find me there—
> *At Ten* for certain, Sir, in Bloomsb'ry-Square—
> Before the Lords *at Twelve* my Cause comes on—
> There's a Rehearsal, Sir, exact *at One*.—[22]

Hurried along by Time, and the times, how shall a man "rhime in this eternal Roar?" And why rhyme at all in an age when men, in their theft of others' reputations, seem to mimic that Time which steals a man's glory from him:

> 'Twas, "Sir your Law"—and "Sir, your Eloquence"—
> "Yours *Cowper*'s Manner—and yours *Talbot*'s Sense."
>   Thus we dispose of all poetic Merit,
> Yours *Milton*'s Genius, and mine *Homer*'s Spirit.
> Call *Tibbald Shakespear*, and he'll swear the Nine
> Dear *Cibber!* never match'd one Ode of thine.[23]

[21] Third ed.; 1683, p. 12. The context of Creech's lines should perhaps be given:
> Lastly none, not the sharpest Eye e're sees
> What parts to make things grow by just degrees
> Nature doth add, nor what she takes away,
> When Age steals softly on, and Things decay. . . .

[22] Lines 92–97. Italics in this passage are mine.

[23] Lines 133–38.

Having arrived at an age and a wisdom that perceive the folly of "Composing Songs, for Fools to get by Heart," both Pope and Horace advocate the abandonment of the art of poetry for an art of living. True enough, the art of the good poet provides, in its own way, a means of rescuing something of value from Time; in the severity of his discipline the good poet will ignore the specious or careless,

> and sometimes, in its stead,
> In downright Charity revive the dead;
> Mark where a bold expressive Phrase appears,
> Bright thro' the rubbish of some hundred years;
> Command old words that long have slept, to wake,
> Words, that wise *Bacon*, or brave *Raleigh* spake. . . .[24]

And good art may transcend, in some sense, not only time past, but also time future, for the poet may "bid the new be *English*, Ages hence." But still there is a "better Art" than that of rhyming, the "better Art to know the good from bad"; and Time, with all the losses it brings, forces upon one an awareness of the art now to be practiced:

> Well, on the whole, *plain* Prose must be my fate:
> Wisdom (curse on it) will come soon or late.
> There is a time when Poets will grow dull:
> I'll e'en leave Verses to the Boys at school:
> To Rules of Poetry no more confin'd,
> I learn to smooth and harmonize my Mind,
> Teach ev'ry Thought within its bounds to roll,
> And keep the equal Measure of the Soul.[25]

Both poets have now realized the need to escape from the tumults and vanities of life in London and in Rome, and both now turn, in the third and last sections of their poems, to meditation on the means of achieving serenity amid the waste and onrush of the years. Both had earlier recounted confiscations of paternal estates, experiences that had underscored for each the impermanence of worldly hopes and possessions, and both now extend and generalize upon these instances of personal loss. Horace writes:

> tanquam
> Sit *proprium* quidquam, puncto quod mobilis horæ,
> Nunc prece, nunc pretio, nunc vi, nunc sorte supremâ
> Permutet dominos, & cedat in altera jura.
> Sic, quia *perpetuus* nulli datur *usus*, & hæres

[24] Lines 163–68.

[25] Lines 198–205.

Hæredem alterius, velut unda supervenit undam:
Quid *vici* prosunt, aut *horrea?* quidve Calabris
Saltibus adjecti Lucani; si metit Orcus
Grandia cum parvis, non exorabilis auro?

Pope's version of this passage fits tightly into his poem's more pervasive scheme of man's subjection to Time, and here as elsewhere he also can be said to "Christianize"[26] the pagan original:

The Laws of God, as well as of the Land,
Abhor, a *Perpetuity* should stand:
Estates have wings, and hang in Fortune's pow'r
Loose on the point of ev'ry wav'ring Hour;
Ready, by force, or of your own accord,
By sale, at least by death, to change their Lord.
Man? and *for ever?* Wretch! what wou'dst thou have?
Heir urges Heir, like Wave impelling Wave:
All vast Possessions (just the same the case
Whether you call them Villa, Park, or Chace)
Alas, my Bathurst! what will they avail?
Join *Cotswold* Hills to *Saperton's* fair Dale,
Let rising Granaries and Temples here,
There mingled Farms and Pyramids appear,
Link Towns to Towns with Avenue, of Oak,
Enclose whole Downs in Walls, 'tis all a joke!
Inexorable Death shall level all,
And Trees, and Stones, and Farms, and Farmer fall.[27]

The sheer mass and weight, and also the pace, of Pope's lines here give to the action of Time a new drama and pathos. Horace, in effect, asks: How can anything be called one's own which, in a brief instant of time, may be snatched away and come into another's possession; and because a perpetual use is given to none, and heir follows heir, what avail material possessions if Death, not to be bribed with gold, cuts down both those who have and have not? Pope deepens the emphasis of the original, and also expands it into a much wider and grander vision: he asks the same questions as Horace, but he also demonstrates that not man alone, but the whole universe, is caught

---

[26] Compare also Pope's lines 278–83, where the Horatian *genius* (that tutelary deity that is born and dies with each individual) is transformed into the Christian God of all mankind:

that Directing Pow'r
Who forms the Genius in the natal Hour;
That God of Nature, who, within us still,
Inclines our Action, not constrains our Will;
Various of Temper, as of Face or Frame,
Each Individual: His great End the same.

[27] Lines 246–63.

up in an earthslide of Time and its inevitable changes. The far horizon of this much expanded vision is reached only in the final couplet of the passage, where the quiet pun on "level," the alliteration and repetition present in the last few words of the last line, and the final dying "fall" achieved by the cadence at the very end of the passage, all include and subdue man within a melancholy pattern that nature itself must endure.

This passage, massive and moving though it is, does not of course constitute the final statement of Pope's poem or his answer to the question of how man may in some sense redeem his time. Near the end of his poem Horace asks:

> Natales gratè numeras? ignoscis amicis?
> Lenior & melior fis accedente senectâ?

Pope enlarges upon this to ask the "Col'nel" of his poem (or the reader) if he is

> Pleas'd to look forward, pleas'd to look behind,
> And count each Birth-day with a grateful mind?
> Has Life no sourness, drawn so near its end?
> Can'st thou endure a Foe, forgive a Friend?
> Has Age but melted the rough parts away,
> As Winter-fruits grow mild e'er they decay?[28]

Pope's lines imply that the answer to his questions is the Shakespearean one of "Ripeness is all." So is Horace's, perhaps, but hardly in the metaphoric terms used by Pope. For these terms Pope may have looked to Shakespeare, but there is a possibility at least that his image of "Winter-fruits" derives from a comment on Horace's lines by Sanadon, the French editor and critic:

210. *Lenior & melior, &c.*] L'âge adoucit nos humeurs. . . . Les réflexions & l'expérience des années passées contribuent à nous rendre meilleurs; voila pourquoi le poète joint ensemble *lenior & melior*. . . . Un vieillar, qui ne chancelle point encore sous le poids des années, est comme un arbre fruitier dans le tems de l'autone: il conserve encore ses feuilles, voila pour l'agrément; & il est outre cela chargé de fruits, voila pour le profit.[29]

The grain of Pope's theme runs out, indeed, only in the concluding lines of his poem, where once again he departs from Horace in order to introduce that most gravid and suggestive of Renaissance images —the stage. "Walk sober off," he says, "before a sprightlier Age/ Comes titt'ring on, and shoves you from the stage." The image had

[28] Lines 314–19.

[29] *Les Poésies D'Horace*, II, 389–90.

been frequently used to stress the brevity and mutability of man's life on earth, most vividly of course by Shakespeare. And Pope's lines, with their evocation of man's "brief hour upon the stage," not only bring to a fitting conclusion his poem about that Time to which all must be lost; they also show how, in the midst of loss, a dignity and a grace may be gained.

As many critics have taken pains to assert, Pope's *Imitations* are indeed "not Horace," and portions of them are not even "out of Horace." But it is because of his very differences from Horace that Pope in these poems acquires the status, not of a mere translator, but of something far more valuable for English readers. Inevitably, Horace's original work will be esteemed more than Pope's imitations of it. Yet, even when all proper admiration is granted to Horace, and so much of it as may be proper is subtracted from Pope, there will still remain truth and force in Gilbert Wakefield's assessment of the *Imitation of the Second Epistle of the Second Book:* "Our country-man's imitation has all the novelty and spirit of original composition."

DAVID DAICHES

The Identity of Burns

ROBERT BURNS IS NOT MERELY the national poet of Scotland; he is
a world-wide symbol, a universal excuse for celebration and sentimentality. Further, the Burns cult developed soon after the poet's death
and has been maintained at a steady level of irrational enthusiasm ever
since. It is a cult participated in by people who do not normally have
any interest in poetry and indeed by not a few who do not even read
Burns's poetry but who cherish his memory, adore his furniture, his
snuffbox, his masonic apron, and his wife's pinkie-ring, memorize the
names of the girls he made love to, and fiercely challenge anybody
who denies that Burns was the greatest poet who ever lived anywhere
in the world. Who was Burns and what was his relation to the Scotland of his day? What kinds of poems did he write and how good are
they and why? What is there about his character and achievement
that can throw light on the way in which he is remembered and celebrated?

Burns was the son of an Ayrshire tenant farmer who had migrated
to this part of Scotland from his native Kincardineshire in order to
improve his prospects. A pious, hard-working, stern but fundamen-
tally kindly man, the elder Burns strove desperately but in the end
vainly to establish himself as a prosperous farmer. This was a bad time
for Scottish farming. Farm rents were grossly inflated, and agricultural methods had not yet properly assimilated the new ideas that
were coming in from England; it was a difficult transitional period,
when increased productivity had not yet caught up with increased
expense. The result was that Burns's father, dogged continually by ill-
luck first on one farm and then on another, died worn out and bank-
rupt in 1784. It was a hard struggle for the whole family: it was
excessive physical work at the plough as a boy, together with considerable periods of undernourishment, that laid the foundations of that

DAVID DAICHES is Professor of English and Dean of the School of English and
American Studies at the University of Sussex.

rheumatic heart disease which plagued Burns as a young man and finally caused his death at the early age of thirty-seven.

If the elder Burns's economic ambitions failed, his educational ambitions for his children were more successful. He joined with other farmers in the neighborhood in hiring a schoolmaster, who lived at different farmhouses in rotation and taught the farm children. The teacher, John Murdoch, was a rather priggish young man of eighteen, who instructed his pupils with pedantic thoroughness in English grammar and syntax, in turning verse into "its natural prose order," and in the genteel English literary taste of the day. It must be emphasized that Burns's formal education was wholly English. The principal textbook used by Murdoch was Arthur Masson's *Collection of Prose and Verse*, which was a purely English compilation, containing passages from the eighteenth-century English poets, including Thomson, Gray, and Shenstone, as well as extracts from Shakespeare, Milton, and Dryden, and prose selections from Addison and from the *Letters Moral and Entertaining* of Elizabeth Rowe. (Thomson, of course, was a Scot, but he had sought his literary fortune in London and made his name as an English poet writing in standard English.) Young Robert also learned the merest rudiments of Latin and acquired a smattering of French. His father managed to borrow other books to round out his children's education. Thus Burns read Salmon's *Geographical Grammar* and William Derham's *Physico-Theology* and *Astro-Theology*, two books that presented the facts and theories of physics and astronomy as evidence for the existence of a beneficent Divine Designer; John Ray's *The Wisdom of God Manifested in the Works of the Creation* also treated science as part of the "argument from design" and helped to lay the foundations of that somewhat genial Deism which was Burns's religion in adult life. From Thomas Stackhouse's *New History of the Holy Bible*, to which the elder Burns subscribed, Burns learned biblical history and geography. His maternal uncle brought home by mistake (he was looking for a different sort of book) "a collection of letters by the Wits of Queen Anne's reign," from which Burns learned to write letters in the formal style of the English Augustans. Gradually, Burns extended his reading, devouring everything he could lay his hands on. He read Pope, Shakespeare, John Locke, as well as theological and agricultural works and—the only books read in his young days that could show him something of a Scottish instead of an English literary tradition— Allan Ramsay's poems and anthologies. His knowledge of Greek and Roman mythology he got from Andrew Tooke's *Pantheon*. Later, in his early twenties, he discovered that archsentimental novel, Henry Mackenzie's *Man of Feeling* ("a book," he once wrote, "I prize next to the Bible"), as well as Sterne's *Tristram Shandy* and that remarkable rhetorical-sentimental compendium of pseudo-Gaelic poetry, Macpherson's Ossian.

Burns's formal education was sporadic and in some measure fragmentary, but he did have a formal education, and he knew Shakespeare, Milton, Pope, and the Bible much better than the ordinary educated man of today knows them. But it was in many respects an artificial education, having little to do with the world he lived in, and the result was that Burns's taste was never certain in English literature. He fell heavily for the sentimental movement that was all the rage at that time, and he read even such a poet as Gray—"the elegantly melting Gray," he called him—for what we would consider the wrong reasons. Indeed, Burns read the later eighteenth-century poets as his age read them, for their tender feeling and proneness to emotional overflow. This really represented something quite alien to Burns's genius, something that every now and again was to come in and corrupt his poetry and falsify his vision. Such writers as Shakespeare and Pope could do him nothing but good—the former helped him to see the potentialities of the poetic use of language and the workings of the poetic imagination, and the latter taught him much about the craft of verse. But Shenstone and Henry Mackenzie did him nothing but harm, and even Gray and Collins were used by him as food for emotional self-indulgence.

If Burns had never broken out of the genteel English education provided by Murdoch, he might have become at best a minor Scottish Shenstone, writing derivative poems in an English he had learned solely from books. But throughout his childhood and youth, he received another kind of literary education, quite different from the formal one he learned from his teacher. The folk tales of the Ayrshire countryside and the Scottish folk songs he heard sung in field and in kitchen represented another tradition altogether from that represented in Masson's anthology. Then there were the poems of Allan Ramsay, and—last and greatest influence of all, which finally revealed to him the possibilities of a poetry that was both Scottish and regional and at the same time universal—the poems of Robert Fergusson, who had died at the age of twenty-four in the public Bedlam of Edinburgh when Burns was a lad of fifteen. The development of Burns as a poet represented the interaction of these Scottish literary forces with the English literature he had studied more formally.

Why should a son of an Ayrshire tenant farmer in the late eighteenth century have been brought up on Gray and Shenstone rather than on the poets of his own country? The answer to this question is a complex one, but it is worth trying to give, however briefly, because it concerns the heart of the problem faced by Burns as a poet and faced by us in trying to understand what he was and how he became what he was.

In the Middle Ages, Scotland was an independent country with a literature and a literary language of its own. That language, which we now know as Middle Scots, was originally the same as the Anglian speech of Northumbria, but eventually, as Scotland matured as a nation, this northern form of English became a language in its own right, with its own relation to Latin and to French and its own characteristic idioms and formations. The great Scottish poets of the fourteenth and early fifteenth centuries, notably Robert Henryson and William Dunbar, developed a rich and complex Scots literary language, which, while arising ultimately out of the ordinary spoken language of the people, reached far beyond it by a consciously artful molding of style and enlargement of vocabulary. It was a language in which thought and emotion could both find expression, in which the full range of utterance from the casual and colloquial to the formal and "aureate" was possible, in which the whole man could speak. In 1603, James VI of Scotland inherited the throne of England and went south to become James I, taking with him many of his Court poets, who henceforth were to write artificial and derivative poems in English. Thus Scottish culture lost at a blow the Court patronage of the arts, which, in an age before commercial publishing and in a country too poor to support lavish private patronage, was essential if a native poetry and music were to flourish. Many other factors—the breakup of the Auld Alliance with France and the turning of a now Protestant Scotland toward England, the prestige of Elizabethan English literature, among others—combined with the loss of a Court center for the Scottish arts to turn Scottish writers' eyes toward England. By 1707, when the Scottish Parliament ceased to exist after having voted an "incorporating union" between England and Scotland, the cultural situation in Scotland had become desperately confused. The language of even educated Scotsmen remained Scots, but more and more the written language was coming to be English. Scotsmen who wanted literary publication wrote in English and sought an English audience. Even David Hume, the great Scottish philosopher and historian, who spoke a broader Scots than Burns did, used to send his manuscripts to an English friend for the removal of Scotticisms; and indeed, in 1761, a visiting Irishman lectured to large Edinburgh audiences on the proper pronunciation of southern English. In 1787, the Aberdeen professor and minor poet James Beattie produced a list of *Scotticisms, arranged in Alphabetical Order, designed to correct Improprieties of Speech and Writing*. Everywhere people were imitating English speech and English style. The Edinburgh critics and leaders of taste, the literati, as they liked to call themselves, considered themselves patriotic Scotsmen, but they felt that Scotland could only vindicate its culture to the world by absorbing English and European culture and beating the English in their own language. They thought of Scots, which in spite of everything most of them continued to speak, as a corrupt dialect of English.

If a nation's literature is written in one language while its daily conversation is conducted in another, then the written language tends to become highly formal and conventional—often well suited for philosophical or historical discourse but less suited for the complex of thought and feeling required by poetry—and the spoken language degenerates into a series of regional dialects. Where there is no national literary language, the national speech will inevitably degenerate into regional dialects, to be transcribed phonetically by local humorists or with antiquarian zeal by backward-looking patriots. Literature in Scots after about the middle of the seventeenth century became more and more literature of low life, the patronizing exhibiting of national customs, or the mock-archaisms of playful scholars. From the early eighteenth century on, the imitation of older Scottish songs and poems became a favorite drawing-room sport, and at the same time editors and anthologists collected for patriotic reasons not only the remnants of traditional Scottish songs but also specimens of older Scottish poetry dating from the time when Scottish literature had a genuine and full literary language of its own. But the elite—the professors and leaders of taste—looked to English and the genteel English tradition. Thus there was no language in which the whole man could express himself; men's public and private selves spoke in different accents, thought and emotion sought different languages, and there was as a result no speech for true contemporary poetry. Allan Ramsay tried hard to use elements of the Scots spoken language in poems descriptive of urban low life and of pastoral activity, and he achieved a limited success. Robert Fergusson made a much more remarkable effort to recreate a genuine Scots poetic tongue and in his Edinburgh poems succeeded in using Scots with a wholeness that had not been seen for generations, but his early death left his work unfinished. It was only when Burns as a young man discovered Fergusson's poems that he was led to continue where Fergusson had left off. But it was natural—indeed, inevitable—that insofar as Burns received a formal education it should have been oriented toward England, not Scotland. Was a true Scottish poetry still possible in Burns's day, or was it the fate of every Scottish poet to become either a rustic purveyor of regional humor, an antiquarian writer of *pastiches,* or to turn south and achieve at best the status of a minor English poet working with only part of his creative self?

Burns, after some hesitation, chose the Scottish rustic mode, refined and enriched by a knowledge of such older Scottish poetry as had been made available by eighteenth-century anthologists and by his study of Ramsay and, more especially, Fergusson—and enriched also by his knowledge of English poetry and his appreciation of poetic craftsmanship in English. Synthesizing his native Ayrshire dialect with literary elements from older Scots and with elements from literary English, he produced a poetic language of surprising flexibility, ranging all the way from neo-classic English to local Scots vernacular and varying continually in the degree to which it drew on each. Burns could of course also write wholly in standard English, and while it would not be accurate to say that when he did so he invariably produced bad poetry, it *is* true to say that his worst poems are sentimental English poems that he wrote with an eye on the genteel Edinburgh audience. Burns's Edinburgh admirers wanted him to be sentimental, edifying, and respectably rustic in an English idiom. His own genius ran to satire, iconoclasm, and a kind of passionate lyrical poetry that seizes the realized moment of experience and renders it without regard for the moral or philosophical consequences. He sometimes allowed himself to be deflected from his true modes of writing by the demands of his audience; but on the whole it is astonishing how this young Ayrshire farmer stuck to his guns in the face of well-meant but thoroughly misguided criticism from friends and well-wishers in high places.

It must be remembered that at the time when Burns published his first volume of poems at Kilmarnock in 1786, there was in educated circles in Edinburgh and beyond a strong cult of the primitive. Edinburgh critics developed theories of poetry based on notions of how primitive man first expressed his passions. Macpherson's Ossian was supposed to show the natural simplicity and high emotional quality of primitive man's experience and expression. Interest in primitive poetry —the term covered an enormous range, from the Bible to the alleged oral literature of Peruvian Indians—had been developing throughout Britain for a considerable time: Percy's *Reliques* and Gray's interest in Norse and Welsh poetry are only the better known aspects of a complex and widespread movement. In Edinburgh this movement was mixed up with the cult of the sentimental as represented by Mackenzie's *Man of Feeling*. Thus when Burns presented a volume of poems "chiefly in the Scottish dialect" to the educated public of Scotland, he was careful to pose as a genuine primitive and to arouse the interest of the literati in the poetry of a supposedly illiterate peasant.

In his Preface he emphasized his lack of education. He overstated the case deliberately. The literati took the bait he offered them with delight. "Whoever will read his lighter and more humorous poems," wrote Mackenzie in reviewing the volume in the *Lounger* of 9 December 1786, ". . . will perceive with what uncommon penetration and sagacity this Heaven-taught ploughman, from his humble and unlettered station, has looked upon men and manners." This was hardly fair to John Murdoch, to Burns's father, and to the other sources that had contributed to Burns's not inconsiderable education, but if Burns was misunderstood it was in some degree because of the part he deliberately chose to play before the literati.

Not that Burns appeared in anything like a deferential pose before the Edinburgh critics when he paid his extended visit to that city after the publication of his poems. Pride and passion, as he once wrote, were the two main elements in his make-up, and he demanded from nobleman and peasant alike recognition of his genius and treatment as in every respect an equal. He frequently gave offense in Edinburgh by resenting the patronizing condescension of well-born ladies and gentlemen. From his earliest years, he had resented the facts of class difference in the Scotland of his day, and when as a small boy he had played with the sons of local landowners, he nursed the bitter grievance that when he and they grew up they would move in different spheres, and he would be expected to touch his cap to people whom he considered no better than himself simply because they happened to own land. Burns was never a man to suffer fools gladly, whatever their rank or profession. So if he paraded himself as an uneducated ploughman in Edinburgh, it was not out of humility, but to emphasize the authenticity of his poetic genius and inspiration. He knew, too, that formal education was no guarantee of wisdom:

> What's a' your jargon o' your schools,
> Your Latin names for horns an' stools;
> If honest nature made you fools,
>   What sairs your grammars?
> Ye'd better ta'en up spades and shools,
>   Or knappin'-hammers.

In verse like this, the true democratic instinct of Burns finds adequate expression: neither rank nor learning can make a natural fool appear any less of a fool—not, at least, in the eyes of Rabbie Burns.

The answer, then, to my first question—"Who was Burns?"—is that he was the proud and ambitious son of a struggling Scottish tenant farmer, born into a Scotland whose culture was deeply divided between a superficial genteel tradition and a half submerged and attenuated national tradition, who captured an audience for his Scots poetry among the educated classes of his day by cashing in on contemporary interest in the primitive sources of poetry and the virtues of the "natural man," and who in considerable degree, but not wholly or consistently, resisted the demands of that audience that he should play up to their sentimental expectations of the ideal peasant poet. The sources on which he drew were the oral folk tradition of his own people, such older Scottish poetry (and it was a fairly small segment) as was available to him in contemporary collections, the Scottish poems of Ramsay and Fergusson, and a variety of anthologies of songs and ballads, all this stiffened by a sense of craftsmanship he learned partly from his study of older English poetry and intermittently threatened by his immersion in the late eighteenth-century sentimental movement.

Though Burns began his poetic career as a song writer (under the joint influence of love, music, and the desire to emulate the son of a local laird who had written a song for *his* girl), it was in the latter part of his life that he wrote most of his songs: his earliest real successes were satirical poems dealing with local church politics, poems projecting with vivid particularization aspects of experience in a farming community, and verse epistles, a traditional Scottish form in which Burns rapidly acquired remarkable skill. His satirical poems— "The Holy Fair," "Holy Willie's Prayer," "The Ordination," among others—show a high technical virtuosity and indicate that Burns had learned his trade from a variety of sources both Scottish and English. Most of them derive from his taking sides with those who believed that the essence of religion was a good heart, against the extreme Calvinists who stressed original sin, the inability of good works to save man, the predestined damnation of the vast majority of all men as a result of Adam's fall and the similarly predestined salvation of a tiny minority not through any virtuous acts of their own but through the arbitrary bestowal of God's grace. "Holy Willie's Prayer" is a dramatic monologue in which the speaker all unconsciously damns the creed he professes by revealing the sanctimoniousness and hypocrisy that it inevitably breeds: it is one of the great verse satires of all time. "The Holy Fair" gives an account, in an old Scottish stanza-form, of an outdoor communion celebration, then a feature of Scottish religious life, mischievously using accepted biblical and religious phraseology to stress the contrast between what really goes on and what is supposed to go on. The whole thing is done in a mood not of bitterness but of joyful exposure of the indomitable claims of the flesh. The brilliance of the ambiguous imagery, the adroit intermingling of the carnal and the spiritual meanings of the same word, the variations of tempo and the manipulation of levels of suggestiveness show a high art: here is no spontaneous bubbling-up of simple peasant emotion but a conscious use of the multiple resources of a complex verse form. On a simpler level, but in its own way equally impressive, is such a poem as "To a Louse," where with affectionately ironic humor Burns reduces to her proper size the proud country lass, masquerading as a fine lady in church because of her new bonnet, by the way he contemplates the louse crawling on the bonnet, visible to the poet as he sits behind her though unknown to the girl herself. It is a perfect little poem, dealing with loving particularization with an aspect of a subject that is the theme of many of Burns's poems, especially of his satires—the relation between appearance and reality, between what is pretended and what really is.

Burns's greatest poetic achievement is his satires. These show a command of a greater variety of poetic skills, a subtler and more complex use of the medium of poetry, than any other kind of poetry he wrote. They are not, however, the poems quoted by orators at Burns suppers. Indeed, such orators generally quote the worst of Burns, the platitudinous or sentimental or jingling or crudely rhetorical Burns. Another important group are his verse letters. This is not a kind of poetry that has ever been popular in England. But in Scotland it had been a tradition since the beginning of the eighteenth century, and Burns learned of the tradition from Ramsay. It represented a handling of language peculiarly suited to his genius, counterpointing the formal and the colloquial, moving out from the carefully localized picture of the poet in a specific time and place to his reflections as they arise naturally from the given situation to a progressively widening circle of comment that culminates in a series of clinching epigrams before the poet returns to himself and his correspondent to sign off in an adroitly turned conclusion. These verse letters show remarkable skill in combining a colloquial ease with a formal pattern in such a way that each brings out new significance in the other.

To Burns the satirist and Burns the writer of masterly verse letters I would add Burns the narrative poet. Even though he wrote only one narrative poem, "Tam o' Shanter," it is enough to enable us to list narrative poetry among his claims to high poetic distinction. This rendering in octosyllabic couplets of a local folk story is a triumph of *pace;* the variations in tempo are handled with the utmost adroitness to achieve not only a narrative style that follows the curve of the action most cunningly but also a wealth of humorously ironic comment on human frailty and human imagination. The opening sets the scene in the local pub where the hero sits happily boozing in a cosy interior while outside the storm rises. This contrast between the cosy interior and the harsh weather outside is an old tradition in Scottish poetry: it can be found as far back as the opening of Henryson's *Testament of Crisseid*, perhaps the first medieval narrative poem to tell the truth about the weather in these islands. (Even Chaucer has his eye on the French rose garden, which in turn derives from the Mediterranean center of secular medieval poetry; his Canterbury pilgrims have no meteorological problems, even in an English April; and when it rains in his *Troilus and Criseyde*, it is only in order to give the hero the opportunity of spending the night with the heroine.) Tam's climax of conviviality is soon reached, and splendidly described. There follows a mock-serious passage in pulpit-English describing the evanescence of pleasure, culminating in a sudden switch back to Scots, this time in a tone of homely proverbial wisdom. Then comes the description of the storm, growing ever more rapid in movement until it has reached the point at which the name of the Devil can be appropriately introduced. The superstitious and drunken imagination of Tam is built up by a remarkable progression of comically horrible images until at last he reaches Alloway Kirk, sees the Devil and the dance of the witches, and, his fancy caught by a "winsome wench and wawlie" dancing in a particularly short shift, he calls out to her in approval and thus betrays his presence. In a flash the witches are after him, and he gallops madly along on his faithful mare Maggie. It looks as though the end has come. But Maggie escapes by crossing a running stream (which witches cannot cross) just as the leader is on her. Her tail, however, has been seized and plucked off. Tam arrives home with a tailless mare. The poem ends with a mock-solemn warning against drink and girls, in language that is a parody of Scottish pulpit moralizing. The whole story can of course be explained by the fact that Tam was drunk and only imagined the witches. But how do we explain Maggie's loss of her tail? Every incident *except one* can be rationally explained. This is a formula for supernatural tales told to a modern skeptical audience that has been followed ever since, notably in Scott's "Wandering Willie's Tale."

So I think we can grant Burns's skill as a narrative poet even though we have only one example to judge by. "Tam o' Shanter" was written in 1790 when Burns was combining farming at Ellisland with his duties as a recently appointed excise officer. He had returned reluctantly to farming after his prolonged visit to Edinburgh—reluctantly, because he knew from experience that the back-breaking work and economic risks of farming at that time would seriously cut down his opportunities of writing poetry. He wanted some sort of government job to enable him to have the leisure for writing and the opportunity for meeting and talking with interesting people that were so important for him. Even after he gave up his farm and settled in Dumfries as a full-time exciseman, he never had the leisure a poet really requires. "Tam o' Shanter" makes us realize what Burns might have done had he had time and opportunity to cultivate all his poetic faculties properly. One single poem in a vein of which he was clearly a past master —it is a tantalizing glimpse of what we might have had if Burns had had health, leisure, and a more congenial environment for poetic creation.

By a more congenial environment, I do not simply mean more educated friends, though it is true that Burns was hampered by the fact that the people he could talk to as intellectual equals (and he found few if any) tended to patronize him socially. I mean a society that did not condemn him to be a performing peasant poet as an illustration of primitivist theories of poetry. I have already suggested that Burns's admirers did him harm, or did their unconscious best to do so. Though Burns resisted the advice that many of them gave him to abandon the Scottish tradition in language and form, he was often content to give them the kind of attitudinizing they wanted. His duty poem in praise of Edinburgh, "Edina, Scotia's Darling Seat!" is a shocking bad performance in a neo-classic English idiom that he was never really able to handle, though some aspects of eighteenth-century English poetic idiom he could use with real skill. If we want to see the real Burns side by side with the bogus Burns, we have only to set "To a Mouse" beside "To a Mountain Daisy." The former recognizes with wry humor the fellow feeling that joins the poet and the little creature and skillfully turns the theme round at the end to project his own unhappy situation. The unsentimental use of diminutives to strengthen the note of friendly concern ("Thy wee-bit housie, too, in ruin!"), the effective introduction of a rustic proverbial idiom that both bridges the worlds of mice and men and sounds an appealing note of rueful wisdom ("The best-laid schemes o' Mice an' Men, / Gang aft a-gley"), the mastery of tone and movement throughout—these show Burns working with a fine assurance in a medium of which he was complete master. But "To a Mountain Daisy" is an exercise in sentimental attitudinizing for the benefit of the tender feelings of his genteel readers. The poetic device known as the pathetic fallacy—the attribution of human thought and feeling to an inanimate object—is a dangerous one at best, and Burns's use of it here, in addressing the daisy, is clumsy and histrionic. In particular, the comparison of the daisy to a country maid betrayed by a rustic seducer—the betrayed maiden is a standard property in sentimental fiction of the period—is grotesquely inappropriate. We know that Burns was attitudinizing when he wrote this poem. He enclosed a copy in a letter to a friend with the remark: "I am a good deal pleased with some sentiments myself, as they are just the native querulous feelings of a heart which, as the elegantly melting Gray says, 'Melancholy has marked for her own.'"

We can see similar defects in parts of "The Cotter's Saturday Night," an attempt to improve on Robert Fergusson's poem on the same theme, "The Farmer's Ingle." But Fergusson's poem remains the more successful, a shrewdly affectionate account of an evening in a farm kitchen set against a sense of the underlying rhythm of the seasons and of agricultural labor. Burns opens the "Cotter" with a monstrous stanza addressed to the prosperous Ayr lawyer Bob Aiken: "My lov'd, my honor'd much respected friend!" And the stanza ends with the suggestion that this bustling and prosperous townsman would be happier in a humble rustic cottage than in his comfortable house in Ayr:

> What Aiken in a Cottage would have been;
> Ah! tho' his worth unknown, far happier there, I ween!

This is sentimental nonsense, and Burns knew it; even the verse echoes dully and mechanically to such forced sentiments. The real opening of the poem is the fine second stanza, setting the time and place with an intimate sense of the quality of living that is involved here, and adding just a suggestion of controlled melancholy in the observation of rustic rest after rustic toil that he got from Gray's *Elegy*. There are other stanzas equally fine; but at intervals Burns the professional sentimentalist showing off his ideal rustics to a genteel Edinburgh audience steps in and wrecks the poem.

I am not maintaining that Burns wrote good poems only when he wrote in Scots and not in English. Many of his finest poems are in an English tipped with Scots, and many of his best songs contain only an occasional Scots word. The linguistic situation in Burns's Scotland was so confused that only by creating a synthetic language of his own, out of his native spoken dialect, standard southern English, and Scots of other times and regions, could Burns have achieved any flexibility in operation at all: this language was in the nature of things neither consistent nor arbitrary, but varied according to the demands of particular kinds of poetic situations. I *am* maintaining, however, that when Burns kept his eye on the literary fashions of educated Scotsmen of his day and wrote for the taste of the literati instead of in one of the ways that he knew suited his own genius, his poetry is generally bad. And there is no doubt that in English literature of his own time his taste was very uncertain. But he was not alone in that. He learned much, however, from English poetry, whose influence we can trace in his work in all sorts of ways. He used what he learned, of course, for his purposes in his own way, sometimes, for example, transforming an elegant piece of Augustan wit into the idiom of Scottish folk song. In the Second Epistle of Pope's "Moral Essays" occur the lines

> Heaven, when it strives to polish all it can
> Its last best work, but forms a softer Man.

Burns gave this thought a completely different kind of expression in the last stanza of "Green grow the rashes O":

> Auld Nature swears, the lively Dears
> Her noblest work she classes, O:
> Her prentice han' she try'd on man,
> An' then she made the lasses, O.

I have claimed Burns as a great poet in virtue of his satires, his verse letters, and his one narrative poem. There remain, of course, his songs. In April 1787, Burns met in Edinburgh James Johnson, a self-educated lover of Scottish songs, who had invented a cheap process for printing by using stamped pewter plates, a combination that led him to project a series of volumes of songs. He enlisted Burns's assistance, and gradually, as Burns became more and more the dominant partner in the project, the original character of the enterprise changed: it became a vast six-volume anthology of Scottish songs, old and new. Later, Burns was approached by George Thomson, a more educated and genteel publisher of Scottish songs, for help in *his* collection. Burns responded to both requests avidly, with the result that the great majority of his own songs were written for and first appeared in either Johnson's *Scots Musical Museum* or Thomson's *Select Scottish Airs*. It is important to understand exactly what Burns did for Scottish song. He found Scottish folk song in a confused and fragmentary state. The decay of the courtly musical tradition after 1603, Presbyterian disapproval of popular secular song, and indeed the whole confused condition of Scottish culture all contributed to this. Scottish airs had been popular since the latter part of the seventeenth century, and many collections of Scottish songs and song tunes appeared both in Edinburgh and London in the eighteenth century. But the great majority of older songs survived only in fragments, as an odd chorus or a few garbled lines. One of the favorite sports of Scottish ladies and gentlemen of the period was writing new words to old airs, and these words were generally frigid and derivative. Burns's aim was to recover as many airs and sets of words as he could and, where the existing words were fragmentary or impossibly coarse or equally impossibly genteel, to re-create the song in the true spirit of the folk tradition. It was a staggering program, nothing less than the single-handed re-creation of the whole body of Scottish folk song. Further, Burns undertook to provide words to tunes which, though they may originally have had words, now existed only as dance tunes. He was anxious that all Scotland should be represented, and in his journeys in Scotland scrupulously collected such songs and fragments as he could find, to rework them into complete songs. We can trace his journeys by the provenance of the songs—a fisherman's song from Fife, an old Aberdeen folk song, a song about an alehouse keeper on the Moray Firth, innumerable love songs connected with particular hills, valleys, streams, and woods in Perthshire, Stirlingshire, Dumbartonshire, Ayrshire, Dumfries-shire, and other Scottish counties. If Burns had not been uncannily in tune with the folk spirit in Scottish song, he would be execrated today for having spoiled the original fragments by bogus improvements. But in fact he did not spoil them; he saved them from total corruption and disappearance and gave them new life and meaning and popularity.

The greater part of Burns's poetic activity in the last years of his life was taken up with these songs. He collected, revised, completed, rewrote, and re-created hundreds of songs, devoting an immense amount of energy to the task and refusing all payment from Johnson or Thomson, declaring that he did it for Scotland's sake. And this was no theatrical gesture: it was true. He regarded this vast work as a contribution to the preservation and renewal of his country's culture. The amount of work he did on a particular song would vary in accordance with the state of the original and the amount of time at his disposal. If only a chorus or a few fragments of verse survived, he might substantially rewrite the whole song. Often the first verse and the chorus survived, and Burns provided more verses. Sometimes he rewrote an old bawdy song as a tender and passionate love song or, as in the case of "John Anderson My Jo," as a poem of married affection. On many occasions, he took a popular dance tune, slowed down the tempo to bring out musical qualities obscured by the fast dancing pace, and wrote a song for it. Burns, though no singer, had an acute ear for melody and a genius for fitting words to music such as few poets have possessed. His correspondence with Thomson about the words and the music of the songs he sent him is full of technical discussions of prosody and of musical rhythm and time.

Burns wrote all his songs to known tunes, sometimes writing several sets of words to the same air in an endeavor to find the most apt poem for a given melody. Roughly speaking, we can divide Burns's songs into three categories: those he rewrote from old fragments, completely new songs he wrote to old tunes, and new songs he wrote for dance tunes which, though they may originally have been song tunes, did not exist as such in Burns's day. But the categories are not always separate and sometimes fade into one another. Many songs that we know from a variety of evidence must have been substantially written by Burns he never claimed as his. He never claimed "Auld Lang Syne," for example, which he described simply as an old fragment he had discovered, but the song as we have it is almost certainly his, though the chorus and probably the first stanza are old. (Incidentally, Burns wrote it for a simple and moving old air, which is *not* the tune to which it is now sung, as Thomson set it to another tune.) Sometimes Burns sent Johnson snatches and fragments, unimproved, sufficient to fit the tune. At other times he hastily produced some provisional words, which, as he explained apologetically, might do to keep the tune alive until better words could be produced. Many of the songs are extremely slight and trivial. But many others are splendid examples of the embodiment of passionate experience in art.

It is the uncanny ability to speak with the great anonymous voice of the Scottish people that must be part of the explanation for the special feeling Burns arouses. But his songs are not all in a simple folk idiom, though most of them have that air of simplicity (whatever the subtleties below the surface) so necessary to a sung poem. There is the symbolic color and imagery of "Open the Door to Me Oh!" which so impressed W. B. Yeats:

> The wan moon is setting ayont the white wave,
> And time is setting with me, oh!

There is that wonderful mixture of tenderness and swagger—so characteristic of the male in love—in "A Red, Red Rose," Burns's rewriting of an old fragment. There is the magnificent abandonment to the moment of experience in "Yestreen I Had a Pint o' Wine":

> The kirk and state may gae to hell,
> And I'll gae to my Anna.

There is the controlled historical melancholy of the Jacobite songs, where Burns gives this romantic lost cause a new meaning in terms of human emotion:

> Now a' is done that men can do,
> And a' is done in vain:
> My Love and Native Land fareweel,
> For I maun cross the main, my dear,
> For I maun cross the main.

There is that splendid drinking song, "Willie Brew'd a Peck o' Maut," with its rollicking chorus:

> We are na fou, We're nae that fou,
> But just a drappie in our e'e; . . .

There is a wonderful counterpointing of folk feeling and high ceremony, of simple emotion and pageantry, in "Go, Fetch to Me a Pint o' Wine," where the whole atmosphere of medieval romance and ballad is concentrated in two stanzas. There is the magical tenderness of "O Lay Thy Loof in Mine, Lass"—though here I would particularly emphasize the importance of taking the words with the tune: it is the tune that lights up the words. There is the lilting love song he composed to one of his wife's favorite airs, "The Posie":

> O Luve will venture in, where it daurna weel be seen,
> O luve will venture in, where wisdom ance has been. . . .

(Again, it is lost without the music.) There is that sprightly piece of ironic self-compliment, "There Was a Lad Was Born in Kyle." There is the moving benedictory cadence, so perfectly wrought together with the music, in "Ca' the Yowes to the Knowes":

> Ghaist nor bogle shalt thou fear;
> Thou'rt to love and Heaven sae dear,
> Nocht of ill may come thee near,
> My bonnie dearie.

A final word on Burns as a man. He was a man of great intellectual energy and force of character who in a class-ridden society never found an environment in which he could fully exercise his personality. After his death, the lively literary lady Maria Riddell wrote a character sketch of him in the *Dumfries Journal* in which she said that his powers of conversation, his impromptu wit, his ability to grasp new ideas, his intolerance of stupidity and arrogance, his capacity for devastating ironic comment, were in her opinion even more impressive than his poetry. "I believe no man was ever gifted with a larger portion of the *vivida vis animi*," she wrote. But it was not only the class structure of his society, which led to his being alternately patronized and sentimentalized over, that constricted him. Coming to Edinburgh between the age of Hume and the age of Scott, Burns found no one really worthy of his mettle. The problem was, however, more than one of personalities. The only substitute for the rejected Calvinism available to Burns in the Scotland of his day was a sentimental Deism, a facile belief in the good heart as all, which though also part of late eighteenth-century English culture, was in

England likely to be involved with other and more profound currents of thought. Let us be clear on one point. In spite of the annual Burns orators, the truth is that Burns in his adult life was not a Christian. He was in a vague sort of way a Deist, who believed in a benevolent designer of the universe and who believed in good-heartedness, generosity, and openness as the supreme virtues. He was also an egalitarian in politics, a sympathizer with the French Revolution, and an unremitting opponent of the class system of his time. He was at the same time a shrewd and penetrating observer of contemporary politics and of human psychology as he found it in the ladies and gentlemen who entertained and patronized him. As for his famous amours, the fact here is that Burns was unable to be on terms of sexual equality with his intellectual equals (or near-equals): the result was that he could only flirt with the well-born ladies, while he sought physical satisfaction with country lasses. His sex life is part of the schizophrenia of the Scottish culture of his time and of the split personality that this forced on him.

I have tried to answer the questions I began with. Who was Burns and what was his relation to the Scotland of his day? What kind of poems did he write and how good are they and why? It remains for me to try and relate what I have said to the Burns cult, which I began by referring to. How can this be explained? I think, very roughly, there are three reasons for the Burns cult. One is the fact that Burns was a humble peasant who stood up for human worth regardless of rank or possessions: he is the most spectacular example in our literature of a humble rustic who really made good in the literary world. Another is that in his songs he identified himself with the folk tradition and spoke with moving authenticity for the daily experiences of men and women as they are encountered in ordinary life. The third reason, which is bound up with the second, is his ability to speak for man's "unofficial self," his total lack—in his best and most characteristic poems—of any idealizing haze or of anything that the reader not professionally interested in literature might regard as pretentious expansion of significance. His love songs are worlds apart from, say, Shelley's *Epipsychidion*, and Shelley is not a poet normally celebrated in country pubs or city clubs. I am not now talking of degrees of poetic merit, but differences in poetic *kind*. The odd thing is that in spite of the fact that the popular feeling about Burns—on which, after all, the Burns cult is based—derives from a true insight into the nature of one side at least of his poetry, the kind of thing spouted annually at Burns suppers does not: it derives from and seeks inspiration in the sentimental-rhetorical Burns, who is not the real Burns at all.

The poet, wrote Wordsworth, is "a man speaking to men." I think we feel this about Burns more than we feel it about any other poet. His voice, when it is his genuine voice, is not the voice of a prophet or a seer or of one who wishes to elevate or edify; it is the voice of man as he is, at work and at play, in love and in hate, sounded with a vibrant clarity it is hard to match elsewhere. Soon after Burns's death, the Industrial Revolution changed the face of much of the part of Scotland he knew best, and later generations looked back from black cities and slag heaps to Burns and saw him through the mists of nostalgia for a lost rustic way of life as the singer of a sentimentalized countryside, the "wee hoose amang the heather" sort of thing. This vulgarization of Burns in the nineteenth century led to his having a bad influence on subsequent Scottish poetry. But that was not Burns's fault. And if we go back, not to what is said about his poetry, but to the poems themselves, especially the great satires, the verse letters, "Tam o' Shanter," and the songs, we shall hear that disturbingly human voice, in mockery, in gaiety, or in passion, laying bare the essence of *la condition humaine* as it is known to daily living. It is a voice that compels assent; and we respond, as Joyce's Molly Bloom responded to life at the end of *Ulysses*, with acquiescence and affirmation: "Yes," we say, "Yes . . . yes."

W. K. WIMSATT, JR.

"Amicitiae Causa": A Birthday Present from Curll to Pope

T HE GIST OF THIS ESSAY consists in two pictures. But a few words are necessary to point their meaning. The pictures are two portraits of Alexander Pope—one engraved perhaps as nearly as possible to his own desire by his favorite artist or "Principal Painter" of the 1730's, Jonathan Richardson the elder, the other a carefully executed replica commissioned by his most persistent antagonist but unfailing abettor, Edmund Curll.

Pope's friendship with the eminent, if somewhat prosy, portrait painter, connoisseur, and theorist Jonathan Richardson the elder, and with his son of the same name, collector and litterateur, can be traced in Pope's letters written during the early 1720's and by other means perhaps even earlier.[1] But Richardson does not seem to have begun portraying Pope in earnest before the 1730's.

Richardson was to die in 1745 at an age near eighty. During the last fifteen years of his life, he seems to have found special comfort in a familial and friendly cult of portrait drawing in pencil and in crayon. Walpole in his *Anecdotes of Painting* remarks that toward the end of his life Richardson was in the habit of drawing his own or his son's portrait every day, and Reynolds told Malone that Richardson "was always drawing either himself or Pope, whom he scarcely

WILLIAM K. WIMSATT, JR., is Professor of English at Yale University.

[1] A number of unsupported statements in this paper, made for the sake of perspective, are summaries of longer expositions which will appear, fully documented, in my book now in progress, *The Portraits of Alexander Pope*.

The following works are referred to in the text and notes below by easily decipherable short titles: Whitwell Elwin and W. J. Courthope (eds.), *The Works of Alexander Pope* (10 vols.; London, 1871-89); R. H. Griffith, *Alexander Pope: A Bibliography* (2 vols.; Austin, Texas, 1922-27); *An Exhibition of the First Editions of Alexander Pope . . . with a Collection of the Engraved Portraits . . .* (The Grolier Club, 1911); George Sherburn (ed.), *The Correspondence of Alexander Pope* (5 vols.; Oxford, 1956).

ever visited without taking some sketch of his face." The nineteen
drawings of Pope by Richardson that are known today may all be
dated, either from their inscriptions or from their resemblance to one
another, between 1732 and 1738. Richardson's oil paintings of Pope
almost all strongly resemble the drawings and seem to belong to the
same period. This is the period too of his portrait etching, practiced
in much the same spirit as his drawings—the subjects being confined
mainly within a small circle of friends and heroes: himself, his son,
Milton, Pope, Bolingbroke, Mead. Richardson seems to have handled
an etching plate much as he did a sheet of paper. I conjecture, though
I cannot prove, that he himself took no hand in those stages so important to the great etchers, the biting of the plate with acid and the
rolling of the impressions.

I am familiar with eleven distinct plates of Pope by Richardson.
These, for the sake of simplification, may be divided into three groups,
each represented conveniently by one of the three fairly well-known
and datable etchings (1736, 1737, 1738: Grolier 32, 34, 33) to which
apparently William Kent refers in his letter to Burlington reporting
a rainy Sunday morning in November 1738 when Pope dragged him
to Richardson's house: "I forgot to tell you that Richerson give me
all the prints he has grav'd, he has given me so many miltons, & three
different popes, the last he has done is write behind his head in greek
letters the English—that's the man, or this is the man, I cannot just
tell."[2]

One of these etchings had been chosen, and no doubt carefully
prompted, by Pope himself for the important role of title-page medallion in the authorized volume of his *Letters* brought out in quarto and
folio by Knapton, Gilliver, Brindley, and Dodsley in May 1737.
Three letters from Pope to Richardson concerning this etched profile
survive, one of them hitherto unpublished. Apparently in February
of 1736 [1737] Pope wrote to Richardson in Queen's Square, Blooms-
bury: "The business of this, next to the Assurances of my true affection, is to desire you to send me inclosd to my Lord Cornburys near
Oxford Chappel the Exact size of the Plate for the title page of my
book. Which is wanted so far as to stop the printing the Title."[3] On
3 March he wrote again, from Twickenham:

I hope your friend has done justice to your Work, in rolling off that
excellent Etching in My Titlepage which will be the most Valuable thing
in the book. As soon as they, together with the Headpiece & Initial letter

[2] *Correspondence*, IV, 150, 28 November 1738. Kent alludes to the motto OYTOΣ
EKEINOΣ, from Aristotle's *Poetics*, which appears on Richardson's better-known etching of Pope dated 1738 (Grolier 33).

[3] *Correspondence*, IV, 54.

to the Preface are done, & the Sheets quite dry, I must desire your Care again to cause them to be very cleanly packed up & sent to the Printer's Mr Wright on St Peter's hill, who should give his Receit for them & return him also the Copper Headpiece & Letter to the Preface. You know the *least Dirt* thrown on the best Work, or best character, will spoil the whole Grace of it. And pray acquaint Mr Knapton, that I will satisfy him in the amplest manner he pleases, as well as be obliged for his Care. . . .[4]

And on 20 April he wrote again: "I desire, you dear Sir, to give the Bearer ye little Plate of my Profile, wch is wanted for another Book."[5]

The *Letters of Mr. Alexander Pope and Several of His Friends* appeared on 19 May,[6] two days before Pope's birthday, in three formats: quarto (Griffith 454, 455), large folio (Griffith 456), and small folio (Griffith 457). The title pages of all three were embellished with the youthful-looking, keen profile to right within a nearly circular linear frame, inscribed beneath: "Amicitiae Causa" and "J. Richardson f." (Later on, this medallion would be flattened out and Pope's head oppressed under a lowered ceiling for the sake of two extra lines of type on the title page of *The Works of Mr. Alexander Pope in Prose, Vol. II*, 1741 [Griffith 531].)

Pope's own preoccupation with portraiture, both verbal and visual, is suggested in a passage of the short "Preface" to the *Letters* of May 1737, where he protests the spontaneity of his letters, ". . . as they flow'd warm from the heart, and fresh from the occasion." "Had he sate down with a design to draw his own Picture, he could not have done it so truly. . . . If an Author's hand, like a Painter's, be more distinguishable in a slight sketch than in a finish'd picture, this very carelessness will make them the better known from such Counterfeits, as have been, and may be imputed to him, either thro' a mercenary, or a malicious design."

And so, what of Edmund Curll? Let us recollect briefly his role as pirate and willing dupe in the publication on 12 May 1735 of the "morning" and "afternoon" editions of the *Letters of Mr. Pope* and subsequently (1735 and 1736) of the four volumes entitled *Mr. Pope's Literary Correspondence*. And let us add that he had all along mani-

[4] *Correspondence*, IV, 58. "Mr. Knapton" is probably the "friend" alluded to in the first sentence of the letter and is probably not John Knapton, the publisher of the *Letters*, but one of his brothers, either George Knapton, the portrait painter (1698–1778), who had been a pupil of Richardson's, or even more likely Charles Knapton (1700–60), known as an engraver of old drawings.

[5] Yale University Library. The letter was brought to my attention by Mr. Herman Liebert at the time of his presenting it to the Yale Library.

[6] Or perhaps 18 May. See Griffith, II, 357, and Elwin-Courthope, I, lxxiii; V, 291; IX, 191, n. 1.

fested a steady interest in the portrait or "head" of his very profitable enemy Mr. Pope. As early as July 1720, in the second volume of Giles Jacob's *Poetical Register,* Curll had provided, to accompany the biographical sketch of Pope, a small line cut ("Clark & Pine Sc."), derived from a painting done by Sir Godfrey Kneller in 1716, Pope half-length, standing, in a cap and unbuttoned coat, with open shirt collar, an image well known through the engraving in mezzotint by J. Smith in 1717.[7] (In this Curll was a step ahead of Pope's legitimate publisher Lintot, who a month later used a similar derivative engraving, "G. Vertue s.," in Volume I of his *Miscellaneous Poems.*[8]) In his public letter about Pope's *Correspondence,* addressed from his shop in Rose Street, Covent Garden, on 22 May 1735, "To the most Noble and Right Honourable the Peers of Great Britain," Curll ended with a flourish: "I have engraven a new plate of Mr. Pope's head from Mr. Jervas's painting; and likewise intend to hang him up in effigy for a sign to all spectators of his falsehood and my own veracity."[9]

By 26 July of the same year, in his letter "E. Curll to the Public" on the same themes, Curll was writing "From Pope's Head, in Rose Street" and boasting, "I have hung up his *Head,* for my *Sign.*"[10] An engraved portrait of Pope beneath the title heading on the first page of Curll's pamphlet catalogue, *Books Printed for E. Curll, at Pope's Head,* published 1 December 1735,[11] suggests that a crude derivative from Kneller's portrait of 1716 (similar to the images mentioned above, by Clark and Pine and by Vertue) was the painted "effigy" that Curll had hung up for his sign.

In copies of the first two volumes of his *Mr. Pope's Literary Correspondence,* published in May and July 1735, Curll was using interchangeably as frontispiece two other small line cuts of Pope, one again of the Kneller 1716 type, "Mr. Pope,"[12] and one after another Kneller painting, "Kneller pinx, 1722. Parr sculp. Mr. Pope."[13] This

---

[7] Clark and Pine's cut faced page 145 of *The Poetical Register.* The same plate appeared again in the second edition, remainder sheets brought out by A. Butterworth and other booksellers in 1723. See Griffith 123. The plate is Grolier 6.

[8] Griffith says the plate was used also in later editions, 1722, 1726–27, 1732, and in Lintot's *The Works of Alexander Pope, Esq., Vol. I,* 1736 (Griffith 124 and 413). It is Grolier 15.

[9] Carruthers, *Life of Pope* (1857), p. 324; Elwin-Courthope, VI, 435–36.

[10] *Correspondence,* III, 476. A slightly earlier date for "Pope's Head" appears in Curll's letter to Broome 22 July 1735 (*Correspondence,* III, 475).

[11] Reproduced facing page 188, Ralph Straus, *The Unspeakable Curll* (London, 1927).

[12] Grolier 10; Griffith 376 and 386. Griffith reports the same plate for No. 385, *Mr. Pope's Literary Correspondence, Volume the First, The Third Edition,* 26 June 1735.

[13] Grolier 20.

PLATE I. Title-page medallion of Pope's *Letters*, *ca.* 19 May 1737 (a copy of the small-paper folio in the Yale University Library). Actual size (plate mark 4 × 3⅞ in.; oval 3⅝ × 3¾ in.).

PLATE II. Frontispiece of Curll's *New Letters of Mr. Pope*, 8 June 1737 (Yale University Library). Actual size (plate mark $3\frac{3}{16} \times 2\frac{15}{16}$ in.).

image of Pope in cap and loose garment with his hand to his forehead was well known through the mezzotint engraving by R. White in 1723. In copies of the third and fourth volumes of *Mr. Pope's Literary Correspondence*, published in September 1735 and March 1736, Curll was using as frontispiece or in other positions yet again two other small line cuts of Pope. One of these was derived from a Kneller painting of 1721, Pope in profile, laureated, in an oval frame formed by a serpent: "Kneller pinx. Parr Sculp. Mr Pope Horatius Anglicanus."[14] This would appear to have been a kind of scoop for Curll, for his rather coarse little line engraving anticipates by three years the mezzotint from the same painting by J. Faber. The other cut, inscribed "Mr. Pope. Parr Sculp.,"[15] is derived from Charles Jervas's oil painting of a cavalier-looking Pope, profile, in long wig and lace neckcloth, which was well known in the large line engraving by Vertue used as the frontispiece of Pope's *Works* in 1717.[16] This little cut by Parr is no doubt the engraving after Jervas to which Curll alludes in his letter to the Peers in May 1735. And the four small line cuts that we have just seen are no doubt what Curll advertises in his catalogue of *Books Printed*, 1 December 1735, page 16, and in an advertisement of 27 November 1736 in the *London Evening Post:* "His Effigies in four Attitudes. price 2 s."[17]

We come now, however, to a fifth and rather different portrait of Pope sponsored by Curll. This appears as a response to Pope's authorized edition of the *Letters*, published in May 1737; it is part of a stage in Curll's approaches to his own *Volume the Fifth* of the *Literary Correspondence* (published in June 1737, Griffith 462). Pope was far advanced in the printing of his book by November 1736,[18] and, though Curll was waiting on Pope for the main part of his vol-

[14] Grolier 31; Griffith 402 and 415.

[15] Grolier 29.

[16] My statement about Curll's four volumes (Griffith 376, 386, 402, 415) is based on the descriptions in Griffith and my own examination of copies in the Yale Library. Griffith reports that in Curll's duodecimo edition of *Volume the Fourth*, published a little later (*ca.* 1 April? Griffith 416), the frontispiece is Parr-Jervas. In a postscript to his letter to Pope in the *St. James's Evening Post*, 12 July 1735, Curll announces yet another picture: ". . . Your Picture from *Richardson* I intend for the Frontispiece of the Third Volume of your *Literary Correspondence*, which is now actually in the Press" (*Correspondence*, III, 472). It is difficult to guess what picture by Richardson Curll has in mind at this date.

[17] See also 30 October–2 November: "And four Prints of him. price 6d. each."

[18] See Pope to Allen, 6 November 1736, *Correspondence*, IV, 41; and Griffith, II, 358 (No. 454). Jacob Isaacs, of Queen Mary College, University of London, has kindly let me photograph a unique print of a profile very similar to that used on the title page of Pope's 1737 *Letters*. This is inscribed beneath in pencil, apparently in Richardson's hand: "Amicitiae Causa// Richardson 1736."

ume, he too was somewhat advanced. In the issue of the *London Magazine* dated 1 November 1736, Curll advertised: "Letters written by Mr *Pope*, and Lord *Bolingbroke*, to Dean *Swift*, in 1725. With his Lordship's Effigies and Character. . . . price 1*s*. 6*d*." And again in the *London Evening Post* for 9–11 November (No. 1402) and for 25–27 November (No. 1409): "This Day is published, (from the Original Manuscripts, transmitted from Ireland) with a curious Print of Lord Bolingbroke, Letters, written by Mr. Pope and Lord Bolingbroke, to Dean Swift, in the Year 1723. Also . . . [letters of Garth, Lansdowne, and William Bromley, posthumous pieces of Walsh, and letters from a Lady in Russia] . . . price 1s. 6 d."[19] In Curll's *Volume the Fifth* of *Mr. Pope's Literary Correspondence*, as published in June 1737 (a volume beginning, but not ending, with the contents just listed), his preliminary "To My Subscribers *encore*" is still dated "5 Nov. 1736." The late R. H. Griffith, who had not seen the longer advertisement in the *London Evening Post*, nevertheless seems to have correctly hypothesized the publication by Curll in November 1736 of a volume (Griffith 429) containing about one fifth the contents of the *Literary Correspondence, Volume the Fifth*, of June 1737. Griffith points out that if his conjecture is correct, this volume (rather than *Volume the Fifth*) prints for the first time the letters of Pope to Swift, August 1723, and Bolingbroke to Swift (postscript to the preceding, but printed by Curll as a separate letter).[20] Echoes of the event can be heard in Pope's letters of this period. On 30 December he wrote, complaining, to Swift: ". . . this last month Curll has obtain'd from Ireland two letters. . . . Your answer to that letter he has not got; it has never been out of my custody."[21] On 4 March 1736 [1737], he sent Lord Orrery a copy of Curll's book, "that you may show him."[22] And Orrery on 18 March duly passed the specimen on to Swift: ". . . part of a fifth Volume of Curl's Thefts, in which you'll find two Letters to You (One from Mr Pope the Other from Lord Bolingbroke) just publish'd with an impudent Preface by Curl."[23] In Dublin, George Faulkner published *Letters from Alexander Pope, Esq.*, dated 1737, apparently a reprint of a part of Curll's volume (Griffith 453).

[19] David F. Foxon has kindly consulted the *London Evening Post* at the British Museum and has verified the text of the advertisement as it appears in the issue of 9–11 November.

[20] *Correspondence*, II, 183 and n. 4; 186 and n. 4; 348 and n. 1. The editor here and at I, xxii apparently follows Griffith in assigning the title *New Letters* to Curll's volume of November 1736.

[21] *Correspondence*, IV, 50 and n. 2.

[22] *Correspondence*, IV, 58–59.

[23] *Correspondence*, IV, 60.

The contents of this early volume of Curll's seem fairly clear from his advertisements and from the actual make-up of the first sixty-six pages of *Mr. Pope's Literary Correspondence, Volume the Fifth*. But a copy of the latter volume in the British Museum having a second title page (*New Letters of Mr Alexander Pope . . .*[24] of which more below) led Griffith to what I believe to have been a mistaken conjecture as to the title page of the November 1736 volume. This title page was in fact an echo of Pope's *Letters of Mr. Alexander Pope*, published in May 1737. This very title page appears in a volume in the Yale Library, which in several respects seems the especially designed setting for it. The contents of this volume, after frontispiece (of which also more below) and title page, are nearly the same, up to page 66, as what Curll had advertised in November 1736 and what Griffith hypothesized for the November 1736 volume.[25] But there is also a great deal more of what would go into the full *Volume the Fifth* of the *Literary Correspondence*—i.e., pages [65]–250, the series of new letters acquired from Pope's *Letters* of 19 May, and pages [251]–242 [*sic*], a verse parody by Curll of Pope's Horatian *Epistle II-ii*. Signatures are the same as those described by Griffith for *Volume the Fifth* (Griffith 462).[26]

Three features of the Yale volume deserve special notice. First, the title page, which reads: "New/ Letters/ of Mr Alexander Pope,/ And Several of his Friends./—/ Vellem Nescire Litteras!/ Cum desiderio Veteres, Revocamus Amores;/ atque olim missas, flemus Amicitias. /—/[ornament]/London:/ Printed, Anno Reformationis, 1737." Vinton A. Dearing, in an article on the 1737 editions of Pope's letters, has reported the significant fact that this title page was printed on the first leaf of signature R—at the end of the section of the book that had had to wait on Pope's publication of 19 May.[27] The two

---

[24] Apparently the same volume as that described in Elwin and Courthope, VI, liv. It reappears in Vinton A. Dearing, "The 1737 Editions of Alexander Pope's Letters," *Essays Critical and Historical Dedicated to Lily B. Campbell* (Berkeley, Calif., 1950), pp. 186–87.

[25] After Curll's advertisement dated "5 Nov. 1736" appears a leaf printed on both sides with a Curll book list—not in Griffith 429 or 462. The portrait of Bolingbroke, which Griffith conjectured as the frontispiece of the November 1736 volume, appears facing page 16.

[26] In this volume, as described by Griffith, Curll adds 106 more pages, in three sequences, containing Walsh's *Works* and twelve lines from Pope's *Essay on Criticism* as a eulogy of Walsh.

[27] Dearing, *op. cit.*, pp. 186–87. He argues that this title page was "designed apparently to be cut out and inserted between the two signatures F, where it would preface the letters reprinted from *Letters of Mr. Alexander Pope* that were new to Curll's *Literary Correspondence* series." But he adds: "It must be admitted that the *New Letters* title page was seldom or never inserted where it would seem logically to belong."

Latin sentences (the first from Suetonius, *Nero* X; the second a couplet misquoted from Catullus XCVI)[28] are lifted by Curll verbatim from the engraved ornaments, done by P. Fourdrinier after Pope's other artist friend William Kent, which appear at beginning and end of the "Preface" (and the second also after the table of "Contents" at top of the first page of the text) in Pope's authorized edition of the *Letters.* The Emperor Nero, asked to sign a death warrant, had exclaimed, "How I wish I had never learned to write!" ("'Quam vellem,' inquit, 'nescire litteras.'") The two Latin quotations are Pope's sardonic and his sentimental summation of feelings about his letters.

In the same vein of mimicry, Curll supplies, secondly, the frontispiece to this volume, which, quite unlike the four crude line cuts of Pope with which he had so far been content, is a very accurate replica etching after the medallion that Pope's friend Jonathan Richardson had supplied "Amicitiae Causa," for the *Letters.* But the full flavor of this polite attention on the part of Curll comes out, I believe, only when, in the third place, we notice the "Advertisement" put at the end of the volume. This consists mainly of a bill of complaints against the "Guinea" edition of the *Letters* and a brief essay on the life and poetry of Crashaw, with the allegation that Pope stole nosegays from him. Then the signature, the concluding words of the volume: "E. Curll/ Rose Street, June 8, 1737./ Die Nat A. Pope,/ Ætat. 49."[29]

Curll himself had earlier published this version of Pope's birthday and was perhaps the original propagator of it—though perhaps too it had been supplied to him by Pope himself either in some way connected with the earlier *Poetical Register* or through the mysterious correspondents, "P.T." and "E.P.," who involved Curll in the publication of Pope's *Letters* in May 1735. In his ". . . Anecdotes of the Life and Family of Mr. Pope," published in July 1735 in *Volume the Second* of *Mr. Pope's Literary Correspondence,* Curll had written: ". . . I shall begin my labour with the account Mr. Pope has given of himself. . . . Mr. Alexander Pope was born in Cheapside, London, on the 8th day of June, in the year 1688; so that one week produced

---

[28] In his letter to Orrery 10 May 1736, Pope quotes this couplet as in the ornament of May 1737 (*Correspondence,* IV, 15). In his letter to Swift 30 December 1736, he quotes the couplet again: "Quo desiderio veteres revocamus Amores, Atque olim amissas flemus Amicitias" (*Correspondence,* IV, 50). R. Ellis (ed.), *Catulli Veronensis Liber* (1867), p. 198, reads: "Quo . . . renovamus . . . missas . . ." with "amissas" a variant.

[29] This advertisement is apparently not repeated in *Volume the Fifth* as described by Griffith. Dearing (*op. cit.,* p. 186) refers to an "Advertisement" printed on [R8], conjugate with [R1] the title page.

both Pope and the Pretender. Memorable era!"[30] Perhaps the allusion to the Pretender (born 10 June 1688) actually explains why somebody had conjured 8 June as Pope's birthday. (Pope and the Pretender were in any event very close to being of an age. An oil painting of Pope, "Anno Aetatis 7," which came to light at Christie's in 1960 and is now in New Haven,[31] has something of a French air in the spirited bearing, the fluffy coiffure, and the bright-colored silks, and if only in such superficials it may strike us by a kind of similarity to Nicholas Largillière's portrait of the Pretender as a child,[32] painted at about the same moment, in 1695.) Curll's date for Pope's birthday gained some currency. It appears incised, along with an incorrect date for Pope's death, under the shoulder of one of the four marble busts of Pope signed by Roubiliac. It appears in the first sentence of William Ayre's *Memoirs of the Life and Writings of Alexander Pope, Esq.* (1745).

But Curll's notion about Pope's birthday is perhaps less interesting in the reason for his mistake (whatever that was) than in the fact that it gives us an approximate date for the publication of his *New Letters*, just eighteen days after Pope's own publication of the *Letters*, and shows the promptitude and solicitude with which Curll had pushed through this meticulous response to new features in the make-up of Pope's birthday present to himself.

---

[30] Elwin and Courthope, VI, 419, 426–27, 439–40; Griffith, II, 309 (No. 386). No day of the month for Pope's birth is given in Giles Jacob's account of him in the *Poetical Register,* 1720, II, 145.

The correct date of Pope's birth, 21 May 1688, is secured by Pope's manuscript entry in his Elzevir Virgil, in the Earl of Mansfield's possession, published in Elwin and Courthope, I, ix. The same date appears in Joseph Spence's *Anecdotes,* ed. S. W. Singer (London, 1820), p. 259.

[31] In the collection of James M. Osborn, to whom I am indebted for good advice in the writing of this essay.

[32] National Portrait Gallery, No. 976.

JOHN ROBERT MOORE

Daniel Defoe: Precursor of Samuel Richardson

At Harvard in September 1914, two graduate students were assigned to adjoining seats in Fred Robinson's class in Chaucer. The arrangement was the chance result of alphabetical sequence in surnames, but there was an affinity in the future interests of the two young men. Alan McKillop went on to achieve high distinction as an authority on Samuel Richardson. His former classmate has been gradually drawn into an absorption in the life and writings of Daniel Defoe.

In some respects Defoe and Richardson may seem utterly unlike. The wiry little horseman and pedestrian, who wore anonymity as a garment as he moved about Great Britain and western Europe, had nothing of the Olympian majesty needed in answering the correspondence of feminine admirers of serial novels. Psychoanalysts have a field day whenever they consider Richardson, but they can make little out of Defoe. Their most ingenious attempts have led to nothing better than suggestions that Moll Flanders continued to steal watches because she felt that the time of youth had slipped away from her—that she robbed pregnant women because she had grown too old for further childbearing. A casual reading of seventeenth- and eighteenth-century newspapers ought to show that watches were stolen because they were valuable and easy to dispose of—that pregnant women were victims of such thefts because they were slow to suspect pickpockets and even slower to defend their property.

Richardson discovered at the beginning of his literary career that his strength lay in the minute development of scenes and characters. Defoe never did learn this, and he continued to promise his readers "strange variety of incidents." It is fortunate that he wrote so few of the many sequels that he promised or suggested; they would all have been "farther adventures." It should have been obvious from the first that his greatest power lay in selection and concentration: in the care-

JOHN ROBERT MOORE is Distinguished Service Professor Emeritus at Indiana University.

ful presentation of political, social, or economic ideas—in the realization of human experience on a desert island, or in the African wilderness, or in the deserted city streets, or in the living room of a Canterbury seamstress, or in the mind of a frightened and homeless little boy.

Richardson gave us his best in *Clarissa*. Defoe wrote or had a hand in at least 552 works of widely different sorts, and he was a pioneer in many significant types of literature and history and journalism; but he went to his grave without knowing his higher capabilities.

Many other dissimilarities might be cited, but the resemblances have more significance for us here. One of the best studies of the later novelist is entitled *Samuel Richardson, Printer and Novelist*. I have no proof that Defoe ever held a stick of type in his hand, but the extent and intimacy of his connection with printers and publishers are unique in literary history. Within his own lifetime, during a recorded period of more than forty-one years, 142 different printers and booksellers (excluding the many pirates, but including John Watts, who never finished setting the type for *The Compleat English Gentleman*) are known to have been concerned in offering his writings to the public, and he had close connections with his publishers in London and Newcastle and Edinburgh.

Often this must have been an unusually personal relationship. When Richard Baldwin died, Defoe continued to employ his widow Abigail as one of his favorite printers and publishers. Long after the elder John Darby's death, Defoe's works were occasionally printed or published by John Darby, Junior. When, during the Sacheverell riots, John Morphew was frightened out of issuing the *Review*, Defoe found a more courageous coworker in John Baker. When the widow of Andrew Anderson was threatened with the loss of her appointment as Printer to the Queen in Scotland, Defoe sought to preserve her official position through his influence with Harley. When Defoe forgot his spectacles at Newcastle, they were sent on to Edinburgh by his printer Joseph Button.

Even outside what he called "the Whole Island of Great Britain," Defoe was not without some relationship to printers and booksellers. We can forget the occasional claim that a tract of Defoe's was first printed by imaginary persons in The Hague or in Cologne; but a few of his political writings were printed or reprinted in Dublin by a careful arrangement from London. Fourteen of his known twenty-nine tracts or books in the first five months of 1715 were printed or sold in London by Samuel Keimer, whom Defoe befriended in the next year by securing his release from the Gatehouse through a personal appeal to Lord Townshend—thereby winning Keimer's expression of gratitude in his *Brand Pluck'd from the Burning*. Later that same Keimer emigrated to Philadelphia, reprinted selections from Defoe's *Religious Courtship* in his own *Universal Instructor*, and gave employment to a recent arrival in Philadelphia—the most famous of young printers, Benjamin Franklin. During his first stay in London, Franklin was for a time employed by one of Defoe's printers, John Watts; and when his friend James Ralph planned a periodical, Franklin introduced him to one of Defoe's principal publishers, James Roberts. The boy Franklin, who so skillfully made the acquaintance of Sir Hans Sloane and secured admission to sessions of the Royal Society, would have had no difficulty in meeting the English author he admired so greatly. The possibility of finding Defoe and Franklin and Richardson at a chance rencounter in a London printing shop is almost as elusive as the song the sirens sang, but it need not be abandoned as beyond all conjecture.

Defoe not only frequented printing houses, he did some of his original writing and at times most of his press correction in the printer's sanctum sanctorum itself. In *The Chimera* he used some of the loose printed sheets as his own authorial copy, and the defective numbering of the later pages resulted from his reliance on the faulty numbering of the sheets to which he referred. Among the leading authors of the early eighteenth century, only Defoe and Richardson wrote directly for the press, with some instructions to the printer on setting the type. *Samuel Richardson, Printer*—yes, most certainly. But *Daniel Defoe: Friend and Collaborator of Many Printers.*

It was once held as common knowledge among all of us who learned the history of English literature from the canonical pages of our textbooks that the modern novel began in 1740 with Richardson's *Pamela*. Long afterward we met with a more discriminating judgment from Bonamy Dobrée, who has pointed out that the novels of Richardson were anticipated by *Moll Flanders:* ". . . it marks the birth of the modern novel. . . . Here for the first time is, as I think, the story of an ordinary person in the work-a-day world. . . . After Defoe we get Richardson, Fielding, and so on, all of them writing studies of society. . . . Here, for the first time, in *Moll Flanders*, we have the unvarnished biography of a person you or I might meet in the street.[1]"

Defoe was Richardson's precursor not only as a novelist of real life; his anticipation of Richardson's narrative method was recognized by two contributors to *Biographia Britannia* before the end of the eighteenth century:

It is observed, in note ZZZ, that the dramatic form, into which De Foe has thrown many parts of his works of imagination, has been evidently imitated by Richardson, in his Pamela, Clarissa, and Sir Charles Grandison. The

[1] *Daniel Defoe* (Groningen, Batavia, 1946), pp. 18–19.

writer of this addition to the article derives the greater pleasure from the remark, as it coincides with an opinion which he has long entertained, that Richardson was formed upon the model of De Foe. Richardson seems to have learned from him that mode of delineating characters, and carrying on dialogues, and that minute discrimination of the circumstances of events, in which De Foe so eminently excelled. If, in certain respects, the disciple rose above his master, as he undoubtedly did, in others he was inferior to him; for his conversations are sometimes more tedious and diffuse; and his works, though beautiful in their kind, are not by any means so various. Both of these writers had a wonderful ability in drawing pictures of human nature and human life. A careful perusal of the "Family Instructor" and the "Religious Courtship," would particularly tend to shew the resemblance between De Foe and Richardson.[2]

I am tempted to develop Kippis's suggestion and to analyze Defoe's use of the dramatic form that was adopted by Richardson not many years later. It is, no doubt, in *The Family Instructor* and *Religious Courtship* that the influence on Richardson is most obvious. But in the present study I shall limit myself to a less familiar subject—Defoe's training in the composition of letters, and his use (in many of his writings) of something of the epistolary method so intimately associated with the novels of his successor.

Of the tens of thousands of letters that Defoe must have written to his chain of correspondents all over Great Britain and western Europe and America, the vast majority can only be surmised. We have specific references to many letters that cannot now be found. In 1706, he gave Harley a list of sixty-three men who served as his agents in distributing one of his pamphlets, but we have extremely few letters that he addressed to them at any time. His personal relations with the American colonies are indicated by his knowledge of American affairs, by the legal records of some of his business dealings, by anecdotes and allusions in his writings, by a letter from Cotton Mather, and by a defense of Governor Eden sent to Defoe from North Carolina, and by the choice of Defoe to speak for the South Carolina Dissenters in London in 1705 and 1706 (when he wrote three pamphlets for them and apparently drew up their successful petition to the House of Lords). But there is no known scrap of any letter from Defoe to his friends on this side of the Atlantic.

For years, he was the trusted agent of William III, and he gave service to the Government under Walpole—but we have no letter from Defoe to either man. His correspondence with Stanhope and Townshend (now lost) is confirmed by statements in his secret com-

[2] Andrew Kippis's addition to the main article signed T ("Daniel De Foe," in *Biographia Britannia* [2d ed.; London, 1793], V, 75).

munications to De la Faye. We might expect a voluminous correspondence with his own large family. His father had sponsored his
admission to the Butchers' Company; his wife was his trusted business
agent during his many absences; his brother-in-law Robert Davis was
his personal representative in confidential missions and a frequent
companion on his travels; of his eight children, six outlived him and
were the objects of his plans for the future. Not one line of Defoe's
writings to any of them is known except in a single letter to his
youngest daughter, which the persistent Henry Baker kept as a record
of his controversy with Defoe over Sophia's dowry.

Only 235 of his letters have been preserved in George Harris
Healey's definitive edition. Nearly all of these have come down to us
by accident—carried off *en bloc* by the Earl of Oxford when he went
out of office, or dug up long afterward by researchers in the Public
Record Office, or stumbled upon among family papers of obscure
correspondents in Norwich or Shrewsbury.

The letters we do have are extremely able as to facts and arguments, woefully careless in style. They were written in hot haste,
often barely literate, frequently in a text hardly better than shorthand.
Sometimes we can date them almost to an hour—dashed off late at
night after a long day in conference with merchants or politicians
or clergymen, or in meetings of the Scottish Parliament or the General Assembly, to catch the early morning post for London. Defoe
wrote faster than most men found it possible to do before the development of mechanical recording, and he rarely made use of an
amanuensis. What he had to say was usually the best that anyone had
to offer on the subject at hand, and we find Harley and Godolphin
and Halifax and Sunderland trying to secure or to monopolize his
services as a roving reporter. The letters of Swift or of Pope are incomparably more finished as literary productions; but Defoe knew—
and wrote—more about the life of his age than any other man in
Europe.

I wish it could be possible to unearth some letter that he wrote to
the friends or relatives who entertained him during his visit to Ipswich
at the age of seven or eight or to some acquaintance he met when he
tried the water at Bath at the age of ten. The only evidence of his
boyhood letters occurs in his recollection of the method of instruction introduced by the Reverend Charles Morton in the academy at
Newington Green, which Defoe attended for about five years in his
teens:

. . . his pupils . . . wrot epistles twice every week upon such subjects
as he prescrib'd to them or upon such as they themselves chose to write
upon. Sometimes they were ambassadors and agents abroad in forreign

Courts, and wrote accounts of their negotiacions and recepcion in forreign Courts directed to the Secretary of State and some times to the Soveraign himself.

Some times they were Ministers of State, Secretaries and Commissioners at home, and wrote orders and instruccions to the ministers abroad, as by order of the King in council and the like. Thus he taught his pupils to write a masculine and manly stile, to write the most polite English, and at the same time to kno' how to suit their manner as well to the subject they were to write upon as to the persons or degrees of persons they were to write to; and all equally free and plain, without foolish flourishes and ridiculous flights of jingling bombast in stile, or dull meanesses of expression below the dignity of the subject or the character of the writer.[3]

It is a curious fact that the first known letter by Defoe was not written until he was forty-two years old; but it was addressed—as his lessons under Morton had taught him to address it—to one of the Principal Secretaries of State.

We know little about the vast personal correspondence of Defoe, and I pass over it hastily as having no direct influence on Richardson's novels. Defoe did compose letters from his youth up, and this constant practice in letter writing had its share in the development of his literary powers. But it is his use of the epistolary method—in his periodicals, tracts, histories, books of travel, novels, and didactic works—that is under consideration here.

The first extant publication by Defoe that has been identified is *A Letter to a Dissenter from His Friend at the Hague*. Published about August 1688, this was an exposure of the Liberty of Conscience granted through an illegal extension of the royal prerogative, which James II sought to confirm by a hand-picked Parliament. Like many of Defoe's later tracts with somewhat similar titles, this was no real letter but an able polemical tract. Often Defoe's so-called "Letters" were so impersonal in manner that they were not recognized as his. For example, on 5 December 1710, the Tory J. Durden informed Harley of his dispute with a Whig who urged him to read *Four Letters* (by Defoe, but not then known as his). Durden agreed to do this if the Whig would read *The Examiner* and [Defoe's] *Essay upon Publick Credit.*[4]

In twenty-six of Defoe's tracts the first significant word of the printed or implied title is "Letter." The titles of five others begin with "Epistle," "Expostulatory Letter," "Remarks on the Letter," "Two Letters," and "Four Letters." In still other tracts, the word "Letter"

---

[3] *The Compleat English Gentleman* (London, 1890), p. 219.

[4] *Hist. Mss. Com. Portland*, IV, 640.

occurs farther along in the title, or at least the author is supposed to be writing a letter. There was some advantage in addressing these tracts to specific persons or groups. But Defoe did not expect his readers to regard them as individual communications, and he felt free to ridicule the device whether it was used by himself or others: "Here you shall see a Pamphlet furnish'd with the Name of the Right Honourable the Countess of —— [alluding to one of his own tracts published during the previous month]; another written by a Person of Honour; a third by the L —— B ——, &c. And for Letters to Lords and Members of Parliament, the Stones on *Salisbury* Plain may as easily be counted."[5]

The least successful of Defoe's projects for publishing letters was a continuation of the widely known *Turkish Spy.* In the summer of 1704, he had proposed to Harley the settling of a resident agent in Paris:

There is a Large Article of Spyes abroad Among the Enemyes. This I Suppose to be Settld, tho' by Our Defect of Intelligence, Methinks it should Not; But It Reminds me of a Book in Eight Volumes Published in London about 7 or 8 yeares Ago Call'd Letters writ by a Turkish Spye— The books I take as They Are, a Meer Romance, but the Morrall is Good, A Settl'd Person of Sence and Penetration, of Dexterity and Courage, To Reside Constantly in Paris, Tho' As tis a Dangerous Post he had a Larger Allowance Than Ordinary, Might by One happy Turn Earn all the money and the Charge be well bestow'd.[6]

No such secret agent was established in Paris by Harley, but fourteen years later one of Defoe's publishers was advertising the first volume of a proposed series:

Just Publish'd, Vol. the 1st. of a Continuation of Letters written by a Turkish Spy at Paris, giving an Impartial Account to the Divan at Constantinople, of the most remarkable Transactions of Europe, and discovering several Intrigues and Secrets of the Christian Courts, especially of that of France, from the Year 1687, to the Death of Lewis the 14th, intermixt with a great Variety of useful Learning; written Originally in Arabick; Translated into Italian, and from thence into English. Printed for W. Taylor at the Ship in Pater Noster-Row; where may be had, the eight former Volumes of the Turkish Spy. . . .[7]

Even in the Preface it is evident that Defoe found it difficult to adhere closely to the original plan of writing history with authorial comments:

[5] *A Letter to a Merry Young Gentleman* (1715), p. 5.

[6] *Letters*, ed. G. H. Healey (Oxford, 1955), p. 38.

[7] *The St. James's Evening Post*, 28–30 August 1718.

If our Correspondent at *Vienna*, to whom *Mahmut* committed his Papers, and to whom they were faithfully delivered by his Successors, does not deceive us, we may expect a yet greater Variety, towards the Conclusion of his Residence, than has yet seen the Light, and perhaps some Remains of things omitted in the Time of former Publication, which, as they come to Hand, shall be communicated with the greatest Exactness, whether they may exactly Correspond with the Chronology of former Publications or no; and tho' there may seem a little Confusion in such a Retrospect, yet I doubt not the Beauty of the Subject shall make full Amends for any Disorder in the Dates.

This has been the Reason why, even in this Volume, some Letters, especially of Speculative Subjects, may come a little out of the Order of Time, which, I think, is a thing of so trifling a Nature, compar'd to the Advantage of their Publication, that it needs not the least Apology for it.[8]

Defoe's *Continuation* has a few passages very characteristic of its author. But the thirty-year-old historical events had little interest for most readers in 1718, the social and political and religious remarks were often commonplace, and the framework of the correspondence proved cumbersome. Mahmut the Turkish Spy is represented by a frontispiece portrait, but he never comes alive in the book. A few months later, the same Taylor was publishing another fictional book by Defoe, but that was a best-seller about an English sailor ship-wrecked on a desert island. The philosophical Mahomet or Mahmut, from whom so much had been expected, was forgotten. Volume I had no sequel, and I have seen no contemporary reference to it except in the newspaper advertisement. W. P. Trent annotated his copy of the *Continuation* with the remark that he had seen only one other; after prolonged search I have located only three more.

The pseudo-Turkish letters, which in 1718 had failed to provide an interesting review of history, had during the two preceding years been successfully employed by Defoe for current events. He had once defined the work of writing a penny paper as "only writing a History sheet by sheet, and *letting the World see it as I go on.* . . ."[9] That sounded easy enough, but as a practicing journalist he was never free of two constant problems: (1) how to use his special information without betraying his secret connection with the Government of the day (in his own terminology, how to write "within doors" so that his readers would suppose that he was only writing "without doors"); (2) how to present an intelligent interpretation of the contradictory nonsense that so often arrived in London as foreign news.

---

[8] *A Continuation of Letters Written by a Turkish Spy* (1718), pp. vii–viii.

[9] *Review*, I (4 April 1704), 49.

The first issue of his *Review* had announced his policy of moderation in pointing out the blunders of other journalists:

Let them please to be careful, not to impose Absurdities and Contradictions in their Weekly-Papers, and they shall meet with no Ill Treatment from this Paper; Nay, we will forgive them small *Errata's*, and slips of the Pen; nor will we always quarrel with them for Errors in Geography; but if they tell us a Lye, that a Man may feel with his Foot, and not only Proclaim their own Folly, but their Knavery too, and tell the World they think their Readers are Fools too, *that is intolerable.*[10]

But at times he found it amusing to reprint one of his rivals' news stories to enliven his own pages, as in a report from the military front in Flanders:

We had planted 11000 *Militia, but when the Enemy appeared, there was not a Fourth Part of them to be Found, and those too ran away in a Fright.*

To which he added a characteristic comment: "No Body at home but the Maid, and she gone to Church."[11]

In August 1716, when London was confused by incoherent reports of a battle between the Imperialists and the Turks, Defoe's *Mercurius Politicus* offered the editor's own detailed analysis of what had happened—in a letter said to be written by Ibrahim Passa, Saraskier of Belgrade, to the Mufti at Constantinople. This had been conveyed to the western world in a letter from Adrianople to a Merchant at Venice, which came by a felucca from Constantinople to Messina. In his monthly journal intended primarily for Tories, Defoe could use such a letter not only to give a skillful discussion of foreign affairs; at times he could also insert innuendoes to delight his readers without causing serious offense to the Government. To leave a loophole for refutation if that became necessary, he added: "Whether this Letter be real or feign'd it seems to express the State of the Turkish Army as they have represented it to the People. . . ."[12]

This new kind of "Turkish letter" aroused an interest which a popular journalist could not ignore. In the next monthly issue, Defoe had no sequel ready to offer, but he promised not to disappoint the public thereafter:

It is Confess'd 'tis very hard to come at any Accounts of Things on the *Turks* side, except what is learn'd by the Effects; but we have found a

[10] *Ibid.,* I (19 February 1704), 4–5.

[11] *Ibid.,* I (13 June 1704), 132.

[12] *Mercurius Politicus* (August 1716), p. 222.

Method by an unexpected Correspondence, to have such Accounts from *Constantinople*, even on purpose for the service of this Work, which we are well assur'd no other Publick Writers can come at; so though they are not come to hand in time for this Publication, we dare assure our Reader, that in our next Month we shall not fail to have an Account of the whole proceedings of the Military Divan or Council of War, after the News of the Battel, with all the Orders issued for their Generals, as well relating to the Siege of *Corfou*, as to the management of their Troops, and the Drawing Supplies for their Grand Army, together with such Views of their farther Measures, as we doubt not shall be as pleasing and entertaining, as profitable and instructing to the Reader.[13]

Although the expected letter from Turkey had not yet arrived, Defoe was able to state in some detail just what it would contain. By October, he was ready to explain why the siege of Corfu had been raised: "It was indeed wondred what oblig'd the *Turks* to Raise their Siege in such haste, and when they were at the Point of Carrying the Place; but it will be easily understood by the following Letter, which we have from good Hands, and which, one said to be written by the Captain *Bassa* to the *Caimacan*, after the Raising the Siege."[14] The next four pages gave an ostensible letter from Ibrahim Skuly Adram, Bassa of the Sea, "TO the Faithful Illustrious Councellor of the invincible ACHMET, *Monarch of the World*, HALI *Bassa, Caimacan*, of the imperial City of *Constantinople*, (*Stambol*)." But even with letters that were professedly so well authenticated, it was the part of wisdom for an English journalist to be cautious: "The Truth is, the Captain Bassa says little in this Letter about the *Venetian* Fleet, but what is confess'd by our own Accounts."[15]

In the month which followed, rival journalists reported (by way of France) that the Turks were preparing to carry on the war. Defoe offered to establish this by his own more direct information: ". . . this will be farther confirm'd by the Credit of a Letter sent by the *Caimacan* of *Constantinople*, to the *Seraskier* of the *Morea* upon that Occasion, the like being as we suppose, sent to the other Commanders of the *Ottoman* Forces in the Frontiers."[16] The highly prized "Turkish Letters" were becoming available more rapidly than Defoe could find space for them, and he concluded his monthly report with an apology: "We have the Copy also of that other Letter mention'd in this, but having not Room to Incert it here, we shall give it in our next."[17] Next month this promise was fulfilled with "A Letter from

13 *Ibid.* (September 1716), p. 222.

14 *Ibid.* (October 1716), p. 370. 16 *Ibid.* (December 1716), p. 532.

15 *Ibid.*, p. 375. 17 *Ibid.*, p. 535.

the *Caimaican* of *Constantinople*, to the Vizier of Belgrade, never printed before."[18]

I shall not attempt to suggest what relationship these "Turkish letters" may have had to the eighteenth-century fondness for Oriental letters. But the pretense of Turkish authorities gave some protection to an English journalist who stood midway between hostile political parties, and it justified a more objective discussion of European events than might otherwise have been possible. In particular, it enabled Defoe to venture an interpretation of foreign military affairs unrivaled in London.

It has been recognized that Defoe served in Monmouth's Rebellion, that he sought to raise a regiment of Dissenters for William III, and that he offered to equip and lead a troop of horse near the beginning of Queen Anne's reign. At times it has been recognized that, as journalist, novelist, and historian, he showed an acute interest in everything concerning the art of war. But the late Charles Dalton, through a confusion with a French Huguenot exile, stated that Defoe himself held a commission as Captain-Lieutenant in Colonel Desborde's Regiment of Dragoons in Portugal, that he was placed on half-pay in 1712, and that he was still drawing his pension in 1722. Dalton suggested that Defoe was more likely to have served as a recruiting officer in Scotland than on active duty in Portugal or Spain. But A. S. White has shown that the Daniel Defaur (or Defoe) of the Army Lists was an altogether different person from the historian and novelist.[19]

However limited the actual military experience of Daniel Defoe, the eighteenth-century predecessor of Liddell Hart and Fielding Eliot, he cared more (and often knew more) about military affairs than any other English writer of his time; and this special interest is almost as apparent in the "Turkish Letters" as in the lives of Charles XII and of Peter the Great, in the *Memoirs of a Cavalier* and the *Memoirs of an English Officer*.

After January 1717, Defoe began to tire of pseudo-Turkish letters as a means af analyzing news from abroad. In the January issue of *Mercurius Politicus* appeared "another Letter from *Constantinople* ... which gives a particular Account of the Preparations of the Turks. ...." But this was said to be "written by a *French* Gentleman."[20] In the March issue, Defoe announced that "we are expecting every Day

[18] *Ibid.* (January 1717), Table of Contents and pp. 53–57.

[19] *English Army Lists and Commission Registers 1661–1714*, ed. and annotated Charles Dalton (reprinted in London, 1960), VI, vii–viii, 268. For this reference, I am deeply indebted to Dr. L. F. Powell and Dr. Esmond de Beer. See also A. S. White, "Defoe's Military Career," *TLS*, 28 January 1926, p. 163.

[20] *Mercurius Politicus* (January 1717), p. 57.

Letters from our Correspondent who sent us the former Account";
but he fell back on "a Letter from an *English* Gentleman in the
Retinue of the Secretary of the *French* Resident now at *Adrianople*."[21] In the June issue he assured his readers: "We have expected
some Weeks to furnish an extraordinary Account of the *Turkish*
Army it self from our usual Correspondent, but doubt not to give it
at large in our next."[22]

Thereafter the Turkish correspondent disappeared from *Mercurius
Politicus*. For the December issue part of the Turkish report was ab-
stracted from a letter the Dutch ambassador at the Porte had written
to the Minister of their High Mightinesses in London. In November
and December 1717, and in May 1718, news about Turkey was provided in omniscient and unsigned letters written in Defoe's own
characteristic style.

Defoe's last use of a pseudo-Turkish letter had appeared in *The
Conduct of Christians Made the Sport of Infidels*, published on 30
July 1717 and excerpted in the August issue of *Mercurius Politicus*.
This pamphlet was not concerned with Turkish affairs, but it satirized
the Bangorian controversy in England.

The essential fairness of Defoe's "Turkish letters" is lacking in the
few contemporary tracts using the same device, for example, the
stupid and brutal attack on Walpole entitled *A Letter from Ibrahim
Bassa, Grand Visier to the late depos'd Sultan Achmet, To Don
Ruperto de Poli, Knt*. In that undated tract, nothing is Turkish but
the names, and vituperation takes the place of fact and argument.

After such foreign correspondence had proved its appeal to Defoe's
public and its usefulness to the editor, there was no reason why confidential letters might not arrive from other countries than Turkey.
In the issue of *Mercurius Politicus* for October 1716, the editor announced that "we shall be able to let our Readers into some such part
of the Secret History of Things, as cannot easily be come at, and
which, at least, we are sure no other publick Writer can furnish them
with; and as this is what we believe will particularly recommend this
Undertaking to the World, so especially it will this Month, perhaps
more than any we have yet wrote of."[23] This preliminary opened the
floodgates for letters from Copenhagen,[24] Paris,[25] Gottenburgh,[26]

21 *Ibid.* (March 1717), p. 203.

22 *Ibid.* (June 1717), p. 405.

23 *Ibid.* (October 1716), pp. 313–14.   25 *Ibid.* (December 1716), pp. 537–40.

24 *Ibid.*, pp. 380–83.   26 *Ibid.* (February 1717), pp. 100–102.

Italy,[27] Russia,[28] Venice,[29] Brussels,[30] Spain,[31] Holland,[32] Stockholm,[33] and Messina.[34] Well might the editor boast that "Our Foreign Affairs are indeed full of infinite Variety, and afford a most agreeable History. . . ."[35]

But when the Pretender removed from Avignon to Italy, Defoe knew where to exercise caution: "It is not our hap to have any Intelligence among his Retinue, and therefore cannot give a certain Account of who are with him and who not. . . ."[36]

Defoe's non-Turkish letters were much less elaborately disguised than those which professed to be Turkish, and they showed little attempt to suggest the atmosphere of the countries from which they were supposed to come. At times there was little pretense that they were anything more than a skillful journalistic interpretation of the situation. After guaranteeing the authenticity of a letter about the affairs of the King of Sicily, Defoe virtually admitted that it represented only the editor's guess: "We desire our Readers to take this whole Account *ad referendum;* That it is a Rational Scheme, both as to the Causes and the Design, we cannot but allow; and if this, or something else very considerable is not concerted there, it is impossible for Humane Reason to comprehend what the King of *Sicily* is doing."[37]

At various times, during a period of forty years, Defoe had some hand in twenty-seven different periodicals. For their news, most of these were largely dependent on domestic or foreign correspondents. If Defoe needed an account of what was happening in an obscure presbytery in Scotland, he could insert a letter that he had actually received from Ross or Sutherland or from a friend in the General Assembly. If he wished to comment on the social foibles of the day, his *Review* could employ real or fictitious letters in the "Advice from the Scandal. Club" or the "Miscellanea" (letters that served as forerunners of *The Tatler* and *The Spectator*). If he sought accounts of foreign countries, he could use communications of many sorts, some of them written by (or modified from letters written by) actual correspondents abroad.

A few of his tracts, like *The King of Pirates*, are bantering letters meant to entertain rather than to instruct his readers. But elsewhere

27 *Ibid.* (October 1717), pp. 739–46.

28 *Ibid.* (February 1718), pp. 132–36.

29 *Ibid.* (December 1717), pp. 826–31.

30 *Ibid.* (May 1718), pp. 311–18.

31 *Ibid.* (October 1717), pp. 753–58.

32 *Ibid.* (July 1718), pp. 401–3.

33 *Ibid.* (January 1719), pp. 14–18.

34 *Ibid.* (July 1719), pp. 473–77.

35 *Ibid.* (January 1719), p. 14.

36 *Ibid.* (March 1717), p. 193.

37 *Ibid.,* pp. 199–200.

he could introduce a genuine letter from North Carolina or Edinburgh, or he could concoct such a convincing narrative as *A True
Account of the Proceedings at Perth*, "Written by a Rebel." *A True
Account* has sometimes been attributed to one of the principal Jacobite leaders; more recently it has been reprinted by an eminent historian in a textbook of authentic historical source material; to this
day it remains the clearest analysis of the collapse of the Jacobite
invasion in 1716. The men who interpret our own news by television
have at their disposal such sums of money as Defoe never knew, as
well as methods of photography and sound recording and wireless
transmission undreamed of in his age. But I have yet to hear one who
excels Defoe in actual insight into the significance of events in his
own time. For Defoe was no graduate of a school of journalism, but
"the Father of Journalism."

His first and most ambitious attempt at current reporting appeared
in *The Storm* (1704, based primarily on authentic letters from correspondents on land and sea. Even more famous was the narrative of
a recent apparition in Canterbury, first published late in 1705. The
apparition of Mrs. Veal perplexed as good a scientist as Dr. John
Arbuthnot[38] and as good a literary scholar as Dr. Samuel Johnson
(until the latter succumbed to the denials apparently set afloat by
Mrs. Veal's brother). Defoe rode to Maidstone with the Colepeper
brothers when those "Kentish Worthies" were released from imprisonment by the House of Commons in 1701; William Colepeper was
Defoe's defense attorney at the trial in 1703; and Defoe wrote a tract
supporting William Colepeper in his controversy with Sir George Rook
in 1704. If the Maidstone Justice of the Peace who in 1705 sent the story
of the apparition "*to his Friend in* London, *as it is here Worded*"
happened to be named William Colepeper, we might possibly come
nearer to the transmission of the story than anyone has yet succeeded
in doing.

Defoe's most extensive work in the form of letters need not concern us here. The *Tour* maintains the tone of an English gentleman,
a devout member of the Church of England who is not intolerant
of Dissenters; but its long letters are expository narratives directed
to the general reader in a pattern already well established for travel
guides. The *Tour* is a work of exceptional merit, but its merits are not
those of epistolary writing. *The Great Law of Subordination Consider'd*, published in the previous month of 1724, professes to be
written by a Frenchman naturalized in England to his brother in

---

[38] Frank Higginbotham, "The Apparition of Mrs. Veal to Mrs. Bargrave at Canterbury, 8th of September, 1705: Two Contemporary Accounts" (*Archaeologia Cantiana*,
LXIII, 154–66).

France; but this is an excuse for remarks on English manners and customs, and the letters are only chapters in a book.

Always Defoe had the gift of seeing life pictorially, as when he ridiculed a famous political opponent of the Queen and the Government: "Pray, Mr. *Steele*, give your self leave to think of this a little when you are in your easie Chair, and after you have stroak'd your Cat."[39]

In numberless anecdotes or episodes he showed his skill in third-personal narrative, and at times he chafed in the strait jacket of a single point of view: "I shall no longer trouble the Story with a Relation in the first Person, which will put me to the Expence of ten thousand *said I's*, and *said he's*, and he *told me's*, and I *told him's*, and the like, but I shall collect the Facts historically, as near as I can gather them out of my Memory from what they related to me, and from what I met with in my conversing with them and with the Place."[40]

But whatever difficulties the fixed point of view may have created for Defoe, all his longer narratives are told in the first person. It was through his constant habit of seeing through the eyes of a single character that he stumbled into writing his novels. In this respect, many of his other compositions have the same essential quality as his fiction. Of *The Shortest Way with the Dissenters*, a controversial tract published as early as 1702, Bonamy Dobrée has written:

It was in this work that he first revealed that element in his genius which, we may well think, is his most distinctive mark; that capacity so to enter into the being of a person he is portraying as seemingly to become that person, to have that person's emotions, to speak with his or her authentic voice. . . . It is this faculty which makes Robinson Crusoe, the saddler of the *Journal of the Plague Year*, Moll Flanders and a dozen others, people in whose reality you believe, and which makes enduring the books which contain them. It is the creative imagination working on actuality raised to the highest pitch; it seems almost to be the complete transference of Defoe's self into his creatures.[41]

If we considered the background of Defoe as a writer of letters, we might be led to expect that he, rather than Richardson, should have sponsored the epistolary novel. But he had served no literary apprenticeship as the author of *Letters Written to and for Particular Friends*, his heroines had no pride in their skill in composition and no need to

---

[39] *The Honour and Prerogative Of The Queen's Majesty Vindicated and Defended* (1713), p. 17.

[40] *The Farther Adventures of Robinson Crusoe* (1719), pp. 43–44.

[41] *Daniel Defoe*, p. 10.

smuggle their thoughts into the outer world, and he had long before worked out a narrative technique that suited his purposes far better than any series of letters could have done.

To Defoe, with his lifelong interest in drama, the natural way of developing a story was along the lines of the *commedia dell' arte*, with some of the main action sketched out in advance and the dialogue developing as the occasion gave rise to it. A reader can see the characters, situations, and incidents developing under Defoe's hand as the spoken words give life to them. It was through this dramatic use of dialogue that Defoe's impact on Richardson was greatest.

However, letters are used in Defoe's didactic works and in the novels—often in one of two ways. Sometimes—to speak in terms of the theater, as Defoe might well have thought of them—they tell of offstage action; sometimes they provide a climax for a scene or a situation.

In *The Family Instructor*, a brother ignores the preliminaries by declaring "I have heard all this by Letters,"[42] and a sister says, "I heard that my Father had written a kind Letter to him, to desire him to come home again. . . ."[43] One letter that serves to create a dramatic scene (although fortunately, to judge from the commonplace words that are quoted from it, it is never read aloud) is the savage attack on the father by his absent and favorite son—a letter that astonishes brother, sister, and servant, and drives the father almost frantic.[44] Perhaps the most interesting letter in the didactic works was sent by a prodigal and half-repentant son after he had been crippled and had sold his military commission:

DEAR SISTER,

While I had a Hand to write to you, I too seldom paid you the Respect, which my Affection and Duty to you requir'd; and now I have neither a Hand to write, or a Heart to dictate; my last gave you an Account of my being wounded at the Siege of Doway, *of which after some Time I was cured; tho' I lay all the Winter sick at* Lisle; *now I am the miserablest Object in the World: I was taken Prisoner of War last Week, and am brought to this Place, having my right Arm broken by a Musquet Ball, and to morrow it must be cut off:* GOD *is just, Sister. I cut off my Father's right Arm, as to his Family, when I broke from him by Violence, and went abroad against his Consent; now I loose my right Arm as a just Retaliation: I insulted my Father upon my having an Estate without him, now I must come a Begging to my Father for Bread, or perish in Misery; for my Estate is gone, and I am out of Commission: God is just,*

[42] *The Family Instructor* (2d ed.; 1720), II, 157.

[43] *Ibid.*, p. 251.

[44] *Ibid.*, pp. 255–56.

Sister! *He is very* just! *I hope you have begg'd my Father's Pardon, and obtain'd his Blessing; tho' I may never live to do it. I have wrote to my Father for some Assistance, but have little Reason to expect it.* Adieu.

Your dying Brother

Cambray————1709.[45]

It is an example of the strange economy practiced by the most fertile and prolific of writers that this letter was supposedly written in 1709 after "the Siege of Doway." In the next year, one of Defoe's ablest political tracts, *A Letter from a Gentleman at the Court of St. Germains*, was said to be "Found at Doway, after the Taking of that Town."

In the novels, there are often special reasons why there should be few or no letters. Colonel Jack is illiterate throughout the most interesting part of his story. Robinson Crusoe spends approximately twenty-eight years (the chronology is a bit defective here, as so often in Defoe) "all alone in an un-inhabited Island on the Coast of America, near the Mouth of the Great River Oroonoque. . . ." Captain George Roberts is for a long time without pen or ink or paper. Bob Singleton is so nearly illiterate that any correspondence for him is carried on by the ship's surgeon or by Quaker William. Moll Flanders does receive letters, but she is so afraid of contact with her past that she lets one of her would-be correspondents suppose that his letters have miscarried.[46] The saddler near Aldgate speaks of going to the post office to mail a letter to his brother in the country—but that is only an excuse for introducing the dramatic incident of the purse of gold that no one would touch until it had been purified by fire.[47] After Captain George Carleton has landed in Spain, he seems to have no friend elsewhere in the world to justify any attempt at correspondence. And poor Robert Drury almost forgets his native language "During Fifteen Years Captivity" on the distant Island of Madagascar.

In the novels, as in the didactic works, letters are likely to be used to explain offstage action. Colonel Jack's last wife procures the knowledge of his pardon through a friend in London, and she keeps him safely out of sight until the sloop brings him letters telling that King George has signed an act of grace that makes him a free man.[48] The narrator of *A New Voyage Round the World* entraps his mutinous sailors at the Cape of Good Hope by letting them present to the

[45] *The Family Instructor* (10th ed.; 1725), I, 348.

[46] *Moll Flanders* (Aitken ed.), II, 117.

[47] *A Journal of the Plague Year* (Aitken ed.), pp. 120–21.

[48] *Colonel Jacque* (Aitken ed.), II, 121.

Governor the damning letter supplied by a Dutch captain.[49] Robinson Crusoe's affairs in Brazil are set in order by correspondence alone, after his return to Europe.[50] Captain Singleton's safe return to England is made possible by the correspondence that Quaker William initiates with his sister in London (Singleton's future wife).[51] The fortuneteller Duncan Campbell—as a deaf-mute—communicates entirely by sign language or by written correspondence,[52] and he is rarely farther away from the materials for writing than Pamela herself.

But the most significant use of letters in Defoe's novels is to express strong emotion or to provide a climax for a situation. When the Cavalier's father is overwhelmed by the kindness of Gustavus Adolphus to his son, the letter in which he expresses his gratitude is reproduced in full.[53] When Singleton and his companions realize the difficulty of reaching the African mainland from Madagascar, they set up a landmark in the Portuguese language which is virtually a letter to all who may come afterward:

> "Point Desperation. Jesus have mercy."[54]

When Singleton wishes to elude his piratical companions in the Persian Gulf, he sends them the message which the ship's surgeon has written for him:

> BOATSWAIN THOMAS,—We are all betrayed. For God's sake make off with the boat, and get on board, or you are all lost. The captain, William the Quaker, and George the reformade are seized and carried away: I am escaped and hid, but cannot stir out; if I do I am a dead man. As soon as you are on board cut or slip, and make sail for your lives. Adieu.—R. S.[55]

When Moll Flanders is reproached by a lover she had wronged, she is "struck by this letter, as with a thousand wounds. . . ."[56] But it is the farewell letter from her adored highwayman that leaves her in despair[57] and that prepares for their final reunion in Newgate and their joint exile to Virginia.

If we were required to single out one letter above all others in

[49] *A New Voyage Round the World* (Aitken ed.), pp. 33, 35–36.

[50] *The Life and Strange Surprising Adventures of Robinson Crusoe* (Aitken ed), pp. 317, 320, 339.

[51] *Captain Singleton* (Aitken ed.), pp. 311–13.

[52] *Duncan Campbell* (Aitken ed.), pp. 6–17, 46–47, etc.

[53] *Memoirs of a Cavalier* (Aitken ed.), pp. 88–89.

[54] *Captain Singleton*, p. 38.

[55] *Ibid.*, p. 299.

[56] *Moll Flanders*, I, 126.

[57] *Ibid.*, pp. 157–58.

Defoe's fiction, perhaps it would be the one delivered to Robert Drury at the seaside, when he finally discovers an English ship, come to take him away from his long captivity:

To Robert Drury on the Island of Madagascar.
Son Robert Drury,   *Loughborough, Feb. 27th 1715.*
I am inform'd by one Mr. Thornbury, *that he left you in Health on the Island of Madagascar?* [sic] *which I was glad to hear: My very good friend Mr.* Terry *hath a Friend, Commander of a Ship, the Bearer hereof, that hath promis'd to do all he can to get you at Liberty, I therefore desire you to do the Captain all the Service that you can in the Country: And in so doing you will oblige our good Friend Mr.* Terry, *and your ever loving Father till Death, John Drury.*[58]

Robert Drury's Journal can be proved, at many points and in many ways, to be totally impossible as an actual journal of one man's experience. But throughout the story, Defoe has exerted much of his old skill in making the impossible seem more plausible than anything that could actually have happened. As long as learned men continue to trace the family background of Robert Drury, most nebulous of heroes, it will perhaps be this fictitious letter more than anything else that will encourage them to persevere in so fruitless an endeavor.

In the preceding pages, I have spoken of the precursor of Richardson—not of the follower of Defoe. The latter topic is worthy of consideration by the leading authority on Richardson. But if Alan McKillop does not care to undertake it,[59] I can explain my present avoidance of the theme by repeating Defoe's words:

. . . I purpose to handle that Subject by it self, . . . and . . . because I have not room to speak effectually to it here, I refer it to another Occasion.[60]

[58] *Madagascar: Or, Robert Drury's Journal* (1728), pp. 429–30.

[59] I am not unmindful of the exceptionally fine chapters on Defoe and Richardson in *The Early Masters of English Fiction* (Lawrence, Kan., 1956). They are not primarily concerned with Defoe's influence on Richardson.

[60] *The Evident Approach of a War* (1727), p. 59.

RICARDO QUINTANA

The Scheme of Collins's Odes on
Several ... Subjects

Today we are all aware of the dangers invited by those who
would approach a poet's poems through what they take to be his intentions. We insist rightly enough that it is the poetry itself that
counts; and we may well go on to ask whether an artist's intentions
are not multiple to the point of rendering explications supposedly
based thereon useless at the least. Yet in certain cases, and up to a certain point, the intentional approach is perfectly sound, and we all
make use of it. For instance, we recognize that in most of his sonnets
Milton chose to use the Italian form, and we see that in doing so he
committed himself to several things—to an attitude toward his theme,
to a particular kind of logical-rhetorical-emotional development of
statement, etc. In this case, be it observed, it is the poetry that indicates
what we have chosen to call the poet's intentions. We have not had to
go outside the poems themselves.

It is my hope to show in what follows that Collins had a scheme
in mind while composing many of the pieces that make up the volume
of his which appeared late in 1746, the *Odes on Several Descriptive
and Allegoric Subjects*.[1] The scheme, to be sure—if I am right about

RICARDO QUINTANA is Professor of English at the University of Wisconsin.

[1] To anyone familiar with Collins scholarship and criticism of the past forty years
or so, my indebtedness to many persons will be apparent throughout my essay. A. D.
McKillop (in "The Romanticism of William Collins," *SP*, XX [1923]) was one of the
earliest to direct attention to Collins's central concern in the odes with the concept
of poetry. In his Warton Lecture on "The Poetry of Collins" (*Proceedings of the
British Academy* [1928]) and in his *Collins* (1928), H. W. Garrod wrote with great
perception about the *Odes on Several ... Subjects*, suggesting the true nature of the
Ode on the Poetical Character, and marking off the patriotic odes from the poems
surrounding them. A. S. P. Woodhouse ("Collins and the Creative Imagination; A
Study in the Critical Background of His Odes [1746]," in *Studies in English, By
Members of University College, Toronto* [1931]) and E. G. Ainsworth (*Poor Collins;
His Life, His Art, and His Influence* [1937]) both enlarged our understanding of the
Odes. S. Musgrove's interesting discussion, "The Theme of Collins's Odes" (*N&Q*,
9 October 1943 and 23 October 1943) may at first seem to be a direct if not a com-

it—was not so elementary a thing as Milton's choice of sonnet form, yet it did have to do with the sort of poetry Collins deliberately set himself to write, and it did condition the poems that were composed. One may, I think, go still further and say that it is the key to the 1746 volume, revealing the shape of the book as a whole, establishing the relationship of the twelve odes to one another, and throwing some light on the way Collins's creative powers were channeled.

It happens that we know from external sources a good deal about the kind of poetic theory Collins was obviously inclined toward. There is Joseph Warton's short Advertisement standing at the front of his *Odes on Various Subjects,* which appeared late in 1746 at about the same time as Collins's *Odes on Several . . . Subjects.* The fact that Warton and Collins had originally planned to publish their odes in a joint volume gives the statements in the Advertisement something more than indirect relevance to Collins. There is the essay "Of the Essential Excellencies in Poetry" in Dodsley's *Museum* of 4 July 1747,[2] which has been attributed to Collins and which—whether his or not—embodies ideas about poetry which were common at the time among Collins's friends. There are passages in Bishop Hurd's writings that bear closely upon the poetic of the Collins-Warton group. And there are both the poems and the critical observations of Joseph Warton and his brother Thomas. These are essential materials if we are called upon to consider the atmosphere, the milieu, in which Collins lived during his working years. But there is nothing here that puts us on to those specific intentions of Collins which constituted what I have called the scheme of the *Odes on Several . . . Subjects.* These intentions are to be found within the body of his poetry. I put it this way because, though the *Odes* seems to me to be self-contained and self-explanatory, there are passages in his other poetry—notably the *Epistle: Addresst to Sir Thomas Hammer* and the *Ode on the Popular Superstitions of the Highlands of Scotland*—which are pertinent and which I shall admit to the present discussion.

II

Collins showed great concern regarding the different "kinds" of poetry. This is not surprising, for such concern was general in the

---

plete anticipation of what I have to say, but I believe that there turn out to be substantial differences between him and myself. There is, finally, McKillop's fine article of 1960 in the *Tennessee Studies in Literature* on "Collins's *Ode to Evening*—Background and Structure," as sensitive criticism of Collins as we have ever had.

[2] See Frederick Page, "An Essay by Collins," *Times (London) Literary Supplement* (11 July 1935). Page's attribution of the *"Essay"* to Collins was questioned by Edmund Blunden (*TLS* [8 August 1935]), who called attention to the many hands concerned in Dodsley's *Museum.*

eighteenth century, present everywhere in criticism and reflected everywhere in the practices of the poets. What distinguishes Collins in this respect is that his views were so distinctly colored by the new aesthetics—and the aestheticism—of his day. His manner of discriminating between different varieties of poetry, the things he went on to analyze, and the conclusions to which he followed through all bear the marks of this order of aesthetic theorizing. However, we do not have to go to external sources to learn what the kinds were that he discerned and what each meant to him. The poems themselves tell us. The more explicit statements are to be found in the *Epistle to Hanmer* and at points in the *Ode on the Popular Superstitions*, and it would be well to look at these two pieces before turning to the *Odes on Several . . . Subjects*.

In the course of the *Epistle to Hanmer*,[3] the poet finds occasion to refer to five kinds of literary art—and in the case of one of these to four different modes thereof—as well as to the art of painting, which is seen as a kind of creative art distinct from letters. The five literary species are Greek tragedy (lines 17–26), Graeco-Roman comedy (lines 27–34), love poetry, Provençal and Italian (lines 35–44), English drama (lines 45–66 and 75–100), and French drama (lines 67–74). Within English drama, the speaker distinguishes Jonson's plays (lines 65–66), those of Fletcher (lines 57–63), Shakespeare's historical drama (lines 75–92), and those plays of Shakespeare in which we find sweet illusion of the cheated mind (lines 93–100). "Expressive Picture" is discussed—with references to Shakespeare's *Julius Caesar* and *Coriolanus*—in two of the latter verse paragraphs (lines 107–40).

Undoubtedly, there were many things that the writer of the *Epistle* could have adduced about what constitutes the differences between these kinds. But what he actually says is pretty much confined to two aspects. The first has to do with the descriptions and imagery characteristic of the particular type. The second is a matter of the psychological effect produced by this kind of art. The distinction between the two aspects—imagery and effect—is not, however, always maintained with consistency. Sometimes the descriptive details and imagery as well as the resulting emotional effect are merely pointed out quickly and objectively; but at other times we are presented with the moving and speaking images created by the artistic imagination,

[3] The first edition of the *Epistle*, entitled *Verses Humbly Address'd to Sir Thomas Hanmer*, was published in 1743. In the following year appeared a second edition, extensively revised and entitled *An Epistle: Addresst to Sir Thomas Hanmer*. All my references are to the revised text of the second edition. Those using the Stone-Poole-Page edition of Collins's *Poems* (Oxford University Press, 1937) will find this on pages 317–22, but they must there renumber the lines, because the numbers given by Stone-Poole-Page refer—to everyone's confusion—to the original text of 1743.

and these figures are allowed to express to us, the onlookers, their actuating emotions. In this way the affective qualities of the imagery peculiar to this kind of art and the psychological effect of the kind and its imagery are merged in one another. The first references are to Greek tragedy. This, we are told, affords "speaking scenes" and these we follow with "kind concern," pity, and overflowing eyes. The writer then devotes a verse paragraph to his second kind, the comedy of Greece and Rome, and we note that here he merely refers to the historical fact that Menander and after him the Latin dramatists practiced this art; he passes over the scenes that bring laughter— he does not tell us why, though we are free to conjecture. The love poetry of the Troubadours and the Florentine lyricists is graceful, wanton, full of "gay description" that "could not fail to move." In the dramatic scenes given us by Fletcher, we find "each flowing thought that warms the female mind" and lovers' sighs and tears. Such scenes we follow "with pleas'd attention." But Shakespeare is manlier than Fletcher, portraying "our rude passions," and the writer of the *Epistle* becomes a spectator at Shakespeare's history plays, watching "with glad surprise" as the "majestic forms of mighty monarchs" take the stage and become expressive figures: "There Henry's trumpets spread their loud alarm," "Here gentler Edward claims a pitying sigh," and in his final hours Richard III experiences horror as the ghost of the murdered Edward V appears before him. Then follows the finest passage in the entire *Epistle* (lines 93–100)—the only one, indeed, in which we are likely today to feel that Collins attains genuine poetry—as we turn from Shakespeare's history plays to the idyllic ones like *The Tempest*, finding everywhere "Some sweet illusion of the cheated mind": humble shepherds, contented in their quiet scenes; twilight fairies; smiling woods and valleys; an enchanted island which "Spring diffusive decks." Finally, the wish is voiced that the expressive power of pictorial art might be united with poetry as powerful as Shakespeare's, and as examples of what might result therefrom we are asked to look at two imaginary canvases, one portraying Anthony at Caesar's bier, the other depicting the scene between Volumnia and Coriolanus:

> Touch'd to the soul, in vain he strives to hide
> The son's affection, in the Roman's pride:
> O'er all the man conflicting passions rise,
> Rage grasps the sword, while Pity melts the eyes.

The *Ode on the Popular Superstitions of the Highlands of Scotland* has much in common with the *Epistle to Hanmer*. Though cast as an ode, it is after all an epistle as well, being addressed to John Home, the dramatist and friend of Collins. And its subject is poetry, or more specifically the different kinds of poetry that Home may fashion from the materials given in Scottish folklore and verse. There is no need to go though the *Ode* passage by passage as we have with the *Epistle to Hanmer*, but the things in it that bear upon our present discussion should be mentioned briefly. In the opening stanza, tragedy is referred to and its power to melt our hearts. Stanza II describes the kind of poetry that Home may command if he chooses to use his Doric quill, that is, a simple, pastoral style, in treating fanciful themes dear to the untutored Scottish peasantry. From Stanza III through Stanza VIII, "strange lays" are described (dirges, tales of war, tales by some "gifted wizzard seer") and the moving stories they contain and the powerful scenes they portray. With "varied stile" (Stanza IX), Home may seek still further themes in "each cold Hebrid isle." The most stirring of all the stanzas, the eleventh, justifies all these "false themes" on the grounds that Shakespeare himself made use of material like this in *Macbeth*. In short, the *Ode* continues the sort of exposition given in the earlier *Epistle:* exposition in terms of different "kinds" and the theme of each kind, the theme being resolved into imagery and psychological effect.

III

It has been said repeatedly that the subject of the *Odes on Several . . . Subjects* is the nature of poetry. This is a statement that needs careful examination, by which I mean that it should send us back to the *Odes* to test the truth of the assertion against what the twelve poems in the volume are able to tell us about themselves. One very obvious thing that they reveal is preoccupation with the kinds. Odes I and II[4] ("To Pity" and "To Fear") concern themselves with tragic drama. Ode III ("To Simplicity") has pastoral poetry steadily in view. The next to the last ode, "The Manners" (XI), addresses itself to what Bishop Hurd was to refer to[5] as that kind of poetry which, in distinction from both the poetry of the heart and the passions and the poetry of the imagination, has men and manners for its theme; it is, in other words, moral and social poetry, akin to comedy in the sphere of drama. "The Passions. An Ode for Music" (XII) is the twelfth and final piece. As has generally been recognized, it is not only an ode *for* music but an ode *about* music—about the evocative power of an art allied, like the art of painting, to the literary arts.

What of the seven remaining odes? Do any of them turn out to be

[4] In *Odes on Several . . . Subjects,* the individual odes are given by title only. The numbers I have supplied for convenience.

[5] In Letter X of his *Letters on Chivalry and Romance* (1762).

similar, in respect of this preoccupation with the kinds, to the five we have just looked at? Only, I think, "On the Poetical Character" (IV). I grant that this ode is a controversial one, but I believe that Garrod was at least going in the right direction when he pointed out that it is really about John Milton.[6] Its title is somewhat misleading in that it may seem to suggest that there is only one sort of poetical "character": namely, that set forth in the poem. It is this ambiguity that has perhaps led so many commentators to the belief that the *Odes on Several . . . Subjects* is about the nature of poetry *tout court* and that in the fourth poem Collins is, as it were, summing up his essential and inclusive poetic. To begin with, it is not Collins who is speaking here but, as we point out when engaging in elementary analysis, the "I" of the poem or, what amounts to the same thing, the poem itself. And in view of the logic that controls the first three and the last two poems in the volume, are we not drawn to the conclusion that "On the Poetical Character" signalizes not John Milton but rather the *kind* of poetry—Sublime Poetry—that Milton created in *Paradise Lost?* The *Odes*, let us remind ourselves, is on "several" "subjects." The "diction" referred to in the epigraph—"May I be a discoverer of diction . . . ," the usual translation of the lines from Pindar's ninth Olympian given on the title page—does not necessarily imply one and only one kind of diction. Indeed, the emblematic wreath that lies immediately below the quotation from Pindar points, whatever the precise interpretation of the different leaves, to distinct orders of poetic art.[7]

Half of the odes are thus accounted for. Reading the other six in search of their self-revealing qualities, there is no reason that I can see for dissenting from Garrod's opinion[8] that five of them constitute a series of patriotic poems, a series interrupted by the "Ode to Evening" (IX). It would be possible, I suppose, to find in the "Ode to Liberty" (VII) some evidence that the poem is giving the shape, movement, and spirit of an exalted kind of patriotic ode, elaborately formal; but I do not think it defines a kind in the way that the first six we have discussed do. It functions in a different way and is similar to the "Ode Written in the Beginning of the Year 1746" (V), the "Ode to Mercy" (VI), the "Ode, to a Lady on the Death of Colonel Ross" (VIII), and the "Ode to Peace" (X). In all of these five pa-

[6] In his Warton Lecture, "The Poetry of Collins" (*Proceedings of the British Academy* [1928]), he calls it an ode on the poetical character of Milton.

[7] Edmund Blunden called attention to the nature of the title page in his introductory study in his edition of *The Poems of William Collins* (1929).

[8] Set forth clearly in his *Collins* (1928).

triotic odes the primary themes are associated less with aspects of creative art than with the qualities of patriotic citizenship.

What of the "Ode to Evening"? Collins's magnificent pastoral—one of the two great artistic achievements in the 1746 volume—may be regarded, to be sure, as a statement about pastoral poetry. Indeed, it opens as though it were going on to define its kind of pastoral music. There is, however, a rapid transition to another music, the music of nature, which by line 10 has completely taken over and is sustained to the end, though it comes to be intermingled with natural sights and colors. All this is merely another way of saying that the triumph of the "Ode to Evening" lies in the fact that analysis of effect has here become, superbly, the effect itself. But what of its position in the midst of the patriotic odes? Does this signify anything? Is any connection being suggested between pastoralism and patriotism? Certainly the "Ode to Simplicity" establishes (stanzas VI and VII) a link between pastoralism and freedom; and "smiling *Peace*" in line 50 of the original version of the "Ode to Evening" brings civic well-being into association with the pastoral mood. The finest of all the patriotic poems is "How Sleep the Brave." Here pastoralism and the emotions felt by those who remember their country's dead have been fused in one of the great imaginative passages in our poetry. It is quite possible, I think, that the position of the "Ode to Evening" is an expression of a close relationship: pastoralism extends itself to include themes that arise from patriotism.

IV

There would seem to be, then, two groups of poems within the *Odes*, the group of six (I, II, III, IV, XI, XII), which point to certain kinds, and the patriotic group of five (V, VI, VII, VIII, X). "The Ode to Evening" (IX) appears to stand midway between the two groups, at once defining the mood of the pastoral and bringing pastoralism and patriotism close to one another.

Looking again to the odes, we may briefly take note of certain of the devices through which are effected the statements that the poems are making. In the six poems that point to the kinds, the most obvious device is, of course, personification. One says "of course," but one recognizes even while saying so that the personifications work at two levels and really operate in two somewhat different ways. In Ode I, for instance, Pity is a rational generalization, a defining term that points to the tragic species of drama. But it is also an allegorical figure on whom a certain existential quality is being bestowed by means of the descriptions of the emblems of Pity. The patriotic poems are not without their figures of personification, but I think these figures will be found to function somewhat differently, as has already been pointed out in Section III above. A clear example of this different manner is to be seen in the "Ode to Mercy," where the figure of Mercy, though she does indeed sing songs to Valour and is therefore among other things a kind of poetry, is not invoked for the purpose of inspiring creative literary effort but rather as a spirit who civilizes the behavior of a warring nation.

Another device, general throughout the volume, is that of expressive and dramatic imagery. In the *Epistle to Hanmer* we have seen how objective description (e.g., "With graceful ease the wanton lyre he strung, / Sweet flow'd the lays—but love was all he sung" [lines 41–42] gives way at times to moving and speaking images (Mark Anthony at Caesar's bier [lines 115–20]; Coriolanus standing over his mother [lines 127–32]). It is when the images in the *Odes* come to life, when imaginative drama takes over, that we have those weird, vivid, unforgettable passages, like the famous one in the "Ode to Fear":

> For lo what *Monsters* in thy Train appear!
> *Danger*, whose Limbs of Giant Mold
> What mortal Eye can fix'd behold?
> Who stalks his Round, an hideous Form,
> Howling amidst the Midnight Storm,
> Or throws him on the ridgy Steep
> Of some loose hanging Rock to sleep:
> And with him thousand Phantoms join'd,
> Who prompt to Deeds accurs'd the Mind. . . .

There would seem to be a good deal less of such arresting effects in the patriotic poems and the "Ode to Evening," enclosed by them. In these the imagery is no less expressive; but as is so strikingly the case with the "Ode . . . 1746" and the "Ode to Evening," it is expressive in that it has become, so fully, so perfectly, that which it is evoking.

The subtlest of all the devices is the matching of odic form to each ode's substance and spirit. The different forms exhibited by the twelve odes have long since been set forth in detail, and commentators have doubtless come to feel that it would be pressing home the obvious to emphasize how form is in each case expressively appropriate. But it is so important that the reader of the *Odes* be alert to what is being conveyed through the formal patterns that this aspect may well be stressed again and again. The shift from Pity in Ode I to Fear in II brings a corresponding shift—I begin with the perfectly obvious —from the six-line stanza and its quiet movement to a form that provides a wider register, one that extends at its upper limits to the frenzied. And we observe that the six-line stanza of the "Ode to Pity" reappears in the "Ode, to a Lady on the Death of Colonel

Ross" and in the "Ode to Peace," each time conferring its special emotional quality. A traditional contrast running through seventeenth- and eighteenth-century poetry had been one between the Pindaric ode and the Horatian, and this is reflected in the *Odes*. We may probably regard the three poems employing the six-line stanza as presenting a variant—a "Greek" one—of the quieter Horatian ode. But it is among the pastoral pieces and the patriotic ones that we find what is more typically Horatian. The "Ode to Simplicity," the "Ode ... 1746" and the "Ode to Evening" are all essentially Horatian, and it is noteworthy that the first and last of these have borrowed their forms from Milton, in the one case from the scheme of the first six lines of the *Nativity* stanza, in the other from the translation of Horace's fifth ode of the first book.

One final point. In the poems that are speaking primarily about the kinds, we have repeatedly in the closing lines that sort of identification between symbolic figure and speaker that occurs in both *L'Allegro* and *Il Penseroso*. In the final stanza of the "Ode to Pity," we have, for instance,

> There let me oft, retir'd by Day
> In Dreams of Passion melt away,
>   Allow'd with Thee to dwell:
> There waste the mournful Lamp by Night,
> Till, Virgin, Thou again delight
>   To hear a *British* Shell!

The action to which the poem looks forward is the action of a creative writer hopeful of directing his talents toward a certain artistic end. The patriotic poems, on the other hand, urge some form of public action, sometimes doing so in quite obvious terms, and once—in the "Ode ... 1746"—with such subtlety and imaginative control that the act is forgotten in the overpowering emotion that attends the commemorative ceremony.

V

All poems, I suppose, if they are in any way worth reading, have to be read in many different ways simultaneously. Assuredly this is true of the twelve poems that comprised Collins's *Odes on Several Descriptive and Allegoric Subjects*. In my present discussion, I have taken as my starting point what I believe to be the scheme of the volume and have tried to confine myself to those things which seem, by the logic of composition, to depend thereon. Such a procedure most emphatically does not, nor is it intended to, yield a full reading that does justice to the polythematic character of any poetry of a higher order. Nor is it a method that lends itself with equal readiness to the poetry of every period. But eighteenth-century poetry is characteristically organized around a core of compositional logic, showing in this respect a kind of ordering that is close to that given in rhetoric. Such organization is true not only of the poetry of the more conventional variety—Pope's, Goldsmith's, Johnson's—but of poetry like Collins's, marked by the new aestheticism.

Which leads to the first of several comments that I should like to make by way of summary. The *Odes on Several . . . Subjects* is not about The Poet, it is not about William Collins, but it is about different kinds of poetry, their different kinds of imagery, their different effects. Was Collins a preromantic poet? The question can be answered in different ways, one of which is by pointing out that his preoccupation with the kinds places him in one important respect within a strictly neo-classical poetic.

The second comment is this. The organizational principle that we have been speaking of, seen not only in the design of the *Odes* as a whole and in the relation of each piece to the others but in the appropriate form disclosed by each poem, might well be kept in mind when we consider the charge so often brought against Collins that he was too often arty in the worst sense. What may strike us at first as overly elaborate and fussy is, we should remember, part of a comprehensive aesthetic purpose. Invariably the form, whether simple as in the case of the great "Ode . . . 1746" or ornate as in the "Ode on the Poetical Character," is an organic part of the achieved effect. There is a clarity about all this which is proof, it would seem, that an art that is essentially rococo and therefore to be regarded by some in a patronizing way is marked nevertheless by an integrity of craftsmanship. Collins's imaginative endowment has never been questioned. But there is not so wide a gap between his intuition and his execution as much of the critical writing on him has assumed.

And finally, let it always be remembered that there are poems in the 1746 volume which, when read with any understanding and sympathy, disclose Collins's deep emotional engagement. The patriotism of the *Odes* is a far-reaching thing. It goes beyond Mercy, Liberty, and Peace to the very soul of the nation. Collins used his art not for self-expression, not for the sheer pleasure of exercising certain aesthetic techniques, but for two purposes that must have seemed to him very close to each other: for exploring the resources of poetry, and for expressing the hopes and desires of a civilized community.

JEAN H. HAGSTRUM

William Blake's "The Clod & the Pebble"

B LAKE'S FAMOUS THREE-STANZA song of experience, "The Clod & the Pebble," has teased some of us out of thought for so many years that it may well be asked why anyone would now wish to add another to the many voices that have spoken about it. The reason is, mostly, that it lives in the memory as a poem with greater unity and a sharper and a less conventionally sentimental meaning than its commentators have usually ascribed to it.

Exactly one half of the poem—six lines—one and one-half stanzas—is devoted to the Clod.

> Love seeketh not Itself to please.
> Nor for itself hath any care:
> But for another gives its ease
> And builds a Heaven in Hells despair.
>
> So sang a little Clod of Clay
> Trodden with the cattles feet: . . .

This portion of the poem is illustrated by the design at the top of the page (Plate I). One ram, two oxen, and several sheep stand by a dead or dying tree and drink at a brook.

The second half of the poem, exactly equal in length to the first, concerns the Pebble.

> But a Pebble of the brook
> Warbled out these metres meet.
>
> Love seeketh only Self to please
> To bind another to its delight:
> Joys in anothers loss of ease
> And builds a Hell in Heavens despite.

These lines are illustrated by a duck on a brook and two frogs on the water's edge, one of whom merely sits while the other leaps as

JEAN H. HAGSTRUM is Professor of English and Chairman of the Department at Northwestern University.

though after prey. A worm or snake lies between the two frogs. Scourge-like leaves and ribbon-like branches connect the top and bottom design; and the visual arrangement of the page implies that, since the animals at the top are on one side of the water and the creatures at the bottom on the other, the text of the poem has taken the place of the brook—a typically Blakean conceit that suggests the organic relation of all elements of his form.

Yeats and Ellis say that the poem brings out a basic principle in Blake that must always be remembered: "the great idea, that everything can be seen in a good or an evil aspect, yet its individuality remains the same."[1] But which is the good, and which the evil, aspect? To most commentators there seems to have been little doubt. The author of the *Songs of Innocence* and the believer in a Christ who will unite all mankind in forgiving love and thus usher in the New Jerusalem must be praising unselfish love. The "pliable" Clod, which has in it "the germs of higher life," is "chosen quite appropriately to represent unselfish love. The Pebble, on the other hand, is completely dead; it lies in the water, which . . . to Blake meant always materialism."[2] Or, again, the Pebble, a symbol of selfhood and the "usurpation of divinity," is related to the God of this world, his priests, and the selfish father with "cold and usurious hand," whereas the Clod represents man's divine desire to love "another as itself."[3] Or, once again, the Clod is the familiar "Clay" of *Thel*—"the pliable earth capable of fertility and growth"—and the hard, rounded Pebble is "incapable of anything, sterile and without plasticity."[4]

Such interpretations, which, without actual count, seem to predominate, have much to recommend them. Blake did believe in unselfish divine love. He began his career hymning its presence in the world of innocent nature and ended his literary work by proclaiming its triumph at the final apocalypse—at "the Great Harvest & Vintage of the Nations" (*Milton*, plate 43). But plausible though the majority view may at first seem, this paper aims to overturn it—to turn it upside down, as a matter of fact, and argue that the Pebble, not the Clay, is Blake's *raisonneur*.

More often than not, commentary on Blake has suffered from excessive exuberance. Dryden, Mrs. Radcliffe, Byron, Shelley, and

[1] *The Works of William Blake* (London, 1893), II, 12.

[2] S. Foster Damon, *William Blake: His Philosophy and Symbols* (London, 1924), pp. 279–80.

[3] Robert F. Gleckner, *The Piper & the Bard* (Detroit, 1959), pp. 75, 25, 259.

[4] Mark Schorer, *William Blake: The Politics of Vision* (New York, 1959), pp. 205–6.

Wordsworth have been quoted to illuminate Blake's meaning, to say nothing of Milton and Shakespeare, those mighty influences upon his genius. But in most of these cases, the meaning of the parallel passage, even when it is demonstrably Blake's source,[5] usually contributes very little to untangling his meaning—so original and even eccentric is his adaptation of what he borrows. Nor, in interpreting his symbols, will the quality of the object, as we see it or as his contemporaries have seen it, help interpretation. Quite the contrary, such an approach may separate us from Blake's own unique angle of vision. The fact that a pebble is round and hard and that a clod of clay is pliant earth in which seeds germinate is of very little relevance. The moon and the stars that drove most romantics to fits of careless rapture were symbols to Blake of Old Nobodaddy's reign—which, Blake said, weakened and even obliterated his imagination. And although it is more useful to ask Blake to illuminate Blake than to turn to Byron or to nature, even here the interpreter must be wary. In the *Marriage of Heaven and Hell*,[6] the eagle represents genius, but in *Jerusalem*,[7] a screaming famished eagle, with bony wings, apparently stands for death and destruction. A man with arms spread out can be either Christ or Urizen. Within the same poem both the hero Orc and the priests who are his antagonists are symbolized by serpents.[8] The horse can mean radically different things: there are the dull and respectable horses of instruction in the *Marriage*,[9] the eternal horses of revolutionary deliverance in the "Song of Liberty" (No. 20), and, on a single page, the "Horse of Intellect" (that is, the Pegasus of Inspiration that leaps into the sky) or the dead horses of instruction that are repelled by the celestial spheres.[10]

Damon says that water, being the old Catholic symbol of death—a fact that has no relevance whatever—always means materialism to Blake. That surely depends on what kind of water Blake is talking about: water in "the cistern that contains" or in "the fountain that overflows."[11] Schorer cites as parallel to the little Clod of this poem the "Clod of Clay" that Thel encounters and that exhales her life in

[5] Damon convincingly cites the *Midsummer Night's Dream*, I, i, 206–7; II, i, 243 (*op. cit.*, p. 279).

[6] ix, 15.

[7] IV, xciv, 15.

[8] *America* viii, 1; xv, 19–20.

[9] ix. 5.

[10] "A Descriptive Catalogue" (1809), Nos. vi and viii, in *The Complete Writings of William Blake*, ed. Geoffrey Keynes (London, 1958), p. 581 (hereafter referred to as *CW*).

[11] *Marriage of Heaven and Hell*, viii, 15 (*CW*, p. 151).

milky fondness over the infant worm. The parallel is striking and may be apposite, for the two poems are not widely separated in date. But Blake's clay can also be selfish and can stand variously for the moon of Enion (that gloomy fallen sea-goddess), for that deceitful daughter of Albion, Gwendolyn, who dances to the timbrel of war, and for Urizen himself. For in the book named after him Urizen provokes this comment by the Eternals, who contemplate his fall and stony sleep:

> What is this? Death.
> Urizen is a clod of clay.[12]

Of all these clods of clay, which is closest to the Clod of this poem? *Urizen* is the nearest in date, for it was published in 1794, the year in which the *Songs of Experience* were combined with the *Songs of Innocence*. It is also the closest in meaning, as the poems that surround "The Clod & the Pebble" in the *Songs of Experience* amply demonstrate. The accompanying design, with a dead or dying tree that forms a border and with ribbon-like vegetation and sharp leaves that surround the text, so unlike the lusher, greener, more appealing vegetation of Innocence, establishes its affinity with other poems written out of disillusioning Experience. The Clod sings that love "builds a Heaven in Hells despair." The pitiable Chimney Sweeper sings that God, the Priest, and the King—and the boy's parents too—"make up a heaven of our misery." Urizen, the "Human Abstract" in the poem of that name, says of two of the virtues that in Innocence Blake had associated with love and peace:

> Pity would be no more
> If we did not make somebody Poor;
> And Mercy no more could be
> If all were as happy as we.

In the same poem, the tyrannous god of the Establishment sits down and waters with his tears the tree of humility that takes root "Underneath his foot." In "The Clod & the Pebble," the Clay is trodden with the cattle's feet as it sings its self-effacing song.

The Pebble, which has been much vilified for being selfish, sings of a love that brings pleasure to the self and loss of ease to another. Its selfishness resembles that of the child in "A Little Boy Lost," who is burned at the stake as a fiend by a priest in a holy place. The lad

---

[12] *Vala*, ix, 629 (*CW*, p. 374); *ibid.*, iii, 395 (*CW*, p. 290); *Jerusalem*, III, lvi, 27–28 (*CW*, p. 688); *Urizen*, vi, 11–12 (*CW*, p. 226).

In the famous color print, entitled "Elohim Creating Adam," now in the Tate Gallery, the Urizenic deity, who hovers over the suffering Adam, picks up a "clod of clay" with his left hand. The clod is here associated not only with Urizen but with the disaster of material creation.

had refused to repeat the pieties about parental love but had instead confessed frankly that "Nought loves another as itself," pointing to the little bird "That picks up crumbs around the door" as an example of healthy natural egotism. In a manuscript poem from the Note-Book of 1793 an angel praises the virtues of mercy, pity and peace, but a devil curses them as the results of poverty and unhappiness. The devil is right:

> And Mercy & Pity & Peace descended
> The Farmers were ruin'd & harvest was ended. . . .
> And Miseries' increase
> Is Mercy, Pity, Peace.[13]

These poems provide the proper perspective of Blake's view in the early 1790's of the mercy and love of Innocence and also of selfish— even aggressive—physical love that the Pebble praises. The *Marriage of Heaven and Hell* and the Lambeth prophecies are also germane. In the *Marriage*,[14] the sneaking serpent walks in mild humility and the good man must roar like Rintrah. Angelic piety can neither sow nor reap, but diabolical energy—the energy of sexual appetite and bodily impulse—can cut a deep furrow. In the *Book of Urizen*,[15] the tyrant sheds the tears of Pity as he weaves and spreads his religious net; and in *Europe*,[16] he feeds his soul with Pity. In the *Song of Los*, those "merciful" institutions of organized Pity and love, the hospitals and churches, are, along with palaces and castles, "nets & gins & traps to catch the joys of Eternity."[17]

If these poems do in fact constitute the proper context for "The Clod & the Pebble," then one must read it in "its infernal or diabolical sense"—the sense in which Blake was trained by the revolutionary devil to read his Bible. Hell is good, heaven is evil; angels are conventional and "established," devils are wise and active. In such a reading of the poem, value resides with the Pebble, who makes a revolutionary hell out of heaven, not with the Urizenic Clod, who makes a conventional heaven out of hell. The poet of Experience perceives that unselfish love is also a passive, acquiescent love, the kind recommended by the wardens of charity schools, the kind that sanctions and entrenches poverty and degradation. The love that the Pebble recommends in a song that the poet calls "meet" is aggressive and selfish and may give pain. But it is as salutary as the corrosives of hell. "Damn braces; Bless relaxes."[18]

---

[13] *CW*, p. 164.

[14] ii, 17–20.

[15] xiv, 52–59.

[16] xii, 4.

[17] iv, 1–2.

[18] *Marriage of Heaven and Hell*, ix, 18.

The accompanying design (Plate I) seems to support the "hellish" meaning we have derived from the words and from their context in Experience. The sheep at the top huddle, their heads bent down toward the earth—in the manner of Experience, not of Innocence. They resemble the herds on the first plate of Blake's *Job* (Plate II), where the family worships a legalistic deity, but not on the last plate, where the redeemed family worships the divine imagination in song and music. The oxen have the open, disillusioned eyes of experience, that anticipate the haunting expressions that Blake gave his Four Zoas, those gods in pain who preside over fallen nature, who in the *Expulsion* ride their staring horses through the sky as Adam and Eve leave Eden (Plate III). More specifically, the staring kine of this page remind us of one of the Zoas, Luvah, the Bull or Ox of Ezekiel's vision, who appears in Blake's *Comus* illustrations, the Genesis fragment, an illustration to Dante, and the painting entitled "Four and Twenty Elders." "The Clod & the Pebble" is too early a poem for the details of Blake's later myth to be relevant in all its refinements. But the cattle do enforce the impression that we are in the world of Experience—of fallen nature and of an oppressive society that calls for passive humility and obedience. But at the bottom of the page the water runs, the pebble warbles, a frog leaps—details that contrast with the death-like positions of the cattle. As on the title page of the *Marriage of Heaven and Hell*, energy rises from below.

Blake's hatred of placid institutionalized pity and his faith in unrepressed, natural, and aggressive love, though peculiarly intense in his revolutionary period, existed before and after the decade of the nineties, when he hoped the flame of revolutionary violence would burn up the Establishment, root and branch. He was capable of expressing these views even when they did not dominate his philosophical and social thought—even during the days when he hailed those four daughters of the Voice of God, Mercy, Pity, Peace, and Love, in one of his loveliest Songs of Innocence. He also carried his revolutionary slant on love into his last period, the period of the great Christian epics and the great Christian art.

Blake's attack on false, Urizenic pity began early, long before he had created Urizen, his solid and unforgettable personification of social and intellectual evil. He had early joined Lavater in his attack on the "pietist who crawls" and had exclaimed, "I hate crawlers." Lavater had said, conventionally, "where pride begins, love ceases." Blake reacts, "Pride may love!" Blake confessed he was unable to love his enemy or to forgive the "frigid, smiling crawler." "Active Evil is better than Passive Good."[19]

[19] Annotations to Lavater, *CW*, pp. 67, 68, 79, 77.

In his latest myth, when he had dedicated himself to "the Divine Pity" as the only force that could heal society and when he declared that "we must not be tyrants also"—a disinclination to fight fire with fire that was not characteristic of his revolutionary period—Blake was greatly occupied with those antithetical twins, false pity and true (even selfish) individuality. Pity is a gate that leads from Beulah to Ulro, the land of materialistic negation of all value. Satan, who in the later epics takes over Urizen's role as the god of this world, is, like his predecessor, impelled by pious pity. Satan, one of the Elect, is a person of "incomparable mildness," a hypocrite capable of "seeming a brother" but "being a tyrant"—a man of mild manners, mild speech, and mild curses. The poet's hero, Los, attacks pity as an unmanly quality, and all in all a considerable number of the many lines in Blake's late epics are devoted to this attack. Even outside the epics, in a poem like "William Bond," the man (who loves ruddy, sunny, daylight affection and selfish, natural, uninhibited love) frightens Mary Green (who loves the piteous, moaning, "moony" love that Blake always found characteristic of fallen nature).[20]

Blake's attack on Christian mildness is so persistent that it must have been mounted from deep within his psyche. Many of his contemporaries he assailed in the same terms he used to denigrate Satan. The despised Reynolds's praise of Blake's culture-hero, Michelangelo, provoked this outburst: " 'Tis Christian Mildness when Knaves Praise a Foe."

Blake, who late in life still refused to profess "Generosity to a Foe," could not resist deriding his patron Hayley's ostensible subservience to the Sermon on the Mount:

> To forgive Enemies H. does pretend,
> Who never in his Life forgave a friend.

Blake liked—or at least could tolerate—Fuseli, precisely because he was not pretentiously and impossibly "Christian":

> The only Man that e'er I knew
> Who did not make me almost spew
> Was Fuseli: he was both Turk & Jew—
> And so, dear Christian Friends, how do you do?[21]

Blake's Jesus was not "Christian" in the manner of Hayley, Reynolds, and the Establishment. The true Jesus, that is—for there

---

[20] *Milton*, I, vii, 27 (*CW*, p. 487); *Vala*, viii, 26–31 (*CW*, p. 341); *Milton*, I, vii, 6, 24 (*CW*, pp. 486–87); *ibid.*, I, viii, 19–20 (*CW*, p. 488); "William Bond," Poems from the Pickering MS (*CW*, pp. 434–36).

[21] MS Note-Book 1808–11 (*CW*, pp. 539, 541, 544, 551).

were two. The first was the unselfish, gentle, humble, chaste, obedient, filial god of conventional religion, the "Yea Nay Creeping Jesus," whom Blake hated to his dying day.[22] The other Jesus, whose portrait is drawn in "The Everlasting Gospel," deserted his parents at an early age, rode a chariot of fire, wielded a scourge, acted with "triumphant, honest pride," and

> His Seventy Disciples sent
> Against Religion & Government.

The first Jesus, "Humble as a Lamb or Ass," is descended from the Clod of Clay in the *Songs of Experience*. The second, who taught us our own humanity to adore and to be guided by the "Spirit of Life," is, though more remotely, descended from the selfish Pebble of the brook.[23]

[22] Blake died 12 August 1827. On 12 April he wrote to George Cumberland: "God keep me from the Divinity of Yes & No too, the Yea Nay Creeping Jesus" (*CW*, p. 878).

[23] *The Everlasting Gospel*, Draft *b*, ll. 1, 34; Draft *c*, ll. 1, 25–26, 29, 40–41; Draft *d*, l. 77; Draft *i*, ll. 37–38 (*CW*, pp. 748, 749, 750, 753, 757).

The CLOD & the PEBBLE

Love seeketh not Itself to please,
Nor for itself hath any care;
But for another gives its ease,
And builds a Heaven in Hells despair.

So sang a little Clod of Clay,
Trodden with the cattles feet:
But a Pebble of the brook,
Warbled out these metres meet.

Love seeketh only Self to please,
To bind another to its delight:
Joys in anothers loss of ease,
And builds a Hell in Heavens despite.

PLATE I. *Songs of Innocence and Experience.* (The Rosenwald Collection, Library of Congress.)

PLATE II. Illustration to the Book of Job (Plate 1). (The Huntington Library, San Marino, California.)

PLATE III. Illustration to *Paradise Lost:* The Expulsion. (The Huntington Library, San Marino, California.)

FREDERICK A. POTTLE

Boswell as Icarus

Among the boswell papers that came to Yale University from Malahide Castle in 1950 is a handsome printed diploma with manuscript additions announcing in very florid Italian that the noble and learned Signor James Boswell, Baron of Auchinleck in Scotland, being vouched for by our well-born and valorous fellow shepherds Carillo Maratonio and Filandro Lampidiano, has been made an Arcadian shepherd with the name of Icaro. He may now recite his compositions in the Parrhasian Grove and in a year's time may petition the learned College of Arcadia to invest him with title to the country that the College is reserving for him. A postscript announces that the College has suspended its ordinance requiring a wait of a year and is forthwith granting to the said well-born and valorous Icaro the Tarsensine countries, so that for the future his style will be Icaro Tarsense (Icarus of Tarsus). The diploma is initialed by the Keeper General Mireo Rofeatico, is signed by the Under Keeper Filillo Lipareo, and is dated from the Store Shed[1] in the Parrhasian Grove on the first day of Sciroforione, the fourth year of the 635th Olympiad, the third year of the nineteenth Olympiad from the founding of the Arcadia.

Discussion of the various delightful puzzles that this document presents can best begin with some account of the College of Arcadia,

FREDERICK A. POTTLE is Sterling Professor of English at Yale University.

[1] "Nella Capanna del Serbatojo." The stem of *serbatoio* (Lat. *serv-*) means "to keep, to preserve, to put by." Baretti in his dictionary glosses the word as "coop, mew, place in which fowls are kept to be fattened; fish-pond, reservoir"; in his review in *Frusta Letteraria*, later to be mentioned, he remarks sarcastically that, though in Rome *serbatoio* may signify the office of a poetic society, in Florence (i.e., in right Tuscan) it signifies a meat-safe ("Stanzino da serbare Uccellami morti, tanto crudi che cotti, insieme con altre derrate mangiative"). The present-day meaning is "reservoir, tank," *serbatoio della benzina* being what in America would be called a gas tank. The Arcadians could not say straight out "repository of the records" or "archives," but had to resort to such language as they supposed shepherds would have used.

an institution still in existence, though now sadly declined in fame.[2] The paucity of information in English concerning it will excuse the detailing of matter that Italian scholars would consider commonplace.

In the year following the death (1689) at Rome of Queen Christina of Sweden, a group of fourteen men of letters who had been accustomed to meet in her palace and under her protection resolved to continue their association, and for that purpose founded the Arcadia. Their announced purpose was to reclaim Italian poetry from the effete Marinism which in their eyes had almost utterly ruined it—we would say that they were revolting from the metaphysicals. To mark their return to ancient simplicity and truth of feeling, they accepted as inspired the remark of one of their number, "It seems to me that we have this day revived Arcadia," and called themselves the learned or judicious (*saggio*) College of Arcadia. The College took the form of a literary republic with an elective president (*Custode Generale*), and devised for itself a great deal of that seriously taken pastoral machinery which to us seems pretty but rather childish and to our ancestors was soon going to begin to look downright silly. The Arcadians chose pastoral names and conferred them on all newcomers. They revived the Olympic calendar and the Olympic games, substituting poetic for athletic contests, and crowned their victors with laurel in the Parrhasian Grove. It was decreed that at meetings and in converse with one another the pastoral mode should always be employed; in poetry, however, pastoralism was not to be unreasonably pursued. In fact, the principal models of the Arcadians were Pindar and Anacreon among the ancients and Petrarch, Costanzo, and Chiabrera among the Italians; as Giulio Natali well says, their positive function was to elaborate forms which they handed on to the neo-classic poetry of the second half of the eighteenth century. "Thus, from the formal classicism of the Arcadia, we pass to the integral classicism of Parini."

The Arcadia, as a national academy ("the first truly national academy" in Italy), founded branches or "colonies" throughout the

---

[2] For an excellent brief account, see the article "Arcadia" by Giulio Natali in the *Enciclopedia Italiana;* for something more comprehensive, E. Portal, *L'Arcadia* (1922). Vernon Lee's essay, "The Arcadian Academy," in *Studies of the Eighteenth Century in Italy* (1880; reprinted with illustrations, 1908), is the best introduction to the subject in English. For the seventeenth and eighteenth centuries, my principal source has been a very useful compendium printed by an English Arcadian whom I know only as Lariso Salaminio: *Storia dell' Accademia degli Arcadi . . . scritta da Gio. Mário Crescimbeni . . . pubblicata l'Anno 1712.* Londra, T. Becket, 1804. In future reference I shall give this book the short title Crescimbeni, though it actually contains matter that Crescimbeni did not write.

land, and became almost at once extremely numerous. Women as well as men were admitted to membership. Though its official activities were almost exclusively poetical, it took in scientists, composers, painters, jurists, clerics, and men of affairs. By the end of the presidency of the first Custode Generale, Giovanni Mario Crescimbeni (d. 1728), practically everybody in Italy who was of any account was a member of the Arcadia. This popularity, very stimulating at first, could hardly fail to produce a reaction.

For thirty-five years, the Parrhasian Grove at Rome, where in summer outdoor contests in verse and solemn crownings were held, was the garden of a succession of Roman nobles who felt honored to play host to the Arcadia; and the Capanna del Serbatoio was some room or hall of shifting location more fit for winter meetings and the storing of paraphernalia. Then, in 1726, through the munificence of King John V of Portugal, a grateful Arcadian, a steep, narrow triangle of land on the Janiculum was purchased as a permanent Grove for the Academy, set out with laurel trees, and fitted up with paths, a grotto, fountains, and amphitheater. An elaborate portico, consisting of two separate pilastered buildings, stood at the foot of the slope fronting on what is now the Via Garibaldi, about a quarter of a mile from the Porta Settimiana, where the Via Garibaldi now takes a sharp turn to the left. Through the opening between the two halves of the portico, one had a fine vista up the slope of symmetrically disposed flights of steps banked by laurels, curving first around the monumental fountains and a tablet recording the munificence of the donor, then around the grotto (another fountain), and finally, at the top of the slope, terminating in the low elliptical amphitheater backed by a columned *skene*. Statues of Pan and Syrinx faced Pallas and Hermes on the portico, recumbent figures of Tiber, Arno, and Alpheus poured water from their urns, and on the top of the *skene* Pegasus pranced against a background of shrubbery.[3] Though the roofed, two-storied portico contained two smallish rooms and the structure that I have called a *skene* contained two more, these were used only as refuges from the rain or for accommodation of "gran personaggi," the Bosco Parrasio being strictly a place for outdoor meetings. The Capanna del Serbatoio, where indoor meetings were held and the records and the growing collection of portraits of illustrious members were kept, was movable: it was originally situated in the house of the Keeper General near S. Maria in Cosmedin, and

---

[3] Portal, *op. cit.*, pp. 37–38; Crescimbeni, *op. cit.*, pp. 75–95, a detailed description, with a fine engraving, extracted partly from *Notizia del nuovo Teatro degli Arcadi*, by Vettorio Giovardi (1727).

from thence was transferred to a series of houses and palazzi. In 1765, it was apparently in the Palazzo Borghese.[4]

We may begin consideration of our puzzles by identifying the "gentillissimi e valorosissimi pastori" who appear in the diploma as Mireo Rofeatico, Filillo Lipareo, Carillo Maratonio, and Filandro Lampidiano. Mireo Rofeatico is easily found in almost any work dealing with the Arcadia. He was Michele Giuseppe Morei (1696–1766), third Custode Generale, an *abate* and poet of no great reputation at the present day. He had been Custode for twenty-three years when he initialed Boswell's diploma and his hand looks old and shaky, though he was only sixty-nine. He died in the year following. Fillillo Lipareo, the Sotto-Custode, is shown by the registers of the Arcadia now preserved in the Academy's office in the Biblioteca Angelica, Piazza S. Agostino, to have been "Abate Enrico Turner, Romano," but I know nothing whatever about him beyond his name, which is obviously English, Scots, or Irish.[5] I rather doubt that he was an expatriate. Boswell never mentions him, and Boswell was in Rome for the better part of six months and got to know most of the resident exiles. Probably, like the Abate Charles Erskine, later a cardinal, he was the son or grandson of some earlier recusant or Jacobite who had settled in Rome and married there.

The Arcadian registers are imperfect[6] and do not list either of Boswell's sponsors, Carillo Maratonio or Filandro Lampidiano. (For that matter, alas! they do not list Icaro Tarsense.) But the correspondence of an American Arcadian, happily preserved, removes the veil from one of the names. In the Gratz Collection of the Historical Society of Pennsylvania is a long and friendly letter, Rome, 31 August 1765, addressed to Dr. John Morgan (1735–89) and signed Filandro Lampidiano. Morgan has endorsed it, "From Abbey Grant." The Reverend Peter Grant figures prominently in Boswell's Roman notes. A Scotsman, he was Agent in Rome for the Scots Mission and apparently out of sociability and pure goodness of heart served as a sort of ecclesiastical *cicerone* to visiting Britons.[7] It was probably

---

[4] Portal, *op. cit.*, pp. 44–45, 76.

[5] Information from my friend and colleague, Robert Warnock, who kindly searched the registers for me in July 1958. Some twenty years ago, the Arcadia gave its valuable library to the Biblioteca Angelica, with an understanding that it could use the chamber of the Angelica for its meetings.

[6] No new state of affairs. Portal (*op. cit.*, pp. 72–73) says that when Francesco Maria Lorenzini, the second Custode Generale, died, no registration could be found for most of the Arcadians admitted during his term of office (1728–43).

[7] The office of Agent is explained in J. F. S. Gordon, *Ecclesiastical Chronicle for Scotland* (1867), IV, 195, 214–15, in the account of the Scots College at Rome which forms chapter xii of the life (by J. A. Stothert) of Bishop George Hay. The same

he who made it possible for Boswell to attend the Palm Sunday services in the Pope's chapel at Monte Cavallo (the Quirinal); he certainly arranged for him to attend the Maundy Thursday services in the Sistine Chapel at the Vatican and to be presented in private audience to the Pope (Clement XIII), again at Monte Cavallo, on 13 May 1765. Boswell on first meeting Grant thought him an "excellent, obliging, hearty character."[8] He was of about the age of Boswell's father.

Proof that Grant was one of the sponsors gives us a basis for not altogether irresponsible guessing as to the identity of Carillo Maratonio. If Grant's vocation is more significant in this connection than his nationality (and the Arcadia seems to have been managed almost exclusively by *abati*), then Carillo might well have been Charles Erskine, whom Boswell certainly knew—who was, in fact, his relation. If Grant's nationality is the deciding factor, then we might look for Carillo among Britons more or less permanently settled at Rome—Jacobites, artists, antiquaries—with whom Boswell associated. He might have been Andrew Lumisden, Secretary to the Old Pretender; or Gavin Hamilton, painter and excavator of Hadrian's villa; or Colin Morison, antiquary, whom Boswell engaged to give him a course in the antiquities and fine arts of Rome; or James Byres, antiquary of similar profession, who sold Sir William Hamilton the famous Barberini (Portland) vase. They were probably all Arcadians, though I have evidence of membership only for Gavin Hamilton.[9]

The two most interesting questions, however, that the diploma poses are those of its date and Boswell's utter silence concerning his Arcadian honors. Since our answer to the second of these may be affected by our answer to the first, it will be best to turn next to con-

---

work (pp. 560–61) gives a biographical sketch of Peter Grant from the Abbé McPherson's MS, and Grant is frequently mentioned in other parts of the life of Bishop Hay. The Agent represented the Scots Roman Catholic clergy, kept an eye on the Rector of the Scots College (who seems most of the time to have been trying to make Jesuits, not secular priests, out of the seminarians), and acted generally as intermediary between the Scots clergy on the one hand and the Cardinal Protector and Propaganda on the other. Boswell's expense account shows no payments to him. Grant's letter to Morgan was called to my attention by Mrs. Judith S. Chernaik and Dr. Whitfield J. Bell.

[8] Boswell MSS at Yale, J7, 25 Feb., 1 April, 5 April, 14 May 1765. Extracts under all but the first of those dates in *Boswell on the Grand Tour: Italy, Corsica, and France, 1765–1766* (1955).

[9] Vernon Lee includes his name in a list of Arcadians chosen to illustrate the "mongrel" or international character of the serious membership of Arcadia in the 1770's (*Studies of the Eighteenth Century in Italy*, p. 60 of the ed. of 1880, p. 96 of that of 1908). She cites no source and says nothing of having searched the registers, but she probably had good authority.

sideration of the Arcadian calendar. It is an ingenious and amusing construction and may give the reader some ideas about the difficulties of calendar making which will be new to him, though he could find them all in Webster or the *Encyclopædia Britannica.*

The Roman Arcadians were well aware that Olympia was in Elis, not Arcadia, but to a group who wished to institute contests and crown victors with laurel, the machinery of the Olympic games was irresistible—and why be pedantic about a distance of only twenty or twenty-five miles? And if you are looking for machinery, what could be more mystifying and delightful than the Olympic calendar itself? Crescimbeni got a distinguished astronomer among the Arcadians, Francesco Bianchini, to help him work it out.[10] I have not attempted to discover how closely Bianchini's construct follows the antique, having spent quite enough time coming to understand Bianchini, but I am prepared to offer, for the first time, I think, in English, a set of rules for converting Bianchini's Arcadian calendar into the Gregorian.

The machine of the solar system provides three grossly obvious recurrences by which to divide time. The rotation of the earth on its axis gives us the succession of light and darkness and the unit day-and-night (the period from noon to noon); the combined motions of moon orbiting about the earth and of earth orbiting about the sun give us the phases of the moon and the unit we call a month or a lunation (average period from new moon to new moon), and the orbiting of the earth about the sun gives us the succession of the seasons and the unit we call a year. These units are incommensurable, indeed are continually varying, and can be co-ordinated only by resort to occasional *ad hoc* corrections. If we are content, as in our current calendar, to make our months merely arbitrary or conventional divisions with no relation to actual lunations, the adjustment is not too difficult. Since the solar year now consists of 365 days, 5 hours, 48 minutes, and 45+ seconds, we call it 365 and add a day in every year the number of which is divisible by 4. This is a slight overcorrection, so we correct the correction by making century-years common years unless they are divisible by 400. This is still an overcorrection, at the present time, of slightly more than 26 seconds a year, but a surplus of that order will take so long to build up to a day that we can safely ignore it—or rather can leave it to the peoples of the future to adjust.[11] If, however,

---

[10] Crescimbeni, *op. cit.,* pp. 19–20.

[11] If the surplus remained constant at 26 seconds per year, it would amount to a day in 3,323 years, and we should be able to provide satisfactory correction for two hundred centuries (as the 14th *Britannica* suggests in an article originally written in 1830 by Thomas Galloway for the 7th) by making the year 4000 and its multiples common years. But in fact the solar year is decreasing slightly in length and at a not

one insists on bringing in genuine lunations, the co-ordination can be only roughly approximate and the corrections have to be larger and more frequent, for 12 lunations amount to only about 354⅓ days, that is, fall short of a solar year by between 10 and 11 days, whereas 13 lunations run between 18 and 19 days over. No method can be devised that will at the same time make each month start off with a new moon and each year begin at the same distance from a fixed solar event like the equinox or the solstice, but if one is content with occasional conformity, the matter can be patched up.

So far as I am aware, we do not have from Bianchini himself an explanation of the principles underlying his calendar, but are dependent on a "Discorso intorno all' Effemeride Arcadica perpetua, fatto l'Anno 1693" by Crescimbeni.[12] Crescimbeni may have understood the system himself, but his account is careless, confused, and inconsistent. I shall follow his directions so far as they will work and shall then pursue what seems to be the logic of the machine.

Bianchini simplified the problem of co-ordinating the lunar and the solar calendars by bringing them together, and that rather loosely, only on the occasion of the Olympic games, which were held in high summer every fourth year, and by requiring the first day of only one month in 48 or 49—the first month of that fourth year—to fall on a genuine new moon. This new moon could not be far distant from the summer solstice (21 June), but it is not easy to state the rule abstractly. Crescimbeni is very confusing here. By inveterate custom, he says, the crowning of the victors in the Olympic games was held "nel xv. d'Ecatombeone [the first month of the year], e nel plenilunio più vicino [*alternatively,* prossimo] al solstizio estivo." Later he attempts to mend matters by the definition "nell xv. giorno del primo mese, e della più vicina lunazione al solstizio della state,"[13] but this does not cover the ground either. I shall not presume to say how the ancient Olympic calendar operated; but in the first cycle of Bianchini's system the New Year's Day of the contest years, starting at 1 July, seesawed backward and forward between 17 June and 31 July, and 15 Ecatombeone showed a parallel oscillation between 1 July and 14 August. Clearly, the full moon of the crowning day was on many occasions neither that nearest the solstice nor that of the lunation that began nearest the solstice. Judging from

---

wholly predictable rate—in 1900 it measured 365 days, 5 hours, 48 minutes, and 45.97 seconds, whereas by 2000 the seconds will have decreased to 45.44—so that it would not be practical to carry constant rules for correction any farther than the Gregorian system does.

[12] Crescimbeni, *op. cit.*, pp. 42–49.

[13] *Ibid.*, pp. 42, 43, 45, 46, 47.

the first cycle, one could say that the crowning day always falls on a full moon and that that full moon is always either the first or the second after 21 June. But as this, if made a general rule, would make insuperable difficulties in the "perpetual" or long-term working of the system, we had better be content at this point not to fix the posterior limit at the second full moon, but to hold open the possibility that 15 Ecatombeone could fall as late as the *third* full moon after 21 June.[14]

The chronology of the third-century Roman grammarian Censorinus equated A.D. 238 with the second year of the 254th Olympiad. By this reckoning, the second half of A.D. 1692 (the year in which the Arcadian calendar was adopted) would have been the first half of the fourth year of the 617th Olympiad. But for convenience of reckoning, 1 July 1685 in the Gregorian calendar was taken as the starting point, that day being a new moon; 1 July 1685, the New Year's, became consequently the neomenia of Ecatombeone of the first year of the 616th Olympiad. The year was divided into 12 months of 30 days each: Ecatombeone, Metaginnione, Boedromione, Mematterione, Pianessione, Antesterione, Posideone, Gamelione, Elafebolione, Munichione, Targelione, and Sciroforione,[15] and the days of each month were grouped in three decades: "standing month," "moving month," and "falling month" (*mese stante, mese andante, mese cadente*). Since, as we have seen, a lunation does not consist of 30 but of 29.5305882 days (29 days, 12 hours, 44 minutes, and 2.82 seconds), the months, at the end of the first 360 days, would have exceeded the actual lunations by 5.63294 days. The calendar required that this difference, in four years' time, be made up to a full lunation, so that 1 Ecatombeone of the first year of the next Olympiad should coincide with a new moon. For this, seven more days ($5.63294 \times 4 = 22.53177$;

---

[14] If 15 Ecatombeone of contest years had to be either the first or second full moon after 21 June, then the theoretical limits of 1 Ecatombeone could be stated as "not more than 13 days before nor more than 44 days after the summer solstice," i.e., the contest year could begin not earlier than 8 June and not later than 4 August. The actual limits of Bianchini's first cycle are stated in the text. If we are permitted, in the long-range working of the system, to make 15 Ecatombeone the first, second, or third full moon after 21 June, the theoretical posterior limit of 1 Ecatombeone would be extended to 74 days after the summer solstice, and the contest year could begin not earlier than 8 June and not later than 3 September. In the Great Cycle of 2,080 years which I shall later propose, the actual limits of 1 Ecatombeone are 17 June and 25 August, and 15 Ecatombeone ranges from 1 July to 8 September.

[15] In Attic Greek, Hekatombaiōn, Metageitniōn, Boēdromiōn, Maimaktēriōn, Puanepsiōn, Anthestēriōn, Poseideōn, Gamēliōn, Elaphēboliōn, Mounuchiōn, Thargēliōn, Skirophoriōn. This is not the order of Liddell and Scott or of the *Encyclopædia Britannica* (*s.v.* "Calendar"), which run, after Boedromion, Puanepsion, Maimakterion, Poseidion, Gamelion, Anthesterion, but may be assumed to be authoritative for Arcadia.

22.53177 + 7 = 29.53177) were needed. Instead of adding these seven days all at once at the end of the fourth year, the calendar distributed them as "projecting" or "anarchic" days, not included in any month, but standing at the end of each of the four years. And to preserve symmetry, instead of adding two anarchic days to the first three years of each Olympiad and one to the fourth, Bianchini added two to each of the four years and subtracted a day from the last month (Sciroforione) of the fourth year, deleting not the thirtieth day, but the second; that is, omitting 2 Sciroforione altogether in the numbering of the days of this month, and counting 1, 3, 4, etc. The first seven years from 1 July 1685, therefore contained 362, 362, 362, 361, 362, 362, 362 days, respectively.

Now, the correspondence of 1,447 days to 49 lunations, as we have seen above, is a close one (only 25.45 seconds too much annually), and if one could actually synchronize the system at its start with a new moon, 1 Ecatombeone of every fourth year would fall on a new moon for almost 3,400 years. But of course since each Arcadian year has been three or four days shorter than a Gregorian year, 1 Ecatombeone has been steadily moving back into June, and if the eighth year had only 361 days, as it would if the scheme continued to be followed, 15 Ecatombeone of the ninth year (a contest year, when the full moon must come right with regard to the solstice) would have receded 28 days and would fall on the wrong side of 21 June. We therefore intercalate an additional month at the end of every eighth year, calling it Second Sciroforione. At the first intercalation, we give this month 29 days and at the next (end of the sixteenth year) 30 days, and so on, turn and turn about.[16] We now have 5,847 days for 198 lunations, which again is a fairly close correspondence: only 0.0564636 days too little in 16 years, an error that would not build up to a day for more than 280 years.

Actually, long before that time, it is proposed to correct by starting the cycle all over again. Anyone who has performed the calculations thus far will have observed that the Arcadian year is on the average a little longer than the Gregorian (365.4375 days, averaged over 16 years). According to Crescimbeni, this gain in 160 years will be just enough so that we can then omit the usual intercalated month, 1 Ecatombeone will fall on 1 July, 1 July will again be a new moon, we shall be back just where we started, and the calendar is perpetual. Since I find insuperable difficulties in this account, it will be better to quote verbatim and at length:

[16] "For ease of writing," regular Sciroforione is actually given 30 days in the years with intercalated months, and Second Sciroforione is given 28 or 29. In the former case, the days run 1, 4, 5, ... , 30; in the latter, 1, 3, 4, 5, ... , 30.

Con simil regola si avrà ogni quattro Olimpiadi, cioè ogni sedici anni, il circolo perfetto della luna, almeno per conseguire il nostro fine; che la coronazione de' vincitori ne' giuochi Olimpici si faccia nel xv. del primo mese, e della più vicina lunazione al solstizio estivo: di modo che ogni sedici anni tornerà la luna al suo sistema, e l'anno lunare al suo principio; ma non già in tal tempo ritornerà a contrapporsi all' anno solare, richiedendosi, perchè ciò segua quaranta Olimpiadi, cioè anni censessanta Gregoriani, dopo i quali tornando il novilunio più vicino al solstizio estivo, e la Neomenia del primo mese dell' Olimpiade nel primo di Luglio dell' anno Gregoriano si renderà in tal guisa perpetua la nostra Effemeride, sì nell' anno lunare come nel solare.

Debbesi finalmente avvertire, che nel fine d'ogni quarantesima Olimpiade non si dovrà intercalare il solito mese, ma solamente un giorno: tanto avanzando, e non più l'anno solare sopra il lunare in tal tempo: anzi in questo primo circolo dal 1685 al 1845, nè meno tal giorno sarà necessario d'intercalarlo, mercè della correzione di Gregorio, che toglie il bisesto all' anno 1700.[17]

Crescimbeni shows that he is confused by implying that 1800 would be a leap year, and in fact his calculation simply does not work out. It would work out as between the Arcadian and the Julian calendars. In the Julian calendar a year averages 365.25 days, and 160 years amount to 58,440 days. If every block of 16 Arcadian years were composed of 5,847 days $[4(362 + 362 + 362 + 361) + 29 + 30$, average 365.4375], ten such blocks would amount to 58,470 days, or 30 days more than 160 Julian years. If we omitted the last intercalary month of 30 days, the Arcadian and the Julian calendars would indeed exactly coincide: 58,440 days. But under the Gregorian calendar during the historical period 1 July 1685–30 June 1845, 1700 and 1800 were not leap years, and consequently the 160 Arcadian years corresponding would run 32 days longer than the Gregorian, and omission of the intercalary month would not square matters. Olympiad 655.4 would end on 2 July, and to begin a new cycle with 1 July, it would be necessary to *omit* two days. And there is no leeway in the lunar calendar for omissions; on the contrary, to keep the lunar calendar abreast of the actual lunations, we should need to *add* a day, partly to supply the missing half-day of the last intercalation (it will be remembered that Second Sciroforione consists alternately of 29 and 30 days), partly to make up the half day that the accumulated error of the system will have produced in 160 years (see above, p. 397). If we do add one day to the last year of Olympiad 655 in place of the usual intercalary month of 30 days, we shall have a very satisfactory adjustment so far as the lunar calendar is concerned, the

[17] Crescimbeni, *op. cit.*, pp. 47–48.

error being less than 50 minutes for the first Arcadian cycle, or (repeating the adjustment at the end of each cycle) 1 day in 4,700 years.[18] But it is not true either that this correction will place 1 Ecatombeone of the first year of the second cycle on 1 July, or that 1 July 1845 was a new moon. 1 Ecatombeone of Olympiad 656.1 would fall on 4 July 1845, and in fact the new moon next after the summer solstice in 1845 fell on 4 July.[19] The calendar cannot be made "perpetual" in the sense of returning to the same starting point of 1 July every 160 years, but must drift forward on the Gregorian calendar one, two, or three days for each cycle.[20] Crescimbeni is hopelessly wrong as to some details of the first cycle, and has omitted some feature essential to the long-term operation of the system. But if the rules would permit 15 Ecatombeone to fall sometimes as late as the third full moon after 21 June, it is not difficult to see how this drift could be regularly arrested and the calendar returned to its starting point. If we allow the drift to accumulate to 29 days, which would occur at the end of the thirteenth cycle, Olympiads 1096–1135, A.D. 3605–3765, and then omit the usual intercalation of Second Sciroforione (29 days) at the end of 1133.4, making the usual substitution of 1 day for Second Sciroforione at the end of 1135.4, 1 Ecatombeone of the first year of the next Olympiad (1136.1) will fall on 1 July, and we shall be back where we started in 1685. The correspondence of 759,704 days to 25,726 lunations (instead of 759,733 days for 25,727 lunations) is very close, an overcorrection of only 2 hours, 6 minutes, and 40.33 seconds for a period of 2,080 years. The adjustment could be repeated for more than 20,000 years before the surplus built up to a day.[21] In order to purchase such regularity, it

18 If the cycle had run to 58,470 days and 1,980 lunations, the error would have been − 0.564636 days. (See above, p. 397.) But if we complete it in 58,440 days and 1,979 lunations, the error is 58,470.564636 − 58,440 − 29.5305882, or 1.0340478 days. If we increase the cycle to 58,441 days, the error is only 0.0340478 day, or, as stated in the text, 49 minutes, 1.73 seconds in 160 years.

19 *La Connaissance des temps . . . pour l'année 1845, juillet:* "N. L. le 4, à 4^h 39^m du soir." The *Nautical Almanac* for the same year: "N. M. 4D 4H 29.8M."

20 One day when the cycle contains 40 leap years (e.g., the fifth cycle, 2325–2485); two days when it contains 39 (e.g., the third, 2005–2165); three days when it contains 38 (e.g., the first, 1685–1845).

21 See above, p. 398 and n. 18. 1,979 × 13 = 25,727; 25,727 − 1 = 25,726. 25,726 × 29.5305882 = 759,703.9120332. 58,441 × 13 = 759,733; 759,733 − 29 = 759,704; 759,704 days − 759,703.9120332 days = 0.0879668 days = 2 h. 6 min. 40.33 sec. The regularity alleged would not continue indefinitely, for in the fourth and fifth Grand Cycles of each group of five (e.g., A.D. 7,925–10,005 and 10,005–12,085) the drift forward on the Gregorian calendar (assuming it to receive no correction in the period) would be 28 days, not 29. But a discrepancy of two days in the solar cycle over a stretch of 10,400 years would presumably be less than the error in the Gregorian calendar itself if it had remained uncorrected to that date. We are not certain enough of the values involved

does not seem shocking to allow an outdoor summer festival to be held sometimes as late as September—really a better month in Rome than July or August.

But this is pure speculation, and speculation of little historical relevance, for it does not seem likely that the Arcadian calendar was used much after the eighteenth century. I therefore come back to the matter in hand and provide a conversion table for the Arcadian calendar through its first cycle, developing its general principles and correspondences through its first 17 years, and then recording only

TABLE 1

Olympiads and Years, Arcadian	Years, Gregorian	Days, Arcadian	Days, Gregorian	Difference	1 Ecatombeone	15 Ecatombeone
616.1	1685–86	362	365	....	1 July	15 July
2	1686–87	362	365	− 3	28 June	12 July
3	1687–88*	362	.366	− 3	25 June	9 July
4	1688–89	361	365	− 4	21 June	5 July
617.1	1689–90	362	365	− 4	17 June	1 July
2	1690–91	362	365	− 3	14 June	28 June
3	1691–92*	362	366	− 3	11 June	25 June
4	1692–93	390	365	− 4	7 June	21 June
618.1	1693–94	362	365	+25	2 July	16 July
2	1694–95	362	365	− 3	29 June	13 July
3	1695–96*	362	366	− 3	26 June	10 July
4	1696–97	361	365	− 4	22 June	6 July
619.1	1697–98	362	365	− 4	18 June	2 July
2	1698–99	362	365	− 3	15 June	29 June
3	1699–1700[a]	362	365	− 3	12 June	26 June
4	1700–1	391	365	− 3	9 June	23 June
620.1	1701–2	362	365	+26	5 July	19 July

[a] Not a leap year.

the Gregorian dates corresponding to 1 Ecatombeone and 15 Ecatombeone of the first year of each Olympiad. It will be seen that the Arcadian years run in an unvarying series of 362, 362, 362, 361; 362, 362, 362, 390; 362, 362, 362, 361; 362, 362, 362, 391 days; and that when every fourth year in the Gregorian calendar is a leap year, 1 Ecatombeone drops back 3, 3, 4, 4; 3, 3, 4 days and then moves ahead 25 (−4 + 29); drops back 3, 3, 4, 4; 3, 3, 4 days and then moves ahead 26 (−4 + 30). In Table 1 leap years are starred.

It is·apparent that if n is the date of 1 (or 15) Ecatombeone in the first year of a group of seventeen such as the above, the dates in the

---

to make confident computations so far ahead. The proposed Arcadian rule would accomplish all that can reasonably be demanded of such a construction: it would keep the two calendars in exact predicted agreement for as long a time as is practical.

TABLE 2

Olympiads and Years, Arcadian	Years, Gregorian	1 Ecatombeone	15 Ecatombeone
616.1	1685–86	1 July	15 July
617.1	1689–90	17 June	1 July
618.1	1693–94	2 July	16 July
619.1	1697–98	18 June	2 July
620.1	1701–2	5 July	19 July
621.1	1705–6	21 June	5 July
622.1	1709–10	6 July	20 July
623.1	1713–14	22 June	6 July
624.1	1717–18	8 July	22 July
625.1	1721–22	24 June	8 July
626.1	1725–26	9 July	23 July
627.1	1729–30	25 June	9 July
628.1	1733–34	11 July	25 July
629.1	1737–38	27 June	11 July
630.1	1741–42	12 July	26 July
631.1	1745–46	28 June	12 July
632.1	1749–50	14 July	28 July
633.1	1753–54	30 June	14 July
634.1	1757–58	15 July	29 July
635.1	1761–62	1 July	15 July
636.1	1765–66	17 July	31 July
637.1	1769–70	3 July	17 July
638.1	1773–74	18 July	1 August
639.1	1777–78	4 July	18 July
640.1	1781–82	20 July	3 August
641.1	1785–86	6 July	20 July
642.1	1789–90	21 July	4 August
643.1	1793–94	7 July	21 July
644.1	1797–98	23 July	6 August
645.1	1801–2[a]	10 July	24 July
646.1	1805–6	25 July	8 August
647.1	1809–10	11 July	25 July
648.1	1813–14	27 July	10 August
649.1	1817–18	13 July	27 July
650.1	1821–22	28 July	11 August
651.1	1825–26	14 July	28 July
652.1	1829–30	30 July	13 August
653.1	1833–34	16 July	30 July
654.1	1837–38	31 July	14 August
655.1	1841–42	17 July	31 July
656.1	1845–46	4 July[b]	18 July

[a] Leap year fails in 1800.

[b] One day only, instead of the usual 30, is added at the end of 655.4. See above, pp. 397–98.

fifth, ninth, thirteenth, and seventeenth places (1 and 15 Ecatombeone of the first year of the succeeding Olympiads) are given by $n - 14$, $n + 1$, $n - 13$, and $n + 3$ if the corresponding Gregorian calendar shows a leap year every four years. When a leap year fails, the Gregorian date will be advanced by 1: e.g., 1 Ecatombeone of Olympiad 620.1 (1701–2) is $n + 4$, not $n + 3$.

These are supposed to be true new moons and true full moons, but the reader who takes the trouble to verify them by contemporary almanacs, as I have done, will probably be puzzled to find that if one takes the Arcadian day as beginning at midnight, the majority of them will be off by one or two days. On the average, 1 Ecatombeone will be found to begin 28 hours before the new moon with which it is supposed to coincide. This, it could be maintained, is not due to any inaccuracy in the system but to coarseness in its discriminations. The new moon with which the cycle started did not actually occur at the first midnight of 1 July 1685 but at 9 o'clock in the evening of that day,[22] and the system provides nothing but integers to locate values that are all fractional. The irregularities are not erratic but systematic, the calendar being like a clock that runs fairly accurately but is so constructed that its hand jerks from pip to pip and was set fast to begin with. An intriguing and perhaps more plausible defense would be that in the Arcadian, as in the Greek calendar on which it was based, the day began at sunset, not at midnight. In primitive times this happened because actual sighting of the young crescent was necessary for fixing the beginning of a new month, and the custom continued after observation had given way to calculation. An added incentive for beginning the Arcadian day at sunset could have come from the fact that the first new moon of the system did occur shortly after sunset on 1 July 1685. If the Arcadian days ran from sunset to sunset, the average advance of the system would be reduced by as much as 20 hours, and the correspondences would be much more striking.

The values for the second, third, and fourth years of each Olympiad may easily be interpolated by subtracting successively 3, 3, and 4 days from 1 Ecatombeone of the first year of the Olympiad (3, 3, and 3 days if the Olympiad contains a century-year that is not a leap year). Table 3 illustrates with Olympiad 635, which includes the year of Boswell's diploma.

The first, second, and third years in each Olympiad always consist

[22] The London Stationers' Company *Almanack* for 1685 gives the time of the new moon (of course in Old Style, 10 days behind Gregorian) as "52 min. past 7 at night" on 21 June. The conventional difference now between the time of Rome and London is 1 hour; the actual difference, 49 minutes, 48.55 seconds (12°27′08″ of longitude).

of 362 days (12 months of 30 days, plus 2 anarchic days). The fourth year has variously 361 days (11 months of 30 days, 1 month of 29 days, 2 anarchic days); 390 days (12 months of 30 days, 1 month of 28 days, 2 anarchic days), and 391 days (12 months of 30 days, 1 month of 29 days, 2 anarchic days). There are several ways of telling which series a given fourth year belongs in, but the simplest is to divide the Olympiads up into groups of four, as I have done in Table 2. Each one of these boxes corresponds to 16 Olympic years. The fourth year of the first and third Olympiads in each box (e.g., 632.4 and 634.4) has 361 days, the fourth year of the second Olympiad (e.g., 633.4) has 390 days, and the fourth year of every fourth Olympiad that does not end a cycle of 160 years (e.g., 635.4) has 391 days. We have assumed that the last year of a cycle has 362 days.

TABLE 3

Olympiads and Years, Arcadian	Years, Gregorian	Difference	1 Ecatombeone
635.1	1761–62	. . . .	1 July
2	1762–63	−3	28 June
3	1763–64	−3	25 June
4	1764–65	−4	21 June

Because of the perfect and unvarying regularity in the first eleven months of the Arcadian year, it is perhaps easier to compute dates forward from 1 Ecatombeone of the year in which they occur than backward from 1 Ecatombeone of the next year. 1 Sciroforione of 635.4 was 330 days forward from 21 June 1764, or 17 May 1765. Figuring backward, it is 2 anarchic days plus 29 days for Second Sciroforione and 30 for Sciroforione, 61 days back from 17 July; again 17 May.

This is not what one would have expected, for the diploma was found folded in a wrapper addressed "All' Illmo Sig^re Sig^re Prone Colmo Il Sig^r Barone Giacomo Boswell, Venezia."[23] Boswell was in Rome on 17 May 1765 and remained there till 13 June. If the diploma was really completed on 17 May, it could have been put directly into his hands by Abbé Grant. Clearly it was *not* ready and was sent after him. Perhaps the date is conventional; perhaps, though the dating is explicit, the neomenia of Second Sciroforione (16 June) is really meant. Or perhaps (the conjecture I myself find most attractive)

---

[23] "All' Ilustrissimo Signore Signore Padrone Colendissimo. . . ."

Boswell was elected on 17 May but the diploma was held up because Morei could not or did not initial it promptly.[24]

We cannot of course be sure that Boswell's Roman diary never mentioned the Arcadia, for there are some gaps in it due to family censorship. It is possible too that he may not have heard of the honor done him till after he had left Rome. But neither of these suppositions will explain the utter silence of all his later records on the subject. Readers of his published journals will remember how he yearned for admission to the Margrave of Baden's Order of Fidelity;[25] should he not have been enchanted with his privilege to attend meetings in the Parrhasian Grove—even to recite his verses there? The Academy still bore an honored name, or at least bore honored names on its roll. Metastasio and Goldoni were members, Angelica Kaufmann was an Arcadian, and Alfieri and Canova later accepted the diploma, as indeed did Goethe. It is true again that Boswell, after he left Holland, adopted a superior attitude toward learned academies: he attended meetings of the Royal Academy at Berlin and of the Della Crusca at Florence, called the first "a poor affair," and was condescending toward the second.[26] But an academy with pastoral names and a Parrhasian Grove ought to have seemed different. I suspect that he was bullied into a low opinion of the Arcadia by a man whom he met at Venice just at the time the diploma came into his hands, a man whom he certainly for a time held in great respect, the terrible-tempered Giuseppe Baretti.[27] Baretti in 1763 had started a literary review with the ominous title *La Frusta Letteraria* ("The Literary Whip"), and the very first book he had applied the scourge to had been the *Memorie Istoriche dell' Adunanza degli Arcadi* by Morei himself. Though Vernon Lee's description of his onslaught seems to me overcharged ("He cried and shrieked at the . . . institution, and sank down exhausted, but triumphant, with the assertion that every intelligent creature knew that Arcadia was the stupidest, most pe-

---

[24] If the membership was really voted "in Piena Ragunzana d'Arcadia, . . . Giorno Lieto per General Chiamata," as the diploma says, it may be possible to date it from records of meetings of the Arcadia. I am investigating this possibility.

[25] *Boswell on the Grand Tour: Germany and Switzerland* (1953), 16 November 1764 and documents following 1 January 1765.

[26] *Ibid.*, 13 September 1764; Boswell MSS at Yale, J7, 23 August 1765 ("Abbé discourse on fire President squinting a little but genteel half an hour thanks & away").

[27] Boswell MSS at Yale, C718, Lord Mountstuart to Boswell, 25 June 1766. In reply to Boswell's proposal to dedicate his law thesis to him, he names some of Boswell's great friends more worthy of the honor: "a Statesman Mr. Pitt. a great Warriour, Gen¹ Paoli. a great Genius, Rousseau. a larn'd man, Johnson. a Compound of them all, L'Abbatè Barretti I believe his name is, I mean your Venetian hero."

dantic, most mercenary, vilest institution in Italy"), it must be granted that his remarks were rude and hilarious. Here is the opening:

Those lovers of useless information, who, not knowing how to use their time properly, spend it in learning nonsense, and who wish to be informed of that most famous piece of literary puerility called the Arcadia, should set themselves to read this handsome book, which gives the clearest of clear accounts of it. . . . The work is divided into ten chapters, which are like ten paste jewels. Here is the substance of those ten chapters.

More telling would have been certain sentiments that Baretti had not yet put into print, but that he would certainly have put into words if Boswell had consulted him about the Arcadia:

Our imaginary shepherds are therefore justly fallen into contempt, as it has been the case these many years. The Arcadian colonists are at last nearly annihilated throughout Italy; and the *Arcadia Romana* consists now only of a few *Abatino's*, who still persist to meet sometimes in order to recite their meagre verses to each other; and they still chuse a *Custode Generale*, or *Chief Herdsman*, whose most important business is to make a penny of his place; and this he chiefly effects by sending Arcadian patents to the English travellers on their arrival at Rome: by which trick he aggregates their lordships and honours to the august body of the Roman Arcadians. Those patents are seldom refused, as they never cost above nine or ten shillings given to the Abatino's who offer them gratis. By means of so small an expence their lordships and honours may become, if they chuse, directly and intimately acquainted with very skilful managers of love-intrigues, as a good many of our present Arcadians are far from being so simple and innocent as the ancient ones of Greece.[28]

To which, as far as Boswell was concerned, we may reply "Nonsense!" Abbé Grant was none of these sordid *abatinos*, nor, I venture to assert, was his brother-shepherd Carillo Maratonio. Boswell could have preened himself on being an Arcadian shepherd, and I, for one, am sorry that he didn't. Though he managed to think well of most people, or at least to treat them with good humor, he later developed something like hatred for Baretti and made no bones of his dislike. The affront—at least the original affront—was probably Baretti's rough invectives against the Corsicans, whose cause Boswell had taken much to heart, and it probably deserved no such resentment. But if it was Baretti who disenchanted him from the Arcadia, who shall say that his dislike of Baretti was unjust?

The Bosco Parrasio still exists and is still the occasional haunt of

[28] Joseph Baretti, *An Account of the Manners and Customs of Italy* (1768), pp. 260–61. Vernon Lee is wrong in saying (*op. cit.*, p. 50 of ed. of 1880, p. 81 of that of 1908) that Baretti "had already, in his English work on Italy, showered abuse on Arcadia." The *Account* appeared five years after the review in the *Frusta Letteraria*.

the Collegio d'Arcadia. At the end of the eighteenth century, it fell into sad decay and was restored and reconstructed in 1839.[29] Vernon Lee, visiting it in the 1870's, found it again much neglected and ruinous. Later (I do not know exactly when) it was rented to a noble family (the Arcadians reserving the right of meeting in the garden) and is now in excellent keeping. The flights of steps, the landings, the grotto and fountain, the amphitheater and the memorial tablets, are apparently all as they originally were; but Pan, Syrinx, and Pegasus are no more, the open "maestoso portone" at the foot of the slope has given way to a less impressive modern wall and gate, too high to see over, and a small villa (part, I suspect, of the reconstruction of 1839) stands at the top of the slope, with entrance on the Via S. Pancrazio. I do not know how much this preserves of the structure of 1726, but the side toward the garden is presumably on the old foundation. The laurels and medlars and ilexes have flourished; the Bosco Parrasio, which in 1726 was chiefly memorable for prospects, is now densely shaded and seems very secluded. It is a delicious place, but much smaller than one expects it to be from having read about it.[30]

[29] Portal, *op. cit.*, pp. 39–44.

[30] I wish to acknowledge the expert assistance of Mr. Brian G. Marsden, graduate student in astronomy at Yale, who has verified my calculations and corrected several of them. I owe to him the suggestion (p. 402) that the Arcadian day possibly began at sunset.

DONALD J. GREENE

The Development of the Johnson Canon

T HE BEST PART OF EVERY AUTHOR is in general to be found in his book," Johnson once remarked.[1] As we all know, this shrewd maxim was ignored in Johnson's own case for a century or more after his death, Macaulay and others having persuaded the reading public that "Johnson the man"—that is, the amusing figure who is the central character in Boswell's great work of art—was all, and "Johnson the writer" nothing. We think we have now recovered from this delusion and come round to Johnson's own view. Yet for all that the "revival of interest" in Johnson's writings has been in process for a number of decades, it is with some surprise and chagrin that we discover how small an acquaintance with Johnson's writings is still thought necessary to qualify the modern critic to "sum up" and pronounce on Johnson's total "achievement." The best of such attempts, W. J. Bate's *The Achievement of Samuel Johnson*, lists in its index only around twenty titles of works by Johnson—to be sure, his most noted and perhaps weightiest ones, *Rasselas*, *The Rambler*, the *Dictionary*, the edition of Shakespeare, *The Lives of the Poets*, and so on; but still, as we shall see, only a fraction of what we now know to be a list of titles running into the hundreds. Other similar books, purporting to assess Johnson for the modern reader, those by Hesketh Pearson, C. E. Vulliamy, and Hugh Kingsmill, for instance, frankly display even less familiarity with his writings or concern for them. An honorable older exception is Joseph Wood Krutch's *Samuel Johnson* (1944), which does make a genuinely systematic attempt to trace Johnson's career as a writer. Yet even it gives only a sketchy account of all but a dozen or so of the "big" titles; and much more has been learned about Johnson's writings in the nearly twenty years since it was published.

DONALD J. GREENE is Professor of English in Victoria College at the University of Toronto.

[1] *Johnsonian Miscellanies*, ed. G. B. Hill (1897), II, 310.

This situation is not one that Johnson scholars can be proud of. Modern standards of serious scholarship would not tolerate a "comprehensive" study of, say, Milton's mind that was based solely on the three major poems, a handful of the best-known shorter ones, and the *Areopagitica,* or of Swift's based on *Gulliver, A Tale of a Tub,* and the usual half-dozen anthology pieces, ignoring the host of less well-known writings by those authors—the formidable *œuvre,* the year-to-year, even month-to-month production, of the great professional writer from which the "big" pieces stand out only as an Everest or Kanchenjunga projects above the rest of a massive mountain range; they do not rise abruptly and unexpectedly, as the novice sometimes thinks, in the midst of a flat and barren plain. If it is argued that many of the lesser writings of Johnson, who made his living during much of his life as a professional journalist, are short and "ephemeral" in nature, we might remember that Johnson himself once wrote a noble (and neglected) defense of the importance of "fugitive pieces." It is true that Johnson's reviews of, say, the reports of Benjamin Franklin's experiments with electricity, or the memoirs of Sully, or the pamphlets in the Byng controversy, are only a few sentences long and were probably dashed off in a quarter of an hour before a printer's deadline. Still, the mere fact that Johnson read in these works, knew what they had to say, and thought them worth publicizing is something the serious historian of the intellect will not find negligible. And in fact the reader will discover something thought-provoking, something that genuinely illuminates our knowledge of Johnson's powerful and far-searching mind, in every one of these. A genuinely satisfying account of the "achievement" of Samuel Johnson will not be possible until the inquirer has attempted, as Johnson said, "to consolidate these Atoms of Learning into Systems, to collect these disunited Rays, that their Light and their Fire may become perceptible."[2]

One reason for the reluctance of critics to familiarize themselves with Johnson's writings is uncertainty as to just what he did write. Johnson set his name only to a bare dozen of his works; that the rest were unsigned is due partly to the fact that he often indulged in ghost-writing for friends, partly to the older tradition of journalistic anonymity, and partly to a perhaps neurotic idiosyncrasy.[3] The result is that the process of bringing Johnson's *œuvre* to light has been a slow and gradual one—just how gradual, this article will demonstrate. And the process is far from complete: though we speak of "the John-

[2] *Proposals for the Harleian Miscellany* (1744).

[3] See *Letters of Samuel Johnson,* ed. R. W. Chapman (1952), No. 124 (to William Strahan, 20 January 1759), offering *Rasselas* for publication: "I will not print my name, but expect it to be known."

son canon," we probably should not. If the canon of an author's works is a comprehensive list of those writings generally agreed on by reputable scholars as authentic, then there is no Johnson canon, for there is no such agreement, and there will probably be none for years to come.

The task of arriving at such agreement has been hampered by a number of causes. One is this very tendency of Johnsonian critics to shy away from the unfamiliar writings and confine themselves to discussing a "Johnson" who is a composite merely of *Rasselas, The Rambler, The Lives of the Poets*, and Boswell. It is a vicious circle: agreement on the authorship of doubtful pieces can be attained only by discussion and debate; but the existing lack of agreement (with Johnson, though not with other major writers) seems to inhibit discussion. Another grave handicap is what Allen Hazen has called, in connection with Johnsonian bibliography, "the curious and rapid obsolescence that overtakes many details of literary history."[4] Hazen was speaking of the dedication of Dr. Burney's *History of Music*, which, he pointed out, "has been long known to be by Johnson," but somehow never found its way into bibliographies of Johnson. One might add the unfortunate example of Johnson's translation of Crousaz's *Commentaire* on Pope's *Essay on Man*, which incorporates much original work by Johnson and is now regarded, rightly, as a work of considerable importance. The report of its "discovery" by L. F. Powell in 1934 was acclaimed as a major "addition" to the canon. Yet as far back as 1785, the *European Magazine*, in a most competent account of Johnson's writing, had affirmed that "we can ascribe to him with confidence" this work.[5] Both the attribution and the account itself were completely ignored by Johnson scholars for 150 years, although files of the *European Magazine* can be found in most large libraries. Third, this "obsolescence" of bibliographical information among Johnson scholars is aggravated by an approach to matters of canon that its practitioners no doubt think of as laudably "conservative" (it seems in fact to have just the opposite effect, of *not* conserving), but that was long ago rejected in the closely analogous field of textual criticism as irrational and invalid—the method of arbitrarily selecting a "best MS" or "best edition" (here a "best canon") and attributing to it an "authority" that it cannot possess. For instance, Johnson's "Observations on a Letter from a French Refugee in America," in the *Literary Magazine*, May–June 1756—one of his most pungent statements of his views on colonies in general and the American colonies in particular—was publicly ascribed to

4 *Samuel Johnson's Prefaces and Dedications* (1937), p. 23.

5 Volume VIII (January 1785), p. 9.

him, with much plausibility, on five separate occasions between 1774 and 1950, and no one has ever shown the slightest desire to controvert the attribution. Yet in a recent listing of journalistic pieces by Johnson, the compiler still feels compelled to annex a question mark to it. His reason, no doubt, is that it does not happen to occur in the list of Johnson's prose writings published by Boswell. "The most authoritative opinion, of course, is Boswell's," he says.[6] The reasons why Boswell's opinion should be so regarded (even if it could be shown that Boswell ever passed an opinion at all on this piece—it probably escaped his notice entirely) would be hard to formulate.

One purpose of this article is to place the list of Johnson's writings furnished by Boswell in its proper perspective in the history of the development of the Johnson canon and so, perhaps, to help keep Boswell's dead hand from inhibiting the urgent work of investigating pieces attributed to Johnson by others. But apart from this, Johnsonian students, and perhaps literary students in general, should find it interesting to see how greatly our picture of a major author has changed from one period to another during the last two hundred years. If the "Johnson" dealt with by the critic is the sum total of the available records of his mind and art, then the "Johnson" of 1962 is an astonishingly larger and more complex figure than the Johnson of, say, 1878, when Leslie Stephen's account in the *English Men of Letters* series was published; and the Johnson of 1878 was a very different one from the Johnson of Hawkins's *Life* in 1787. It would be pleasant to be able to say that the successive "summings up" of Johnson over the last two centuries have reflected the steady increase in our knowledge of Johnson's career as a writer: unfortunately, it cannot be said, although, as what follows shows, the material has been available for critics had they wished to make use of it. What follows is a listing, in chronological order, of the earliest published attributions to Johnson of most of his known and presumed writings. It is a preliminary and to some degree selective list. It does not pretend to be perfectly complete or infallible: the chances of discovering, among the newspaper and magazine items of the eighteenth century, an earlier attribution than the one I give of, say, Johnson's *Adventurer* essays are quite large. Still, this listing may clear up misconceptions that the "Johnson canon" sprang more or less full-armed from the brain of Boswell (and because of its origin ought not to be tampered with); and it should be useful in indicating to the student just what "Johnson"—the sum total of his known writings—consisted in for the generations of 1750, 1800, 1850, 1900, and 1950. Perhaps it would

---

[6] Edward A. Bloom, *Samuel Johnson in Grub Street* (1957), p. 121.

have been well, if only to indicate that more than a dry bibliographical exercise is involved here, to entitle this article "The Search for Samuel Johnson."[7]

I

ATTRIBUTIONS DURING JOHNSON'S LIFETIME (TO DECEMBER 1784)

A. *Works First Published with Johnson's Authorship Mentioned on the Title Page or Elsewhere in the Work*

1731 *Messia.* In J. Husbands's *A Miscellany of Poems.* Preface: "by Mr. Johnson, a commoner of Pembroke College in Oxford."

1735 Proposals for publishing *Angeli Politiani poemata Latina . . . quibus notas, cum historia Latinae poeseos . . . et vita Politiani addidit Sam. Johnson.* Lost; title given in Hawkins, *Life of Johnson* (1787).

1739 Proposals for publishing a translation of Sarpi, *History of the Council of Trent, and a Life of Sarpi.* "By S. Johnson." (Recently recovered.)

1747 *The Plan of an English Dictionary.* Signed "Sam: Johnson."

1749 *The Vanity of Human Wishes.* Title page: "by Samuel Johnson."

Irene produced and published. Title page: "by Samuel Johnson."

[1753 *The Works of Virgil,* ed. Joseph Warton. "Advertisement": "To my learned and ingenious friend Mr. Samuel Johnson I am very much obliged; not only for his elegant essay on Pastoral Poetry"—a reprint of *Rambler* 37—"but for several most judicious remarks and observations scattered thro' the whole."][8]

1755 *A Dictionary of the English Language.* Title page: "by Samuel Johnson, A.M."

---

[7] The list below is based on the longer and more detailed listing of all published attributions to Johnson that I have been working on for some time. In this (surprisingly complex) project, I have had much kind assistance from many Johnsonians; I must mention in particular Arthur Sherbo and Jacob Leed, some of whose suggestions are incorporated in the following list. To save space, I have here omitted the titles of some very small, presumably authentic pieces and a large number of obviously erroneous attributions. Still, the inclusion of a title in the present list does not mean that I affirm its authenticity: it is a list of *attributions,* not my own attempt at compiling a "canon." Although I include letters intended for publication (e.g., in the columns of the *GM*), I do not include private letters and private diaries: these have been competently dealt with by R. W. Chapman (1952) and E. L. McAdam, Jr., and Donald and Mary Hyde (1958).

GM = Gentleman's Magazine; EM = European Magazine; LM = Literary Magazine; J = Johnson.

[8] Arthur Sherbo has suggested (*Johnsonian News Letter,* December 1958, March 1959) that Johnson's "contributions" to these items may simply be general critical remarks reprinted from earlier published work of Johnson's, e.g., *The Rambler.*

1756   Sir Thomas Browne, *Christian Morals*. Title page: "with a life of the author, by Samuel Johnson."

Proposals for printing . . . the dramatick works of William Shakespeare, corrected and illustrated by Samuel Johnson.

1759   *The Greek Theatre of Father Brumoy. Translated by Mrs. Charlotte Lennox.* "Advertisement" to Vol. III: "The Discourse on the Greek Comedy, and the General Conclusion, are translated by the celebrated author of the Rambler."

1765   *The Plays of William Shakespeare . . . to which are added notes by Sam: Johnson.*

[1767   *The Idylliums of Theocritus*, trans. and annotated by Francis Fawkes. Preface: "The celebrated Mr. Samuel Johnson has corrected part of this work and furnished me with some judicious remarks." Noted in 1939 by R. W. Chapman and A. T. Hazen, *Supplement to Courtney*.][8]

1779–   *Prefaces, Biographical and Critical, to the Works of the English*
81   *Poets. By Samuel Johnson. (The Lives of the Poets.)*

1783   "On the Death of Dr. Robert Levet." *GM* (August): "By Dr. Johnson."

I have excluded from this portion of the list publications signed merely "S. J." or "S. J——n"; a few friends, but not the general public, would have been able to expand the letters. They are included below.

B. *Earliest Published Attributions to Johnson of Works Printed Anonymously or under Names of Others*

1741   *London* (pub. 1738). Attributed in *GM* (October), p. 551 n.

1748   Prologue at the opening of the Drury Lane theatre (spoken and published 1747). Printed with Johnson's name in Dodsley, *A Collection of Poems.*

1750   *The Rambler.* Never published with Johnson's name in his lifetime, but attributed almost immediately in magazines.

Prologue to *Comus. General Advertiser* (April 4): "There will be a new prologue, written by the author of *Irene*."

1753   *Life of Richard Savage* (1744). J's authorship mentioned in obituary notice in *GM* (October, p. 491) of Mrs. Brett, Savage's putative mother.

1756   Editorship of Sir Thomas Browne, *Christian Morals* (1756). *GM* (April): "Many allusions to philosophical principles and historical facts . . . are explained by the editor, Mr. Samuel Johnson."

1758   *The Idler.* Attributed almost immediately in magazines. Title page of 3d collected ed., 1767: "by the author of the Rambler."

1759   *Rasselas.* Attributed almost immediately by magazines.

1750's Various short poems, often appearing first in *GM* in 1740's,
to   published with J's name in anthologies of poetry: e.g., "Epitaph
1770's on Claudy Phillips" (*GM*, 1740), assigned to J in J. Hackett, *Select and Remarkable Epitaphs* (1757).

1760 "Of the Duty of a Journalist" (*Universal Chronicle*, 1758). Excerpts in "A Praxis of sentences collected from the works of my friend and instructor Mr. Samuel Johnson," in Baretti, *A Grammar of the Italian Language.*

1766 William Kenrick, *A Defence of Mr. Kenrick's Review of Dr. Johnson's Shakespeare* (p. 13): J "advised and assisted" Charlotte Lennox, *Shakespeare Illustrated* (1753); "Dissertation on Pope's Epitaphs" (1756).

1767 In 3d collected ed. of *The Idler* ("by the author of The Rambler"): "Essay on Epitaphs" (1740); "On the Bravery of the English Common Soldiers" (1760).

In 3d ed. of *Life of Savage* ("by the ingenious Author of the *Rambler*"): lives of Blake, Drake (1740).

1770 *The False Alarm.*

1771 *Thoughts on . . . Falkland's Islands.*

1774 *The Patriot.* All three almost immediately attributed in reviews and attacking pamphlets.

Review in *GM* (Nov.) of T. Davies (ed.), *Miscellaneous and Fugitive Pieces*, 1773–74: lives of Boerhaave (1739), Barretier (1740), Burman, Sydenham (1742), Cave (1751), Frederick the Great (1756–57), Ascham (1761); Introduction to the Harleian Miscellany ("On . . . Small Tracts and Fugitive Pieces") (1744); Preface to *The Preceptor* (1748); *The Vision of Theodore* (1748); "Introduction to the Political State of Great Britain" (1756); "Observations on a Letter from a French Refugee" (1756); reviews of *Letters from Newton to Bentley*, Blackwell, *Memoirs of the Court of Augustus*, Jenyns, *Nature and Origin of Evil* (1756); "Preliminary discourse" to *London Chronicle* (1757); introduction to *The World Displayed* (1759); to *Proceedings of the Committee for Cloathing French Prisoners of War* (1760); to *Catalogue of Exhibition of the Society of Artists* (1762); prologue to Goldsmith, *The Good-Natur'd Man* (1768).

"Academicus" in *GM* (Dec.): "Character" of Collins (1763); life of Cheynel (1751; signed "S. J——n").

1775 *Marmor Norfolciense* (1739); reprinted with hostile dedication to J. by "Tribunus," making his authorship clear.

Taxation No Tyranny, A Journey to the Western Islands of Scotland. Almost immediately attributed in reviews and attacking pamphlets.

1777 Prologue to Hugh Kelly, *A Word to the Wise.* Immediately attributed in newspapers.

1779 Epilogue (Latin and English) to Baretti and Philidor's cantata, *Carmen Seculare*. Attributed by George Colman in *Monthly Review* (April).

1780 Francis Blackburne, *Memoirs of Thomas Hollis:* "Milton an Imitator of Masenius" (signed "William Lauder," 1747) and other material in the Lauder controversy, 1747–54.

1781 William Cooke (ed.), *The Beauties of Johnson:* "Further Thoughts on Agriculture" (1756); "Reflections on the Present State of Literature" (1756); *An Account of an Attempt to Ascertain the Longitude at Sea* (Z. Williams, 1755); *The Convict's Address to His Unhappy Brethren* (William Dodd, 1777).

Even without Johnson's co-operation, a fair start had been made on the beginning of a "canon" before his death. The most important contribution was, of course, the three volumes of Tom Davies's unauthorized *Miscellaneous and Fugitive Pieces* (its title inspired by Johnson's essay on "Fugitive Pieces," which it reprinted), and the analysis of the authorship of its contents by the *GM's* reviewer. Neither is infallible: as the reviewer complains, Davies omits the life of Blake and the "Observations on a Letter from a French Refugee" (Davies prints the letter, but not Johnson's observations). He might also have complained that Davies prints Rolt's "Thoughts on Agriculture" but not Johnson's continuation, "Further Thoughts on Agriculture." At the same time, the reviewer fails to note that the life of Sarpi, printed by Davies, is by Johnson (it was signed "S. J." in its first appearance in the *GM*), and he attributes the "Character of Collins" to Warton; a correspondent, "Academicus," corrects him in the next number of the *GM*. It is worth noting that as early as 1750 someone on the *GM*—perhaps Cave or Hawkesworth—had begun to worry lest Johnson's early pieces for the *GM* be forgotten: a note appended to its reprinting of *Rambler* 60 "confirms the truth" of the famous statement "I have often thought that there has rarely passed a life of which a judicious and faithful narrative would not be useful" by mention of "the lives of several persons in different stations, inserted in our magazines, which we find to have been singularly acceptable to our readers"—those of Sarpi, Boerhaave, Blake, Drake, Barretier, Morin, Burman, and Sydenham. In spite of this broad hint, it was not until 1785 that Johnson's translation of Fontenelle's *éloge* on Morin was formally attributed to Johnson.

The item listed under 1760 is interesting; it is noted in Hazen's *Prefaces and Dedications* (p. 207 n.) as communicated by D. C. Gallup. The full contents of Baretti's "Praxis"—more than a hundred pages—should be analyzed; new early attributions and, conceivably, wholly new attributions might come to light.

It is worth noting that during Johnson's lifetime it was apparently not known to the general public that he was the author of the translation of Lobo, the *Complete Vindication of the Licensers of the Stage*, the Parliamentary Debates, and a sizable part of the *Adventurer*, to mention nothing else.

II
NEW ATTRIBUTIONS, 1784–91

1784   Thomas Tyers, *Biographical Sketch of Dr. Samuel Johnson* (*GM*, Dec.): Epitaph on a Duckling (1712? 1715?);[9] Parliamentary Debates (1740–42; simultaneously attributed by the *EM*); trans. in part of Sarpi's *History of the Council of Trent* (1738); preface to, and work in, *Catalogue of the Harleian Library* (1742); preface to Anna Williams, *Miscellanies* (1766); life of Sarpi (1738; signed "S. J."); dedication to George Adams, *Treatise on the Globes* (1766); preface to Alex. Macbean, *Dictionary of Ancient Geography* (1773).

John Nichols in *GM* (Dec.): life of Styan Thirlby (first pub. *GM*, April).

An Account of the Writings of Dr. Samuel Johnson (*EM*, Dec.; continued to April 1785): essays for *Birmingham Journal* (1735 [sic]; lost); trans. of Lobo-Le Grand, *A Voyage to Abyssinia* (1735); "Ad Urbanum" (1738; signed "S. J."); *A Compleat Vindication of the Licensers of the Stage* (1739)—"attributed on the authority of an old bookseller who remembered the publication of it"; trans. and ed. of Crousaz, *Commentary on Pope's Essay on Man* (1739) (independently reattributed in 1934 by L. F. Powell); trans. of Fontenelle, *Éloge* on Louis Morin (1741); *Miscellaneous Observations on Macbeth, with Proposals for a New Edition of Shakespeare* (1745); preface to Sir Walter Raleigh, *The Interest of England with Regard to Foreign Alliances Explained* (1750; an attribution that needs investigation); dedication of Charlotte Lennox, *Shakespeare Illustrated* (1753); introductory essay and editorship, *Literary Magazine* (1756); "Observations on the Anglo-Russian and Anglo-Hessian Treaties" (1756); "Observations on the Present State of Affairs" (1756); editorship of *Works of Roger Ascham* (ostensibly by James Bennet) (1761); dedication of Thomas Percy, *Reliques of Ancient English Poetry* (1765).

1785   John Nichols in *GM*: letter "on Du Halde's *History of China*" (1738); speech on the expedition to Rochefort (1757).

[9] In the original version in the *GM*, Tyers gives Johnson's age for this precocious feat as "three." In the revised version, published as a separate pamphlet (reprinted, ed. Gerald D. Meyer, in the Augustan Reprint Series, 1952), he sensibly changes it to "five."

1785   Tyers, additions to *Biographical Sketch* (*GM*): dedication of
        Charlotte Lennox, trans., *Memoirs of Sully* (1755); review of
        Tytler, *Enquiry into Evidence . . . against Mary, Queen of Scots*
        (1760); sermons ("He composed forty sermons").
        William Shaw, *Memoirs of Dr. Samuel Johnson:* preface to James
        Fordyce, *Sermons to Young Women* (1766).
        William Cooke, *Life of Samuel Johnson:* numerous writings for
        (and ostensibly by) William Dodd (1777).
        James Boswell, *Journal of a Tour to the Hebrides:* Latin poems on
        Skye, to Mrs. Thrale, etc. (1773); "Meditation on a Pudding"
        (parody of James Hervey) (1773).

1786   Hester Lynch Piozzi, *Anecdotes of the Late Dr. Samuel Johnson:*
        "Epitaph on Hogarth" (1771); "To Mrs. Thrale on Her Thirty-
        fifth Birthday" (1776); "To Sir John Lade" (1780); and many
        other short poems.

1787   Sir John Hawkins, *Life of Johnson:* prize poem for the Earl of
        Berkshire (*ca.* 1722; lost); "View of the Controversy between
        Crousaz and Warburton" (1743); proposals for publishing the
        Harleian Miscellany (1743); contributions to *The Adventurer*
        (1753–54)—I have discovered no earlier published attribution;
        review of Jonas Hanway, *Eight Days' Journey* and *Essay on Tea*
        (1757); "Considerations on Plans for Construction of Blackfriars
        Bridge" (1759); "Account of the Imposture in Cock-Lane"
        (1762); dedication of John Kennedy, *Complete System of As-
        tronomical Chronology* (1762); epitaph on Oliver Goldsmith in
        Westminster Abbey (1776; no doubt generally known); trans.
        of part of Sallust, *De Bello Catilinario* (uncertain date; un-
        published).
        The Works of Samuel Johnson (11 vols.): preface to Richard
        Rolt, *New Dictionary of Trade and Commerce* (1756); "ΓΝΩΘΙ
        ΣΕΑΥΤΟΝ" (1772), and much hitherto unpublished poetry,
        chiefly Latin and from later years.
        John Nichols in *GM:* "Considerations on the Case of Trapp's Ser-
        mons" (1739; now first published).

1788   *Works*, Supplementary Vol. XIV (ed. Isaac Reed?): dedications
        of Robert James, *Medicinal Dictionary* (1742); Charlotte Len-
        nox, *The Female Quixote* (1752); W. Payne, *Introduction to the
        Game of Draughts* (1756); Baretti, *English-Italian Dictionary*
        (1760); James Bennet, *Works of Ascham* (1761); J. Gwynn,
        London and Westminster Improved (1766); reviews of three
        pamphlets on case of Admiral Byng (1756–57); contributions to
        J. Gwynn, *Thoughts on the Coronation* (1761); "The Fountains:
        A Fairy-Tale" (1766).
        Sermon for the Funeral of Mrs. Samuel Johnson (1752).
        Sermons [25, including the above] *Left for Publication by the Rev.
        John Taylor, D.D.* (dates?).

1789 *Works*, "Supplementary Vol. XV" (ed. George Gleig): Preface: "The following are ascribed to him by a lady to whom he was long known, whose mind he successfully cultivated, and whose name, were it mentioned, would remove every suspicion"—reviews (1756) of Russell, *Aleppo;* Lucas, *Essay on Waters;* Lennox,. *Memoirs of Sully;* Evans, *Essays on America;* J. Warton, *Essay on Pope;* dedication of John Lindsay, *Evangelical History* (1757).

This, the period of the early biographies of Johnson, is the real beginning of the scholarly investigation of the "canon." And it represents an impressive contribution. The neglected "Account of the Writings" in the *European Magazine* is particularly striking. Its attribution of the Crousaz *Commentary* (which it carefully distinguishes from the dubious *Examen*) has been noted. It seems to furnish our only authority for the ascription of the *Complete Vindication of the Licensers,* that very fine early expression of Johnson's "libertarianism." It first attributes the *Miscellaneous Observations on Macbeth* and the early proposals for a Shakespeare edition, the editorship of the *Literary Magazine,* and the dedication of Charlotte Lennox's *Shakespeare Illustrated*—most important items in Johnson's literary biography. Nor are Tyers's and Hawkins's contributions by any means negligible. The contents of the 1787 *Works*, together with the 1788 and 1789 supplements, of course provide the first really "official" canon of Johnson's writings—some years before Boswell's list appeared, it must be emphasized.

III

New Attributions, 1791–99

1791 James Boswell, *Life of Johnson:* much juvenile poetry (e.g., translations of Horace, Virgil, etc.); prefaces to *GM*, 1738, 1741, 1743, 1744, and various editorial notes in *GM;* "Debate between Cromwell and Committee of the House of Commons" (1741); trans. of Guyon, *Dissertation on the Amazons* (1741); proposals for James, *Medicinal Dictionary* (1741); for works of Charlotte Lennox (1775); for William Shaw, *Analysis of the Scotch Celtic Tongue* (1777); "The Jests of Hierocles" (1741); Foreign History (*GM*, Nov. 1742); reviews of *Memoirs of Duchess of Marlborough* (1742); Birch, *History of the Royal Society;* Murphy, *Gray's Inn Journal;* Hampton, *Polybius;* Borlase, *Isles of Scilly;* Browne, *Christian Morals;* Home, *Experiments on Bleaching;* Keith, *Catalogue of the Scottish Bishops;* P. Browne, *History of Jamaica; Philosophical Transactions,* 1755; *The Cadet; Some Further Particulars in Relation to . . . Byng* (all these 1756); James

Grainger, *The Sugar-Cane* (1764); Goldsmith, *The Traveller* (1764); "Observations on the Militia Bill" (1756); part of introduction to Sir William Chambers, *Designs of Chinese Buildings* (1757); address of the painters, etc., to George III (1761); dedication of Hoole, trans., Tasso's *Jerusalem Delivered* (1763); "character" of Rev. Z. Mudge (1769); contributions to Goldsmith, *The Deserted Village* (1770); to T. Davies, *Life of Garrick* (1780); preface to Baretti, *Easy Phraseology* (1776); revisions to Lord Hailes, *Annals of Scotland* (1776); to Crabbe, *The Village* (1783); "legal arguments" requested by Boswell in connection with his own cases (various dates); election address for Henry Thrale (1780); pamphlet against Sir Charles Hanbury Williams (1740's; lost); defense of Lord Charles Hay (1750's; lost); dedication of "musick for the German flute" to Edward, Duke of York (not located; 1760's).

Letter by Johnson (first printed in Boswell, *Life*, I, 155): "An historical account of Parliament" (lost; 1742).

Thomas Warton, in Boswell's *Life:* obituary notice of Z. Williams (1755).

1794 "G." in *GM:* Foreign History (*GM*, Nov. 1747).

1799 Boswell or Malone, *Life*, 3d ed.: Foreign History (*GM*, Nov. 1748; probably an error for the above).

As we have seen, the vast majority of the writings listed in Boswell's *Life* had been earlier publicly attributed to Johnson, though some readers of Boswell seem to have acquired the impression that Boswell worked his list up entirely independently and from scratch —something quite impossible, of course, with Tyers, Hawkins, and the 1787–89 *Works* in front of him. I list above the writings mentioned by Boswell which had not previously been publicly attributed to Johnson and of which alone he may claim the credit of "discoverer." It is still an impressive list; Boswell can apparently continue to hold the title of the scholar who has attributed the largest single number of new titles to the "canon"; though, when one examines the list, not too many of them are of great importance—the review of the Duchess of Marlborough's *Memoirs* and the "Debate between Cromwell and the Committee of the House of Commons" (a skilled abridgment of a seventeenth-century pamphlet) are perhaps the most distinguished. On the basis of the total importance of the works ascribed, rather than merely the number of titles, the author of the *Account* in the *EM*, 1784–85, certainly contributed more than Boswell to our knowledge of Johnson's writings; so perhaps did Tom Davies and Tom Tyers.

Boswell's list—there are actually two, one in the text of the *Life*, and the other in the "Chronological Catalogue" prefixed to it; the two do not always agree—was unquestionably a good compilation for its time. But for the modern student to rely on it to the neglect of other information about Johnson's writings or to endow Boswell with some mystical "authority" not possessed by other investigators is only to retard the progress of canonical study. Boswell's account of Johnson's literary career contains many errors: the beginning of *The Idler* and the end of *The Rambler* are misdated; the preface to Rolt's *Dictionary* is assigned to 1761 instead of 1756; the date of Charlotte Lennox's *The Female Quixote*, actually 1752, is given as 1751 in the "Chronological Catalogue" and as 1762 in the text of the *Life*. Boswell does not know the date of the essay "The Bravery of the English Common Soldiers," except that it was reprinted with the 1767 collected edition of *The Idler;* so with fine absence of logic he lists it under 1758, the year *The Idler* began to be published. The attribution of the Foreign History in the *GM* for November 1748 is clearly an error of transcription. And as a glance at the earlier pages of this essay will show, Boswell's list has many important omissions—for instance, the "Observations on a Letter from a French Refugee" and the translation of Crousaz's *Commentary*. His failure to note these pieces, combined with the subsequent uncritical acceptance of his list as "authoritative" or "the best," resulted in their being ignored for a century and a half, to the detriment of Johnson studies.

Further confusion has been added by Boswell's appending "acknowl." or "intern. evid." to the titles he lists. It has been frequently assumed that a piece distinguished by his "acknowl." (or its equivalent, an asterisk) is *ipso facto* entitled to greater credence than one not so marked. But there seems to be no basis for this assumption. Boswell nowhere says that "acknowl." means "acknowledged to me, Boswell, by Samuel Johnson personally." He gives three differing accounts of the significance of the mark: (*a*) *Life*, I, 16 (Hill-Powell): "N.B. To those which he himself acknowledged is added *acknowl.*"; (*b*) I, 112–13, n. 4: "[I] shall mark with an asterisk (*) those which he acknowledged to his friends"; (*c*) I, 309: "some of them I know he avowed, and have marked them with an *asterisk* accordingly." The three accounts seem to be in descending order of force: "he acknowledged *to his friends*" (Boswell not necessarily being present) is a weaker statement than the categorical "he himself acknowledged"; and "I know he avowed" is still weaker, since Boswell does not reveal just *how* he knows this. My own considered guess is that Boswell's "acknowl." or asterisk often means little more than "I have seen this piece earlier attributed, with an air of confidence, by Tyers or Davies or Hawkins or some other 'friend,' from which we may infer that Johnson probably acknowledged it as his." As anyone who has carefully inspected his list knows, Boswell's use of the marks is not consistent. In the text of the *Life* (I, 464), the life of Ascham and dedication of Bennet's edition of Ascham bear an obelus, meaning that they have been attributed on "internal evidence." Yet by the time they reach the "Chronological Catalogue," they have been promoted to "acknowl." The translations from Brumoy are marked as having been attributed from "intern. evid." Yet they are specifically attributed to Johnson by name in the text of the work itself. More serious, Boswell marks as "acknowl." the "Considerations on the Case of Trapp's Sermons" and *A Compleat Vindication of the Licensers*—meaning, he says, "Johnson himself acknowledged them" or "acknowledged them to his friends" or "I, Boswell, know he avowed them." The "Considerations," a private memorandum written by Johnson for Cave in 1739, was found by Nichols in the files of the *GM* after Johnson's death, and it was printed and attributed for the first time in the *GM* in 1787. The first, and only independent, attribution of the *Vindication* was made by the *EM* in January 1785, where, as we have seen, "this pamphlet is ascribed to Dr. Johnson on the authority of an old bookseller who remembered the publication of it." No evidence has yet emerged that either work was connected with Johnson during Johnson's lifetime.

To sum it up, the listings in Boswell's *Life* of the prose works attributed to Johnson are an ambitious, but sometimes confused, inaccurate, and misleading compilation of the titles of a hundred or so prose works previously ascribed to Johnson in print, with the addition of some thirty-five or forty titles of (mostly very short) pieces attributed by Boswell himself. The amount of inaccuracy in the compilation makes it dangerous to rely on it, or use it as a primary reference, in investigation into problems of the Johnson canon; the only sound procedure is for the investigator to go back and trace the history of the attribution of each individual item he is dealing with to its source—which, in most cases, is not Boswell. There is no reason to think Boswell a better judge of the probable authenticity of a doubtful piece than any other serious student of Johnson's writings; where he adduces evidence, or provides argument, to support his judgment of the authorship of a certain piece, that evidence and argument must, of course, be considered and weighed; but Boswell's bare statement of *opinion*, where not so supported, carries no special "authority" (and the mere omission or inclusion of an item in the list is not necessarily an expression of opinion—it may indicate simply ignorance of the existence of the piece, or, as with the Foreign History for November 1748, a clerical error). That is to say, we must treat

Boswell exactly as we should treat Tyers or Davies or Hawkins or any other student of the canon: and why not? A study of Boswell's markings of "acknowl." and "intern. evid." shows that they cannot be relied on to convey any trustworthy information; the only safe practice is to ignore them.

IV

NEW ATTRIBUTIONS, 1800–1925

1805 J. Wright, ed. *Account of Samuel Johnson's Life:* review of Edward Moore, *The Gamester* (*GM*, 1753).

1806 Alexander Chalmers, ed. *Works of Samuel Johnson:* preface to John Payne, *New Tables of Interest* (1758).

1807 A. Chalmers, ed. Boswell's *Life:* proposals for printing *Miscellanies* of Anna Williams (1750); obituary notice of Edward Cave (*GM*, 1753).

1808 Edmond Malone, ed. W. G. Hamilton, *Parliamentary Logick:* "Considerations on Corn" (found in J's handwriting in Hamilton's papers; 1766?).

1812 [Stephen Jones?] *Biographia Dramatica:* review of Hawkesworth's adaptation of Southerne's *Oroonoko* (*Critical Review*, 1759).

1813 Advertisement of Thomas Maurice, *Westminster Abbey and Other Poems:* "Dr. Johnson condescended to write the preface . . ."— dedication of Maurice, *Poems . . . with a Translation of Sophocles Oedipus Tyrannus* (1779).

1821 John Nichols, Preface to Vol. III of *General Index to GM:* preface to *General Index* to *GM*, 1753 (noted by L. F. Powell, 1943).

1822 A. Chalmers, ed. Boswell's *Life:* letter on the fireworks at celebration of Peace of Aix-la-Chapelle (*GM*, 1749; signed "O. N."); review of Edward Moore, *Gil Blas* (*GM*, 1751); prefaces to *GM*, 1751, 1753, 1754.

1826 Samuel Parr, in Charles Marsh, "Recollections of Dr. Parr," *New Monthly Magazine:* dedication of Burney, *History of Music* (1776) (independently reattributed by L. F. Powell, 1934).

1828 Samuel Parr, in E. H. Barker, *Parriana:* "J certainly revised and improved" preface to James Hampton, trans. of Polybius, *History* (1756).

W. Field, *Memoirs of Samuel Parr:* "Parr attributed, from internal evidence" dedication of Zachary Pearce, *Commentary on the Four Evangelists* (1777).

1831 J. W. Croker, ed. Boswell's *Life:* two sets of Latin verses and two of Latin prose (college exercises; from MSS); paragraph concerning Sir Joseph Mawbey, M.P. (*GM*, 1769).

1834 W. Roberts, *Memoirs of Hannah More:* revision of stanza in Hannah More's "Sir Eldred of the Bower" (1776).

1842   John Mitford, in *GM:* Book IX, Chapter XI of *The Female Quix-ote*, by Charlotte Lennox (Chapter heading, "Being in the Au-thor's Opinion the Best Chapter in This History") (1752).

1843   T. B. Macaulay, review of Mme. D'Arblay, *Memoirs:* revisions to Fanny Burney, *Cecilia* (1782). Controverted by G. B. Hill, ed. Boswell's *Life* (1887); defended by George Saintsbury, essay on Mme. D'Arblay, 1895.

1852   James Crossley, in *Notes and Queries:* preface and notes to Baretti, *Introduction to the Italian Language* (1755).

1856   *Autobiography of Sylvanus Urban*, in *GM:* "Venus in Armour," "From the Song of Solomon," "The Logical Warehouse" (*GM*, 1738).

1861   H. G. Bohn, in Lowndes, *Bibliographer's Manual:* preface to Wil-liam Guthrie, *General History of the World* (1764).

1885   C. Welsh, *A Bookseller of the Last Century:* part of advertisement by Dr. Robert James for *A Vindication of the Fever Powder* (1777).

1887   G. B. Hill, ed. Boswell's *Life:* dedication of Reynolds, *Seven Dis-courses before the Royal Academy* (1778); review of James Grainger, *The Sugar-Cane* (*Critical Review*, 1764); of Charlotte Lennox, *The Female Quixote* (*GM*, 1752).

1897   G. B. Hill, *Johnsonian Miscellanies:* work (apart from preface) on Richard Rolt, *Dictionary of Trade and Commerce* (1756).

1907   James Hill, *Bookmakers of Old Birmingham:* preface to Edward Brodhurst, *Sermons* (1733).

1918   Wilbur L. Cross, *The History of Henry Fielding:* "Hill . . . was held up to public scorn by Dr. Johnson in the *GM* of the same month"—review of Dr. John Hill, *The Impertinent* (*GM*, 1752).

Although the nineteenth century and the early twentieth were the heyday of the cult of "Johnson the personality," a respectable amount of inquiry into the canon went on. The list for this period contains some of the most controversial attributions—the preface to Hampton's *Polybius* and the theatrical criticisms for the *GM*, for instance. The attributions of the Guthrie and Brodhurst prefaces are interesting but probably wrong. Macaulay's excursus into Johnsonian attribution is quite fantastic: a glance at the examples he gives to prove his case shows how very little he was acquainted with Johnson's prose style. Saintsbury's support of him is even more fantastic. The chapter Johnson is thought to have contributed to Charlotte Lennox's novel ought to be better known. Cross's attribution is most interesting. The matter-of-fact way in which he mentions the work sounds as though he were simply taking his information from another source, but I have not yet found an earlier one.

V

NEW ATTRIBUTIONS, 1925–62

1926 R. W. Chapman, ed. from MS: J's writings for William Dodd (1777; see above, 1785, Cooke).

1928 L. F. Powell, in *The Library:* assistance with editorial work in Thomas Percy, *Reliques of Ancient Poetry* (1765).

1929 R. B. Adam, *The R. B. Adam Library:* dedication of Charlotte Lennox, trans. of Brumoy's *Greek Theatre* (1759); trans. of Horace, *Odes* II, 20 (1725 or 1726; from MS); "short scheme" for *Dictionary of the English Language* (1746; printed in facsimile); dedication of William Payne, *Introduction to Geometry* (1767).

1930 Catalogue of Sotheby and Co.: dedication of John Hoole, trans. of *Works of Metastasio* (1767).

   R. W. Chapman, ed. of facsimile reprint: proposals for *The Publisher* (1744).

1933 Medford Evans (Yale doctoral dissertation): editorial note on pirating by *Common Sense* (*GM*, 1739).

   R. W. Chapman, *Times* (London): MS sermon in Yale library (in Taylor's hand, with corrections by J).

1934 L. F. Powell, ed. Boswell's *Life:* advertisement concerning *The World Displayed* (1759); dedication of Charles Burney, *Account of the . . . Commemoration of Handel* (1784).

   R. W. Chapman, in Powell, ed. *Life:* preface to Baretti, *Italian Library* (1757).

1935 Miriam Small, *Charlotte Ramsay Lennox:* dedication of *Philander* (1757); of *Henrietta* (1767); of trans. of De la Beaumelle, *Memoirs of Mme. de Maintenon* (1757).

   A. T. Hazen and E. L. McAdam, Jr., Yale exhibition catalogue of J's works: proposals for printing *Le Poesie di Giuseppe Baretti* (1750's?).

1936 Dorothy Moody, in *Modern Language Notes:* about 50 lines, from recovered MS, of verse trans. of Addison, "Battle of the Cranes and Pygmies" (1725 or 1726).

   A. T. Hazen, *Bulletin of the Institute of the History of Medicine:* nine articles in Dr. Robert James, *Medicinal Dictionary* (1742) (earlier mentioned, but not specifically identified, by Boswell, 1791).

1937 A. T. Hazen, *Johnson's Prefaces and Dedications:* dedication of John Hoole, *Cyrus* (1768); of William Payne, *Elements of Trigonometry* (1772); preface to Hoole, *The Present State of the English East India Company's Affairs* (1772); ed. *Monarchy Asserted* (1741); preface to Thomas Flloyd, trans. of Lenglet du Fresnoy, *Chronological Tables of Universal History* (1762);

opening sentence of Baretti, *Guide through the Royal Academy* (1781); introductory essay to *Universal Chronicle* (1758).

1938 L. F. Powell, *Times* (London): Henry Hervey Aston, *A Sermon Preached at St. Paul's before the Sons of the Clergy* (1745).

C. L. Carlson, *The First Magazine:* introduction and abridgment of George Anson, *Voyage Around the World* (*GM*, 1749–50).

1940 E. L. McAdam, Jr., and A. T. Hazen, in *Huntington Library Quarterly:* four paragraphs in Thomas Talbot, *Address to the Nobility . . . of Herefordshire*—a project for an infirmary at Hereford (1774).

1941 J. L. Clifford, *Hester Lynch Piozzi:* electoral addresses for Henry Thrale (London newspapers, 1765–80).

D. Nichol Smith and E. L. McAdam, Jr. (eds.), *Poems of Samuel Johnson:* "Upon the Feast of St. Simon and St. Jude" (1725–26; from MS); "first draft" of *Irene* (1736–37; from MS).

1942 Boylston Green, *Yale Library Gazette: Observations* (on current affairs; five weekly instalments in *University Chronicle*, 1758).

Hester Lynch Piozzi, *Thraliana*, ed. K. C. Balderston: sermon or sermons for George Strahan (not yet found); "a poem in Dodsley's collection" (not identified).

E. L. McAdam, Jr., in *Review of English Studies: The Weekly Correspondent* ("periodical essays" running for three weekly instalments in *Public Ledger*, 1760); preliminary address to *Public Ledger* (1760).

1947 H. W. Liebert, in *Publications of the Bibliographical Society of America:* revisions to Henry Lucas, *The Earl of Somerset* (1779).

Mary Knapp, *Times Literary Supplement:* prologue to Garrick, *Lethe* (1740).

1951 E. L. McAdam, Jr., *Dr. Johnson and the English Law:* contributions to Sir Robert Chambers, Vinerian lectures on the English law at Oxford (*ca.* 1766–67; from MS; earlier reported by McAdam in *Review of English Studies*, 1939–40); legal argument in connection with entail of Salusbury property (1782; lost—some 28 pages were known to have existed).

A. L. McLeod, in *Notes and Queries:* letter (signed "Pamphilus") on inscription on Gay's monument in Westminster Abbey (*GM*, 1738). Controverted by H. W. Liebert, 1952; reattributed (independently) by Jacob Leed, 1958.

C. J. M. Lubbers van der Brugge, *Giuseppe Baretti:* assistance with various writings of Baretti.

1952 R. W. Chapman (ed.), *Letters of Samuel Johnson*, frontispiece to Vol. I: school exercise in Latin prose, dated 1725 (from Congreve MSS; see below, 1955, Chapman).

D. J. Greene, in *Review of English Studies:* reviews of William Mason, *Elfrida* (1752); Edward Young, *The Brothers* (1753);

Macnamara Morgan, *Philoclea* (1754); Philip Francis, *Constantine* (1754; all in *GM*).

1953 E. L. McAdam, Jr., in *Review of English Studies:* assistance with Saunders Welch, *Proposals* (1758).

B. B. Hoover, *Samuel Johnson's Parliamentary Reporting:* advertisement for *Proposals for Publishing Anagrammata Rediviva* (*GM*, 1738). Jacob Leed has discovered a copy of the actual *Proposals*, but has not yet published a notice of them.

1954 E. L. Ruhe, in *Notes and Queries:* letter by Cave defending his project of translating Sarpi's *History of the Council of Trent* (1738).

1955 R. W. Chapman, in *Bodleian Library Record:* six school exercises (Latin) (from Congreve MSS).

J. L. Clifford, *Young Sam Johnson:* school exercise (Latin), "To harbor malefactors is hardly safe"; "On a Daffodil" (J's first known English poem; before 1725); "Ode on a Lady Leaving Her Place of Abode"; trans. of Virgil, *Eclogue* V (part) and an epode of Horace, not II (these last three items not yet published); dedication and assistance, Henry Hervey Aston, trans. into English verse of Lord Hervey's Latin epitaph on Queen Caroline (1738).

1956 D. J. Greene, in *Review of English Studies:* some thirteen additional reviews in *LM* (1756).

Arthur Sherbo, *Samuel Johnson, Editor of Shakespeare, with an Essay on the Adventurer:* numerous translations into English verse of Latin mottoes in *The Adventurer* (1753).

Jacob Leed, in *Modern Philology:* letter on "condolence," signed "Pamphilus" (*GM*, 1738).

1958 Gwin J. Kolb, in *Studies in Bibliography:* advertisement for *Public Ledger* (1760).

D. J. Greene, in *Notes and Queries:* ten short prefaces (signed "J") in *Harleian Miscellany* (1744).

1959 Arthur Sherbo, in *New York Public Library Bulletin:* "An Essay on Elegies" (*Universal Museum*, 1767).

D. J. Greene, in *PMLA:* Foreign History, *GM*, August-December 1741; January-March, August, September, November, 1742; April 1743; Foreign Books, *GM*, November 1741 to September 1743; editorial comment on "Dissertations on Wool," *GM*, 1740–43; Parliamentary Debates, *GM*, May-September, and Supplement, 1744; letter on swearing, signed "S. J.," *GM*, 1740; "Some Account of the Present State of the Controversy concerning Milton's Imitation of the Moderns," *GM*, 1750.

1960 Laurence C. McHenry, Jr., in *Bulletin of the History of Medicine:* article "Oribasius" in James, *Medicinal Dictionary* (1742).

Jacob Leed, in *PBSA:* abridgment of *The Art of Deciphering* (*GM*, 1742).

1960   F. W. Gibbs, in *Ambix:* trans. of Boerhaave, *Elements of Chemistry* (1732).

1961   Gwin J. Kolb, in *Studies in English Literature:* Foreign History, *GM*, February 1749, December 1750; review of *The Reduction of Louisbourg, GM,* December 1758; advertisement of new ed. of *Pilgrim's Progress* (1759); review of *The Honour and Advantages of Agriculture, GM,* 1760.

1962   Arthur Sherbo, in *Johnsonian Studies* (Cairo): review of William Shirley, *The Black Prince;* of Charlotte Lennox, *Life of Harriot Stuart* (*GM*, 1750); review of *Remarks on Mr. Mason's Elfrida* (and other short reviews) (*GM*, 1752); Foreign History, November (first paragraph); review of Glover, *Boadicea,* and of Richardson, *Sir Charles Grandison* (and other short notices) (*GM*, 1753); reviews of William Whitehead, *Creusa,* Hogarth, *The Analysis of Beauty, The Day of Doom, The Day of Judgment* (*GM*, 1754); review of *Select Epitaphs* (ed. W. Toldervey), Joseph Nichol Scott, *Essay towards a Translation of Homer's Work* (*GM*, 1755). (The above is only a selection from this long article.)

The number of new attributions to Johnson made during the past thirty-five years is remarkable. Yet it should not be too surprising. Johnson, after all, was a professional writer, lived a long life, and during much of it had no other source of income than his pen. He was interested in every subject under the sun, and he had the born journalist's urge to see something about it in print, however prone he may have been to complain of the pain of actual writing and of his own slothfulness. Rather, it would have been surprising had the list of Johnson's writings before 1925, thin and spotty for a writer of his potential, containing inexplicable chronological gaps (what *could* he have been living on in 1745?), continued to survive under the scrutiny of such shrewd literary detectives as Chapman, Powell, Hazen, and McAdam. The recovery of such important documents as the early poems, two new sermons, two new sets of periodical essays (abortive, to be sure), new (medical) biographies, and, above all, the substantial contributions to Chambers's law lectures (to mention only some of the hundred or so new titles in the list for this period) renders earlier accounts of Johnson's literary career obsolete and necessitates their being rewritten. At least, they would if it were Milton we were dealing with, not Johnson; and it seems difficult to argue that Johnson deserves the application of less rigorous standards of literary criticism than Milton.

Many of these recent attributions need to be further investigated and discussed (as, indeed, do many older ones); a number of those listed above (like a number of those listed in the earlier periods) are highly unconvincing. But each of them should be freely investigated and discussed, on its own merits, not subjected to the lazy procedure of saying, "Since it is not already in the 'received'—i.e., generally, Boswellian—canon, the presumption is against it, and I shall gain credit for my 'conservatism' by ignoring it." "Authority," says J. P. Postgate in his classic essay on "Textual Criticism" in the eleventh edition of the *Encyclopaedia Britannica*, "has properly no place in textual criticism," and, again, "The received conjectures which make this [the 'received' or vulgate] text acceptable have no more authority in themselves than equally good conjectures which have not yet won their way into the text, and it is clearly illogical to treat a text largely built on conjecture as if it were now beyond the reach of conjecture." For "text" read "canon" throughout. The practice, in investigations into the canon, of "starting with" Boswell's list (or Courtney's, which is little more than Boswell's), arbitrarily endowing it with prescriptive authority, and placing the onus of proof on the investigator who proposes a modification of it is closely similar to the older practice, in textual criticism, of selecting and adhering to a "best MS" or "best edition" and then requiring that proposed deviations from that text demonstrate a greater degree of probability than is inherent in the readings of the "best MS" themselves—a practice long ago discredited and abandoned. As Postgate, Housman, and others have pointed out with great emphasis, there is nothing "conservative" or "cautious" in such a practice; on the contrary, the abdication of the investigator's critical faculties in favor of the existing "readings" of the arbitrarily chosen "authority" is incautious and irresponsible. To confer such authority on Boswell is not a "safe" but a reckless proceeding, like surrendering one's control over the steering wheel of an automobile to a chauffeur whose record already contains a number of convictions for incompetent and dangerous driving. True, the other available chauffeurs have similar convictions. So the only answer, painful as it seems to human inertia, is for the "canonical" investigator to do his own driving—that is, to collate all the available evidence for and against the authenticity of each attribution in question, and, using with consistency accepted general principles for the assessment of scholarly evidence, make his decision independent of mere "authority." After all, the textual scholar had to learn to do so many decades ago.

Compiled by STUART WILSON

The Publications of Alan Dugald McKillop

1919 "Festus and the Blessed Damozel," *MLN*, XXXIV, 93–97.
1920 "Illustrative Notes on Genesis B," *JEGP*, XX, 28–38.
1921 "Some Early Traces of Rabelais in English Literature," *MLN*, XXXVI, 469–74.
"Jane Austen's Gothic Titles," *N & Q*, N.S. IX, 361–62.
1922 "A Poem in the Collins Canon," *MLN*, XXXVII, 181.
1923 "A Bibliographical Note on Collins," *MLN*, XXXVIII, 184–85.
"The Romanticism of William Collins," *SP*, XX, 1–16.
"Sir Daniel Fleming and His Account Book," *Texas Review*, VIII, 285–93.
Review of Edward Bungert, *The Dependence of Part I of Cynewulf's Christ upon the Antiphonary*, in *JEGP*, XXII, 162–64.
1924 "Some Details of the Sonnet Revival," *MLN*, XXXIX, 438–40.
"The Power of Byron," *New Republic*, XXXVIII, 201–3.
Review of A. S. Cook, *Possible Begetter of the Old English Beowulf*, in *JEGP*, XXXII, 305–7.
1925 "Richardson, Young, and the *Conjectures*," *MP*, XXII, 391–404.
"A Victorian Faust," *PMLA*, XL, 743–68.
Review of J. Duncan Spaeth, *Old English Poetry*, in *JEGP*, XXIV, 279–81.
1926 Review of Howard S. Buck, *A Study in Smollett*, in *PQ*, V, 369.
Review of Arnold Whitridge, *Tobias Smollett: A Study of His Miscellaneous Works*, in *PQ*, V, 369–70.
1927 Review of John W. Draper, *William Mason*, in *MLN*, XLII, 478–79.
1928 "The First English Translation of *Werther*," *MLN*, XLIII, 36–38.
"The First English Translation of *Werther*—a Correction," *MLN*, XLIII, 467.
"A Lost Poem by Collins," *TLS*, 6 December, p. 965.
"Notes on Smollett," *PQ*, VII, 368–74.
Review of Marion K. Bragg, *The Formal Eclogue in Eighteenth Century England*, in *MLN*, XLIII, 213.

STUART WILSON is Assistant Professor of English in the State University of New York, College at Fredonia.

1928 Review of Thomas Gray, *Poetry and Prose*, ed. J. Crofts, in *MLN*, XLIII, 213.

Review of Eric Partridge, *A Critical Medley*, in *MLN*, XLIII, 213–14.

1929 Review of Brian W. Downs, *Richardson*, in *PQ*, VII, 199.

Review of H. W. Garrod, *Collins*, in *PQ*, VIII, 186.

1930 "Smollett's First Comedy," *MLN*, XLV, 396–97.

Review of Norman Foerster, ed., *Humanism and America*, in *University of California Chronicle*, XXXII, 384–87.

1931 "The Personal Relations between Fielding and Richardson," *MP*, XXVIII, 423–33.

Review of H. Dorken, *Lord Byron's Subjectivismus*, in *MLN*, XLVI, 279.

Review of J. M. Horner, *The English Woman Novelists*, and Frances Brooke, *Lady Julia Mandeville*, in *MLN*, XLVI, 554–55.

Review of A. Latz, *Sklaverei, Staatskirche and Freikirche*, in *MLN*, XLVI, 279.

1932 "Mrs. Radcliffe on the Supernatural in Poetry," *JEGP*, XXXI, 352–59.

"Goethe and Literary Criticism," *RIP*, XIX, 84–108.

Review of P. Harting and W. Schellberg, *Handbuch der Englandkunde*, in *MLN*, XLVII, 69.

Review of Paul Dottin, *Samuel Richardson*, in *MLN*, XLVII, 120–22.

1933 "A Critic of 1741 on Early Poetry," *SP*, XXX, 504–21.

"Richardson's Early Years as a Printer," *RES*, IX, 67–70.

"Sir Walter Scott in the Twentieth Century," *RIP*, XX, 196–215.

Review of F. L. Lucas, *Thomas Lovell Beddoes: An Anthology*, in *MLN*, XLVIII, 138.

1934 "English Circulating Libraries, 1725–1750," *The Library*, N.S. XIV, 477–85.

1935 "Charles Lamb Sees London," *RIP*, XXII, 105–27.

Review of Louis I. Bredvold, *The Intellectual Milieu of John Dryden*, in *PQ*, XIV, 375–76.

1936 *Samuel Richardson: Printer and Novelist*. Chapel Hill.

"Collins's 'Ode to the Passions,' " *TLS*, 7 March, p. 204.

1937 "Stockton Axson: A Memorial Address," *RIP*, XXIV, 1–36.

Review of R. J. Allen, *The Clubs of Augustan London*, in *MLN*, LII, 602–3.

1938 " 'The Hero; or the Adventures of a Night,' " *MLN*, LIII, 414–15.

"An Iconographic Poem on *Tom Jones*," *PQ*, XVII, 403–6.

Review of Katherine Hornbeak, *Richardson's Familiar Letters*, in *MLN*, LIII, 551.

Review of William M. Sale, Jr., *Samuel Richardson: A Bibliographical Record*, in *MLN*, LIII, 218–20.

1939 Editor, with Louis I. Bredvold and Lois Whitney, *Eighteenth Century Poetry and Prose*. New York.

"The Authorship of 'A Poem to the Memory of Mr. Congreve,' " *MLN*, LIV, 599.

1940 Review of Daniel Defoe, *Review*, ed. A. Secord, in *MLN*, LV, 218–20.

1942 *The Background of Thomson's "Seasons."* Minneapolis and London,

"The Poet as Patriot: Shakespeare to Wordsworth," *RIP*, XXIX, 309–35.

Review of John Dyer, *Grongar Hill*, ed. Richard C. Boys, in *MLN*, LVII, 481–82.

Review of René Wellek, *The Rise of English Literary History*, in *PQ*, XX, 195–97.

1943 "Samuel Richardson's Advice to an Apprentice," *JEGP*, XLII, 40–54.

Review of Hoxie N. Fairchild, *Religious Trends in English Poetry*, Vol. II: *1740–1780, Religious Sentimentalism in the Age of Johnson*, in *JEGP*, XLII, 443–45.

Review of Louis L. Martz, *The Later Career of Tobias Smollett*, in *MLQ*, IV, 118–20.

Review of Eric S. Taylor, "James Thomson's Library," *TLS*, 20 June, 1942, p. 312, in *PQ*, XXII, 179–80.

Review of Geoffrey Tillotson, *Essays in Criticism and Research*, in *MLN*, LVIII, 650–51.

Review of Paul Van Tieghem, "Le Roman sentimental en Europe de Richardson à Rousseau (1740–1761)," *Revue de littérature comparée*, XX, 129–51, in *PQ*, XXII, 188.

Review of Claude E. Jones, *Smollett Studies*, in *PQ*, XXII, 173–74.

1944 "Thomson's Visit to Shenstone," *PQ*, XXIII, 283–86.

Review of John T. Taylor, *Early Opposition to the English Novel*, in *PQ*, XXIII, 154.

1945 Review of Alfred O. Aldridge, "The Eclecticism of Mark Akenside's 'The Pleasures of Imagination,' " *JHI*, V (1944), 292–314, in *PQ*, XXIV, 135–36.

Review of Rae Blanchard (ed.), *Tracts and Pamphlets by Richard Steele*, in *MLN*, LX, 204–5.

Review of Catherine Macdonald Maclean, *Born under Saturn*, in *South-Central Bulletin*, V, No. 1, 3.

1946 Review of George M. Kahrl, *Tobias Smollett: Traveler-Novelist*, in *PQ*, XXV, 162–63.

1947 "The Mock Marriage Device in *Pamela*," *PQ*, XXVI, 285–88.

Review of Marjorie Hope Nicolson, *Newton Demands the Muse*, in *JEGP*, XLVI, 218–21.

Review of J. M. S. Tompkins, " 'In Yonder Grave a Druid Lies,' " *RES*, XXII (1946), 1–16, in *PQ*, XXVI, 113–14.

1948   *English Literature from Dryden to Burns.* New York.

"The Early European View of Old China," *RIP*, XXXV, No. 3, 1–19.

"A Letter from Samuel Richardson to Alexis Claude Clairaut," *MLN*, LXIII, 109–13.

"James Thomson, 1748–1948," *Johnsonian News Letter*, VIII, No. 3, 1–3.

"Some Newtonian Verses in *Poor Richard*," *New England Quarterly*, XXI, 383–85.

"Luxury Versus Liberty–an Eighteenth-Century Pattern," *South-Central Bulletin*, VIII, No. 1, 14–15.

1949   "Bonnell Thornton's Burlesque Ode," *N & Q*, CXCIV, 321–24.

"Ethics and Political History in Thomson's *Liberty*," in *Pope and His Contemporaries: Essays Presented to George Sherburn*, ed. James L. Clifford and Louis A. Landa (New York: Oxford), pp. 215–29.

"Nature and Science in the Works of James Hervey," *TxSE*, XXVIII, 124–38.

"Wedding Bells for Pamela," *PQ*, XXVIII, 323–25.

"Rice Institute," in *Houston: Text by Houstonians* (Marrero, La.), pp. 97–102.

Review of George Sherburn, "The Restoration and Eighteenth Century (1660 to 1789)," *A Literary History of England*, ed. A. C. Baugh, in *PQ*, XXVIII, 373–75.

1950   Editor, *Critical Remarks on Sir Charles Grandison, Clarissa, and Pamela (1754).* (Augustan Reprint Society Publication No. 21.) Los Angeles.

"The Early History of Thomson's *Liberty*," *MLQ*, XI, 307–16.

"Thomson and the Jail Committee," *SP*, XLVII, 62–71.

Review of John Arthos, *The Language of Natural Description in Eighteenth-Century Poetry*, in *JEGP*, XLIX, 120–24.

Review of Bonamy Dobrée, "The Theme of Patriotism in the Poetry of the Early Eighteenth Century," reprinted from *Proceedings of the British Academy*, XXXV (1949), in *PQ*, XXIX, 252–53.

Review of Lewis M. Knapp, *Tobias Smollett: Doctor of Men and Manners*, in *PQ*, XXIX, 297–98.

Review of Robert E. Moore, *Hogarth's Literary Relationships*, in *JEGP*, XLIX, 421–22.

1951   *The Background of Thomson's "Liberty"* (Monograph in English), *RIP*, XXXVIII, No. 2.

"Epistolary Technique in Richardson's Novels," *RIP*, XXXVIII, No. 1, 36–54.

"Allusions to Prose Fiction in Jane Austen's *Volume the Third*," *N & Q*, CXCVI, 428–29.

Review of William M. Sale, Jr., *Samuel Richardson: Master Printer*, in *PQ*, XXX, 285–87.

1952 "Charlotte Smith's Letters," *HLQ*, XV, 237–55.

"Epistolary Technique in Richardson's Novels," in *Studies in the Literature of the Augustan Age: Essays Collected in Honor of Arthur Ellicott Case*, ed. R. C. Boys (Ann Arbor), pp. 199–217.

"The Struggles of the Scholar" (Presidential Address: South-Central Modern Language Association, 1951), *South-Central Bulletin*, XII, 1–4.

"Peter the Great in Thomson's *Winter*," *MLN*, LXVII, 28–31.

Review of Douglas Grant, *James Thomson: Poet of "The Seasons,"* in *PQ*, XXXI, 307–8.

1953 "The Geographical Chapter in *Scriblerus*," *MLN*, LXVIII, 480–81.

"The Reception of Thomson's *Liberty*," *N & Q*, CXVIII, 112–13.

"William Ward Watkin," *Proceedings of the Philosophical Society . of Texas*, XVII, 27–29.

Review of Samuel Kliger, *The Goths in England*, in *PQ*, XXXII, 247–50.

1954 "Letters from Aaron Hill to Richard Savage," *N & Q*, CXCIX, 388–91.

"Richardson's Early Writings—Another Pamphlet," *JEGP*, LIII, 72–75.

"The Reinterpretation of Laurence Sterne," *EA*, VII, 36–47.

Review of Ernest Tuveson, "The Importance of Shaftesbury," *ELH*, XX, 267–99, in *PQ*, XXXIII, 296–97.

1955 "Shaftesbury in Joseph Warton's *Enthusiast*," *MLN*, LXX, 337–39.

"Two 18th Century 'First Works': 1. Samuel Richardson's First Book. 2. James Thomson's Juvenile Poems," *Newberry Library Bulletin*, IV, 10–23.

"Johnson and Ogilvie," *Johnsonian News Letter*, XV, No. 4, 7–8.

Review of Sidney Gecker, *English Fiction to 1820 in the University of Pennsylvania Library*, in *PQ*, XXXIV, 228–29.

Review of Henry Pettit, "A Bibliography of Young's *Night Thoughts*," *University of Colorado Studies* (1954), 1–52, in *PQ*, XXXIV, 330.

Review of Alexander Pope, *Minor Poems*, ed. Norman Ault and John Butt, in *PQ*, XXXIV, 307–9.

Review of John Traugott, *Tristram Shandy's World: Sterne's Philosophical Rhetoric*, in *SR*, LXIII, 687–90.

1956 *The Early Masters of English Fiction*. Lawrence, Kansas.

Editor, with Louis I. Bredvold and Lois Whitney, *Eighteenth Century Poetry and Prose*. 2d ed. New York.

"On the Acquisition of Minor English Fiction, 1740–1800," *Newberry Library Bulletin*, IV, 70–74.

Review of Chester F. Chapin, *Personification in Eighteenth-Century English Poetry*, in *PQ*, XXXV, 254–55.

1956   Review of Alice G. Fredman, *Diderot and Sterne*, in *PQ*, XXXV, 327–29.
1957   "The Context of *Sense and Sensibility*," *Studies in English, Honoring George Wesley Whiting*, *RIP*, XLIV, 65–78.
       Review of William Collins, *Drafts and Fragments of Verse*, ed. J. S. Cunningham, in *PQ*, XXXVI, 352–54.
       Review of *The Poetical Works of Charles Churchill*, ed. Douglas Grant, in *PQ*, XXXVI, 351–52.
1958   Editor, *James Thomson (1700–1748): Letters and Documents*. Lawrence, Kansas.
       "Armstrong's Anecdotes of Thomson," *N & Q*, CCIII, 376.
       "Mrs. Centlivre's *The Wonder:*—A Variant Imprint," *Book Collector*, VII, 79–80.
       "Ornaments Bearing Printer's Names," *Book Collector*, VII, 299.
       "Some Heroic Couplets by James Thomson," *MLN*, LXXIII, 12–14.
       "Thompson and the Licensers of the Stage," *PQ*, XXXVII, 448–53.
       "Critical Realism in *Northanger Abbey*," in *From Jane Austen to Joseph Conrad: Essays Collected in Memory of James I. Hillhouse* (Minneapolis), pp. 35–45.
       Review of Nelson S. Bushnell, *William Hamilton of Bangour, Poet and Jacobite*, in *PQ*, XXXVII, 334–35.
       Review of Johannes Kleinstück, "Zur Form und Methode des Tristram Shandy," *Archiv für das Studium der neueren Sprachen und Literaturen*, CXCIV, 122–37, in *PQ*, XXXVII, 353.
       Review of Ian Watt, *The Rise of the Novel*, in *MP*, LV, 208–10.
1959   "Some Recent Views of *Tom Jones*," *CE*, XXI, 17–22.
       "Supplementary Notes on Samuel Richardson as a Printer," *SB*, XII, 214–18.
       "Asa Crawford Chandler, 1891–1958," *Proceedings of the Philosophical Society of Texas*, XXII, 26–28.
       Review of Jean H. Hagstrum, *The Sister Arts*, in *MLQ*, XX, 198–99.
       Review of Joyce Hemlow, *The History of Fanny Burney*, in *MLR*, LIV, 98–99.
       Review of Alan B. Howes, *Yorick and the Critics*, in *PQ*, XXXVIII, 349.
       Review of Robert Newcomb, "Franklin and Richardson," *JEGP*, LVII (1958), 27–35, in *PQ*, XXXVIII, 346.
       Review of Karl W. Deutsch *et al.*, *Science and the Creative Spirit*, in *University of Toronto Quarterly*, XXVIII, 200–203.
1960   *Samuel Richardson: Printer and Novelist* (reprint of 1936 ed.). Hamden, Conn.
       "Collins' 'Ode to Evening'—Background and Structure," *Tennessee Studies in Literature*, V, 73–83.

1960 "Giffard's *Pamela: A Comedy*," *Book Collector*, IX, 455–56.

"The Living Burns," *RIP*, XLVII, No. 3, 1–16.

Review of Bonamy Dobrée, *English Literature in the Early Eighteenth Century, 1700–1740*, in *PQ*, XXXIX, 293–95.

Review of Bernard Kreissman, *Pamela-Shamela*, in *CE*, XXII, 205.

Review of Marjorie Hope Nicolson, *Mountain Gloom and Mountain Glory*, in *MP*, LVII, 206–7.

1961 Editor, James Thomson, *The Castle of Indolence and Other Poems*. Lawrence, Kansas.

The Background of Thomson's "Seasons" (reprint of 1942 ed.), Hamden, Conn.

"Griffith's Pioneer Study of the Progress Piece," in *The Great Torch Race: Essays in Honor of Reginald Harvey Griffith*, ed. Mary T. Osborne (Austin, Texas), pp. 45–47.

"James Ralph in Berkshire," *SEL*, I, No. 3, 43–51.

Review of Thomas Crawford, *Burns: A Study of the Poems and Songs*, in *PQ*, XL, 375–77.

1962 *The Early Masters of English Fiction* (reprint of 1956 ed.). London.

Editor, *An Essay on the New Species of Writing Founded by Mr. Fielding (1751)*. (Augustan Reprint Society Publication No. 95.) Los Angeles.

Editor, *An Essay on the New Species of Writing Founded by Mr. Fielding (1751)*. (Augustan Reprint Society Publication No. 95) Los Angeles.

Editor, Laurence Sterne, *Tristram Shandy*. (Harper's Modern Classics.) New York.

"The Early History of *Alfred*," in *Studies in English Drama Presented to Baldwin Maxwell* (Iowa City), pp. 311–24; also in *PQ*, XLI, 311–24.

Review of Louis F. Peck, *A Life of Matthew G. Lewis*, in *JEGP*, LXI, 426–28.